# A SURVEY OF HINDUISM

# A SURVEY OF HINDUISM

*Third Edition*

KLAUS K. KLOSTERMAIER



STATE UNIVERSITY OF NEW YORK PRESS

**Published by**
STATE UNIVERSITY OF NEW YORK PRESS,
ALBANY



Printed in the United States of America



For information, contact State University of New York Press, Albany, NY
www.sunypress.edu

Production by Marilyn P. Semerad
Marketing by Anne M. Valentine

**Library of Congress Cataloging-in-Publication Data**

Klostermaier, Klaus K., 1933–.
A survey of Hinduism / Klaus K. Klostermaier. -- 3rd ed.
p. cm.
Previously published: Albany : State University of New York Press, c1994. 2nd ed.
Includes bibliographical references and index.
ISBN-13: 978-0-7914-7081-7 (hardcover : alk. paper)
ISBN-13: 978-0-7914-7082-4 (pbk. : alk. paper)
1. Hinduism. I. Title.
BL1202.K56 2007
294.5--dc22

2006021542

10 9 8 7 6 5 4 3 2 1

# Contents

# Illustrations

**Figures**

## PHOTOGRAPHS

## Maps

# Preface to the Third Edition

The *Survey of Hinduism* in its preceding two editions has gained wide acceptance and has received much encouraging comment in scholarly reviews. It was especially gratifying for me to see it appreciated by Hindu students and scholars—a token for the fulfilment of my ambition to present Hinduism in such a way that Hindus would recognize their own traditions in it. Many of the suggestions of reviewers have been taken up and incorporated in this new edition.

While most of the structure and content of the previous edition has been left unchanged, except for some updating, adding, and correcting, a number of new chapters have been added: the first chapter deals in more detail with the current controversy concerning the beginnings of Hinduism and takes a more decisive stand on it in the light of recent research. Chapters have been added on the relationship of Hinduism with the three major non-Hindu religions with substantial followings in India: Buddhism, Christianity, and Islam. A new section has been added, dealing with issues that are important but that did not fit into the preceding sections such as the history of the relationship of India with the West, the accomplishments of Hindus in the sciences, Hinduism and Ecology, Indian measures of time, including the Calendar, and an extended chronology.

India is fast emerging as a modern economic and military superpower and its popular culture, represented prominently by the colorful creations of Bollywood, is attracting more and more fans across the globe. Interest in its rich traditional culture, its philosophy, and spirituality is growing worldwide too. India is the only major modern country that in its contemporary culture has preserved a substantial part of its ancient cultural traditions, a heritage that will prove an invaluable contribution also to our emerging global culture.

The author is grateful to State University of New York Press for the opportunity of bringing out a new revised and enlarged edition of the *Survey* and wishes to express his thanks to its dedicated staff for the care taken in the production. He also expresses his appreciation to Canada Council for continued support.

# Abbreviations

| | |
|---|---|
| ALB | *The Adyar Library Bulletin (Brahmavidyā)* |
| ABORI | *Annals of the Bhandarkar Oriental Institute* (Poona) |
| BSOAS | *Bulletin of the School of Oriental and African Studies* (London) |
| CHI | *The Cultural Heritage of India* (H. Bhattacharya, general ed.) |
| ER | *Encyclopedia of Religion* (M. Eliade, ed.) |
| ERE | *Encyclopedia of Religion and Ethics* (J. Hastings, ed.) |
| HASA | *Historical Atlas of South Asia* (J. Schwartzberg, ed, 2d edition) |
| HCIP | *The History and Culture of the Indian People* (R. C. Majumdar, general ed.) |
| HDhs | *History of Dharmaśāstra* (P. V. Kane) |
| HIL | *A History of Indian Literature* (J. Gonda, general ed.) |
| HIPh | *History of Indian Philosophy* (S. N. Dasgupta) |
| HOS | *Harvard Oriental Series* (Cambridge, Mass.) |
| HR | *History of Religion* (Chicago) |
| IFR | *Indian and Foreign Review* |
| IJHS | *International Journal of Hindu Studies* |
| IJHSc | *Indian Journal of History of Science* |
| JAAR | *Journal of the American Academy of Religion* |
| JAOS | *Journal of the American Oriental Society* (New Haven) |
| JAS | *Journal of the Asian Society* (Ann Arbor) |
| JBRS | *Journal of the Bihar Research Society* (Patna) |
| JIES | *Journal of Indo-European Studies* |
| JIPH | *Journal of Indian Philosophy* |
| JOIB | *Journal of the Oriental Institute* (Baroda) |
| JRAS | *Journal of the Royal Asiatic Society* |
| JVS | *Journal of Vaiṣṇava Studies* |
| KSBCCV | *Kuppuswamy Sastri Birth Centenary Commemoration Volume* (Madras: Kuppuswami Research Institute) |
| RS | *Religion and Society* (Bangalore/Delhi) |
| SBE | *Sacred Books of the East* (Oxford University Press) |

| | |
|---|---|
| SBH | *Sacred Books of the Hindus* (Allahabad: Panini Office) |
| WZKSA | *Wiener Zeitschrift für die Kunde Südasiens* |
| ZDMG | *Zeitschrift der Deutschen Morgenländschen Gesellschaft* |
| ZRGG | *Zeitschrift für Religions—und Geistesgeschichte* |

# Note on Transliteration and Pronunciation

The internationally adopted system of transliteration of Sanskrit into English has been followed throughout. Sanskrit vowels have by and large the same value as their Italian counterparts. A macron above a vowel sign indicates a doubling of the length: *ā* = *aa*. Consonants broadly correspond—with some exceptions—to their English equivalents. Among the more notable differences are the numerous aspirates: *th* is not pronounced like the English *th* in *theater* but is a double consonant like the *t-h* in *hot-house*; *j* and *c* and their aspirates are pronounced like *dsh*. There are different *t* and *d* sounds (indicated by dots underneath the letters) for which there are no exact equivalents in English; *ś* and *ṣ* are pronounced like *sh*. While English does not have equivalents for some of the consonants indicated by diacritics (a dot above or below the letter) diacritics have been retained for the sake of correct rendering of the words (in Sanskrit the word meaning will change if *d* is exchanged for *ḍ*, *t* for *ṭ*, *n* for *ṅ*).

Since this work is not primarily intended for the specialist in the field, Sanskrit words have been rendered in their uninflected stem forms rather than with their case endings (e.g., *hetu* for *hetuḥ*; *mandapa* for *mandapam*, etc.) Words, like *karma*, *yoga*, etc., which have become part of the English vocabulary have been left in the customary form of writing. I have also followed the fairly common practice of adding an English plural ending (-s) to Sanskrit words, neither separating the -s through a hyphen, as is done in some scholarly journals, nor using the grammatically correct Sanskrit plural formations: thus I have rendered, for example, the plural for Purāṇa as Purāṇas, and not Purāṇa-s or Purāṇāni.

Indian names of authors have usually been left as they were found in the documents quoted; no attempt has been made either to transcribe them or to provide them with diacritics. Tamil names and words have not been consistently transliterated according to the most recent conventions; for the sake of easier identification, the Sanskritized form of some names has been retained (e.g., Sundaramūrti instead of Cuntaramurti, and so forth).

In the bibliography Indian names have usually been dealt with as if they were European names. While this is technically not always correct—Śastrī, Iyengar, and others are really titles and not proper names—it makes it easier to identify authors.

Transliterations from Hindī have been treated in the same way as those from Sanskrit, since it uses the same script. Although in spoken Hindī the short *-a* of the last syllable of a word is usually not articulated (a Hindī speaker will say Rām instead of Rāma, Śiv instead of Śiva) the syllable letters are the same in Devanāgarī as in Sanskrit and thus have been fully transliterated.

Although there is no upper/lower case distinction in Indian alphabets, proper names of persons, places, rivers, mountains, titles of books, and so forth, have been capitalized according to English-language conventions.

# Introduction

More than eight hundred million of India's over one billion people call themselves Hindus.[1] In addition, some fifty million Hindus are living outside India: eighteen million in Nepal, the only country that has declared Hinduism its state religion, fifteen million in Bangladesh, three million in Sri Lanka, two million in Pakistan, the rest all over the world. North America is by now home to about 2.5 million Hindus, and most major cities have Hindu temples, often replicas of classical Indian temples executed by traditional Indian craftsmen.[2] Hindu gurus have become very visible in the West during the past few decades as promoters of a faith that many young Westerners adopted as their own. The establishment of fairly large, permanent Hindu communities around temples in North America is already leading to what has been called the *Hinduization of America*,[3] the incorporation of the landscape, mountains, and rivers of North America into Hindu sacred spaces and localities.

Hinduism is not only one of the numerically largest but also the oldest living major tradition on Earth, with roots reaching back into prehistoric times. It has preserved beliefs and practices from times immemorial, and it has developed new expressions under the influence of many other traditions.

For many centuries India had been a distant and mysterious land to Westerners. Since the Age of Discovery—and it is an interesting coincidence that the discovery of America took place as the result of Europe's search for India—India has become increasingly familiar to the West. The West realized that India had more to offer than spices and markets, and in turn India gave up its initial reserve, opening up its treasures of literature and culture to Western scholars. India's ancient heritage is readily accessible today.

Hinduism, while offering many striking parallels to other great religions, nevertheless cannot be easily compared to any of them. That has as much to do with its history as with its present adherents, with the way religion has been conceived in India, and the way it is understood today in the West. Hinduism, while certainly circumscribing Indian religiosity, has many other specific historic-cultural and socio political dimensions. It both represented and

Photo 1. Temple scene in Mathurā (Uttar Pradesh)

always found itself in a situation of cultural and religious pluralism. Hinduism has aroused the curiosity not only of scholars of religion but equally that of sociologists and anthropologists, political scientists and archaeologists, philosophers and historians, not to forget the philologists who were the first to get seriously interested in Hindu literature. We must remind ourselves, however, that Hinduism was not primarily created by its sages and saints to provide material for doctoral dissertations for European and American scholars or to enable anthropologists and sociologists to do their obligatory field work but for the physical and spiritual sustenance of its population: it interprets the world to Hindus, makes life meaningful to them, provides them with a theoretical and practical framework for their individual and corporate existence, educates them intellectually and morally, and finally, fulfills their aspirations for transcendent freedom and salvation.

In contrast to Ancient Greece and Rome, whose classical literatures and traditions have been the major inspiration of Western humanities, but whose modern successor nations have little in common with them, India is a modern country in which much of its ancient tradition is still alive. It is alive not only in the age-old rituals that continue to be performed, in its ancient temples and places of pilgrimage that attract millions of worshipers, or in the popular stories from epics and Purāṇas that are still enjoyed by contemporary audiences in theaters and films, but also in the structure of its society and many of its laws, in its institutions as well as in its popular customs. It would be wrong, however, to portray Hinduism as a relic of a fossilized past, a tradition unable to change, a museum exhibit that must not be touched. On the contrary, Hinduism in its long history has undergone many changes, rapidly adapting to modern times, constantly bringing forth new movements, and taking new directions. Hinduism has always been more than a religion in the modern Western sense, and it aims at being a comprehensive way of life as well today, a tradition by which people can live.

Much scholarly writing on Hinduism focuses on the past of India—the literary and architectural monuments, the practices and institutions of ancient India. A great amount has been written—and continues to be written—on Vedic ritual and ancient Indian kingship, topics no doubt of great historic significance but of very marginal relevance today. Many a book on Hindu mythology, on the gods and goddesses of India more often than not does not attempt to tell the reader how contemporary Hindus understand these divinities and how and why they worship them, but frequently tries to prove a Freudian, a Jungian, or some other psychological or anthropological thesis, playing around with structuralist, functionalist, or other theoretical models which are clever and appear plausible to Western intellectuals, but explain little and often distort a great deal of Hindu reality. Given the enormous mass of writings associated with Hinduism, it is very easy to find supportive quotes for each and every thesis. It is another question whether the thesis would be acceptable to Hindus and whether it fits the context in India. Hindu resentment against the "endless

Photo 2. Gaṇeśa: Khajurāho (Madhya Pradesh)

psychoanalyzing of our Gods, Goddesses and heroes" erupted in February 1991 in one of the unlikeliest of places, in the Department of South Asian Studies at the University of California at Berkeley.[4] Individual American scholars were criticized for considering Rāma a symbol of "the type of Indian son who makes a passive homosexual identification with his father" or taking Ganesa as an "example of a story representing the primal Oedipal triangle of a son, father and mother."[5]

The aim of this *Survey* has been to describe Hinduism as the living tradition of the Hindus; a tradition with its own logic and with a dynamic of its own. The intention was to portray Hinduism in such a way that contemporary Hindus would be able to recognize their own tradition and outsiders will understand something of the Hindu tradition, when they encounter it.

The method adopted reflects the purpose of the book: to offer reliable information on Hinduism as a whole and to make a modern Westerner understand some of its meaning. As for information: this has to be selective. Hinduism with its long history and its many manifestations is simply too large a subject to be exhaustively dealt with in a volume of this size. Much has been written about Hinduism that need not be repeated here but can be referred to. As for understanding: this can, obviously, only be communicated to the extent that it is available. Understanding usually implies a translation of foreign concepts into more familiar categories. The choice of the categories into which one translates is crucial and must not be arbitrary. Understanding takes place within certain systematic contexts, and it always operates with certain presuppositions.[6] Thus an interpretation of a phenomenon like Hinduism in modern Western categories takes place within a given philosophical or theological, sociological or anthropological, historical or political framework. These frameworks facilitate the integration of information, but they also may hinder us from seeing the specifics and those aspects for which there is no parallel. As L. Dumont remarked: "Hindu religion, or philosophy, is at least as all-embracing in its own way as any sociological theory may be."[7] The same can be said about any philosophical or psychological theory.

In some areas of interpretation of Indian history and its intellectual and religious meaning a notable rift has emerged between "Western" and "Indian" scholars.[8] There is no doubt that much early Western scholarship on India was influenced not only by prevalent European historical and philological methodologies but also by colonial interests. There is equally little doubt that some contemporary Indian scholarship is motivated by an urge to prove Indian popular traditions right and by an effort to establish intellectual priority or moral superiority. Over and above such unscholarly tendentiousness and prejudice there is, of course, a cultural context that influences both the choice of topics and the aim of investigations. Typical "Western" investigators may consider their task accomplished if a text has been philologically and grammatically analyzed, without commenting on the meaning expressed. A typical "Indian" scholar would identify with the issues with which the text is dealing, would

Photo 3. Richly decorated *gopura*: Tirupati (Andhra Pradesh)

take sides in controversies dealt with in the text, and argue for a particular school of thought. While the former would be satisfied with a purely historical account of religious notions, the latter would internalize them and see their existential implications. As "Insider-Outsider" I have attempted to pay attention to both concerns, fully aware of the fact that it is not always possible to avoid taking sides.

Intentionally I did not choose the framework of any one particular contemporary Western academic discipline.[9] That made my task at one and the same time easier and more difficult: easier because I did not have to justify with the concepts of a particular discipline what obviously does not fit into its schema,[10] more difficult because the range of phenomena to be dealt with becomes so much larger, the choice of vocabulary more problematic, the risk of overreaching one's competence so much greater.

The study of other cultures is no longer just the hobby of a few leisured academics, it has become a major component of general education. The world of today is connected through multiple networks of trade and commerce, political and military alliances, and through large-scale migrations of populations. If we consider each other as belonging to one and the same human family we cannot consider cultures and races eternally immovable barriers between peoples. Nor can we ignore them. I agree with L. Dumont that "cultures not only *can* be made to communicate, they *must*."[11] Through that communication we will doubtlessly also become capable of sharing other cultures' viewpoints, seeing their logic from within, and valuing as precious what was merely exotic to us before. In this particular case: we will not only learn *about* Hinduism but also learn *from* Hinduism.

Hinduism, as a way of life embraces all aspects of Indian culture. This *Survey*, while focusing on those expressions of Hinduism that are "religious" in a more specific sense, cannot leave out other aspects of life and culture that in the West are no longer connected with religion. Hindu "religion" has a metaphysical core, and it provides a spiritual interpretation to life in its entirety. Hinduism always left much freedom to its adherents to choose among many options, and it exerted—except in matters that had to do with sectarian discipline and caste rules—little pressure on its followers in matters of faith and belief. India has at all times accommodated a great variety of races and cultures within its boundaries, varieties of languages, customs, gods, and traditions of worship. In spite of the emergence of All-India expressions of Hinduism, the regional roots of particular branches of each of these are very much in evidence, and local practices vary markedly from one place to the other. At all times the flexibility of Hinduism also showed in the very obvious difference between theory and practice, a difference that makes it all the more unlikely to understand Hinduism by merely paying attention to its verbalized theory without having observed its living practice.

Serious Western study of India began as Sanskrit philology with the establishment of chairs for Sanskrit in major European universities in the early

Photo 4. Dispensing free drinking water as charity: Vṛndāvana (Uttar Pradesh)

Photo 5. Wayside shrine in Chennai (Tamilnadu)

nineteenth century. It concentrated on classical drama and epics, on Vedānta, Veda, and grammar, and eventually on the Prakrits, which were part of the Sanskrit dramas and which are also the canonical languages of the Buddhists and Jains. The study of modern Indian languages and especially the study of South Indian languages developed only very recently in the West, and with it the interest in popular religion, in the Purāṇas and in medieval literature in Indian vernaculars. There would be few Indianists today who doubt the importance of these languages and literatures for an understanding of almost all aspects of Indian culture. But work is still scarce. Many more Western scholars know Sanskrit than Tamil, and again there are many more translations of ancient Pali and Ardhamāgadhī works available than of medieval or modern Hindī, Marathī or Bengalī texts. Things are slowly changing and it is encouraging to see many of the younger generation of Indianists, especially in North America, devoting their talents and energies to translating such vernacular literature.[12]

Nobody will deny the importance of knowing Sanskrit and the intrinsic value of Sanskrit literature for Indian studies. After all, Sanskrit was the language of Brahmin scholarship for thousands of years, and Sanskrit literature constitutes an irreplaceable treasure-house of the literary achievements of many generations of Indian poets, scholars, and thinkers. One must not forget, however, that several times in Indian history successful attempts were made to break the monopoly of Sanskrit learning by expressing important ideas and lofty thoughts in other languages. An impressive vernacular literature has developed that embodies and further develops the ancient culture and by virtue of being vernacular reaches much larger strata of the population. Thus the Hindī re-creation of the *Rāmāyana*—Tulāsidāsa's free rerendering of Vālmīki's Sanskrit work in the medieval Hindī *Rāmacaritamānasa*—has become immensely more popular than the Sanskrit original, and it has influenced the thoughts and values of a much larger number of people. Contemporary translations of epics and Purāṇas in Indian vernaculars and religious journals in Hindī, Marathī, Gujaratī, Bengalī, Tamiḷ and other languages reach a much wider audience than the classical Sanskrit treatises. To some extent modern vernacular religious literature keeps repeating and exposing the content of the classical texts. But it is not *mere* repetition and exposition. A popular religious monthly in modern Hindī like *Kalyāṇa*, which has a circulation of over two hundred thousand, also deals with contemporary problems and offers a fairly faithful mirror of recent developments within Hinduism. It is not only simple folk who write letters and express their religious sentiments in journals like this, scholars and religious leaders address a large readership through this medium as well.

As a young man and as a student of Indian religions at a European university, I made a quite deliberate decision not to publish anything on Hinduism unless I had seen Indian reality for myself and experienced Hinduism *in loco*. Looking for an opportunity to immerse myself in the Hindu milieu after I had earned my doctorate, I accepted an invitation from the late Swami Bon Mahārāj to join his Institute of Indian Philosophy in Vṛindāvana,[13] Uttar Pradesh. Vṛndāvana has since become quite well known due to the spread of the Hare Krishna movement (ISKCON) and their preaching of Caitanya Vaiṣṇavism. ISKCON has built a large center and a beautiful temple in Vṛndāvana, and the sight of foreign visitors has now become quite common. When I joined Swami Bon's Institute I must have been the only resident non-Indian. The extended sojourn in Vṛndāvana, the daily experience of a vibrant and intense Hinduism, the many contacts with pious and learned Hindus intensified my motivation to read and study the sources.[14] Vṛndāvana then was a small town of perhaps thirty-five thousand permanent residents with a large influx of pilgrims, surrounded by numerous villages, largely untouched by modern developments, in many ways still living in the Middle Ages.

When I left Vṛndāvana after two years, I moved to Bombay, now called Mumbāī, a modern metropolis, the most Westernized of India's big cities, with a population then of about eight million people, now fifteen million. Hinduism was flourishing also in Bombay and I learned to appreciate the new ways in which it appears and the appeal it has for sophisticated modern people.[15] I spent six years there and left with a PhD in Ancient Indian History and Culture from Bombay University. During that time I had the opportunity to see many famous places and participated in many festivals and pilgrimages. A year spent in Madras while on sabbatical leave from the University of Manitoba

Photo 6. Holy Cows in Vṛndāvana

opened my eyes to the quite distinct Dravidian tradition within Hinduism—a tradition whose distinctiveness is emphasized also through contemporary political developments.

Life in India—for most people—is quite unromantic. To provide for the daily necessities, be it in the villages or in the big cities, is for the majority of Indians an exhausting, competitive task. In India, as everywhere, there is a good deal of poverty, unemployment, and disillusionment among the youth. There were natural calamities and social tensions, language riots and religious confrontations. To experience all this for ten years had a sobering effect on my youthful enthusiasm and kept me from unduly romanticizing India—past or present. Yet living in India nevertheless also made me aware of being part of a great old civilization, of the influence of great figures and movements from the past and the present, of the pervasive presence of religion in all aspects of daily life, for better or worse. No amount of reading texts can replace the immediacy of recognition given through an encounter with a *samnyāsi* who has spent a lifetime in pursuit of *moksa*. No theory of art can do what a visit to a place like Elephanta or Ajanta does to a sensitive person. No description can adequately express the sensation of participation in a major temple feast in a place like Madurai or Tirupati.

While over 80 percent of India's population are Hindus,[16] with a total population estimated at 1.3 billion, that leaves a considerable number of non-Hindus who in some way or other interact with the Hindu majority.

The largest group, no doubt, are the Muslims. Even after partition, which was intended to give to Indian Muslims a homeland of their own in Pakistan, over 120 million Muslims live in today's India. The coexistence of this large minority with the Hindu majority often is an uneasy one: centuries of conflict have created a permanent, latent tension that, at the slightest provocation, flares up into a riot—often with great loss of life and property on both sides.

The Sikhs, long counted as close to Hindus, have also been asserting their own religious and cultural identity. They constitute only about 2 percent of India's population. They are strongly concentrated in the Punjab, where they claim to have a majority. Not all Sikhs are convinced that they need a separate Khalistān, but the more extremist faction did not shy away in the last decades of the twentieth century from terrorism and murder to press the claim. Happily the situation has calmed down now.

Around thirty million Indians are Christians, divided into a great many different churches and denominations. Tensions between Christians and Hindus have increased over the past decades, mainly over the issue of Christian missions. There are about seven million Buddhists, four million Jains, a few hundred thousand Parsis and Jews—all of them with a long Indian history of their own.

*Ādivāsis*, the original inhabitants of the country, divided into a large number of tribes, make up a sizeable minority of over sixty million. They comprise hundreds of different groups, strongly concentrated in Central India, but they can be found throughout the subcontinent. They are in varying degrees influenced by Hindu culture and often have lost their own languages, but they, in turn, have also contributed to the development of Hinduism. Many castes—especially among the lower ones—were formed by assimilating tribes to Hindu society. Many local Hindu traditions can be linked to tribal origins: tribal forms of deities merged into larger Hindu gods, tribal places of worship and sacred spots were taken over by Hinduism as *tīrthas* and places where Hindu temples were built.[17] In a countermove to the so-called Sanskritization—a term coined by the sociologist M. N. Srinivas to describe the trend among low castes and tribals to heighten their status by employing Brahmin priests and by adopting high-caste rituals—a reassertion of tribal culture is taking place in India. To some extent this is the result of a deliberate policy encouraged by the Central Government, to protect the cultures of the tribes. It also is a reaction against what tribals perceived to be Hindu aggressiveness and exploitation. It is worth noting that tribals are in the forefront of India's ecological movement; they initiated the Chipko movement to protect the forests in the Himalayan foothills, and they launched massive and effective protests against the Narmada development scheme.

Furthermore, an estimated two hundred million Indians are and are not Hindus. These are the people whom Gandhi had called *Harijan*, "God's People," and who were otherwise known as outcastes, scheduled castes, or Untouchables. Strictly speaking they had no rights within traditional Hindu society, but they lived and functioned at the margins of it.[18] They even patterned their own society along caste structures, observing higher and lower, clean and unclean among themselves. Under Dr. Ambedkar, as a Māhār a member of one of the scheduled castes, several million outcastes abandoned Hinduism and adopted Buddhism as their religion. Many are by now organized under the banner of Dalit, "oppressed," associations; some of these are virulently anti-Brahmin, attacking in their publications also the notion of a unified Hinduism and of a cultural Hindu identity of India.

The Indian government made special provisions for the "scheduled castes" by reserving places in schools and positions in government for them. Some have done economically fairly well. The majority, however, still live on the margins of Hindu society—quite literally so. Atrocities against Harijans are still quite commonplace and a caste-Hindu backlash is noticeable against what is seen as "pampering" of the "scheduled castes" by the government. In connection with recommendations on their behalf by the Mandal Commission, this led to riots and self-immolation by caste Hindus some years ago.

India is a large country and has always contained a considerable part of the earth's population, roughly one-sixth at present. India's civilization in all its aspects—material, intellectual, artistic, spiritual—is a major component of world civilization and has been so for the past five thousand years at least. Learning about India widens our horizons and makes us better understand what it means to be human and civilized.

When I conceived the structure of the *Survey of Hinduism*, I deliberately did not follow the schemata of the then-used textbooks but developed, based on my own life experience, a topical approach that, I felt, not only was closer to actual Hinduism but also avoided the superimposition of Western categories and schemata on Eastern culture and thought.

Indian scholarly books often end with a *kṣamā-prārthana*, a statement in which the writer requests the readers' indulgence for the shortcomings of the work. It may be appropriate to begin this *Survey* with such a *kṣamā-prārthana*, directed not so much at those who look for information about Hinduism in this book, but at those about whom the book is written. The very idea of writing, as an outsider, about the life and religion of a people as large and as ancient as the Hindus, requires, I believe, an apology. It has been done before, of course. That does not say much about the appropriateness of the endeavor. Quite articulate critiques of Western "Orientalism" have been voiced by Orientals and Westerners alike. Orientalist constructions of India[19] have evidently much to do with constructions of reality in general undertaken by the systematizing Western mind. Sociological, psychological, economical, and historical constructions of Europe or America fall into the same category.

Hindus are quite capable of speaking for themselves. This is acknowledged in the *Survey* by letting Hindu voices speak for Hinduism and by keeping outsiders' voices and interpretations to a minimum. Hinduism is not a "case" to be scientifically studied and to be reduced to preset categories taken from Western culture but an expression of human nature and culture to be accepted on its own terms.

# Part I

## Hinduism: Sources and Worldview

The long history, the vastness, and the heterogeneity of Hinduism offer enormous challenges to each and every description of the tradition. The very question of identifying the beginning of Hinduism has become one of the most controversial topics in Indian studies. For the time being two irreconcilable notions are being heatedly discussed in scholarly and popular literature. The first chapter attempts to weigh the merits of these.

The identity of Hinduism rests primarily on the particular line of verbal revelation on which the Hindu tradition is grounded. The Vedas and the other books, which are held sacred as scriptures by Hindus, differentiate Hinduism from other religions possessing their own specific holy books, and they permit at least in a negative way a definition of the essentials of Hinduism over against what is not Hinduism.

While acceptance of the Veda as revealed is certainly the most basic criterion for declaring oneself a Hindu—the preferred self-designation of Hinduism in Indian languages is *Vaidika dharma*, the "Vedic Law"—there is another genre of literature that has shaped the minds and hearts of present-day Hindus much more profoundly: the two great epics, *Mahābhārata* and *Rāmāyana*, and the voluminous *Purāṇas*, the true Bibles of Hinduism. Typical for Hinduism, it has not just one, but eighteen such scriptures, accepted as revealed by the followers of the various greater traditions. They exalt Viṣṇu, Śiva, Devī to the highest position; they contain the colorful myths for which Hinduism is famous; they instruct their readers in matters of worship and hygiene, promise health, wealth, and eternal salvation to all who recite them. The *itihāsa-purāṇa* literature is enormous—it has hardly any parallel in another culture. While not all Hindus are fully acquainted with it, many know surprisingly much from it.

There is one book, however, that virtually all Hindus know and many recite daily by heart: the *Bhagavadgītā*, the Song of the Lord. It has become a classic also in the West; there are scores of translations in English and other

European languages available. It is a Kṛṣṇa book, but it articulates much that is typical for all of Hinduism, and it contains advice and hopes, that most Hindus accept as expressing their own aspirations.

The relative geographic isolation of the Indian subcontinent facilitated the development over long periods of time of a civilization that was little influenced from the outside. Cosmological and other ideas developed and found fairly universal acceptance throughout India. Together these could be termed the *Hindu world-picture*. The Hindu worldview appears in a number of variants, but it also shows a surprisingly large number of common features—features distinctive enough to set it off against the worldviews of other civilizations.

All observers—including Hindus themselves—would describe Hinduism as polytheistic. Nowhere else in the world do we find such a profusion of gods and goddesses, of semidivine beings and demons, ramifications of genealogies of gods and manifestations of divinity in human and animal forms. But that is only the surface of Hinduism, the colourful appearance of a tradition, which has enormous depths. While Hinduism could never be conceived as a parallel to biblical or Islamic monotheism, it has developed its own sophisticated notions of the unity of the highest principle, and many forms of Vaiṣṇavism, Śaivism, or Śāktism have theologies, in which One Supreme Being is given the title and role of Lord or Mistress, the creator, preserver, and destroyer of the whole universe and the savior of those who believe in him or her.

CHAPTER ONE

# The Beginnings of Hinduism

> The modern archaeological record for South Asia indicates a cultural history of continuity rather than the earlier 18th through 20th century scholarly interpretation of discontinuity and South Asian dependence upon Western influences.
>
> —J. G. Shaffer and D. A. Lichtenstein, "Migration, Philology and South Asian Sociology"

The ancient Persians, who occupied the lands west to the Indus River called the whole country lying across the Indus River *Sindh* and its inhabitants *Sindhus*, a designation that was later taken over by the Greeks who succeeded them and resulted in the now commonly used designations of India and Indians. The Muslims, who began invading India from the eighth century onward, used the term *Hindu* as a generic designation for non-Muslim Indians, identical with "idol worshipers." In the 1830s Englishmen, writing about the religions of India, added *-ism* to *Hindu* and coined the term *Hinduism*, making an abstract and generic entity out of the many diverse and specific traditions of the Hindus.[1] While Hindus have appropriated the designation *Hindu* and use it today to identify themselves over against Muslims or Christians, they have expressed reservations with regard to the designation of *Hinduism* as the "religion of the Hindus." They see a certain disrespect in the *-ism* suffix and emphasize that the Hindu *dharma* is more comprehensive than the Western term *religion*: it designates an entire cultural tradition rather than only a set of beliefs and rituals. With these reservations in mind, we are going to use the widely introduced term *Hinduism* in describing the majority religio-cultural tradition of India in spite of the impossibility of defining it in any precise manner.

## THE BEGINNINGS OF HINDUISM

The Vedas, the oldest literary monument of the Indian people, a collection of hymns composed in an archaic Sanskrit, are universally considered the foundational scriptures of Hinduism. The authors of these hymns called themselves *Āryans*, "Noble People." The date of the composition of these hymns and the original habitat of the Aryans have become one of the most contested issues in Indian studies. The polemical literature has reached such dimensions and the emotions have been raised to such heights that only a sketch of the controversy and some hints about its ideological background can be given in this place.[2]

Around 1860 a group of European Sanskritists suggested that the best explanation for the many common features of what later were called the Indo-European languages was the assumption of an invasion of a band of Aryan warriors, who till then had been living somewhere between Central Asia and Western Europe, into India. Did not the *Ṛgveda*, the oldest Sanskrit source, describe the battles, which the Āryas, under their leader Indra, the "fort-destroyer," fought against the Dasyus, whose land they occupied? Making the self-designation *ārya* (noble) a racial attribute of the putative invaders, every textbook on Indian history began with the "Āryan invasion" of northwestern India, the struggle between the "fair-skinned, blonde, blue-eyed, sharp-nosed Aryans on horse chariots" against the "black-skinned, snub-nosed indigenous Indians."

This putative "Aryan invasion" was dated ca. 1500 BCE, and the composition of the hymns of the *Ṛgveda* was fixed between 1400 and 1200 BCE. The Aryan invasion theory was conceived on pure speculation on the basis of comparative philology, without any archaeological or literary evidence to support it. It was resisted as unfounded by some scholars from the very beginning.[3] In the light of recent archaeological finds, it has become less and less tenable. Nevertheless, the Aryan invasion theory, recently downgraded to an Aryan migration theory, is still widely defended and forms part of many standard histories of Hinduism. In the following, the arguments pro and con will be presented, and it will be left to the reader to judge the merits of the case.

## THE ARYAN INVASION THEORY

Eighteenth- and nineteenth-century European attempts to explain the presence of Hindus in India were connected with the commonly held biblical belief that humankind originated from one pair of humans—Adam and Eve, created directly by God in 4005 BCE—and that all the people then living on the earth descended from one of the sons of Noah, the only family of humans to survive the Great Flood (dated 2350 BCE). The major problem associated with the discovery of new lands seemed to be to connect peoples *not* mentioned in chapter 10 of Genesis, "The Peopling of the Earth," with one of the biblical genealogical lists.

With regard to India this problem was addressed by the famous Abbé Dubois (1770–1848), whose long sojourn in India (1792-1823) enabled him to collect a large amount of interesting materials concerning the customs and traditions of the Hindus. His (French) manuscript was bought by the British East India Company and appeared in an English translation under the title *Hindu Manners, Customs and Ceremonies* in 1897 with a prefatory note by the Right Honorable F. Max Müller.[4] Addressing the origins of the Indian people, Abbé Dubois, loath "to oppose [his] conjectures to [the Indians'] absurd fables," categorically stated: "It is practically admitted that India was inhabited very soon after the Deluge, which made a desert of the whole world. The fact that it was so close to the plains of Sennaar, where Noah's descendants remained stationary so long, as well as its good climate and the fertility of the country, soon led to its settlement." Rejecting other scholars' opinions that linked the Indians to Egyptian or Arabic origins, he ventured to suggest them "to be descendants not of Shem, as many argue, but of Japhet."[5] He explains: "According to my theory they reached India from the north, and I should place the first abode of their ancestors in the neighbourhood of the Caucasus."[6] The reasons he provides to prove his theory are utterly unconvincing—but he goes on to build the rest of his "migration theory" (not yet an Aryan invasion theory) on this shaky foundation.

When the affinity between many European languages and Sanskrit became a commonly accepted notion, scholars almost automatically concluded that the Sanskrit-speaking ancestors of the present-day Indians had to be found somewhere halfway between India and the western borders of Europe—Northern Germany, Scandinavia, southern Russia, the Pamir—from which they invaded the Punjab.[7] When the ruins of Mohenjo Daro and Harappa were discovered in the early twentieth century, it was assumed that these were the cities the Aryan invaders destroyed.

In the absence of reliable evidence, they postulated a time frame for Indian history on the basis of conjectures. Considering the traditional dates for the life of Gautama, the Buddha, as fairly well established in the sixth century BCE, supposedly pre-Buddhist Indian records were placed in a sequence that seemed plausible to philologists. Accepting on linguistic grounds the traditional claims that the *Ṛgveda* was the oldest Indian literary document, Max Müller, a greatly respected authority in Veda studies, allowing a time span of two hundred years each for the formation of every class of Vedic literature and assuming that the Vedic period had come to an end by the time of the Buddha, established the following sequence that was widely accepted:

- *Ṛgveda*, ca. 1200 BCE
- *Yajurveda*, *Sāmaveda*, *Atharvaveda*, ca. 1000 BCE
- *Brāhmaṇas*, ca. 800 BCE
- *Āraṇyakas*, Upaniṣads, ca. 600 BCE

Max Müller himself conceded the purely conjectural nature of the Vedic chronology, and in his last work, *The Six Systems of Indian Philosophy*, published shortly before his death, admitted: "Whatever may be the date of the Vedic hymns, whether 1500 or 15000 BC, they have their own unique place and stand by themselves in the literature of the world."[8]

There were already in Max Müller's time Western scholars, such as Moriz Winternitz, and Indians, like Bal Gangadhar Tilak, who disagreed with his chronology and postulated a much earlier date for the *Ṛgveda*. Indian scholars pointed out all along that there was no reference in the Veda to a migration of the Āryas from outside India, that all the geographical features mentioned in the *Ṛgveda* were those of northwestern India and that there was no archaeological evidence whatsoever for the Aryan invasion theory. On the other side, there were references to constellations in Vedic works whose time frame could be reestablished by commonly accepted astronomical calculations. The dates arrived at, however, 4500 BCE for one observation in the *Ṛgveda*, 3200 BCE for a date in the *Śatapatha Brāhmaṇa*, seemed far too remote to be acceptable, especially if one assumed, as many nineteenth-century scholars did, that the world was only about six thousand years old and that the flood had taken place only 4500 years ago.

Present-day defenders of the Aryan invasion/migration theory are displaying what they believe to be an impenetrable armor of philological detail research: in addition to the *Ṛgveda* and the *Avesta*, whole libraries of literary documents pertaining to dozens of languages are marshalled and "laws of scientific linguistics" are adduced to overrun any opposition.[9] The scholarly debate has largely degenerated into an ideological battle. The defenders of the Aryan invasion theory call everyone who is not on their side "fundamentalist Hindu," "revisionist," "fascist," and worse, whereas the defenders of the indigenous origin of the Veda accuse their opponents of entertaining "colonialist-missionary" and "racist-hegemonial" prejudices.

Many contemporary Indian scholars, admittedly motivated not only by academic interests, vehemently reject what they call the "colonial-missionary Aryan invasion theory." They accuse its originators of superimposing—for a reason—the purpose and process of the colonial conquest of India by the Western powers in modern times onto the beginnings of Indian civilization: as the Europeans came to India as bearers of a supposedly superior civilization and a higher religion, so the original Aryans were assumed to have invaded a country that they subjected and on which they imposed their culture and their religion.

As the heat around the Aryan invasion theory is rising, it is also emerging that both sides return to positions that were taken by opposing camps more than a hundred years ago. The difference between then and now is the evidence offered by a great many new archaeological discoveries, which clearly tip the balance in favor of the "Indigenists."

## ARGUMENTS FOR AN INDIAN INDIGENOUS ORIGIN OF THE VEDA.

One would expect the proponents of an event to provide proof for its happening rather than demanding proofs for a non-event.[10] The controversy about the Aryan invasion of India has become so bizarre that its proponents simply assume it to have taken place and demand that its opponents offer arguments that it had not taken place. In the following a number of reasons will be adduced to attest to the fact that the Aryan invasion of India—assumed by the invasionists to have taken place around 1500 BCE—did not take place.

1. The Aryan invasion theory is based purely on linguistic conjectures, which are unsubstantiated.

2. The supposed large-scale migrations of Aryan people in the second millennium BCE first into western Asia and then into northern India (by 1500 BCE) cannot be maintained in view of the established fact that the Hittites were in Anatolia already by 2200 BCE and the Kassites and Mitanni had kings and dynasties by 1600 BCE.

3. There is no hint of an invasion or of large-scale migration in the records of ancient India: neither in the Vedas, in Buddhist or Jain writings, nor in Tamil literature. The fauna and flora, the geography, and the climate described in the *Ṛgveda* are those of northern India.

4. There is a striking cultural continuity between the archaeological artifacts of the Indus-Sarasvati civilization and later phases of Indian culture: a continuity of religious ideas, arts, crafts, architecture, and system of weights and measures.

5. The archaeological finds of Mehrgarh dated ca. 7500 BCE (copper, cattle, barley) reveal a culture similar to that of the Vedic Indians. Contrary to former interpretations, the *Ṛgveda* reflects not a nomadic but an urban culture.

6. The Aryan invasion theory was based on the assumption that a nomadic people in possession of horses and chariots defeated an urban civilization that did not know horses and that horses are depicted only from the middle of the second millennium onward. Meanwhile archaeological remains of horses have been discovered in Harappan and pre-Harappan sites; drawings of horses have been found in Paleolithic caves in central India. Horse drawn war chariots are not typical for nomadic breeders but for urban civilizations.

7. The racial diversity found in skeletons in the cities of the Indus civilization is the same as in today's India; there is no evidence of the coming of a new race.

8. The *Rgveda* describes a river system in North India that is pre-1900 BCE in the case of the Sarasvatī River and pre-2600 BCE in the case of the Dṛṣadvatī River. Vedic literature shows a population shift from the Sarasvatī (*Ṛgveda*) to the Ganges (Brāhmaṇas and Purāṇas) for which there is also evidence in archaeological finds.

9. The astronomical references in the *Ṛgveda* are based on a Pleiades-Kṛttika calendar of ca. 2500 BCE. Vedic astronomy and mathematics were well-developed sciences: these are not features of the culture of a nomadic people.

10. The Indus cities were not destroyed by invaders but deserted by their inhabitants because of desertification of the area. Strabo (*Geography* XV.1.19) reports that Aristobulos had seen thousands of villages and towns deserted because the Indus had changed its course.

11. The battles described in the *Ṛgveda* were not fought between invaders and natives but between people belonging to the same culture.

12. Excavations in Dvārakā have led to the discovery of a site larger than Mohenjo Daro, dated ca. 1500 BCE with architectural structures, use of iron, and a script halfway between Harappan and Brahmī. Dvārakā has been associated with Kṛṣṇa and the end of the Vedic period.

13. There is a continuity in the morphology of scripts: Harappan—Brahmī—Devanāgarī.

14. Vedic *ayas*, formerly translated as "iron," probably meant copper or bronze. Iron was found in India before 1500 BCE in Kashmir and Dvārakā.

15. The Purāṇic dynastic lists, with over 120 kings in one Vedic dynasty alone, date back to the third millennium BCE. Greek accounts tell of Indian royal lists going back to the seventh millennium BCE.

16. The *Ṛgveda* shows an advanced and sophisticated culture, the product of a long development, "a civilization that could not have been delivered to India on horseback." (160)

17. Painted gray ware culture in the western Gangetic plains, dated ca. 1100 BCE, has been found connected to earlier Indus Valley black and red ware.

It would be strange indeed if the Vedic Indians had lost all recollection of such a momentous event as the Aryan invasion in supposedly relatively recent times—much more recent, for instance, than the migration of Abraham and his people, which is well attested and frequently referred to in the Hebrew Bible.

## INDUS CULTURE OR SARASVATĪ CIVILIZATION?

The Sarasvatī is frequently praised as the mightiest of all rivers, as giving nourishment to the people and, unique among them, flowing pure from the mountains to the ocean.[11] It is the most often mentioned river in the *Ṛgveda*—and it no longer exists. Its absence led to the suggestion that it might have been a symbolic rather than a real river, an idea supported by the later identification of Sarasvatī with the Goddess of Wisdom and Learning. More recent satellite photography and geological investigations have helped to reconstruct the ancient riverbed of the Sarasvatī and also established that it had dried out completely by 1900 BCE due to tectonic shifts. Of the 2,600 archaeological sites so far discovered that were connected with the Indus civilization, over 1,500 were found located on the Sarasvatī River basin, including settlements that exceeded in size the by now famous Indus sites of Mohenjo Daro and Harappa.[12] It is hardly meaningful to assume that the invading Vedic Aryans established thousands of settlements on its banks four centuries after the Sarasvatī had dried out.

When the first remnants of the ruins of the so-called Indus civilization came to light in the 1920s, the proponents of the Aryan invasion theory believed to have found the missing archaeological evidence: here were the "mighty forts" and the "great cities" that the warlike Indra of the *Ṛgveda* was said to have conquered and destroyed. Then it emerged that nobody had destroyed these cities and no evidence of wars of conquest came to light: floods and droughts had made it impossible to sustain large populations in the area, and the people of Mohenjo Daro, Harappa, and other places had migrated to more hospitable areas. Ongoing archaeological research has not only extended the area of the Indus civilization but has also shown a transition of its later phases to the Gangetic culture. Archaeo-geographers have established that a drought lasting two to three hundred years devastated a wide belt of land from Anatolia through Mesopotamia to northern India around 2300 BCE to 2000 BCE.

Based on this type of evidence and extrapolating from the Vedic texts, a new theory of the origins of Hinduism is emerging. This new theory considers the Indus valley civilization as a late Vedic phenomenon and pushes the (inner Indian) beginnings of the Vedic age back by several thousands of years (see Figure 2.1). Instead of speaking of an Indus Valley civilization the term *Sarasvatī-Sindhu* civilization has been introduced, to designate the far larger extent of that ancient culture. One of the reasons for considering the Indus civilization "Vedic" is the evidence of town planning and architectural design that required a fairly advanced algebraic geometry—of the type preserved in the Vedic *Śulvasūtras*. The widely respected historian of mathematics A. Seidenberg came to the conclusion, after studying the geometry used in building the Egyptian pyramids and the Mesopotamian citadels, that it reflected a derivative geometry—a geometry derived from the Vedic *Śulvasūtras*. If that is

Figure 2.1. Prehistoric rock drawings: Bhīmbhetka (Maharashtra)

so, then the knowledge ("Veda") on which the construction of Harappa and Mohenjo Daro is based cannot be later than that civilization itself.[13]

While the *Ṛgveda* has always been held to be the oldest literary document of India and was considered to have preserved the oldest form of Sanskrit, Indians have not taken it to be the source for their early history. *Itihāsa-Purāṇa* served that purpose. The language of these works is more recent than that of the Vedas, and the time of their final redaction is much later than the fixation of the Vedic canon. However, they contain detailed information about ancient events and personalities that form part of Indian history. The Ancients, like Herodotus, the father of Greek historiography, did not separate story from history. Nor did they question their sources but tended to juxtapose various information without critically sifting it. Thus we cannot read *Itihāsa-Purāṇa* as the equivalent of a modern textbook of Indian history but rather as a storybook containing information with interpretation, facts and fiction. Indians, however, always took genealogies quite seriously, and we can presume that the Purāṇic lists of dynasties, like the lists of *guru-paramparās* in the Upaniṣads, relate the names of real rulers in the correct sequence. On these assumptions we can tentatively reconstruct Indian history to a time around 4500 BCE.

G. P. Singh defends the historical accuracy of the Purāṇic dynastic lists and calls the Purāṇas "one of the most important traditions of historiography in ancient India."[14] These lists he says "disprove the opinion that the ancient Indians (mainly the Hindus) had no sense of history and chronology."

A key element in the revision of ancient Indian history was the recent discovery of Mehrgarh, a settlement in the Hindukush area, that was continuously inhabited for several thousand years from ca. 7000 BCE onward. This discovery has extended Indian history for thousands of years before the fairly well datcable Indus civilization.[15]

Nobody has as yet interpreted the religious significance of the prehistoric cave paintings (Figure 2.2) at Bhīmbetka (from ca. 100,000 to ca. 10,000 BCE), which were discovered only in 1967, and we do not know whether and how the people who created these are related to present-day populations of India.[16] These show, amongst other objects, horses clearly readied for riding—according to the "Invasionists" horse breeding and horse riding were an innovations that the Aryans introduced to India after 1500 BCE.

Civilizations, both ancient and contemporary, comprise more than literature. It cannot be assumed that the Vedic Aryans, who have left a large literature that has been preserved till now, did not have any material culture that would have left visible traces. The only basis on which Indologists in the nineteenth century established their views of Vedic culture and religion were the texts that they translated from Ancient Sanskrit. Traditionally trained philologists, that is, grammarians, are generally not able to understand technical language and the scientific information contained in the texts they study. Consider today's scientific literature. It abounds with Greek and Latin technical terms, it contains an abundance of formulas, composed of Greek and Hebrew letters. If scholars with only a background in the classical languages were to read such works, they might be able to come up with some acceptable translations of technical terms into modern English, but they would hardly be able to really make sense of most of what they read, and they certainly would not extract the information that the authors of these works wished to convey through their formulas to people trained in their specialties. Analogous to the observations, which the biologist Ernst Mayr made with regard

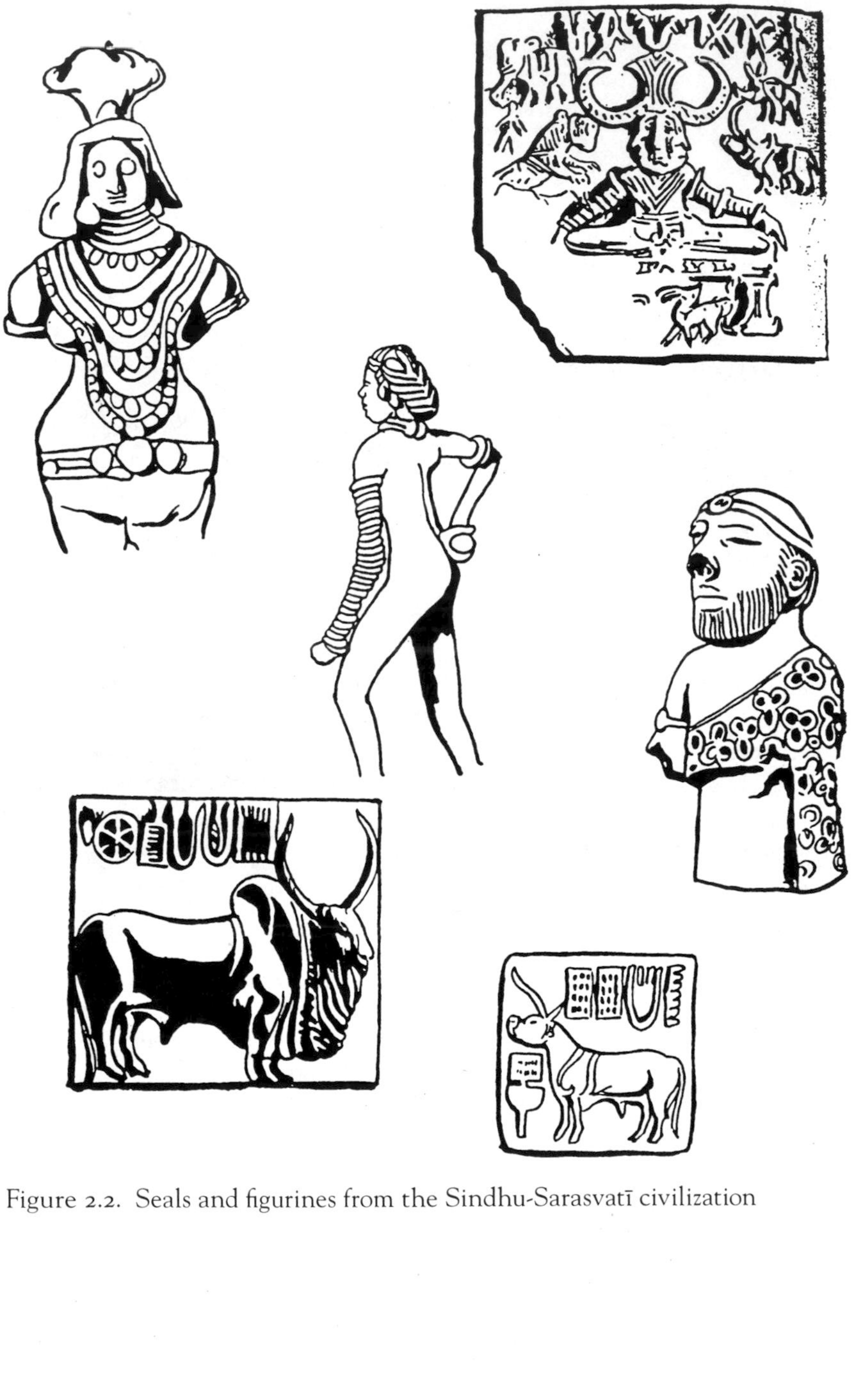

Figure 2.2. Seals and figurines from the Sindhu-Sarasvatī civilization

to translations of Aristotle's works, namely, that sixteenth-century humanists misunderstood and mistranslated his scientific terminology, we must also expect new insights to come out from new translations of ancient Indian technical texts that are more adequate than those made by nineteenth century European philologists.[17]

The admission of some of the top scholars (like Geldner, who in his translation of the *Ṛgveda*—deemed the best so far—declares many passages "darker than the darkest oracle," or Gonda, who considered the *Ṛgveda* basically untranslatable) of being unable to make sense of a great many Vedic texts—and the refusal of most to go beyond a grammatical and etymological analysis of these—indicates a deeper problem. The ancient Indians were not only poets and literateurs, but they also had their practical sciences and their technical skills, their secrets and their conventions that are not self-evident to someone who does not share their world. Some progress has been made in deciphering technical Indian medical and astronomical literature of a later age, in reading architectural and arts-related materials.[18] However, much of the technical meaning of the oldest Vedic literature still eludes us. It would be enormously helpful in the question of the relation between the *Ṛgveda* and the Indus civilization if we could read the literary remnants of the latter: thousands of what appear to be brief texts incised on a very large number of soapstone seals and other objects, found over large areas of north-western India and also in Western Asia. In spite of many claims made by many scholars who laboured for decades on the decipherment of the signs, nobody has so far been able to read or translate these signs.[19]

## THE *ṚGVEDA*—A CODE?

Computer scientist Subhash Kak believes to have rediscovered the "Vedic Code," on the strength of which he extracts from the structure as well as the words and sentences of the *Ṛgveda* considerable astronomical information that its authors supposedly embedded in it.[20] The assumption of such encoded scientific knowledge would make it understandable why there was such insistence on the preservation of every letter of the text in precisely the sequence the original author had set down. One can take certain liberties with a story, or even a poem, changing words, transposing lines, adding explanatory matter, shortening it, if necessary, and still communicate the intentions and ideas of the author. However, one has to remember and reproduce a scientific formula in precisely the same way it has been set down by the scientist, or it would not make sense at all. While the scientific community can arbitrarily adopt certain letter equivalents for physical units or processes, once it has agreed on their use, one must obey the conventions for the sake of meaningful communication.

Even a nonspecialist reader of ancient Indian literature will notice the effort made to link macrocosm and microcosm, astronomical and physiological processes, to find correspondences between the various realms of beings and to

Photo 7. Nāga: Khajurāho

order the universe by establishing broad classifications. Vedic sacrifices—the central act of Vedic culture—were to be offered on precisely built, geometrically constructed altars and to be performed at astronomically exactly established times. It sounds plausible to expect a correlation between the numbers of bricks prescribed for a particular altar and the distances between stars observed whose movement determined the time of the offerings to be made. Subhash Kak has advanced a great deal of fascinating detail in that connection in his essays on the astronomy of the Vedic altar. He believes that while the Vedic Indians possessed extensive astronomical knowledge that they encoded in the text of the *Ṛgveda*, the code was lost in later times and the Vedic tradition was interrupted.

## INDIA, THE CRADLE OF CIVILIZATION?

Based on the early dating of the *Ṛgveda* (ca. 4000 BCE) and on the strength of the argument that Vedic astronomy and geometry predates that of the other known ancient civilizations, some scholars have made the daring suggestion that India was the "cradle of civilization."[21] They link the recently discovered early European civilization (which predates ancient Sumeria and ancient Egypt by over a millennium) to waves of populations moving out or driven out from northwest India. Later migrations, caused either by climatic changes or by military events, would have brought the Hittites to western Asia, the Iranians to Afghanisthan and Iran, and many others to other parts of Eurasia. Such a scenario would require a complete rewriting of ancient world history—especially if we add the claims, apparently substantiated by some material evidence, that Vedic Indians had established trade links with Central America and East Africa before 2500 BCE. No wonder that the "new chronology" arouses not only scholarly controversy but emotional excitement as well. Much more hard evidence will be required to fully establish it, and many claims may have to be withdrawn. But there is no doubt that the "old chronology" has been discredited and that much surprise is in store for students not only of ancient India, but of the ancient World as a whole.

An entirely new twist to the question has been added by a recent suggestion that modern humankind did not originate circa one hundred thousand years ago in Africa, as was long assumed, but in Asia: and if in Asia, why not in the Indus Valley?[22] To answer that question, much more archaeological work is necessary and many more pieces of the puzzle will have to be put together.

CHAPTER TWO

# Hindu *Dharma*

## *Orthodoxy and Heresy in Hinduism*

> All those traditions and all those despicable systems of philosophy, which are not based on the Veda, produce no reward after death; for they are declared to be founded on darkness. All those [doctrines] differing from [the Veda] which spring up and [soon] perish, are worthless and false, because they are of modern date.
>
> —*Manusmṛti* XII, 95

Translations can sometimes be quite revealing. If we try to find an Indian synonym for the term *religion* (admittedly difficult to define even within the Western tradition!) we have to choose from a variety of terms, none of which coincides precisely with our word. The most common and most general term is *dharma*, today usually translated as "religion."[1] Another important aspect of religion is expressed by the term *sādhana*, frequently rendered in English as "realization." In its sociological sense *religion* may often have to be understood as *saṃpradāya*, mostly (and erroneously) translated as "sect," which describes the great Hindu traditions of Vaiṣṇavism, Śaivism, and Śāktism and their subdivisions. The term *mārga* ("path") is also frequently used as synonymous with "religion" in the sense of a path to salvation. Thus the *tri-mārga* scheme organizes the entire range of religious affiliations into *karma-mārga*, *bhakti-mārga*, and *jñāna-mārga*, the path of works, the path of loving devotion, and the path of knowledge, respectively. The representation of Hindu religion will differ again according to the affiliation of the writer with regard to caste or position in society; thus a Brahmin householder will offer a different presentation of religion from that of a *samnyāsi* who has given up all caste affiliation and all ritual.

## THE MEANING OF *DHARMA*

*Dharma*, etymologically from the root *dhṛ-*, "to sustain" or "to uphold," has been given diverse meanings in various Indian schools of thought. At one end of the spectrum we have the grammatical or logical use of the term *dharma* as merely an element of a word or of a sentence.[2] At the other end is the ontocosmological interpretation of *dharma* as that "which gives sustenance to the universe or the universal principle of all things."[3] Generally, however, it is used with reference to "religion" in the specific sense of socioethical laws and obligations. P. V. Kane thinks that *dharma* is "one of these Sanskrit words that defy all attempts at an exact rendering in English or any other tongue".[4] He eventually circumscribes the term by saying that it comprises "the privileges, duties and obligations of a man, his standard of conduct as a member of the Aryan community, as a member of one of the castes, as a person in a particular stage of life."

*Manusmṛti*, the Laws of Manu, the most important authority on the subject, identifies the sources of *dharma* as "the Veda in its entirety, the traditions (*smṛtis*) fixed by men conversant with the Vedas, the customs of righteous people and one's own conscience (*ātmanastuṣṭi*)."[5] The promise is held out to the man who follows all the rules laid down in Manu's Law that "he will obtain fame here on earth and supreme bliss beyond."[6] The same book also condemns as *nāstikas* those who place their own reasoning above the authority of tradition.[7] *Nāstika* is normally translated as "atheist," though it does not quite correspond to its English equivalent.[8] In India followers of atheistic systems like that of the Sāṁkhya are *āstikas* or orthodox, because they do not explicitly question or reject the Vedas; whereas Buddhists and Jains or the followers of any non-Vedic religions are *nāstikas*, including also the solidly materialistic and hedonistic Lokāyatas. The *dharma* of the *Manusmṛti* is also geographically defined:

> The land between the two sacred rivers Sarasvatī and Dṛṣadvatī, this land created by divine powers is the Brahmavārta. The customs prevailing in this country, passed on from generation to generation that is called the 'right behavior' (*sādācara*). From a brahmin born and raised in this country, all men should learn their ways. The country where the black antelope naturally moves about is the one that is fit for sacrifice—beyond is that of the *mlecchas* (the barbarians, the unclean!). A twice-born (viz. a Brahmin, a Kṣatriya, a Vaiśya) should resort to this country and dwell in it; a Śūdra, however, may, for the sake of gaining his livelihood, live anywhere.[9]

From the point of view of content, this *dharma* comprises social classification and the division of society into four *varṇas*, each with its particular functions and rights; the whole complex of sacrifices and rituals; the *saṃskāras*, performed at the critical periods of life; marriage laws, right of succession, the regulation of the relationship between men and women, parents and children, teachers and pupils; the definition of sin and atonement, pilgrimages and vows, feasts and celebrations—including the myths concerning the creation of the universe, transmigration, and final emancipation.[10]

Since, according to Hindu tradition, Manu is the mythical ancestor of all of humankind, his ordinances are *mānava dharma* or "the law of humankind," *sanātana dharma*, or "eternal" and "natural" religion. Modern Hindu scholars try to justify this claim in terms of the many religions and systems of law prevailing in the world as well as to specify how it relates to Hindu law. Thus Śrī Nārāyanjī Puruṣottama Saṅgani explains:

> Upon which as a fundament everything is built and which gives to the whole world its order, that which provides man in this world with blessed peace and in the next with supreme bliss and helps to attain to complete emancipation, that is *sanātana dharma*, the eternal religion. It is of the nature of God, because it has developed through God himself. As God has no beginning, middle, or end, so the *sanātana dharma* has no beginning or end. It is beginningless, of hoary antiquity, always the same, in it there is no development or change. This religion is from God and therefore God is its Lord.[11]

He continues to state in detail that this religion of humankind exists in a general form, comprising the duties of firmness, forgiveness, restraint, abstention from stealing, purity, control over the senses, forbearance, knowledge, truth, and freedom from hatred and anger, and in a specific form as absolute truth "revealed only to Hindus, different according to the *caturvarṇāśrama* scheme of life." The concept of *svadharma* is a very crucial one: *dharma* is right conduct not in a general moral sense but specified for each caste and for each situation in life. Time and again the rule laid down in the *Bhagavadgīitā* is quoted: "It is better to fulfill one's own duty (*dharma*), however imperfectly, than to do that of another, however perfect it may be."[12]

Thus *dharma* presupposes a social order in which all functions and duties are assigned to separate classes whose smooth interaction guarantees the well-being of society as a whole, and beyond this maintains the harmony of the whole universe. *Dharma* has its roots in the structure of the cosmos, and the socioethical law of mankind is but one facet of an all-embracing law encompassing all beings. Thus we can also appreciate the frequently quoted maxim: "The 'law' when violated destroys—when preserved protects: therefore *dharma* should not be violated lest the violated *dharma* destroy us." [13] Thus *dharma*, at least theoretically, is its own justification: *dharma* does not depend on a personal authority that could also make exceptions and pardon a transgressor; it is inherent in nature and does not allow modifications. *Dharma* guarantees the continued existence of India; the *avatāras* appear in order to rescue *dharma* from corruption and thus restore the country. In the strictest and fullest sense, *dharma* coincides with Hinduism. That did not prevent certain developments from taking place within what was considered "law" in Indian history, nor did it exclude the treatment of many moral questions on a rational and universal basis.[14]

Figure 3.1. Sapta Ṛṣis: The Seven Vedic Sages

## THE WEIGHT OF *DHARMAŚĀSTRA*

*Dharma-śāstra* as a literary genre is undoubtedly the largest in the whole of Indian literature.[15] That is due to both the importance of the subjects dealt with under it and the inherent difficulty of applying its principles to concrete instances. According to Indian tradition, *dharma* is hidden and had to be revealed by competent persons. Since *dharma* was supposed to be the overarching rule of life, everything came under its purview and great care had to be taken to find expressions of *dharma* in particular circumstances. The universal nature of *dharma* also explains the absence of the division between a "religious" and "secular" sphere, so fundamental to the modern West.

The meaning of the word *dharma* has undergone many changes in the course of the millennia,[16] and its revival in the context of today's *Hindu jāgaran* is felt as a threat by Indian secularists. As J.D.M. Derret points out, *dharma* is not the result of theoretical or logical conceptualization but of experience lived through by several generations and interpreted in the spirit of these experiences.[17] It is very malleable and beyond the grasp of outsiders, who do not share this life experience. It is group centered and group oriented. It is based on notions of authority, of duty, of consensus. It is in many ways the very opposite of "law" as understood in the modern West, with its emphasis on equality, rights, and majority votes.

Though from an absolutist, Vedāntist standpoint good and evil are relative, the two sides of one coin as it were, the *dharmaśāstra* tradition of India has labored continuously to separate sharply *dharma* from *adharma*, to spell out quite unambiguously what *righteousness* and *unrighteousness* mean and what they lead to.

Thus the fourth-century logician Vātsyāyana analyzed the elements of both in the following manner: *adharma* as well as *dharma* depend either on body, or speech, or mind. Unrighteousness related to the body is threefold: violence, theft, and unlawful sexual indulgence. Correspondingly righteousness connected with the body consists in charity, succor of the distressed, and social service. The vices originating from speech are: telling lies, caustic talk, calumny, and absurd talk. The corresponding virtues of speech are: veracity, talking with good intention, gentle talk, and recitation of scriptures. *Adharma* connected with the mind is threefold: ill will, covetousness, and irreligious thinking. *Dharma* originating in the mind is kindness, disinterestedness, and faith or piety.[18]

Patañjali's *Yogasūtras* offer a less systematic, but more popular series of virtues necessary for the attainment of peace of mind and are an exposition of *dharma* under the two categories of *yama* and *niyama* (restraints and observances). The *yama* comprise nonviolence, veracity, abstinence from theft, continence, and abstinence from avariciousness; and the *niyama*, purity, contentment, ritual actions, study and "making the Lord the motive of all action."[19] Through these and similar analyses of *dharma* there emerges quite clearly the universal validity of *dharma*, though its motivation and particular application may be typically Hindu. The voluminous *dharmaśāstra* literature that has developed over the centuries contains, as well as casuistry and local law, much that has been at the center of ethical reflection in the West too.[20] As liberal forces in the West fought to change laws, which were defended by conservative institutions as divine or natural laws, so modern Hindus have often found the custodians of *dharma* obstructing the path toward social justice and progress.[21] The defenders of the traditional law allowed the burning of widows, the frequently inhuman ways in which the upper castes treated the outcastes, the superstitions and vices of the past. It is for this reason that many of those who fought for a better lot for the masses became bitter enemies of the

Figure 3.2. Symbols of Hinduism

established order. In recent times voices could be heard from within the tradition advocating reform without overthrowing the entire structure. "Hinduism is not a static structure, but a dynamic force," wrote A. D. Altekar, adding:

> Unfortunately, the truth of this proposition is not sufficiently realized by the Hindus themselves. The orthodox Hindu believes that Hinduism is once and for all time fashioned by the pristine *śāstras* of hoary antiquity; the educated

> Hindu is not sufficiently acquainted with the history of his culture and religion to know their true nature. It was a dark day when the non-official change-sanctioning authority, the Daśāvara Pariṣad of the Smṛti, was replaced by a government department presided over by the Minister for Religion. For, when Hindu rule came to an end in the thirteenth century, this department also disappeared, and during the last six hundred years Hinduism has remained more or less static. With no authoritative and intelligent agency to guide him, the average Hindu believes that religious beliefs, philosophical theories and social practices current in the twelfth century comprise the whole of this tradition and it is his conviction that these beliefs and practices are sanctioned by the scriptures (which he does not understand), and that to depart from them is an unpardonable sin. This utter and pitiable ignorance of the real nature of Hinduism is at the root of the amazing opposition, which measures like the Hindu Code have evoked in the recent past even in educated circles.[22]

There is no doubt that "modernity" has made inroads into traditional Indian *dharma*, and a respected authority like Laxman Shastri Joshi finds that "the moral foundations of Indian society appear to be crumbling rapidly."[23] He sees, to his distress, that "nationalism appears to be taking the place of the old socio-religious consciousness," which he considers "not a healthy product of the new human civilization." He takes a bold stance, however, when he declares: "The need has arisen today for laying the foundations of a new ethics without invoking the aid of collectivity, God or any supernatural or transcendental principle. We need an ethics that will give man the confidence in his powers of creating his own social existence. . . . Morality is the beauty of human existence, it is the rhythm of human life."

Reflections about *dharma* do not, however, remain in the sphere of ethical theory, they enter into very practical issues: laws for the new Indian Republic that would be binding for all the diverse groups of Hindus, who had so far been following a multitude of traditional laws sanctioned by various *śāstras*, and codes of conduct for all those who engage in public activities. India in fact abrogated traditional law in certain sectors, when it declared untouchability to be abolished and discrimination on account of caste to be punishable. As daily life shows in countless instances, the transition is not easy and it can by no means be considered to have been completed.[24]

We shall have constant need to refer to *dharma* when describing the various aspects of Hindu life and doctrine. A few other key concepts for the understanding of religion in the Indian sense will be introduced at this juncture.

## REACHING INDIVIDUAL PERFECTION THROUGH *SĀDHANA*

*Sādhana*, derived from the root *sādh-*, "to finish" or "to accomplish", denotes the "means of realization." One who practices a *sādhana* is a *sādhaka*, a word closely related to the word *sādhu*, the "just man" or "saint." While *dharma* is imposed on persons by nature or by society, they are free to choose their own *sādhana*. While, therefore, there is basically only one *dharma*, there are countless *sādhanas*, which differ considerably and essentially. They are connected insofar as according to the classical *caturvarṇāśrama* scheme the last stage in the life of a brahmin was to be that of *saṃnyāsa*, the life of the wandering ascetic, wholely dedicated to *sādhana*, the pursuit of complete emancipation. The scheme has been departed from quite frequently even in former times; in fact any man or woman can become a member of a *saṃpradāya* (a religious order) and practice the *sādhana* that agrees with his or her condition.[25] Though the classical schema of the three ways is usually applied, there are in fact many more ways; almost every sect and subsect has its own ideas about *sādhana*. All agree, however, in the basic conviction that one is not born free but must liberate oneself through discipline. The analysis of the nature of bondage determines also the nature of the *sādhana*: for the followers of Śaṅkara, bondage consists in an illusion about the real nature of the Self; for the followers of Rāmānuja, it is forgetfulness of the Lord; for many *bhakti* schools it is a wrong emotional attitude toward world and God, and for *śakti* schools a separation from the Mother. *Sādhana* entails bodily as well as mental and spiritual practices. It is usually practiced under the guidance of a guru, through whom the disciple has to search and whom he has to serve. The general name for the ascetic practices is *tapas*, literally, "heat." Some of those practices must go back to prehistoric times; ancient Vedic texts already use the term and sometimes the creation of the universe itself is ascribed to *tapas*. *Tapas* may mean anything, from real self-torture and record-breaking austerities to the recitation of sacred syllables and the chanting of melodies. Fasting, *prāṇayama* (breath control), *japa* (repetition of a name of God or a short *mantra*), and study of scriptures are among the most common practices. At the *melās* one can observe other varieties of *tapas*: lying on a bed of thorns or nails, prolonged standing on one leg, lifting one arm for years till it is withered, looking straight into the glaring sun for long hours, and similar sportive feats. Many ascetics keep silent for years. This is one of the most powerful means of storing up spiritual energy. Although perhaps under Christian influence the practices associated with *sādhanas* are often associated with theistic ideas not very different from the ideas of the value of voluntary suffering and self-mortification, originally they had nothing to do with either ethical perfection or pleasing God. *Tapas* used to be seen as generating psychophysical energy, the accumulation of which determined one's position in the universe. The aim, therefore, was to reach a higher position with greater power through *tapas*. There are numerous stories in Indian literature about forest hermits who had accumulated so much *tapas* that the gods, and even the highest among them, Indra, became afraid of losing their positions. The gods usually sent to the ascetic as their ultimate weapon a bewitchingly beautiful heavenly damsel to confuse his thoughts, or a rude fellow to make him lose his temper in an outburst of anger, thereby burning up all his stored up *tapas* energy. The ascetic would then have to start afresh, unless he decided to embrace another vocation. Those who had gathered enough *tapas* could compel a *deva* to appear, who would have to offer an absolutely effective boon, opening up infinite possibilities for the imagination of authors and poets. The boons are limited by the power of the god, and the *tapasvi* has to make the right choice. If the god is not quick witted enough, the ascetic who called him can also turn the boon against the god. The gods, therefore, usually grant boons with built-in precautions, stipulating the conditions under which the boon will be effective.

A telling story is that of Vikra, who, after practicing severe *tapas* for many years, called on Śiva, asking him to grant the boon that whosoever's head he would touch, that person should die instantly. Śiva laughingly granted the boon, realizing his folly only when Vikra chased his wife and him, to try out the new art. Śiva in his despair sought refuge with Viṣṇu, asking for advice. Viṣṇu cunningly induced doubt in Vikra. Śiva, he told Vikra, cannot always be taken seriously. He might have been joking or lying—so better try it first on yourself. Vikra did so, and thus killed himself with the boon he had received. The story has as its main theme the superiority of Viṣṇu over Śiva, who has to appeal to Viṣṇu to save his life.

## ORTHODOXY BATTLING HERESY

This incident reveals something of the rivalry that exists between the different *saṃpradāyas*, the various churches and sects of Hinduism. The great majority of Hindus belong either to Vaiṣṇavism, Śaivism, or Śāktism; all of them have countless subdivisions, springing from local traditions, cults and a great many religious teachers.[26] Between them there had often been competition for the dominance of Viṣṇu, Śiva, and Devī; not seldom also intolerance and fanatical zeal. In the nineteenth century the *Kumbha Melās*, the occasions when a large number of *sādhus* of all *sampradāyas* congregate, witnessed regular battles between Śaivas and Vaiṣṇavas in which many lost their lives.[27] The immediate reason for the quarrels was usually a question of precedence in the ritual bath at the most auspicious time, but there always lurked a much larger and more important issue: the right belief! Vaiṣṇavas are absolutely sure that Viṣṇu alone is the Lord and that placing Śiva above Viṣṇu is the grossest heresy and unbelief. And Śaivas, of course, know that only Śiva is the Great Lord, whom all must adore and serve and for whose glory they expend themselves. The *Liṅgapurāṇa* promises Śiva's heaven to one who kills or tears out the tongue of someone who reviles Śiva.[28] The Vaiṣṇava scriptures contain not only barbed stories, such as the one about Vikra, but also venomous invectives against all who do not follow Viṣṇu.[29] Considerable friction existed also between the followers of these Purāṇic traditions and the orthodox Vedic Brahmins. The Pāñcarātrins, one of the prominent sects of Vaiṣṇavas, were labelled great sinners, whose existence was the result of killing cows in some former birth. They were accused of being absolutely non-Vedic; further, it was held by the orthodox, that the literatures of the Śāktas, Śaivas, and Pāñcarātras were for the delusion of humankind.[30]

Both Śaivas and Vaiṣṇavas considered the "atheistic" Buddhists and Jains their common enemy. [31] Numerous are the historical instances of persecution of people who refused to conform to the idea of orthodoxy that demanded the acknowledgment of Brahmanical authority and Vedic revelation.[32]

Some authors seem to think that the reception of Buddha among the *avatāras* of Viṣṇu would express a spirit of tolerance. But the way in which this Buddha-*avatāra* is described in the *Viṣṇupurāṇa* and the general Hindu attitude of considering both good and evil as coming from the same Supreme Being would suggest that we have here an early and unmistakably hostile Hindu text dealing with Buddhism.[33]

Buddha is introduced as one of many forms of the *māyā-moha* (delusive power) of Viṣṇu: he engages in what may be termed psychological warfare against the *daityas* on behalf of the *devas*, who have come to take refuge with him. He is sent to destroy the enemies of the Vaiṣṇavas from within. He is characterized as *raktāṃbara*, dressed in a red garment, as *mṛdvalpamadhurākṣara*, speaking gently, calmly and sweetly. The teachings, which he communicates for the self-destruction of the *daityas*, considered as pernicious and heretical by the Hindus, are:

1. The killing of animals for sacrifices should be discontinued.
2. The whole world is a product of the mind.
3. The world is without support.
4. The world is engaged in pursuit of error, which it mistakes for knowledge.

As a result of this teaching the *daityas* abandon the *dharma* of the Vedas and the *smṛtis*, and they induce others to do the same. The same *māyā-moha* of Viṣṇu had appeared before Buddha as "a naked mendicant with shaven head and a bunch of peacock feathers in his hands" and he is to appear again as the preacher of the Cārvāka doctrines.

The *Viṣṇupurāṇa* calls the Ṛk, Yajus, and Sāmaveda the "garments" of a man: a man is naked if he goes without them. The *daityas*, seduced by Buddha, are in such a position. Whereas the *devas* were unable to dislodge the *daityas* before, they now defeat them: "The armor of *dharma*, which had formerly protected the *daityas* had been discarded by them and upon its abandonment followed their destruction."

The *Viṣṇupurāṇa* follows up the story of the defeat of the *daityas* by establishing general rules concerning the treatment of heretics. The text calls them naked, in tune with the aforementioned idea, and sinners. The criterion of orthodoxy is behavior in conformity with the rules laid down for each one of the four *āśramas*. There is no fifth *āśrama*, the text categorically states. Our

Purāṇa shows special concern for the conscientious performance of the daily rites prescribed for the householder; the most prominent features of Buddhists being the neglect of them. A neglect of the daily rites for a year is considered so grave a sin that there is no expiation for it: "There is no sinner upon earth more culpable than one in whose dwelling the *devas*, the *ṛṣis*, the *pitṛs*, and the *bhūtas* are left to sigh without an oblation."

The *Viṣṇupurāṇa* suggests complete excommunication of the Buddhists: all social contact must be broken even; looking at a heretic necessitates lengthy expiations. The Hindu who dines with a Buddhist goes to hell. Buddhists are to be considered as unclean, whatever their caste affiliation may have been. Not only is the Hindu told to have nothing to do with the Buddhist, he must discourage the Buddhist from associating with him: if a heretic observes a faithful one in his rituals, these remain without fruit.

To illustrate its teaching the *Viṣṇupurāṇa* tells the story of king Śatadhanu and his pious wife: the mere conversation of the king with a *pāṣaṇḍa* suffices to let him be reborn as a dog, a wolf, a vulture, a crow, and a peacock before assuming a human body again. The instrument of his salvation is his wife who looked away from the heretic when the king conversed with him and thus remained undefiled.

According to an old tradition it was Śaṅkarācārya who tried to reconcile the rival Hindu traditions in the eighth century by introducing the so-called *pañcāyātana-pūjā*, the simultaneous worship of Gaṇeśa, Sūrya, Viṣṇu, Śiva and Devī, explaining that all deities were but different forms of the one Brahman, the invisible Supreme Being.[34] That this attempt was not well received by all is illustrated by a story in which the followers of Madhva, the "Hammer of the Jainas," explain their master's negative relationship to Śaṅkara and his followers:

> The demon Manimat was born as the illegitimate child of a widow and was therefore called Śaṅkara. He studied the *śāstras* with Śiva's blessings and the depraved welcomed him. He really taught Buddhism under the guise of Vedānta. He seduced the wife of his Brahmin host and used to make converts by his magic arts. When he died, he asked his disciples to kill Satyaprajñā, the true teacher of Vedānta; the followers of Śaṅkara were tyrannical people who burnt down monasteries, destroyed cattle, and killed women and children. They converted Prajñātīrtha, their chief opponent, by force. The disciples of Prajñātīrtha, however, were secretly attached to the true Vedāntic doctrine and they made one of their disciples thoroughly learned in the Vedic scriptures. Acutyaprekṣa, the teacher of Madhva, was a disciple of this true type of teacher, who originated from Satyaprajñā. Madhva was an incarnation of Vāyu for the purpose of destroying the false doctrines of Śaṅkara, which were like the doctrines of the Lokāyatas, Jainas, and Paśupatas, but were more obnoxious and injurious.[35]

The same Śaṅkara is said to have had the Kārpātikas whipped because they were non-Vedic. He founded the Daśanāmi order and established *maṭhas* at four strategic points in India, allocating to each a quarter of India for missionary purposes. Śaṅkara, as described in the *Digvijaya*, "the conquest of space," conformed to the current idea of the *ācārya*, the "doctor" who had to be able to defend his own position against all objections and to defeat his opponents in public debate.

Though quite often the existence of "six viewpoints," accepted as orthodox, is taken as a sign of doctrinal tolerance within Hinduism, each author necessarily identifies himself with one of them and tries to prove the others either wrong or defective. The decision to call a system orthodox or heretical is often based on subjective criteria and sectarian affiliations. Thus Mādhava, a fourteenth-century Advaitin, arranges his *Sarvadarśanasaṁgraha*, the summary of all systems, in such a way that each following system cancels out the preceding one; in the end Advaita Vedānta as expounded by Śaṅkara emerges as the only truth.[36] The Cārvākas—unabashed materialists and hedonists and enemies of the Vedic-Brahmanic religion—are defeated by the Buddhists who in turn are proved wrong by the Jainas. These have to give way to the Rāmānujists, who in turn are superseded by the followers of Madhva. Four schools of Śaivism, the Pāśupata, the Śaiva, the Pratyabhijñā, and the Raseśvara systems, cancel each other out successively. The truth of the next, the Vaiśeṣika system, is overthrown by the Naiyāyikas, who suffer defeat at the hands of the Mīmāṃsakas. These in turn have to give way to the followers of Pāṇini, who are ousted by the Sāṁkhya system. The Yoga system finally comes closest to the truth, which is fully present in Śaṅkara's Advaita Vedānta.

The *Brahmasūtras*, as understood by Śaṅkara, are largely a refutation of non-Vedāntic systems of thought. Not only do they reject the four major schools of Buddhism but also Sāṁkhya and Bhāgavatism. Śaṅkara explains the need for the exposition of Brahman knowledge by stating that "there are many various opinions, partly based on sound arguments and scriptural texts and partly on fallacious arguments and scriptural texts misunderstood. If people would embrace one of these opinions without previous consideration, they would bar themselves from the highest beatitude and incur grievous loss."[37]

Synopses of the various systems from other standpoints will choose a different sequence in order to prove their views right—the accusation hurled against rival sects of not being Vedic or being ignorant of the correct methods of interpretation of texts results either in the insinuation that the doctrines in question reveal crypto-*nāstikas*, or in the "tolerant" opinion that the others have some glimpses of truth mixed with untruth, while the system held by the writer is the whole and sole truth.

Religious Hinduism is unanimous, however, in rejecting the system known as Cārvāka or Lokāyata, a solidly materialistic system that, as part of India's 'realistic' philosophical tradition, has also engaged the attention of Western scholars more recently.[38] The above-mentioned Mādhava writes that he thinks most of his contemporaries in 14th-century India to be Cārvākas, regarding wealth and pleasure as the only aim in life and living according to the motto: "As long as you live enjoy yourself—nobody can escape from death. Once this body is consumed by fire—how will you ever return?" The only reality they acknowledge is material: the four elements—earth, water, air, and fire, together with their combinations. The so-called soul is only a by-product of these, similar to the emergence of alcohol in the fermentation of certain substances. The soul dies with the body. They even quote scripture to corroborate their theories: "Arising from out of these elements, one also reenters into them. When one has departed, there is no more knowledge," says the *Bṛhadāraṇyaka Upaniṣad*.[39] Wisdom consists in aiming at the maximum enjoyment with the least trouble and avoiding grief. To the more pious contemporaries who are asking why one should go to such lengths in organizing sacrifices and religious celebrations, they coolly reply: Religion is only of use for the priests as their means of livelihood; the Vedas are full of untruth and contradictions. The Vedic pandits defeat each other and the authority of the way of knowledge is cancelled by those who advocate the way of works. The Vedas are nothing but the incoherent rhapsodies of swindlers and impostors. It is difficult to surpass the cynicism of the Cārvākas, as illustrated in the following quotation from an otherwise lost work by a certain Bṛhaspati:

> There is no heaven, no spiritual liberation, nor any soul in another world. The good deeds of the various classes do not leave any trace. The *agnihotra*, the three Vedas, the *samnyāsi*'s three staffs, the ashes on one's body are all inventions, made for gaining a livelihood by those who lack vigor and intelligence. If an animal slaughtered in the *jyotiṣṭoma* goes to heaven, why does the sacrificer not immediately kill his father? If *śrāddha*, the sacrifice for the deceased, does profit the dead, then the traveler does not need to take any provisions on his journey. If sacrifice nourishes the beings in heaven, why not those who stand on a rooftop? Let people enjoy their life and let them eat *ghī* even if they have debts. Once the body is burnt, how should he return? Why does one who leaves his body not return for the sake of his relations? I tell you why: all these ceremonies are without value, they have been introduced by the Brahmins for the sake of gain. The authors of the three Vedas were frauds and humbugs. The well-known formulae of pandits, priests and their like, and the obscene ritual prescribed for the queen in the *aśvamedha* were all invented by rogues and demons.[40]

As almost everything else in Hinduism, so also the dichotomy between orthodox and heretics operates differently on different levels. On one level—the level of caste-regulated behavior—the distinction between *āstika* and *nāstika* is quite clear. *Nāstikas* are excommunicated. On another level—the level of personal religiosity and devotion—the distinction is blurred; as caste is not observed in the gatherings of *bhaktas*, so *bhakti* religion offers salvation also to those who are *nāstikas*. It introduces, however, its own criteria for excommunication: sins against the "name" are unforgivable.

The two levels on which Hinduism moves—not only the level of the absolute and the relative—are in constant interaction. The observation of caste rules and Vedic propriety alone would not qualify a person for salvation by Viṣṇu—one needs to be elected by him, an election that has to be earned through acts of devotion and service—but also Vaiṣṇava writers insist on it. However—and here we again switch levels—the perfect one, the saint, the guru, can take liberties with rules and regulations: divine license suspends human law. And again: in a devotional context a person may be considered a saint, a soul close to God, and may still be denied those rights that come from observing caste regulations.

Hindus are used, of course, to compartmentalizing society and accepting a corresponding compartmentalization of right and wrong behavior. The devotee, in *satsaṅg*, moves temporarily into another society—the community of believers, which operates under its own laws. The termination of the *satsaṅg* brings about the termination of this status—all move back into the caste they were born into.

Though it may be impossible to establish criteria of "orthodoxy" that would find acceptance by all Hindus, it would not be correct to conclude that such an idea is absent from Hinduism and that we have to substitute for it instead an idea of "orthopraxy."[41] Doctrinal issues have been discussed by Hindus throughout the ages with tenacity and also with the understanding that there is always an aspect of absolute truth reflected in any particular religious doctrine. While there has never been one central authority in Hinduism strong enough to decide the issue categorically, the numerous heads of the various Hindu churches have nevertheless established very rigorous canons from within which their understanding of orthodoxy is defined.[42] Thus they clearly determine which books have to be considered as revelation, which authors may be used as commentators, and which line of tradition must be followed. Students of religion in traditional institutions were not supposed to read other books or to listen to any other teacher. This often makes them incapable of appreciating or understanding any version of Hinduism that differs from their own; even today the debates between pandits of different schools are often quite acrimonious and filled with narrow-minded attempts to "defeat" each other. The more recent history of Hinduism is also not free from intolerance: the Ārya Samāj and its offspring, the Hindū Mahāsabhā and the Rāṣṭrīya Svayaṃsevak Saṅgh, and similar organizations have intimidated and often provoked non-Hindus. They have been responsible for inciting riots and for atrocities in the name of the one true religion. The Hindutva agitation, leading up to the infamous destruction of the Babri Masjid in Aydhoyā and the subsequent riots in many places have opened the eyes of many to the large potential of intolerance present in today's political Hinduism.[43]

In a nonviolent, but nevertheless very effective, way the caste *pañcāyats* and the leaders of *saṃpradāyas* have always exercised control over their members, carefully watching them and enforcing their views of orthodoxy, if necessary through imposition of penances or expulsion from the community. Hinduism may appear to be very vague and extremely tolerant to the outsider, but the insider must conform to very precise regulations of life within the group. *Svadharma*, everyone's peculiar set of duties and obligations, orders and restricts each person's life. Those who have achieved freedom from social duties by choosing *samnyāsa* must conform to the precise rules of their own particular *saṃpradāya*, if they do not want to risk being reprimanded by zealous colleagues. When *sādhus* meet they first ask one another about the *saṃpradāya* and their guru; quite often they remonstrate with one another, pointing out violations of rules and customs. There is a *yati*-dharma, a code of behavior for *samnyāsis* that everyone has to follow. As long as someone lives with a guru one has to serve her or him conscientiously and loyally, without showing any sign of an independent opinion. For many the guru represents God; to contradict the guru would be blasphemy; blind faith and unquestioning service are considered to be the way to eternal bliss, and the attitude of certain gurus toward the rest of humanity consists, at an advanced age, of a mixture of limitless arrogance, naive self-deceit, and megalomania, not infrequently supported by European and American admirers.

Rivalries between different denominations of Hinduism acquire in our time, quite often, political overtones. Thus a recent takeover of the Vaiṣṇa Devī shrine by an independent board supported by the governor of Kashmir resulted in a bitter exchange between Karan Singh, the President of the Virāt Hindū Samāj and Governor Jagmohan. Karan Singh accused Jagmohan of being an Ārya Samājist, and as such being against image worship, whereas he himself defended the rights of the Dharmārth Trust that is "responsible for the advancement and promotion of Sanātana Dharma."[44] In early 1993 members of the RSS who had been in the forefront of the Ayodhyā agitation forcibly installed Rama pictures in Kṛṣṇa-temples and disturbed a popular Kṛṣṇa festival in Kerala.[45]

CHAPTER THREE

# The Veda

## *Revelation and Scripture in Hinduism*

> Let the scriptures be your standard for what should be done and what should not be done. Knowing the regulations of the scriptures you should do your work here.
>
> —*Bhagavadgītā* XVI, 24

No other living tradition can claim scriptures as numerous or as ancient as Hinduism; none of them can boast of an unbroken tradition as faithfully preserved as the Hindu tradition. The sources of Hinduism are not only historical materials to be worked up by the scholar of antiquity; they have been recited and studied by the faithful throughout the ages. The reading of a Hindu religious scripture is always carried out with some kind of solemnity in a worship setting. In order to ward off all unfavorable influences and to create an auspicious disposition, a so-called *maṅgala-śloka* is recited before the text proper begins, hymns of praise and devotion to a number of deities, to the guru, and to the text to be read. Time, place, and the external circumstances of the recitation are regulated, and the reading itself is usually done in a prescribed recitative.[1] It is essential to observe all these rules in order to obtain the fruits of the reading, which are quite often spelled out concretely at the end of the scripture itself.[2] The reading is not terminated abruptly either. The last sentence is read twice, thus indicating the end of the reading. The gods who were addressed in the beginning are now implored to forgive all inattention, disrespect, and incorrect or imperfect reading; this is the so-called *aparādha kṣamā pañca stotra*, marking the conclusion of the recitation. The book of scripture itself is always treated with reverence; it is never laid on the bare floor and is carefully guarded against all disrespect. In former times Hindus did not allow people from low castes or foreigners to read or to possess their sacred books; nowadays anyone can buy printed copies (and quite often translations also) of Hindu scriptures in a bookstore. Though secular Western scholarship has begun to analyze and dissect the Hindu scriptures, Hindus continue to regard them as revelations,[3] given to their ancestors as special privilege, and they resent the secularist view that sees in them only ancient literature. Before the sacred lore was written down, it existed for untold centuries as an oral tradition handed down from generation to generation.[4] It was committed to writing only at a relatively late period in its history—and even now the proper study consists in memorizing the texts. The authentic Hindu tradition consists of that chain of authorities in which the oral tradition has been kept alive.[5]

The various sacred books of the Hindus are not all considered to hold the same degree of revelation. Hindu scholars developed early on a precise and widely accepted theological epistemology, according to which all authoritative literature is categorized. The *prasthāna trayī*, the triad of instruments for the attainment of religious knowledge for the sake of salvation, consists of *śruti*, *smṛti*, and *nyāya*. From Śaṅkara (Eighth century CE) onward, the Vedāntins identified these with the Upaniṣads, the *Bhagavadgītā* and the *Brahmasūtras*. Other schools, for example, the Mīmāṃsakas would not agree with this. As the different branches of Hinduism differ in their ideas concerning orthodoxy and heresy, so they differ also in their recognition of certain classes of scriptures and their relative position in this scheme.

## REVELATION PROPER: *ŚRUTI*

*Śruti* literally means "that which has been perceived through hearing"; it is "revelation" in the most immediate sense. As a technical term it comprises the scriptures with the highest theological value, containing supreme and unquestionable authority. *Śruti* may be commented upon, but it can never be questioned. In theological debates discussion is carried on only for the purpose of establishing the meaning of *sruti*. Hārīta, an author of an early *Dharmasūtra*[6] holds the opinion that *śruti* is of two kinds, the Vedic and the Tantric or Āgamic. He thereby acknowledges the fact that in his time the non-Vedic traditions had become powerful enough to claim a position equal to that of the Veda, which originally had held this title exclusively. Even now the *sanātanists*, the followers of the Vedic *dharma*, refuse to acknowledge the *Āgamas*, the scriptures of the Vaiṣṇavas, Śaivas, and Śāktas as *śruti*. This is a rather unrealistic position, since for more than a thousand years Hindu religion has been much more influenced by the *Āgamas* than by the Vedas, and even the acknowledged *ācāryas* of Vedānta accepted the *Āgamas* and shaped their interpretation of Vedic texts accordingly.[7]

For all practical purposes, then, we have to accept two mainstreams of *śruti*, though no Hindu will allow that all the scriptures accepted by the one or the other Hindu *saṃpradāya* are revelation and therefore are of any consequence to him.

The Veda, sacred knowledge, comprises several categories of literature: *saṃhitās, brāhmaṇas, āraṇyakas,* and (early) *upaniṣads.* The date of the final codification is controversial—it took place after hundreds of years of oral transmission.[8] The earliest part, the Veda in the strict sense, is divided into four *saṃhitās* or collections: *Ṛgveda,*[9] a collection of more than a thousand hymns addressed to various gods; *Sāmaveda,*[10] a collection of extracts from the former with the appropriate musical instructions for recitation; *Yajurveda,*[11] the book of Vedic ceremonies; and *Atharvaveda,*[12] a heterogeneous collection of hymns and spells. The four Vedas are neither sacred history nor doctrine; they are the instruments for the performance of the *yajña,* the sacrifice, which stood at the center of Vedic religion.[13]

Traditional scholars correlate the secular learning of the Hindus as *Upavedas,* or supplementary knowledge, with the four Vedas: *Arthaveda,* the science of statecraft and politics with the *Ṛgveda; Gandharvaveda,* music and the fine arts with the *Sāmaveda; Dhanuṣveda,* the art of archery (and warfare in general) with *Yajurveda;* and *Āyurveda,* medicine and biology, with the *Atharvaveda.*[14]

Despite the existence of four Vedas, the *Ṛgveda* occupies a special position as *śruti.* Because of the importance given to the exact wording, to the very sounds and syllables of the text itself, a series of auxiliary sciences for the study of the Veda, the *Vedāṅgas,* came early into existence as an essential part of the Brahmin's training.[15] Among them *Śīkṣā* deals with precise and faultless pronunciation; *Kalpa* discusses the details of ritual; *Vyākaraṇa* is the

Photo 8. Contemporary Vedic fire altars: Vṛndāvana

study of grammar, including some linguistics and philology; *Nirukta* treats the etymology of unusual and rare words; *Chaṇḍa* specializes in the explanation and practice of verse meters; and *Jyotiṣa* teaches planetary science—astronomy and astrology together—which was (and is) the instrument for determining the right moment for religious acts.[16] Though the *Vedāṅgas* are not part of the *śruti*, they are indispensable for those who have to perform Vedic rituals.

The thoroughness of these auxiliary sciences is quite extraordinary: in order to hand down the text of the hymns of the *Ṛgveda* orthologically, special mnemonic and reading techniques were developed. In addition to memorizing the text of the *samhitās*, the Vedic student had to learn the *pada-pāṭha* (the "word text", where the words were given in their original and complete form) the *krama-pāṭha* ("step text," where each word was connected both with the preceding and the following word), the *jaṭa-pāṭha* ("braided text," involving a reverse recitation); and the *ghana-pāṭha* ("dense text," involving a complicated series of combinations and retrocombinations of words). A class of works called *Pratiśākhyas* described all the grammatical changes necessary for constituting the *saṃhitā* text out of the *pada-pāṭha*.[17]

The hymns themselves were never simply read aloud, but they had to be recited in an exactly prescribed pitch. Through Vedic recitation, "Brahmins gain merit and perfection and contribute to the sacred order of the universe."[18] Although the text of the *Ṛgveda* remained unchanged throughout India for thousands of years, different styles of recitation developed and were preserved in different parts of the country. The recitation had to be accompanied by precisely studied movements of the right arm and of the fingers according to accent and pitch. A young Brahmin had to go through many years of intensive training before he was qualified to officiate at a sacrifice. Since it was believed that a single mispronounced syllable could spoil the entire costly arrangement, extreme care was taken to perfect the Brahmin's training. Harsh punishment awaited the offender: a Brahmin who read the Veda without the correct movements of the hand faced expulsion from his caste; one who did not pay attention to the exact length of the syllables, to cadences and tunes, was threatened with being reduced to ashes and being reborn as a vile animal. The effect of the mantra was supposed to depend on its correct pronunciation rather than on the meaning of a sentence or the action of a deity. The *Śatapatha Brāhmaṇa* relates a telling myth: Tvaṣṭṛ, whose son Viśvarūpa had been killed by Indra, is about to conjure up, with a soma-libation, *Vṛtra indraśatruḥ*, the one who cannot fail to kill Indra because in him the powers of all *devas* are combined. Because of a wrong accent in the infallible mantra, the one who intended to kill Indra is destined unfailingly to be killed by Indra.[19] This belief in the literal efficacy of the mantra was analyzed and systematized in one of the recognized orthodox schools, the *Pūrva Mīmāṃsā*.

The *Brāhmaṇas*, a voluminous collection of writings, deal mainly with explanations of the sacrifice and contain early versions of many myths. They are also considered part of *śruti*,[20] as are the *Āraṇyakas*, the forest-treatises and the Upaniṣads. The two latter classes of writings are sometimes intermingled[21] and they contain similar materials. The Upaniṣads are also called the *Vedānta*, the end of the Veda: they mark the latest part of the Veda, and they are regarded as the end and aim of the Veda. Within *śruti* a twofold division obtains: *Karmakaṇḍa* and *Jñānakaṇḍa*. The Vedic *Saṃhitās* and the *Brāhmaṇas*, which center around the sacrifice, make up the "part of action", systematized by *Pūrva Mīmāṃsā*; the *Āraṇyakas* and the Upaniṣads, with their emphasis on speculation and intuitive knowledge, form the *Jñānakaṇḍa*, the part of wisdom. This has found its systematic development in the numerous schools of Vedānta philosophy. The most authoritative Vedāntins quote from about fifteen Upaniṣads; whereas popular modern editions contain 108 Upaniṣads.[22] Besides these at least one hundred more *Upaniṣads* have been composed in recent centuries; even today certain sects and schools mold their teachings in the form of an Upaniṣad to lend it greater authority with the orthodox.[23] Each one of the Upaniṣads belongs to one of the Vedic *Saṃhitās*; thus there are *Ṛgveda Upaniṣads*, *Sāmaveda Upaniṣads* and so on. Among the *Saṃhitās* again, different traditions are distinguished, pointing out the fact that Vedic religion developed within, and was handed over by, a number of families, each of which kept its own particular traditions and rites within the general frame of Vedic religion.[24] The Upaniṣads in their imagery show quite clearly the specific family relationship. Thus the *Bṛhadaraṇyaka Upaniṣad*, belonging to the white *Yajurveda*, begins its cosmogonic and soteriological speculations with a metaphorical explanation of the horse sacrifice, which is the specific symbol of the white *Yajurveda* and treated prominently in the *Śatapatha Brāhmaṇa*, which belongs to the same school. The Upaniṣads contain a good deal of "mystical" practice and theory, but they have also numerous allusions to the rites and ceremonies of the Vedas.

The later Upaniṣads are compendia of doctrines of various schools of Hinduism and really belong to the Āgamas, a class of literature considered as authoritative and as ancient as the Vedas by the followers of Vaiṣṇavism, Śāivism, and Śāktism—that is, by the majority of Hindus.

The term *āgama*, used to describe traditional teachings, is often used to denote all writings that are considered revealed by the Hindus. More specifically the term is used in connection with non-Vedic scriptures, considered to be revelation by particular Hindu sects. Thus we have traditional lists of 108 *Pāñcarātra* or Vaiṣṇava Āgamas (also called Saṃhitās), 28 Śāiva Āgamas and 77 Śākta Āgamas (also called Tantras). Each of these branches of Hinduism has numerous subdivisions, and the recognition of a scripture depends on one's affiliation with one of them.[25] In the most specific sense the scriptures of the Śaivites are called *Āgamas*. They normally consist of four parts: *jñāna* or knowledge, *yoga* or concentration, *krīya* or rituals, and *cārya* or rules for daily life. The latter two parts are considered to be the most important and are usually the most extensive, since they affect worship and life in a major way. This class of scriptures had been for a long time neglected by Western scholars.

After the pioneering work of F. O. Schrader,[26] others followed, and a steady stream of text editions and translations has been appearing lately. The Āgamas have been found important not only as sources for the beliefs and practices of the sects by which they have been adopted as scriptures but also for the study of the cultural history of India. They often contain detailed information on temple building, image making, and performance of public festivals. According to G. S. Murti:

> The *Āgama* is fundamentally a *Sādhana śāstra* . . . it prescribes a particular way of life and a practical course of self-discipline in conformity with the theoretical teachings of its philosophy. It also governs, to a considerable degree, the forms of worship performed in the temples and the forms of rituals performed in the homes. . . . For the past hundreds of years the Vedic sacrifices or *yajñas* have largely given place—especially in South India—to resplendent rituals of temple-worship based on the *Āgamas* . . .[27]

The Purāṇas—another large class of sacred books of Hinduism, about which more detail will be provided in the next chapter—are sometimes considered scriptures too. Thus Vaiṣṇavas would quote the *Viṣṇu Purāṇa* and the *Bhāgavata Purāṇa* side by side with the Upaniṣads as equal in authority. *Purāṇas* as well as *Āgamas* make claims to be direct revelations of the god, with whom they are affiliated and contain numerous passages in which the Supreme God is the speaker and promulgator of commands. More general Hindu practice would assign them a place within *smṛti*.[28]

The *Bhagavadgītā* has acquired a special position within Hinduism: it calls itself an Upaniṣad, claiming the authority of the *śruti*. It no doubt comes from the Vedānta tradition, but it also shows strongly *āgama* influences; traditional authorities of Vedānta philosophy consider it the *smṛti-prasthāna*.

In between *Śruti* and *smṛti* come the numerous *sūtras*, with regard to authority. They are short compendia summarizing the rules concerning public sacrifices (*Śrautasūtras*), domestic rites (*Gṛhyasūtras*), and general religious law (*Dharmasūtras*)—collectively called the *Kalpasūtras*. Since they do not usually contain new revelation, they are not quoted in doctrinal arguments.[29]

## SACRED TRADITION: *SMṚTI*

*Smṛti*, literally, "that which has been remembered," tradition, constitutes the second highest religious authority. The term *smṛti* is used in either a narrower sense, comprising only the *Dharmaśāstras*, or in a wider sense, including *Itihāsa* and *Purāṇa*. The *smṛtis* in the narrow sense are associated with specific family traditions within Vedic religion. Their rules are therefore not always identical, and in case of doubt each Brahmin was bound to follow his own *smṛti* rather than any other authority. The *smṛtis* as we have them today must have been preceded by centuries of development: the many references to former lawgivers and scholars establish again an unbroken succession of *dharma*.[30]

Among the *smṛtis* the *Manusmṛti* occupies a special place and has been more widely accepted than any other such code. Manu is considered the ancestor of the entire human race and the lawgiver for all humankind; he did not make the law but promulgated the revealed *dharma* as it applied to different classes of society. Their main castes and the regulation of life according to the *caturvarṇāśrama* scheme are connected with creation itself, the description of which forms the first part of the book. After dealing with what one expects from a law book—rules for castes, duties of individual classes of people, civil and criminal law, sacrifices and atonements—the book concludes with an excursus on transmigration and supreme bliss.[31] Although it certainly allows us glimpses of social life in ancient India we must bear in mind that such books often do not reflect the actual conditions but an ideal aimed at by the authorities.[32] Among the numerous other *smṛtis*, *Yājñavalkyasmṛti* and *Viṣṇusmṛti* deserve special mention. The latter already includes a Vaiṣnava interpretation of *dharma*.[33]

For daily life *smṛti* is often of greater importance than *śruti*; it affects the life of every Hindu in many details. The most orthodox Hindus are called the *smārtas*, followers of tradition, which still influences Indian society to a very large degree.[34] A good deal of the material of both *śruti* (in the Vedic sense) and *smṛti* has been incorporated into *Itihāsa-Purāṇa*, literally "ancient history." It comprises the two great epics, the *Mahābhārata* and the *Rāmāyaṇa*, as well as the eighteen *Mahāpurāṇas*; some schools claim the title also for a large number of so-called *Upapurāṇas*.[35] Since these books are written in a more popular style, containing many stories and examples, they have found a place in the heart of the Indian masses and even today probably exert a much greater influence on the mind and imagination of the majority of Indian people than any other literature. The *Mahābhārata* and the eighteen *Mahāpurāṇas* are said to have been composed by Vyāsa Kṛṣṇadvaipayana: the same ṛṣi who, according to tradition, compiled the Veda in response to revelation (see Figure 4.1). This enhances the authority of these books as sources of religion and law. It is in the Purāṇas, however, that the split between the various branches of Hinduism becomes most pronounced, and many chapters in them are narrowly sectarian in character.[36]

The core of the *Purāṇas* may well be as old as the Vedas; we read in some Upaniṣads that *Purāṇas* were narrated during the protracted sacrificial sessions. The *Purāṇas* quite frequently contain the full or expanded versions of myths alluded to in the Vedic hymns, and tales of heroes and gods even antedating the Veda may have been preserved in them. Attempts to reconstruct the *Ur-Purāṇa* or the "Original *Purāṇa Saṃhitā*" have not been very successful, and therefore scholars have concentrated on studies of the *Vāyu-Purāṇa* as most probably containing most of its ancient form.[37]

The texts of the epics and Purāṇas that we have in our printed editions have been fixed only between the fourth and the tenth centuries CE, but the materials contained in them belong very often to a much earlier period. The

Figure 4.1. Sage Vyāsa dictating the *Mahābhārata* to Gaṇeśa

Purāṇas had been long neglected by modern scholars; only recently has their value as sources for historical and geographical information been vindicated. For a knowledge of popular Hinduism as it is, and has been for some centuries, they are indispensable.

The *Itihāsa Purāna* has, in the course of time, absorbed almost the entire religious literature, including the philosophical speculation of the *darśanas*, so that pious Hindus could claim to have *śruti*, *smṛti*, and *nyāya*—the whole religion—while reading their *Purāṇa*.

## THE INTERPRETATION OF THE REVEALED WORD

*Nyāya*, *pramāṇa*, or *yukti*—logical argument or rational proof—is the third avenue of religious knowledge in Hinduism. *Nyāya* too is used in a general sense of logical proof and as the specific name of a school of thought, which specialized in logic and epistemology.[38] All Hindu theologians clarify at the beginning of their treatises their evaluation of the traditional six sources of knowing, determining which of them they consider as means for religious knowledge. These modes are: *pratyakṣa*, or sense perception, *anumāna*, or inference, *śabda*, or authority (especially of scriptures), *upamāna* or analogy, *arthāpatti*, or hypothetical supposition, and *abhāva*, or nonperception. Religious knowledge derives mostly from *śabda*, the Word. Centuries before the West had developed its own brand of linguistic analytical philosophy, Indian theologians had evolved the most sophisticated philosophy of language, in whose controversies many interesting problems of a theological nature are raised. As T. R. V. Murti says:

> Indian philosophy has rightly considered language and thought as intimately related. The *Nyāya-Vaiśeṣika* is essentially a philosophy of *padārtha*, the meaning of words. As in Aristotle, here also categories of language are categories of Being. . . . Both the *Pūrva* and *Uttara Mīmāṃsā* do not profess to be anything more than an exegesis of the Revealed Word (the Veda).[39]

The most important contributions to the elucidation of the Word have been made by the Pūrva Mīmāṃsakas and the grammarians. For the Brahmanical tradition language itself is of divine origin, the Spirit descending and embodying itself in phenomena, assuming various guises and disclosing its real nature to the sensitive soul.[40] The *Mīmāṃsakas* analyze the problem: What makes a word meaningful? They found as answer that it is the connection of the word with *akṛti*, the Uncreated Idea that as such is incomprehensible and never exhausted by the individual word. *Śabda* is in this form ever-present and eternal. We do not always perceive it, because its perception depends on its manifestation through the physical word sound. If it were not eternal the word could not be understood every time it is uttered. The word, which we speak and hear, is only a partial manifestation of an eternal, meaningful reality; it is not produced by our utterance. Since the word is not an effect, it is not perishable either.[41]

The school of Pāṇini, the grammarian, developed this *śabda* philosophy further in the theory of *sphoṭa*. Etymologically *sphoṭa* means a boil that, when opened, suddenly ejects it contents. Applied to the problem here, it illustrates the fact that the meaning of a word appears suddenly after the syllables have been pronounced—none of the individual syllables convey either part or the whole of the meaning. Thus they say:

> The eternal word, called *sphoṭa*, without parts and the cause of the world, is verily Brahman. Thus it has been declared by Bhartṛhari: "Brahman without beginning or end is the indestructible essence of speech—it shines forth in the meaning of all things and out of it comes the whole world"![42]

Ultimately, according to this school, all words denote the Supreme Brahman and they maintain that "one who is well-versed in the Word-Brahman attains to the Supreme Brahman."[43]

Language had been one of the main concerns of Indians throughout the ages. Pāṇini, probably in the sixth century BCE wrote "the first scientific grammar, "unsurpassed as a single-handed achievement even today. His *Aṣṭādhyāyī*[44] introduces a perfect phonetic system of the Sanskrit alphabet, offers an astonishingly complete analysis of the contemporary linguistic materials, and is the first work to trace words to a limited number of verbal roots.[45] There were grammarians before him as his references reveal, and there followed others, notably Kātyāyana and Patañjali[46] to complete and develop the work. Similarly the Dravidians occupied themselves with linguistic studies of which the *Tolkāppiam* is particularly renowned for its age and its perception.[47] Language itself, and not only the scriptures, was considered "divine," an attribute that even extended to the characters in which it was written.[48]

## VEDIC INTERPRETATION

It is in the study of the Veda in the strict sense where Western and Indian scholarship disagree most sharply. Modern Western Veda scholarship was initiated by Eugéne Burnouf in Paris (1801–1852) and reached a first peak in the work of his two pupils Rudolph Roth (1821–1895) and Friedrich Max Müller (1823–1903). Roth provided the educated European public with the first detailed and accurate knowledge of the Veda but he also held on to European aims in the study of the Veda: according to him the study of the Veda was not meant "to ascertain the meaning that Sāyaṇa or Yāska attributed to the hymns"[49] but to read the hymns as "lyrics" separate from the "theological" background. Müller was the first to edit and print the entire Ṛgveda Saṃhitā together with Sāyaṇa'a commentary, and he received respect from the Indian pandits for this. His translations, however, were "Western" in outlook and intention. Among Western scholars, R. Pischel (1849–1908) and K. F. Geldner (1852–1921) were the only ones to consider the "Ṛgveda as a purely Indian document to be interpreted, not with the help of comparative linguistics or mythology, but with the later, even classical literature of the subcontinent."

There are, by now, several complete translations of the Ṛgveda into Western languages. Each of them is unsatisfactory.[50] Jan Gonda considers the Ṛgveda an "untranslatable corpus" and concludes:

> The distance in time, space and cultural environment between the authors of the Veda and modern Indologists, the incompleteness of our sources, the reinterpretation suggested by the Indian traditionalists and the prejudices and limitations of modern scholarship itself have contributed to a deplorable state of affairs. The very plurality of meanings so frequently given in our dictionaries show that a modern language cannot in many cases offer one single equivalent of an ancient Indian term.[51]

According to traditional Indian rules, the Veda could be interpreted in three ways—the choice being left to the interpreters, which of the three alternatives they choose. Thus one could understand the hymns either as relating to sacrificial rites (*adhiyajña*), or to deities (*adhidaivata*), or to the Self (*adhyātma*). To explain the widely divergent interpretations of the Veda—some modern Hindus believe that the Vedas contain the principles of nuclear physics or that Western scientific progress was due to the "stealing of the Veda" from India in the nineteenth century—it may be helpful to remember with R. N. Dandekar that "though the Veda was regarded as the final authority, complete freedom was allowed in its interpretation."[52]

In the period of perhaps close to six thousand years since the hymns of the Veda came into existence, and through which the text has been preserved with unparalleled fidelity, the meaning given to the words of the Veda has undergone several drastic changes. The very use of the word *vid*—from which the name Veda is derived—in the hymns themselves suggests that the Vedic texts were "viewed as being verbal expressions of sacred knowledge".[53] The hymns describe and praise the (Vedic) gods whom to know was the privilege of the Āryans, and whose worship secured their protection. Speaking was considered a very important activity, and addressing the gods counted as prerogative of the highest class of people, the Brahmins, who took the very name of their *varṇa* from the designation of the sacred word. *Brahman*, derived from the root *bṛh* = to grow, to become great, was originally identical with the Vedic word, that makes people prosper: words were the principal means to approach the gods who dwelled in a different sphere. It was not a big step from this notion of "reified speech-act" to that "of the speech-act being looked at implicitly and explicitly as a means to an end."[54] Viśvamitra claims that his powerful words (*brahman*) protect his Bhārata clan. In contrast to the speakers of false speech—the non-Āryans—whose words are like a barren cow and bear neither flowers nor fruits,[55] the Veda is the source of everything good and beneficial. No wonder, since the "gods themselves created the godly speech."[56] Vedic prayer—*brahman*—reified and personified, resulted in the figures of the creator god Brahmā, and later in the Upaniṣadic notion of Brahman as the metaphysical principle of everything and the hidden ground of reality.[57] The word—*vāk*, of feminine gender—appears in the famous *Vāk-sūkta* of the *Ṛgveda* (125) as the Goddess singing her own praises as sustainer of the gods and preserver of the world. When the texts of the Veda were used exclusively in the context of the Vedic sacrifice (*yajña*), the sacrifice was considered the source of the three Vedas and they were used instrumentally as part of the mechanism of the sacrifice, for which it did not matter what intrinsic meaning the words had. Kautsa, a teacher mentioned in the *Nirukta* by Yāska (ca. 500 BCE), a work devoted to an etymology of Vedic words that were no longer understood by ordinary people, held that the word of the Veda was no longer perceived as meaningful "normal" speech but as a fixed sequence of sounds, whose meaning was obscure beyond recovery. While the text itself was preserved through a variety of mnemonic devices (*vikṛrtis* = modifications), the preservation of its meaning obviously was more difficult. The difficulty had much to do with changing paradigms of thought. Since writing was considered sacrilegious, efforts were made to transmit the sounds of the text in their proper sequence without paying as much attention to its understanding.

Subhash Kak has recently come up with a fascinating attempt at "decoding" the *Ṛgveda* that might have immense implications for our understanding not only of the *Ṛgveda*. According to him "the *Ṛgveda* is a Stonehenge in words", an astronomical code. Using clues from the *Śatapatha Brahmaṇa*, that refer to the "Veda as an altar of words" and comparing instructions for the building of Vedic fire altars with astronomical data, he arrived at startling conclusions concerning the observational skills of the Vedic Indians and the astronomical information contained in the *Ṛgveda* as a whole and in some hymns in particular. In his opinion "altars were man's way of trying to reach the sky. So is this book. Its entire makeup represents space and sky. It is clearly a symbolic altar."[58] Kak believes that the astronomical paradigm was lost about three thousand years ago and replaced by a different one, which made it impossible to recognize the astronomical information contained in the *Ṛgveda*.

The effort of the grammarians went in the direction of preserving and interpreting the Vedic texts for ritual application, not for cosmological understanding. Patañjali, the author of the *Mahābhāṣya*, declares *veda-rakṣa*, preservation of the Vedic text, the first and foremost task of Sanskrit grammar. Its second most important task was to supply rules for the modification of Vedic texts in ritual settings. It was the duty of Brahmans to study the text and to learn its proper pronunciation. A purely instrumental use of the Veda was promoted through *Mīmāṃsā*. As M. M. Deshpande has it: "The Vedas have come a long way from being living speech-acts of certain Aryan priests of ancient India, and the Indian tradition now reveres them mostly as preserved sacred texts which are chanted in ritual performances and which remain only in a theoretical sense the basic texts of modern Hinduism."[59]

## THE POWER OF THE REVEALED WORD

Words of blessings and of curses were always taken seriously by the Hindus, and an almost material substantiality was attached to them that would bring about their realization almost automatically. The mantra, used in connection with the Vedic sacrifice, works without fail. The Word is a power that makes the gods subject to the will of man. "Brahman is the word" and the Brahmin its keeper and lord. Speech itself was addressed as a deity already in the *Ṛgveda*.[60] In later Hinduism the body of a divinity was considered to consist of mantras that are identical with cosmic processes. No sacrifice could be performed without words. The *Atharvaveda* has mantras for and against everything: there are mantras to cure fever and illness, to awaken love and affection, to raise enmity and hatred, and to sicken and kill an enemy. Tantric Hinduism operated with esoteric syllables that were meaningless for the non-initiate but full of significance and power for the one who had received *dīkṣā*.[61]

The most famous most powerful and most mysterious of all mantras is OM (AUM) also called *prāṇava*, the primeval mantra. Many expositions have been brought forward, none of them fully convincing. The texts that speak of OM suggest that it has to be understood from within the context of the mantra theory. A mantra need not have an intelligible word meaning; it is the sound equivalent of reality and at the same time the medium by which this otherwise transcendent reality is reached. OM is not a concept of something but it is the *Śabda-brahman*, the Supreme Being in the form of sound. It is the primeval sound, the medium between pure, spiritual *brahman* and the concrete material world. The *Chāṇḍogya Upaniṣad* calls OM the "all-word."[62] Through the identification of important concepts and beings, the mantra OM, otherwise empty, is filled with concepts and meaning. The recitation of OM on the one hand reduces all beings into the nothing of OM, "the image of the supreme reality." On the other hand the recitation makes OM itself meaningful without, however, identifying it with any particular being. The *Māṇḍūkya Upaniṣad* identified AUM with the four stages of consciousness: A stands for the waking state, *U* for dream, M for deep sleep; AUM in its totality corresponds to *turīya*, the transcendent state. There is no logical proof for the statement "Om is Brahman"[63]—it is *Śruti*, revelation! "OM—this syllable is the whole world. Its further explanation is: the past, the present, and the future—everything is just the word OM. And whatever else that transcends threefold time—that too is just the word OM . . . OM is the *ātman* . . ."[64] OM stands at the beginning of every hymn and every religious action, as well as of every recitation of a sacred text. With OM everything finds its conclusion.

Since the sacred texts themselves have the quality of *mantras*, the opinion could develop that it is ultimately unimportant whether their meaning is understood or not. Many Brahmins who traditionally function at the occasions where the recitation of Vedic mantras is required, such as at marriage and cremation, do not really understand their meaning. The blessing derived from scripture does not depend on its comprehension, as the example of the *Śrimad Bhāgavata Māhātmya* explains:

> One who daily recites the *Bhāgavata*, with the uttering of every single letter gathers as much merit as one would get by the gift of a brown cow. One who daily listens to half or even a quarter of a verse from the *Bhāgavata* gathers merit as from the gift of a thousand cows. It is better to keep half or quarter of a verse from the *Bhāgavata* in one's house than a collection of hundreds and thousands of other holy books. The glorious and holy *Bhāgavata* confers long life, freedom from disease and good health. One who recites it or listens to it is freed from all sins. To the one who prostrates before a copy of the *Bhāgavata* I give wealth.[65]

Following this exhortation, rich merchants arrange frequently for the reading of holy books over loudspeaker systems. Hired Brahmins recite the whole book without interruption. Hardly anyone listens—it is enough to recite the text faithfully in order to gain merit.

The whole life of a Hindu is enveloped in mantras. According to the most orthodox rules the conception of a child is supposed to be accompanied by the recitation of mantras; mantras are spoken over the expectant mother before birth; birth itself, name giving, initiation and marriage, purification and temple visits, death and cremation, all have to be performed with *mantras*. At the time of initiation ascetics receive a personal mantra, whispered into the ear by the guru. This will be *their* mantra, their *daimonion*, through which they distinguish themselves from all the others: it is a name that nobody knows but devotee and master. They are not permitted to divulge this secret word unless they themselves have to give *dīkṣa* to their disciples. Many Hindus carry mantras written on tiny pieces of paper in small capsules of copper, silver, or gold, fastened to arms, legs, or necks to protect themselves from certain illnesses or as a safeguard against the evil eye.

Time and again this faith in the effectiveness of mantras leads to scurrilous happenings. Some years ago a businessman had lodged a complaint with the police against a *sādhu* who had boasted of a miraculous mantra through which he could double any given amount of money. With great expectations the businessman gave the holy man two thousand rupees. The *sādhu*, however, disappeared with the amount before he had doubled it.[66]

The understanding of Scripture as mantra[67] should neither obscure the importance of the understandable content nor the tremendous effort of countless generations of Hindus to derive meaning from it and to build up a coherent system of philosophical religious thought. The desire for comprehension led at a very early stage to the elaboration of the *sūtras*, in which the essentials of certain branches of knowledge are condensed and systematized. One of the most important works of this kind is the *Brahmasūtra*, also called *Vedāntasūtra*, a compendium of 550 short statements that purport to render pithily the rich content of the main Upaniṣads. In it the attempt is made to reconcile the apparent contradictions between different Upaniṣadic doctrines.[68] The voluminous commentaries written in the course of centuries upon this text are the main works of Vedānta. Similarly there are *sūtras* and *bhāṣyas* in all the other areas of Hindu thought. The desire to understand and to grasp the meaning of revealed truths has helped to produce some of the most penetrating works of philosophical theology. All questioning has definite limits; to question too much is to destroy the foundation upon which one stands and that alone allows one to engage in meaningful conversation.

CHAPTER FOUR

# *Itihāsa-Purāṇa*

## *The Heart of Hinduism*

*Śruti* and *smṛti* are the two eyes of *dharma*, but the *Purāṇa* is its heart—on no other foundation does it rest but these three.

—*Devībhāgavata Purāṇa* XI, 1, 21

*Itihāsa*, history/story, is the collective term for the *Rāmāyaṇa* and the *Mahābhārata*, in Western publications usually called the *Great Epics*.[1] Related to them in character and importance are the Purāṇas, "ancient books," of which eighteen are accepted as *Mahāpurāṇas*, important scriptures of the major Hindu traditions. *Itihāsa-Purāṇa* is often called collectively the *fifth Veda*, the Holy Book of the mass of people who were not entitled to study the four Vedas. Western scholarship has for a long time played down the importance of *Itihāsa-Purāṇa*, partly because of its largely mythological contents, partly also because the existing texts and editions offered such a bewildering variety of readings, claiming ancient origins for obviously very recent interpolations and on the whole lacking the unity of theme and structure of epic or historical works in the Western sense. Indian tradition has always claimed great antiquity and authority for these writings and though the more critical approach of modern Indian scholarship[2] has had to dismantle some of the cherished legends surrounding these books, it has tended on the whole to reinforce the traditional view and lent it greater importance.[3] As in several areas studied before, in the field of *Itihāsa-Purāṇa* studies too one has to respect the typically Indian character of this literature and its subject matter in order not to approach it with models of epics or history taken from elsewhere. *Itihāsa-Purāṇa* is in a very real sense the heart of Hinduism, with all its strengths and weaknesses. Although the core of *Itihāsa-Purāṇa* may possibly go back to the seventh century BCE or even earlier, it is much more popular and much more alive today in India than any folk literary tradition of Europe.

Indian languages are strongly influenced by the vocabulary and the imagery of *Itihāsa-Purāṇa*; the numerous rewritings of these texts in the Indian vernaculars are quite often the first major literary works in those languages. They have shaped Hindu religious and theological terminology and have become the medium for imparting secular knowledge as well. They are the source for much of Indian sociology, politics, medicine, astrology, and geography. Reading *Itihāsa-Purāṇa* one can recognize the character of the Indian people, enlarged, typified, idealized—true in an uncanny sense. The personalities described, their wishes and fantasies, their joys and sorrows, their emotions and ideas are much closer to the India of our own time than the venerable age of the books would suggest. Many Indians bear the names of the heroes and heroines of *Itihāsa-Purāṇa*; most of them are familiar from early childhood with the stories contained in them, stories that combine entertainment with moral education. School readers in the Indian vernaculars are full of tales from them. Countless films and dramas take their subjects, often with very little modification, from these ancient books. Even simple people in the villages can speak with such enthusiasm and earnestness about Rāma and Sītā, about Kṛṣṇa and Arjuna, Hanuman and Rāvaṇa, Bharata and Lakṣmaṇa that one realizes that contemporary India also identifies with the tradition expressed in *Itihāsa-Purāṇa*. Broadcasting and television, printing presses and professional *Kathā* performers, films and musicals keep this "true history of India" alive, "history not of events, but of the urges and aspirations, strivings and purposes of the nation."[4] Whatever critical literary scholarship may or may not find out about the texts and their history, Hinduism without them would not be what it is. Anyone interested in the real religion of the Indian people today would find in *Itihāsa-Purāṇa* the source for all aspects of the contemporary living religion of the masses.

## THE GREAT EPIC

> The *Mahābhārata* represents a whole literature rather than a single homogeneous work; it constitutes a veritable treasure-house of Indian lore, both secular and religious. No other single work gives such insight into the innermost depths of the soul of the people. It is a "Song of Victory," commemorating the deeds of heroism in a war fought to avenge insults to womanhood and to maintain the just rights of a dynasty that extended the heritage of Bhārata and knit together the North, East, West and South of India into one empire. It is a *purāṇa-saṃhitā* containing diverse stories of seers and sages, of beautiful maids and dutiful wives, of valiant warriors and saintly kings. It is also a magnificent poem describing in inimitable language the fury of the battlefield, the stillness of the forest-hermitage, the majesty of the roaring

> sea dancing with billows and laughing with foam, the just indignation of a true daughter of a warrior line, and the lament of the aged mother of dead heroes. It is an authoritative book of law, morality, and social and political philosophy, laying down rules for the attainment of *dharma*, *artha* and *kāma*, called *trivarga*, and also showing the way of liberation expounding the highest religious philosophy of India.[5]

Since the sixth century CE the *Mahābhārata* has been called *śatāsahasrī saṃhitā*, the collection of one hundred thousand stanzas. In Western terms, this means that this huge work is four times as voluminous as the whole Bible, or eight times the text of the *Iliad* and the *Odyssey*, the greatest Greek epics, together. A work of this magnitude has its history. Generations of scholars have been busy trying to find the *Ur-Mahābhārata* within the huge mass of literature of the great epics. Attempts to strip away the various layers of narrative and arrive at the original saga have had as little success as the endeavor to explain the whole work as an invention designed to illustrate maxims of law.[6] The critical edition of the *Mahābhārata*, one of the greatest literary enterprises of any time in any language, did not even try to reconstruct the "original *Mahābhārata*" but aimed at constituting an "accepted text" by retaining all that was common to the numerous recensions, relegating to notes and appendixes those portions that on account of their weaker textual evidence could be supposed to have been added after the final redaction around 400 CE.[7] On the whole the traditional view has gained strength through the failure of modern criticism regarding the origin and development of the *Mahābhārata*. Thus many scholars today accept the view that the *Mahābhārata* underwent two major recensions: it began as *Jāya*, a poem about the victory of the Pāṇḍavas over the Kauravas of about seven thousand *ślokas*. This is supposed to have been the work of Vyāsa, also known as Kṛṣṇa Dvaipayana, the son of Parāśara and Satyavatī: it was augmented to about three times its former length in the *Bhārata* by Vaiśampayana, who recited it at the snake sacrifice of Janamejaya. The *Sūta*, who heard it there, related it as *Mahābhārata* of one hundred thousand verses to the assembly of sages in the Naimiṣa forest during the sacrifice performed by Śaunaka.

The present edition of the *Mahābhārata* itself speaks of three beginnings:[8] *manvādi*, beginning from Manu, corresponding to the first twelve *upa-parvans* (sections) of the present work; *āstikādi*, beginning with Astika, comprising *upa-parvans* thirteen to fifty-three; *uparicarādi*, from *upa-parvan* fifty-four onward.

The text of the *Mahābhārata* which emerges in the critical edition is the form which the work took after the Bhārgavas, a family of learned Brahmins, claiming descent from the Vedic sage Bhṛgu, who had specialized in *dharma* and *nīti*, rewrote it completely, thus making it primarily into a sourcebook of instruction on religious law. The new didactic materials were incorporated mainly in the *Śānti* and *Anuśāsana Parvans*, which now cover almost one-fourth of the whole *Mahābhārata*, thus raising the work to the rank of a *smṛti*. After this *Bhārgava-Mahābhārata* had become popular in India, the different regions developed their own recensions of it, incorporating material that seemed to be of local importance. The so-called northern and the southern recensions are the principal ones, differing by as much as a third of the full text. At some point, as yet unknown, the *Mahābhārata* was subdivided into eighteen *parvans* (parts) of varying length: the smallest is the *Mahāprasthānika*, the seventeenth, with only 120 *ślokas*; the longest the *Śānti*, the twelfth, with 14,525 *ślokas*. Of greater importance is the subdivision into ninety-eight sub-*parvans* that topically subdivide the whole work into more congruous sections. As *khila-bhāga*, supplement to the *Mahābhārata*, the *Harivaṃśa*, a Kṛṣṇaite work, is very often added in the editions; in itself it is a rather voluminous work of some sixteen thousand *ślokas*.[9]

The *Mahābhārata* consequently became a veritable encyclopedia, and it carries this verse about its own scope: "Whatever is written here may also be found elsewhere; but what is not found here, cannot be anywhere else either."[10]

Not content with the sheer mass of writing contained in it, which covers all possible aspects of secular and religious culture, traditional Hindu interpreters have widened the scope of its teaching exponentially, by explaining the *Mahābhārata* to have three different layers of meaning in each of its words. Thus Madhva, commenting on the aforementioned verse of the three beginnings, writes:

> The meaning of the *Bhārata*, in so far as it is a relation of the facts and events with which Śrī Kṛṣṇa and the Pāṇḍavas are connected, is *āstikādi*, or historical. That interpretation by which we find lessons on virtue, divine love, and the other ten qualities, on sacred duty and righteous practices, on character and training, on Brahmā and the other gods, is called *manvādi*, or religious and moral. Thirdly, the interpretation by which every sentence, word or syllable is shown to be the significant name, or to be the declaration of the glories, of the Almighty Ruler of the universe, is called *auparicara* or transcendental.[11]

A modern scholar, the initiator of the critical edition, took up this idea to explain the three planes on which the *Mahābhārata* must be understood in its complete meaning: on the mundane plane, the story is the realistic account of a fierce fratricidal war of annihilation with its interest centerd on the epic characters. On the ethical plane, the war is seen as conflict between *dharma* and *adharma*, good and evil, justice and injustice, with the final victory of *dharma*. On the transcendental plane, the war is fought between the higher and the lower self in man.

> Arjuna, the superman under the guidance of Kṛṣṇa, the Super-self, emerges successful in this conflict, after he has destroyed with the sword of knowledge the ignorance embodied in his illegitimate desires and passions symbolized

> by his relatives, teachers, elders and friends ranged on the other side. In this interpretation Śrī Kṛṣṇa is the *Paramātman*, and Arjuna the *Jīvātman*. Dhṛtarāṣṭra is a symbol of the vacillating egocentric self, while his sons symbolize in their aggregate the brood of egocentric desires and passions. Vidura stands for *Buddhi*, the one-pointed reason, and Bhīṣma is tradition, the time-bound element in human life and society.[12]

The main story of the *Mahābhārata* can be sketched out in a few lines:[13] Vicitravīrya, a king of the lunar dynasty, has two sons: Dhṛtarāṣṭra and Pāṇḍu. According to custom Dhṛtarāṣṭra, the elder son, is to succeed his father; but being born blind, his younger brother Pāṇḍu is made king instead. Pāṇḍu dies after a brief reign, leaving five minor sons from his two wives behind.[14] Thus the blind Dhṛtarāṣṭra assumes kingship. His hundred sons, the Kauravas, are growing up together with the five Pāṇḍavas, whom Dhṛtarāṣṭra appears to consider the rightful heirs. Duryodhana, the eldest among the Kauravas, however, claims the throne and attempts to eliminate the Pāṇḍavas through a series of criminal tricks. He refers to the fact that his father had been the eldest son and rightful heir to the throne and succeeds in exiling the Pāṇḍavas together with their common wife Draupadī. Duryodhana, thinking them to be dead, takes over the kingdom from his father. During their sojourn in the forest, the Pāṇḍavas, however, win allies and challenge Duryodhana to battle. In order to avoid a war, blind old Dhṛtarāṣṭra divides the kingdom into two parts, leaving one half to his own sons and giving the other half to the Pāṇḍavas. Yudhiṣṭhira, the eldest among the Pāṇḍavas, is installed as king of Indraprastha, identified with the later Delhi, whereas Duryodhana remains king of Hastinapura, the elephant fortress some sixty miles to the north. An uneasy peace prevails, riddled with quarrels and fights. During a visit to Indraprastha, Duryodhana falls into a pond. Draupadī finds the situation absurdly comical and breaks out in laughter. This loss of face has fatal consequences: Duryodhana challenges Yudhiṣṭhira to a game of dice where the winner takes all. Yudhiṣṭhira is carried away by his passion for gambling and loses everything to the Kauravas: his kingdom, his private possessions, his elephants, his brothers, himself, and finally Draupadī. Draupadī, on being called into the gambling den, refuses to come. The Kauravas rudely pull her in by the hair and tear her clothes off to humiliate her—miraculously her hair grows long to give her cover. Bhīma on seeing this takes a terrible oath: "May I never enter the resting place of my fathers unless I have torn open the breast of this stupid dog of a Bhārata in battle and drunk his blood!" Again, blind old Dhṛtarāṣṭra intervenes and prevails upon Duryodhana to return the kingdom to the Pāṇḍavas. This time Duryodhana does not give in: he demands that another round of dice be played with the imposition that the loser would have to go into the jungle for twelve years, remain incognito for one more year in the country, and only then be allowed to be free to return openly. If during the thirteenth year they were found out, they would have to go back into exile for another twelve years. The Pāṇḍavas again lose the game and have to leave for the forest. The *Mahābhārata* fills the twelve years in the forest with beautiful stories through which the numerous hermits living there edify the refugees. They manage, in the thirteenth year, to get employment in the court of Virāṭa without being recognized and appear at the beginning of the fourteenth year before the king to reclaim their kingdom. But Duryodhana is no longer willing to give up his empire. Thus both parties prepare for an all-out war.

The Great War, lasting for eighteen days, is described in six hundred chapters. Using means both fair and foul, the Pāṇḍavas emerge as the victors. Very few, however, of those who entered the war on both sides remain alive, and the survivors' weeping and lamenting overshadows any joy that might accompany this hard-won victory. The Pāṇḍavas, although victorious, leave the kingdom in the hands of a younger relation and start toward the Himalayas to go to Indra's heaven. Four of the five brothers die on their way: only Yudhiṣṭhira reaches the goal. According to Indian tradition the Great War marks the beginning of the *Kaliyuga*, the Age of Strife, the age in which righteousness has given place to unrighteousness, where *dharma* is only one footed and humankind goes toward its inevitable doom. To give an example of one of the typical stories that abound in the *Mahābhārata*, one of the episodes from the *Āraṇyakaparvan*, the time when the Pāṇḍavas dwelt in the forest, may be related here.[15]

Toward the close of the Pāṇḍavas' exile, it happened that a deer carried away the firestone of a devout hermit. The man began to lament: "How shall I now offer my fire sacrifice, unable to light a fire?" He approached the Pāṇḍavas for help. They pursued the deer, but they could not catch it, because it was not an ordinary deer. Exhausted and miserable they sat under a banyan tree and bewailed their fate: "So helpless and weak have we become; we cannot even render a small service to a Brahmin." Bhīma said: "Yes, it is true. We should have killed those scoundrels when they dragged Draupadī into the hall by her hair. Because we have not done it we have been reduced to such weakness!" Arjuna agreed with him: "I watched in silence while the vulgar creature insulted her. We have deserved our fate." Since Yudhiṣṭhira felt great thirst, he asked Nakula to climb a tree to see whether there was a river or a pond close by. Nakula saw cranes and water plants in not too great a distance, so he went to fetch water. When he reached the pond he at once lay down to drink. No sooner had he dipped his hand into the water than he heard a voice: "Do not hurry! This pond is mine. Answer first my questions, then you may drink!" Nakula's thirst was too strong, he drank at once; immediately he dropped down lifeless. When Nakula did not return for a long time, Yudhiṣṭhira sent Sahadeva to fetch water. He met with the same fate as Nakula. Arjuna and Bhīma too, sent after Sahadeva, did not return. Finally Yudhiṣṭhira had to go by himself. Seeing his four brothers dead beside the water, he began to lament: "Is this to be the end? You have been taken away just when our exile was coming to its end! The gods themselves have forsaken me in my unhappy state!" Still grieving he stepped into the pond to drink. The voice was heard again: "Your brothers died, because they would not listen to me. First give an answer to my questions, then drink, for this pond is mine!" Yudhiṣṭhira asked for the questions. The *yakṣa* said: "What makes the sun shine each day?" Yudhiṣṭhira replied: "The power of Brahman."—"What saves a man from every danger?" "Courage saves a man from all dangers!"—"Studying which science does a man become wise?" "Not through the study of any science but by living in the company of wise men does a man become wise!"—"Who is a more noble protector than the earth?" "The mother who brings up the children she has given birth to, she is a more noble protector than the earth."—"Who is higher than heaven?" "The father."—"Who is swifter than Wind?" "The mind!"—"Who is more miserable than a straw blown about the wind?" "A careworn heart!"—"Who is the traveler's friend?" "The willingness to learn!"—"Who is the husband's friend?" "The wife."—"Who is man's companion in death?" "*Dharma* alone accompanies a man on his lonely journey after death!"—"Which is the largest vessel?" "The earth, for it contains all other vessels!"—"What is happiness?" "Happiness is the result of proper conduct!"—"What makes a man popular by abandoning it?"—"Pride! Because if a man renounces it, he will be loved by all!"—"Which loss brings joy and not mourning?"—"Anger! If we give up anger we are no longer subject to suffering."—"What makes a person rich if he loses it?"—"Desire! If we give it up we shall be rich!"—"What makes a man a Brahmin? Is it birth, good conduct or erudition? Answer rightly!"—"Birth and erudition do not make a man a Brahmin, only good conduct does. No matter how erudite a man may be, if he is the slave of bad habits he is no Brahmin. Even if he is well-versed in the four Vedas, if he has got bad habits he belongs to a low class!"—"Which is the most surprising thing in this world?"—"Every day people see other creatures leave for the abode of Yama, yet those that remain behind behave as if they were going to live forever. This really is the most astonishing thing in this world." In this manner the *yakṣa* asked many questions and Yudhiṣṭhira replied to them. In the end the *yakṣa* addressed him thus: "O King! One of your brothers will return to life. Which one do you want?" Yudhiṣṭhira thought for a while and then said: "May Nakula, he who is of the color of a dark cloud, lotus-eyed, broad-shouldered, long-armed, he who lies here like a felled oak tree, may he return to life!" The *yakṣa* was content and asked: "Why did you prefer Nakula to Bhīma, who has the strength of sixteen thousand elephants? I have heard that Bhīma is your favorite! And why not Arjuna, whose skill with weapons is your protection? Tell me, why did you chose Nakula and not these two?" Yudhiṣṭhira replied: "*Dharma* is the only protection of man, not Bhīma and not Arjuna. If *dharma* is violated man will be annihilated. Kuntī and Mādrī were my father's two wives. I am a son of Kuntī: she is not entirely bereft of children. To fulfill the law of righteousness I pray that Mādrī's son Nakula be returned to life!"

The *yakṣa* liked Yudhiṣṭhira's sense of justice and returned all his brothers to life. In fact, he was Yama in disguise, the lord of death who had adopted the form of the deer and the *yakṣa* to test his son Yudhiṣṭhira, whom he now embraced and blessed: "Only a few days and the twelve years will be over. The thirteenth year will also pass and your enemies will not find you out. Your undertaking will be brought to a happy end!"

The story ends with a familiar promise: "Those who listen to the story of Yudhiṣṭhira's meeting with his father Yama will never tread on evil paths. They will never seek discord with their friends nor envy others for their wealth. They will never be victims of lust and will never set their hearts on things that pass away."

## THE HINDU'S FAVORITE BOOK

The *Rāmāyaṇa*, since ancient times considered the composition of Vālmīki,[16] is shorter, more unified, more appealing, and even more popular than the *Mahābhārata*. In its present form it comprises about one-quarter of the volume of the *Mahābhārata*, namely about twenty-four thousand *ślokas*. Western scholars have for over a century applied a good deal of textual criticism to this work. Some assumed that the original core was identical with the Buddhist *Daśaratha Jātaka*[17]—a theory that was given up when it was proved that this *Jātaka* is a much later work. The traditional Indian view seems to emerge as historically substantially correct: before being reduced to writing, the story of Rāma, the Prince of Ayodhyā, was sung as a ballad by wandering bards in the assemblies of kings. The *Rāmāyaṇa* itself says that the first recitation took place in the forest before a gathering of sages, the second in the streets of Ayodhyā, and the third and final one in the palace of Rāma, after the horse sacrifice, through which Rāma confirmed his enthronement. It is not difficult to discern in the present *Rāmāyaṇa* text interpolations that often interrupt the flow of the narrative: Purāṇic stories, genealogical lists, imitations of motifs from the *Mahābhārata*, repetitions and, perhaps again under Bhārgava influence, additions of ethical, philosophical, and other didactic materials.[18]

In its numerous reworkings in the vernaculars the *Rāmāyaṇa* has become an inspiration for millions of Hindus. Mahātmā Gandhi praised the *Rāmacaritamānasa* of the 16th century poet Tulasīdāsa[19] as the greatest work in the entire religious literature of the world; countless Indian villagers know a large number of its *dohas*, summarizing not only the story of Rāma but also epigrammatically expressing the accumulated wisdom of India. Scholars have hailed it as the perfect example of the perfect book.

The *Vālmīki Rāmāyaṇa*, also called *Ādikāvya*, or first epic poem, has also recently appeared in a critical edition. Work on this edition has brought to light a great number of recensions in various parts of the country, which can be grouped into a northern and a southern family of texts, with considerable differences. The southern text, which is less smooth and polished than the northern one, seems to be the older one.[20] The hypothesis of an *Ur-Rāmāyaṇa*, from which both recensions stem, has been considered quite valid. The present text is divided into seven *kāṇḍas* (parts) of fairly equal length.[21] Most scholars assume that the first and the last are later additions to the core of the story. As regards the interpretation of the Rāma story, most Western scholars consider the original tale as a ballad about a human hero, later made into an *avatāra* of Viṣṇu when the *avatāra* doctrine had become popular. Indians are inclined to consider Rāma a historical figure who lived and ruled around 3500 BCE. They also assume that Vālmīki considered Rāma as a divine being from the very beginning.[22]

The basic Rāma story as told by Vālmīki is quite brief:[23] in the *Bālakāṇḍa* we hear about the birth and childhood of Rāma, son of king Daśaratha and queen Kauśalyā, one of the three wives of the king, besides Kaikeyī, who bore Bhārata, and Sumitrā, the sons of whom were Lakṣmaṇa and Śatrughna. The marriage of Rāma with Sītā, the lovely daughter of King Janaka of Videha, is narrated at great length. The king had offered his daughter in marriage to any hero who would be able to bend the bow of Rudra that was in his possession. The bow, which no previous suitor was even able to lift from the floor, becomes a willing instrument in Rāma's hand.[24] Rāma and Sītā spend a brief, happy time at Ayodhyā after their marriage. Daśaratha, feeling the burden of his age, intends to crown Rāma king and to retire. Everything is prepared and there is general rejoicing among the people of Ayodhyā, for Rāma has been a very popular prince. The very night before the *abhiṣeka*, however, Mantharā, the hunchbacked, evil-minded servant of Kaikeyī, Daśaratha's favorite wife, succeeds in poisoning Kaikeyī's mind by suggesting that if Rāma became king, he would try to kill his potential rivals—the first of whom would be Bharata, Kaikeyī's only son. Worried, Kaikeyī looks for means to prevent the coronation, and Mantharā comes up with some devilish advice: a long time ago Kaikeyī had carried the unconscious Daśaratha from the battlefield, thus saving his life. Daśaratha, recovered, promised to fulfil any two wishes that Kaikeyī would utter. Kaikeyī had stored up this credit; now she wants to make use of it. Rāma should be banned for fourteen years into forest exile and her own son Bharata should be crowned king. Daśaratha pleads and threatens, entreats and curses Kaikeyī, to no avail. He must keep his word. Bharata is not in Ayodhyā at the time of this tragic happening, he has no hand in it. Rāma receives the bad news with a manly spirit; he consoles his father and expresses his willingness to go into the forest exile, in order to help his father keep his promise. He even visits Kaikeyī to show that he does not bear a grudge against her. Sītā and Lakṣmaṇa ask to be allowed to share Rāma's exile. When the three of them leave, the whole town of Ayodhyā is plunged into grief and Daśaratha dies soon afterward of a broken heart. Bharata on his return to Ayodhyā learns what has happened; he refuses to accept the kingship and proceeds with Śatrughna into the forest to persuade Rāma to return as king. Rāma refuses: his father's word is sacred to him. Bharata then places Rāma's sandals upon the throne, considering himself as his trustee till the time of Rāma's return.

Figure 4.2. Scenes from *Vālmīki Rāmāyaṇa*

Rāma's sojourn in the forest is filled with many incidents similar to those narrated in the *Mahābhārata* about the Pāṇḍava's exile. Fights against *rakṣasas*, the hobgoblins and forest spirits of Indian folklore, interpreted by many Western scholars as the dark-skinned aboriginals, entertaining and edifying stories from forest hermits, and a variety of other adventures fill the *Āraṇyakāṇḍa*. Vālmīki is a master of poetical painting in his descriptions of the beauty of the forests. Because Rāma kills many of the *rakṣasas*, making the forest a safe and peaceful place to live for pious hermits, he befriends many Brahmins and becomes the enemy of the *rakṣasas*. One day Śūrpaṇakhā, "nails-like-winnowing-fans," the sister of Rāvaṇa, the powerful king of the *rakṣasas*, comes to Rāma's dwelling place. She is infatuated with Rāma and has turned herself into a beautiful woman. She asks Rāma to marry her. Rāma tells her that he is already married and counsels her to try her luck with his brother Lakṣmaṇa. When he, too, refuses her, she returns to Rāma. That makes Sītā burst out laughing. Śūrpaṇakhā is enraged, assumes a terrible form, and threatens to devour Sītā. Lakṣmaṇa cuts off her ears and nose and sends her home in disgrace. Rāvaṇa is infuriated and bent on vengeance. On his insistence, the demon Marica transforms himself into a gold-spotted deer, appearing before Rāma's hut, so beautiful and enticing that Sītā pleads and weeps, threatens and curses Rāma to get the deer for her. Rāma, suspecting an evil trick of a *rakṣasa*, prevails on Lakṣmaṇa to guard Sītā and not to leave her alone under any circumstances. Rāma meanwhile pursues the elusive gold-spotted deer, killing it at last with an arrow. Dying, the demon cries out: "O Lakṣmaṇa, O Sītā," sounding as if Rāma was in mortal danger. True to Rāma's word Lakṣmaṇa does not want to leave Sītā. But Sītā, quite mad with fear for Rāma, accuses Lakṣmaṇa of evil intentions and threatens to kill herself. Lakṣmaṇa now goes in search of Rāma, finds him quite unharmed and returns with him to the hermitage only to find Sītā gone. Rāvaṇa, disguised as a pious hermit, had invaded the place in Lakṣmaṇa's absence and had carried her off to Laṅkā, his kingdom.[25] Rāma and Lakṣmaṇa begin their search for Sītā. Many animals and trees give them clues. Jaṭāyu, an aged bird who has been mortally wounded in his fight against Rāvaṇa, informs them about the identity of the abductor. They win numerous allies, of which the most important of them is Hanuman, the monkey general, with his numerous troops. Hanuman's magic tricks are ultimately responsible for the success of the search. He can jump for miles, has the power to make himself as small as a mouse or as tall as a mountain. He finds out that Sītā is kept prisoner in Rāvaṇa's palace at Laṅkā. Rāvaṇa, tries to woo her with flatteries, promises, and threats; at one time he even produces a severed head that looks like Rāma's. Sītā is unimpressed and remains faithful to Rāma. Hanuman visits Sītā, comforts her, and carries messages between Rāma and his wife. At last Rāma prepares for war against Rāvaṇa. The monkeys build a bridge between Rāmeśvara and Laṅkā (the line of islands between India and Śrī Laṅkā is even now called Hanumansetu, Hanuman bridge) across which the entire army invades Laṅkā. A long and bloody battle ensues, in which both sides suffer heavy losses. Rāvaṇa has many powerful magic weapons at his disposal and if it were not for Hanuman, who fetches healing herbs from the Himalayas, Rāma and his friends would all be dead. Finally the monkey army storms Rāvaṇa's fortress city: Laṅkā goes up in flames and Sītā is reunited with Rāma. When the fourteen years of exile are over, Rāma triumphantly re-enters Ayodhyā as king. But the happy end of the story, at which every reader rejoices, is not the real end, after all. Because people entertain gossipy suspicions about Sītā's fidelity, having spent a long time in another man's house, Rāma had asked Sītā to undergo a fire ordeal in order to prove her innocence. Sītā submitted to it, passed the test, but despite her proven fidelity nevertheless was sent off to the forest. Vālmīki offers her refuge in his hermitage where she also gives birth to her two sons, Kuśa and Lava. After a long time she returns from the forest with her two sons and takes a final oath of purification: "I have never thought of another man but Rāma; may the earth receive me to confirm this! I have always worshiped only him in words, thoughts, and deeds; may mother earth receive me to confirm this! I have never known any man but Rāma; may the goddess earth accept me!" After these words the earth opens up and Sītā disappears in her.

The last chapters of the *Rāmāyaṇa* relate how Rāma, Bharata, Śatrughna, and all the citizens of Ayodhyā leave the city and go to the River Sarayū. There Rāma and his brothers physically enter the body of Viṣṇu, thus proving their divine origin.

The beautiful language and the poetry of the *Rāmāyaṇa* alone would suffice to make it a favorite of the Hindus; as well as this, they also admire Rāma's obedience toward his father, his generosity towards Kaikeyī, Sītā's fidelity in following Rāma into the jungle and during her captivity, Bharata's and Lakṣmaṇa's brotherly loyalty and the greatness and strength of Rāma. If ever there was an ancient literary work that is alive in our time, it is the *Rāmāyaṇa*! It is read and sung every day by numberless Hindus, humble and high; it is worshiped and held sacred and performed in *Rāma-Līlās* every year in small and big towns. After the monsoon rains are over, at the time of the Dasserah festival, people in villages and cities gather to reenact the drama of Rāma and Sītā. The killing of Rāvaṇa and his retinue is the main attraction for small and big children. Depending on their means, each community erects tall figures on bamboo sticks, fills them with straw, and covers them with colored paper, stuffing the limbs with crackers. At nightfall these demons are lit and explode to the delight of all; the forces of good, embodied in Rāma, have again proved victorious over the forces of evil, symbolized in Rāvaṇa. "The *Rāmāyaṇa* will be read in this country of Bharata as long as its rivers continue to flow and its mountains remain in their place" reads one verse, and the Hindu who cherishes the *Rāmāyaṇa* does so also in order to gain the award promised in one of its concluding *ślokas*: "Whoever reads this noble work that tells of Rāma's deeds will be free from all faults and sins, and with all kin and relatives he will go to heaven."[26] The *Mahābhārata* and the *Rāmāyaṇa* have much in common; as well as having certain sections that have been borrowed from the *Rāmāyaṇa* and transposed into the *Mahābhārata* or vice versa, they reveal a common fund of mythology and a common mentality.[27]

## THE PURĀṆAS—THE BIBLES OF HINDUISM

The Purāṇas, for a long time neglected and rejected by Western Indological scholarship,[28] have always occupied a central place in living Hinduism.[29] According to Purāṇic tradition Brahmā uttered the Purāṇas as the first of all the scriptures; only after this did he communicate the Vedas. Some major schools of Hinduism accord the status of *śruti* to several of the Purāṇas, attributing equal age and authority to both Purāṇas and Vedas. According R. C. Hazra, a great authority in the field, "it is difficult to say definitely how and when the Purāṇas first came into being, though their claim to great antiquity next only to that of the Vedas cannot be denied."[30] The word *purāṇa*, perhaps not yet in the precise sense of later time, occurs already in the *Atharva Veda*, the *Śatapatha Brāhmaṇa*, the *Bṛhadāraṇyaka Upaniṣad*, and other early works.[31] According to Hazra,

> The way in which the *Purāṇa* has been connected with sacrifice as well as with the *yajus* in the *Atharvaveda*, the theory of the origin of the universe from sacrifice as expounded in the *Puruṣa-sūkta* of the *Ṛg-Veda* and the topics constituting the *pāriplava ākhyānas* or recurring narrations in the *aśvamedha* sacrifice, tend to indicate that the *Purāṇa*, as a branch of learning, had its beginning in the Vedic period and originated in the narrative portion (*ākhyana bhāga*) of the Vedic sacrifice, which, in the *Brāhmanas*, is repeatedly identified with the god Prajāpati, the precursor of the later Brahmā, the creator.[32]

All the extant *Mahāpurāṇas*, eighteen in number, with, as tradition has it, altogether four hundred thousand *ślokas*, are said to have Vyāsa as their author. Textual criticism of the Purāṇas is even more complicated than in the case of the great epics; the sheer mass of material, the sectarian claims connected with quite a few of them, and the great liberty taken by writers of all ages of interpolating passages into the Purāṇas, make any serious scholarly study of the Purāṇas at the present stage seem an almost hopeless undertaking.

The Purāṇas, representing the popular religious traditions, were never subjected to the process of codification through which the Vedic *sūktas* went, who were the official text at the official functions of state and had to be uniform. Having existed for centuries in oral versions, with many local variants at one and the same time, reduced to writing at very different times without following any strict rules, they probably cannot be brought out in any meaningful critical edition. Written Purāṇa texts, with many variants, have been around for many centuries, and some sort of received text has developed that is often available in several printed editions. The Delhi publisher Motilal Banarsidass has recently reprinted all *Mahā-Purāṇas*, parallel to a series of complete English translations of all of them. The undertaking of the Kashiraj Trust to bring out critical editions of the *Purāṇas* must be understood as an attempt to collate existing manuscripts and editions and establish some sort of accepted version, embodying what most text witnesses have in common. L. Rocher's argument against the possibility of critical editions is quite convincing: the Purāṇas were not meant to be books. There is a widely shared opinion among Indian scholars that several centuries before the beginning of the Common Era there was an "original *Purāṇa Saṃhitā*." According to V. S. Agrawala, Lomaharṣana, the original teacher of the Purāṇa taught the *Mūlasaṃhitā* to six pupils, the authors of the *Parasaṃhitās* of four thousand to six thousand *ślokas* each, dealing with essentially the same four topics, each constituting a *pāda*: *sarga* or creation of the world, *pratisarga* or dissolution, *manvantara* or world ages, and *vaṃśa* or genealogies. This original *catur-pāda* form is preserved in the extant *Vāyu Purāṇa* and the *Brahmāṇḍa Purāṇa*. The *Vāyu* is usually considered to come closest to the *Ur-Purāṇa* and Agrawala thought he could recover from the present text of the *Vāyu* Purāṇa the *Mūlasaṃhitā* by eliminating some eighty spurious, interpolated chapters.

The *Amarakośa*, an ancient Sanskrit lexicon[33] defines *purāṇa* as *pañca-lakṣaṇa*, having five characteristic topics—namely, the preceding four plus *vaṃśānucarita* or stories about the deeds of the descendants of the dynasties glorified in it.

The *Viṣṇu Purāṇa*, one of the oldest, conforms best to this pattern; but even here quite a number of additional topics are dealt with. In many other Purāṇas the "five topics" are barely touched; altogether the material illustrating *pañca-lakṣaṇa* constitutes only about one-fortieth of the present texts. Important topics in addition to those already mentioned are the *puruṣārthas*, the four aims of life—namely, *artha* or wealth, *kāma* or enjoyment, *dharma* or rules for life, and *mokṣa* or spirituality—the *vratas* or religious observances, *śrāddha* or rites for departed ancestors, *tīrtha* or description of places of pilgrimage, *dāna* or gifts, *vṛtti* or means of subsistence, *rakṣa* or manifestations of higher beings, *mukti* or release, *hetu* or the potential *jīva*, and *apāśraya* or Brahman as the refuge.

R. C. Hazra thinks that from the third to the fifth century those matters have been added to the *Ur-Purāṇa* which formed the subject matter of the early *smṛtis*, whereas from the sixth century onward new topics were added dealing with holy places, image worship, astrology, and so forth, which now form the bulk of Purāṇic lore. The oldest and most original part of the Purāṇas seems to be their mythology and history. Quite a few scholars are inclined to consider the Purāṇic lists of dynasties as of considerable historical value. F. E. Pargiter spent the better part of his life in a reconstruction of the ancient Indian historical tradition[34] according to Purāṇic records and has come up with some very interesting suggestions as regards the earliest history of India.[35]

According to one theory the various *Purāṇas* came into existence as an attempt to provide each of the Vedic *śākhas* with a Purāṇa of its own; another theory, no less plausible—especially in view of the numerous *Sthala Purāṇas* or local chronicles—connects the various Purāṇas with different parts of India: "The *Brahmā Purāṇa* may represent the Orissan version of the original work, just as the *Padma Purāṇa* may give that of Puṣkara, the *Agni* that of Gāyā, the *Varāha* that of Mathurā, the *Vāmana* that of Thaneśvar, the *Kūrma* that of Banares, and the *Matsya* that of the Brahmans on the Narmadā."[36] A Vaiṣṇava schema divides the 18 *Mahāpurāṇas* according to the three *guṇas* into *sāttvika* or Viṣṇu, comprising the *Viṣṇu, Bhāgavata, Nāradīya, Garuḍa, Padma*, and *Varāha*; *rājasa* or Brahmā, comprising the *Brahmā, Brahmāṇḍa, Brahmavaivarta, Mārkaṇḍeya, Bhaviśya*, and *Vāmana*; and *tāmasa* or Śiva, comprising the *Śiva, Liṅga, Skanda, Agni, Matsya*, and *Kūrma*. That this schema is entirely inadequate becomes apparent when one considers the fact, quite evident in the present texts, that several *Purāṇas* have been reworked more than once from different sectarian standpoints, combining Vaiṣṇava, Śaiva, and Śākta features. The *Upapurāṇas* lend themselves even less than the *Mahāpurāṇas* to a satisfactory classification. Not even their number can be determined exactly. A few of them claim to be, and have the status of, *Mahāpurāṇas*, that is, they are *śruti* for the followers of the particular group in question.[37]

In a general way one can state that the texts of the *Mahāpurāṇas*, as they have been printed, have been fixed between the time of 400 CE and 1000 CE, the *Viṣṇu Purāṇa* being closest to the earlier date, the *Bhāgavata Purāṇa* nearer to the latter; but it is not possible to assign any specific date to any one of these works, containing as they do materials from hoary antiquity together with quite recent chapters, dealing, amongst other things, with Akbar's court and the British in India.[38] Most of the Purāṇas have been translated into English, some several times, by different scholars and it is quite easy for anyone interested in this literature to get acquainted with the contents and style of this class of writings "whose importance for the development of Hinduism can never be overrated."[39]

The Purāṇas, like all Hindu scriptures, give at the end the succession of sages and saints through which they have been transmitted concluding with a *phala-śloka*, the promise of reward for reading them:

> Whoever hears this great mystery that removes the contamination of the Kali age, shall be freed from all sins. Who hears it every day redeems all obligations toward *devas, pitṛs*, and men. The great and rarely attainable merit that one acquires by the gift of a brown cow, one derives from hearing ten chapters of this Purāṇa. Who listens to the entire Purāṇa obtains assuredly the reward that attends the uninterrupted celebration of the *Aśvamedha*. Who reads and retains with faith this Purāṇa acquires purity as exists not in the world, the eternal state of perfection.[40]

Apart from the texts in the *Purāṇas* that extol the merits of reading them, there are *Māhātmyas*, Praises of the Greatness of each Purāṇa, very often printed together with the texts in the available editions. They pour lavish praise on the texts themselves and promise untold happiness and reward to all who even recite as little as a fraction of a verse or keep a part of the book in their dwellings. As the *Bhāgavata Mahātmya* says:

> It is better to preserve in one's house one-half or even one-quarter verse copied from *Śrīmad Bhāgavata* than a collection of hundred and thousands of other scriptures. There is no deliverance at any time from the noose of Yama for one whose house does not contain a copy of the *Śrīmad Bhāgavata* in the Kali age. I, the Lord, take up my abode in the house that contains a verse, one half of a verse or even a quarter verse of the *Śrīmad Bhāgavata* written by hand. I never forsake the person who daily narrates my stories and is intent on hearing them and whose mind delights in them.[41]

*Itihāsa-Purāṇa* is great literature, and with more adequate translations becoming available these books may become quite popular also in Western countries. They contain fantastic stories that delight Western as well as Indian children, and they offer entertainment also to the more sophisticated lover of literature. Dealing as they do with timeless human experiences, the joys and tragedies of humankind anywhere, they speak to a Western audience as well as an Indian one.[42]

Students of myths and symbols will find them an inexhaustible source not only of materials but also of interpretations and theories; students of comparative law and ethics will find some of the most interesting resources in them. Their vastness and their overall lack of a specific ideology make them very adaptable to changing circumstances and provide them with great strength and resilience, the sign of vigorous life.[43]

CHAPTER FIVE

# The *Bhagavadgītā*

I consider myself worshipped through the sacrifice of knowledge by the one who reads this our sacred conversation. And a person who listens to it with faith and without scoffing shall be liberated and attain to the happy realm of the righteous.

—*Bhagavadgītā* XVIII, 70ff.

Throughout the last thousand years of the history of Hinduism, the popularity and authority of the *Bhagavadgītā*, the "Song of the Lord," has been, and still is, unrivalled.[1] The Vedāntins accepted it as the third of the *prasthānas* and it has also been received by the masses as a book of spiritual guidance and comfort. Whoever reads it for the first time will be struck by its beauty and depth. Countless Hindus know it by heart and quote it at many occasions as an expression of their faith and of their own insights. All over India, and also in many places of the Western hemisphere, Gītā lectures attract large numbers of people. Many are convinced that the *Bhagavadgītā* is the key book for the re-spiritualization of humankind in our age. A careful study of the Gītā, however, will very soon reveal the need for a key to this key-book. Simple as the tale may seem and popular as the work has become it is by no means an easy book, and some of the greatest scholars have grappled with the historical and philosophical problems that it presents.

The *Bhagavadgītā* in its present form constitutes chapters 23 to 40 in the *Bhīṣmaparvan* of the *Mahābhārata*, one of the numerous philosophico-theological interpolations in the Great Epic.[2] Since we possess Śaṅkarācārya's commentary on the *Bhagavadgītā*, which presupposes the same text that we possess today,[3] we know with certainty that the Gītā has not been changed in the last twelve hundred or more years. The very fact that Śaṅkara commented upon it, despite its obvious theistic and Kṛṣṇaitic bias, would permit the conclusion that at the time it already enjoyed a very high standing among philosophers and ordinary people alike. Little is known about the text before that date, and this is the reason why we find the most extraordinary range of views among scholars, both as regards the age and the original form of this poem.

R. D. Ranade, one of India's greatest religious scholars of the recent past, in a study entitled *The Bhagavadgītā as a Philosophy of God-Realization, Being a Clue through the Labyrinth of Modern Interpretations*[4] offered a critique of dozens of different opinions on the date and message of the *Bhagavadgītā*. There have been numerous Western scholars who have tried to explain the obvious inconsistencies of the present text by stripping the *Ur-Gītā* from later additions and interpolations. According to G. Holtzmann, the original Gītā was Vedāntic in character and the unorthodox *bhakti* doctrines have been grafted upon it; according to Garbe, the original Gītā was a devotional and sectarian (Kṛṣṇaite) tract, to which the Vedāntic portions were tacked on under the influence of Brahmanism. E. W. Hopkins thought that our Gītā was a Kṛṣṇaite version of an older Viṣṇuite poem, and this in turn was at first a nonsectarian work, perhaps a late Upaniṣad.[5] W. Garbe proceeded on philological grounds to sift out what he considered the additions and kept of the 700 *ślokas* only 530 as genuine, all of them non-Vedāntic.[6] H. Oldenberg, a widely respected Sanskritist, thought that the original Gītā comprised only the first twelve of the present eighteen chapters, the last six being a later addition. R. Otto came to the conclusion that the original Gītā consisted of only 133 stanzas; the rest was added and interpolated later. The original text did not contain any doctrinal matter, whereas the eight tracts that were added brought in sectarian dogma. Several Western scholars—bitterly opposed by Indians—maintained that the Gītā betrayed Christian influence.[7] The most articulate of these was probably F. Lorinser, who in 1869 published a metrical version of the *Bhagavadgītā*. He tried to prove that the author of the Gītā had used the New Testament, especially the Pauline epistles, weaving Christian ideas and conceptions into his system. A. Weber, a reputable Sanskrit scholar, saw in the *Nārāyaṇīya* section of the *Mahābhārata* a report of an Indian's visit to a Western, Christian country and attributed the Gītā to the authorship of such Brahmins that had familiarized themselves with Christianity at Alexandria. Necessarily these authors had to give to the *Bhagavadgītā* a fairly recent date, usually around 200 CE. In the opinion of most scholars today the *Bhagavadgītā* in its major portions antedates the Christian era. Some decades ago a Kashmiri Buddhist published a study in which he tried to prove that the Gītā was a Buddhist work or at least that it borrowed heavily from Buddhism.[8] In our own day numerous practical interpretations of the *Bhagavadgītā* have been given. The one that attracted the most attention and criticism may have been B. G. Tilak's *Gītārahasya*, in which the Gītā is interpreted as "a Gospel of action."[9] Mahātmā Gandhi spoke quite frequently on the *Bhagavadgītā*, which he called his mother; and his secretary published a Gītā translation-cum-interpretation that reflects Gandhi's own thoughts.[10] Mahātmā Gandhi sees in the *Bhagavadgītā* an allegory of human life that has to fight out the dilemma between divinely ordained duty and personal preference. Sri Aurobindo Ghose finds in the *Bhagavadgītā* all the major points of his own philosophy: the ascending grades of consciousness, the gnostic ideal, the superman, and the transformation of matter into spirit.[11] S. Radhakrishnan, finally, whose edition synthesizes all the great classical interpretations of the *Bhagavadgītā* into a modern philosophy of life, eventually comes up with a modernized version of Advaita Vedānta as the original purport of the *Bhagavadgītā*.[12]

Without claiming to be able to solve all the questions raised by the many scholars who have written the most contradictory comments on the *Bhagavadgītā*, we may briefly summarize the views of S. K. Belvalkar, the editor of the *Bhīṣmaparvan* in the critical edition of the Mahābhārata, who also on other occasions has demonstrated his thorough knowledge of the problems related to the Gītā. Belvalkar assumes that, as the *Mahābhārata* underwent at least two recensions before it was fixed in the "modern" form, thus the Gītā also underwent a certain degree of rewriting. On the other hand he maintains that the Gītā in its main contents has always been what it is today, that is, there has never been any original Gītā to which foreign and substantially different elements were added. He explains, quite plausibly, that the Gītā is a pre-Buddhist work, representing a heroic Brahmanical effort to reunite a people, exposed to the most radical and most diverse religious ideas.[13] This reunion had to include all the acceptable streams of religiosity of the time—Brahmanic ritual, Upaniṣadic knowledge and devotional forms of cult and worship with the firm frame of *varṇāśrama dharma* as the unifying bond—a concept also found in modern times, when everyone could call himself a Hindu, regardless of the particular religious beliefs or rituals that one followed, as long as one remained within the caste structure. Belvalkar calls the *Bhagavadgītā* the "swansong of the centuries of Śrauta religion" and thinks that

> the peculiar achievement of the *Bhagavadgītā* as a philosophical poem consisted precisely in having successfully gathered together under one banner the Brahmanic ritualists and the Upaniṣadic Vedāntists, the Sāṁkhya pacifists and the Yoga activists, the devotees of Kṛṣṇa and the free-thinking recluses, as also the majority of the average adherents of established institutions—not excluding women and the depressed classes, whom Brahmanism had denied the right of Vedic sacraments—requiring each of its constituents to give up or modify a part of their dogma in the interest of a compromise on a common platform with the other constituents. The ultimate position reached was philosophically quite self-consistent, special efforts being made to modulate the current opposition between *jñāna* and *bhakti*, between *karman* and *samnyāsa*, and between Ritualism and the Ātmanism.[14]

It may be easier for Indian scholars, who have grown up in the thought patterns of their own tradition, to see harmony where Westerners, trained in analytical thinking, see contradiction. Since the *Bhagavadgītā* is very much an Indian book, we should respect the traditional Indian attitude toward it and read it as a Hindu scripture rather than dissect it as an ordinary work of literature.

Notwithstanding the critical approach of many Western Indologists, the *Bhagavadgītā* has become a favorite book of many Westerners as well. Sir Charles Wilkins made the Gītā known in Europe through his English translation, which appeared in 1785. August von Schlegel produced a critical text edition and a Latin translation in 1823. Wilhelm von Humboldt, who read this Latin version, was so enthusiastic that he declared that "this episode of the *Mahābhārata* is the most beautiful, nay perhaps even the only true philosophical poem which we can find in all the literatures known to us."[15] Several good English translations have appeared in the last few decades, and one can suggest that the *Bhagavadgītā* should be read by everyone who claims to have more than a provincial education. W. M. Callewaert and Shilanand Hemraj in their *Bhagavadgītānuvāda*[16] not only try to trace the original text of the *Bhagavadgītā*, but they also mention scores of commentaries and hundreds of translations into virtually all the major—and some minor—languages of the world. The *Bhagavadgītā* was one of the texts that every Vedāntācārya had to comment upon. In addition many others wrote commentaries both in Sanskrit and in Indian vernaculars as well as in European languages. New translations into English keep appearing almost every year—apparently none of the existing versions is found satisfactory to all of those who use and study it.

In the narrative of the *Mahābhārata* the *Bhagavadgītā* is inserted just before the outbreak of the actual battle between the Kauravas and the Pāṇḍavas. The two related clans are fighting for their kingdom; the Kauravas, who have usurped the reign, are defending their claim against the Pāṇḍavas, the rightful heirs, who have been cheated out of their possession. Arjuna, the hero of the *Bhagavadgītā*, is the leader of the rightful claimants. With him is Kṛṣṇa as his charioteer, a befriended king of Dvārakā, whose divine character is to become manifest only during the narration of the Gītā itself. Kṛṣṇa has sent his army to help the Kauravas who are also his friends. Just when both armies are fully arrayed against each other, Arjuna realizes what he is going to do: he is about to fight and kill his relations, teachers, friends—and realizing that, he is ready to give up the war altogether, telling Kṛṣṇa: "I would not kill these, though killed myself, not for the rule over the three worlds—how much less for the sake of this earthly kingdom? What pleasure should we have after having slain the sons of Dhṛtarāṣṭra, our brothers? Only sin will we reap if we kill them!"

He repeats the tenets of the traditional *dharma* that teaches that killing members of one's own family leads to the destruction of the whole family and to punishments in hell. "Far better would it be for me if the sons of Dhṛtarāṣṭra, with weapons in hand, should slay me in battle, while I remain unresisting and unarmed." Arjuna then throws away his bow and arrow, depressed and overwhelmed by grief. In the second chapter, Kṛṣṇa begins to speak. The message itself is quite brief: "You have to fight, Arjuna!" Kṛṣṇa, however, persuades

Figure 5.1. Kṛṣṇa instructing Arjuna

Arjuna with arguments taken from the various established viewpoints, appearing in the process not only as the charioteer of Arjuna but as the great teacher of wisdom, nay, as the Supreme One revealing himself and his plans. He begins by telling Arjuna that his attitude is *anārya*, ignoble, that it is not conducive to *svarga*, the old Vedic heaven, and that it leads to dishonor; it is unmanly not to fight here and now! Since Arjuna is familiar with these thoughts, they do not impress him as a solution to his problem; he plainly admits his confusion and asks Kṛṣṇa to teach him as a *guru* teaches his disciple, and he again declares: "I will not fight!" Slowly Kṛṣṇa comes out with the New Philosophy that does not solve Arjuna's moral dilemma, but leaves behind the Old Morality: Wisdom, he says, consists in realizing that the *ātman* is permanent, while the body by its very nature is doomed to die: there is no reason to grieve for either the dead or the living.

> Never was there a time when I was not nor you nor these lords of men,
> nor will there ever be a time hereafter when we shall cease to be. . . .
> He who thinks that this slays and he who thinks that this is slain, both of them fail to perceive the truth; this one neither slays nor is slain.
> He is never born nor does he die at any time, nor having once come to be does he again cease to be.
> He is unborn, eternal, permanent and primeval.
> He is not slain when the body is slain.
> Just as a person casts off worn-out garments and puts on others that are new, even so does the embodied soul cast off worn-out bodies and take on others that are new. (BG IV, 12.19–22)

This philosophical argument by itself would be insufficient to justify fighting a war; it just helps eventually to get rid of feelings of guilt over the action itself by suggesting that it does not involve the *ātman*, neither actively nor passively, but remains on the periphery of reality, in the sphere of change and inevitable death. The motivation to fight is supposed to come from the appeal to the *kṣatriya-dharma*, the iron rule that tells everyone what is right and wrong. As Kṛṣṇa puts it: "There exists no greater good for a *kṣatriya* than a war enjoined by dharma; happy the *kṣatriyas*, for whom such a war comes of itself as an open door to heaven." A violation of this duty would be sinful and would bring shame, because it would make people think Arjuna is a coward—the worst that could happen to a professional warrior! Both the possibilities that the risk of war entails are preferable to the abstention from war: "If you are killed you will go to heaven; if you win, you will enjoy the earth; treating alike pleasure and pain, gain and loss, victory and defeat, get ready for battle; thus you will not incur any sin!"

Kṛṣṇa calls the teaching that he has given so far, Sāṁkhya, and he is now ready to teach also the wisdom of Yoga, which, if accepted, frees from the bondage that karma imposes. And here he now speaks words that are really the gist of the whole *Bhagavadgītā* and that have influenced practical ethics in India throughout the centuries: "Your rightful claim[17] extends to actions only, not to the results; the fruits of action should not be your motive but also do not cling to inaction. Established in Yoga, do your work after abandoning attachment, unmoved by success or failure."

In order to drive away the idea of renouncing that has fascinated Arjuna so far and appeared to him as a solution of the dilemma, Kṛṣṇa tells Arjuna that Yoga is neither inaction nor mere action but *karmasu kauśalam*, skill in action, action with understanding. He then describes the "wise man," the true Yogi, as one who has given up all desires and whose *ātman* is content in the *ātman*. Untroubled in the midst of sorrows and free from lust amid pleasures, free from passion, fear, and anger, without attachment of any kind, neither rejoicing in the good nor dejected by evil, drawing away the senses from the objects of sense as a tortoise draws in his limbs under the shell, acting free from self-interest—this is the "divine state" that brings supreme happiness.

The basic message is thus given in the second chapter; most of the rest is a further explanation of the main points. Arjuna asks for a motivation of action, when Kṛṣṇa explains the insight of Yoga as the highest way of life. Kṛṣṇa clarifies the matter by pointing out that he had been of yore the teacher of two different ways of salvation: a way of knowledge for the contemplatives and a way of works for the actives. Nature, so he says, depends on continued work: "Do your alloted work, for action is better than inaction; even bodily life cannot go on without action. All work, except sacrificial action, causes bondage: therefore do your work as a *yajña*, free from all attachment."

The work of the perfect person is not done with a view to further her own interests but in the interest of *loka-saṅgraha*, the good of the world. Kṛṣṇa points to his own example: he has no desire unfulfilled and yet he continually engages in action in order to give an example to humankind: "If I should cease to work, these worlds would fall in ruin and I should be the creator of disordered life and destroy these peoples."

Kṛṣṇa's teaching is not absolutely new at the time of the discourse with Arjuna; he refers back to Īkṣvāku, who taught it and who had received it from Manu via Vivasvān—Kṛṣṇa had taught it to him! Arjuna does not quite understand how Kṛṣṇa, who is about his own age, could possibly have been the teacher of mythical ancestors! Kṛṣṇa now explains his repeated coming into the world:

> Many are my lives that are past. . . . Though I am unborn and my Self is imperishable, the Lord of all creatures, establishing myself in my own nature I become embodied through my *māyā*.
>
> Whenever *dharma* declines and *adharma* rises up, I create myself (a body); for the protection of the good, for the destruction of the wicked, and for the establishment of *dharma* I come into being in every age. (BG IV, 5–8).

Kṛṣṇa is the creator of the *caturvarṇāśramadharma*: though himself unchangeable, he has ordained action; action, however, that is not what ordinary people usually understand by that word: "One who in action sees inaction and in inaction action is the wise, the *yogi*, the one who has fulfilled his duty." Doing one's duty because of duty, *niṣkāma karma*, action free from desire, is the ideal; and this activity does not entangle one in further karma but is in itself liberating, because it is centered on Kṛṣṇa, who is free from karma and who destroys it.

The *Bhagavadgītā* explains Yoga in several chapters in very much the same way, often with the same words, as Patañjali in his *Yogasūtra*, and it also describes the origin of the world in the Sāṁkhya style, repeating the traditional two-way theory of the soul's course after death. It reaches its religious peak, however, in chapters 9 to 11 where Kṛṣṇa pronounces his divine self-revelation, the *rāja-vidyā*, the regal wisdom, *rāja-guhyam*, the royal secret, *pavitram idam uttamam*, this most holy subject, open to realization and, within the traditional religion, the only way to escape from rebirth.[18] Kṛṣṇa says:

> This whole universe is permeated by me through my unmanifest form (*avyakta mūrti*). All beings are grounded in me but I am not grounded in them. My *ātman* sustains all things but is not established in them. As the air moves everywhere in space, thus are all things established in me because I support them. At the end of each *kalpa* all beings return into my *prakṛti*, from where I send them forth again at the beginning of the *kalpa*. Under my instructions *prakṛti* gives birth to all things and thus the world revolves."[19]

It is foolishness to despise God in a human body and wisdom to recognize him in all things:

> I am the ritual action, I am the sacrifice, I am the ancestral oblation, I am the medicinal herb, I am the sacred hymn, I am the *ghī*, the fire and the offering. I am the father of this world, the mother and the support. I am the object of knowledge, the sanctifier. I am the OM, the *ṛk*, the *sāma* and the *yajus*. I am the goal, the support, the lord, the inner witness, the secret abode, the

> refuge, the friend. I am the origin and the dissolution, the ground, the resting place and the imperishable seed. I give heat, I withhold and I send forth the rain. I am immortality and also death, I am *sat* and *asat*."[20]

Because Kṛṣṇa is the pervading and omnipresent Supreme Being, he is also the recipient of all devotion and offering. It is in the instructions for worship that the *bhakti* character of the Gītā appears clearest:

> Whosoever offers me with *bhakti* (devotion), a leaf, a flower, a fruit or water, that offering of *bhakti*, of the pure-hearted I accept. Whatever you do, eat, offer, give, suffer—dedicate it as a *tarpaṇa* (offering) to me. Thus you will be freed from the good and evil results that accompany actions. I am alike to all beings; none is hateful to me, none a favorite. But those who worship me with *bhakti* are in me, and I in them. Those who take refuge in me, be they lowborn, women, *vaiśyas* or *śūdras*, attain the highest abode. On me fix your mind, be devoted to me, worship me and revere me; having yoked yourself to my self you will attain me.[21]

The entire tenth chapter deals with the *vibhutivistara-yoga*,[22] the description of the manifestations of God in visible objects—important for the time in which it was written because here Kṛṣṇa is explaining himself as the core and essence of Vedic religion and life. The eleventh chapter, called *viśva-rupa-darsana*, the vision of the cosmic form of God, is the most powerful, and quite overwhelming.

Arjuna, impressed by the oral revelation of God's greatness has one great desire: *drāṣṭum icchāmi te rūpam aiśvaram puruṣottama*: "I wish to see your divine body, Supreme Being!"[23] Kṛṣṇa is willing to fulfill this wish—but Arjuna is unable to see God with his natural vision; Kṛṣṇa has to endow him with divine eyes to see the divinity. What Arjuna then sees, terrifies him:

> In your body, O Lord, I see all the *devas* and the hosts of beings, Brahmā seated on the lotus throne and the *ṛṣis* and *nāgas*. I behold you, infinite in form on all sides, with numberless arms and bellies, faces and eyes, but I do not see your end or your middle or your beginning. (XI, 3)

More relevant for the concrete situation of the war into which Arjuna is about to enter, he sees how all the warriors whom he knows

> are rushing into your flaming mouths as torrents rushing into the ocean. As moths rush swiftly into a blazing fire to perish there, so do these men rush into your mouths with great speed to their own destruction. Devouring all the worlds on every side with your flaming mouths you lick them up. Your fiery rays fill this whole universe and scorch it with their fierce radiance, O Visnu!

Kṛṣṇa responds with a profound revelation of the relativity of time:

> *Kālo'smi*, time am I, world destroying, come to the end to subdue the world. Even without you all the warriors arrayed in the opposing armies shall not

> live on. Therefore arise and fight and win glory. Conquering your enemies, enjoy a prosperous kingdom. They have been slain by me already, you be the instrument alone. Slay Drona, Bhīṣma, Jayadratha, Karṇa and the other heroes who are doomed by me. Be not afraid. Fight! You will conquer your enemies in battle!

Arjuna then falls prostrate and praises Viṣṇu under many titles, asking him at the end of his prayer to assume his familiar form again, because he is terrified by the *viśva-rūpa*, the All-form.

The twelfth chapter contains a brief discourse on the superiority of *bhakti* to *jñāna* and a description of the true *bhakta* repeating what had been said before. The thirteenth chapter, entitled *kṣetra-kṣetrajñā-vibhāga-yoga*, the discrimination between the "field" and the "knower of the field," develops a *puruṣa-prakṛti* theory that agrees in many points with Sāṃkhya, assuming however that there is only one *puruṣa*, Viṣṇu-Kṛṣṇa. All the following chapters are occupied with demonstrating the applicability of the *tri-guṇa* scheme to various spheres of life and describing consequently three kinds of faith, of food, of sacrifice, of austerities, of gifts, of knowledge, of work, of doers, of understanding, of steadiness and of happiness—implying always that the follower of Kṛṣṇa partakes of the *sattva-guṇa*, the nature of Viṣṇu. This, incidentally, is good āgamic-purāṇic Vaiṣṇavism. From these chapters emerges the picture of the true Kṛṣṇaite as being fearless, pure of mind, steadfast in knowledge and concentration, charitable, devoted to the study of scriptures, dedicated to austerities, upright, nonviolent, truthful, free from anger, peaceful, forgiving, compassionate, gentle, modest, and humble. There is a touch of Advaita in the last passages where Kṛṣṇa describes the blessed state of the perfect sage:

> Endowed with pure understanding, firmly restraining oneself, turning away from sound and other objects of sense and casting aside affection and aversion, dwelling in solitude, eating but little, controlling speech, body, and mind and ever engaged in meditation and concentration and taking refuge in renunciation, casting aside egoism, violence, arrogance, desire, anger, avarice, tranquil in mind he becomes worthy to become one with *brahman*. Having become one with *brahman*, tranquil in spirit, he neither grieves nor desires. Regarding all beings as alike, he attains supreme *bhakti* to me. Through *bhakti* he gains knowledge of me, having gained knowledge of me in truth he enters into me.[24]

The *Bhagavadgītā* ends with a renewed injunction of Kṛṣṇa for Arjuna to fight, promising him final liberation:

> You are dear to me, I shall tell you what is good for you: Fix your mind on me, be devoted to me, sacrifice to me, prostrate yourself before me, thus you will come to me. I promise you truly, for you are dear to me. Abandon all reliance on [traditional] *dharma* and take your refuge (*śaraṇam*) alone to me. Do not worry, I shall release you from all sins![25]

The Gītā attaches the customary blessings for all those who read it—an untold number of Hindus over twenty-five centuries. Many Hindus—and increasingly many non-Hindus too—have considered the Gītā not only a book to be read and studied, but they take it as a guide in their lives. A need for such guidance is felt especially in times of crises and confusion like ours, when the established institutions are no longer able to provide orientation and when there are no longer commonly accepted values and standards.

The Gītā is a book of crisis. Without referring to the Gītā, a modern writer describes the symptoms of the manifestation of crisis—and he clearly means our own time—in terms that could be taken straight out from the Gītā: "loss of meaning, withdrawal of legitimation, confusion of orientations, anomie, destabilization of collective identities, alienation, psychopathologies, breakdowns in tradition, withdrawal of motivation."[26]

A direct modern Western reference to the *Bhagavadgītā* occurred in a context that to call historical is almost an understatement: it may better be called apocalyptic. In the course of his trial Robert J. Oppenheimer, who was accused of having passed on atomic secrets to the USSR described the thoughts that passed through his mind when he witnessed the first atomic test bomb explosion in the desert of New Mexico.[27]

In the stage version by Heinar Kipphart that closely follows the official protocol, the conversation between State Prosecutor Evans and defendant Oppenheimer reads like this:[28]

> EVANS: "I am addressing myself to the moral scruples, the contradiction that on the one hand you were prepared to go ahead with the matter of which you were, on the other hand, afraid of. When did you experience this contradiction for the first time?"
>
> OPPENHEIMER: "When we ignited the first atomic bomb in the desert of Alamogordo."
>
> EVANS: "Could you be more precise?"
>
> OPPENHEIMER: "On the sight of the fire-ball two ancient verses came to my mind. The one: 'Of a thousand suns in the sky if suddenly should burst forth the light, it would be like unto the light of that Exalted One' (*BG* XI, 12). The other: 'Death am I, cause of destruction of the worlds, matured and set out to gather in the worlds there' "(*BG* XI, 32).
>
> EVANS: "How do you know that a new idea is really important?"
>
> OPPENHEIMER: "By the sense of a deep horror gripping me."

While the prophetic dimension of the Bhagavadgītā can be clearly perceived as applicable to our own time—a time of crisis, a time of disorientation, a time of foreboding of universal doom—it is not so easy to establish the universal applicability of the ethics of the Gītā. Everybody can understand and even, up to a degree, practice freedom from desire and selfless action. However, the promised effect can only be had within the *varṇāśrama-dharma*: only by selflessly following one's *svadharma* can one be united with the creator of *dharma* and the rewarder of self-surrender. *Dharma*, as the Gītā understands it, is irrevocably tied up with *varṇāśrama-dharma*: as the eternal world order it has ontological, inbuilt sanctions which simply do not apply to those who have no birth place in it. The mutuality of *ethos* and *polis*, of ethics and society, requires that there first be an embodiment of an *ethos* before there can be an articulation of ethics.

India, too, has built its atom bomb and the prospect of another Great War of infinitely larger proportions than that described by the Gītā looms large not only over India but over the whole world. The modern world is not guided by *varṇāśrama-dharma*: Today's decisions concerning war and peace are not preceded by dialogues between the main actors and their God. Questions of ethics, of moral right or wrong, do not enter into the power calculus of today's mighty. If religion is brought in, it is only used as an instrument to placate emotions or to motivate the populace for an undertaking that all too clearly serves only the interests of big business and party politics.

Rewriting the *Gītā* from such a perspective Rikhi Jaipaul, an Indian diplomat and poet, composed a kind of *Upagītā*, which no longer offers transcendental hope in the face of a universal cataclysm. The new version of the final apocalypse is short:[29]

**Kurukshetra Revisited**

Clear-eyed Arjuna scanning the ruin ahead
his heart overcome with sorrow asked
which will be worse—to win or lose,
will the few with limitless power
condemn the many to karmas not their own,
will the mind that moves the soul prevail?
Pondering deep into the darkening night
of the long journey of man to his doom,
the silent Krishna had reason to lament
and washed his hands in innocence divine.
Soldiers and airmen will not fall with glory
like autumn leaves to sprout again in spring,
souls of sailors will not return as sea gulls,
warmongers will no longer sit on moonbeams
reaching to the stars for their profits;
no more the chivalries and virtues of war
nor hopes of living to fight another day,
foes and friends and neutrals alike
will perish together in the white nuclear night,
their fathers' souls will rise to die again.

Nevermore the ways of our fathers, nevermore
for in one mad act man can outwit his God
and attain the nirvan of his own oblivion;
in his final fling of self-defense there lies
the destruction of his world to make a legal point
of supervening sovereignty in pursuit of security;
helpless in the iron grip of cause and effect,
his means shape his end, baring the moral flaw
and epic pride that feed the fires of his pyre;
alas that which may save him will die with him.[29]

CHAPTER SIX

# The World of the Hindu

> I wish to hear from you how this world was, and how in future it will be. What is its substance, and whence proceeded animate and inanimate things? Into what has it been resolved and into what will its dissolution again occur? How were the elements manifested?
>
> —Maitreya in *Viṣṇu Purāṇa* I, 1

Hinduism, like all traditional religions, offers a comprehensive world view in which everything has its place and where all individual parts contribute to a meaningful total picture. All astronomical, geographical, historical, cultural information that was available at a given time is overarched by a philosophy that anchored its ethics, its anthropology, and its sociopolitical laws ultimately in a creator and ruler of the universe. Throughout its long history, under the influence of expanding horizons and growing detail knowledge, the worldview of the Hindus has changed and developed. After the formation of sectarian Hinduism, differing notions of the identity of the Supreme Being and varying sets of sectarian mythologies brought about sectarian worldviews, which were laid out in the sectarian Purāṇas. In all their forms, however, Hindu world views maintained their influence on the daily life and thought of Hindus, and contemporary efforts to integrate contemporary scientific knowledge into the traditional framework—often backed by Indian scientists of repute—prove how important it has always been for Hindus to possess a workable and viable worldview.

## VEDIC CREATION MYTHS

In the *Ṛgveda*, *pṛthvī-dyaus*, Earth-and-Heaven, are divinities.[1] India shares this heaven-earth division and religion with a good many other peoples, who similarly explain the whole world as having originated from a pair of world parents. "Which was the former, which of them the later? How born? O sages, who discerns? They bear of themselves all that has existence. Day and Night revolve as on a wheel. . . ."[2] But this simple scheme could not accommodate the numerous new developments in Vedic religion, which uses a basic partition of the universe into *tri-loka*, "three-worlds," the combination of the places for gods, ancestors, and men. To each of the worlds eleven *devas* were assigned, with various functions. As S. Kramrisch explains:

> Heaven and earth, as dyadic monad, are a closed unit. It must be violated, split into its components, and these must be separated, lest they fall together and the world-to-be collapses. The act of creative violation and the power of keeping apart the pair so that they become Father Heaven and Mother Earth between whom all life is engendered is the test by which a creator god establishes his supremacy. He makes the Dyad into Two. He is the One and at the same time the Third, who plays the leading part in the cosmic drama. He is hero and artist in one.[3]

Speculation about the origin of the world is one of the staples of almost all religions, and quite frequently much of the rest of their philosophies is derived from this starting point. The earlier Vedic hymns have many scattered references to the origin of the world, involving a variety of gods; it is only in the later hymns that anything like a definite doctrine emerges. One hymn is addressed to *Viśvakarman*, The One-who-makes-all.[4] He is called mighty in mind and power, maker, disposer, and most lofty presence, the Father who made us, the One beyond the seven *ṛṣis*. He is described as not to be found, "another thing has risen up among you."[5]

The two best-known Vedic descriptions of creation, however, are the so-called *puruṣa sūkta* and the *nāsadīya sūkta*. The former, true to the basic Vedic philosophy, derives everything from a ritual sacrifice. Thus it goes:

> Thousand-headed was the *puruṣa*, thousand-eyed, thousand-footed. He embraced the earth on all sides, and stood beyond the breadth of ten fingers. The *puruṣa* is this all, that which was and which shall be. He is Lord of immortality, which he outgrows through (sacrificial) food. One fourth of him is all beings. The three fourths of him is the immortal in heaven.

This *puruṣa* begets *virāj*, the "widespread," and both together bring forth *puruṣa*, the son, who becomes the sacrificial victim of the great sacrifice of the gods. From this great sacrifice originate the verses of the Vedas, horses, cattle, goats, and sheep. The four castes, also, have their origin in him, the sacrificial victim. The brahmin was his mouth, out of his two arms were made the *kṣatriyas*, his two thighs became the *vaiśyas* and from his feet the *śūdras* were born.[6] From his mind was born the moon, from his eye the sun, from his mouth Indra and Agni, from his breath Vāyu, from his navel the sky, from his head the heaven, from his feet the earth, from his ears the four quarters.

*Yajñena yajñam ayajanta devāḥ*[7]—the gods offered the sacrifice through the sacrifice. The *yajña* is the great creative force. We find here the germ of the later *Pāñcarātra* system, the idea that Viṣṇu is also the material cause of the universe, out of which everything is fashioned. A more speculative treatment of the topic of creation is found in the *nāsadīya sūkta*, in the last book of the Veda:

> Neither being, nor nonbeing existed: there was no air, no sky that is beyond it. What was concealed? Wherein? In whose protection? And was there deep unfathomable water? Death then existed not, nor life immortal, of neither night nor day was there any token. By its inherent force the One breathed windless: no other thing existed beyond that. There was at first darkness, by darkness hidden; without distinctive marks, this all was water. That which, becoming, was covered by the void, that One by force of heat came into being. Desire entered the One in the beginning: it was the earliest seed, the product of thought. The sages searching in their hearts with wisdom, found the kin of being in nonbeing. . . . Who knows for certain? Who shall declare it? Whence was it born, and whence came this creation? The gods were born after this world's creation: then who can know from whence it has arisen? None can know from whence creation has arisen and whether he has or has not produced it: he who surveys it in the highest heaven, he only knows, or, perhaps he does not.[8]

Several key words of Vedic religion are employed here: *tapas*, heat, the power of the *yogi*, is said to be responsible for the first stirring of creation; *kāma*, desire or lust, the cause of both the multiplicity and the inherent impermanence of things. The terms *asat*, nonbeing, and *sat*, being, do not have the Greek meaning we connect with them, but the Indian one, which differs considerably: *asat* is an entity without determination, akin to chaos, unstructured matter in the modern sense. The asymmetry of *sat* and *asat*, which is, as it were, complementary, is of a similarly fundamental nature as that between chaos and order, as understood by modern science, expressed in terms of entropy and negentropy. *Sat* and *asat* are the positive and the negative poles, complementary, whose tension produces and maintains the many things. As will become still clearer from later accounts, the Hindu idea of creation presupposes some kind of uncreated substratum, and the account is concerned more with the molding and ordering of this basic material than with its absolute beginning. As S. Kramrisch sees it:

> The three ontological moments in the relation of *sat* and *asat* correspond to different levels in the structure of creation. The dark Un-create on high has for its lower limit the first streak of the dawn of creation in the highest heaven. . . . Sunk below creation, the non-existent is negativity; the existent is the cosmos, the ordered world, the world of *ṛta*, a work of art. The non-existent is chaos, decomposition, the absence of *ṛta*, the domain of *nirriti*. It is the counterpart, *apud principium*, by the act of creation and separation, of the Darkness that was—and is—before the beginning of things.[9]

The Upaniṣads offer a great variety of theories to explain both the beginning of the universe and its structure. According to the *Bṛhadāraṇyaka Upaniṣad*, in the beginning the *ātman*, the Self, was alone, in the form of a *puruṣa*, a male being. He looked around and saw nothing beside himself. He said: "I am." He was afraid and he had no joy; he longed for another being. He was as large as a man and woman embracing. He divided himself into two: husband and wife. Thus human beings were created. She turned into a cow; he became a bull. She turned into a mare; he became a stallion. And thus the various kinds of animals came into existence.[10] The account given here reveals the first traces of the Sāṁkhya system, in which everything owes its origin to the interaction between *puruṣa* and *prakṛti*, the uncreated principles, one male, the other female, spirit and matter, passivity and activity.

Another ancient motif is that of the world egg, which floats on the primordial ocean and from which spring the many creatures on earth.[11] According to some texts, the first being to come forth from the primeval egg was Viśvakarman, the Vedic creator-god. The world egg, and the origination of the universe from it, is a favorite theme of many later Hindu works, notably the Purāṇas.

Manu's account of creation is informed by his endeavour to derive the socio-ethical law of dharma from the nature and structure of the universe itself. In the beginning the world was in chaos, without distinguishable forms and attributes, as if in sleep. Then appeared the *svayambhu bhagavān*, the Lord-who-is-of-Himself, invisible and without distinguishing characteristics; he removed the darkness. This *paramātman* was filled with a desire to create beings. He created water and put the seed *śakti-rūpī*, power-form, into it. This seed shone with the splendour of a thousand suns. It then became an egg, as bright as gold, and from it issued Brahma who shaped all the worlds. He, who is the origin of everything, eternal, of the form of *sat* and *asat*, *puruṣa* who issued from it, he is called Brahmā. For a whole year he remained in the form of an egg, and then, through concentrated thought (*dhyāna*), he divided himself into two. From the two halves were created heaven and earth, and space in between them: the eight points of the compass, the place of water and the sea. From the Self he produced mind (*manas*),[12] containing in him both *sat* and *asat*; from this came individuality (*ahaṁkāra*),[13] with pride and dominion.[14] The following chapters in *Manusmṛti* enumerate the successive creation of the twenty-four principles from which, according to the Sāṁkhya system, everything is made: *mahat*, The Great Principle, all that contain the three *guṇas* in themselves, the five sense-organs and so on. The various celestial beings are then created, along with *yajña*, the sacrifice. For it *Ṛk*, *Yajur*, and *Sāmaveda* were produced out of Agni, Vāyu and Sūrya. *Tapas*, heat/power, as well as *rati*, erotic pleasure, *icchhā*, desire, and *krodha*, anger, are created. Dharma and *adharma* and all other pairs of opposites like *hiṃsa* and *ahiṃsā*, cruelty and kindness, are apportioned to the various beings by Brahmā himself.

The origin of the four castes is explained in the same terms as the account in the *puruṣa-sūkta*. Brahmā divides his body into two parts. Out of their union springs up the first human being, *Virāṭ*. *Virāṭ* practices *tapas* in order to create Prajāpati, who brings forth ten *Maharṣis* as well as seven Manus, Devas, and the various kinds of good and evil spirits: the *yakṣas* and *piśācas*, *gandharvas* and *āpsaras*, *nāgas* and *garuḍas*.

## WORLD AGES

In the *Manusmṛti* we find already the idea of a periodical creation and destruction of the world, as well as all the divisions of time from the-winking-of-an-eye to the world ages.[15] One day and night is made up of thirty *muhūrtas*, each *muhūrtas* of thirty *kālas*, each *kāla* of thirty *kāṣṭas*, and each *kāṣṭa* of eighteen *nimeṣas*.

> The sun divides days and nights, both human and divine; the night is for the repose and the day for work. A month is a day and night of the departed ancestors; the dark fortnight is their day of work, the bright fortnight their time of sleep. A year is the day and night of the *devas*; the half year during which the sun progresses to the north will be their day, that during which the sun goes southward, the night. (I, 65–68)

There follows a description of the day and night of Brahmā and of the world ages: the *Kṛta-yuga* consists of four thousand years of the *devas*; the twilight preceding it consists of as many hundreds and the twilight following it of the same number. In the other three *yugas* with their twilights preceding and following, the thousands and hundreds are diminished by one each.

> These twelve thousand years are called one age of the *devas*. One thousand ages of the gods make one day of Brahman, and his night has the same length. . . . At the end of that day and night he who was asleep awakes and, after awaking, creates. . . .[16]

The *Manusmṛti* as well as the Purāṇas use the term *Manvantara*, an age of Manu or age of humankind, calculated as seventy-one ages of the *devas*. "The *Manvantaras*, the creations and destructions of the world, are numberless; sporting as it were, Brahman repeats this again and again." Throughout we find what we might term *historical pessimism*: the world is in constant moral decline.

> In the *Kṛta* age dharma is four-footed and complete: and so is truth—nor does any gain accrue to men by unrighteousness. In the other three ages dharma is successively deprived of one foot, and through theft, falsehood, and fraud the merit is diminished by one fourth. Men are free from disease, accomplish all their aims, and live four hundred years in the *Kṛta* age, but in the *Tretā* and the succeeding ages their life is lessened by one quarter. (I, 81–83)

Dharma too is different according to the ages: in the *Kṛta* age austerity is the chief virtue, in the *Tretā* age wisdom, in the *Dvāpara* the performance of sacrifices, and in the *Kali* age, in which we now live, *dāna* or liberality.[17]

In all the Purāṇas our present age is described as being close to universal chaos and final destruction. The laws that governed and upheld humankind in former ages have broken down, humankind has become weak, oppressed by numerous calamities, and short lived.

## PURĀṆIC COSMOGRAPHY

Before dealing with details of traditional history that concern almost exclusively the *Kali* age, it may be worthwhile to mention some features of the traditional world description offered mainly in the *Purāṇas*, and presupposed in all historical or mythical narrations.[18] The Hindus certainly had a quite accurate knowledge of those parts of India in which they lived, and at certain times they also ventured forth across the seas. Not content with their experiences, they constructed a complete world model in which everything found its exact place. Though these models as described in various texts differ in a number of substantial details, all of them begin with Mount Meru as the center of the world, around which Jambudvīpa, the known world (mainly India) is situated. The *Mahābhārata* has preserved an older version of the world model in which four *dvīpas* or continents were arranged around Mount Meru, with the Ocean of Salt as the southern border of the world and the Ocean of Milk as the northern.[19] The fully developed Purāṇic model is much more complex: it knows of seven *dvīpas* surrounded by and surrounding seven concentric oceans. In the center of this world stands Mount Meru, forming with *Jambudvīpa* the innermost circle. Its boundary is formed by a vast ring of salt water, the *lavana-sāgara*, followed by another concentric ring of land and so on, according to the scheme presented in Figure 6.1.[20]

The middle column indicates the width of each ring of sea or land, using the diameter of *Jambudvīpa* (given as 100,000 *yojanas*)[21] as the basic unit. The whole map has to be imagined as consisting of concentric circles, whose center is Mount Meru, the pivot of *Jambudvīpa*. *Jambudvīpa* consists in detail of the following parts shown in Figure 6.2.[22]

*Bhārata-varṣa* (India) again is divided into nine parts, ruled over by kings from the dynasties descended from Satajit,[23] going back through various illustrious rulers to Pṛthu, from whom the earth (*pṛthvī*) took her name, since he "subdued the earth," levelling it and beginning to cultivate it. Whereas the other eight parts of *Jambudvīpa* are described as "places of perfect enjoyment, where happiness is spontaneous and uninterrupted, without vicissitude, without age and death, without distinction of virtue or vice, without any change brought about by the cycle of sages," *Bhārata-varṣa* is subject to the deterioration which is brought about by the succession of the four *yugas*; it knows suffering and death. But it is praised nevertheless as "the best of the divisions of *Jambudvīpa*, because it is the land of works" enabling people to gain heaven or even final emancipation. The gods themselves praise the good fortune of those born in *Bhārata-varṣa*.[24] The description of the several parts

| | | |
|---|---|---|
| Aṇḍakaṭaha<br>Tamas | 128 | Shell of the World Egg<br>Darkness |
| Lokālokaśaila<br>Kañcanībhūmī | 128 | World-No-World Mountains<br>Land of Gold |
| Jalasāgara<br>Puṣkaradvīpa | 64<br>64 | Sea of Sweet Water<br>Blue-Lotus Land |
| Kṣirasāgara<br>Śākadvīpa | 32<br>32 | Milk Ocean<br>Teak Tree Land |
| Dadhisamūdra<br>Krauñcadvīpa | 16<br>16 | Buttermilk Ocean<br>Heron Land |
| Sarpisamūdra<br>Kuśadvīpa | 8<br>7 | Melted-Butter Ocean<br>Kuśa Land |
| Surāsamūdra<br>Śālmaladvīpa | 4<br>4 | Wine Ocean<br>Silk-Cotton-Tree Land |
| Ikṣurasasamūdra<br>Plakṣadvīpa | 2<br>2 | Sugar-Cane-Juice Ocean<br>Fig-Tree Land |
| Lāvaṇasamūdra<br>Jambudvīpa | 1<br>1 | Salt-Water Ocean<br>Roseapple-Tree Land |
| | 510 | Mount Meru |

Figure 6.1. The Purāṇic world model

of *Jambudvīpa* contains much valuable information about the geography and ethnology of ancient India. Mount Meru, the Golden Mountain, stands in the center of *Jambudvīpa*. Its height is given as eighty-four thousand *yojanas*, its depth below the surface of the earth as 16,000. Its diameter at the summit is thirty-two thousand *yojanas* and at its base sixteen thousand *yojanas*; "so that this mountain is like the seed-cup of the lotus of the earth." From the base of Meru extend mighty mountain ridges; on its summit is the vast city of Brahmā, extending over fourteen thousand *yojanas*. And around it, at the cardinal points and in the intermediate quarters, is situated the stately city of Indra and the cities of the other regents of the spheres. The capital of Brahmā is enclosed by the River Ganges: issuing from the foot of Viṣṇu[25] and washing the lunar orb, it falls here from the skies. After encircling the city it divides into four mighty rivers.

The Purāṇas describe in detail not only *Jambudvīpa* but also the other continents with their geography and history. In the five continents outside *Jambudvīpa* the lives of people last for five thousand years; they are happy, sinless, and enjoy uninterrupted bliss. They have their own system of classes, corresponding to the four castes in *Bhārata-varṣa*, but this division does not result in any friction or any deprivation of one group of people compared with the other. In *Puṣkaradvīpa* people live a thousand years, free from sickness and

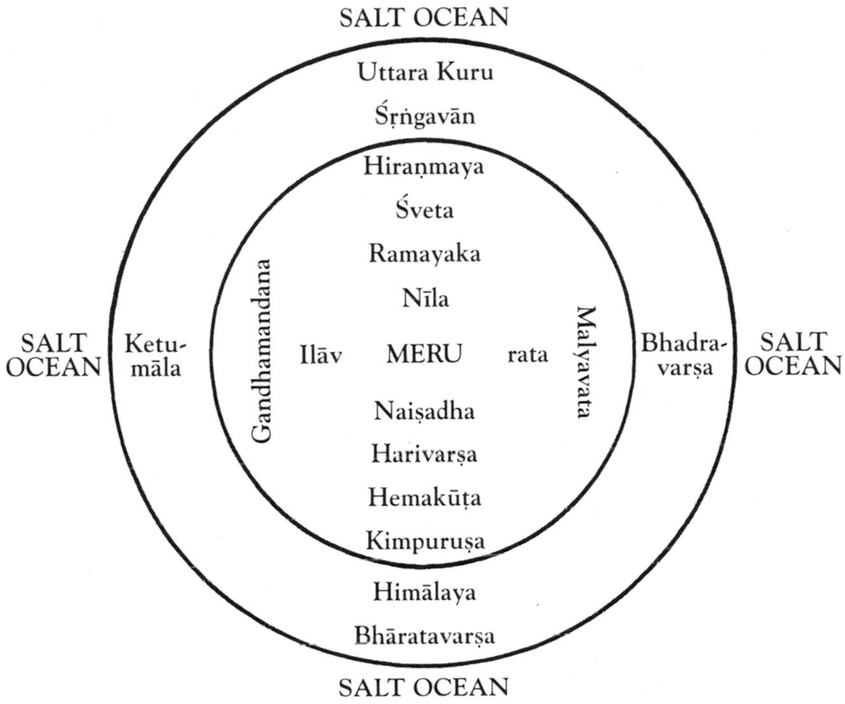


Figure 6.2. Map of Purāṇic world model

sorrow and unruffled by anger and affection. There is neither virtue nor vice, neither killer nor slain; there is no jealousy, envy, fear, hatred; neither is there truth or falsehood. Food is spontaneously produced there. There is no distinction of caste and order, there are no fixed institutes, nor are rites performed for the sake of merit. The three Vedas, the Purāṇas, ethics, policy, and the laws of service are unknown. It is, in fact, a terrestrial paradise where time yields happiness to all its inhabitants, who are exempt from sickness and decay. A *Nyāgrodha* tree grows on this land, which is the special abode of Brahmā, and he resides in it, adored by *devas* and *asuras*.[26]

> Beyond the sea of fresh water is a region of twice its extent, where the land is of gold and where no living beings reside. Thence extends the *Lokāloka* mountain, which is ten thousand *yojanas* in breadth and as many in height; and beyond it perpetual darkness invests the mountain all around; which darkness is again encompassed by the shell of the world egg. Thus the universe with its exterior shell is five hundred million *yojanas* in extent. It is the mother and nurse of all creatures, the foundation of all worlds, and the principal element.[27]

The universe as described in Hindu cosmology is geocentric: the earth is the center of the entire universe, though not its best part as regards enjoyment. It is, however, best suited for "work," for the possibilities, which it opens to gain the supreme end, liberation. The Hindu world is, however, less ethnocentric than the world view of, for instance, the ancient Near Eastern peoples. Mount Meru, the center of the Hindu world, is far away from *Bhārata-varṣa*. Only later Hindu sects identify the center of the world with their centres of worship. Thus some Śaivites consider Cidāṁbaram as the world center, some Vaiṣṇavas identify Vṛdāvana with the pivot of the world. The Purāṇic accounts are also quite modest when comparing their own country with other countries; the people in other countries are described as materially much better off, they are free from most of the hazards that beset the people of Bhārata-varṣa.

A vertical section produces the following layers or sheaths of the world egg, the *brahmāṇḍa*:[28]

| | |
|---|---|
| *Satyaloka* | |
| *Tapoloka* | |
| *Janaloka* | |
| *Maharloka* | |
| *Svarloka* (planets) | Regions of the consequences of work |
| *Bhuvarloka* (sky) | |
| *Bhurloka* (earth) | |
| *Atala* (white) | Netherworlds |
| *Vitala* (black) | |
| *Nitala* (purple) | |
| *Gabhastimat* (yellow) | |
| *Mahātala* (sandy) | |
| *Sutala* (stony) | |
| *Pātāla* (golden) | |
| *Śeṣa* (the world-snake) | |
| *Raurava*, etc. | (28 *nārakas* or hells) |

Beginning with the Earth as the centre, the *Viṣṇu Purāṇa* explains the netherworlds, not to be confused with hells or with the idea of netherworlds in the West. Each of the seven nether worlds extends ten thousand *yojanas* below the surface of the one preceding. "They are embellished with magnificent palaces in which dwell numerous *danavas, daityas, yakṣas,* and great *nāgas*. The Muni Nārada, after his return from those regions to the skies, declared among the celestials that *Pātāla* was much more delightful than Indra's heaven."[29] Below these is *śeṣa*, the "form of Viṣṇu proceeding from the quality of darkness," also called *ananta*, the endless one, with a thousand heads, embellished with the *svāstika*. *Śeṣa* bears the entire world like a diadem upon his head. When *ananta*, his eyes rolling with intoxication, yawns, the earth, with all her woods and mountains, seas and rivers, trembles. The hells "beneath the earth and beneath the waters" are the places of punishment for sinners—specified according to their crimes.[30] The sphere of the earth (moving upward) "extends as far as it is illuminated by the rays of the sun and moon; and to the same extent the sphere of the sky extends upward, till the beginning of the sphere of the planets." The solar orb is situated a hundred thousand *yojanas* from the earth and that of the moon an equal distance from the sun. At the same interval above the moon occurs the orbit of all lunar constellations. *Budha* (Mercury) is two hundred thousand *yojanas* above the lunar mansions. *Śukra* (Venus) is at the same distance from *Budha*. *Aṅgāraka* (Mars) is as far above *Śukra*; *Bṛhaspati* (Jupiter) as far from *Aṅgāraka*, while *Śani* (Saturn) is two hundred and fifty thousand leagues beyond *Brhaspati*. The sphere of the *Seven Ṛṣis* is a hundred thousand *yojanas* above *Śani*, and at a similar height above these is the *Dhruva* (polestar), the pivot of the whole planetary circle. *Bhur*, *Bhuvar*, and *Svar* form "the region of the consequence of works"—the region of the works that bring merit is *Bhāratavarṣa* alone.[31]

Above *Dhruva*, at the distance of ten million *yojanas*, lies *Maharloka*, whose inhabitants dwell in it for a *kalpa* or a Day or Brahmā. At twice that distance is *Janaloka*, where *Sanāndana* and other pure-minded sons of Brahmā reside. At four times the distance, between the last two, lies the *Tapoloka*, inhabited by the *devas* called *Vaibhrajas*, whom fire cannot harm. At six times the distance, *Satyaloka* is situated, the sphere of truth, whose inhabitants will never know death again. *Satyaloka* is also called *Brahmāloka*. Some of the sectarian texts add above *Brahmāloka*, *Viṣṇuloka* (or *Vaikuṇṭha*) and *Śivaloka* (or *Kailāsa*), assigning the supreme place to the deity of their own choice.[32]

The world egg (with its seven *dvīpas* and *samudras*, its seven *lokas* and its seven netherworlds, *Śeṣa* and the hells beneath—all within the shell of *brahmānda*) is but the center of a greater universe, which is stratified according to the following scheme:

*Pradhāna-Puruṣa* (Primeval matter and spirit)

*mahat* (the first principle)

*bhutādi* (the gross elements)

*nabhas* (ether)

*vāyu* (wind)

*vahni* (fire)

*ambu* (water)

The World Egg (earth)

The *Viṣṇu Purāṇa* explains in detail.[33] The world is encompassed on every side and above and below by the shell of the egg of Brahmā, in the same manner as the seed of the wood apple is encircled by its rind. Around the outer surface of the shell flows water, for a space equal to ten times the diameter of the world. The waters are encompassed by fire, fire by air, air by ether, and ether by the gross elements, these by the first principle. Each of these extends in breadth ten times the layer that it encloses, and the last is enveloped by *pradhāna*, which is infinite and its extent cannot be enumerated: it is therefore called the boundless, the illimitable cause of all existing things, supreme nature, or *prakṛti*; the cause of all world eggs of which there are thousands and tens of thousands, and millions and thousands of millions. Within *pradhāna* resides *puman*, diffusive, conscious, and self-irradiating, as fire is inherent in flint. Both are encompassed by the energy of Viṣṇu (*Viṣṇu-śakti*), which is the cause of the separation of the two at the period of dissolution, and the cause of their continuance in existence, as well as of their recombination at the time of creation.

## PAST AND FUTURE WORLD RULERS

The Hindu universe is peopled by all possible degrees of being: inanimate objects, plants, animals, demons, *devas*, semidivine beings, humans, et cetera. The Purāṇas contain poetic genealogies for all of them. For our purpose it will be of interest to outline briefly the history of the human race, as reported in traditional Hindu literature. Several scholars have tried to reconstruct ancient Indian history with the names and dates supplied in epics and Purāṇas; so far they have not come to an agreement as regards the most important dates, especially with regard to the Bhārata War, which is considered the central landmark in ancient Indian history.[34] Since we are here not directly concerned with history in the modern Western sense, we may content ourselves with a summary of the opinion of one authority in this area.[35] Without necessarily accepting his chronology, we nevertheless get an idea of a historically probable calculation and also gain some familiarity with the more prominent names in Indian history and mythology.

From Brahmā, the creator, was born Manu Svayambhuva,[36] who divided into a male and a female and produced two sons, Priyavrata and Uttānapāda, and two daughters, Prasūti and Ākūti. From these were born Dharma and Adharma and their progeny, Śraddhā (faith), *Lakṣmī* (good fortune), Krīya (action), Buddhi (intelligence), Śānti (peacefulness) as well as Hiṃsā (violence), Anṛta (falsehood), Nikṛti (immorality), Bhaya (fear), Māyā (deceit), Mṛtyu (death), *Duḥkha* (pain), *Śoka* (sorrow), Tṛṣṇa (greed), Krodha (anger), and so forth.

We move into the realm of protohistory with the story of Vena, the grandson of Caksuṣa, in the line of the sixth Manu.[37] Apparently Vena offended the religious feelings of his subjects by proclaiming himself to be God and forbidding all other forms of worship. The *ṛṣis* who were worshippers of Hari (Viṣṇu) did not accept his claim to divine kingship and killed Vena, who left no heir.

In the period following the death of the king, anarchy spread terror among the people, who clamored for a ruler. The *ṛṣis* drilled the left thigh of the dead king; out of it came a dwarfish black being, whom they called Niṣāda and who became the ancestor of the Niṣādas in the Vindhya Mountains. They drilled the right arm of the dead king and produced Pṛthu, at whose birth heaven and earth rejoiced. His consecration is described at great length; he is celebrated as the initiator of agriculture, of road construction, and city building. From his line sprang Manu Vaivaśvata, the savior of humanity at the time of the Great Flood. We have several accounts of the deluge, which also plays a great role in the popular traditions of other cultures.[38] Pusalker accepts the flood as a historical event that occurred around 3100 BCE. In Hindu mythology it is connected with the *Matsya-avatāra* of Viṣṇu. A small fish swam into Manu's hands when he was taking his morning bath, asking for protection. Manu put it first into a jar, then into a pond, and, when it was fully grown, back into the sea. The fish gave Manu a warning about the coming flood and advised him to prepare a ship and enter it at an appointed time. Manu did so and when the flood finally came, the fish appeared again and pulled Manu's boat to the Northern Mountains. After the water had subsided, Manu was ordered to disembark and descend from the mountain, whose slope is called *Manoravatāraṇam*, Manu's descent. He was the only human being saved, and with him humankind took a new beginning. He was also the first lawgiver and first tax collector. His eldest offspring had a double personality as the male Ila and the female Ilā. From Ilā, who married Budha, was born Pururavas, the originator of the Aila or Lunar dynasty. From Ila's eldest son, Ikṣvāku, who had his capital at Ayodhyā , sprang the Aikṣvāka or Solar dynasty. The other eight sons of Manu also became founders of peoples and dynasties whose lines are recorded.

According to the most famous kings in the lists, Pusalker divides the history after Manu into a *Yayāti* period (3000–2750 BCE), a *Māndhāṭr* period (2750–2550 BCE), a *Paraśurāma* period (2550–2350 BCE), a *Rāmacandra* period (2350–1950 BCE), and a *Kṛṣṇa* period (1950–1400 BCE). The end of this era coincides with the great Bhārata War, which according to Indian tradition marks the beginning of the *Kali-yuga*, the last and most evil of all the ages of humankind.[39]

The *Purāṇas* have lists of dynasties of kingdoms that flourished at the end of the Bhārata War and continued until they were absorbed by the great Nanda Empire of Magadha in the fourth century BCE.[40] One of the prominent figures in the Purāṇas is Parīkṣit, a Paurava king who lived after the Great War. Largely from Buddhist accounts we are informed about the kingdoms of Kośala and Kāśī. The kings ruling over Magadha gradually extended their influence till they were the only great power in northern India.

Between Manu, the savior of humankind, and the Bhārata War, the Purāṇas list ninety-five generations of kings, on whom they report in the past tense. From Parīkṣit, "the ruling king,"[41] onward they use the future tense, thus giving these genealogies the character of prophecies and enhancing their authority. They offer quite precise information regarding names and important details of their lives and deaths up to the time of the Guptas in the fourth century CE. Then again the names and stories are fanciful, further developing the idea of a constant deterioration of the quality of life during the *Kali-yuga*, which lasts for three hundred sixty thousand years from the death of Kṛṣṇa.[42] After enumerating a large number of names, the *Purāṇa* states:

> These will all be contemporary monarchs, reigning over the earth; kings of churlish spirit, violent temper, and ever addicted to falsehood and wickedness. They will inflict death on women, children, and cows; they will seize upon the property of their subjects; they will be of limited power and will, for the most part, rise and fall rapidly. Their lives will be short, their desires insatiable, and they will display but little piety. The people of the various countries will follow their example. . . . Wealth and piety will decrease day by day, until the world will be wholly depraved. Then property alone will confer rank; wealth will be the only source of devotion; passion will be the sole bond of union between the sexes; falsehood will be the only means of success in litigation; and women will be objects merely of sensual gratification. Earth will be venerated but for its mineral treasures, dishonesty will be a universal means of subsistence, presumption will be substituted for learning. No person's life will exceed three and twenty years. Thus in the Kali age shall decay constantly proceed, until the human race approaches its annihilation.

At the end of times *Kalki*, a divine descent, will arise, who "will destroy all the *mlecchas* and thieves and all whose minds are devoted to iniquity. He will then reestablish dharma on earth, and the minds of those who live at the end of the Kali age shall be awakened. . . . The men who are thus changed by virtue of that peculiar time shall be as the seeds of human beings and shall give birth to a race who shall follow the laws of the *Kṛta* age." (IV, 24, 122) The Purāṇa adds some astronomical information from which the end of the times can be foretold; also included is the prophecy that Devapī of the race of Puru and Maru of the family of Īkṣvāku will outlive all others and constitute the germ of the renewal of the *Kṛta* age, after twelve hundred years of Brahmā's night have elapsed.[43]

Hindus in more recent times have also become acquainted with geography and history in the modern sense, which in many details is in conflict with traditional teaching. There are some who tenaciously cling to the literal truth of their scriptures and reject modern scholarship as biased and ignorant. In a number of cases, scholarship has vindicated the ancient traditions over against the rash assumptions of former generations of historians. There are also some who try to harmonize the scriptural accounts with modern scientific ideas in geology or biology, often in a somewhat forced way.[44] Others have compromised between tradition and modernity, sometimes demythologizing and allegorizing the scriptures so as to uphold their truth and to sound modern at the same time.

In a manner typical of modern enlightened Hinduism, S. Radhakrishnan demythologized Hinduism in a speech before the *Viśva Hindū Sammelan* in New Delhi,[45] stating that there was nothing sectarian or dogmatic about Hinduism, which was but the reconciliation of all paths to God. The Hindu myth of the creation of the world, he continues, implies that life came out of matter, animal life out of plant life, and gave rise in time to human reason. The famous myth of the churning of the Milk Ocean out of which the gods derived *amṛta*, the nectar of immortality, he interprets as the "churning of the spirit" from which comes purity of heart.

Hinduism has shown throughout its long history ambivalence with regard to the reality of the physical universe. This is probably most clearly articulated in the positions assumed by Śaṅkara and Rāmānuja. For Śaṅkara as well as Rāmānuja the visible world has its origin in *brahman*, the Absolute. But while for Śaṅkara the world is *māyā*,[46] a kind of illusion or appearance and an alienation of the Self, for Rāmānuja it is the body of God, sharing some of the qualities ascribed to the Supreme One, real and sacramentally necessary.

Over against the One Supreme the world is characterized by duality. The opposites of dharma and *adharma*, of good and evil, of hot and cold, of gods and demons are possible only in the world, and the world is constituted by them. This fundamental structure is articulated in the seemingly naive creation stories of the Purāṇas as well as in the sophisticated cosmological speculation of the *darśanas*. It appears in the self-partition of *brahman* in the Upaniṣads and

Figure 6.3. *Amṛta manthana*: Churning of the Milk Ocean

in the *sura-asura* contest of the Churning of the Milk-Ocean, in the *puruṣa-prakṛti* dualism of Sāṁkhya, and in the *vyavahāra-paramārtha* distinction of Śaṅkara. Within the dualism a tripartite schema supplies the dynamics of development: the Pṛthvī-Dyaus polarity of the Veda becomes sacrificially relevant as *triloka*—three worlds. The *puruṣa-prakṛti* polarity is actualized toward liberation through the *tri-guṇa* dynamics. The *vyavahāra-paramārtha* dichotomy includes the active pursuit of the triad of the *puruṣārthas*. Behind the colorful and seemingly naive stories in which the traditional Hindu worldview is often described there are profound ideas and structural insights that could well be expressed in modern abstract mathematical terms—as has been done.[47]

CHAPTER SEVEN

# The Many Gods and the One God of Hinduism

> "Yes," said he, "but just how many gods are there, Yājñavalkya?" "Thirty-three." . . . "Yes," said he, "but just how many gods are there, Yājñavalkya?" "One!"
>
> —*Bṛhadāraṇyaka Upaniṣad* III, IX, 1

About a score of different Sanskrit words are rendered by the one English word *god*.[1] We have to look at some of them in order to find out how Hindus can at one and the same time have many gods and believe in One God.

## VEDIC *DEVAS*

When English publications on Vedic religion speak about *gods*, they use this term as translation for the Vedic word *deva* or *devatā*.[2] Thus they enumerate faithfully the eleven celestial gods, the eleven atmospheric gods, and the eleven terrestrial gods. F. Max Müller was struck by the evident fact that in a number of Vedic hymns, the *deva* to whom the song was addressed was praised as the only one, the supreme, the greatest, and that praise was not restricted to one and the same *deva*, but given to various *devas* in various hymns. This did not conform to the classical notion of *polytheism*, so Müller coined the new term *henotheism* (from the Greek term *hen[os]* = one) to distinguish this religion from *monotheism*, the revealed Biblical religion. The Hindu *deva* is not God—at the most *deva* could be loosely translated as a "divine being." Etymologically it means "shiny," "exalted"; and thus we find that the term *deva* covers everything that has to do with the supernatural: all figures, forms, processes and emotions, melodies, books and verse meters—whatever needs the explanation of a transcendent origin or status—are called *devas* or *devatā* in one place or another.[3] The functions of different parts of the body, symbols, and syllables are explained as *deva*. In Vedic religion we find the term used in a relatively restricted way; but even there we are not entitled to equate it with *god*, but rather with *supernatural powers* in a general sense.

Anthropologists have become aware of the importance of the idea of "power" in tribal religions. R. N. Dandekar attempted to show that behind the Vedic *deva* worship lies such an idea of an all-pervading ultimate power, of which the *devas* partake without being quite identical with it. According to him most of the Vedic *devas* are created for the myths and not the myths for *devas*. Mythology is thus primary and *devas* are secondary. The Vedic *ṛṣis* had a message that they conveyed in images for which they created the concretized figures of *devas*. Thus we can see that Vedic mythology is evolutionary, implying a change of the character of a *deva* according to changed circumstances. Much more important than the variable figure of the *deva* was the basic underlying potency of which the individual *devas* were only expressions and manifestations; the Vedic counterpart to the *mana* power is the *asura* power, which is shared by all beings, especially the *devas*. That is also the explanation of the highly variable and flexible anthropomorphism of the Vedic *devas*. There is, strictly speaking, no Vedic pantheon in the sense in which there is a Greek or a Roman one.[4]

The Vedic seer did not share the outlook of moderns. Though *agni* is the term for "fire" in the most general sense, to the Vedic religious mind the reality of *agni* is not simply the chemical process of carbonization of organic matter that modern scientists would associate with the term *fire*. In fire the *ṛṣi* sees a *deva*, a transcendent aspect that makes *agni* fit to be used as an expression that hints at a something beyond the material reality investigated by modern chemistry. *Agni* is a *deva*, not a "personification of a natural phenomenon" as nineteenth-century Western scholarship would describe it, but the manifestation of a transcendent power. The physical reality of fire is so obvious and so necessary that the Hindu would not think of spiritualizing it away; but there is more to it than meets the senses—the *ṛṣi* is inspired to "see" and express the mystery behind all visible reality. Objective natural science never found *devas* nor will it find God in the physical universe; it requires the sensibilities of a *kavi*, the poet and the prophet to discover divine reality in it.

Granting that the hymns of the *Ṛgveda* in their present form are an ancient revision of a still more ancient text,[5] and keeping in mind what has already been said about the evolutionary character of Vedic mythology, we find it quite acceptable that at different stages there were different *devas* at the center of Vedic religion. In our present Veda text Indra dominates, a rather late arrival in Vedic religion who is difficult to circumscribe because he assumes at least three different roles: Indra the cosmic power, Indra the warlike leader of the Aryans, and Indra the ancient mythical dragon-killing hero.[6] Popular books on Indian religion still carry the nineteenth-century cliché of

Indra as "personification of the rain storm" or "weather god." Quite apart from the misunderstanding of the nature of a *deva* we must also reject this idea, because "most of the descriptions of Indra are centered round the war with, and subsequent victory over, Vṛtra. A proper understanding of this point, would, therefore, serve as an adequate starting point for a critical study of Indra's personality and character."[7] What a study of this myth reveals is that Indra, contradictory as many of his single features may be, is the manifestation of the saving divine power defeating the opposing demonic power.[8]

Of the more than one thousand hymns of the *Ṛgveda*[9] about a quarter are addressed to Indra alone. While not exhaustively dealing with all the questions surrounding the nature of Indra, we can get an impression of the nature of Vedic devotion to Indra by quoting one of them expressing Indra's greatness. The titles given to Indra in this hymn, such as *maghavān*, *mahāvīra*, *deva eka*, *rājā*, are essential attributes of the High God, titles given to the Savior God in later developments of Indian religion. The hymns do indeed allude to historical events and historic personalities when describing the personality of Indra, but the sum total of attributes given to him is more than just the apotheosis of a warrior hero. That the slaying of Vṛtra by Indra is more than the victory of a warrior over his enemy seems to suggest itself to us when we read that the effect was that Indra "raised the Sun for all to see." It is the work of the High God to "chase away the humbled brood of demons," to "encompass the worlds from all sides," and to "divide day and night." It is the High God alone "before whom even the Heaven and Earth bow down," "without whose help our people never conquer," who is "the bestower of food and wealth," "man's helper from old, not disappointing hope, friend of our friends, rich in mighty deeds." His authority as High God is finally established through his victory over the demon whom no human being would be able to defeat. Only if Indra is understood as a symbol for, and a manifestation of, the High God do the attributes given to him make sense, especially since the same attributes are given to other *devas*, the same deeds are ascribed to Agni, to Soma, to Varuṇa and others. "They call him Indra, Mitra, Varuṇa, Agni and he is heavenly-winged Garutman. To what is One, sages give many a title."[10] Indra is only one of the names given to the Savior God. The Supreme was first, and only under specific circumstances did he receive the name of Indra. The Supreme is nameless—men give names to him, variously describing him in categories taken from cosmic events, from history, or from their own experience.

> He, who as soon as he was born became the first among the high-minded *devas*, their protector on account of his power and might, he who made the worlds tremble before his breath on account of his valor, he, you people, is Indra!
>
> He who fixed fast and firm the earth that staggered, and set at rest the agitated mountains, who measured out the air's wide middle region and gave the heaven support, he, you people, is Indra!

Who slew the dragon, freed the seven rivers and drove the cattle forth from Vala's cave, who generated fire between two stones, the spoiler in warriors' battle, he, you people, is Indra!

By whom the universe was made to tremble, who chased away the defeated host of dark-skins, and like a gambler gathering his winnings, seized the foe's riches, he, you people, is Indra!

Of him the terrible, they ask: Where is he? They also say: He is not. He sweeps away like birds, the enemies' possessions. Have faith in him, for he, you people, is Indra.

Inciter to action of the poor and humble, of the priest and the suppliant singer, fair-faced he gives his favors to the one who pressed Soma between two stones, he, you people, is Indra!

He under whose supreme control are horses, all chariots, the villages and cattle, he who gave being to sun and dawn, who leads the water, he, you people, is Indra!

To whom two armies cry in close encounter, both enemies, the stronger and the weaker, whom two invoke upon one chariot mounted, each for himself, he, you people, is Indra.

Without whose help our people never conquer, whom, battling, they invoke to give them succor, who became the universe's likeness, who shook the unmovable [mountains], he, you people, is Indra.

He who struck before they knew the danger, with his weapon many a sinner, who does not give pardon to one who provokes him, who slays the *dasyu*, he, you people, is Indra.

Even the Heaven and the Earth bow down before him, before his breath the mountains tremble. Known as the Soma-drinker, armed with thunder, he who wields the bolt, he, you people, is Indra![11]

Indra emerges as power that increases even more through the sacrifice and the *mantras*. *Devas* also depend on mortals: religion is a two-way road to power![12]

Next to Indra, Agni is the *deva* most often addressed in the Vedic hymns; he is indispensable in the all-important business of sacrifice! The very first hymn of the *Ṛgveda Saṃhitā* and some two hundred more are addressed to him.

I praise Agni, the *purohit* (priest), the divine *ṛtvik* (another class of Vedic priests), the *hotar* (a third class of Vedic priests) and lavisher of wealth. Worthy is Agni to be praised by the living as by the ancient *ṛṣis*. He shall conduct the *devas* to this place. Through Agni man obtains wealth.[13]

Agni-fire is the medium through which the material gift of the sacrifice is transformed into the spiritual substance of which the gods can partake and from which they draw their strength!

One of the most impressive and beautiful hymns is addressed to Savitṛ, the "inspirer," sun, light, intelligence, the luster of beauty.

Photo 9. Agni: Khajurāho

> Agni I first invoke for prosperity, I call on Mitra and Varuṇa to come to help, I call on night who gives rest to all moving life, I call on Savitṛ, the divine helper. Throughout the dusky firmament advancing, laying to rest the mortal and the immortal, borne in his golden chariot he comes, the divine Savitṛ who looks upon every creature. The *deva* moves by the upward path, the downward, with two bright bays, adorable he journeys. Savitṛ comes, the helper from afar, and chases away all distress and sorrow.[14]

Heaven and Earth are hymned as *devas*; Aditi, "Mother Earth," is also mentioned separately; the Maruts, the storm winds are a group of *devas* frequently invoked; rivers and waters appear as divinities; the *soma* juice and the *kuśa* grass, both indispensable for the sacrifice, are variously referred to as *deva*.

The *devas* are not the moral ideals for men to follow, nor are they considered lawgivers. The hymns speak of *ṛta*, "the law," as independent of the *devas*, standing apart and above them as an impersonal and infallibly effective power. The word *ṛta* is connected with *ṛtu*, the seasons, the regular round of spring, summer, rain, autumn, and winter. Beyond that we can understand *ṛta* as the principle of order behind all things and events. In a way *ṛta* foreshadows both the later *karman* and *brahman*.

Several *devas*, especially Mitra and Varuṇa, are invoked as the guardians of *ṛta*, never as its creators. Both are also thought to reward good and punish evil.[15] The central role of Varuṇa in Vedic religion became the focus of H. Lueders's lifework. He intended to show that Varuṇa was originally the ocean surrounding the world by whom oaths were taken already in prehistoric times. During the Indo-Iranian period the notion of *ṛta* developed; "truth" as ruling power. Its seat was placed in the ocean and Varuṇa became its protector.[16]

Kubera, the Vedic god of treasures and riches and the *lokapāla* of the North, was and still is a very popular deity. In Vedic mythology he is also the king of *yakṣas* and *kinnaras*.

We have largely lost the ability to appreciate nature as a symbol of the divine, and that makes many of us unable to appreciate Vedic *deva* worship without using categories drawn from a mechanized world. It is not just a superstitious remnant if today Hindus offer praises and prayers to the rising sun at the time of their morning prayer. There may be many a modern, educated Indian among those sun worshippers who knows about the physical properties of the sun, its surface temperature and its chemical composition. Worship is not addressed to the astronomical body, not to a symbolized idea but to the *sūrya-deva*, the metaphysical reality through which an aspect of the supreme reality becomes relevant for humans. Quite frequently one may observe a pious person worshipfully saluting the electric light after switching it on in the evening. The Indian peasant regards the cow as the seat of many *devas* and worships her; factory workers offer worship to their machines on certain days, to the *deva* of technology by whose operations they live. They all may grasp in their own way

Photo 10. Kubera: Khajuraho

what many of us have not yet quite understood—that all things, whether made by humans or not, manifest a power that is beyond us.

## UPANIṢADIC *BRAHMAN* AND PURĀṆIC *ĪŚVARA*

In the *Bṛhadāraṇyaka Upaniṣad* we read a dialogue in which Yājñavalkya is asked the crucial question: *Kati devāḥ*, how many are the *devas*? His first answer is a quotation from a Vedic text: "Three hundred and three and three thousand and three." Pressed on, he reduces the number first to thirty-three, then to six, then to three, to two, to one-and-a-half and finally to One. "Which is the one *deva*?" And he answers: "The *prāṇa* (breath, life). The Brahman. He is called *tyat* (that)."[17] Though *devas* still figure in sacrificial practice and religious debate, the question "Who is God?" is here answered in terms that have remained the Hindu answer ever since. *Brahman*, untranslatable, identified with the revealed word uttered by the Brahmins, with the soul of everything, with the creator and maintainer of the world, with the inner principle of the universe—*brahman* becomes the term around which the loftiest religious speculation has revolved for thousands of years and it is still the term used to designate the supreme being. *Brahman* has always retained an aura of the not quite concrete, the spiritual that escaped the grasp of the ordinary worshipper. The terms used to express the Supreme Being in its concreteness are equally old: *Īśa* or *īśvara*, the Lord, or *bhagavān*, the Exalted One, are titles given to the Supreme Being by Hindus even now. The name, which is associated with this title, now becomes rather crucial. Whereas the Vedic *ṛṣi* was casual in associating names with the title *deva*, because a plurality of *devas* seemed quite natural and even necessary to grasp different facets of the nameless one, to the new theologians a plurality of Lords seems intrinsically impossible and they insist that the One, with whom they associate the title *īśvara* or *bhagavān*, is the only One—as *brahman* is by necessity one only, ultimately identical with the Lord.

The exclusive association of the title *Lord* with one particular name has led to the development of mutually exclusive religions whose worship and mythology centered on the One God, dismissing in this process the gods of the others as minor beings. Later attempts to unify different traditions (at least theoretically) and to consider their rival Lords as equal sharers of one divine power in the *trimūrti* have sometimes led to wrong conclusions among Western students of Hinduism. Hindu texts do indeed speak of the triad of Brahmā as creator, Viṣṇu as preserver, and Śiva as destroyer, fulfilling the functions of the One God, but all those texts belong to one of the traditions in which the Supreme is identical with one of those names and the three separate names are but different aspects of the same being.[18] Some of the famous *trimūrtis* are quite clearly recognizable as artistic expressions of different modalities of one and the same *īśvara*.[19]

Brahmā, the first of the three, has no following worth mentioning today; only a few temples in India are known to offer worship to him. There are several sectarian accounts that try to explain why he has receded into obscurity. According to an ancient Śaivite myth, he was born with five heads. When he became interested in Pārvatī, Śiva's consort, the latter chopped one of Brahmā's heads off. Since that time he has been shown with four heads only. In his four hands he carries a manuscript symbolizing the Vedas, a water vessel, a ladle and a string of beads. In the *Mahābhārata* he is addressed as *Pitāmahā*, the grandfather, who instructs the *ṛṣis* on religious matters. In Vaiṣṇava mythology he has the role of the demiurge: enthroned on the lotus, which grows out from Viṣṇu's navel, he shapes the world. The Śaivite tale that Brahma was deprived of worship because of a lie may be understood as a blackmail of the Brahmins, whose special Lord he must have been and who did not at first recognize the Śaivites as orthodox.[20]

Within the present-day practice of the *pañcāyata-pūjā* among nonsectarian Hindus, introduced by Śaṅkarācārya, the worship of Sūrya, Śiva, Viṣṇu, Devī and Gaṇeśa takes place simultaneously.

Sūrya is possibly the most Vedic of the five; we find his worship already in the *Ṛgveda*, under the title of Savitṛ. As the source of life, light, and warmth he is the natural "Lord of creation." He is also the source of inner enlightenment as the famous *Gāyatrī mantra* suggests.[21] Purāṇic accounts associate Manu, the ancestor of mankind, and Yama and Yamī, the god and goddess of the netherworlds and of death, with *Sūrya* as his children.[22] The same Purāṇa has given him four wives: *samjñā* (knowledge), *rajñī* (splendor), *prabhā* (light), and *chāyā* (shade). At certain times there had been a strong movement of worshippers of Sūrya as lord, as evidenced by Sūrya temples and *Saura Purāṇas*.[23]

Śiva figures as the One God and the Lord for many millions of Hindus today. A separate chapter will be devoted to him, obviating the need to go into much detail here. The worshippers of *Bhairava*, the fearsome form of Śiva, who are quite numerous in Mahārāstra, derive their motivation from the myth of Dakṣa, who, from being an enemy of Śiva, was converted by Śiva's forceful intervention in the form of *Bhairava* into a devotee, reciting with his goat head the thousand names in praise of Śiva.[24]

The most celebrated Śiva motif mainly known in the West through omnipresent artistic representations is that of the *Naṭarāja*, the King of the Dance. The Purāṇas mention a *tāṇḍava*, a dance of world destruction, and a *līlā*, the dance of the enamored Śiva. A South Indian text records the following details of the myth: Followers of the orthodox Brahmin school of Mīmāṃsā tried to destroy Śiva by successively creating a fierce tiger, a serpent, and an elephant, whom Śiva killed. Finally they sent the embodiment of evil in the form of a dwarf, Muyalaka, the *Apasmāra puruṣa* to overthrow Śiva—but Śiva began his cosmic dance, subduing the dwarf and thereby liberating the world. In this pose *Śiva Naṭarāja* has been immortalized in countless beautiful sculptures, especially in South India. Śaivite theology has invested each and every detail of this image with meaning. Thus it symbolizes today for the pious the divine activities of God: "Creation arises from the drum, protection proceeds

Photo 11. Śiva Sadāśiva (Maharashtra) [Heras Institute]

from the hand of hope, from fire proceeds destruction, from the foot that is planted upon Mulayaka proceeds the destruction of evil, the foot held aloft gives deliverance."[25] His smile shows his uninvolved transcendence, the three eyes are interpreted either as sun, moon, and fire, or as the three powers of Śiva: will, knowledge, and action. The garland of skulls around his neck identifies him as time, and the death of all beings. The single skull on his chest is that of Brahmā, the creator of the world—all beings are mortal, only Śiva is eternal.[26]

Quite often one finds representations of Śiva with five heads. The famous *Śivāṣṭamūrti* combines eight forms of Śiva. Those combinations may be the reflection of amalgamations of individual local or tribal cults that were unified into Śaivism in historical times. A frequent representation shows *Śiva ardhanārī*, half man-half woman in one figure, symbolizing the inseparable unity of Śiva and Śakti.[27]

Śiva's abode and paradise is *Kailāsa*, open to all who worship Śiva, irrespective of caste or sex.[28] *Śaiva Purāṇas* abound in descriptions of hells and in means to escape from them. Śiva himself revealed the famous *mṛtyuñjaya-kavaca*[29] to his devotees so that they might overcome the fear of death.

The most important manifestation of Śiva, his presence and the object of worship for his devotees is the *liṅga*. This is the only "image" of Śiva, the formless absolute Being that is found in the innermost sanctuary of a Śiva temple. The most ancient sculpture of a *liṅga* that still receives public worship is found in Guḍimally, South India and dates from the second century BCE. Its phallic origin is established beyond doubt, but it also can be safely said that it does not evoke any phallic associations in the minds of the worshippers. Many local myths describe the *Śiva liṅgodbhava*, Śiva's appearance from within an icon of this kind. The twelve famous *Jyotir-liṅgas*, each the centre of a pilgrimage, are said to have come into existence by themselves, without human hand, and thus manifest special potency. Many miraculous events are reported from those places.[30] An ancient custom associated with Śaivism is the wearing of a garland of *rudrakṣa* beads, used for *Śiva-japa*, the repetition of the bliss-giving name of Śiva and a sign of belonging to Śiva. Also numerous Śaivites smear their bodies with white ashes—Śiva is said to have a white body!

One of the great Śiva centers is Cidambaram, a town not far from modern Chennai, the former Madras. For the devotees it is the very center of the world. In its thousand-pillared hall daily festivals are arranged for the worship of Śiva—splendid and awesome spectacles. Here in Cidambaram Śiva is said to dance his cosmic drama—but, as the Śiva mystics say: Cidambaram is everywhere! Thus speaks Tirunāvukkaraśu Swami:

> He is difficult to find, but he lives in the heart of the good. He is the innermost secret of the scriptures, inscrutable and unrecognized. He is honey and milk and the bright light. He is the king of the gods, within Viṣṇu and Brahmā, in flame and wind, in the roaring seas and in the towering mountains.[31]

In front of Śiva temples one usually finds the image of *Nandi*, a bull—quite often of huge proportions. The bull is Śiva's mount, associated with Śiva from time immemorial. This again may be one of the remnants of a formerly independent animal worship that became part of Śaivism.

Numerically, Viṣṇu commands the largest following: statistically about 70 percent of Hindus are Vaiṣṇavas, split into numerous sects and schools of thought. Viṣṇu, too, is given a complete chapter later on—here only a few observations are offered.

Viṣṇu is one of the *devas* of the *Ṛgveda*; certain passages in the *Brāhmaṇas* suggest that Viṣṇu is of solar origin.[32] But here too the name Viṣṇu, translated as the "all-pervading one," may be only a Sanskritization of an older Dravidian name, *viñ* = the blue sky, an opinion that receives confirmation from the fact that Viṣṇu even now is always painted a dark blue color.[33] The totemism of tribal cults may have led to the development of the doctrine of the *avatāras*, the descents of Viṣṇu, as may also the Buddhist teaching of the *bodhisattvas*, appearing at different ages. The *Nārāyaṇa* and the *Vāsudeva Kṛṣṇa* cults merged into Vaiṣṇavism in pre-Christian times and gave it perhaps the most powerful stimulus for further development. It seems fairly certain that the basis for the latter was a historical Kṛṣṇa, a hero from the Vṛṣṇi clan of the Yādava tribe residing in and around Mathurā, one of the oldest cities of India. Pāṇini mentions "*bhakti* to *Vasudeva*," and we have the testimony of Megasthenes that Kṛṣṇa worship was established already in the fourth century BCE in the region. Possibly this Kṛṣṇa is also the founder of Bhāgavatism which found its literary expression in some of the favorite scriptures of the Hindus, especially the *Bhāgavata Purāṇa*. The Viṣṇu tradition is perhaps the most typical of all the forms of Hinduism and the greatest books of Indian literature reflect it strongly. The *Mahābhārata* is mainly a Vaiṣṇava book; the *Rāmāyana* treats of Rāma, the *avatāra* of Viṣṇu. One of the most ancient of the Purāṇas is the *Viṣṇu Purāṇa* and the numerous *Vaiṣṇava Saṃhitās* have been the models on which the sectarian works of other religions have been based. The most popular book of the entire Hindu literature, the *Bhagavadgītā*, is a Kṛṣṇa scripture. Countless inspired devotees of Viṣṇu have composed throughout the ages an incomparable store of *bhakti* hymns that live in the literally incessant *bhajans* and *kīrtans* throughout India even today.[34] Viṣṇu *bhakti* knows all shades of love, from the respectful devotion of the servant to his masters, through the affectionate relationship between parent and child, to the passionate eroticism of Kṛṣṇa and Rādhā.

The images of Viṣṇu are of particular importance; they are the real and physical presence of the god, who has the earth and the individual souls as his body. Viṣṇu, too, is being praised by his devotees in a litany of a thousand names that glorify his mythical exploits and enumerate his divine qualities.[35] *Hari* is the most common name under which he is invoked. *Nārāyaṇa*, *Keśava*, *Puruṣottama* are other favourite names that are not only signs of identification but also powerful spells in themselves. Ekanāṭha, a sixteen-century Mahratta poet, sings:

Photo 12. Viṭhobā (Maharashtra) [Heras Institute]

> How sweet is the curdling of liquid *ghī*. So blissful is the seeker, when the hidden one reveals his form. Dark is he, dark is the totally unknown and locked is the way to thoughts and words: the scriptures are silent and the Vedas do not utter a word. Not so the revealed one. How bright! How near! Our thirst is quenched if only he appears, who is so dear to our heart. The ever-perfect one, eternal bliss, being and thought—see it is Govinda, source of ecstasy and rapture. Strength, courage, honor and exalted spirit—see, we witness our God sharing all this. If I but catch a glimpse of God, my eyesight is restored. I have escaped the net of life; the guilt of my senses is cancelled. In the light of the lamp all hidden things are made apparent—so it is when I think of my God: the God from faraway is here![36]

Viṣṇu's heaven is called *Vaikuṇṭha*; but the various subdivisions of Vaiṣṇavism have also introduced new heavens such as Kṛṣṇa's celestial Vṛndāvana or Goloka and Rāma's heavenly Ayodhyā. Viṣṇu's *vahana* is the winged Garuḍa; a special landing post is available for him in South Indian temples.

Usually Śiva and Viṣṇu are represented together with their wives, Pārvatī and Śrī, around whom the Purāṇas have also woven a rich mythology. In Śāktism, however, it is the Goddess who assumes the role of the Supreme Being, whether depicted without a male consort or as superior to him.

*Śakti* means "power" personified in the Goddess, the Divine Mother to whom are ascribed all the functions Viṣṇu has for the Vaiṣṇavas or Śiva for the Śaivas: creation, maintenance, and destruction of the world, illusion and liberation. The female terra-cotta figures found in many sites of the Sindhu-Sarasvatī civilization so much resemble the *Devī* images kept in the homes of today's Indian villages that one may safely infer that they bear witness to a cult of the Goddess. This civilization again may be considered part of a larger culture, spreading from the Mediterranean in the West to Central India in the East, in which the Great Mother was the creator, the Lady of humans, beasts, and plants, the liberator and the symbol of transcendent spiritual transformation.[37] The very name Umā, as well as her association with a mountain and the lion, seems to connect her with Babylonia, Accad, and the Dravidian culture.[38] Another important current of Devī religion comes from indigenous village cults, "the most ancient form of Indian religion."[39] The Goddess is implored to drive away the evil spirits that cause diseases and is asked to help grow vegetables.

Many ancient Indian tribes also had goddesses whose worship coalesced in the course of time with that of the Great Mother. The forms of worship practiced by the tribes—bloody, including human, sacrifices—are still associated with Devī worship. Very often the worship of deceased women of a village merges with the worship of the Great Mother, a process of "making religion" that can still be observed in Indian villages. Many of the names of the Goddess, found in the litany of a thousand names, are probably the names of these local village goddesses. Also many of her functions are taken unmistakably

Photo 13. Durgā: Khajurāho

from village religion. Generally the Aryans must have been hostile toward the cult of the Mother, but already in the *Mahābhārata* we find Durgā established as war goddess, superseding Indra in this function.[40] The goddess of war also played a major role in Tamilnāḍu.[41] There are, no doubt, Vedic elements also in Devī religion—the worship of the Earth (*pṛthvī*) as a goddess for instance, or the worship of *vāk*, the Word, as pointed out. But it is in the Purāṇas and Tantras, which perhaps already show influences from Inner Asia, that Śāktism becomes fully developed in its mythology and cult.

In Śāktism *prakṛti* or *māyā* becomes the active principle of the universe, both as a metaphysical principle and a concrete personality. The most important center of Śakti worship was, and still is, Kāmarūpa in today's Assam. Also the great rivers of India, principally the Gaṅgā and the Yamunā, have been worshipped as goddesses since ancient times.[42] The most important Devī-myth, her killing of *mahiṣāsura*, the embodiment of evil in buffalo form, is the focus of the immensely popular *Durgā-pūjā* celebrations, which are still held in Bengal. Devī is represented figuratively in many forms, particular depictions usually alluding to one of her mythological exploits. A peculiar feature of Tantricism, however, are the *yantras*, symbolic diagrams considered by Śāktas to be representations of Devī.[43]

Gaṇeśa, one of the most popular deities today in India, is also associated with Śiva's family.[44] But it seems that the elephant-headed, pot-bellied patron god of businessmen and scholars comes from an older stratum of religion, in which animal worship was predominant. This may also be the case with Hanuman, the monkey-god, who in the *Rāmāyaṇa* is made the general of the chief ally of Rāma and thus comes to be associated with Viṣṇu worship. The genealogies and family trees of the main deities that we meet so frequently in the Purāṇas are attempts, not always successful, to coordinate the various popular deities and to make them appear, if not as manifestations of the one God, then at least as his children or servants.[45]

God is not dead in India and not a mere memory of the past. There are numerous "living Gods" and "Incarnations" everywhere in India today; some of them claim to continue the ancient line of Viṣṇu or Śiva or Devī *avatāras*, while others simply assume that they are the Supreme in a human body. It is not uncommon in India to get an invitation "to meet God the Father in person," to listen to the latest revelation through an *avatāra* of God, or to be confronted by someone who utters the word of God in the first person singular.

Many Hindu homes are lavishly decorated with color prints of a great many Hindu gods and goddesses, often joined by the gods and goddesses of other religions and the pictures of contemporary heroes. Thus side by side with Śiva and Viṣṇu and Devī one can see Jesus and Zoroaster, Gautama Buddha and Jīna Mahāvīra, Mahātmā Gandhi and Jawaharlal Nehru, and many others. But if questioned about the many gods, even illiterate villagers answered: *bhagavān ek hai*—the Lord is One. They may not be able to figure out in theological terms how the many gods and the one god hang together and they may not be sure about the hierarchy obtaining among the many manifestations, but they know that ultimately there is only One and that the many figures somehow merge into the One.

Hindu theology has many ways of explaining the unity of *brahman* in the diversity of *Iṣṭa-devātas*: different psychological needs of people must be satisfied differently, local traditions and specific revelations must be accommodated, the ineffable can only be predicated in—quite literally—thousands of forms. Among the *sahasra-nāmas*—the litanies of a thousand names that are recited in honor of each of the great gods—the overlap is considerable: each one would be named creator, preserver, destroyer of the universe, each one would be called Truth[46] and Grace and Deliverance. Each one, in the end, is the same: One.[47]

# Part II

## *Trimārga*: The Three Hindu Paths to Liberation

One of the oldest, most popular, and most important ways of viewing Hindu religiosity is the distinction of three "paths": *karmamarga*, the path of works, *jñānamārga*, the path of knowledge and *bhaktimārga*, the path of loving devotion. Some conceive of these as representing a kind of evolution of Hinduism—depending on which of the paths one considers the highest, the sequence would be altered accordingly.

While it is a historical fact that the prevalence and full recognition of *bhaktimārga* took place after that of *jñānamārga* and that Ancient Vedic religion placed a major emphasis on karma or sacrificial ritual, the three paths coexisted for a long time side by side, and they also merge at many points. The actual Hindu practice contains elements of all with emphasis given to one of them according to personal preference.

The idea of "religion" as a "path" is found in other cultures too—the idea of a plurality of equivalent paths is fairly unique to Hinduism. True, there is also rivalry between adherents of different Hindu paths, and some are suggesting that only one of them is the true path, the others being lower or incomplete—but the general understanding is that of equally valid options. Within each *mārga* the latitude varies. *Karmamārga* is a discipline that has to be followed fairly uniformly allowing only for minor local variants. *Jñānamārga* comes in various shapes: already the Upaniṣads specify thirty-two different *vidyās*. However, the need to have a teacher and the requirement of absolute loyalty toward the guru restrict individual choices once the guru has been selected. *Bhaktimārga* leaves personal choices wide open. Not only can one choose one's *Iṣṭa-devatā* and call oneself a devotee of Viṣṇu, Śiva, Devī or another *deva*, one can also choose, within each sect, a variety of interpretations and practices. It is especially the *bhaktimārga* that constantly brings forth new developments and movements.

In spite of the many options between and within the different paths, Hindu religion is highly structured and tends to embrace a person's entire life with its regulations. Hinduism is basically very conservative and many of the regulations going back to Vedic times are still effective in shaping the daily routine of millions of Hindus. Some of this routine is described in the chapter on *karmamārga*: the path of works.

Hinduism, like all traditional religions, was always aware of the ethical dimension of life and of the fact that the moral universe is fragile and in need not only of being preserved but also of being constantly restored. Notions of guilt and sin play a great role in Hinduism and devices for righting wrongs and for the atonement of sins occupy a large place in the life of many Hindus.

Rites of passage are fairly universal—Hinduism has designed elaborate rituals in its *saṃskāras* not only to accompany its members into the next stage of life but also to augment their spiritual powers and to ensure personal fulfillment.

More than anything else it was the *jñānamārga*, the path of knowledge, that was found attractive by non-Hindus, who admired the deep wisdom and spiritual insights of the Hindu sages. The Upaniṣads and the literature based on them deal with human universals, the discovery of one's true self and the soul of the world, liberating knowledge, and the final emancipation.

While the *karmamārga* presupposes high-caste standing and the *jñānamārga* is largely for an intellectual elite, the *bhaktimārga*, the path of loving devotion, has universal appeal: it promises salvation and heaven also to low-caste people, to women and children and even to animals. Great waves of God love have swept over India periodically and have left behind large congregations of devotees, an enormous treasure of inspired poetry, thousands of beautiful temples, and millions of images in which the deities are physically present to their worshippers. Only some moments of this history of God intoxication can be recalled in the chapters on Viṣṇu, Śiva, and Devī—only a small amount of literature can be referred to, and only very inadequately can the fervor be described that animates Hindus who celebrate the great feasts in honor of their deities in the major centers of devotion.

Although all of India has in the course of the last three thousand or more years come under the influence of, first, Vedic, and then, Purāṇic and Tantric Hinduism, and while all regions of India have preserved some of their own local traditions in temple architecture, festivals, and songs, one region stands out in India for its distinct culture and its independent tradition: Tamiḷnāḍu, the Land of the Tamils, in South India. Tamil belongs to a family of languages different from Sanskrit and the rest of the North-Indian Aryan languages. Tamilians claim that both their language and their culture are older than that of the North. There is no doubt that in spite of the extensive Sanskritization that took place and that resulted in most of the Tamils today being Śaivites or Vaiṣṇavas recognizing the same sacred books and traditions as the rest of India, Dravidian elements are strong and distinctive enough to warrant a special chapter on the gods of the Tamiḷs. This too, of course, is an incomplete sketch of a rich and colorful tradition within Hinduism. It may serve as a first introduction to a large subject and as a further reminder that traditional Hinduism has, beside its Vedic and Sanskritic heritage, important non-Vedic and non-Sanskritic components.

CHAPTER EIGHT

# The Path of Works

## *Karmamārga*

> In ancient days the Lord of creatures created people along with sacrifice and said: "By this shall you bring forth and this shall be unto you that which will yield the milk of your desires."
>
> —*Bhagavadgītā* III, 10

In February 1962 Indian newspapers were carrying numerous articles describing measures to meet a predicted *aṣṭagraha*, a particular astronomical conjunction of earth, sun, moon, and the five major planets. The astrologers were unanimous in considering it an exceedingly evil omen—possibly the harbinger of the end of the world. Some journalists were serious; others tried to joke a little; none dared to call the whole thing a humbug. Quite apart from the fact that astronomically speaking the *aṣṭagraha* was not quite accurate, millions of Hindus were frankly worried, expecting a ghastly catastrophe. Many sold all their belongings and went to Prayāga or Kāśī or to some other holy place from whence one goes directly to heaven at the time of death or where one can attain *mokṣa*. The rich engaged thousands of Pandits and Brahmins to organize Vedic *yajñas* that would go on for weeks and weeks on end, reciting millions of Vedic mantras. The dreaded event passed without a major disaster. What had happened? The world had been saved through the creation of the auspicious karma produced in the ritual appropriate for the occasion.

Ritual is one of the most prominent and most important features of Hinduism, and it has two main sources: the Vedic and the Āgamic traditions.[1] For the sake of a more methodical presentation a separate treatment of Vedic ritual, as it emerges from the classical texts, will be given here before describing other forms that are more popular today. The rationale of both of these forms of ritual, as expressed in the Pūrva-Mīmāṃsā system ad the Āgamic treatises is quite different too, as shall be seen.

## THE VEDIC WAY TO HEAVEN

Quite early in the Veda the distinction was drawn between the *karma-kāṇḍa* and the *jñāna-kānda*, the part dealing with "works" and the part dealing with "knowledge," different not only in their contents but also in their ultimate aims. The aim of the *karma-kāṇḍa* is found within *triloka*, the tripartite universe of heaven, earth, and netherworlds. It promises bliss and wealth, and a sojourn in *svarga*, a heaven with earthly pleasure, as the highest goal after death. *Jñāna-kāṇḍa* is neither interested in things of this earth nor in heaven; it wants insight into, and communion with, a reality that is nonsensual and not transient: *brahman*. It was meant for those who had given up all worldly liabilities, with interests that went beyond wife and children, house and property, business and entertainment. The householder living within his family circle had to choose *karmamārga* to secure for him what he needed and wished for, and also in order to conform to the social pattern established upon a firm basis of ritual. Later theorists try to demonstrate that the two elements, the life of the householder and the life of the houseless, constituted the even balance of an ideal social order. In reality there was and is considerable friction and competition between the two. There are texts in which the householder is praised as the one who provides nourishment for all, and there are other texts that speak of the spiritual merit that the whole society derives from the *samnyāsis*' efforts; but there is also ample evidence of householders' polemics against *samnyāsa*, which was considered by many an exaggeration, said to go against the *śāstras* and to be a violation of the basic duties ordered by the Vedas.[2]

The householder knew that everything depended on his work; what was true for food and drink and shelter was assumed to be true of sunshine and rain, of happiness and ill luck too. Religion for him was work that, when properly done, produced its fruits. From that basic consideration there developed an intricate system and a theology of sacrifice, which explained everything as being the result of ritual, *yajña*, including the creation of the universe.[3] As the importance of the proper performance of religious work rose, so did the importance of the Brahmins, the professionals of ritual *sacrifice*. An explanation may be required to prevent a possible misunderstanding of the term sacrifice. In the fully developed Vedic system it had little to do with the devotion with which Hindus today offer their *pūjā*. *Yajña* in Vedic tradition is an act that has its own intrinsic power and "exercises compulsion not only over the gods but also over natural phenomena without requiring the cooperation of the gods."[4] When we understand the nature of the *devas* as manifestations of a power greater than themselves and not wholly identical with any of them, we may also appreciate the Vedic analysis of the *yajña* as requiring four components: *dravya* or sacrificial matter, *tyāga* or the relinquishing of the object sacrificed,

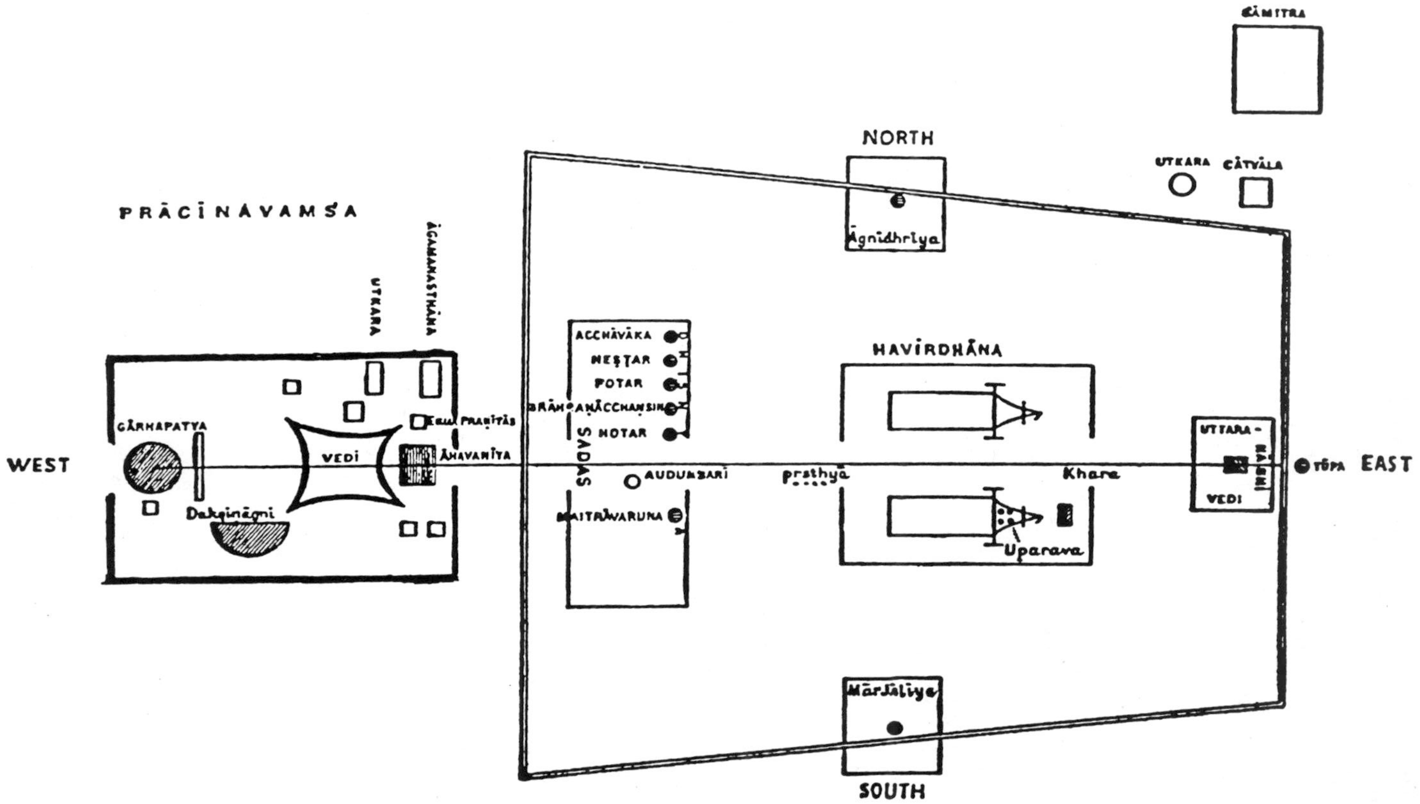


Figure 8.1. *Māhāvedī*: Vedic sacrificial area

a *devatā* to be addressed as the recipient and a mantra, or effective word, none of which may be omitted. As a reality the *yajña* is more comprehensive than a *deva*: it has power over the *deva*.[5] A businesslike atmosphere prevails in Vedic sacrificial religion: every desired object has its specified sacrifice; every sacrifice has its price. Because the *devas* are believed to depend on *yajñas*, the Vedic sacrificer can tell them quite openly: "If you give me what I want, I shall give to you. If you don't give to me, I shall not give to you. If you take something away from me, I shall take away from you."[6]

Offering sacrifices (Figure 8.1) was part of dharma, of the established world order and the particular social order. Kings had to arrange for public *yajñas* for the welfare of their people; householders had to maintain domestic sacrifices for the wellbeing of their families. The expense involved in performing *śrauta* sacrifices, especially the elaborate ones, like the *aśvamedha*, was so high that it could strain the resources of an entire kingdom and ultimately was the major cause for their discontinuance.[7] However, even in ancient times the possibility of substitution existed. Material substitution was regulated through specific texts—supplements to ritual texts such as the *Mūlādhyayapariśiṣṭa* of Kātyāyana[8]—which gave precise monetary equivalents for cows and bulls mentioned as *dakṣina* in the texts themselves, usually fixed at a nominal level, such as one rupee for one cow or bull. Spiritual substitution mentioned especially in *bhakti* texts of later times went so far as to equal the spiritual worth of reciting the name of God, or of a *pūjā* to a *mūrti*, to a great many of the most expensive *śrautas*, such as the *aśvamedha*.

Public sacrifices were splendid and costly events in former ages; they have become relatively rare but they are still occasionally performed. At the occasion of the aforementioned *aṣṭagraha* quite a number of such public Vedic sacrifices were performed by thousands of Brahmins, paid for by rich businesspeople and industrialists who alone were able to afford the hundreds of thousands of rupees required. On November 27, 1957, the *Times of India* reported, under the headline "Sādhus Perform *Mahā Yajña* to Fight Menace of H-Bombs," a public sacrifice arranged by a former Governor of Bombay. More than 500 *sādhus* and paṇḍits gathered in Bombay for a *Mahā Yajña* to reconcile the *devas* and to increase the spiritual strength of mankind, "to purify the evil, morbid, and dangerous atmosphere pervading the world because of atom bombs and H-bombs."[9] The Indian weekly *Blitz* carried a report about a Vedic sacrifice ordered by Jana Sangh politicians with the intent to kill Indira Gandhi through spells.[10]

In 1975 the Dutch-American Indologist Frits Staal had a group of Kerala Sambudri Brahmins perform an ancient Vedic sacrifice, the *agnicayana*. The whole procedure, the preparations including the burning and laying of the bricks for the fire altar, the putting up of the *paṇḍal*, the performance of the *yajña* itself, and the demolition of the fire altar after its use are shown on the hour-long film that was made by the experts, who also set down their observations and reflections in an impressive two-tome study.[11] The subsequent

Figure 8.2. Vedic fire sacrifice

controversy arising around the performance—the challenge to the claim that what we see in the film is exactly what Vedic Brahmins did three thousand years ago—need not be dealt with here. The point Staal has proved is that Vedic traditions are preserved in some parts of India and that the detail laid down in ancient ritual works is observed on occasions like this—and also how enormously expensive such grand sacrifices are.[12]

According to a Upaniṣadic teaching humans owe their existence to the "five fire sacrifices,"[13] and the classical *śāstras* circumscribe with the term *pañca mahāyajña*, five great sacrifices, the routine of daily duties of the Brahmin. When a Brahmin had no other obligations, the execution of these occupied all of his time; under the pressure of changing circumstances the five sacrifices were reduced to mere symbolic gestures. Thus *deva-yajña*, the sacrifice to the gods, could be performed by throwing a stick of wood into the fire; *pitṛ-yajña*, the sacrifice to the ancestors, could be fulfilled by pouring a glass of water onto the floor; *bhūta-yajña*, sacrifice to all creatures, can be reduced to throwing out a small ball of rice; *manuṣya-yajña*, the sacrifice to humans or hospitality in the widest sense is fulfilled by giving a mouthful of rice to a Brahmin; *brahma-yajña*, the mantra sacrifice or study of the Veda, may consist in the recitation of one single line of scripture. Those, however, who can afford the time, frequently perform the elaborate ceremonies detailed in the *śāstras* and fill their days with holy ritual and sacred chant. The ideal daily routine of the Brahmin as outlined in the law books may be followed in its entirety by very few people in India today, but surprisingly many practice part of it quite regularly.

## THE VEDIC WAY OF LIFE

Vedic tradition endows also the biological facts and necessities of hygiene with a religious meaning and provides for a detailed regulation of everyday life.[14] The Hindu householder is enjoined by his *śāstras* to rise at dawn. The first word he speaks should be the name of his *Iṣṭa-devatā*, the chosen deity. He should direct his eyes toward the palms of his hands to behold an auspicious object as the first thing every morning. Then he is to touch the floor to perform as the first work of the day an auspicious action and then bow before the images of gods in his room. The mantras and prayers vary according to denomination and family tradition. Various scriptures enjoin the householder to begin the day by thinking what he is going to do today to increase dharma and *artha*, righteousness and wealth, and about the efforts he will take toward this end.

The scriptures provide very detailed rules for daily hygiene. In an age concerned about environmental pollution, we can appreciate the great subtlety of the ancient Hindus in promoting physical cleanliness when we see how they surrounded the vital functions with many religious thoughts and rules. The daily bath is a necessity in India as well as a religious precept. While pouring water with the *loṭha* (brass vessel) over himself the pious Hindu is supposed to recite a mantra, such as the following: "O you waters, the source of our fortune, pour strength into us so that our vision may be wide and beautiful. Let us enjoy here your auspicious essence, you who are like loving mothers. Be our refuge for the removal of evil. O waters, you delight us, truly you have created us."

*Tarpaṇa* as part of the morning ablutions must be specially mentioned. The bather folds his hands to hold some water, then lets it flow back into the river while reciting mantras to *devas* and *pitṛs*. Each day after the bath clean clothes are put on. The sacred thread, called *yajñopavita* or *janëu*, is never removed at bath but according to the different occasions worn differently. After sipping some water from the hollow of his hand the Hindu, if he belongs to one of the more recent *saṃpradāyas*, applies the specific marks of his denomination to his body. This spiritual makeup is done very lovingly and carefully: vertical lines on the forehead for the Vaiṣṇavas, horizontal lines for the Śaivas, with many variations according to the particular subsect. Many write the name of their God or short mantras with white paste on their skins. According to many religious books all ceremonies and prayers are fruitless if the devotee does not carry the signs of his God on his body.

The Śaivite *Bhasmajābala Upaniṣad* is exclusively concerned with the preparation and significance of the *tripundra*, the three lines in honor of Śiva. It describes how the sacred ashes are to be prepared from the dung of a brown cow and how the markings are to be applied.

> For Brahmins the wearing of *bhasma* (ashes) alone is the right conduct. Without wearing the sign one should not drink nor do anything else. He who has given up the sign out of negligence should neither recite the *gāyatrī mantra* nor put offerings into the sacred fire, nor worship the gods, the *ṛṣis* or the *pitṛs*. That alone is the right path to destroy all sin and attain the means of salvation. . . . He who makes use of this sign of ashes in the early morning is delivered of the sin he may have committed during the night and of the sin that originates in the stealing of gold. He who resorts to this at midday and looks, meditating, into the sun, is freed from the sin of drinking intoxicating beverages, the stealing of gold, the killing of Brahmins, the killing of a cow, the slaying of a horse, the murder of his guru, his mother and his father. By taking his refuge to the sign of ashes three times a day, he attains the fruit of Vedic studies, he attains the merits of ablutions in all the three and a half crores of sacred waters; he attains the fullness of life.[15]

The morning prayer that follows called *saṃdhyā* is still observed by millions of Hindus every day. It is to take place before sunrise and to end when the sun's disk is fully above the horizon. The main text is the *gāyatrī mantra*, which is to be repeated several times; the scriptures recommend to the faithful to prolong it as much as possible because the ancestors had attained long life, understanding, honor and glory by this means. One of the strangest rites still practiced today is the daily "driving out of evil." The Brahmin takes water into the hollow of his right hand, brings it close to his nose, blows onto the water through the right and the left nostrils, repeats the mantra three times, and pours the water out. The *saṃdhyā* rites have been lengthened in later schools by the inclusion of many texts from *Purāṇas*; very few people use those long versions.

The orthodox *Smārta* is enjoined to proceed to *agniṣṭoma* after his *saṃdhyā* is completed, to redeem the first of his debts, with which every man is born. Most ordinary Hindus will perform *japa* instead, the repetition of a brief mantra or of one of the names of God. These vary according to the religious affiliation; but all believe that the name of their own God, if recited often, would confer blessing and ultimate redemption. If *japa* is to be effective, the recitation has to be done with the help of a *mālā*, a string of beads, different again according to the different sects. Vaiṣṇavas use a *mālā* made up of beads from the wood of the *tulasī* tree; Śaivites are obliged to put their faith in the *Rudrākṣa-mālā* made from the seeds of a shrub. Usually the *mālās* have 16, 32, 64, or 108 beads. Numerous treatises explain the merits of the *mālās* and recommend their use through an account of their divine origin. Thus the Śaivite *Rudrākṣajabala Upaniṣad* writes:

> Thus spoke the Lord Kālāgnirudra: "In order to bring about the destruction of Tripura, I had to close my eyes. From my eyes fell water drops. These drops turned into *rudrākṣas*. For the sake of the deliverance of all living beings I have disposed that by the mere uttering of their names as much merit is gathered as by the gift of ten cows, and by looking at them and touching

them twice as much. . . . If worn by the pious the *rudrākṣas* absolve of all sins committed by day or by night."

Precise instructions follow, how many of these beads to wear, what kind of beads to choose, and so on.[16]

Every morning All-India Radio used to broadcast *śahnai* music; not necessarily because the oboe-like instrument was a favorite with the program director, but because its sounds are traditionally considered auspicious and the Hindu is enjoined to listen to such in order to ensure a happy day for himself. The radio morning programme also included recitations from the *Mahābhārata* or the *Rāmāyaṇa*. Hindus devote much care to the separation of auspicious from inauspicious objects, sights, sounds, and times. Hindī newspapers usually contain a daily extract from the *pañcāṅga*, with an indication of the astrological data, lists of auspicious and inauspicious colours and directions. There are differences of opinion on many of these, but some are universally recognized. A Brahmin, a cow, fire, gold, clarified butter (*ghī*), the sun, water, and a courtesan, for instance, are considered to be auspicious objects to behold, and one may look forward to a good day if any of them is seen first thing in the morning. Quite serious people delay a long-planned journey or postpone an important decision if they happen to meet a cripple, a madman, a drunkard, a bald-headed man, or a *samnyāsi*, considered to be inauspicious sights.

## A BRAHMIN'S DUTIES

The orthodox Brahmin is supposed to fill the first part of his day with these religious exercises. After that he is to study or to read his Veda, do his *svādhyāya*, to gather firewood, flowers, and grass for worship. The third part of the day should be devoted to earning money. In the olden days there were strict rules for it, a distinction between permitted and forbidden occupations. Formerly the nonobservance of such rules entailed punishment like expulsion from the caste; today, especially in big cities, much of this has been forgotten. Since ancient times the teaching of the Veda had been the Brahmin's privilege; he was not allowed to ask for payment, but the student was bound to give regularly to his guru presents according to the wealth of his family. "Receiving gifts" is the Brahmins' privilege even today and many insist on it. The common expression "to honor a Brahmin" means to make a gift to him. Today Brahmins are found in a great many different professions. They are farmers, government officials, lawyers, and teachers—but also cooks, soldiers, and employees are found among them. Since by tradition Brahmins had an educational privilege, they have been able even in modern times to occupy relatively more influential posts, and to some extent today's India is still Brahmin-dominated.[17]

After midday the orthodox Brahmin was instructed to take another bath and to offer an elaborate *tarpaṇa* to the *devas*, the *pitṛs*, and *ṛṣis*: "May the *devas*, *ṛṣis*, *pitṛs*, the human beings, all beings from Brahmā right down to the blade of grass be satiated; likewise all ancestors, the mother, the maternal grandfather and the rest, may this water do good to the millions of families of bygone days who live in the seven *dvīpas*."[18] The longer formula takes up a great deal of time, enumerates thirty-one *devatās* singly, and includes a long list of *ṛṣis* and relations. At the mention of each single name water is sprinkled, with the invocation "may he be pleased with it."

The *deva-yajña* used to be an elaborate ritual. As regards the domestic rites, it has been largely replaced by *pūjā*, the worship of an image according to Āgamic scriptures. Official Vedic worship did not make use of images, as far as we know, but popular religion was certainly not totally identical with Vedic orthodoxy, as the *Atharva Veda* already shows. Purāṇas, Saṃhitās, Āgamas and Tantras have taken over a good deal of Vedic terminology and regulations and combined these with material from other traditions. Thus we find countless chapters detailing the obligatory daily domestic rites that are followed by many households. The average Hindu family keeps a *mūrti* before which daily worship is offered quite formally several times a day. The particulars—such as vessels to be used, materials to be employed, colour of flowers—vary from sect to sect. In its elaborate form *pūjā* consists of sixty-four individual ceremonies; in daily ceremonies at home usually only part of them are performed. These are: *āvāhana*, invitation of the *Iṣṭadevatā*, *āsana*, offering a seat to the deity; *pādya*, offering water to wash the feet; *arghya*, offering water for washing the hands; *ācamanīya*, offering water to rinse the mouth, *snānīya*, water for a bath; *vāstra*, leaves for clothing the deity, *yajñopavita*, offering a sacred thread, *candana*, sandalwood paste; *puṣpa*, flowers, *dhūpa*, incense; *dīpa*, a lighted lamp; *naivedya*, offering of cooked food; *tāṃbūla*; a betel nut; *dakṣina*, some money; *nāmaskāra*, a solemn greeting; *pradakṣinā*, circumambulation; and *mantrapuṣpa*, scattering a handful of blossoms before the image while reciting some honorific mantras. Each individual gesture is accompanied by appropriate *mantras*, varying from sect to sect. Many of the ancient *śāstras* give explicit order to distribute food to different deities in various parts of the house, to gods and to *caṇḍālas*, the outcastes,[19] to lepers and cripples, to crows and insects. Eating is considered to be a "sacrifice to the gods who dwell in the body."

Almost all nations consider hospitality a virtue. *Manuṣya-yajña*, one of the basic duties of the Brahmin, is interpreted by Manu as "honoring guests." There is a possibility of understanding it in an allegorical sense too. *Agni*, the fire, is the "guest of the householder," and whatever is thrown into the fire is considered to be an offering of food "to the guest." On the other hand there are also Hindus who retain the literal meaning of the precept and make it a point to invite at least one guest to every major meal. The interpretation of *atithi* (guest) that is given in the *śāstras* says that only a Brahmin can be, properly speaking, a guest, that hospitality is restricted to one meal and one overnight stay if he arrives late in the evening and cannot return to his village. A guest who has been disappointed or turned away can unload all his sins upon the householder and can take away from him his *puṇya*, his merit.[20] If a *samnyāsi* turns up as a guest, the host has—according to Hindu theory—to consider himself lucky; it is not the guest who should be grateful for hospitality, but the host must thank the *saṃnyāsi* for the opportunity to earn merit. The practice, at least today, is less than ideal though, and few *saṃnyāsis* would approach an unknown family for hospitality. However, the invited guest, especially a svāmi, is showered with effusive attention. India still has a tradition of hospitality that has no parallel. Wealthy, pious Hindus of the past and the present have established numerous guesthouses in places of pilgrimage; those *dharmaśālas* offer usually free shelter and quite frequently also free food to travelers and pilgrims, irrespective of their creed or color.

"Who goes to a meal without having performed the various sacrifices consumes only sin and does not really eat," says an old proverb. Only one who fulfills the rules of dharma gains strength from his food. "All beings live by food. The Veda explains: 'Food is life; therefore one should give food, eating is the supreme sacrifice!'" Thus say the Upaniṣads.[21] *Anna* (food) and *bhojana* (eating) occupy the first place among the topics of conversation of the average Hindu. Mahātmā Gandhi's writings convey some impression of the solicitude and anxiety Hindus bestow on their daily meals, on diet and preparation. There is good reason behind it, of course. India has known famines and times of scarcity throughout recorded history and the Indian climate makes it necessary to take care of one's health far more than in moderate zones. Many a Hindu knows hundreds of health rules from home, and it is common for religious books to give instruction also with regard to food and meals. The traditional Indian housewife spent most of her time in the kitchen preparing the meals. Indian cuisine has a not undeserved reputation, although the majority of the population has to be satisfied with a somewhat monotonous routine. The Upaniṣads even offer a theology of food: "If food is pure, the mind becomes pure. When understanding is pure it allows strong concentration (on the Self). If this is safeguarded, all the knots (which fetter the Self to the world) are loosened."[22]

Next to the treatment of marriage, food in all its aspects takes up the broadest space in the *dharma-śāstras.* Caste rules concern primarily intermarrying and interdining, specifying who may receive food from whom and who may not, thereby drawing very close social borderlines between different groups of people. Whereas the ancient Vedic Indians seem to have had but few food taboos—according to recent research they were meat-eaters, not excluding beef—under Buddhist and Jain influence meat-eating became considered irreligious. Several Hindu rulers (and even some Muslims) forbade the slaughter of animals: animal sacrifices were replaced by flower *pūjās* and meat dishes by vegetarian food. The majority of Hindus today are vegetarians for religious reasons that are frequently fortified by hygienic arguments. The religious books specify the kinds of food that may be taken by particular groups of people. The rules also have regional variations. The Brahmins of Uttar Pradesh avoid all meat, fish, eggs, and many other things; the Brahmins of Bengal must have a piece of fish with their rice, and they also eat eggs. The strictest rules have been devised by the Vaiṣṇavas, who classify all foods into *rājasika*, exciting, *tāmasika*, foul, and *sāttvika*, pure: only the last category is permitted, excluding thereby not only all meat and fish but also onions, garlic, red fruits like tomatoes, and many other things. Special rules obtain for the frequent days of fast observed by different groups at different times.[23]

## THE THEORY OF VEDIC *YAJÑA*

The understanding of Hinduism as a whole calls for a somewhat more thorough study of the public Vedic sacrifices, though most of them belong irrevocably to the past. Indological scholarship has done an enormous amount of work in this area, editing and translating virtually all the preserved texts and making detailed studies of many historical problems.[24] The Vedic *saṃhitās* were exclusively meant for use at the public sacrifices and official rituals; the highly technical *śrauta-sūtras* lay down with great precision the details of the public sacrifices. We read in Hindu literature of *yajñas* to which thousands of Brahmins were invited and at which hundreds of sacrificial animals were slaughtered, *yajñas* lasting for months, even years, that cost so much that they could impoverish the richest man.[25] Since the effect of the Vedic sacrifice depended on the correct pronunciation of the mantra, the precision of the ritual, and the observance of hundreds of minute circumstances, it very soon became the exclusive domain of sacrificial specialists, the Brahmin priests. The significance of priesthood increased in proportion as the sacrifice became more complicated. Even for the humblest of Vedic sacrifices four to five Brahmin specialists were required, hundreds for the major ones.

The efficacy of the Vedic sacrifice was supposed to depend on the offering: several remarks in Vedic works give some reason to assume that the most noble and most efficacious sacrifice was the *puruṣa-medha*, the human sacrifice.[26] It made the sacrificer equal to Prajāpati, the creator. The accounts we have give the impression that this was a real sacrifice according to an elaborate ritual, not just a symbolic ceremony.[27]

Animal sacrifices were very common; one proof of this is the opposition of early religious reformers like Buddha and Mahāvīra against them. The greatest was the *aśva-medha*, the horse sacrifice, to be performed by kings as part of their assuming "universal power."[28] It was highly regarded, even in later times when its performance had become extremely rare.[29] Thus the *Bhāgavata Purāṇa* declares that the extermination of the whole of humankind could be atoned for by one single *aśva-medha*. It was also taken as the highest unit for religious merit in describing the *puṇya* accruing from pilgrimage to certain holy places. The Daśāsvamedha Ghāṭa in Vārāṇasī has been so named because a bath in the Ganges at this particular spot is supposed to bring as much merit as the performance of ten horse sacrifices. The animal most often sacrificed, however, was the goat. The *Brāhmaṇas* give the following explanation for it: "When the *devas* had killed a human being for their sacrifice, that part of him that was fit to be made an offering went out and entered a horse. Thence the horse became an animal that was fit to be sacrificed. From the horse it went into the ox; from there it went into the goat. In the goat it remained for the longest time: therefore the goat is the most fitting sacrifice."[30] The goat contains the most *medha* (sacrificial substance), that is required for ensuring the proper result in sacrifice. The common daily oblation consisted of rice, barley-cakes, butter, curds, and milk, in short the *devas* were supposed to have the same taste as humans.

A very important ingredient of most sacrifices was *soma*, the intoxicating sap of a plant.[31] It is often called *amṛta*, nectar of immortality; an entire section of the *Ṛgveda* consists of nothing but *soma* hymns. According to tradition an eagle brought it to Indra; by partaking of it the *devas* gained immortality. *Soma* is called "child of heaven" and is supposed to have healing powers, to drive away blindness and lameness. In one hymn we read: "We have drunk *soma*, we have become immortal; we have gone to the light, we have found the *devas*. What can hostility now do to us, and what the malice of mortal men, O immortal one!"[32]

The Vedic sacrifices are intimately connected with the course of time and with the movement of the heavenly bodies. They are an expression of an awareness that human existence is precarious and time bound. Over and over the sacrifice is equated with the year, the month, the day, or the various seasons and the sacrifice itself is considered essential for maintaining the flow of time. The full-moon and new-moon sacrifices have always been, and still are, of fundamental importance; their ritual became the model for all the other *Iṣṭis*. If the new-moon sacrifice were not offered, there would be no more moon. Even today, the religious calendar of the Hindus is a united lunar-solar calendar, with all the complications and difficulties that result from such a combination. The lunar month is divided into thirty *tithis*, fifteen *tithis* of the dark half and fifteen *tithis* of the bright half, which do not coincide at all with the "days" of our calendar and have to be learned from the indispensable *pañcāṅga*. Since the "auspicious time" in which important events must take place—the marriage ceremonies, the opening of great buildings, the beginning of the parliamentary sessions—is calculated according to *muhūrtas*, subdivisions of the lunar *tithis* (there are 30 *muhūrtas* in each *tithi* of approximately 45 minutes duration), the specialists acquainted with the *pañcāṅga* who sit on the pavements of small and big cities are never without a clientele in need of their services. As a historical curiosity it may be mentioned that the reason for choosing midnight of August 15, 1947, for the official Declaration of Independence of India was the official astrologer's finding that that was the only auspicious time.

## NEW MEANINGS OF SACRIFICE

Whereas the Vedic sacrifice gives the impression of a transaction in which little or no emotion is invested—the *devas* do not have to be won over through any sign of affection or love—in later times the emotional content of the sacrifice becomes predominant. The value of the gift offered may be insignificant, the sacrificer may be ignorant of Vedic mantras and ceremonial, what counts is devotion to the God, whose grace is sought and who only considers the heart. As Kṛṣṇa tells Arjuna in the *Bhagavadgītā*: "Whosoever offers to me with devotion (*bhakti*) a leaf, a fruit, a flower, a cup of water—that offering of love, of the pure of heart, I accept."[33] The Purāṇas compete with each other in telling the masses, who could never hope to participate in a Vedic public ceremony, that it is devotion alone that counts. This devotion may be expressed in a symbolic gesture, perhaps the repetition of the name of God, or the offering of an incense stick or a flower. But inevitably the formalism at work in the Vedic religion also entered the Āgamas: they abound in detailed regulations for worship, ordering and forbidding certain acts and words as firmly as the Vedic sūtras did.[34] Worship at the major temples follows a very strict ritual, which according to tradition has been usually instituted by the God himself through a revelation to a leading *ācārya* who codified it.[35] The basic pattern of worship follows the pattern of personal attention devoted to an honored guest or a king.[36] Whereas the *deva* in the Veda is but a transitory symbolic fixation of the ultimate power, the *īśvara* of the Purāṇas is the Ultimate in person, present in the image, ready to give grace to every worshipper. The rationalization of karma, the ritual act, in this "new devotion" is quite different from that of the Vedic sacrificial religion.

According to the *Pūrva Mīmāṃsā*, the school of orthodox Vedic interpretation, each Vedic sacrifice, duly performed, produced an incorruptible substance called *apūrva*, independent of *devas*, which was at the sacrificer's disposal after his death. Whatever else the sacrificer might have done, if he had the *apūrva* from a sacrifice that ensured a sojourn in heaven, he would come to heaven, whether or not the *devas* were willing. In the "new religion" the devotee had to be constantly on the alert to remain in his or her God's favor; eternal salvation could be gained or lost even in the last moment of life. Popular stories tell of great sinners, who according to all the Vedic rules would be condemned to the lowest hells, winning immediate eternal bliss through an even inadvertent utterance of the name of Hari or Śiva.[37] The Purāṇas insist on regular worship of God as a means to win God's grace, and a good deal of the activity of the pious is directed toward gaining *puṇya* by performing actions that are described in the holy books as ordained by God for this end: *japa*, the repetition of names of God, singing the praises of God, reading holy books, attending temple services, worshipping the image, going on pilgrimages and so on. Though there are constant reminders of the affection and emotion with which a devotee has to do the daily worship in order to "fulfil the law," quite frequently these actions are performed mechanically, as if they could become effective automatically and magically.

Comparative studies of ritual have pointed out a great many parallels between the Vedic Indian and other peoples' notions of sacrifice and cult.[38]

Anthropologists and ethologists speak of "ritual behavior" even in animals, assuming that not only human societies but also animals feel an urge to perform acts that among humans are called ritual. The implications are far reaching. For one, the beginnings of ritual would not lay in rational deliberation and conscious reflection but in the subconscious psyche, perhaps even in the biological sphere. The other conclusion to be drawn would be that rituals are likely to continue, in spite of periodic major enlightenments, which belittle and ridicule them as meaningless and unable to achieve their purpose. Meaningless they may be, as F. Staal has tried to prove,[39] but not purposeless. Cārvākas and Buddhists derided Vedic ritual and succeeded to some extent in interrupting Vedic sacrificial tradition. New forms of ritual developed within the Hindu communities and also among the Buddhists. Nineteenth-century reformers debunked old as well as new forms of ritual and sacrifice. And again, other forms developed and have found acceptance among contemporary Hindus.

CHAPTER NINE

# Purity and Merit

## *The Twin Concerns of* Karmamārga

> Pure, Maruts, pure yourselves, are your oblations; to you, the pure, pure sacrifice I offer. By Law they came to truth, the Law's observers, bright by their birth, and pure, and sanctifying.
>
> —*Ṛgveda* VI, 56, 12

Although certain aspects of purity in Hinduism certainly have to do with bodily fluids and their discharge—menstruating women are considered ritually impure, to mention the most obvious of such instances—it would be wrong to identify the issue of purity in Hinduism totally with this, as some, under the influence of a recent school of anthropology, seem to do. In addition to the materially conditioned purity there is a very sophisticated notion of a higher purity, partly ethical, partly spiritual. Thus the central theme of the teaching of the present Śaṅkarācāryas—the *jagad-gurus*, or "world teachers," who are listened to with great seriousness by a great many Hindus and whose words carry authority—is purity of mind. "Purity of mind is thought to bring the mind to greater understanding. Purity of mind, requisite for devotion and meditation, leads on to religious knowledge. Two classic qualifications for self-knowledge are freedom from desires and purity of mind."[1] To some extent the notion of auspicious-inauspicious, which is central to Hinduism runs parallel to that of purity-impurity. Here, as in most other cases, Hindu practice and belief do not simply follow from a logical extension of one basic idea: there is a plurality of basic notions from which—quite logically, but not always in mutually compatible fashion specific beliefs and practices flow. The Hindu notion of merit is also multidimensional. Besides the Vedic idea of *apūrva*—the merit accruing from a sacrifice that can be stored up for later use in heaven, we find Purāṇic notions of gaining merit by either reciting the names of a deity or by performing *pūjā*. Quite different, but not unrelated, is the idea, very widespread too among Hindus, that *tapas*, self-mortification, self-imposed and voluntary, both purifies and confers merit. Equally, the idea of gaining purity and merit not only for oneself but also for ancestors and others, by going on pilgrimage and bathing in a *tīrtha* is fairly universally acceptable to Hindus.[2] It is not really a Vedic idea but it combines with Vedic ideas in the practical life of Hindus. More will be said in a later chapter that explains how gaining of purity and merit is tied to specific times and places.

The inextricable conjunction of the rather impersonal Vedic and the highly personal Purāṇic traditions make it impossible to clearly differentiate in the activities of traditional Hindus between acts done to obtain ritual purity, to gain merit, or to win the grace of God—which, in a certain sense, obviates everything else.

Hinduism certainly did preserve archaic and magical elements, but it integrated those with ethical reflection and theological thought. It will be good if besides observing what can be observed by way of ritual action one also reads, or listens to, reflections on ethical issues by learned and thoughtful Hindus, past and present. The Upaniṣads already throw doubt on the efficacy of Vedic ritual—they recommend asceticism and introspection as means to gain purity and earn merit.

Throughout the history of Hinduism there is on the one hand an insistence of performing the prescribed ritual for reasons of achieving and maintaining one's status within the *varṇāśramadharma*, and there is on the other hand the clearly expressed conviction that rituals alone are not sufficient and that the purity that they effect is not enough to reach the ultimate aim of life, *mokṣa*. Numerous Hindu saints and singers denounced ritualism and ridiculed the belief that ritual purity would win a person entry to the realm of God. Personal virtues as well as social engagement, genuine devotion, and service of God are stressed as means to reach purity and to gain merit.

The majority of today's Hindus would agree. The equivocal nature of the Hindu notions of purity and merit is underscored by the fact that most Hindus make use of all available means offered to earn merit and to purify themselves, regardless from which source they come. Devout Hindus will accept the blessing of a Christian priest as well as the *aśīrvāda* of a Hindu *pūjāri*, they will visit places of pilgrimage regardless of which religion they belong to, and they will participate in all forms of worship that appeal to them. They will, however, follow their own traditional, Vedic practices where religion intersects with their standing in society and will undergo the prescribed *saṃskāras*.

## ETHICAL STANDARDS OF HINDUISM

Hindu tradition has devoted a great deal of intellectual work to the clarification of moral and ethical issues; in this context it is impossible even to mention all the important authors and views.[3] As the brief discussion of dharma has shown, religion and the morality connected with it are defined within the framework of the *varṇāśrama* scheme as *svadharma*, morality appropriate to each class and to each stage in a person's life. Certain moral precepts, however, are supposed to be common to all humankind. The so-called *sādhāraṇa-dharma* has a number of features in common with the Ten Commandments of the Bible or the Natural Law of the Western classical philosophical tradition. Hindu ethics as a whole, however, shows so many peculiar features that it would be misleading to represent it in Western terminology. Nor is the Hindu tradition united in the articulation of its ethical thought. Numerous schools have produced sometimes radically different views on important matters. Only some of these will be described here; for others, more specialized works will have to be consulted.[4]

Hindu ethics generally speaking is strongly scriptural, that is, it orients itself on the mandates given in recognized *śruti*. The Vedic tradition was largely replaced and absorbed by the Purāṇic-Āgamic tradition, which in addition to general rules and precepts has numerous special provisions for the followers of each individual sect and group. Combined with what we would call moral and ethical principles we find rules relating to forms of worship, ritual purity, and also items of practical wisdom and hygiene.

The supreme ideal of most branches of Hinduism is the sage, who is unperturbed, free from affection and hatred, not influenced by good or bad luck. For the sage there is, strictly speaking, no more morality, being "beyond good and evil" in a literal sense, because *pravṛtti*, volition, the spring of action, has dried up. This is the situation of the fully realized person, as Vedānta describes it. Not-too-well-informed people derive from such statements the impression that Hinduism as a whole does not care for ethics. Good and evil are relative according to the teaching of the Upaniṣads—relative to the whole world of *karma*. As long as humans participate in it through their own actions, they are bound by it as by an absolute rule!

There has been a discussion going on in India for many centuries, whether righteousness affects the innermost self or whether it is just accidental to it. Many Indians consider morality a quality of the *ātman* and as a subjective category to depend also on the intentions of the doer.[5] In order that a moral rule may qualify as a precept apart from its scriptural basis, its inherent goodness must usually also be proved. Since scriptural precepts, which also include rituals, are of such great importance, Hindu thinkers have devoted much thought to finding out the reasons for their validity. According to the orthodox Mīmāṃsā, the scriptural laws express something like a Universal Moral Imperative, which produces *ātmākūta*, an impulse in the self, to do what has been prescribed, together with an insight into the rightness of the precept.[6] According to the Naiyāyikās, the professional logicians,

> whatever the Lord commands is good and is good *because* the Lord commands it. Similarly, whatever the Lord forbids is evil and is evil because the

> Lord forbids it. The authority of the scriptural prescriptions on the will of the agent is such a *vyāpara* or process in the agent himself: it is the desire for the good and aversion toward the evil involved in the injunctions and prohibitions of scripture as the Lord's commands. It is these desires and aversions in the agent that are the real operative forces, and moral authority is the operation of good and evil through the agent's subjective desires and aversions.[7]

Many authors operate with a basic distinction of *sukha* (agreeable)—*duḥkha* (painful), or *hita* (wholesome)—*ahita* (unwholesome), which may be considered as a rule of thumb for moral decisions in concrete situations. Thus for instance the precept of truthfulness has to be realized within this situational ethics, as expressed by a leading contemporary Indian thinker: "The final standard of truth is the amount of good that is rendered to people by one's words. Even a misstatement or a false statement, if beneficial to all beings, should be regarded as preferable to a rigorous truthful statement."[8] That this is not just the isolated opinion of an avant-garde thinker is proved by numerous sayings and proverbs in popular scriptures. A different, absolute, standard is introduced by the *Bhagavadgītā* with *niṣkāma karma*, the disinterested pursuit of the Lord's command as duty for duty's sake.[9]

## VICE AND VIRTUE IN HINDUISM

Both popular and scholarly books describe *moha*, *lobha*, *krodha*—delusion, greed, and anger—as the root of all vices: "the gates to hell," as the *Bhagavadgītā* says.[10] Some authors try to reduce the first two into one, but all are unanimous in considering the deeds performed under the influence of these passions as sinful.

Jayanta specifies the three roots further[11] and identifies with their help the most common vices. *Moha* is given the title *pāpatama*, "head sin," because without delusion, he says, there cannot be greed and anger. The direct consequences of delusion are misjudgment, perplexity, conceit, and heedlessness. The consequences of desire are sexual craving, extreme niggardliness, worldliness, thirst for life enjoyment, and greed. Aversion produces anger, envy, jealousy, malevolence, and malice.

Before proceeding with a detailed description of the system of vices in the classical *śāstras* it may help to quote some popular scriptures, the source of the common Hindu's ethical education, to see what a Hindu considers to be the life a good person should live. Since a great deal of traditional Hinduism is quite patently patriarchal, it is no use to apply inclusive language: many of the texts speak of men only and highlight male ideas and ideals, virtues and vices of men rather than of all humans. The *Viṣṇu Purāṇa* enjoins the respectable man to worship gods, cows, Brahmins, *sādhus*, elders, and teachers. He should dress in neat garments, use delicate herbs and flowers, wear emeralds and other precious stones, keep his hair smooth and neat, scent his person with agreeable perfumes and always go handsomely attired, decorated with garlands of white flowers. He should never appropriate another's belongings nor address anyone in an unkindly way. He should speak amiably and truthfully and never make public another's faults. He should not mount a dangerous vehicle, nor seek shade under the bank of a river. He should not associate with ill-famed people, with sinners or drunkards, with one who has many enemies, with a harlot or her gallant, with a pauper or a liar, with a slanderer or a knave. He should not swim against the current of a rapid stream, not enter a house on fire, nor climb to the top of a tree. When together with others he should not grind his teeth or blow his nose or yawn with uncovered mouth, he should not clear his throat noisily nor cough or laugh loudly nor break wind noisily; he should not bite his nails nor scratch the ground, nor put his beard into his mouth. He should avoid going by night to a place where four roads meet, to the village tree, to the cemetery or an ill-famed woman's house. He should not cross the shadow of a venerable person, of the image of a deity, of a flag, or of a heavenly body. He should not travel alone through the forest nor sleep by himself in an empty house. He should stay away from hair, bones, thorns, filth, and remnants of offerings, ashes, chaff, and the bathing place of someone else. He should not go near a beast of prey and should rise from his bed as soon as he awakens. He should avoid exposure to frost, wind, and sunshine. He should not bathe, sleep, or rinse his mouth when naked. He should not offer any oblations or greetings with only one garment on. He should not engage in a dispute with superiors or inferiors because, the text says "controversy and marriage are to be permitted only between equals." He must never circumambulate the temple on his left hand,[12] nor spit in front of the moon, fire, the sun, water, wind, or any respectable person; he must neither urinate while standing, nor upon a highway. He must not treat women with disrespect, but he also should not trust them completely. He is to be generous toward the poor. He should carry an umbrella for protection against sun and rain, a staff when walking by night, and also wear shoes. He should speak wisely, moderately, and kindly.

> The earth is upheld by the truthfulness of those who have subdued their passions and are never contaminated by desire, delusion, and anger. Let therefore a wise man ever speak the truth when it is agreeable, and when the truth would inflict pain let him hold his peace. Let him not utter that which, though acceptable, would be detrimental; for it would be better to speak that which would be salutary. A considerate man will always cultivate, in act, thought, and speech, that which is good for living beings, both in this world and the next.[13]

Detailed instructions are given for each activity and situation in life, giving guidance in a very practical form, interspersed with religious precepts. A very similar list is provided in the *Cāraka Saṃhitā*, a classical text on medicine, which as well as dealing with technical medical matters provides general rules for a good and healthy life.[14] That health and religion go hand in hand is a commonly accepted truism among the Hindus. There attaches, therefore, also a moral stigma to people afflicted with leprosy or other deforming diseases, which makes their lot still more miserable. But generally the Hindu has a quite sound moral sense—old-fashioned, perhaps, and tinged with sectarian overemphasis on ritual, in some cases—but practical and sure in the essentials. To introduce also sources in languages other than Sanskrit, a few verses from the *Tirukkuṟaḷ*, the sacred book of the Tamiḷs, which the Hindus in South India treasure as the "Tamiḷveda," may be quoted here.

> People without love think only of themselves; people who have love free themselves of the self for the sake of others.
> Heaven and earth are not enough reward for a friendly service that is given without any thought of gain.
> The joy of the revengeful lasts but a single day, but the peace-lover's joy lasts forever.
> Those who fast and mortify themselves are great, but greater are they who forgive wrongdoing.
> This is wisdom supreme: do not repay with evil, evil done to you.[15]

## DEADLY SINS AND LESSER SINS:

The classical *dharma-śāstra* developed a fairly comprehensive casuistry, classifying and cataloguing sins and their appropriate penances. Sins have their special consequences, and thus social sanctions as well as religious ones. It is worth noting that the digests of Hindu law treat *prāyaścittas*, penances and atonement for sins, after dealing with purity and impurity.[16] The principal division of sin that obtains in the *śāstras* is that between *mahā-pātakas*, great sins, and *upa-pātakas*, minor sins. The former are generally given as five, interpreted differently by various authors.

*Brāhmaṇa-hātya*, the killing of a Brahmin, was considered the most grievous of all offenses, unforgivable and expiated only by death. Some pandits hold that it includes all members of the upper three castes who have studied the Vedas. The killing of an unborn child and of a pregnant woman was considered equally vile. The killing of a man of a lower caste or of an outcaste is treated by some law books only as a minor offence, a far lesser crime than the killing of a cow. The *śastras* provide also for non-Brahmins by saying that it would be a *mahā-pātaka* for a *Kṣatriya* to flee from the battlefield or to mete out, as a rule, unjust punishment; for a *Vaiśya* to use false scales and false weights; for a *Śūdra* to sell meat, to injure a Brahmin, to have sexual intercourse with a Brahmin woman, and to drink milk from a *kapila* (brownish) cow, reserved for the Brahmins. There is no dharma proper for the casteless; from the orthodox point of view they are on a level with the animals as far as religious merit is concerned. Accordingly, offenses committed by them against people belonging to a caste were punished with disproportionate harshness, and crimes against them by people from higher castes were absolved very easily with a merely formal penance.

The second *mahā-pātaka* is *sūra-pāna*, drinking of intoxicating beverages. It is the object of long treatises, classifications, restrictions, and excuses, to find out what exactly was meant by *sūra*. Strict interpreters forbid all alcoholic drinks and all drugs. Most pandits allow the *Śūdras* to drink their toddy and liquor without incurring sin. Among *sādhus*, especially the uneducated ones, it was common practice to improve their capacity for meditating by using drugs.

*Steya*, stealing, is the third grave sin; but this is a qualified theft defined as "stealing a large amount of gold from a Brahmin." Long treatises specify quantity, persons and circumstances. Generally speaking, traditional India did not know the capitalist idolization of personal property and even the *śāstras* formally allow theft of food for cows, of materials for sacrifice, or of modest quantities of food for one's personal use. Again, almost daily occurrences of brutal punishment meted out to Harijans for minor theft show that the law was written by, and for the benefit of, the higher castes.

The fourth *mahā-pātaka* is *guru-vaṅganā-gama*—relations with the preceptor's wife. Some authorities interpret *guru* in this context as father and not as religious master and the prohibition would relate to incest, applicable also to the spiritual father.

The last of the deadly sins is *mahā-pātaka-saṃsārga*, association with a great sinner. The law forbids one to eat with one, live with one, ride with one, or accept one as a friend or a pupil.

Some of the later texts broaden the concept of "great sin" and add a series of offenses that they consider as equivalent: kidnapping, horse stealing, theft of diamonds or of land, sexual relations with members of the lowest castes, relatives or a holy person.

All the *mahā-pātakas* are technically unpardonable and there is no penance that would make persons, who have incurred one of these sins, acceptable again in their caste. From the religious point of view some *śāstras* say that such sinners could expiate through their death the offenses they have committed. The Purāṇas, however, handle such cases quite easily by recommending some religious practice associated with the Lord, who, if properly worshipped, forgives and condones everything.

As regards the *upa-pātakas*, the minor offenses, there is wide discrepancy and lack of an accepted classification. One authority mentions five: relinquishing the sacred fire, offending the guru, atheism (*nāstikya*, disregard for the traditional religion), gaining one's livelihood from an unbeliever, and sale of the *soma* plant. Others add: forgetting the Veda, neglecting the Veda study, violation of *brahmacarya*, the vow of celibacy. Longer lists enumerate more than fifty minor sins, many of them quite serious offenses that can, however, be made good by performing the prescribed penance. Thus offenses like the preparation of salt (the breaking of a state monopoly), accepting money for teaching the Veda, the study of false *śāstras*, killing a woman, marrying off a younger son before the elder brother, installation of devices that kill living organisms or cause injury, like an oil press, and the sale of one's wife are mentioned together with common theft, adultery, cruelty toward parents, unrestrained pleasure seeking, and the usurpation of the priestly office.[17]

## PENANCE AND ATONEMENT

Manu decrees that a person who causes pain to a Brahmin, steals, cheats, and commits unnatural venery loses caste. One who kills a donkey, a horse, a deer, an elephant, a snake, or a buffalo is transferred to a mixed caste.

The *śāstras* underline the importance of undergoing the prescribed penances by pointing out the evil consequences a sin may have in another rebirth, if it has not been washed away through *prāyaścitta*. Thus, according to Manu, gold stealing shows in diseased nails, and spirit drinking in black teeth; Brahmin murder in consumption; violation of the guru's wife in skin disease; calumny in stinking breath; stealing of cloth in leprosy: "Thus, in consequence of a remnant of the guilt are born idiots, dumb, blind, deaf, and deformed people, despised by the virtuous."[18]

In addition to possible consequences in rebirth, Hindu scriptures quite frequently give detailed descriptions of the hells in which individual sinners are punished for their sins: people who have injured living beings have to suffer being cut with sharp blades for ages, people who have committed adultery are punished by being tied to a red-hot image that they have to embrace for many years; liars are hung with their mouth in pools of foul matter.[19] The ancient *śāstras*, which belong to a period in which religious and secular authority were one, have, however, quite precise rules in their criminal code; for the sake of preserving society they could not be as extravagant or as lenient as the Purāṇas. They distinguish between unintentional and intentional acts; the former are usually expiated by reciting Vedic texts, the latter demand special penances.[20] Those special penances constitute in fact the criminal code of ancient India and are still of great importance in traditional jurisprudence. Some of the modes of atonement have gone out of practice, other still apply.

Manu, for instance prescribes for unintentional murder of a Brahmin "to make a hut in the forest and dwell in it for twelve years, subsisting on alms and making the skull of a dead man his flag," or to try to expose oneself in a battle to archers or to surrender one's whole property to a Brahmin or to sacrifice one's life for the sake of Brahmins or cows—or verbal absolution from three Brahmins.[21] Austerities, recitation of Vedic texts, performance of special sacrifices, breath control, gifts, pilgrimages, ablutions, and rituals are among the means imposed by religious authorities even now for offenses; if performed properly they are supposed to take away the sins and their consequences in this and future births. Thus Manu says: "By confession, by repentance, by austerity and by `reciting the Veda a sinner is freed from guilt, as also by liberality. . . . Insofar as his heart loathes his evil deed, so far is his body freed from that guilt.

He who has committed a sin and has repented is freed from that sin, but only by ceasing with the promise: 'I will do so no more.'"[22] Normally, in addition to repentance, an actual atonement is demanded. One of the most widely practiced penances is *prāṇayama*, breath control. The "person of sin" is "burnt" by regular controlled inhalation and exhalation and retention of air.

*Tapas*, literally "heat," designating all sorts of austerities, is the general means for making reparation for wrongdoing. It may include sexual continence, truthfulness, frequent bathing, wearing of wet clothes, sleeping on the floor and fasting for a specific length of time. "*Tapas* quickly consumes all sins," goes the proverbial saying. Under certain circumstances *tapas* can also be won by proxy: devout widows perform penances that are meant to profit their deceased husbands. The rich pay the poor to perform *tapas* on their behalf. Merit bestowed upon another is lost to oneself; therefore one can read in popular books moving stories of the ultimate penance somebody performs by giving away as a gift the whole store of *tapas* acquired in many years of hard work.

*Agniṣṭoma*, a gift consumed by fire, is one of the traditionally accepted means of atonement. It is to be accompanied by the shaving of head and beard, bathing in holy water, muttering of mantras, pouring *ghī* into the fire, abstinence and truthfulness in speech. The sin is thrown into the fire and burnt along with the offering.

*Japa* may be the most common and most widespread means of atonement for Hindus today. It can be of three kinds: *vācika*, an audible murmuring, is the lowest; *upāṃṣu*, inaudible lisping, confers ten times more merit; *mānasa*, a mental recitation, is worth a hundred times as much. For the purpose of atonement the books prescribe a high number of recitations of certain formulae or names. In ancient times *japa* was accessible only to the upper castes that had the right to recite the Veda. It was forbidden to the *śūdras* and outcastes; if they practized it nevertheless, it remained without effect. Later a special kind of *japa* was created for *śūdras* and women. The Purāṇas again are full of mantras and *stotras* that carry with them the promise of expiating all sins if recited even once by anyone; the mere utterance of the revealed name of God frees many generations from hells and punishments.

*Dāna*, the offering of gifts to Brahmins, is among the acts most often recommended in the *śāstras* to atone for crimes. The gift of gold is especially effective, and so is the gift of a cow, a horse, land; gifts are even potent enough to annihilate the accumulated guilt of former lives. There are numerous copperplates preserved that document the gift of land for the purpose of gaining religious merit for the donor and his ancestors. Even today industrialists build temples and rest houses for pilgrims for the same purpose; hundreds of beggars and cripples give to the pious Hindus who visit a temple ample opportunity to rid themselves of their sins by distributing money, food, and cloth.

*Upavāsa*, fasting, is another popular form of penance. In its strict sense it entails total abstinence from food and drink and even at present there are numerous Hindus who keep up a total fast on a good number of days in a year. For the more sophisticated and theologically astute Hindus *upavāsa* often means nothing more than observing certain restrictions in the kind of food they take, with the same religious merit attached to it. Thus the Vaiṣṇavas, who are strict vegetarians, keep *ekādaśī*, every eleventh day in each half of the lunar month, as a fasting day. On those days they are not supposed to eat cereals grown above the ground such as rice, wheat, barley, or pulses. Whatever grows below the ground, all roots and tubers, as well as milk and other dairy products may be eaten.

*Tīrtha-yātra*, pilgrimage to holy places, is another popular penance. The *Mahābhārata* mentions already the "seven holy cities": Kāśi, Prayāga, Mathurā, Ujjainī, Haridvāra, Ayodhyā, and Gāyā; each of them is the goal of millions of Hindu pilgrims seeking to make atonement for their own sins and the sins of their ancestors. The *Purāṇas* carry numerous *Mahātmyas*, praises of those holy places, in which the merits of visiting the sacred spots are described in detail. Even in the modern India of steel combines, jet travel, and political parties millions of people are constantly on the move to wash away their sins: many people retire to one of the holy cities in their old age and quite a few arrange to be brought to Vārāṇasī to die there, because then one does not have to fear punishment or rebirth.

Many Hindus undertake these penances of their own accord; others are told to do so, often by the caste *pañcāyat*, which oversees the affairs of its members and interferes, if necessary. Crimes with social implications were punished by the secular authority. According to Manu, Brahmins could, however, take the law into their own hands, because they were superior to the Kṣatriyas. But that they, too, had in reality to abide by the decisions of the ruler, becomes clear when we hear that they may "punish through their own weapon, which is the word of the Veda" and use the spells of the *Atharvaveda* against those who have offended them.[23]

## THE IDEAL OF HOLINESS

It is only natural that the sin consciousness of a person is the more acute the more aware one is of the holiness of the Lord. Thus we find in texts that were meant for the more exclusive circles of religious professionals a far more scrupulous determination of sins and a greater urgency for acts of atonement. Vaiṣṇavas, who consider *sevā* or service of the Lord Viṣṇu the sole aim of life, have special lists of "sins against service." These include: entering the temple in a car or with shoes on, neglecting to celebrate the feasts of Viṣṇu, greeting the image of Viṣṇu with one hand only, turning one's back toward it, stretching one's feet toward the image, laying down or eating before the image, gossiping before the image, eating one's food without first having offered it to Viṣṇu, and so forth. All signs of disrespect or negligence before the bodily presence of the Lord in his image are thus considered sins, to be atoned for through the repetition of the name of Viṣṇu.

The "sins against the name," however, cannot be atoned for. They are ten according to the authorities: Scolding a Vaiṣṇava; thinking that both Viṣṇu and Śiva are (equally) Lord; thinking that the guru is a mere human being; reproaching the Vedas, Purāṇas and other scriptures; interpreting the name; speaking or thinking ill of the name; committing sins on the strength of the name; considering other good works as equal to the recitation of the name; teaching the name to people who have no faith; and disliking the name even after having heard about its greatness.[24]

## NEW DEPARTURES ON THE PATH OF WORKS

A new understanding of the path of works developed from the late eighteenth century onward—possibly under the influence of contact with the British and a socially conscious Christianity. The eagerness with which Ram Mohan Roy responded to New Testament ethics and with which he successfully fought against cruel traditions like *satī* and infanticide did not lead to a large-scale Hindu conversion to Christianity but to a "Hindu Renaissance" with clearly social and ethical overtones. The call to action of Kṛṣṇa in the *Bhagavadgītā* was interpreted as a call to remedy the social ills of Hindu society—and eventually as a call to liberate the homeland of the Hindus from foreign domination. B. G. Tilak's commentary on the Gītā—"the Gospel of Action"—gives an explicitly sociopolitical slant to the old notion of *karmamārga*. So did Mahātmā Gandhi and many others in his footsteps.

CHAPTER TEN

# *Saṃskāras*

## *The Hindu Sacraments*

> With holy rites, prescribed by the Veda, must the ceremony of conception and other sacraments be performed for the twice-born, which sanctify the body and purify in this life and after death.
>
> —*Manusmṛti* II, 26

The *saṃskāras*, often called the sacraments of Hinduism, are rituals by means of which a Hindu becomes a full member of the socioreligious community.[1] They begin with conception and end with cremation, "sanctifying the body and purifying it in this life and after death."[2] The classical *śāstras* list a great number of *saṃskāras* that apparently were in use in former times; nowadays only a few are practiced, but an immense importance attaches to these in the practical life of Hindus. Manu explains the effect of the different *saṃskāras* (see Figure 10.1) thus:

> In the case of the twice-born[3] the sins that come from seed and womb are redeemed through *homas* during pregnancy, through *jātakarma*, the ritual performed at birth, through *cauḍa*, the tonsure of the whole head leaving only one lock at the crown of the head, and the girdling with *muñja* grass. This body is made fit for the attainment of Brahmā through *svādhyāya*, the study of scripture, by observance of *vratas*, holy vows, through the so-called *traividyā*, by worshipping the *devas*, *pitṛs*, and *ṛṣis*, by begetting a son and through the daily performance of the *pañca mahāyajñas* as well as public *yajñas*.[4]

Hindus associate great significance with the ceremonies surrounding the birth of a child and the name giving. Popular works such as the *Viṣṇu Purāṇa* offer instructions like these:

Figure 10.1. Some *samskāras*

> When a son is born, let his father perform the ceremonies proper on the birth of a child. . . . Let him feed a couple of Brahmins and according to his means offer sacrifices to the *devas* and *pitṛs*. . . . On the tenth day after birth[5] let the father give a name to his child; the first shall be the appellation of a god, the second of a man: Śarma for a Brahmin, Varma for a Kṣatriya, Gupta for a Vaiśya, and Dāsa for a Śūdra. A name should not be void of meaning: it should not be indecent, nor absurd, nor ill-omened, nor fearful, it should consist of an even number of syllables, it should not be too long nor too short, nor too full of long vowels, but contain a due proportion of short vowels and be easily articulated.[6]

Manu adds that the names of women should be easy to pronounce, not imply anything dreadful, possess a plain meaning, and be auspicious, ending in long vowels and containing a word of blessing (*aśīrvāda*).[7] In the fourth month the "leaving-of-the-house" ceremony should be celebrated, in the sixth the first feeding with rice and other family customs. In the first or third year all males of the three upper castes are supposed to get *cauḍa* or tonsure.

## THE SECOND BIRTH

*Upanayana*, initiation, is among the most important *saṃskāras* still in fairly universal use, even in liberal Hindu families. According to the *śāstras* it is to take place in the eighth year for a Brahmin boy, in the eleventh for a *Kṣatriya* boy, and in the twelfth for a *Vaiśya* boy.[8] The investiture with the *yajñopavita* or *janëu*, the sacred thread, marks the end of the young twice-born's childhood and innocence as he enters the first of the four *āśramas* or stages of his life: studentship. From now onward he is held responsible for his actions. As a child he had no duties and could incur no guilt; he did not have to observe restrictions regarding permitted and prohibited food, he was free in his speech, and his lies were not punished. In ancient time the young *brahmacāri* took up residence with his guru to be taught in the Vedas; nowadays the boys normally remain with their families and continue attending the same school as before. Nevertheless it marks an important occasion in the life of a Hindu boy, since it is often the first personal and conscious encounter with his religion as part of his own life. Most families keep contact with their traditional Pandit who instructs the boys in their *dharma*.

The exact time for the ceremony of *upanayana* is determined by the family astrologer. The occasion still retains something of an initiation ceremony; a crucial rite of passage that in olden times could result in the death of the candidate. The boy is given a wooden staff and dressed with a belt of *muñja* grass. The head is shaved, except for the *śikhā*. The Brahmin who performs the ceremony recites mantras to Savitṛ, asking him not to let the boy die. Then the sacred thread is put on for the first time, to be worn henceforth day and night. It consists of three times three single threads about two yards long, and normally is worn over the left shoulder (during the last rites it is worn over the right). The origin of the *janëu* has not been explained as yet; many believe it to be the remnant of a garment. Neglect of the *janëu* can lead to expulsion from the caste, and good works without the *janëu* bring no fruit. Traditionally also the *gāyatrī-mantra* was imparted to the young Brahmin at this occasion; its repetition was meant to be the common means of expiation for sins. The ancient *śāstras* contain a complete *brahmacāri-dharma* for the boys, to be observed from the time of initiation till marriage. The reformist Ārya Samāj attempts to revive it in its *gurukulas*, where young boys and girls are kept under strict discipline from the age of four to twenty. There are also still a few Vedic schools in India where young boys spend several years in the manner prescribed by the *śāstras*: mornings and evenings the boys chant Vedic hymns in chorus, the daytime is devoted to memorizing the Veda, studying the *Vedāṅgas*, and collecting firewood. Quite strict rules must be observed with regard to food. The boys have to be very respectful toward the guru, never addressing him without certain honorific titles. Complete sexual continence was of the essence; the very name of this mode of life was synonymous with chastity. A *brahmacāri* who failed in this respect had to submit to very humiliating, painful, and lengthy penances. Manu says he must go around clad in the skin of a donkey for a whole year, beg food in seven houses while confessing his sin, eating only once a day and bathing three times daily. Usually this stage of life ended with marriage at the age of around twenty. But there had always been *naiṣṭhika brahmacāris* who continued to live as such without ever marrying.[9]

## A SACRAMENT FOR MEN AND WOMEN

The most important *saṃskāra* had always been, and still is, *vivāha*, marriage. Hindu law knew eight forms of marriage of which it recognized four as legal, though not all of them equally worthy.[10] Besides the normal case of arrangement through the parents, Hinduism knows also legalized forms of love marriage. Monogamy is the rule today, though traditional Hindu law permitted a man to marry up to four wives. After many years of work—and against the opposition of many traditional Hindus—the Government of India passed in 1955 the Hindu Marriage Act, which, with several amendments, became in 1976 the official marriage law for Hindus, replacing earlier legislation. It unified Hindu marriage law, which had existed in a number of regional variants and it also brought it closer to modern Western law by recognizing civil marriage and allowing divorce, also at the request of the wife. Its enactment was not universally welcomed, not even among Western experts in Hindu law.[11] The *Mahābhārata* describes a society in which polyandry was practiced; Draupadī is the wife of the five Pāṇḍava brothers. A few tribes in the hills around Tehrī Garhvāl practice it even now.

Popular books and *śāstras* alike give advice about the "auspicious" and "inauspicious" signs to look for in one's marriage partner. Thus we read that a man should select a maiden "who has neither too much nor too little hair, is neither black nor yellow complexioned, neither a cripple, nor deformed." He must not marry a girl who is vicious or unhealthy, of low origin, ill-educated, with a disease inherited from father or mother, of a masculine appearance, with a croaky voice, a harsh skin, with white nails, red eyes, fat hands, too short, or too tall. She also should be "in kin at least five degrees removed from his mother and seven from his father."[12]

The actual ceremonies of the marriage culminate in a feast very often so sumptuous that poor families take up ruinous loans in order to meet the expenses and provide food for all those who expect to be invited. Depending on status, a richly decorated horse or an elephant must be hired, dancers and musicians must entertain the numerous guests, Pandits and Brahmins must be paid their *dakṣiṇās*. The ceremonies differ from one region to the other, but everywhere they follow a certain pattern that is meaningful and rests on ancient traditions.[13]

One of the texts details the following ritual. To the west of the fire on the altar, there is to be placed a grinding stone, to the northeast a water jug. The bridegroom sacrifices while the bride holds his hand. He faces west, the woman looks toward the east, while he says: "I take thy hand in mine for happy fortune."[14] He takes her thumb only, if he wishes only for sons, the other fingers only, if he wishes only for daughters, the whole hand, if he wants both boys and girls. Three times the bridegroom leads the bride around the fire, murmuring: "I am *amā* (this), you are *sā* (she); I am heaven, you are earth; I am *sāma*, you are *ṛk*. Let us marry each other, let us beget sons and daughters. Kind to each other, friendly, with well-meaning mind may we live a hundred years." Each time he makes her step onto a stone with the words: "Step on this stone, be firm as stone, overcome the enemies, trample down the adversary." Then the bridegroom pours *ghī* over the bride's hands, the bride's brother sprinkles grains of rice over their hands, three times. The bridegroom loosens the hair band of the bride with the words: "I deliver you from the bonds of Varuṇa." He asks her to take seven steps toward the north, saying: "May you take a step for power, a step for strength, one for wealth, one for fortune, one for descendants, one for good times. May you be my friend with the seventh step! May you be faithful to me! Let us have many sons. May they reach a ripe old age!" The officiating Pandit moves the heads of bride and bridegroom close together and sprinkles them with water. The bride is supposed to spend the three nights following the wedding ceremony in the house of an older Brahmin woman whose husband and children are still living. When the bride has seen the polestar, the star *arundhatī* and the *Seven ṛṣis* (Ursa Major), she must break her silence by saying: "May my husband live long and may I bear him children." When entering her own house she is to say: "May your happiness increase here through your sons and daughters." The bridegroom then kindles, for the first time, their own sacred fire. The bride sits on a bull's hide and is first given curds to eat with the mantra: "May all gods unite our hearts."

There are countless variations and additions to the ceremony just described. Some prescribe that the couple should look into the sun, that the bridegroom should carry the bride over the threshold, that he should touch her heart with mantras, that he should offer silver and gold before the statues of Śiva and Gaurī. Depending also on the patriarchal or matriarchal tradition prevailing in the area the relative importance of bride or bridegroom is expressed in the wedding ceremonies and the homecoming, too.

According to the *Ṛgveda* the goal of marriage is to enable a man to sacrifice to the *devas* and to beget a son who will ensure the continuity of the sacrifice. Woman was called "half of man"; the domestic sacrifice could only be performed by husband and wife jointly. The son, *putra*, is so called, the scriptures say, because he pulls his parents out (*tra*) from hell (*pu*). He is necessary not only for the pride of the family to continue its line but also for its spiritual welfare in the next world. *Śrāddha*, the last rites, could be properly performed only by a male descendant. Without *śrāddha* the deceased remains forever a *preta*, a ghost.[15]

There are special sections in Hindu law, called *strī-dharma*, that regulate the rights and obligations also of married women, who even in traditional patriarchal Hindu India were not simply the slaves of men. Manu has some flattering remarks about the mother being the goddess of the house and the gods showering happiness on the house where woman is honored.[16] To underline this he says: "The house, in which female relations, not being duly honored, pronounce a curse, perishes completely as if destroyed by magic. Hence men who seek happiness should always honor women on holidays and festivals with gifts of jewelry, clothes, and good food. In that family where the husband is pleased with his wife and the wife with her husband happiness will assuredly be lasting."[17]

On the other hand, Manu also warns men against woman, the perpetual temptress[18] and decrees that she should never be independent: "In childhood a female must be subject to her father, in youth to her husband, when her lord is dead to her sons. She is not to separate from her husband. Though destitute of virtue, seeking pleasure or devoid of good qualities, a husband must be constantly worshipped as a god by a faithful wife."[19] She must always be cheerful, clever in her household affairs, careful in cleaning her utensils, economical in expenditure, and faithful to her husband not only as long as he lives but until her own death.[20] In former times the highest test of fidelity was the voluntary self-immolation on the husband's funeral pyre; occasionally it is still performed, though it has long been forbidden by law. In places of pilgrimage numerous widows spend the rest of their lives attached to temples and religious establishments, singing *bhajans* for some wealthy donor who provides them with food and shelter.

## PROVIDING FOR THE BEYOND

*Antyeṣṭi*, the last rites, also called *mṛtyu-saṃskāra*, the sacrament of death, is still performed today by practically all Hindus, orthodox as well as liberal.

Hindus usually burn their dead, except in times of great disasters. Some sects like the Vīraśaivas practice burial. Also small children and *samnyāsis* are buried; the bodies of poor people, for whom nobody is willing to pay the expenditure of cremation, are often unceremoniously thrown into the nearest river. But ordinarily Hindus will provide for a *śrāddha* to be performed according to the *śāstras*. Details of the rites vary greatly according to the status of the departed, but there is a basic pattern followed by most.

After the hair and nails of the dead person have been cut, the body is washed, the *tilaka* applied to the forehead, and it is wrapped in a new piece of cloth and garlanded with flowers. The one who performs the rites, normally the eldest son, washes his feet, sips water, does *prāṇayama*, and prays to the earth. Then the litter is carried by some men or on a cart drawn by cows to the *smāsana*, the cremation grounds. The eldest son then circumambulates the place prepared for cremation and sprinkles water over it. With an iron rod he draws three lines on the floor, saying: "I draw a line for Yama, the lord of cremation; I draw a line for *Kāla*, time, the lord of cremation, I draw a line for *Mṛtyu*, death, the lord of cremation." Some sesame seeds are put into the mouth of the deceased and the body is put upon the funeral pyre. After several minor rituals during which five little balls made of flour are placed on different parts of the dead body, the pyre is lit by the eldest son. Rich people burn their dead with sandalwood, which spreads a powerful and pleasant scent, strong enough to cover up the smell typical of the cremation grounds. While the pyre is burning lengthy sections from the "hymns for the dead" are recited.[21] Yama is called upon to give the deceased a good place among the ancestors, the *pitṛs* are invoked as patrons of the living, Agni is invited not to harm the deceased but to carry him safely across with his body into the kingdom of the fathers. Pūṣan, the creator, the life of the universe, is besought to keep the departed in safety. Finally, the earth is besought to be good to the dead. One of the mourners is appointed to lift a filled earthen water jug onto his left shoulder, make a hole in the back of the jug and walk three times around the burning corpse. The jug is knocked three times and then completely broken. The relatives (no other people are allowed to participate) then turn to the left and leave the cremation grounds without looking back, the youngest child in front.

Old taboos attach to the last rites; dealing with corpses causes ritual impurity and thus the relations first go to a place where there is a brook or river, immerse themselves three times, facing south (the direction of Yama, the god of the netherworlds), sip some water, and deposit the stone used for breaking the jug on the shore. They then sacrifice water mixed with sesame, saying: "O departed one, may this water, mixed with sesame, reach you." On the threshold of the house they sip water and touch auspicious objects like fire, cow dung, and water before entering. The burning place is cooled with a mixture of milk and water under recitation of *Ṛgvedic* verses. On one of the following days the skull is shattered and the remnants of the bones are gathered into an earthenware jar that after some time is either thrown into a holy river, preferably the Gaṅgā or Yamunā, at some *tīrtha*, to ensure the felicity of the departed, or buried with some ritual on a piece of land set apart for that purpose.

*Samnyāsis*, those who have received *dīkṣā*, which anticipates cremation, are buried in a yoga posture. Frequently a chapel-like memorial called *samādhī* is erected over the tombs of famous and popular *sādhus*, and people keep coming to those places, seeking advice and assistance from the heavenly master.

Cremation rites are only the first part of *antyeṣṭi*: for ten days after the burning, water mixed with sesame is offered every day together with the leaves of certain trees. On the tenth day the eldest son, who officiated at the cremation, goes to the cremation ground and offers a *piṇḍa*, a small ball of rice, saying: "May this *piṇḍa* benefit the *preta* of so-and-so of this family so that his ghost may not feel hunger and thirst." According to the belief of many Hindus it is important that crows should come and peck at the *piṇḍas*; if they do not come the relatives believe that the deceased has left the world with wishes unfulfilled. Often they try to attract the crows for hours, with promises to fulfill the wish of the departed. The stone upon which the sacrifice was offered is anointed and thrown into the water. A handful of water is then offered to the *preta*. There is a popular belief that persons for whom the proper *śrāddha* ceremonies have not been performed have to remain forever *piśācas*, evil ghosts, even if numerous sacrifices are offered on their behalf at some later date. In the Purāṇas we read that immediately after cremation every person receives a *yatanīya-śarīra*, a body that will be subject to tortures and suffering in relation to the sins committed; the *bhaktas* of Viṣṇu, however, receive an incorruptible body like Viṣṇu's, with four arms, in which to enjoy forever the presence of Viṣṇu and serve him eternally. The subtle body of the deceased, so another story goes, in which they live for some time before the next rebirth in another body, is built up by means of the funerary rites.

Present Hindu practice constitutes a synthesis of various strands of belief relating to the afterlife: on the one hand the Purāṇas faithfully describe the Vedic cremation ritual without adding anything sectarian,[22] on the other hand they abound in descriptions of rebirths, heavens, and hells that are quite obviously irreconcilable with the Vedic conception,[23] which aims at transforming the dead soul into a venerated ancestor, without any hint at rebirth or sectarian heaven-and-hell.

According to the sūtras the admission of the *preta* into the circle of the *pitṛs* is obtained through the *sapiṇḍi-kāraṇa*, which normally takes place one year after death. On every new-moon day until then a special *śrāddha* called *ekoddiṣṭa* is performed for the benefit of the deceased. Four earthen vessels are filled with a mixture of water, sesame seeds, and scents, one for the *preta* and one each for father, grandfather, and great-grandfather. The contents of the pot for the *preta* are poured into the other three pots while mantras are recited. From now on the new *preta* ranks as the first of the *pitṛs*; the great-grandfather drops out from the list according to the Vedic rule: "There can be no fourth *piṇḍa*." Now the "ghost" has become a "father," regularly mentioned in the numerous ancestor libations throughout the year.

Thus, through the last sacrament, the meaning of the *saṃskāras* is fulfilled: the Brahmin, transformed into a twice-born being through *upanayana*, attaining the fullness of manhood in *vivāha*, becomes a "complete being" who is worthy of worship, through *śrāddha*, and is thus able to provide blessings for his descendants.

It is through the performance of *saṃskāras* that all Hindus practice the *karmamārga*, the path of works, though as far as their beliefs and intellectual convictions are concerned they may choose to follow the *bhaktimārga* or the *jñānamārga*, the ways of devotion and knowledge.

CHAPTER ELEVEN

# The Path of Knowledge

## *Jñānamārga*

Those who know Brahman as *satyam* (real), *jñānam* (knowledge), *anantam* (infinite), set down in the secret place (of the heart) and in the highest heaven, obtain all desires, together with the allknowing Brahman.

—*Taittirīya Upaniṣad* II, 1

The Upaniṣads, also called *Vedānta*, "the end of the Veda," are the basis for the mainstream of the Indian philosophical and mystical tradition, which refers to them as to its source and ultimate authority. The hymns from the Vedic Saṃhitās today mainly serve a practical purpose as part of the ritual; very few draw their personal religion and beliefs from them. The Upaniṣads, however, are studied, quoted, and used even now in arguments, and in attempts to build up a contemporary philosophical spirituality.

Chronologically the Upaniṣads constitute the last part of *śruti* connected via specific Brāhmaṇas and Āraṇyakas to the Saṃhitās.[1] It has become customary, however, to consider them as a class of texts by themselves and to publish them independent of the rest of *śruti*.[2] Some authors treat them as a kind of protestant countercurrent to the prevailing Vedic sacrificial religion, others as a plain continuation of the same tradition. Both views have their merits and their evident shortcomings: the Upaniṣads quote the Vedas quite frequently and make use of Vedic ideas; they also contain anti-Vedic polemics and represent unorthodox viewpoints.[3] There is, however, a difference between the Saṃhitās and the Upaniṣads, recognized since early times by the Hindu interpreters: the Vedas and Brāhmaṇas center around the sacrificial ritual whose ultimate goal is *svarga* or heaven; the Upaniṣads proclaim an esoteric teaching, the dispensability of ritual, and the attainment of freedom and immortality through a process of concentration and spiritual interiorizing—a difference that prompted ancient writers to classify the religion of the Upaniṣads as *jñānamārga*, "the way of knowledge," over against *karmamārga*, "the way of works," propounded by Saṃhitās and Brāhmaṇas. The Upaniṣads vary considerably in length; among the ten or twelve Upaniṣads normally considered as the authentic or principal ones, the longest amounts to about one hundred printed pages, the shortest to only about three pages.

## THE PRINCIPAL UPANIṢADS: THEIR AUTHORS AND THEIR TEACHINGS

The following chronology has been fairly commonly accepted by scholars: *Bṛhadāraṇyaka* and *Chāndogya* form the oldest group, then come *Īśa* and *Kena*; the third group is made up of *Aitareya*, *Taittirīya*, and *Kauṣītakī*, the fourth of *Kaṭha*, *Muṇḍaka*, and *Śvetāśvatara* with *Praśna*, *Maitrī*, and *Māṇḍukya* concluding the "principal Upaniṣads."[4] This chronology does not take into account the different strata in each of the more lengthy texts, pertaining to different eras. The rest of the 108 Upaniṣads, which are commonly considered as canonical in one way or other, belong partly to much later times and normally represent sectarian teachings of various groups that would preclude their universal acceptance.

Quite frequently the *Īśa(vasya) Upaniṣad* is described as the most important one, the essence of all Upaniṣadic teaching; this may be due partly to its brevity, partly to its concentrated contents, but the Upaniṣads mentioned before contain much that differs in content from the *Īśa* and much that adds to it.

The designation *upaniṣad* is usually explained as derived from *upa* (close by), *ni* (down), and *ṣad* (sit), implying a form of teaching from the teacher's mouth to the pupil's ear, a secret doctrine, or at least a teaching that was not common knowledge of the people. No precise information about their authors' identities can be given. The Upaniṣads do mention a great number of names both in the texts and in the lists of *guru-paraṃparā* at the end of the texts, and we must assume that many of those names do refer to actual historical personalities that might be called Upaniṣadic philosophers.[5]

In certain parts of the Upaniṣads intended to convey a teaching through hyperbole or metaphor, the names of *devas* and *ṛṣis* are mentioned as authors of certain doctrines or practices, an ascription that does not allow any historical verification. Other parts of the Upaniṣads have over the centuries been transmitted anonymously; numerous individual theories and exercises, however, are connected with definite names, most probably representing eminent historical personalities.

Maitrī, after whom one entire Upaniṣad is called, must have been a great mystic who lived and taught the things laid down in his Upaniṣad. Kauśītakī, another name connected with an entire Upaniṣad, could have been the author of the doctrine of the three meditations and the first to have identified *prāṇa*, life breath, with *brahman*. Jaivali can well be considered the author of the *pañcāgni vidyā*, the understanding of the entire cosmic process as being a symbol of, and the model for, sacrifice in the Vedic sense.[6] Uddālaka can be identified from the *Chāndogya Upaniṣad* as the author of a quite interesting cosmology, differing in his views from other early cosmologists whose names are mentioned as well.[7] Kauśala Aśvalāyana is an early psychologist whose teachings are recorded briefly in the *Praśna Upaniṣad*.[8] Aśvalāyana is superseded by the psycho-metaphysician Pippalāda, who developed the doctrine of *rayī* and *prāṇa*, the Indian equivalent of the Aristotelian *hylē* (matter) and *morphē* (form) dualism. A Vāmadeva appears as a master theoretician of the doctrine of rebirth, who held that a human is born three times: at the time of conception, at the time of the birth of one's own child, and at the time of rebirth after death.

The most important group of Upaniṣadic philosophers are those connected with spirituality, the real core of Upaniṣadic teaching. We have the teaching of Śaṇḍilya preserved in a section of the *Chāndogya*,[9] that of Dadyac in a section of the *Bṛhadāraṇyaka* expounding the *madhu-vidyā*,[10] and the interdependence of all things. Another famous name is that of Sanatkumāra, introduced as the preceptor of Nārada in the *Chāndogya*: for him bliss, *ānanda*, is the centre of all human effort.[11] Aruṇi and Yājñavalkya, his pupil, emerge as the two most frequently mentioned and most important Upaniṣadic teachers. Both develop what might be called a *metaphysical psychology*, a rigorous method of realization and an appropriate theory of its working. Gārgī, one of the two wives of Yājñavalkya, plays a major role in a section of the *Bṛhadāraṇyaka Upaniṣad*. She is the first Indian woman philosopher we know of.[12]

Before reading any of the Upaniṣad texts it is necessary to familiarize oneself with the method of teaching used by them, which is often so different from our current philosophical or theological presentation as to bar any true understanding of it. The Upaniṣads are fond of riddles and enigmatic comparisons,[13] employing images and illustrations drawn from ancient Indian experiences and theories rather than from ours. Often one must familiarize oneself with a great deal of background before being able to follow the argument of the Upaniṣads. Sometimes the Upaniṣads also employ the aphoristic method, condensing an entire world view into one sentence or even one syllable.[14] Closely connected is the apophatic method, the way in which Socrates preferred to teach: instead of a positive answer the student is given a question or a piece of purely negative information about what is *not* truth, thus compelling him to transcend the merely verbal and conceptual understanding and to see the proper answer to the truly important questions as consisting in silence rather than in talk.[15]

Quite often the Upaniṣads derive certain teachings from an etymology of keywords; those etymologies, too, do not always follow the paths of contemporary Sanskrit scholarship but employ certain models that demand some study of the historical background beyond mere linguistics. Myths are quite frequently employed, and these often constitute (in literary terms) the most beautiful portions of the Upaniṣads.[16] Analogies are utilized to lead the student gradually to the level of insight required to understand the teacher's perception of reality. Monologues are not absent, though they are much less frequent than in later philosophical and theological teaching. The most interesting and potentially most valuable method is the dialectics employed in some of the major Upaniṣads.

The ancient Indians certainly were great debaters, as we know also from other sources. They sharpened their dialectical skills in protracted controversies with exponents of other views, as the accounts in the Pali canon, for instance, show. Buddhists actually were largely responsible for the refinement in dialectical skills used by the Hindus to overthrow them. It was an ancient Indian practice to challenge an adversary to a public debate that had to end with the defeat of one of the two contestants; the one who lost the argument, at the same time usually lost all of his disciples who went over to the conqueror. Thus the biographer of the great Śaṇkara entitles his work the *Digvijāya*, the conquest of the four quarters by his hero, who was successful in debate after debate against his rivals.

With regard to the contents of the Upaniṣads, a reader should not expect them to contain a systematic treatise of philosophy but a string of more or less developed insights, theories, and principles. The *Vedantasūtra* (also called *Brahmasūtra*) ascribed to Bādarāyaṇa attempts to summarize and systematize the basic philosophy of the Upaniṣads in four *adhyāyas* or treatises, containing altogether 550 aphorisms. It has become the basic text of all the schools of Vedānta philosophy, and the *bhāṣyas*, or commentaries, written upon it constitute the main works of the different systems, often offering diametrically opposed interpretations of the same brief sutra. As research has shown quite convincingly, this *Vedāntasūtra* represents largely the position taken by the *Chāndogya Upaniṣad*, with a few additions here and there; it leaves out much of the contents of the other Upaniṣads, which can hardly be brought together under one system.

## MAJOR THEMES IN THE UPANIṢADS

The problems raised by the Upaniṣads do not coincide with the approaches developed by recent Western academic disciplines, but they can be related to later physics, biology, psychology, religion, and philosophy as well as with mythology and astrology.

One of the threads that runs through much of the Upaniṣadic quest is the enquiry into the hidden ground of being and the root of one's existence, the essence of things and the bond that keeps them together. This search concerns as much the physical structure of material things as the spiritual dimension of human existence. Like the philosophizing of the pre-Socratics of ancient Greece the Upaniṣadic approach is neither purely physical nor purely metaphysical, neither purely psychological nor purely logical according to modern categories; we are able again to appreciate the holistic approach that allows us to put the elements of knowledge acquired through different methods into one mosaic of our world, rough in its details, but impressive in its totality.

We have mentioned before some of the Upaniṣadic ideas concerning the origin of the universe. The search for the substratum common to all beings and its source and origin is one of the main themes dealt with in different Upaniṣads. As well as the attempts to understand water, air, fire or *ākāśa*, ether or space as the ur-element we have the interesting theory of the *Taittirīya*, which assumes five basic elements: fire, water, earth, wind, and space. The whole universe is structured in pentads, corresponding to the elementary pentad, resulting in an ontic interrelationship, a true cosmic harmony: "Fivefold verily, is this all, with the fivefold indeed does one win the fivefold."[17] This theory gains importance in connection with rebirth. At the time of death the faculties and organs of the body return to their respective places in the cosmos: the eye to the sun, the vital breath to the wind, the flesh to the earth, the fluids to the water, thought to space.

We cannot overlook the relevance of the *pañcāgni vidyā* here, the doctrine of the five fires, which explains the entire creation as an interlocking succession of five sacrifices. This connection gains again importance in Yoga philosophy where an attempt is made to establish real connections between the corresponding parts of the microcosm and the macrocosm, ideas that, incidentally, are not foreign to the Western tradition either.[18]

Imagined contests between the individual organs of the body and the various functions, concerning their relative importance for the others, look like entertaining children's stories; in fact they are quite serious philosophy, attempting as they do to reduce the fivefold reality of the microcosm to the One, which in its turn must be the principal element of the universe itself, sustaining all being. The conclusion that it is *prāṇa*, the breath of life that supports the life of all the other functions, brings us very close indeed to the central *ātman-brahman* speculation, which we shall examine more closely in the next chapter.[19]

A different Upaniṣadic seer derives the existence of all being from hunger, the equivalent of death.[20] Knowing means controlling; thus the Upaniṣads set out to teach the conquest of death. It cannot take place in the sphere of phenomena, where rebirth and re-death are necessarily part of nature; it must reach beyond. The conquest of the inner space, the opening of the seemingly closed world of nature, constitutes the most precious portion of the Upaniṣads for us today. The "ultimate," the "point of rest," the "immutable," the Upaniṣads find, is the inner core of all things, the reason for their existence. Though invisible, it is more powerful than the visible. It is delicate and subtle, impervious to the senses but "self-evident." It cannot be made into the object of objective reasoning, but exists only as the identity found in introspection. The ultimate, to be sure, is unborn, unchanging, and immortal. Its abode is "the abode of the heart"—seemingly manifold, but in fact one. It is not identical with any thing, it is no-thing; it is neither the object seen nor the faculty of seeing: it is the seeing of the seeing, the hearing of the hearing, and the thinking of thinking. As such it is inscrutable, and yet it is present in everything and realizable in all situations. It is the truth and the reality of things, not only *satyam* but: *satyasya satyam.*[21]

## THE QUEST FOR REALITY BEYOND APPEARANCE

Reality is the term that stands at the center of all the endeavor of Indian philosophy; the differentiation between the obvious and the real, the conditional and the essential, the apparent and the true. The quest for Reality finally leads to the discovery that Reality cannot be found outside but only inside. Thus the *jñānamārga*, the path of knowledge, does not constitute a system of objective conceptual statements but a way toward self-discovery. The ground of the universe and the ground of our own existence are identical.

This self-discovery takes place in stages, of which the Upaniṣads usually enumerate four. The most systematic exposition of this four-step process of cognition is given in the *Māṇḍukya.*[22]

The first and lowest stage of awareness is *jāgarita-sthāna*, the normal state of being awake and hence open to sense perception and rational thought. The human spirit is poured out into a multitude of objective things, bound to space and time and to the laws of the physical universe.

*Svapna-sthāna*, the dreaming state, "in which one cognizes internal objects" is already higher, because the human spirit is no longer subject to the laws of the physical world or bound to space and time. A person now herself creates the world in which she moves, she steps out of the limitations of physical nature by creating whatever the mind conceives.

*Suṣupti*, profound and dreamless sleep, is the third state, higher again than the dream. It is a "blissful state," a state of unification in which the spirit is no longer scattered over a profusion of objective and subjective things, but there is no consciousness of this unification and bliss.

*Turīya*, the fourth state, is beyond all that: it is neither perception of external nor of internal objects, neither knowledge nor ignorance, it is without describable qualities, it is supreme consciousness of consciousness, a cessation of all movement and all multiplicity, complete freedom. It is the self. And it is the knowledge of the self, which is the same, because the self, as the Upaniṣads understand it, is pure knowledge-being-obliss. The knowledge, which we ordinarily possess, is knowledge of something. The knowledge of *turīya* is knowledge of nothing in particular, but of the ground of all things and all knowing. It is the self, knowing itself as the self, not the function of an isolated capacity of the mind, but pure awareness, the lighting up of the subject itself as pure perception. Thus *jñāna* is not a conceptual synthesis of a subject-object polarity but the experience of the subject as reality as such. The aporia of the coexistence of the finite and the infinite, the real and the unreal, the temporal and the eternal, the subjective and the objective is not resolved but seen as nonexistent. *Jñāna* is the self-enlightenment of reality as such, the self-consciousness of reality. In *jñāna* consciousness rests in itself, knowing nothing beyond this self-consciousness that has no objective content. The difficulty lies in interpreting and communicating this knowledge through concepts whose validity is negated in this very knowledge. The concepts are all taken from the sphere of objective knowledge, in which *jñāna* cannot happen. On the level of the perception of the ultimate as reality there cannot be any concepts, because there is no more multiplicity, no thing with which this knowledge could be identified. It is not possible to have some of this knowledge; either one has it fully or one does not have it at all. Perception of *ātman* is indivisible. There is, however, scope for growth: the knowledge may be dimly perceived first before becoming overwhelmingly clear.

The *Muṇḍaka Upaniṣad* distinguishes between a *para*, a higher, and an *apara*, a lower knowledge. The lower is the knowledge of the Vedas and *Vedāṅgas*, or traditional knowledge. The higher is that "wherewith the imperishable is grasped." Thus it says: "That which is invisible, incomprehensible, without family or caste, without eye and ear, without hand or foot, eternal, all permeating, omnipresent, extremely subtle: that is the imperishable recognized by the wise as the source of all beings. Just as the spider emits a thread and absorbs it again, or as grass sprouts from the earth or as hair grows on a living body, thus everything has its roots in the imperishable."[23]

## THE PECULIARITY OF VEDĀNTIC KNOWLEDGE

It is very difficult to express Vedāntic knowledge, or the way leading to it, in Western terminology, which is heavily dependent on Greek thought.[24] Knowledge and way in the Indian understanding have stages, not set side by side, but within each other, in depth, within consciousness itself. Its aim is to reach reality itself, not to abstract a concept from it. This means the training not only of the mind, but the development of a lifestyle of inwardness, from within which life then develops in a new way, whose knowledge is simply incommensurable with the knowledge achieved through sense perception and abstraction from it. The closer this knowledge comes to reality, the less concepts can express it adequately. It is possible to make statements about this knowledge—as well as about the *ātman* and about *turīya*, all ultimately identical!—statements that are to be understood as dialectical approximations only: it is immanent and transcendent at the same time and neither immanent nor transcendent nor a combination of both. Every concept employed must at once be negated. Affirmation and negation at the same time, the *neti neti*, not thus, not thus, leads to a higher level of consciousness, where there is neither affirmation nor negation.

Human existence has not only a horizontal, historical dimension, but a vertical, nonhistorical dimension as well. To cope with actual human existence this movement toward the center, the attainment of a level of consciousness of the self, is indispensable. In our age of popularized technology all problems seem to be understood as questions concerning quantifiable material entities. Our "soul science" declares all ultimate questioning as sickness because it presupposes the negation of a transcendent reality. Upaniṣadic thinking "rests" and is static as far as the outward movement and change in topic is concerned; for people unused to probing the depths this vertical movement does not "lead further" and is considered uninteresting. There is no visible progress and one needs time and patience. There are signs that some of our contemporaries have realized that technological toys cannot serve as substitutes for the soul and that technical progress does not simply spell happiness. They have taken up ideas developed three thousand years ago in a materially far less developed culture in which nevertheless dissatisfaction with things could be strong enough to come to understand the no-thing as supreme bliss and ultimate fulfillment. In the Upaniṣads the specific knowledge is always emphasized as being new and different; *brahma-vidyā* as compared to sacrificial knowledge is considered to be much higher and incomparably better. Vedic ritual religion is, in the light of *jñānamārga*, ignorance and darkness, a shaky raft unable to cross the ocean of existence. But the Upaniṣads know well that a knowledge boasted of becomes an expression of ignorance, worse even than plain and naive not-knowing. Thus the *Iśa Upaniṣad* says: "Into blind darkness enter they that worship ignorance; into darkness greater than that, as it were, they that delight in knowledge."[25]

Compared to the way of work and its solid factual knowledge of the mechanism of sacrifices the way of knowledge means a turning toward the subject and the correct realization that the subject can never be understood as part of something else, but only as a self-contained totality; it cannot be grasped in a concept but only in a realization. The realization is not *of* the ultimate, but it *is* itself the ultimate. He who knows himself knows Reality. The *method* of knowing reality is what the Upaniṣads can teach. They cannot teach Reality. All have to find it for themselves individually, using the method taught.

There are outward conditions to be fulfilled; according to some Upaniṣads the membership in the Brahmin caste is absolutely required and the disciple must have gone through the Vedic *saṃskāras*, especially the *upanayana*, before taking up the *jñānamārga* with a reputed teacher. Then the student has to undergo a long process of physical, mental, and moral preparation before being led to the formulae of knowledge. The preparation seems to be the more impressive part—the realization may be imparted in a sentence, a word—even in silence at the very end of the period of training. It is not the acquisition of some outward knowledge but an awareness of actual reality, the removal of so many layers of nonreality. Basically it is nothing new that is made known in realization; it is a subjective change to see everyday things and happenings as manifestations of the absolute; to see the self not as the individual "I" with physical needs and demands but as reality in the ultimate sense. The imparting of *jñāna* does not have the characteristics of an instruction but of a revelation. Therefore it is important not only to approach a scholar of all the traditional sciences but someone who has received revelation through a chain of bearers of this same light, a guru standing in the *guru paramparā*. The teacher does not choose his students; the students come and ask the teacher to be admitted. The students must serve their master faithfully and submit to strict discipline; little of the long time is spent in oral instruction, most of it is *tapasya*, ascetical training, which sharpens the energies of the intellect, especially the power of discrimination that is most essential. A person must learn to distinguish the self from what is not the self, reality from appearance; one must be strong enough to reject all that is nonessential and nonreal. Through this the students gain access to new depth and new horizons that enable them to understand the true meaning of the words used to express the higher knowledge. Self-realization can be neither gained nor taught vicariously; everyone has to gain it personally. The guru points the way, supervises the training, and clarifies doubts.

The discussions between master and pupil as recorded in the Upaniṣads are very often a Socratic kind of questioning, to bring to light truth from within the disciple. Words are imperfect instruments through which to discover the unspeakable. They can be understood only when realization has already taken place; and by then they are redundant. They serve to repudiate wrong conceptions and to prevent false identifications. The common instruments of logic—to arrive at conclusions from certain premises by way of syllogisms—are considered to be inadequate: they can only provide particular and finite object knowledge, never an all-encompassing subject realization. The means therefore for finding truth is not discursive reasoning but meditation. The Upaniṣads differ in their methods of meditation; some begin with gradually widening cosmic contemplations, others utilize the Vedic religious symbolism, others employ mantras like the OM; from the audible sound the aspirants reach out to the soundless until they can finally say: "OM is *brahman*, OM is the universe."

The Upaniṣads are not only records of ancient India, they are part of the living Hindu tradition. Quite often they are recited as other scriptures are, memorized and quoted by people who do not spend all of their time as disciples of a guru. The recitations are quite frequently begun by the following *śloka*, which in itself sums up the essential teaching of the Upaniṣads:

> *Pūrṇam adaḥ pūrṇam idam pūrṇat pūrṇam udacyate*
> *Pūrṇasya pūrṇam ādāya pūrṇam evāvaśiṣyate*

> "Fullness is this, fullness is that. Fullness proceeds from fullness. Having taken out fullness from fullness, fullness itself remains."

The conclusion of the Upaniṣad, again recited, is often a promise of liberation as the following:

> This Brahmā told to Prajāpati, Prajāpati to Manu, Manu to humankind. He who has learned the Veda from the family of a teacher according to rule, in

> the time left over from serving his teacher, he who after having returned to his family settled down in a home of his own, continued to study what he has learned and has virtuous sons, he who concentrates all his senses in the self, who practices kindness toward all creatures, he who behaves thus throughout his life reaches the Brahmā world, does not return hither again, verily he does not return hither again.[26]

The Upaniṣads are the great book of principles, India's *prōtē gnōsis*, its basic philosophy, from which branch out the many systems of Vedānta of later centuries.

CHAPTER TWELVE

# *Ātman* and *Brahman*

## *Self and All*

Verily, this body is mortal. It has been appropriated by Death. But it is the standing ground of the deathless, bodiless Self.

—*Chāndogya Upanisad* VIII, XII, 1

A great number of important topics are dealt with in the Upaniṣads but their central concern is undoubtedly the knowledge of, and path to, *ātman* and *brahman*. The great amount and the diversity of the statements relating to *ātman-brahman* in even the principal Upaniṣads makes it impossible to offer a synthesis. All we can do is to mark major trends of thought. One of these is the attempt, made repeatedly in the Upaniṣads, to arrange the seemingly infinite plurality of things in a limited number of categories, coordinating macrocosm and microcosm, and to understand manifold reality as a combination of relatively few primordial elements. By means of a progressive reduction a person can finally arrive at the One, which is further reduced to an immaterial essence pervading everything without being identical with any one object: the Real is the ultimate support of all phenomena. To grasp this Real, there are, in the main, two distinct paths. One begins with the outside world and the manifold objects, and reduces them to five elements, to three, and finally to one. The other begins with a person's subjective consciousness and discovers in its depths the Real, which proves to be the source of everything. Finally the realization dawns that the immanent *ātman* is identical with the transcendent *brahman*: *ātman* is *brahman*.

We possess the record of a lively discussion between the great philosopher Yājñavalkya and his wife Gārgī Vacaknavī in which the first of those two ways is demonstrated.

"Yājñavalkya," said Gārgī, "since all this world is woven, warp and woof, on water, on what is the water woven, warp and woof?" "On wind, O Gārgī!" "On what is the wind woven?" "On the sky, O Gārgī." The questioning goes on, and Yājñavalkya explains the "warp and woof" of each world within the cosmology of the time, which we saw before: the sky is "woven" on the world of the *Gandharvas*, this on the sphere of the sun, this on the sphere of the moon, this on the world of the planets, this on the world of the *devas*, this on the realm of *Indra*, this again on the *Prajāpati-loka*, the world of the creator of all beings. "On what then is the world of the Lord of Creation woven?" "On the world of *brahman*, says Yājñavalkya. Gārgī tries to press on, wanting to know about the source of *brahman*, but Yājñavalkya rejects the question: "Gārgī, do not question too much lest your head fall off. Really, you are asking too much about the divine being, about which we are not to question too much. Gārgī, do not question too much!" Thereupon Gārgī Vacaknavī kept silent.[1]

Before proceeding with texts, it may be of some help to give a brief etymological explanation of *ātman* and *brahman*, though an understanding of both terms emerges, better perhaps, from the texts themselves, which let us appreciate the deep ambiguity of these notions and the impossibility of really defining them.

*Ātman* is the grammatical form of the reflexive pronoun in Sanskrit; according to the context, it can mean the body, anything that one considers as mine or myself, a meaning that leads on to the probing question of what this "myself," the subject of all feelings, thought and wishes, really consists of.

*Brahman* has many meanings. It is commonly derived from the verbal root *bṛh-*, to grow, to become great. In the Vedas, *brahman* means sacred utterance: that through which the *devas* become great. Later it came to be used as a term denoting ritual and also those who were in charge of it, the Brāhmaṇas. The Upaniṣads, finally, use it as a designation for the ultimate reality, to be understood as the life breath of the universe and everything in it.[2] But it is also used more loosely, in an analogous way; the word, the eye, the ear, the heart, the sun, space are all called *brahman*. Elsewhere every identification with any concrete object is denied and *brahman* became a synonym for the unfathomable, the unthinkable, the mysterious that has no name. The popular Hindu traditions equate *brahman* with Viṣṇu, Śiva or Devī respectively, giving it the attributes of the creator, the preserver and the destroyer, seeing in it a Supreme Person with numerous divine qualities that are described in detail. Advaita Vedānta refuses to identify *brahman* with any activity or quality, and rather prefers to draw a distinction within *brahman* to express the conviction that the ultimate ground of all being is without any qualities or activities, since that would denote change; it is therefore *nirguṇa*.

A word of caution may be appropriate here: it would be misleading to translate *ātman* as "soul" and *brahman* as "supreme being," as is done quite frequently in popular books. Both words have a Western philosophical or religious background and already reveal a specific solution of a problem that is left open in the Upaniṣads, namely the question of the oneness and the plurality of reality. We can avoid a wrong identification of *ātman* and *brahman* with non-Indian concepts by considering in some detail how the authors of the Upaniṣads arrive at their *ātman-brahman* realization.

> OM. The brahman-knower obtains the supreme. As has been said: he who knows *brahman* as the real (*satyam*, which also means truth), as knowledge (*jñānam*) and then as the infinite (*anantam*) placed in the secret cave of the heart and in the highest heaven realizes all desires along with *brahman*. From this *ātman*, verily arose *ākāśa*, (space or ether, a fine and subtle substance permeating the universe); from this came air, from air fire, from fire water, from water the earth, from the earth herbs, from herbs food, from food *puruṣa*, the "person." . . . From food (*anna*) verily are produced whatsoever creatures dwell on the earth. By food alone they live. And at the end they pass into it. Food is verily the firstborn of the being. . . . Verily those who worship *brahman* as food obtain all food. Different from, and within that sphere that consists of food (*anna-rasa-maya*), is the self that consists of life breath (*ātma prāṇa-maya*) by which it is filled. This has the form of a *puruṣa*. . . . The *devas* breathe this life breath (*prāṇa*), as also do men and beasts; *prāṇa* is the life (*āyus*) of all. They who worship *brahman* as *prāṇa* attain a full life . . . this is the *ātman* of the former. Different from it and within the *prāṇa*-sphere is the self, made of mind (*ātma mano-maya*), by which it is filled. This (again) has the form of a *puruṣa*. . . . Different from and within it, is the self that consists of understanding (*ātma vijñāna-maya*), by which it is filled. This too has the form of a *puruṣa*. Faith (*śrāddha*) is his head, order (*ṛta*) its southern side, truth (*satyam*) its northern side, yoga its self (*ātma*), and the great one (*mahā*) its foundation. Understanding directs the sacrifice and the actions. All *devas* worship the *brahman*, which is understanding as the foremost. . . . Different from and within that, which consists of understanding is the self, consisting of bliss (*ātma ānanda-maya*), by which it is filled. This too has the form of a *puruṣa*: his body is bliss (*ānanda ātma*), *brahman* the foundation. . . . He who is here in the *puruṣa* and yonder in the sun, he is one. Who knows this, on departing from this world, reaches the *ātman* consisting of food, of life breath, of mind, of understanding, of bliss. Where words do not reach and the mind cannot grasp, there is the *brahman* full of bliss; who knows it does not fear anything.[3]

We can learn from this one text—among other things—the rather complex meaning of the term *ātman* that would not allow us to equate it with the term "soul" as popularly understood.

The distinction of the five strata of *ātman*, corresponding to five different *brahman* realities is quite instructive: each reality is the inner core of the one preceding it till we reach the very heart of being, which is *ānanda*, bliss, which cannot be further qualified as having an "exterior" and an "interior." The self of a person needs nourishment that builds up a material self; it requires life breath that builds up a subtle material self; it requires mind that develops the intellectual self; further on, it requires understanding, developing the sphere of deep insight. The core and the heart of reality, finally, is the sphere of bliss, where *ātman* is seen as consisting of, and resting on, *brahman*. For each sphere of the self there is a corresponding ultimate, to be realized as relative, step by step, till the true ultimate is reached.

What is *brahman*? We have seen one answer to the question. Another approach is given in the *Chāndogya Upaniṣad*. A father, whose son has just returned from his guru full of pride in his Vedic knowledge, questions him about the *brahman*. The son has to admit his ignorance and has to hear from his father that unless he knows *brahman*, he knows nothing at all. The father tries to teach him by way of practical experiments: "Bring a fig," says the father. Śvetaketu, the son, brings it. "Divide it. What do you see?" "Tiny seeds," is the answer. "Divide one of the seeds. What do you see?" "Nothing." Now follows the essential teaching: "My dear, that subtle essence which you do not perceive, that is the source of this mighty Nyagrodha tree. That which is so tiny (*aṇimā*) is the *ātman* of all. This is the true, the self, that you are, Śvetaketu!"[4]

The teaching drawn from the next experiment is the same: Śvetaketu is asked to throw a handful of salt into a vessel filled with water, to taste it in different places, and then to try to separate salt again from water. The salt is one with the water, it cannot be separated, though Śvetaketu knows that it is different from it. This is the *ātman*, all pervading, and inseparable from objects, not identical with them. And his father concludes this lesson with the same formula: *Tat tvam asi*, that you are! The invisible substance that makes the Nyagrodha tree grow is the life of humans too, even more—the one who knows it, is it! The same Upaniṣad has another well-known instruction on *brahman*: Prajāpati, the Father of all that is born announces: "The *ātman* that is free from all evil, free from old age, free from death, free from worry, free from hunger and thirst, whose desire is truth, whose purpose is truth, that should be sought, that one must strive to understand. Who has found this *ātman* and understands it, attains all worlds and the fulfilment of all desires." *Devas* and *asuras* hear this; they too are without this ultimate fulfillment, they, too, have everything to learn. Indra, the king of the *devas*, and Virocana, the chief of the *asuras*, approach Prajāpati for instruction. For thirty-two years they live as *brahmacāris*; they serve their guru without hearing a word about *ātman*. After the time is up, Prajāpati asks them for what purpose they had originally come. They repeat the words that Prajāpati had used and state that they were seeking the sorrowless, deathless *ātman*. Now Prajāpati instructs them. They are told to look at themselves in the mirror of a sheet of water and to report their impressions. They find that they see themselves, "a picture even to the very hairs and nails." Prajāpati asks them to put on their best clothes, adorn themselves, and look again in the mirror and to report about it. The two say that they see themselves well dressed and neat. And Prajāpati concludes: "That is the immortal, fearless *brahman*." The two leave, satisfied that they have got what they wanted. Prajāpati looked after them and said to himself: "They go away, without having perceived, without having known the self. All who follow such a doctrine will perish." Virocana declared to the *asuras* that bodily happiness is the one-and-all there is. Indra, however, before returning to the *devas* realized an objection: if the *ātman* is identical with the bodily reality, it will suffer as the body suffers, become blind, lame, crippled as the body, perish together within the body. "I see no good in this," he concludes and returns to Prajāpati. He serves him another thirty-two years and is asked at the end of this long term the same question, but gets a different answer: "The one that happily moves about in a dream is the *ātman*, the immortal fearless *brahman*." At first Indra is satisfied and takes leave; before reaching his heaven he discovers the fault in this answer, too: someone who dreams of being chased and tortured, of mourning and dying, suffers sorrow and cannot be called happy. And back he goes to serve again for thirty-two years. Now Prajāpati comes up with a new secret: "He who dwells in deep, dreamless sleep is the *ātman*, the immortal fearless *brahman*." Indra, after a brief satisfaction with this answer, becomes sceptical again: One who sleeps is not aware of himself and his bliss. It is as if he did not exist at all. Prajāpati commends Indra's sharp mind and tells him to serve him for only another five years, after which time he will really impart the ultimate secret to him. When the time has come he instructs him as follows: "Mortal, indeed, is this body. It is held by death; but it is the support of his deathless bodiless *ātman*. Verily with a body one cannot have freedom from pleasure and pain. But pleasure and pain do not touch the bodiless. Bodiless are air, clouds, lightning, and thunder. . . . Even so that serene one, when rising up from this body and reaching the highest light appears in his own form. Such is the Supreme Person. . . . Who finds this *ātman* obtains all worlds and the fulfilment of all wishes."[5] Indra, the king of heaven, had to wait for 101 years before he was given the full insight; a human should not desist, therefore, from his effort, even if realization is not reached at the first attempt.

A fairly systematic treatment of the *ātman-brahman* theme is provided in the *Muṇḍaka Upaniṣad*. After demonstrating the social and secular necessity of Vedic rites and sacrifices and their intrinsic inadequacy to save from repeated old age and death, it develops the exigencies and methods of *brahman* knowledge. Realization of *brahman*, the imperishable, the *puruṣa*, the true, the real, can only be attained through a guru.

> That is the truth: as from a fire, blazing, sparks like fire issue forth by the thousands, so many kinds of beings issue forth from the imperishable and they return to it. Splendid and without a bodily form is this *puruṣa*, without and within, unborn, without life breath and without mind, higher than the supreme element. From him are born life breath and mind, all the sense organs, also space, air, light, water and earth, the support of all. Fire is his head, his eyes are the sun and the moon, the regions are his ears, the revealed

> Vedas are his speech, air is his life breath and his heart is the universe. Out of his feet the earth is born, indeed he is the soul of all beings.

One by one, the text explains how everything issues out of this *brahman*. *Brahman* must be known both as being (*sat*) and nonbeing (*asat*), as the support of everything, upon whom the sky, the earth, and space is woven.

> In the highest sphere, made of gold, is *brahman* without stain, without parts, pure, the light of lights. The sun does not shine there, nor the moon nor the stars, nor the lightning either, whence then this fire? Everything has its shine from this shining one: his shine illumines the world. *Brahman* indeed is immortal, in front, behind, to the right and left is *brahman*. It spreads forth below and above. *Brahman*, indeed is this all, the greatest. . . . A seer, who sees the creator of golden color, the Lord, the *puruṣa*, the womb of *brahman*, becomes a knower, freed from good and evil.[6]

The *Bṛhadāraṇyaka Upaniṣad* explains the immanence of *brahman* in all things as the result of its entering into them after creating them. "He entered into them even to the tips of the nails, as a razor is hidden in the razor case. They do not see him. When breathing, he is called *prāṇa*, breath, when speaking he is called *vāk*, speech, when seeing he is called *cakṣus*, eye, when hearing he is called *śrotra*, ear, when thinking he is called *manas*, mind." The Upaniṣad instructs us also that by meditating on the *ātman* one realizes all things to be one and oneself to be one with it: "Whosoever knows thus, *aham brahmāsmi*, I am *brahman*, becomes this all. Even the *devas* cannot prevent him from becoming thus, for he becomes their *ātman*."[7]

Here we have one of the four *mahāvākyas*, Great Sayings, which according to Śaṅkara express the gist of the Upaniṣadic teaching in a short formula and whose understanding is equated with ultimate liberation. Earlier another one was quoted: *tat tvam asi*, Uddālaka's teaching: "that you are."[8] Elsewhere we read: *ayam ātma brahman*, this Self is *brahman*,[9] and *prajñānam brahman*, Wisdom is *brahman*.[10] The *mahāvākyas* cannot be applied to the three lower stages of consciousness: they are true only of *turīya*. In our waking state, in our dreams and in our sleep the I-consciousness and the awareness of the Ultimate are not identical—only in the "Fourth State" do Consciousness and Reality coincide.

It is difficult to understand the Upaniṣadic teaching of *ātman-brahman* from within Western philosophical thought: we must make a serious attempt to find the appropriate framework of interpretation. To call the Upaniṣads *pantheistic* and thus have done with the question is not good enough. The Upaniṣads never state that the world, as it is and as it is normally perceived, is simply identical with the absolute. The Upaniṣads demand first of all a movement of the mind into another level of being and consciousness. It would also be wrong to compare the Upaniṣads with a rationalist theology. If any comparison can be made, it would be with what is commonly and vaguely called mysticism. The difficulty, however, is that there are various forms of *mysticism*, not all of which would be comparable with the Upaniṣadic approach to reality. The Upaniṣads do not present us a systematic theology but they offer inner experiences and visions.

The Upaniṣadic *ātman* is not unequivocally identical with *brahman*: only in *turīya*, the ultimate stage of consciousness, which is not easily accessible. Only persistent meditation efforts open up the depths of the self. Reality, once discovered, appears as "self-evident," but before we come to this conclusion we have to go through a long and time-consuming process of *neti neti*, of physical and spiritual discipline, rejecting inadequate substitutes for the absolute that are offered by a great many diverse ideologies. We recognize our self and the absolute, *ātman* and *brahman*, as one and the same reality, only after having penetrated to the state of being wherein we are stripped of our so-called identity. If we follow the steps outlined in the *Kena* and *Bṛhadāraṇyaka Upaniṣads* to realize the *satyasa satya*, the Reality of Reality, we will be led into an *aporia*, a perfect darkness, a last portal, which we find ourselves unable to pass, unless it be opened from within.

As the *Kaṭha Upaniṣad* says: "This Self cannot be attained by instruction, nor by much thought nor by listening to many scripture readings: the Self is only attained by one who is chosen: to such a one the *ātman* reveals itself."[11]

CHAPTER THIRTEEN

# *Karma, Vidyā, Mokṣa*

## *Liberation from Rebirth*

> From the unreal lead me to the Real,
> From darkness lead me to light,
> From ignorance lead me to knowledge,
> From death lead me to immortality.
>
> —*Aitareya Brāhmaṇa* II, 1

Thus does the *Bṛhadāraṇyaka Upaniṣad* describe the process of dying:

> Just as a heavily loaded cart moves creaking, so the *ātman* of the body with the *ātman* of wisdom on it moves creaking, when breathing becomes small through old age or disease then just as a mango or some other fruit loosens itself so this *puruṣa* frees himself from these limbs and returns again to the womb. . . . When this *ātman* becomes weak and confused, as it were, all the *prāṇas*, the life breaths gather round him. He takes into himself those sparks of light and recedes into the heart. When the eye *puruṣa* departs, he cannot recognize forms any more. "He is becoming one, he does not see," so they say; "he is becoming one, he cannot smell," they say; "he is becoming one, he does not taste," they say; "he is becoming one, he does not speak," they say; "he is becoming one, he does not hear," they say; "he is becoming one, he does not think," they say; "he is becoming one, he does not feel," they say; "he is becoming one, he does not know," they say. The point of his heart becomes lighted up and by that light the *ātman* departs either through the eye or through the head or through other apertures of the body. And when he thus departs, the *prāṇas* depart after him. He becomes understanding, he follows after understanding. His knowledge and his deeds follow him as does also his previous wisdom. Just as a caterpillar, when it has come to the end of

> one blade of grass, and after having made its approach to another one, draws itself together toward it, so this *ātman*, after having thrown away this body and after having dispelled ignorance, draws itself together. And as the goldsmith, taking a piece of gold, turns it into another, newer and more beautiful shape, even so does this *ātman*, after having thrown away this body, make unto himself newer and more beautiful shapes like that of the Pitṛs, the *gandharvas*, the *devas*, of Prajāpati, of Brahmā or some other being. This *ātman* indeed is *brahmaṇ* consisting of understanding, mind, life, sight, hearing, earth, water, air, space, light and darkness, desire and desirelessness, anger and freedom from anger, righteousness and unrighteousness and all things. This is what is meant by saying: "It consists of this and consists of that." As one acts and as one behaves so one becomes. The one who does good becomes good; the one who does evil becomes evil. One becomes righteous by righteous action, unrighteous by unrighteous action. Others, however, say: a *puruṣa* consists of desire (*kāma*). As his desire is, so is his determination (*kratur*); as his determination is such deed he commits; whatever deed he commits, that he attains.
>
> On this there is the following verse: The object to which the mind (*manas*) is attached, the subtle self (*liṅga*) goes together with the deed, being attached to it alone. Exhausting the results of whatever works he did in this world he comes again from that world to this world for work. This is true for the mind with desires. The mind who is free from desire, whose desire is satisfied, whose desire is the *ātman*, his *prāṇas* do not depart. Since he is *brahman*, he goes into *brahman*.
>
> On this there is the following verse: "When all the desires that dwell in the heart are cast away, then does the mortal become immortal, then he attains *brahman* here."[1]

Death is a theme that looms large in the Upaniṣads. Death is the creator and the destroyer of all that is. Death, especially in the form of re-death (*punarmṛtyu*)[2] is the greatest evil that threatens the human existence. Belief in rebirth seems to be accepted in the Upaniṣads without further argument. Scholars generally assume that it forms part of the religion of the indigenous peoples of India, which influenced Vedic religion quite heavily. According to the Upaniṣads the Vedic *yajña* cannot save from repeated death, to which even the *devas* are subjected in one way or another. At the root of the Upaniṣadic search for the liberation that goes beyond the attainment of the status of *devas*, there is already a certain skepsis with regard to the nature of the *devas*: for the Upaniṣads, they are in the sphere of sense-experience and therefore in the lower ranges of consciousness and reality. The process of liberation does not, therefore, depend on any intervention from the side of the *devas*. The Upaniṣads do not deny a Supreme God; certain texts quite clearly speak of the *puruṣottama*, of grace and election as essential for liberation;[3] but their concern is the immanent process of liberation in the subjective consciousness. Death is a happening on the periphery of external consciousness, as are all physical and psychical ills, and so one is affected by these only so long as one is caught up in the lower stages of consciousness. Reality and consciousness are identical, a unity of bliss and immortality, freedom from change, freedom from rebirth and redeath.[4]

The most important synonym for death in the Upaniṣads is *kāla*, time. Everything that is created by time must also find its end in time: *manas*, *apas*, *arka*, *prithvī*, *tejas*, the body and the senses, sun and earth and water, everything must die. Only that which is not born from death-time, the *ātman*, is not liable to die. The dialogue between Naciketas and death in the *Kaṭha Upaniṣad*, a most beautiful and profound passage, makes it quite evident that the basic aim of the Upaniṣads is to show a way of escape from repeated death.[5]

Fundamental to the Upaniṣadic understanding of death and liberation is the metaphysical anthropology presupposed in it, which differs substantially from both the popular and the academic philosophical understanding in the West. We have seen before the five different *ātman* corresponding to five different components or "sheaths" of human existence. Barring more detailed subdivisions, Vedantic anthropology considers the human person to be composed of *sthūla śarīra*, *sūkṣma śarīra*, and *ātman-brahman*. The gross body is destined to disintegrate at the time of death. The subtle body with all the imprints of deeds and thoughts of the previous life, is preserved and clings to its *ātman*; this results in intermediate existences in heavens or hells, depending on the quality of the deeds, and finally in an earthly rebirth. *Karma* keeps in motion the vicious circle of action, desire, reward, and new action. The karma of former births, called *prārabhda*, is worked out in the present birth; and karma acquired in this birth, good or bad, works toward a future birth. The Upaniṣads have several similar accounts of the route that the departed take before they are reborn as human beings; these texts, often elaborated, have found a place also in the *Purāṇas* and other popular Hindu scriptures. The Upaniṣads generally describe a *deva-yāna* and a *pitṛ-yāna*, the former leading to no-return, the latter leading to relatively enjoyable rebirths on earth; those who go neither way are reborn as animals or demons, before slowly ascending the ladder of being again. Thus says the *Bṛhadāraṇyaka Upaniṣad*:

> Those who meditate on the truth in the forest with faith, pass into the light, from the light into the day, from the day into the half-month of the waxing moon, from the half-month of the waxing moon into the six months that the sun travels northward, from these months into the world of the *devas*, from the world of the *devas* into the sun, from the sun into the lightning. Then one of the mind-born goes to the sphere of lightning and leads them to the *brahma-loka*. In the *brahma-loka* they live for a long time. For these there is no return. Those who, through *yajñas*, gifts, and austerities, conquer the worlds, pass into the smoke, from the smoke into the night, from the night into the half-month of the waning moon, from the half-month of the

> waning moon into the six months during which the sun travels southward, from these to the world of the fathers, from the world of the fathers into the moon. Reaching the moon they become food. There the *devas*, as they say to King Soma, increase, decrease even to feed upon them there. When that is over, they pass into space, from space into wind, from wind into rain, from rain into the earth. Reaching the earth they become food. Again they are offered in the fire of man.[6] Thence they are born in the fire of woman with a view to going to other worlds. Thus do they go round. But those who do not know these two ways, become insects, moths, and whatever there is here that bites.[7]

Other texts describe rebirth as the search for a womb of the *puruṣa*, the thumb-sized *homunculus* made up of subtle body and *ātman*.

The cause of rebirth is karma, inherent in the subtle body; the cause of liberation from rebirth is the cutting of the bond that ties *ātman* to the subtle body and with it to karma. Though it is easy to give a correct etymology of karma from the root *kṛ-*, to do, to act, and although the word has become one of the favorite terms of the present generation, its meaning is difficult to explain.[8] Literally, it is simply the deed done, a work performed. But the deed is not terminated when a certain action comes to an end; the accomplished deed itself is a new entity that as such continues to exert its own influence, even without the will and activity of the doer. The whole *karmamārga* is based on this teaching of the objective efficacy of the accomplished deed; the *apūrva* of the Mīmāṃsakas, the suspended latent causality of ritual actions, is quite an ingenious invention in this direction; it allows substantiated causality to accumulate like a bank account for later use in heaven. Karma is neither material nor spiritual in the usual sense of those terms. It can be produced and annihilated, it can lead to good and to evil consequences, but it is always finite, however powerful its influence may be. It is, in a sense, the law of nature; universal, because it applies to all of nature, but finite, because nature itself is finite.

Karma is often popularly understood as fate[9] and compared to the Greek notion of *moīra*. But we must take note of a very important difference: the *moīra* of the Greeks cannot be influenced: karma can be manipulated! To the Greek mind, this helplessness makes tragedy possible, tragedy being the ultimate and inevitably fatal clash of man's will with fate. Indian literature does not know tragedy; karma can be influenced or even totally neutralized through religion! The aspect of life, so prominent in Western thought, that decisions once made cannot be revoked, that there are immutable laws that even the Supreme cannot change, is absent from Indian thought; the round of rebirths, of world creations and destructions in an endless series, offers the possibility of ever new changes in decisions made, of ever new developments, so that no being's downfall is final and irredeemable. Karma does not cancel free will and genuinely free decisions; nor do free will and one's own decisions neutralize karma. Modern Indians call karma a "scientific" concept, and serious investigations into claims of karma transmitted from former lives have been made by Indian and Western psychologists and medical doctors. The University of Virginia Press published a series of volumes by Dr. Ian Stevenson, an American physician, who critically examined dozens of "Cases of the Reincarnation Type" and who came to the conclusion that reincarnation was the most plausible explanation for the astonishing phenomena reported and described.

The Upaniṣads maintain that they have found a way to deal with karma that is better than that of the Vedas: not to produce good karma as counterbalance for bad karma, but to eliminate karma altogether!

> Unsteady, verily, are these boats of the eighteen sacrificial formulas, which are said to be the lower karma. The deluded, who delight in these as leading to good existences, fall again into old age and death. Abiding in the midst of ignorance, wise in their own esteem, thinking themselves to be learned, fools, afflicted with troubles, they go about like blind men led by one who is himself blind. The immature, living variously in ignorance, think "we have accomplished our aim." Since those who perform sacrifices do not understand because of their attachment, they sink down, wretched, when their *lokas* are exhausted. These deluded men, regarding sacrifices and works of merit as most important, do not know any other good. Having enjoyed heaven won by good karma they enter this world again, or a lower one. But those who practice *tapas* and *śrāddha* in the forest, the *śānta*, the tranquil and peaceful ones, knowers, who live the life of a mendicant, depart free from sin, through the door of the sun to the place where dwells the immortal, imperishable *ātman*.[10]

The Upaniṣads contain a sacred teaching that accomplishes what Vedic work could not do. The Vedas give to the *āryas* the means to influence karma and they are thus far above the *mlecchas* who are excluded from it; but the knowledge contained in the Upaniṣads grants a degree of happiness and freedom and light that makes the Vedas look like a fetter, like night and unhappiness. Far from providing only a temporary relief from the ills of the world, the knowledge of the Upaniṣads uproots the weed called *karma* and deprives it of its soil, the body. The body is where karma operates and from whence it comes. At the level of the *dvandvas*, the pairs of opposites, which make up the world—heat and cold, pleasure and suffering, birth and death—it is impossible to obtain pure and eternal bliss and life. The body cannot be redeemed, because it is part of the world of the *dvandvas* itself. Freedom implies freedom from the pairs of opposites, from the body. The one who is completely free is "beyond good and evil" in an ontological sense. "As water does not cling to the lotus leaf, so evil deeds do not cling to one who knows *brahman*."[11] There is no transformation of the finite into the infinite, of the mortal into the immortal; there is only a separation of the finite from the infinite, of the mortal from the immortal, of the subtle body with its karma from the *ātman* that is by nature free, infinite, immortal. "The knot of the heart is cut, all the doubts are dispelled and karma comes to an end when He is seen."[12]

The path of the Upaniṣads was and is that of an elite that could afford to cut all ties with society and devote itself to the spirit. For the majority of Hindus, in ancient as well as in contemporary India, the path of works is what religion is understood to be: pilgrimages, almsgiving, recitation of prayers and other good works are supposed to create *puṇya*, which allows one to dwell for some time in heaven and attain a good rebirth. The *Purāṇas*, however, in an attempt to assimilate Vedāntic teaching as well as popular practices, promise "enlightenment" as the result of the uttering of the name of God or of devotional worship of the image, and assure the devotee that the Supreme God will take upon himself all the karma of his devotees. The *bhakta* is freed from rebirth, not so much through the process of gradual sublimation, as through an act of grace of God.[13]

There is no longer any meaning in ritual actions if one has wholly transcended the sphere of karma. But the *Brahmasūtras* enjoin those who have achieved knowledge to continue performing the usual rituals, lest they be considered irreligious. *Nitya karma*, the daily obligatory ritual, does not result in karma for those who perform it with wisdom, but augments *vidyā*. Work done in a disinterested way, as *niṣkāma karma*, does not entangle in this world, but is a symbol of freedom to act without considering the results of one's actions.

The Upaniṣads know the notion of a *jīvanmukta*, the one who is completely free while still living in a body: like a potter's wheel that turns for some time after the pot has been shaped, due to the impetus given to it by the potter, so the physical life of the free person is carried on without any connection to the *ātman* that has found its meaning in itself.

*Mokṣa* or *mukti*, liberation, the key term of Vedāntic philosophy, is hardly ever used by the Upaniṣads to describe the ultimate condition; they prefer expressions like *immortality*, *bliss*, becoming *brahman*.[14] This freedom is "not a new acquisition, a product, an effect or result of any action, but it always existed as the Truth of our nature; we are always emancipated and always free."[15] In the Upaniṣadic doctrines a person is given the means to remove the obstacles, the wrong notions; liberation itself is an event that comes from the *ātman*'s own interiority. This is the deeper truth beneath apparently paradoxical statements.

The Upaniṣads say that release from old age and death, bliss and immortality consists in "knowing the unknowable *brahman*."[16] It entails both a separation of consciousness from sense-object knowledge and an extension of consciousness until it finally includes everything. The Upaniṣads say "the liberated becomes everything."[17] The statement "*ātman* is *brahman*" is the liberating truth itself and as such it is immortality. From the standpoint of objective knowledge the ultimate knowledge is a negation of knowledge: *brahman* is not to be seen, not be heard, not to be thought, but those who understand the seeing of the seeing, the hearing of the hearing, the innermost principle underlying all, know *brahman* also in a positive way. The discrimination between the Self and the not-Self is in itself enlightenment about the Self; there is no further need to prove the nonexistence of not-being. The supreme human condition, true freedom, is identical with Truth-Reality-Being-Bliss: it is "self-awareness" that has no object-subject polarity but is everything as pure consciousness.[18]

There is no further need to cleanse the *ātman* from sin and to make it perfect: being free from sin, incapable of sin, incapable of being perfected, is a result of the fact that it *is*. "Deathlessness," then, consists in becoming conscious of the innermost support of the personality, in gaining unity with the Ultimate.[19] Whatever has been created goes back to its source, the body with all its parts and faculties is dissolved into the elements from which it was derived. The *ātman* withdraws its support to these its creations and thus they fall back into their nonexistence, into their difference from *ātman* that proves them to be nothing by themselves. By leaving everything it gains the whole, and by reducing its consciousness to the barest subject-awareness it becomes all-consciousness.[20]

*Mokṣa* is but the recognition of a situation that always existed as such; it is a psychological breakthrough, not an ontological change. It is not a quickening of the dead, not a resurrection and transfiguration of the body, but its rejection. It is not heaven but the overcoming of heaven, making all objective bliss redundant.

Liberation is beyond happiness and unhappiness, beyond heaven and hell. Who wants something must take its opposite into the bargain; who seeks redemption as a positive reality must accept bondage with it. For the Upaniṣads the way out from the tragic hopelessness that sees human life as a constant frustration, is given by the insight that sorrow and death do not touch the innermost core of a person. The way of knowledge is, therefore, strictly speaking, not a path to salvation but a method of discrimination; the *jīvanmukta* is not a saint, but a wise person. As the Upaniṣad says: "Such a one, verily, the thought does not torment: Why have I not done the right? Why have I committed sin? One who knows this, saves oneself from these. Truly, from both of these one saves oneself—one who knows this."[21]

However, it would be a mistake to conclude that the Upaniṣads are amoral. On the contrary, they contain many passages with rigorous ethical commands. Thus the *Taittirīya Upaniṣad* contains the following instruction to a pupil: "Speak the truth! Practice dharma! Do not neglect the study of the Veda! Be one to whom mother, father, teacher, and guest are like *devas*! Do not do what others find reproachable!"[22] The very prerequisite for being accepted as a student was a high moral standard, and the life of the student itself demanded a more rigorous self-discipline than would normally be considered necessary. But morality is only a precondition; it is a matter of course for the one whose interests are no longer directed toward sense gratification and possession of material goods. There comes a point when a person realizes that real goodness is not to be found in the accidental quality of a finite act, but in the heart of being itself, at one with the ultimate reality.

Although several other ideas are at work in the *karmamārga*, as we have seen earlier, and in the *bhaktimārga*, which will be described in the following chapters, the Upaniṣads as the basis of the *jñānamārga* had, and have, a tremendous impact on Hinduism as such and are representative of one of its major themes: the acceptance of the aloneness of human existence not only as inevitable but as fulfilling, the overcoming of suffering and sorrow by realizing their nonreality, liberation through insight into one's true nature, the negation of redemption from outside because of a profound recognition of its intrinsic impossibility. It is useless to try to save a human—all are saved, if they would only see it! "Just as the flowing rivers disappear in the ocean casting off shape and name, even so the knower, freed from name and shape, attains to the divine *puruṣa*, higher than the high. One who knows the Supreme *brahman* becomes *brahman*."[23]

CHAPTER FOURTEEN

# The Path of Loving Devotion

## *Bhaktimārga*

Fix your mind on Me; be devoted to Me, sacrifice to Me; prostrate yourself before me; so will you come to Me, I promise you, for you are dear to Me!

—*Bhagavadgītā* XVIII, 65

The majority of Hindus today are followers of the *bhaktimārga*, whose exterior manifestation in temples, images, processions, feasts, and popular gurus characterize so much of present-day India. The term *bhakti*, used so frequently as the keyword in this form of religion, defies an exact and adequate translation.[1] In addition to the general difficulty of translating crucial words from Sanskrit into English, the problem is compounded by two quite peculiar handicaps. First, the etymology of the word is not quite clear. Grammatically, *bhakti* is an abstract noun formed by adding the suffix *-kti* to one of two different verbal roots: if derived from the root *bhañj-*, to separate, *bhakti* would have to be translated as *separation*. That makes sense insofar as *bhakti* presupposes that the individual human person is separated from and not identical with the Supreme Being. In this view inner longing for reunion is the characteristic of human life and the *bhakta* is one who is aware of the painful separation between humans and God and tries to overcome it. The majority of Indian scholars, however, derive *bhakti* from the root *bhaj-*, to worship, to be devoted to. This, too, makes sense, since *bhakti* religion consists of acts of worship and loving devotion towards God.

Vallabha, the sixteenth-century founder of the *puṣṭimārga*, explains that the suffix *-kti* means *love* and the root *bhaj- service*. *Bhakti* thus means the action of service (*sevā*). *Sevā* is a bodily affair; in order that it may be complete it implies love, and without love the service would be troublesome, but not desirable; love also for its completion requires service.[2]

The second problem in trying to find an English equivalent for *bhakti* is the diversity of definitions given to *bhakti* by the numerous different schools of thought and groups of worshippers, providing many subtle specifications and subdivisions of *bhakti*, considered by the adherents of various sects to be of the very essence of *bhakti*.

There are two classical texts that call themselves *Bhaktisūtras*, purporting to present the authoritative definition of *bhakti* and quite openly imitating the style of the *Vedāntasūtras* in order to impress those for whom these were the supreme authority.[3] Thus Śāṇḍilya begins: *Athāto-bhakti-jijñāsa*," now, then, an enquiry into *bhakti*." He continues, defining it as "passionate longing for the Lord from one's whole heart," and he says that in it one finds immortality. In it is contained the knowledge of God; but since also haters of God have this knowledge, only loving devotion combined with knowledge can save a person.[4]

Nārada, the author of the other *Bhaktisūtra*, defines *bhakti* as *parama premā*, highest affection for the Lord, possessing immortality in itself "gaining which a person becomes perfect, immortal and satisfied, attaining which a person does not desire anything, does not hate, does not exult, does not exert himself of herself (in furtherance of self-interest). Having known that, a person becomes intoxicated; becomes motionless, becomes one who enjoys the self."[5]

The *Bhagavadgītā*, probably the best known *bhakti*-scripture, sees the essence of *bhakti* in concentration of attention on Kṛṣṇa and worshipping him; it is probably this description which would cover most of the general features of the different kinds of *bhakti*.[6]

## THE DEVELOPMENT OF *BHAKTI*

In its full development and almost complete domination of the Indian religious scene, historically the *bhaktimārga* comes as the last path for the attainment of salvation, after *karmamārga* and *jñānamārga*. However, it would be wrong to set the three paths into some sort of evolutionary sequence; in all probability all three *mārgas* were present throughout Indian religious history, though their official recognition and preference varied. P. V. Kane sees in many hymns of the *Ṛgveda* evidence of Indra *bhakti* or Varuṇa *bhakti*. The fact that Varuṇa is in many respects the Vedic equivalent of the Purāṇic Viṣṇu may be understood as a first stage of Viṣṇu *bhakti*, which later became so prominent.[7] We do not find the word *bhakti* in the principal *Upaniṣads*, but the *Kaṭha* and the *Muṇḍaka Upaniṣad* speak of the necessity of divine grace to obtain liberating insight—a teaching that is typical for *bhakti*.[8] Similarly the frequent use of the term *puruṣa uttama*, the Supreme Person, to describe *brahman* in the Upaniṣads—a term that became a proper name of Viṣṇu in *bhakti* religion—would indicate the presence of *bhakti* ideas in Vedic times.[9]

The *Śvetāśvatara Upaniṣad*, which is a fairly early text, expounds a fully developed Śiva *bhakti*; certainly this attitude took time to mature into such a systematic treatise. The later Upaniṣads are in fact mostly *bhakti* treatises, quite close in terminology to the Saṃhitās and Āgamas, the recognized scriptures of Vaiṣṇavism and Śaivism. The most popular class of literature in India, the *Mahābhārata*, the *Rāmāyaṇa*, and the *Purāṇas* are the sources from which *bhakti* religions have drawn their inspiration for centuries. These books constitute encyclopedic summaries of the entire religious heritage of India, seen from the viewpoint of a *bhakta*.

*Bhakti* movements have produced inner Indian missionary thrusts and are now also reaching out for Western converts. The best known—but not only—contemporary Hindu *bhakti*-movement in the West is ISKCON (International Society for Kṛṣṇa Consciousness, popularly known as the Hare Krishna Movement) which did much to translate and distribute classical *bhakti* literature and especially the teachings of the Caitanya school of Gauḍīya (Bengal) Vaiṣṇavism, to which it is affiliated.

*Bhakti* has inspired Indian poets and singer-saints, whose hymns are popular with large masses of Hindus. Even illiterate Indian villagers are familiar with the songs of the Āḷvārs and Nāyanmārs in South India, or with couplets from Tulsīdās, Kabīr, Sūrdas, Tukārām, Rāmprasād, and many others from the North, whose stanzas they chant and quote as summaries of their own religious wisdom.[10]

Some Western scholars have recently taken up the study of what is termed the *Sant* tradition,[11] which is held to be "the universal path to sanctity,"[12] including not only Vaiṣṇavas like Tulsīdās and non-sectarian poet-saints like

Photo 14. Members of ISKCON at a sacred tank in Govardhana (U.P.)

Kabīr, but also most of the Sikh-gurus and several Muslim *pīrs*. "Who were the *Sants*?" Charlotte Vaudeville asks, and answers:

> Socially, they belonged to the lower strata of Hindu and Muslim society: nearly all were Śūdras, some of them even Atiśūdras, i.e., Untouchables. They were poor, mostly uneducated or even illiterate; quite a few were women. They had no access or right to Brahmanical knowledge, were not acquainted with Sanskrit and could only express themselves in the local languages of the people, the archaic Indo-Aryan vernaculars of Hindustan and central India. With the possible exception of Marathī, these languages were still in a state of infancy, apparently not suited to the expression of metaphysical or mystical truth. The poetry of the Sants largely contributed to the development of the northern vernaculars into "literary" languages. It was especially the case with Hindī, which was to become the national language of India in modern times.

*Bhakti* had a wide appeal from the very beginning, not only because it recognized the emotional approach to God as fully valid, but also because it broke down all the barriers of privilege that had kept out large groups of the population from *karmamārga* and *jñānamārga*. *Bhakti* became the way of salvation for everyone: women and children, low castes and outcastes, could become fully recognized members of the *bhakti* movement. Some of the great *bhaktas* are saints for Hindus, Muslims, and Sikhs alike. Even Christians in India are beginning to accept them as theirs, finding the religiosity of these *bhaktas* to be deep and genuine and utilizing their hymns in their services. Some of the universally revered *bhaktas* were outcastes, like Nanda and Cokamela, some were women like Mīrābāī and Āṇṭāl; others were great sinners for whom orthodoxy could not find means of salvation. Kabīr, one of the finest Hindi poets of medieval India, reputedly was a Muslim weaver; his songs are a favorite with countless Hindus in northern India even today. He says in one of them:

> It is foolish to ask a saint about his caste. The *brahman*, the *kṣatriya*, the *vaiśya*, and the *śūdra*, all seek but God. The barber has looked for God, too, and so did the washer man and the carpenter; even Räidās was a seeker after God. Ṛṣi Svapaca was a tanner. Hindus and Muslims have equally realized God; there is no scope of distinction in the ultimate aim.

Kabīr may even move beyond *bhakti* in its more specific sense when he sings:

> My true guru has shown me the way: I have given up all rites and ceremonies and I no longer bathe in holy rivers. I have become aware that I alone am mad, the whole world is sane. I had been disturbing those intelligent people! No longer could I live in the dust of subservience; no longer do I ring the temple bells, nor do I enthrone a divine image. I no longer offer flowers. Mortification does not please the Lord; we do not reach Him by going about naked and torturing ourselves. Those who are kind and righteous, who do

> not get entangled in this world's dealings, who consider all creatures on earth as their own self, they attain to the Immortal, the true God is with them forever. Kabīr says: Those attain the true name[13] whose words are pure, who are devoid of pride and self-deceit.

Vaudeville considers Kabīr an exponent of *nirguṇa bhakti*, a seeker of the absolute, closer to the Upaniṣadic tradition than to the popular Purāṇic religion of *avatāras* and a plurality of *Iṣṭa devatās*. Nevertheless, he is a *bhakta* insofar as he conceives the Absolute in terms of a person, and understands life as an ethical challenge to be met in a spirit of devotion to God and service to others. Summarily Vaudeville concludes:

> Whether they be born Śaiva, Vaiṣṇava, or Muslim, all the *Sant* poets stress the necessity of devotion to and practice of the divine Name (*nāma*), devotion to the Divine guru (*satguru*), and the great importance of the 'company of the *Sants*" (*satsaṅg*). The Name, the Divine Guru, and the *satsaṅg* are the three pillars of the *Sant sādhana*.[14]

## THE PRACTICE OF THE *BHAKTIMĀRGA*

Most of what Kabīr rejects constitutes the daily religious practice of the average *bhakta*, and we will have to deal in some detail with this worship routine to draw a sketch of a follower of the path of devotion.

The majority of *bhaktas* belong to one of a large number of specific worship traditions, a *saṃpradāya*—a term often (incorrectly) translated "sect" or "denomination." Certain features are common to all of them and the popular *Stotra-ratnas*, Hindu prayer books, contain hymns to all the main deities who form the object of loving devotion and adoration of many groups of *bhaktas*. Included are prayers to Gaṇeśa, Viṣṇu, Śiva, Sūrya, Devī, Dattā, Rāma, Kṛṣṇa, besides hymns to Gaṅgā and Yamunā, the planets and various less popular *avatāras* of the main deities.[15] Numerically the Viṣṇu *bhaktas* with their many subdivisions are the most important group. Śiva *bhaktas* come second and Devī *bhaktas* or *Śāktas*, rank third, followed by the rest. Though there are enough differences between the various groups to make mutual vilification, or even persecution, far from uncommon in Indian religious history, they all have so much in common with regard to practices and beliefs that it is possible to provide a general description of *bhakti* without referring in every instance to a particular *saṃpradāya*.

The promise of salvation for all resulted in a tendency to simplify the requirements for it, so that all might be able to fulfill the essence of righteousness, however poor and unlearned they might be. This has led practically all the *bhakti* schools to teach that the name of God is sufficient to bring salvation to everyone who utters it. The story of Saint Ajamila, very popular with Viṣṇu *bhaktas*, is typical: Ajamila was a Brahmin who had married a wife of his own caste according to the proper rites. After some time, he fell in love with a low-caste woman, repudiated his rightful wife, and had ten sons from the concubine. He wasted his whole life in gambling and thieving. When he reached the age of eighty he felt that he was going to die. Before his death he wanted to see his youngest son and called out with a loud voice: Nārāyaṇa! Nārāyaṇa also happens to be one of the popular names of Lord Viṣṇu, and though Ajamila had not thought of Him, the utterance of the Name wiped out all his sins and he was given a place of honor in Viṣṇu's heaven.[16]

In several places the *Bhāgavata Purāṇa* underlines this belief when it teaches: "The utterance of the Lord's name completely destroys all sin, even when it is due to the name being associated with something else, or is done jocularly, or as a result of involuntary sound or in derision."[17]

A contemporary "Appeal for *Japa* of the Divine Name" exhorts its readers to recite the "mantra of the sixteen names," which is the "Great Mantra" for the *japa* of Kṛṣṇa *bhaktas*:

> *Hare Rāma Hare Rāma Rāma Rāma Hare Hare*
> *Hare Kṛṣṇa Hare Kṛṣṇa Kṛṣṇa Kṛṣṇa Hare Hare.*

It carries the following message:

> The whole world is groaning inwardly at present. Tyranny, persecution, immorality, disputes, sin, war, and destruction are on the increase everywhere. The mounting irreverence towards religion and God is turning humanity into a race of cannibals. As a result natural calamities have also multiplied. Earthquakes, floods, drought, famine, food scarcity, and epidemics have become alarmingly frequent. None knows where they will lead us to. Under such circumstances, resorting to God is the only way out of this inferno of calamities. Taking to the repetition of the Divine Name is essential for complete self-surrender to God. There is no calamity that will not yield to the Divine Name and there is nothing that cannot be achieved by the Divine Name. Powerful counterforces might delay the achievement, but the Divine Name is infallible in bringing its reward. In this dark age of Kali the Divine Name is our only resort. Therefore for the good of India and the world at large everybody should repeat and sing the Divine Name both for worldly gains and otherworldly peace and happiness, nay even for reaching the ultimate goal of our existence, viz. God-Realization.

There follows an appeal to the readers of the magazine to make a vow to perform *japa* and to send in an account of the number of times the complete mantra has been recited, aiming at 20 crores of repetitions.[18] "Persons of all castes and communities and of every age and sex can undertake this *japa*. Everyone should repeat the mantra at least 108 times every day. Intimation of the *japa* should be sent to the *nāma-japa* section of *Kalyāṇa* office, Gorakhpur, U. P."[19]

Śaivites and Śāktas attribute similar powers to the name of Śiva or Devī, though usually the wearing of certain marks and signs also is considered essential in order to benefit from *japa*. The great devotion to the "name" has led to the composition of litanies of thousand names of God, the *sahasranāmas*; a large number of the names given in these to Viṣṇu, Śiva, and Devī by their followers are identical. Apart from the great popularity of the practice among the masses of Hindus, the theologians of the *bhaktimārga* have developed theological arguments for it, too. In order to be effective, the *nāma-japa* must be undertaken with a name that God himself has revealed in the scriptures; with such a self-revealed name, God's *śabda*, God himself is identical and that lends power to the sound of the name itself. Repetition of the name is the most powerful remedy against all sins and faults; the sins against the name itself, however, are unpardonable and exclude a person from the community of *bhaktas* as a heretic.[20]

However generous the *bhaktimārga* might be toward the traditionally unorthodox, it has created its own divisions between orthodox and heretics. The *Varaha Purāṇa*, a Vaiṣṇava scripture, declares that at Viṣṇu's instance Śiva proclaimed the *Śaiva-siddhānta* in order to lead astray those who should not be saved.[21] The *Padma Purāṇa*, another Vaiṣṇava scripture, declares all non-Vaiṣṇavite doctrines to be paths leading to hell. Thus it says:

> Hear, O goddess, I declare now the *tāmasa-śāstras*, the scriptures of darkness, through which a wise man becomes a sinner even if he only thinks of them. At first I declared through my *moha-māyā*, my deluding form, the Śaiva teachings such as the *Pāśupata* system. The following doctrines were laid down by Brahmins who were deluded by my illusionary power: Kaṇāda proclaimed the great *Vaiśeṣika* system; the *Nyāya* and *Sāṃkhya* systems were taught by Gautama and Kapila; the much maligned Cārvāka system was explained by Bṛhaspati, while Viṣṇu took on the form of Buddha to destroy the *Daityas* who proclaim the false teachings of the Buddhists and go about naked or in blue garments. I myself, O goddess, took on the body of a Brahmin and in *Kaliyuga* proclaimed the wrong *śāstras* of the *māyā*-doctrine (i.e. Śaṅkara's *Advaita Vedānta*), which is but Buddhism in disguise. The Brahmin Jaimini composed the great system of *Pūrva Mīmāṃsā* which is worthless because it advocates atheistic doctrines.[22]

*Bhakti* means not only love for God, but also enmity toward those who do not love him in the same way. Even a saint like Tulasīdāsa, whose verses generally are expressing a very humane form of religiosity, teaches the Rāma *bhaktas*:

> Avoid those who do not love Rāma and Sītā, as your most bitter enemies, no matter how near of kin they may be. Prahlāda resisted his father, Vibhiṣāna left his brother and Bharata his mother. Bali dispossessed his guru and the *gopīs* left their husbands in order to come to the Lord and their mode of conduct became a source of joy and happiness for the whole world. Only insofar as they are related to God are children and relations worthy of one's love.

So, too, the *Bhagavadgītā*, often quoted as a document of Hindu tolerance, also condemns the people who are not Kṛṣṇa *bhaktas*, as evildoers and bewildered fools.[23]

## THE THEORY OF DEVOTION

The extreme conclusions drawn from a dogmatic understanding of *bhaktimārga* should not make us blind to the very great contribution *bhaktas* have made to religious thought and practice. They represent a Way that has recently been gaining great popularity in the West: the activation of emotions as a genuine path to God and to personal fulfillment. The teachers of *bhakti* have developed systems that reveal great psychological insight. They usually distinguish different degrees in *bhakti*; love has to grow and mature over the years, and it has to permeate gradually the whole life of the *bhakta*.

Thus Nārada in his *Bhaktisūtras* enumerates eleven degrees of *bhakti*: *bhakti* begins with the glorification of Kṛṣṇa's greatness; then the *bhakta* proceeds to the love of Kṛṣṇa's beauty, to worship him according to the traditional rituals, remembering him constantly, considering oneself first as the Lord's slave, then as his companion, as his parent; finally evoking the love that a wife has toward her husband, surrendering completely to him, feeling completely absorbed in him and—sensing nothing else but the pain of separation from the Lord! Nārada considers the pain that lovers experience when they are separated from each other as the highest form of love.[24]

The *Bhāgavata Purāṇa* has a more popular enumeration of nine steps of *bhakti* that begins with listening to talks about Viṣṇu, continues with the recitation of his name, remembrance and veneration of his feet, offering *pūjā* before his image, prostrating oneself before him, considering oneself a slave of Viṣṇu, a friend, and finally surrendering completely to him.[25]

Rāmānuja, the greatest *bhakti* theologian so far, enumerates six prerequisites for someone embarking on the *bhaktimārga*: a *bhakta* has to observe certain dietary rules, has to show complete disregard for worldly objects, continue faithfully all religious activities, must perform *pūjā*, has to behave virtuously and to be free from depression.[26]

The central act of *bhakti* is *prapatti*, self-surrender, which consists of five individual components: the intention of submitting to the Lord, the giving up of resistance to the Lord, the belief in the protection of the Lord, the prayer that the Lord may save his devotees, the consciousness of utter helplessness.

Taking refuge in the Lord, the *śaraṇāgatī* of both popular and theological *bhakti* writings, is considered the act that makes the person a *bhakta*. Some, like Madhva, wish the devotees to proclaim their surrender to God outwardly, too, by branding themselves with the *cakra*, the sign of Viṣṇu, or by stamping their bodies with his name.[27]

Bengal has produced in Gauḍīya-Vaiṣṇavism the most emotional and also the most subtle form of *bhakti* teaching.[28] It makes use of the concept of *rasa*, a key term in literary criticism in which a scale of emotions and their conditions have been developed.[29] Nine basic *rasas* are usually given, corresponding to as many fundamental "feelings." The most intense of these is *śṛṅgāra*; erotic love. Then come *hāsya*, laughter, derision, followed by *karuṇa*, compassion. *Krodha*, anger, and *bibhatsa*, vexation, are important as well as firmness and steadfastness (*vīrya*). *Bhayānaka*, fearfulness, *adbhuta*, admiration, and *śānta*, tranquillity, conclude the classical scheme. For the Caitanyites Kṛṣṇa is the *akhila-rasāmṛta-mūrti*, the embodiment of the essence of all sentiments. Their method of realization is a gradual development of feeling to such a high pitch that only Kṛṣṇa and Kṛṣṇa alone can be its object. Even more, the devotee realizes that ultimately the love he has for Kṛṣṇa is just a sharing of Kṛṣṇa's own *hlādinī-śakti*, Kṛṣṇa's power of joyful love.

The fully developed teaching of this school distinguishes between three grades of *bhakti*, each again subdivided several times. *Sādhana-bhakti*, the first stage, contains *vaidhi-bhakti*, ritualistic devotion, and *rāgānugā*, or passionate following. It begins with having faith in Kṛṣṇa, enjoins association with good people, participation in worship, avoidance of the worthless, steadfast devotion and real liking of the Lord, which results in attachment and love. The next major stage is *bhāvana-bhakti*, emotional devotion, in which the theory of *rasas* finds a masterful application. Beginning with the sentiment of peacefulness, continuing through servitude, companionship, parental love, and culminating in *madhu-rasa*, sweet love, the authors expound a complex system of religious psychology at the center of which is Kṛṣṇa's divine bodily presence.

When emotional devotion has fully matured it develops into the third stage of *bhakti*, *premā*, which is simply love at its highest level. This is considered to be permanent and cannot be taken away from the devotee under any circumstances.[30] One who has reached this stage may be called an ideal *bhakta* according to the description in the *Caitanya-caritāmṛta*:

> In pure love the *bhakta* renounces all desire, all ritual, all knowledge and all actions and is attached to Kṛṣṇa with all powers. The true *bhakta* wants nothing from the Lord, but is content with loving him. A Kṛṣṇa-*bhakta* is kind and truthful, treats all people alike, hurts no one and is generous, tactful, pure, selfless, and at peace with self and others. A *bhakta* does much good to others and clings to Kṛṣṇa as the only support. A *bhakta* has no wishes, makes no efforts except to honor Kṛṣṇa, is constant and controls all passions. A *bhakta* is always ready to give honor to others, humble, and willing to bear grief without a complaint. A *bhakta* seeks the company of the truly pious and gives up association with those who do not adhere to Kṛṣṇa.[31]

The same text describes the true Vaiṣṇava as "more humble than a blade of grass, more patient than a tree, honoring others without seeking honor" and says: "such a one is worthy of uttering Kṛṣṇa's name."

1. Śravaṇa: Listening

2. Kīrtana: Singing

3. Smaraṇa: Remembering

5. Pādasevana: Serving

4. Arcana: Worshipping

Figure 14.1. The nine degrees of *bhakti*

6. Vandana: Praising

8. Sakhya: Companionship

7. Dāsya: Servitude

9. Ātmanivedana: Self-Surrender

Figure 14.1. (continued)

Photo 15. Playing Kṛṣṇa's flute in Sevakuñja: Vṛndāvana

The ethical overflow of the loving devotion to God is stressed by Puruṣottamācārya, a teacher of the Śrī Vaiṣṇava school of South India, who considers the six constituents of *bhakti* to be: treating everyone with good will and friendliness and discarding what is contrary to it; refraining from all malice, backbiting, falsehood, and violence; having strong faith in the protection of the Lord; praying to the Lord; discarding all false pride and egotism; completely entrusting oneself and whatever belongs to oneself to the Lord, being convinced that such complete resignation earns God's grace and mercy.[32]

Śaiva and Śākta schools have developed systems of Śiva and Devī *bhakti*. These are often quite similar to the Vaiṣṇava *bhakti*, which we have briefly discussed. Thus the *Pāśupatas* prescribe certain activities designed to express and augment a person's love for Śiva. One is told to repeat the name of Śiva, to meditate on Śiva's nature, to bathe in ashes, to behave like a madman, to sing, to laugh, and to shake.[33]

The most sophisticated system of Śiva *bhakti*, however, is known as Śaiva siddhānta, a living faith for millions of Hindus in Tamiḷnādu to this very day. According to its main texts *bhakti* to Śiva develops in four stages: *Dāsamārga*, the slave's way, consists of practices such as cleaning a Śiva temple, smearing its floor with cow dung, weaving garlands of different kinds of flowers for the decoration of the image of Śiva, uttering the praises of the Lord, lighting the temple lamps, maintaining flower gardens and offering one's services to any devotee of Śiva. This is the beginner's form of Śiva *bhakti*. The next stage, *satputramārga*, the true son's way, prescribes the preparation of the articles necessary for Śiva *pūjā* and meditation on Śiva as of the form of light. The third stage is called *sahamārga*, the associate's way, and consists of *yoga*: withdrawal of the senses from their objects, breath control, suspension of mind activities, recitation of mantras and directing the vital breaths through the six body centers. The last and highest stage is called *sanmārga*, the way of truth and reality: *bhakti* in the form of Śiva knowledge has now been fully developed and is identical with liberation and bliss.[34]

As just one example of devotion to the Goddess, a hymn by the famous Bengali Śākta poet Rāmprasād may be given here:

> Mind, worship her who saves on the other side of the Ocean of the World. Know once and for all what worth is in the trash of wealth. Vain is hope in men or money; this was said of old. Where were you, from where have you come, and whereto will you go? The world is glass, and ever amid its snares delusion makes men dance. You are in the lap of an enchantress, held fast in thy prison. Pride, malice, anger, and attachment to your lovers, by what wisdom of judgment did you divide the kingdom of your body among these? The day is nearly gone: think therefore in your heart, the resting place of Kālī, that island filled with jewels, think of the things that day has brought you. Prasād says: the name of Durgā is my promised Land of Salvation, fields flowing with nectar. Tell your tongue ceaselessly to utter her name.[35]

Figure 14.2. Implements for daily *pūjā*

## THE IMPORTANCE OF GOD'S NAME

"Taking the Name" is perhaps the most essential step in the process of becoming a *bhakta*. Since *bhakti* teachers do not lay stress on traditional scholarship or ascetic practices that require long training and above-average strength of will and intellect, they have developed an entire *sādhana* around the name, and individual *japa* as well as congregational *saṁkīrtan* have become the most typical expressions of *bhakti*. At the centres of *bhakti* religion hundreds of people, often paid, chant day and night, in special Bhajana Āśramas the names that spell merit and salvation. One of the better-known saints of our time, Swami Rama Tirtha says:

> As creation owes its origin to the "word" (OM) so the sacred names of Rāma, Kṛṣṇa, Hari are the vehicle that brings the individual back to him. Keep to them and you can obtain *sākṣāt-kāra*, or vision, of the *iṣṭa-devatā*, your chosen deity, whose name or mantra you have chosen, as well as his *dhāma*, his sphere. The chanting of OM goes on in all eternity in the tiniest atom of creation and it acts instrumentally in *pravṛtti*, the expansion and in *nivṛtti*, the contraction of the worlds. If we would trace back the steps and catch the sound and precede *nivṛtti* on its return, we would arrive at the eternal *Vaikuṇṭha*, Viṣṇu's heaven. It is our aim to reach this world of divine bliss where all rebirth ends, and this we hope to attain through *saṁkīrtan*.[36]

*Bhaktas* attribute to *saṁkīrtan* an infallible effect: the great saints Caitanya, Mīrābāī, Kabīr, and Tukārāma entered Viṣṇu's body without leaving behind their physical bodies on earth. They find effusive praise for the practice of the singing of the name: "The name of the Lord is truly a drop of nectar, a heavenly taste in my mouth. My guru has taught me the greatness of the name; today I have experienced its power."[37]

Traditionally five rules have to be followed in the recitation of the name: the name must express the supreme divinity, it must be given by a guru at the time of initiation, it must be practiced in a spirit of devotion, and it must be accompanied by a saintly life. The name must also be sung melodiously with a heart full of love and longing. The various tunes correspond to various spheres and it is necessary to choose the appropriate melody.

The guru has been mentioned repeatedly in connection with the name—for the *bhakti* schools, he or she is of the utmost importance. *Bhaktas* see in the guru the personal representative of the Supreme Lord himself; contrary to the *samnyāsis* they keep a lifelong connection with, and dependence upon, the guru. Quite often the guru is considered an incarnation of God, already during lifetime receiving formal worship. More frequently still, he or she is worshipped after death in a sanctuary built over the tomb. One school of thought is inclined to put the *guru* even above the transcendent God. A text says: "The guru must always be worshipped; the guru is exalted because the guru is one with the mantra. Hari is pleased if the guru is pleased. Millions of acts of

Photo 16. Platform for *rasa-līlā* dance in Vṛndāvana

worship are otherwise rejected. If Hari is angry, the guru is our defense; but from the guru's wrath there is no protection."

Gurus in the *bhakti* schools are usually surrounded by groups of devotees who serve and worship them as their guides and gods. Often this is quite beautiful and one can meet really religious families around spiritual fathers or mothers, but quite frequently, if the guru is an unbalanced, moody and capricious person, the resulting forms of religious life are grotesque and hardly edifying. Devotees then are told that they have to consider the whims and temper tantrums of their gurus as Kṛṣṇa's own *līlā*, His play, which cannot be rationalized but has to be accepted as divine manifestation. Because according to the *bhaktas*' understanding serving God, *sevā*, is the essence of religion, the service offered to the guru—cooking, sweeping, obeying their orders, and so forth—forms the exercise of religion in an immediate sense.

True and genuine religion, beginning with a fascination for God, who is Truth, Goodness, and Beauty, results in genuine humility, joy, and contentment. In the words of Nārada: "Those who have attained love of God have no more desire for anything else; they are free from grief and hatred. They do not get excited over anything; they do not exert themselves to further their self-interest; they become intoxicated and enthused, as it were, because they are completely immersed in the enjoyment of the bliss of *ātman*."[38]

CHAPTER FIFTEEN

# Lord Viṣṇu and His Devotees

Viṣṇu is the instructor of the whole world: what else should anyone learn or teach, save Him, the Supreme Spirit?

—*Viṣṇu Purāṇa* I, 17

Worshipping and praising God is the most prominent activity of Viṣṇu *bhaktas*. Doing so, they place themselves in the company of all beings in a universe that owes its very existence to him.

> Praise to you, lotus-eyed, praise to you, Supreme Being! Praise to you, the soul of all worlds, praise to you, armed with the sharp discus. Praise to him, who created the universe as Brahmā, supports it as Viṣṇu, and destroys it as Rudra at the end of times. Praise to the one who exists in these three forms. Devas, Yakṣas, Asuras, Siddhas, Nāgas, Gandharvas, Kinnaras, Piśācas, Rakṣasas, men and beasts, birds, immovable things, ants and reptiles; earth, water, fire, ether and air, sound, touch and taste, sight, smell, mind intellect, ego, time and the qualities of primeval matter—of all these you are the support; you are the universe, changeless one! Knowledge and ignorance, truth and untruth, poison as well as nectar, are you. You are the deed that leads to bondage and also the deed that leads to freedom as taught by the Vedas. The enjoyer, the means and the fruits of all actions are you, O Viṣṇu. The Yogis meditate on you and to you the pious offer sacrifice. You accept the sacrificial oblations to *devas* and the food offered to the *pitṛs*, assuming the form of *devas* and *pitṛs*. The whole universe before us is your all-form; a smaller form of yours is this world of ours. Still smaller forms of you are the different kinds of beings, and what is called their inner self is an exceedingly subtle form of yours. Praise without end to the Lord Vasudeva, whom no one transcends but who transcends all![1]

In those and similar words countless people praise Viṣṇu, whom they have accepted as their one and supreme Lord. The hymn mentions a few of the fundamental tenets of Vaiṣṇava faith—especially the immanence of Viṣṇu in all beings and his transcendence—and we shall consider a few more, without claiming to be able to exhaust the wealth of imagery and speculation produced in the long history of the various schools of Vaiṣṇavism.

Contemporary Vaiṣṇavism, the largest section of all Hindu traditions, comprising about 70 percent of Hindus today, has many sources. According to R. N. Dandekar, it did not develop primarily out of the Vedic worship of Viṣṇu but began as Vāsudevism: the cult of the deified Vṛṣṇi hero Vasudeva, and later, of his elder brother Saṁkarṣaṇa. A second source was Kṛṣṇaism, the worship of the glorified leader of the Yādavas, also venerated as Gopāla, the Protector of Cows. At some later stage Vāsudevaism and Kṛṇṣaism merged into the cult of Vāsudeva Kṛṣṇa, as it is found in the Mahābhārata. Pāṇcarātra, which developed in the South, merged the cult of Nārāyaṇa with Kṛṣṇaism.[2] The *Mahābhārata* is the most important source for early Vaiṣṇavism. The sources of Bhāgavatism, which merged with it at a later date, are the early Viṣṇu Purāṇas and the Vaiṣṇava *Saṃhitās*.[3]

Vaiṣṇavism has developed the most variegated and the richest mythology of all the schools of Hinduism. The core of Vaiṣṇavism, however, is Lord Viṣṇu as savior, a belief that, again, has found expression in countless myths. The oldest, and perhaps most basic myth of this kind is that of Viṣṇu *trivikrama*, "Viṣṇu who took the three steps," later combined with a myth of one of the *avatāras*, *Vāmana* the dwarf-descent. Allusions to it are found in the *Ṛgveda*,[4] establishing a connection of a Viṣṇu cult with the worship of the sun in the morning, at noon, and in the evening. It is embellished in the epics and Purāṇas and is designed to give a basis to the claim that Viṣṇu's is the whole universe!

Bali, the ruler of the earth, invited *devas* and princes to a great sacrifice. As was the custom, each guest could express a wish that the king was eager to fulfill. Viṣṇu in the form of a dwarf appeared and asked for nothing more than as much ground as he could cover with three steps. Bali wanted him to demand more, half of his kingdom, if he liked, but no, *Vāmana* wanted just that and nothing else. Bali resigned himself to the guest's wish; it was his own fault, after all, if he did not receive more. Before Bali's eyes, however, the dwarf began to grow: his first step covered the whole earth, the second reached out to the sun, and there was no more room for the third: humbly Bali offered his head for Viṣṇu to step on, thereby acknowledging Viṣṇu's rule and supremacy.

A Vedic hymn,[5] the famous *Puruṣa-sūkta*, has become the basis of all later Vaiṣṇava speculation about Viṣṇu as the material cause of all beings.

The very important, and most probably very old, *Nārāyaṇīya* section of the *Mahābhārata*[6] tells about the revelation of a religion of salvation given in ancient times to two sages, Nara and Nārada in *Śveta-dvīpa*, the White Island, situated to the north and inhabited by a race of white, wise beings, all of them worshippers of Nārāyaṇa. It was this interesting text that around the turn of the century prompted some scholars to suspect Christian influence in Vaiṣṇavism.[7]

## VIṢṆU *AVATĀRAS*

The most popular and consequently the most important part of Viṣṇu mythology is focused on the *avatāras*, the bodily descents of Viṣṇu exercising his function as saviour of the world.[8] The *Bhagavadgītā* explains that the Supreme One comes down to earth whenever dharma is in danger, to save the good and to destroy the wicked.[9] Generally one speaks nowadays of the *daśāvatāras*, ten descents of Viṣṇu, though some texts mention a large number, including a good many historical figures like Buddha and Kapila, the founder of the Sāṁkhya system. In all probability the systematization of the *avatāras* belongs to a relatively late period: the animal forms such as *matsya*, the fish, *kūrma*, the tortoise, and *varāha*, the boar, are possibly Vedic Prajāpati transformations and reminiscences of old tribal totems; the human forms like Rāma and Kṛṣṇa may represent deifications of historical persons, while other forms may go back to local gods and tribal deities.[10] Vaiṣṇavism, taken as a more or less unified religion, represents the constant effort to bring the growing mass of mythology together in one principle and to harmonize the heterogeneous elements from various local traditions.

The ten most widely recognized *avatāras* are described in so many texts that it will suffice to merely mention them and some features of the myths connected with them without going into details.[11]

*Matsya*, the fish, defeated the *asuras* who had stolen the Vedas, and returned them to the Brahmins. *Ekaśṛṅga*, the unicorn, saved Manu from the flood in which the whole of humankind perished. *Kūrma*, the tortoise, supported the Mountain Maṇḍara that was used by the gods to churn *amṛta*, nectar, from the milk ocean. *Varāha*, the boar, lifted the earth from the waters into which she had sunk and thus saved her. *Nṛsinha*, the man-lion, saved the *bhakta* Prahlāda from his father and persecutor Hiraṇyakaśīpu and in doing so he saved the whole world. *Vāmana*, the dwarf, defeated Bali, the King of the Earth, and regained the three worlds for the *devas*, who had been exiled form it. From his feet arose the Ganges. *Paraśurāma*, Rāma with the battle-axe, saved the Brahmins by annihilating the Kṣatriyas. The *Rāma* and *Kṛṣṇa avatāras* (Figure 15.1) are the most popular and they occupy a category by themselves. They are universal saviors, not limited to a particular epoch as the others are: they save everyone who surrenders to them.

*Balarāma*, the brother of Kṛṣṇa, is remembered as the killer of Pralamba and a host of other demons. *Kalki* is the only one to come in the future: as the eschatological manifestation of Viṣṇu on a white horse, he is to be the final liberator of the world from *kali*, the embodiment of strife, and all his evil influences. Apart from these, a number of other *avatāras* play a certain role in some of the Vaiṣṇava scriptures and cult centers.[12]

The *Bhāgavata Purāṇa* teaches the famous *Nārāyaṇa-kāvaca*, the prayer called the "protective shield of Viṣṇu" in which all the *avatāras* of Viṣṇu are invoked, remembering their great deeds in the past as a guarantee for present and future salvation.[13]

Photo 17. Varāha *avatāra*: Khajurāho

Figure 15.1. Rāma and Kṛṣṇa: Viṣṇu in human form

*Rāma* was worshipped locally as a hero and a divine king probably long before he came to be considered as an *avatāra* of Viṣṇu,[14] and he is certainly older than the *Vālmīki Rāmāyaṇa*, the celebrated ancient epic narrating his adventures. But his worship as a Viṣṇu *avatāra* may be comparatively late, certainly later than that of Vāsudeva Kṛṣṇa. Even now the human features of Rāma and Sītā, his consort, seem to be more in the foreground of popular religious consciousness than his divinity. There is a late (perhaps twelfth century) work, the *Adhyātma Rāmāyaṇa*, which explains Rāma and his exploits as manifestations of the supreme Viṣṇu in the following manner: "The Lord of Jānakī, who is intelligence itself and, though immutable, being requested by the *devas* to remove the afflictions of the world, took the illusory form of a man and was apparently born in the solar dynasty. After attaining to fame eternal, capable of destroying sins by killing the foremost of the demons, he again took up his real nature as *brahman*."[15] Ayodhyā, the city of Rāma, has become the center of the Rāma *bhaktas* with millions of devotees flocking to the sacred sites each year. Ayodhyā, the "City without War," has also become the focus of worldwide attention through the agitation of the Hindu political parties that clamored for years for a restoration of the legendary birthplace of Rāma, which since Babur's time was partly occupied by a mosque. Plans for a new Rāma temple were drawn up and made public through the media, and millions were mobilized in the *Rām-śilā* movement, which encouraged people to contribute one brick inscribed with the name of Rāma toward the future temple. The agitation reached its apex when, on December 6, 1992, a group of *kārsevaks* (RSS activists) demolished the Babri-Masjid and reclaimed the area for the Rāma temple. The widespread outbreak of Hindu-Muslim rioting that followed all over India, leaving thousands dead and hundreds of thousands homeless, has tarnished the name of Rāma, whose rule was always extolled as *dharma-rājya*, the kingdom of justice and peace.[16]

The most popular among the Viṣṇu *avatāras* is, undoubtedly, Kṛṣṇa, "the black one," also called Śyāma.[17] Many of his worshippers consider him not only an *avatāra* in the usual sense, that is, Viṣṇu appearing in a human disguise, but as *svayam bhagavān*, the Lord Himself in His eternal body. The many scriptures inspired by the Kṛṣṇa cult do not tire of emphasising that Kṛṣṇa is the savior, the ultimate and definite manifestation of Viṣṇu, for the benefit of all who choose to become his devotees.

Present-day Kṛṣṇa worship is an amalgam of various elements.[18] According to historical testimonies Kṛṣṇa-Vāsudeva worship already flourished in and around Mathurā several centuries before Christ. A second important element is the cult of Kṛṣṇa Govinda, "Kṛṣṇa the Cowfinder," perhaps the tribal deity of the Ahirs. Still later is the worship of Balakṛṣṇa, the Divine Child Kṛṣṇa—a quite prominent feature of modern Kṛṣṇaism[19]. The last element seems to have been Kṛṣṇa Gopīvallabha, Kṛṣṇa the lover of the *gopīs*, among whom Rādhā occupies a special position.[20] In some books Kṛṣṇa is presented as the founder and first teacher of the Bhāgavata religion. The question of Kṛṣṇa's historicity, which formerly was of little interest to Hindus, if not simply assumed as a fact, has become the object of quite serious scholarly studies.[21]

Popular myths reveal a faith in Kṛṣṇa as a manifestation of God, capable of liberating mankind. His birth is surrounded by miracles. As a little baby he already gave proof of his divine power. As a young man he lifted up Govardhana to protect the cowherds from torrential rainfalls and thus defied Indra. He is the object of passionate love, which inspired some of India's greatest poets to unrivalled masterpieces, like Jayadeva, who wrote the immortal *Gītāgovinda*. He also is the teacher of the way of salvation in the *Bhagavadgītā* and the *Bhāgavata Purāṇa*, certainly the most popular religious books in the whole of India.[22]

Not only was Kṛṣṇaism influenced by the identification of Kṛṣṇa with Viṣṇu, but also Vaiṣṇavism as a whole was partly transformed and reinterpreted in the light of the popular and powerful Kṛṣṇa religion. Bhāgavatism may have brought an element of cosmic religion into Kṛṣṇa worship; Kṛṣṇa has certainly brought a strongly human element into Bhāgavatism. He is not a God enthroned in distant majesty, inaccessible to humans, but he appears as a sweet child, a naughty boy, a comrade in youthful adventures, an ardent lover—a universal savior! The center of Kṛṣṇa-worship has been for a long time *Brājbhūmī*, the district of Mathurā that embraces also Vṛndāvana, Govardhana, and Gokula, associated with Kṛṣṇa from time immemorial. Many millions of Kṛṣṇa *bhaktas* visit these places every year and participate in the numerous festivities that reenact scenes from Kṛṣṇa's life on earth.[23]

Though there is not even a mention of Śrī, the consort of Viṣṇu, in the earlier sources, in later Vaiṣṇavism Śrī becomes part and parcel of Viṣṇu religion. Apparently also Śrī was worshipped independently before her cult was integrated into Vaiṣṇavism. Now she is considered inseparable from Viṣṇu: Viṣṇu has on his body a mark called *śrī-vatsa*, ineradicably representing his consort. In later Vaiṣṇavism she is identified with Rādhā, and Caitanya, the sixteenth-century Bengali Kṛṣṇa mystic, is held by his followers to be an *avatāra* of Kṛṣṇa and Rādhā together. The most prominent form of South Indian Vaiṣṇavism is called Śrī-Vaiṣṇavism because of its strong emphasis of the role of Śrī. It draws heavily on the popular *bhakti* religion of the Āḷvārs, so that we can see in Śrī worship an element of popular Indian religion, in which worship of goddesses always occupied a prominent place.[24]

## VAIṢṆAVA THEOLOGY

Vaiṣṇavism is intimately connected with image worship. The rationale for this is provided in *Pāñcarātra*[25] theology, which has been fairly commonly accepted by all groups of Vaiṣṇavas. The following sketch offers the description found in a widely acknowledged handbook of Vaiṣṇava theology. *Īśvara*, the Lord Viṣṇu, is the ruler of all, the giver of all gifts, the preserver of all, the cause of all effects, and he has everything, except himself and his own consciousness, as his

Photo 18. Keśighata in Vṛndāvana

body. *Īśvara* is thus the material cause of the universe, becoming through the act of creation the efficient cause as well as the concomitant cause of all things, insofar as he is immanent in time. *Īśvara*, who animates the whole world, is not touched by its imperfections. He is omnipresent through his form, through his knowledge of all things and events, and through his body. He is free from the limitations of space, time, and objects. He is *sat-cit-ānanda*, being, consciousness and bliss, and he is free from sin. He is the refuge and the protector of all beings, having the qualities of gentleness and mercy.

*Īśvara* exists in five different forms: as *para*, *vyūha*, *vibhava*, *antaryāmi* and *arcāvatāra*. Viṣṇu in his own supreme and transcendent form is called *para*: expressed in names like *Parabrahman*, *Paravāsudeva*. He is endowed with a divine body having four arms and adorned by the insignia of his supreme Lordship, seated on *śeṣa*, the infinite world-snake, residing in *Vaikuṇṭha*.

He manifests his powers severally in four *vyūhas*, whose names are Vāsudeva, Saṁkarśaṇa, Pradyumna, and Aniruddha, and who exist for the purpose of creation and worship. Vāsudeva is filled with the six divine qualities; the others have two each, namely *jñāna* and *bala*, knowledge and strength; *aiśvarya* and *vīrya*, lordship and heroism; *śakti* and *tejas*, power and splendor. Each of them descends into three sub-*vyūhas*, such as Keśava, among others who are the presiding deities of the twelve months, each having his special insignia and powers. Keśava shines like gold, and he carries four *cakras* or discuses. The dark-skinned Nārāyaṇa carries four *śaṅkhas*, conches. Mādhava, who is bright like a sapphire, holds four *gaḍas* or clubs; Govinda, who shines as the moon, carries four *śārṅgas* or bows; Viṣṇu, of the color of the blue lotus, has four *halas* or ploughs; Madhusūdana, who is like a bright-hued lotus, carries four *muśālas* or hammers; the fire-colored Trivikrama bears four *khadgas* or swords; Vāmana, radiant like the dawn, holds four *vajras* or thunderbolts; Śrīdhāra, alike to a white lotus, bears four *paṭṭīśas* or spears; Hṛṣikeśa, brilliant as the lightning, carries four *mudgaras* or axes; Padmanābha, effulgent as the midday sun, bears five *audhas*, or shields. Damodāra, red-white like an Indra-gopa beetle, holds four *pāśas*, or nooses.

Under the category *vibhava* come the *avatāras*, which were mentioned before. The text distinguishes between full and partial *avatāras*. It also teaches: "The cause for the descent of an *avatāra* is only the free will of *Īśvara* and not karma. Its fruit is the protection of the good people and the destruction of the wicked."

*Antaryāmi* is the form of *Īśvara*, which resides in the human heart. He stays with the *jīvātman* as friend in the experiences of heaven and hell and is recognizable by the yogi.

For practical religious purposes the *arcā avatāra*, the visible image of God, is the most important. The text describes it as follows:

> The *arcā avatāra* is that special form that accepts as body, without intervention of spatial or temporal distance, any kind of matter that the *bhakta* might

> wish to choose, descending into it with an *aprākṛta śarīra*, a nonmaterial body; he then depends on the devotee concerning bathing, eating, sitting, sleeping, etc. He is filled with divine qualities and tolerates everything, being present thus in houses, villages, towns, holy places, hills, and so forth. He is fourfold on the basis of the difference as *svayam vyakta*, self-manifest, *daiva*, manifest through *devas*, *saiddha*, manifest through saints, and *mānuṣa*, manifest through ordinary human beings.[26]

Images, understood as a physical presence of Viṣṇu, are a very important part of Vaiṣṇavism. The fame of a temple depends on the power of its *mūrti*, and each devout Vaiṣṇava family maintains at least one figure of Viṣṇu or one of the *avatāras* in the house, which receives regular worship. Apart from the anthropomorphic images, the *tulasī* plant, usually kept in a pot in the yard of the house, and the *śālagrāma*, an ammonite found in the Gandakī River in Nepal, are worshipped as embodiments of Viṣṇu.

Vaiṣṇavism has also highly developed temple architecture. Some of the most impressive buildings in the world, such as the Śrīraṅgam temple near Tiruchirapalli, are consecrated to Viṣṇu. In most images Viṣṇu is represented either standing upright or laying on his couch, the world snake *śeṣa*, and usually accompanied by Śrī. The *avatāras* are represented quite frequently in the poses described in the myths. Feasts observed in honor of Viṣṇu are so numerous that it is impossible to mention them all; a few will be described in a later chapter. Nowadays the feasts of the *avatāras* are in the foreground, especially Kṛṣṇa's and Rāma's birthdays.

Despite the prevalence of a highly emotional *bhakti* and often quite unstructured forms of worship we must not overlook the very rich systematic theological heritage of Vaiṣṇavism and its compendious, minutely ordered liturgies.

Vaiṣṇavas generally insist that *their* interpretation of the great scriptural classics, which are universally accepted by Hindus, is the only correct one, rejecting for instance Śaṅkara's Advaitic interpretation of the Upaniṣads as heretical. There is good reason to assume that the first commentary on the *Brahmasūtras*, the lost gloss by Bodhāyana, had indeed been theistic. Vaiṣṇavas, then, interpret many passages in the Vedas and the Upaniṣads in a Vaiṣṇava way. According to Rāmānuja, for instance, all words in the Veda like *power, form, splendor, body* and similar expressions mean Viṣṇu, and similarly Viṣṇu is intended by the Upaniṣads when they mention *the soul of all, the highest brahman*, the *supreme reality* and so on. The earliest attempts to systematize Vaiṣṇavism seem to rely upon the Sāṁkhya system, as testified to by the *Pāñcarātra Āgamas*. The difference of Vaiṣṇava Sāṁkhya lies in its attributing to Viṣṇu the authorship of *prakṛti* and of liberation. The *Bhāgavata Purāṇa*, which considers Kapila an *avatāra* of Viṣṇu, contains the fullest account of Vaiṣṇava Sāṁkhya, concluding with the exhortation: "Therefore through devotion, dispassion, and spiritual wisdom acquired through a concentrated

Photo 19. Viṣṇu Upendra: Khajurāho

mind, one should contemplate the Inner Controller as present in this very body, though apart from it."[27]

## VAIṢṆAVA VEDĀNTA

In the more recent Vaiṣṇava theology, the systems deriving from Vedānta and developing from the tenth century onward are most prominent. They originated with the *ācāryas* of Śrīraṅgam who combined the fervour of the popular religion of the Āḷvārs with Upaniṣadic *jñāna*. Natha Muni (ninth century), the first of them, was the son of the great *Pāñcarātra* master Īśvara Muni. He gave to the Tamil *Prabandham* of the Āḷvārs the status of *śruti* in Śrīraṅgam and established himself as the supreme teaching authority. His successor Yamunācārya (tenth century) was a great Vedāntin who left several systematic works. According to a legend, he kept three fingers bent on his death bed, interpreted by Rāmānuja (1017–1137), his successor, as three unfulfilled wishes that he was going to redeem, namely to give to the Vaiṣṇavas a commentary on the *Brahmasūtras*, to perpetuate the memory of Parāśara, the father of Vyāsa—the author of the *Viṣṇu Purāṇa*—and to spread the glory of Nammāḷvār (see Figure 15.2), considered to be the greatest among the Āḷvārs.[28] He proved to be a great organizer and a great writer. He made the most successful attempt to establish a theistic Vedānta interpretation over against Śaṅkara's Advaita. In addition to the commentary on the *Brahmasūtras*, called *Śrībhāṣya*, Rāmānuja wrote a commentary on the *Bhagavadgītā*, as well as several minor independent and valuable works. Perhaps the best known of these is the *Vedārthasaṅgraha*, a veritable compendium of Vaiṣṇava Vedānta, written in beautiful language.[29]

In Rāmānuja's theology *brahman* is identical with Viṣṇu, who is described as *rakṣaka*, Redeemer. Viṣṇu comes down from his heavenly throne to enter *saṃsāra* for the sake of assisting the struggling *jīvas* to attain salvation; he suffers and endures pain with them and leads them by the hand like a friend. This guidance is given through the medium of the *avatāras* and the guru, the "fully trustworthy person" who tells the lost *jīvas* about their real identity and returns them to their father.[30] Though in their original nature the *jīvas* are particles of the divine nature, due to certain limitations, described as "heedlessness," they become entangled in *saṃsāra* and thereby unhappy. The Lord remains with the *jīvas* as *antaryāmi* to guide them, without taking away the *jīvas*' freedom to follow their own ways. "The Lord then, recognizing those who perform good actions as devotees who obey His commands, blesses them with piety, riches, worldly pleasures, and final release, while those who transgress His commands He causes to experience the opposite of all this."[31] Viṣṇu himself is the *muktidātā*, the giver of salvation, and the role of humans is to prepare the way for God to meet them, to dispose themselves for God's grace. The central act is *prapatti*, self-surrender.

The following text, in Rāmānuja's own words, gives in a nutshell the way to salvation:

Figure 15.2. Nammāḷvār

The pathway through which the supreme *brahman* is to be attained is as follows: By an accumulation of great merit the sins of the past lives are destroyed. Thus liberated, a person will seek refuge at the feet of the Puruṣottama. Such self-surrender begets an inclination toward Him. Then the aspirant acquires knowledge of reality from the scriptures aided by the instruction of holy teachers. Then by a steady effort the *bhakta* develops in an ever-increasing

> measure the qualities of soul like the control of mind, sense control, austerity, purity, forgiveness, sincerity, fearlessness, mercy, and nonviolence. The *bhaktas* continue with the ritual duties and offer their very own self at the lotus-like feet of the Puruṣottama. They ceaselessly worship Him with dedication. The Puruṣottama, who is overflowing with compassion, being pleased with such love, showers His grace on the aspirant, which destroys all inner darkness. In such a devotee there develops *bhakti*, which is valued for its own sake, which is uninterrupted, an absolute delight in itself, and which is meditation that has taken on the character of the most vivid and immediate vision. Through such *bhakti* is the Supreme attained.[32]

Rāmānuja underscores the importance of the guru with the beautiful parable of a young prince, who in the course of his boyish play loses his way in the forest and is then reared by a good Brahmin who knows nothing about the boy's background. When the boy has reached his sixteenth year, a "fully trustworthy person" tells him who his true father is, and that he longs to see him. The boy is exceedingly happy and starts on his way to his real home; his father has gone out from his palace to meet him halfway. Rāmānuja sees in the "fully trustworthy person" a model of the true *guru*. The first among the gurus is Śrī, mediating between God and *bhakta*. She is the embodiment of divine grace and mercy, whose entreaties win the forgiveness of Viṣṇu for the *jīva*. The human guru should be like her: entirely free from egotism, always desirous of the welfare of others, not swayed by the love of fame or profit.[33]

Rāmānuja's concern for his fellow-humans is illustrated in a popular anecdote: Shortly after his secret initiation into the three *rahasyas*, the great mysteries of the Vaiṣṇava tradition, he climbed to the top of a *gopura*, one of the tall towers over the entrance of a temple precinct of Śrīraṅgam, and loudly shouted the three sacred texts so that all people might be saved by them, though he risked his own condemnation for divulging the mysteries.[34]

Shortly after Rāmānuja's death the unity of Śrīvaiṣṇavism was disrupted and two major schools developed, based on dogmatic as well as on linguistic tenets. The *Vaṭakalais*, or Northerners, established their center in Kāñcīpuram. Their best-known *ācārya* was Vedānta Deśika (1269–1370). They maintained that Sanskrit scriptures were the only true sources of their religion. The *Tenkalais*, or Southerners, held on to Śrīraṅgam as their center. Their principal master was Pillai Lokācārya (1205–1311). They held the Tamil textual tradition represented by the Āḷvārs as equally inspired as the Sanskrit scriptures.

The two branches are also known as the "monkey school" and the "cat school," respectively, because the Northerners likened the process of salvation to the activity of a young monkey who must by his own effort cling to his mother if he is to be carried away from a fire, whereas the Southerners saw the best illustration of the process of salvation in a young kitten, which its mother simply picks up to save.[35]

So great was the prestige of Vedānta Deśika, the Vaṭakalai *ācārya*, that he was invited by the Tenkalais to take over the seat of Rāmānuja in Śrīraṅgam, in the hope that the two branches of Śrīvaiṣṇavism might be reunited.[36]

One of the most uncompromising of all Vaiṣṇava *ācāryas* was Madhva (1238–1317), the exponent of Dvaita Vedanta, who thought that Rāmānuja had not been decisive enough in his rejection of Śaṅkara's Advaita. He considered stigmatization of the Viṣṇu *bhakta* with a *cakra* as a prerequisite for salvation. Madhva considered himself the third *avatāra* of Vāyu, a mediator between Viṣṇu and humankind. According to him the *jīva* is an image of Viṣṇu like a reflection in a mirror and the relationship between God and person is described as *biṃba-pratibiṃba*, image and reflection. His doctrine of predestination is quite unique in Indian religion: there are persons who are destined never to become liberated and to remain in eternal bondage. He also assumed differences in the bliss experienced by those who have reached heaven, as there are different capacities of vessels. The at-oneness of the perfect *bhakta* with Viṣṇu he described in a beautiful image: "The released takes everything with the hand of Hari, sees through the eye of Hari only, walks with the feet of Hari." The perfectly free ones even enter into Viṣṇu at will and issue out from him.[37]

Another great master of the Vaiṣṇava tradition is Niṃbārka (1125–1162); with him the role of the guru becomes all-important. "Surrender to the guru" is the central act of saving faith, and the disciple makes a statement to the effect that the guru is considered the only savior from mundane existence.[38]

## "THE WAY OF GRACE"

Vallabha (1481–1533), a Telugū Brahmin belonging originally to the Viṣṇuswāmi school[39] became the founder of a distinct *saṃpradāya* with a specific doctrine of salvation, which became known as *puṣṭimārga*, the way of grace.[40] It counts several million followers especially in northern India, and maintains hundreds of vibrant centres of worship. It became first known in the West through the unsavory "Mahārāja-case"[41] and became tainted through unfavourable early 19th century reports.[42] Recently Indian and Western scholars as well as adherents of the Vallabha *saṃpradāya*, have published text translations and studies of various aspects of Vallabha's teachings.[43] Both the size of the membership of the Vallabha *saṃpradāya* and the weight of the writings of Vallabha and his followers warrant a more extensive treatment of this branch of Vaiṣṇavism.[44]

Vallabha is elevating the *Bhāgavata Purāṇa* to the position of most authoritative scripture; his school considers it to be the only authentic commentary on the *Brahmasūtras*.[45] Vallabha discredits all attempts—especially those made by Advaitins—to use reason for probing the nature of *brahman*.[46] His is a "revelation-only" theology, a teaching that prefers to put up with what appear to be inconsistencies and contradictions in scriptural statements rather than to judge these by reason and fitting them into a logically coherent system.

The *Puṣṭimārga* is also a "family religion," both in the sense that Vallabha himself was a family man and in the sense that his teaching emphasizes the virtues of family life as means to earn God's grace. "The worship of the Lord requires the services of all members of the family, and they are promised the highest bliss that always results from worship, or *sevā*. This mode of worship makes the whole family free from worldly ties even when leading a householder's life, and their whole life becomes divine."[47]

Vallabha was convinced that in his time and age the duties of the *varṇāśrama-dharma* could no longer be properly fulfilled and that formal *samnyāsa*, far from being of spiritual help, would be spiritually harmful if not undertaken in response to the love of the Lord. What was important, however, and what was demanded of each and every member of the *saṃpradāya*, was *ātma-nivedana*, self-surrender and surrender of all of one's own to the guru. There is no doubt that this teaching lead not only to misunderstandings but also to malpractice.

Vallabha understands his *puṣṭimārga* not only as different from *karmamārga* and *jñānamārga*, but also as superior to the *bhaktimārga* of other schools of Vaiṣṇavism. *Puṣṭi* is the uncaused grace of God, for which the devotee prepares, but which he cannot direct or influence: "It is impossible to say for what reason God is pleased to extend his grace; it cannot be for the relief of suffering, for there are many sufferers to whom God does not do so."[48]

On the human side, *puṣṭi* means doing things out of pure love and not because an action is enjoined by the Veda, and also not because the intellect recognizes the majesty and exalted nature of God. The *puṣṭimārga* is open to all, including to women and low-caste people, even the *patitā*, the "fallen," for whom other schools of Hinduism hold out no hope of salvation. It is free from Vedic command and is only interested in establishing a relationship between the soul and its Lord—even if this relationship is one of anger and resentment.[49]

Vallabha distinguishes between *mokṣa* and *nitya līlā* as ultimate aims. Without denying the possibility of Vedāntic *mokṣa*, he holds that *nitya līlā*, eternal enjoyment of the company of God is much preferable.

> When the Lord desires to favor a particular soul—and be it remembered that in showing His favor He is not guided by any other consideration but His own will—He brings out the soul from Himself, gives him a divine body like His own, and plays with him for all time. In this play, which is called *nitya līlā*, the Lord, remaining subordinate to the devotee, gives him the pleasure of His company, which is generally known as *bhajānanda* (bliss of devotion) and *svarūpānanda* (the bliss of the Lord Himself), which is referred to in the *Taittirīya Upaniṣad*, the *Bhāgavata*, and other *Purāṇas*.[50]

The uncaused grace of God and the enjoyment of His company are best exemplified by the *gopīs* of Vṛndāvana, who are the models for the followers of the *puṣṭimārga*. The highest title of God is *Gopī-jana-vallabha*, the Darling of the Milkmaids. Becoming such a devotee is the highest aim of a follower of Vallabha:

> One who thinks of God as all and of oneself as emanating from Him and who serves him with love, is a devotee . . . the highest devotee leaves everything, with the mind filled with Kṛṣṇa alone . . . the *bhakta* is wholly absorbed in the love of God. No one, however, can take the path of *bhakti* except through the grace of God. Karma itself, being of the nature of God's will, manifests itself as His mercy or anger to the devotee . . . the law of karma is mysterious . . . we do not know the manner in which God's will manifests itself; sometimes, by His grace He may even save a sinner who may not have to take the punishment due to him.[51]

Vallabha seems to assume that the seed of *bhakti* exists as *premā*, through the grace of God, in all human beings. It has to be nurtured and increased by self-surrender, by listening to the scriptures, and by chanting His name. It becomes strong if, while leading a householder's life, one remains absorbed in Kṛṣṇa and performs one's duties with a mind fixed on God. This love of God may develop into such a passion (*vyasana*) that one feels unable to do anything else but sing His praises. *Vyasana* is the "inability to remain without God"; under its influence a householder may leave his home and become a *samnyāsi*.[52] "The firm seed of *bhakti* can never be destroyed; it is through affection for God that other attachments are destroyed, and by the development of this affection, that one renounces the home. It is only when this affection for God grows into a passion that one attains one's end easily."[53]

*Sevā*, "service," is very central to the *puṣṭimārga*. It is a distinctive feature of Vallabha's *saṃpradāya* because it denotes the worship of *Śrī Govardhananāthajī* alone. All worship rendered to other manifestations of the Lord is called *pūjā*, and is directed to the Lord's *vibhutis* only, not to his embodiment as *Śrī Nāthajī*. The original image, supposedly revealed to Vallabha on the hill of Govardhana, is the only full presence of the Lord.

Vallabha's *puṣṭimārga* emphasizes the sovereignty of the Lord as no other religion does: those whom He has chosen attain a state almost like His own, while those whom He does not choose remain in bondage and *saṃsāra* forever.

## GAUḌĪYA OR BENGAL VAIṢṆAVISM

Caitanya is one of the most renowned figures in modern Vaiṣṇavism, who also became known to many Westerners as *Mahāprabhu*, the Great Lord of the Hare Krishna movement.[54] Though not really the initiator of the emotionally refined Gauḍīya Vaiṣṇavism, he and his learned disciples made it into an important religious movement, influential far beyond the boundaries of Bengal. He knew the *Bhāgavata Purāṇa*; he had read the Kṛṣṇa poetry of Caṇḍīdāsa and Vidyāpati; he was familiar with Bilvamaṅgala's *Kṛṣṇakarṇāmṛta* and Jayadeva's

*Gītāgovinda*; and the practice of *kīrtaṇa* was already widespread in his time. Caitanya never wrote a book,[55] but among his disciples he had very able men who formulated the theology of the movement that Caitanya initiated. Rūpa Goswāmi's *Hari-bhakti-rasāmṛta-sindhu* is the authentic *summa theologica* of the Caitanyites, and Gopāla Bhaṭṭa's *Hari-bhakti-vilāsa* codifies the accepted form of their ritual.[56]

Caitanya's is a pure Kṛṣṇa religion. At its center stands Kṛṣṇa as the full manifestation of God and the continued presence of Kṛṣṇa in Vraja, more specifically the Kṛṣṇa of Vṛndāvana, the great lover of the *gopīs*, the perfect partners in this love. According to the followers of Caitanya the *Bhāgavata Purāṇa* is *śruti* as well as the only authentic commentary on the *Brahmasūtras*. Nevertheless Baladeva Vidyābhuṣana felt impelled to write a formal *bhāṣya* on the *Brahmasūtra* as well, called *Govinda Bhāṣya*.[57]

## THE POPULAR POETS AND SINGERS OF VIṢṆU *BHAKTI*

The real source of the continued vitality and popularity of Vaiṣṇavism lies in its poets and singers who for centuries traveled up and down the subcontinent to kindle *bhakti* to Viṣṇu in the hearts of their compatriots.[58] Their concern was not theology or liturgy, but *bhakti* for the sake of liberation. Their main topic was the misery of this life and the glory of the life of God. A very striking feature of their teaching is the insistence on the cultivation of a high moral standard: purity, truthfulness, patience, forbearance, love, renunciation, giving up of all selfishness, contentment with one's state of life, self-control, pity, freedom from greed and from hypocrisy, sincerity, and humility—all taught in simple language as the prerequisite and sign of true *bhakti*. They recommend the traditional Vaiṣṇava practices of *nāma-japa*, *saṁkīrtana*, *mūrti-pūjā*, submission under a guru, and so on.[59]

Simple as their words may be, understood by each and everyone, their thoughts are reaching great depth and their devotion is grounded in philosophical insight. Some samples must suffice. For those who know Indian vernaculars there are literally hundreds of books to draw from; for English-reading students of *bhakti*, an increasingly rich amount of translations and scholarly studies are becoming available.[60]

Sūrdās (1478 to ca. 1560) was, according to tradition, blind from birth.[61] Yet his poetry, aflame with the love of Kṛṣṇa, was so famous all over North India that the Muslim Emperor Akbar invited him to his court to converse with him and listen to his recitation. Besides a massive work, the *Sūr-sāgar*, "Sur's Ocean" that recreates in contemporary *braj-bhāṣa* the tenth canto of the *Bhāgavata Purāṇa*, Sūrdās wrote many couplets that are still sung at popular *bhajan* sessions. The translation offered cannot convey the musicality of the original, its clever use of double meanings of words or of closely related sound images, its rhythm and its color. It will, however, reveal some of the content and give an impression of the down to earth metaphors used to deliver the transcendental message. It should also be mentioned that as a sort of copyright the author, following an Indian convention, inserted his own name in the last verse.[62]

> Misguided by illusion after illusion
> Stuck like a fly in the juice of sense-objects, yet far from understanding things
> You have lost the jewel Hari inside your own house.
> You are like a deer that sees mirages
> Unable to quench thirst even if approached from ten different directions
> Having produced in one life after another
> Much karma in which you have entangled yourself
> You resemble the parrot who pinned his hope on the fruit of the silk-cotton tree.
> Having set his mind on it day and night,
> He took it in its beak and found its shell empty—
> The cotton had flown up and away.
> You are like a monkey who is kept tied on a rope
> By the juggler who makes him dance for a few grains at every crossroads.
> Sūrdās says: without devotion to God you will make yourself just into a morsel to be eaten by the tiger Time.[63]

In spite of its use of Vaiṣṇava history and scriptures, this kind of *bhakti* is quite transectarian. At *bhajana* gatherings one may hear poems by Rāma *bhaktas* and *Kṛṣṇa-bhaktas*, recited side by side with those of Kabīir, who did not follow any particular Vaiṣṇava affiliation at all.

What those *bhaktas* search for is true experience.[64] Their basic experience is that God is reality. For Kabīr the religious experience is "penetrating to the heart of reality"; Mīrābāī speaks of Viṣṇu as "the invaluable jewel of reality." Quite frequent are reports about supra-sensuous phenomena, which accompany realization, the most prominent being the hearing of the *anahaṭ-śabda*, the transcendent sound. Kabīr speaks of the "sky-reaching sound" that breaks forth from the full lake of mellifluous nectar, the means of illumination. Some also describe a taste of sweetness perceived in ecstasy, called *Rāmras* or *Hariras*: partaking of it equals immortality. Most *bhaktas* firmly believe that one can have *sākṣātkāra*, a bodily vision of God in this life that seals the love to God with the assurance of final deliverance.

Vaiṣṇavism had and has a deep appeal to women. One of the woman-saint Mīrābāī's songs may help to appreciate the depth of feeling that is Viṣṇu *bhakti*:

> The Name is gone deep into my mind.
> Day and night do I chant it.
> O Lord, I am humble and low, can I sing thy praises?
> I am encaged in the agony of separation.

I gain solace only by repeating thy name!
Guided by the grace of the guru, I have turned out evil thoughts from my mind.
I stretch the arrow of the Name on the bow of Love,
I arm myself with the shield of wisdom and sing my Lord's praises cheerfully all the time.
Making my body a sound-box,
I play on it many notes with the mind in order to wake up my slumbering soul.
I dance before my Lord to gain a place in his divine abode.
O Giridhāra, confer thy blessing on me, who sings of thy sports,
And let me place the dust of thy lotus-feet on my head, for that boon I cherish the most.
So sings Mīrābāī.[65]

Vaiṣṇavism has not lost its attraction in our time. Not only do the centuries-old *saṃpradāyas* continue and intensify their activities, but new movements have also arisen to reactivate *saṁkīrtana* and regular *pūjā*. Swāmi Rāma Tīrtha has carried the message of Lord Viṣṇu to the West. Swāmi Bhaktivedānta founded ISKCON, a movement to propagate Gauḍīya-Vaiṣṇavism not only in India, but also throughout the whole world. Ronald Nixon, an Englishman, who under his Indian name Kṛṣṇa Prem became the guru of Indian as well as Western *bhaktas*, may still be rather an exception, but there is no denying the fact that Vaiṣṇavism, in its many forms, with its basic message of love, has universal appeal to religiously minded persons.

Vaiṣṇavism is also increasingly engaging Western religious scholarship, as the numerous book publications mentioned above indicate. While many scholarly journals carry articles that deal with specific aspects of Vaiṣṇavism, there is also a *Journal of Vaiṣṇava Studies* that since its inception in 1992 has carried important scholarly as well as devotional articles. In 1997 the Oxford Center for Hindu and Vaiṣṇava Studies began offering lecture courses on Vaiṣṇavism and provides opportunity for graduate students to earn degrees in its study. In 1994 the World Vaiṣṇava Association was founded in Vṛndāvana. It maintains a website with an Internet address and also tries to bring the various Vaiṣṇava sects together and to spread Vaiṣṇava teachings.

CHAPTER SIXTEEN

# Śiva

## *The Grace and the Terror of God*

Śiva, you have no mercy. Śiva you have no heart. Why did you bring me to birth—wretch in this world, exile from the other?

—*Basavanna*, quoted in R. K. Ramanujan, *Speaking of Śiva*

Śiva worshippers all over India every day recite hymns to their Great God in many languages. The Sanskrit hymn that follows summarizes a variety of motives that make him dear to his devotees:

> Praise Viśvanātha, the Lord of the City of Banares, whose locks are the charming ripples of the Ganges, adorned on his left by Gaurī, the beloved of Nārāyaṇa, the destroyer of the god of love.
>
> Praise Viśvanātha, the Lord of the City of Banares, beyond speech, the repository of different qualities, whose feet are worshipped by Brahmā, Viṣṇu and the other *devas*, with his wife to the left.
>
> Praise Viśvanātha, the Lord of the City of Banares, the wielder of the trident, adorned by a snake, wearing a tiger skin and matted locks, the Three-eyed one, who keeps in two of his hands the noose and the goad and offers blessing and grace with the two others.
>
> Praise Viśvanātha, the Lord of the City of Banares, wearing a crown with the moon, who burnt the Five-Arrowed-One to ashes with the fire emerging from his third eye on the forehead, whose ears are adorned with the shining rings of *śeṣa*, the king of the snakes.
>
> Praise Viśvanātha, the Lord of the City of Banares, the Five-faced-one, the lion destroying the mad elephant of sin, the Garuḍa destroying the vicious

> demons, the world fire that burns to ashes the jungle of birth, death, and old age.
>
> Praise Viśvanātha, the Lord of the City of Banares, who is effulgent, who is with and without qualities, the One without a second, bliss itself, the unconquerable one, the unknowable one, who is dark and bright and the form of the soul.
>
> Praise Viśvanātha, the Lord of the City of Banares, after you have given up all desires, all reviling of others and all attachment to sinful conduct, enter into *samādhi* and meditate on the Lord, seated in the lotus of the heart.
>
> Praise Viśvanātha, the Lord of the City of Banares, who is free from all emotion such as attachment and others, who is fond of his devotees, the abode of austerities and bliss, the companion of Girija endowed with his throat stained with the poison.
>
> Whoever recites this hymn to Śiva, the Lord of the City of Banares, attains in this life learning, prosperity, immense happiness and eternal fame and after death liberation.[1]

To *Viśvanātha*, Śiva, the Lord of the Universe, also the most sacred of all the temples of the most holy city of Vārāṇasī is consecrated; only Hindus are allowed to enter it.

## SOURCES OF ŚAIVISM

Śiva worship has been traced back to the Sindhu-Sarasvatī civilization, in which it appears to have been an established tradition. *Liṅgas* have been found there, the main object of Śiva worship to this day, as well as figures on seals interpreted as Śiva Mahāyogi and Śiva Paśupati.[2]

The historical homeland of Śiva religion in more recent times, however, has been the Tamil country. Both Śiva's name and his main mythology seem to come from there; the "Red God" was only later given a Sanskrit name, phonetically close to the Tamil one, which is translated as "the graceful one." Tribal religions of northwest India have contributed other features. The ambivalence of this Great God (see Figure 16.1) shows in the identification of "gracious" Śiva with "fearsome" Rudra, the howler. In the Vedas, Rudra is treated as "an apotropäic god of aversion, to be feared, but not adored."[3]

Features of some tribal gods, especially those of the mountains, may have been fused with him as well, as evidenced by the arguably oldest and most popular Śiva myth: Śiva's uninvited appearance at Prajāpati Dakṣa's sacrifice. Dakṣa, the father of Pārvatī, Śiva's consort, established at a hermitage close to the place where the Ganges breaks free from the mountains, had invited all other *devas* and prepared offerings to them, except for Śiva, whom he disliked. When Pārvatī's pleading did not succeed to change Dakṣa's mind, Śiva in his

Photo 16.1. Śiva Trimūrti from Gharapuri [Elephanta]

fury descended from the mountains, destroyed the sacrifice, and killed Dakṣa. Bringing him back to life by providing him with a goat's head, he converted Dakṣa from a Śiva hater into a Śiva worshipper and ensured for himself a permanent portion of the sacrifice.[4]

The myth relating to the destruction of Dakṣa's sacrifice by Śiva—according to all sources the first of Śiva's exploits—may in fact have a historical core: the conquest of Kanakhala, a *tīrtha* close to modern Hardwār, which was of great importance to Śaivites, Vaiṣṇavas, and Śāktas alike, and which was linked to an important Vedic settlement associated with the famous patriarch Dakṣa. As a story of the occupation of a holy place beyond the range of the high Himalayas—the region where Śaivism was at home before it entered the plains of India—it provided legitimacy to the Śaivas, who were originally shunned by the Vedic priests.[5]

*Śivabhagats* are already mentioned by Pāṇini in the fourth century BCE, and the Indian worshippers of Dionysos referred to by Megasthenes a little later may possibly have been Śiva devotees. The oldest Śaivite sect about which we know anything with certainty is that of the *Paśupatas*, whose teachings are largely identical with the even now flourishing Śaiva Siddhānta. Their founder was, according to legend, Śiva himself in the form of Lakuliṣa. Modern research is inclined to see in Lakuliṣa a historical personage of the second century CE.[6] The epics are full of references to Śiva; the *Rāmāyaṇa* usually contains the oldest versions of Śiva myths. In the *Mahābhārata* we find several hymns to Śiva and the mention, even at this early stage, of four different Śiva sects.

The *Śiva Purāṇas* and Āgamas, the main sources of "modern" Śaivism, seem to be comparatively late compositions, though they contain much ancient material. Some Śiva mythology and theology seems to be an imitation of earlier Vaiṣṇava material.[7] That Śaivism had become by then a major stream of Hinduism is proven by the fact that several powerful kings in the Indian Middle Ages were Śaivas. They sometimes forced Śaivism on their subjects and built magnificent sanctuaries in honor of Śiva.[8] Between 700 and 1000 CE Śaivism appears to have been the dominant religion of India, due largely to the influence of the sixty-three Nāyanmārs who flourished during this time and propagated Śaivism among the masses in the form of Śiva *bhakti*. The greatest among India's theological philosophers, Śaṅkarācārya, was according to an ancient tradition "an incarnation of Śiva, born for the purpose of consolidating Hindu dharma in answer to the imploring of Śaivaguru and Āryandā."[9] In the twelfth century a powerful reformist Śaiva movement arose in Karṇātaka, the Liṅgāyats, who still exercise great influence.

The *Ṛgveda* contains but a few hymns to Rudra, mainly imploring him to stay away and not to come to do harm,[10] occasionally beseeching him as "the great physician who possesses a thousand medicines" to give health and remove sorrow. Doris N. Srinivasan holds that Rudra was one of the Vedic *asuras*, "a primordial group which includes both gods and demons possessing the potential to create the truly wondrous, including life itself."[11] Rudra is associated with the North and he is given offerings that are defective. Omniscience is ascribed to him, the possessor of a thousand eyes. Rudra has a special relationship to Soma, even forming a dual deity Soma-Rudra. Soma-Rudra is implored in *Ṛgveda* VI, 74 to provide medicines and to drive away all sins. Soma-Rudra shows the ambivalence of the later Śiva: on the one hand he is gracious and helpful, on the other he is vengeful and possesses deadly weapons. Rudra is called a "promoter of the sacrifice"[12] and "priest of two worlds."[13] In some predominantly agricultural rituals Rudra is prominent too.[14]

The *Yajurveda* offers one of the most interesting texts concerning Rudra, the so-called *Śatarudriya*.[15] It displays many features of classical Śaivism: Śiva is described as both terrifying and also as gracious. The hymn constantly switches from one Rudra to many Rudras, from praise to earnest prayer not to do any harm. "Innumerable Rudras are on the face of the earth," the text says, but names given to them are quite often identical with titles given in later Śaivism to Śiva, the only Lord. Apart from names like Nīlakaṇṭha, Śārva, Paśupati, Nīlagrīva, Bhava, and so on, Rudra is described as the one who stretched out the earth, who is immanent in places and objects, in stones, plants, and animals. There is also the paradoxical ascription of contradictory attributes: after being praised as the Great Lord of all beings, he is called "cheat" and "Lord of thieves," he is fierce and terrible and also the source of happiness and delight. The singer asks Śiva-Rudra to turn away his fearful form and approach the worshipper in his auspicious, friendly form.

The *Vrātya* section of the *Atharvaveda*[16] contains hymns that use the well-known Śiva titles *Bhava*, *Bharva*, *Paśupati*, *Rudra*, *Mahādeva* and *Iśāna*.[17] In Vedic ritual, as described in the *Śatapatha Brāhmaṇa*, Rudra is treated differently from the other *devas*. At the end of the sacrifice a handful of straw is offered to him for propitiation; at the end of a meal the leftovers are placed to the north for Rudra. The *Aitareya Brāhmaṇa* states that "Rudra is an embodiment of all the dread forms of whom *devas* are afraid."[18] The bull that is to be sacrificed to him must be killed outside the village.

We find a fully developed *Śiva-Vedānta* system in the *Śvetāśvatara Upaniṣad* a text, which plays a comparable part in Śaivism to that of the *Bhagavadgītā* in Vaiṣṇavism.[19] It rejects at length a large number of different theological opinions, a sign of its rather late date. Śiva is identified with *brahman*. Thus it teaches: "The immortal and imperishable Hara exercises complete control over the perishable *prakṛti* and the powerless *jīva*: the radiant Hara is one alone." Śiva manifests himself in many forms: as *viśva-rūpa* in the universe, as *liṅga-śarīra* in the hearts of all beings, as omnipresent on account of his all-pervasiveness, as *antar-ātman* of the size of a thumb, to be realized by the Yogis. It also says that in reality all beings are Śiva, and it is due to an illusion that people perceive a difference. "One attains peace on realizing that self-effulgent, adorable Lord, the giver of blessings, who, though one, presides over all the various aspects of *prakṛti* and into whom this universe dissolves and in whom it appears in manifold forms."[20]

We can here already notice the trend in Śaivism towards developing a monistic world view, in contrast to the Vaiṣṇavas, who always maintain an essential difference between Viṣṇu and all other beings.

The *Rāmāyaṇa* of Vālmīki, though pertaining primarily to the Vaiṣṇava tradition, mentions several Śiva myths: Śiva destroying Dakṣa's sacrifice, Śiva's marriage with Umā, Śiva drinking the poison, Śiva killing the demon

Andhaka, Śiva destroying Tripura, and Śiva cursing Kaṇḍarpa. All of them have remained vital within Śaivism, and some of them also became the focus of Śaiva theology.

The *Mahābhārata* tells the strange story that Kṛṣṇa was initiated by Śiva and remained his whole life a *Śivabhakta*. It also explains that *Hari* (Viṣṇu) and *Hara* (Śiva) are one and the same and that among the thousand names of Viṣṇu there also are Śiva, Śārva, Sthānu, Iśāna, and Rudra.[21]

In the *Purāṇas* Śiva mythology reaches its fullest development and also its exclusivity: Śiva is the Only Lord, Viṣṇu and Brahmā are inferior to him.[22] Śiva is even described as the killer of Yama, the god of death, and the mantra that celebrates him as the *mṛtyuñjaya*, the victor over death, is used by his devotees to gain liberation.[23]

The celebrated motif of *Śiva Naṭarāja*, the lord of dance, is immortalized in many sculptures and bronzes.[24] The Śiva *avatāras*— twenty-eight of them, the legendary authors of the Śaivite Āgamas—were probably conceived after the Vaiṣṇava model and play a relatively minor role.[25]

Though anthropomorphic images of Śiva are very numerous and very often of high artistic quality, the object of veneration in the temples is usually the amorphous *liṅga*, an image of Śiva's formlessness. *Śiva-rātrī* is the most solemn festivity of the Śaivas, commemorating the graceful appearance of Śiva to a hunter, who inadvertently dropped some dew on a Śiva *liṅga*.[26]

The Śaiva Āgamas detail the mode of worship that has to be followed in Śaiva temples and homes; largely the ritual resembles that followed by the Vaiṣṇavas, except for the fact that Śaivas still observe animal (and occasionally human) sacrifices.[27] From very early times Śaivism has been connected with rigorous asceticism. Yogis are traditionally Śaivas, seeing in Śiva himself the Mahāyogi. Mādhava describes a group called the *Raseśvaris* who had the peculiar habit of consuming mercury in order to build up an immortal and incorruptible body.

## ŚAIVA ORDERS AND SCHOOLS

Śaivism has developed a great number of different worship traditions and schools of thought—the presentation here is restricted to the most important ones: more detailed information is offered in a number of monographs and articles in encylopedias.[28]

The *Paśupatas* are subdivided into numerous sub-groups that share a common philosophy. They consider Lakuliṇ, an *avatāra* of Śiva, their founder and have in their *Paśu-pata-sūtra* a scripture of their own, dealing mainly with ritual. According to this text Śiva taught five subjects, the knowledge of which is essential for the total annihilation of sorrow: *kārya*, the condition of bondage, *kāraṇa*, the lord and liberator, *yoga*, the means to liberation, *vidhi*, the ritual, and *duḥkhānta*, the final liberation. The person in bondage is also called *paśu*, an ox, whose Lord is Śiva, kept in bondage through *pāśa*, a noose formed through illusion, unrighteousness, attachment, and ignorance. In order to free oneself practices like *japa* and meditation are recommended, as well as bathing in ashes, laughing and dancing like a madman, singing, muttering hum, hum, "like the bellowing of a bull,"[29] snoring, trembling, limping, in general behaving not quite normally. This theology insists on the complementarity between one's own efforts and Śiva's gracious help.

The most important of all the Śaiva systems up to the present time is *Śaiva Siddhānta*, "the final truth of Śiva." It is based upon the recognized twenty-eight Āgamas and the teachings of the sixty-three *Nāyanmārs*, the most famous among whom are Appar, Jñānasambhandar, Sundaramūrti, and Manikkavācakar. Meykaṇḍa's *Śiva-jñāna-bodha* has acquired high authority and has often been commented upon.[30]

Śaiva Siddhānta acknowledges three principles: *pati*, *paśu*, and *pāśa*, the Lord, the person, and bondage. In order to gain freedom, four elements are necessary: *vidyā* or knowledge, *krīya* or ritual actions, *yoga* or austerities, and *cārya* or a virtuous way of life. Śiva is the supreme reality: he is greater than the *trimūrti* of Viṣṇu-Brahmā-Rudra and the only eternal being. He has eight qualities, namely, independence, purity, self-knowledge, omniscience, freedom from sin, benevolence, omnipotence, and blissfulness. The most comprehensive terms to circumscribe the essence of Śiva are *sat* and *cit*, being and consciousness. Śiva is immanent in the five elements, in the sun, the moon, and in sentient beings as *aṣṭa-mūrti*. He is male and female and neuter.

According to Śaiva Siddhānta, Śiva cannot have any *avatāras*, because this would involve him in both life and death, which contradicts the very nature of Śiva. He appears in a bodily form as the guru out of his great love for humans to save them from *saṃsāra*. "Śiva is Love" is the most precise description, and Śaiva Siddhānta has only one great theme: the grace of Śiva. Śiva exercises his fivefold activities, *anugraha* or attraction, grace; *tirobhava*, concealment; *samhāra*, taking away, destruction; *sthiti*, preservation; *sṛṣṭi*, creation; through his form of *Sadā-Śiva*, often represented in art.

Bondage is of three kinds: "*Karma*, *māyā*, and *aṇava*, like sprout, bran and husk hide the real nature of the soul and delude it. They cause enjoyment, embodiment, and the state of being the enjoyer."[31] *Māyā* comprises the whole process of evolution and involution. Karma leads to the fruition of heaven and hell, as ordained by Śiva. "Pleasures and pains are the medicines administered by Śiva, the physician, to cure the diseases and delusions caused by *mālā*."[32] *Aṇava*, beginning-less and eternal, is the primary bondage of the souls: if *aṇava* is removed, the souls will be restored to their essential nature as pure spirits. In the *kevala* state the soul's cognitive, conative, and affective functions are entirely thwarted by *aṇava*; in the *sakala* state humans do exert their powers, but only under the influence of *moha*, delusion, *mada*, intoxication, *rāga*, passion, *viṣāda*, depression, *śoṣa*, dryness, *vaicitriya*, distraction, and *haṛsa*, (improper) merriness.

The process of liberation itself is a chain of interlinking conditions. *Dīkṣā*, initiation, is the direct cause of liberation; but *dīkṣā* is not possible without knowledge. Knowledge presupposes yoga; yoga requires ritual acts, and ritual acts are not possible without proper life. There are three different kinds of knowledge: *paśu-jñāna* and *pāśa-jñāna* give only the knowledge of the soul, of words and things. It is only *pati-jñāna* that gives liberation. The way to it leads through the guru's teaching; it is Śiva who appears in the form of a guru, opens the eyes of the devotee, performs the purificatory rites, and removes the obstacles.

Śaiva Siddhāntins emphasize that it is only in a human birth and only as a Śaiva that one has the possibility of putting an end to the cycle of births and deaths. Only a human being can worship Śiva in the five modes essential to liberation: contemplating him with the mind, praising him with the mouth, exerting the body in different ways in his worship. If a human being does not realize liberation in this life, it might be hard to get another chance. The Siddhāntins claim that only *their* faith is *siddhānta*, that is, final truth. All other beliefs and philosophies lead their followers to one of the thirty-six *tattvas*, below Śiva. Ignoring the *siddhānta* would be a great sin and foolishness, and those despising it have to suffer in hell.

Liberation is but the appearance of the hidden *Śivatva* in the soul through *jñāna*: in the free state humans realize their true and original Śiva nature, which was hidden and curtailed through sin. There can also be *jīvanmukti*, full Śiva realization, while still in this physical body. *Jīvanmuktas* are one with Śiva in their innermost being while *prārabhda* of different kinds still works itself out in their bodies: "*Śiva-jñānis* may do any good or bad deed—they remain unaffected by the changes and never leave the feet of the Lord. It is difficult to determine the nature of the *jīvanmuktas*: some of them may be short-tempered, some sweet-tempered, some free from desires, some lustful." One of the more famous examples is Saint Sundaramūrti, "who was free from attachment, though outwardly he seemed to live a life of sensual pleasures." Those, who have achieved *jñāna niṣtha* "knowledge establishment," are beyond good and evil. Engaging in activities, they do not care for the results. They need not practice austerities nor observe any religious duties nor do they have to engage in meditation or wear external signs of their religion. "Coming to have the qualities of children, of mad people, and people possessed by evil spirits, they may even give themselves up to singing and dancing by reason of their ecstasy."[33]

Śiva resides in the soul always, but only the enlightened will consciously live a Śiva life according to his grace. Whatever the enlightened one does is Śiva's deed, be it good or evil. Śaiva Siddhānta knows of seven different degrees of *jīvanmukti*, liberation while still in a body, likening them in their bliss to the sweetness of sugarcane, fruit, milk, honey, candy, sugar, and nectar. It also describes the love of God and love of neighbor as mutually complementary. A person's love for the devotees of Śiva is a sign of love for Śiva. Because Śiva is in all souls, those who love him truly will also love all beings. All the activities of God are ordered toward the liberation of humans. God's essence is it to be "full of grace."

Śrīkaṇṭha's *Śaiva-Vedānta*, classified with the Vedānta systems as *bheda-abheda*, difference-and-no-difference, may be considered as a special form of Śaiva Siddhānta. Śrīkaṇṭha aims at reconciling the Upaniṣads with the Āgamas, quoting extensively from both sources. For him Śiva Nīlakaṇṭha is the symbol for God showing care. He differs slightly from classical Śaiva Siddhānta in his assertion that the liberated ones are completely free and enjoy the same bliss and freedom that Śiva himself enjoys. Thus he says:

> The place of the husband of Umā is like millions of suns, the first, full of all objects of desires, pure, eternal, indestructible. Having attained that celestial place they become free from all miseries, omniscient, capable of going everywhere, pure, full. Further they come to have pure sense organs and become endowed with supreme Lordship. Then again they assume bodies or discard these at will. Those engaged in the pursuit of knowledge and yoga concentration who attain this supreme place, do not return to the frightful earthly existence. The liberated ones have Śiva as their souls and shine forth with Śiva in all places at all times.[34]

Despite the similarity in conception to the Vaiṣṇava Vedāntists, Śrīkaṇṭha proves to be a staunch sectarian Śaiva: liberation begins only after the souls have crossed the river *virajā*, the boundary between *Viṣṇu-loka* and *Śiva-loka*. Viṣṇu's heaven is still within *saṃsāra*. Beyond *Viṣṇu-loka* is *Śiva-loka*, where the soul finds final liberation and fulfillment.

*Kashmīr Śaivism*, the most important North-Indian school of Śaivism, also called *Śaiva-Advaita*, *Trika*, and so forth, is represented today by only a few living masters.[35] The earliest writings belong to the eighth or ninth centuries, but the roots of the system may be several centuries older. Its two main branches, Spaṇḍa-śāstra and Pratyābhijñā, have much in common. Some of the most respected names in Indian philosophy, like Abhinavagupta, are associated with Kashmīr Śaivism, which must have been quite popular in former centuries, if the extensive treatment accorded to it in the *Śiva Purāṇa* is any indication.[36] Whereas in most other systems *adhikāra*, the fulfillment of certain qualifications, is important, here it is stated explicitly that no prerequisites are asked for from students wanting to enter this school. Since all reality, Śiva and Śakti, and their union, is mirrored in one's own *ātman*, liberation is introspection and recognition of this mirrored image—an idea that is expressed in the very name of the system. Since one of the qualities of Śiva is *ānanda*, bliss, one also acquires Śiva's blissfulness by recognizing one's own Śiva-nature. The follower of this system aims at becoming a slave of Śiva, "one who is being given everything according to the pleasure of the Lord."[37] The reason for human unhappiness lies in the five hindrances through which Śiva-nature is restricted: the All becomes an atom; the universal, omniscient, eternal, blissful Śiva becomes a finite, ignorant, limited, and unhappy *puruṣa*. One is bound by *karma*, *māyā* and *aṇava*—terms we encountered before. Bondage is a work of *śakti*—*śakti* also helps to liberate a person. In individuals *śakti* is present as *Kuṇḍalinī*, represented as a coiled, dormant snake. The innermost core of a human being is *caitanya*, consciousness, identical with Śiva. *Śakti-patā*, descent of *śakti*, is the advent of grace. Though under the influence of bondage, the five essential activities of Śiva are at work, developing a person toward "becoming Śiva." The state of awakening while still in the body is called *samaveśa*, a "contemplative experience of unity consciousness, in which the entire universe is experienced as identical with the self." As Abhinavagupta says: "It is Śiva himself of unimpeded will and pellucid consciousness who is ever sparkling in my heart. It is his highest *Śakti* herself that is ever playing at the edge of my senses. The entire world gleams as the wondrous delight of pure I-consciousness. Indeed I know not what the sound "world" is supposed to refer to."[38]

The stage of consciousness that the Pratyābhijñā system claims to achieve is beyond the *turīya* of the Upaniṣads and therefore called *turyātīta*, divided into "broken" and "unbroken" consciousness. The means to reach this stage is the specific yoga of the school that has much in common with later Kuṇḍalinī yoga.

The youngest among the major Śaiva schools is *Vīra-śaivism*, "heroic Śiva religion," which is closely connected with the name of Basava.[39] The tradition itself seems to go back to a more remote time about which however, we have no reliable information. Under Basava's inspiration Vīraśaivism developed into a vigorous missionary movement. Vīraśaivas are recognizable by the *liṅga* around their neck, which they always wear and which for them is the real presence of Śiva. It is worn in order to make the body a temple of Śiva. As the sources of their religion they recognize the twenty-eight Āgamas and the Tamil Nāyanmārs, as well as later writers. They have a Vedāntasūtra commentary of their own in Śrīpati's *Śrīkara Bhāṣya*.[40] The system is also called *Śakti-viśiṣṭādvaita*, the essence of which is: "There is no duality between the soul and the Lord, each qualified by *Śakti*." The *jīva* is the body of Śiva; *Paraśiva* is both the material and the instrumental cause of the universe. *Śakti* resides eternally in *Parama-Śiva*: it is the creative principle, also called *māyā*. At creation all things issue forth from *Śakti*; at the time of the destruction of the world all return into it and remain there in a seminal form. *Jīva* is in fact a part of Śiva; on account of his ignorance he imagines himself to be different from him. *Bhakti*, which is a part of Śiva's own *śakti*, is the means of final deliverance, subdivided into many stages and steps. Vīraśaivas lay great stress on rituals, which are considered indispensable.

*Pañcācāra*, "fivefold worship," comprises daily worship of the *liṅga*, moral and decent life and work, amity towards all Liṅgāyats, humility, and active struggle against those who despise Śiva or treat his devotees badly.[41]

*Aṣṭavāraṇa*, the eight-fold armour, comprises obedience towards the guru, wearing a *liṅga*, worship of Śiva ascetics as incarnations of Śiva, sipping water

Photo 20. Śiva Tāṇḍava: Khajurāho

in which the feet of a guru have been bathed, offering food to a guru, smearing ashes on one's body, wearing a string of *rudrākṣa* beads and reciting the mantra: *Śivāya nāmaḥ*.[42] Whereas for the ordinary Vīraśaiva release is the result of the faithful observance of all these commandments, Śrīpati introduces a Vedāntic element into the faith, teaching that in the end, through worship and meditation, full oneness with Śiva is attained.

Vīraśaivas are social reformers and constitute quite a vigorous community today in the state of Karṇāṭaka. They have abolished caste differences and are generally quite progressive in economic and social matters. Also, instead of burning their dead as do most other Hindus, they bury them.

Almost from the beginning of Indian history severe austerities and self-mortification have been connected with Śiva and Śaivism. Yoga itself, as expounded by Patañjali, is traced back to the teaching of Śiva, the *mahāyogi*.

## ŚAIVA SAINTS AND SINGERS

Śaivism has brought forth a large number of popular saints, of which the historical sixty-three Nāyanmārs of South India are probably the best known.[43] Maṇikkavācakar is the author of the celebrated *Tiruvācakam*. He suffered persecution for his faith and Śiva appeared in person to him, an event that he celebrates in a song: "O highest Truth, you came to the earth and revealed your feet to me and became the embodiment of grace." His poetry is an ardent appeal for Śiva's grace. Thus he sings:

> Madman clad in elephant's skin, Madman with a hide for his garb.
> Madman, that ate the poison, Madman on the burning-ground fire,
> Madman that chose even me for his own.
> Whether I adore you or revile you, I crave your forgiveness for my evil deeds, which I rue.
> Leave me not, O you who took mercy on the gods and drank the poison in order to save them. How much more do I stand in need of your loving mercy![44]

In a beautiful stanza Maṇikkavācakar describes the perfection he is hoping for:

> I shall raise my hands in prayer to you; I shall clasp your holy feet and call on your name. I shall melt like wax before the flame, incessantly calling out 'My Beloved Father.' I shall cast off this body and enter the celestial city of Śivapura. I shall behold your effulgent glory. In joyful bliss shall I join the society of the true devotees. Then I shall look up to hear you say with your beauteous lips: 'Fear not!' The assurance of your all-embracing love alone can set my soul at ease and peace.[45]

Appar became a martyr for Śiva's sake. Sambandhar vehemently fought the Jainas and Bauddhas as enemies of Śiva. Tirumular wanted to reconcile in

Photo 21. Śiva Bhairava: (Maharashtra) [Heras Institute]

his songs the Vedas and the Āgamas.[46] Sundaramūrti is a favourite with the Tamils even today.

From relatively early times there had also been certain rather unsavory Śaiva sects with "horrible, almost demoniacal practices, which form a ghastly picture of the wild aberrations of the human intellect and spirit."[47] They took their origin from the worship of the Rudra nature of Śiva; though not completely extinct, they play a minor part in today's Śaivism. The most notorious are the Kāpālikas and the Kālamukhas. Kāpālikas worship Bhairava, the terrible form of Śiva, and eat disgusting stuff; they drink wine and are known to have performed human sacrifices. Kālamukhas believe that they may attain salvation by eating their food from a human skull, smearing their bodies with the ashes of the dead and also eating those ashes. But those extremists should not unduly darken the image of Śaivism, which is generally characterized by serious asceticism and genuine devotion, combined with a high degree of sophisticated speculation.

While the popularity of Śaivism in India was never seriously in doubt since it found acceptance by Vedic orthodoxy and while Śaivism provided the background for much of India's speculative theology—from the *Śvetāśvatara Upaniṣad* to Kashmīr Śaivism, from Śaṅkara to Śaiva Siddhānta—the intense interest for Śaivism among Western scholars is something new.

Śaivism used to be the form of Hinduism upon which most abuse was heaped by early Western observers: imagine the worship of the phallus, the ritual slaughtering of animals, the frenzied dancing! By contrast, contemporary Western scholars look with much more sympathy and understanding upon this expression of Hinduism. Stella Kramrisch, whose *The Presence of Śiva* is the undisputed masterwork of its genre, a veritable summa of Śaivite mythology and theology, was reputedly initiated into a Śaiva community.[48] Also A. Daniélou whose *Hindu Polytheism* is a monument of insight, became a member of a Śaivite *sampradāya* while in Banares. Wendy Doniger (O'Flaherty) has devoted much of her life's work to the study of Śiva.[49] A Śaiva Siddhānta mission is operating in the West; it seems to be quite successful in Australia. An American convert to Śaivism, who founded under his adopted name Śivaya Subramuniyaswami a Śaivite monastery in Hawaii, did much to propagate a kind of reformed Śaivism through his books.[50] As founder-editor of *Hinduism Today*, an illustrated monthly, he became the single-most advocate of Hinduism outside India. Kashmīr Śaivism has attracted the attention of Western scholars, especially after Gopi Krishna introduced its more popular teachings to the West, who aroused the interest also of the philosopher-scientist C. F. von Weizsäcker.[51]

CHAPTER SEVENTEEN

# Devī

## *The Divine Mother*

The Mother is the consciousness and force of the Divine, or, it may be said, she is the Divine in its consciousness force. The *Īśwara* as Lord of the cosmos does come out of the Mother who takes her place beside him as the cosmic *Śakti*—the cosmic *Īśwara* is one aspect of the Divine.

—A. Ghose, *Śrī Aurobindo on the Mother*

It is in the very nature of the *bhaktimārga* to elevate the deity to whom worship is rendered to the highest position in the universe and to identify the object of one's praise with the principle of creation and salvation. Followers of the Goddess, the Śāktas, adore Devī and give to her all the attributes of divinity, as the following hymn shows. This *stotra* is recited every year at the time of *Durgā-pūjā* by millions of Hindus, especially in Bengal. Brahmā addresses the Goddess in these words:

> By you this universe is borne and by you this world has been created; by you it is protected and you, O Devī, shall consume it at the end.
>
> You are the Great Knowledge and the Great Illusion; you are Great Power and Great Memory, Great Delusion, the Great Devī and the Great Asurī.
>
> You are Primordial Matter, you are the ground of the three principles, you are the Great Night of the end of the world and you are the Great Darkness of delusion.
>
> You are the goddess of good fortune, the ruler, modesty, and intelligence with knowledge, bashfulness, nourishment, contentment, tranquillity, and forbearance.

> Armed with the sword, the spear, the club, the discus, the conch, the bow, with arrows, slings, and iron mace you are terrible and also more pleasing than everything else and exceedingly beautiful.
>
> You are above all, the supreme Mistress. You are the *śakti*, the power of all things, sentient and others; you are the soul of everything. Who is capable of praising you who have given form to all of us, to Viṣṇu, Śiva, and myself?[1]

We have encountered the Goddess before as the consort of Viṣṇu or Śiva; for the Śāktas she is the real Ultimate Power; the other great gods are merely her instruments and servants. This chapter intends to sketch some of the more important myths concerning Devī, and to give some idea of the highly technical literature known as Tantras, which are considered by the Śāktas as scriptures in addition to the universally accepted *śruti*.[2]

## DEVĪ MYTHS AND FEASTS

Devī mythology appears fully developed in the Purāṇas associated with Śāktism—all of them *Upapurāṇas*, indicating their comparatively late origin. The most important is the *Devī Bhāgavata Purāṇa*, a treasury of Devī lore and speculation.[3] Some of the *Mahāpurāṇas* contain important sections concerning Devī, which may be later interpolations, as for example the famous *Devī-māhātmya*, which forms part of the Śaivite *Mārkaṇḍeya Purāṇa*. The Devī Purāṇas themselves very often restructure otherwise popular Viṣṇu or Śiva myths in such a way as to show the supremacy of the Goddess.[4]

The most prominent and most popular myth connected with Devī is her killing of the buffalo demon (see Figure 17.1). It is narrated in several Purāṇas, with significant differences, and even in village religion it seems to figure quite prominently.[5] It may in fact constitute an ancient myth connected with an ancient ritual.[6]

The *Mārkaṇḍeya Purāṇa* (Ch. 81) reports how for a hundred years *devas* and *asuras* fought against each other. The *devas* were defeated and Mahiṣāsura, the buffalo demon, became the Lord of heaven. The defeated *devas* approached Śiva and Viṣṇu for help, who had to concede that they were powerless against the Great Demon.

On hearing the voices of the *devas*, Viṣṇu's anger knew no bounds, nor did Śiva's, and their faces became distorted. A great light sprang from Viṣṇu's countenance, full of anger, and also from the faces of Śiva and Brahmā. This light merged into one, bright as a burning mountain, filling the whole universe with flames. This powerful blast piercing the three worlds took the shape of a woman: Śiva's splendor became her face, Yama's her hair, Viṣṇu's her arms, Candra's her breasts, Indra's her body, Varuṇa's her thighs, the Earth's her hips, Brahmā's her feet, Sūrya's her toes, Vasu's her fingers, Kubera's her nose, Prajāpati's her teeth; through Agni's light her three eyes took form.

Figure 17.1. The Goddess slaying the buffalo demon

Śiva drew out a trident from his own weapon, Viṣṇu a discus from his, Varuṇa gave her a conch shell, Agni a spear, Maruta a bow and quivers filled with arrows, Indra a thunderbolt and a bell, Yama the staff of death, Varuṇa a rope, Brahmā a string of beads and a water vessel, Sūrya the rays of the sun, Kāla a sword and a shield. The heavens were filled and trembled with her incredibly powerful and terrible roar, all the world was in an upheaval, the sea was in turmoil. Devī's "loud roar with a defying laugh" is the sign for the beginning of the battle between Devī and Mahiṣāsura. With the numerous weapons, which she carries, she kills thousands of demons. Before Mahiṣasura falls, all the demon generals are killed.

> Mahiṣāsura terrified the troops of the Goddess with his own buffalo form: some he killed by a blow of his muzzle, some by stamping with his hooves, some by the lashes of his tail, and others by the thrusts of his horns, some by his speed, some by his bellowing and wheeling movement, some by the blast of his breath. Having laid low her army, Mahiṣāsura rushed to slay the lion of Mahadevī. This enraged Aṃbikā. Mahiṣāsura, great in valor, pounded the surface of the earth with his hooves in rage, tossed up high mountains with his horns and bellowed terribly. Crushed by his wheeling the earth disintegrated, and lashed by his tail, the sea overflowed all around. Pierced by his swaying horns the clouds broke into fragments. Cast up by the blast of his breath, mountains fell down from the sky in hundreds.

This description of the evil embodied in Mahiṣāsura provides the backdrop for the appreciation of the greatness of Devī's deed, which saved the universe from destruction. First the Goddess uses the noose to capture Mahiṣāsura. He sheds his buffalo form. The Devī uses her sword to cut down the lion-form, which he assumes. Then the demon appears as a human being. Devī assails him with bow and arrows. The demon assumes an elephant form, which the Goddess attacks with her mace. Finally the demon assumes again his original buffalo form. Now the final battle takes place. "Enraged, Caṇḍikā, the Mother of the Universe, quaffed a divine drink again and again and laughed so that her eyes became red."

She now kills the buffalo demon, pressing down his neck with her foot and striking him with her spear, finally cutting off his head with her sword. Thus the salvation of *devas* and humans has been accomplished and Devī receives due praise as the resort of all, as *Durgā*, the boat that carries men across the ocean of worldly existence, as *Vidyā*, which is the cause of liberation, as *Śrī*, who has taken her abode in the heart of Viṣṇu, and as *Gaurī*, who has established herself with Śiva. The *devas* ask her to grant delivery from all evil whenever necessary. Devī fulfills her promise by appearing again and again to slay demons who are too powerful to be overcome by Viṣṇu or Śiva. The result of Devī's victory is cosmic relief: "When that evil-natured one was slain the universe became happy and regained perfect peace and the sky grew clear. Flaming portent clouds that were in evidence before became tranquil and the rivers kept within courses. Favorable winds began to blow and the sun became very brilliant. In the final hymn the *devas* praise Devī as the Mother of the Universe, the cause of final emancipation, the giver of enjoyment and liberation, the one who removes all sufferings, who frees from all fear and from all evils.

Devī then prophesies her repeated incarnations in different ages as Vindhyavāsinī, the one who wells in the Vindhya mountains, as Raktadantā, the one with red teeth, as *Śatākṣī*, the hundred eyed, as Śakambharī, the provider of vegetables, as Durgādevī, the goddess who is difficult to approach, as Bhīmadevī, the terrible goddess, and as Bhrāhmaradevī, the bumblebee goddess. All these names are titles under which the Goddess is still worshipped in India. To those who keep her feasts and praise her, Devī promises protection, riches, and victory.

> The chanting and hearing of the story of my manifestations removes sin and grants perfect health and protection from evil spirits. One who is in a lonely spot in a forest or is surrounded by forest fire, or who is encircled by robbers in a desolate spot, or who is captured by enemies, or who under the orders of a wrathful king is sentenced to death, or has been imprisoned, or who is tossed about in a boat by a tempest in the vast sea, or is in the most terrible battle under showers of weapons, or who is amid all kinds of dreadful troubles, or who is afflicted with pain—such a person, on remembering this story of mine, will be saved from all straits.[7]

Countless Hindus recite this hymn of the greatness of the Goddess every year at the time of the great *Durgā-pūjā*, the greatest feast of Bengal.[8] It also carries reminiscences of a time in which the structure of society was matriarchal: all the girls who have married away from home, gather at their homes and celebrate *Durgā-pūjā* with their own parents. Statues of paper pulp and plaster, representing Devī in the act of killing *Mahiṣāsura*, are placed in public places and in homes; special local committees are formed for the consecration and worship of these images. Processions and a series of individual feasts are celebrated for eight days; on the ninth day *Durgā-pūjā* proper commences. It ends with interminable processions to the sea, the Ganges, or another river nearby: the figures of Devī are thrown into the water after Devī has departed from them.

It is quite impossible to bring all the different names and forms under which the Goddess appears in the Purāṇas into one system. By and large the various names are local varieties of Devī. One text in the Devī Purāṇa clearly states that Devī is worshipped as Maṅgalā in the region between the Vindhyas and the Mālāyas, as Jayantī in the coastal area between Vindhyas and Kurukṣetra, as Nandā between Kurukṣetra and the Himālayas, as Kalikā, Tāra, and Umā in the mountains, as Kālarātrī in the Sākya mountains, as Aṃbā in Candhamadanā, as Ujjainī in Ujjain, and as Bhadrakālī in Vaideha.[9] Similar to Viṣṇu and Śiva *avatāras*, Śāktism has also developed the notion of Devī *avatāras* for different ages.[10]

वीरभद्र Vīrabhadra | १ ब्राह्मी Brāhmī | २ माहेश्वरी Maheśvarī | ३ कौमारी Kaumārī

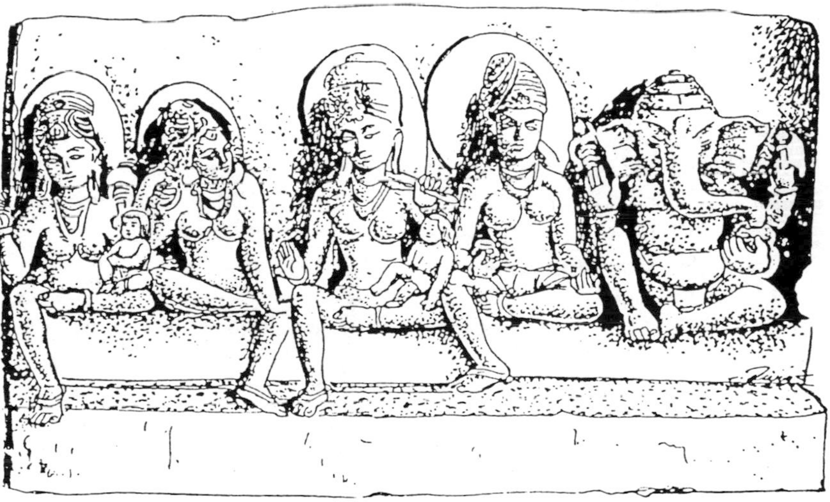

४ वैष्णवी Vaisnavī | ५ वाराही Vārāhi | ६ ऐन्द्री Aindrī | ७ चामुन्डा; Cāmundā | गणपती Gaṇapatī

Figure 17.2. *Saptamātrikas*: The Seven Mothers

The Mātrikās, the divine Mothers, are a class apart, worshipped as a group, especially in the villages, as protectors against all kinds of ills, and particularly those that befall children. The worship of Manasā, the snake-goddess, and of Śītalā, the goddess of smallpox, is very widespread. The *Kālikā Purāṇa* has a peculiar system of differentiating the Goddess according to the different parts of her body. It describes how Satī, without having been invited, attends Dakṣa's (her father's) sacrifice, how she is hurt by Dakṣa's insult of her husband Śiva, and how she voluntarily gives up her life. Śiva then takes Sati's body on his shoulders. Brahma, Viṣṇu, and Sanaiścara enter into it, cut it into pieces and let these fall to earth. Wherever one of the fifty-one parts of her body touched the earth a sanctuary of Devī would be founded, called *Śakta-Pītha*, named after the particular limb of her body.[11]

## DEVĪ IN THE TANTRAS

It is in the Tantras that the Goddess comes to occupy the supreme place: according to the Tantras, *brahman*, being neuter and incapable of creation, produced Śiva and Śakti. Śiva is the cause of bondage, śakti the cause of liberation. She is the life power of the universe; without her, who is symbolized in the letter *i*, *Śiva* is *Śava*, a dead corpse.[12] A large number of texts bear the title Tantras; numerous Purāṇas also contain sections (probably added after the 8th century CE) that are unmistakably Tantric. Tantricism is not restricted to Hinduism only. Possibly Hindu Tantras have influenced the development of Buddhist Mahāyāna cults connected with the goddess Tārā. Tārā, the "one who saves," is the personification of Buddha's kindness. According to the Tantras, people in our Kali age have become too weak to practice any other kind of religion than the worship of the Goddess, who offers salvation without demanding austerities.

Tāntrikas distinguish three *mārgas*, subdivided into seven stages altogether. The first three are identical with practices found among all Hindus: common worship, devotion to Viṣṇu and meditation on Śiva. From the fourth onward we have the peculiar Śākta-Tantra forms of worship. *Dakṣinācāra* "right-handed worship," consists of worshipping Devī as the Supreme Goddess with Vedic rites, including a *japa* with the name of the Goddess on the *Mahāśaṅkhamālā*. *Vāmācāra*, "left-handed worship," consists of the "worship with *cakras*" in which the five *m*'s play a great role.[13] As one author says, "it requires proper training at the hands of a *guru* and the acquisition of the necessary courage to disregard social conventions about sexual purity, to defy taboos about food and drink and to look upon all women as manifestations of Śakti and all males representatives of Śiva."[14]

The next stage is *Siddhāntācāra*, "perfect worship," in which the aforementioned practices are no longer kept a secret, because for the realized one there is no longer any distinction between pure and impure, good or bad. The highest stage is reached with *Kulācāra*, the "divine way of life," when

Photo 22. Lakṣmī: Khajurāho

> the aspirant transcends the likes and dislikes of earthly life like God himself to whom all things are equal. Pity and cruelty are equally meaningless in an ultimate reference and so too are approved and unapproved conduct. Just as one of the Upaniṣads has said that to one who has attained the knowledge of Brahman no sin attaches for any kind of antinomian act, so also the Tantras place the Kaula above every moral judgment and put no prohibitions and restraints in his way as being unnecessary for one who has pierced the veil of space and time, process and differentiation. A Kaula roams in all *ācāras* at will—being at heart a Śākta, outwardly a Śaiva and in social gatherings a Vaiṣṇava. He sees himself in all things and all things in himself.[15]

*Dīkṣā* becomes of utmost importance in Tantricism: a special initiation is necessary for anyone who wishes to enter the Tantric way. It is open to all without distinction of caste or sex, but even a Brahmin has to apply for it, otherwise he is not entitled to take part in the Tantric mysteries. Terrible punishment is in store for those who invite anyone not initiated. The purification of the *pañca mā-kāras* plays a great role. The Tāntrikas are aware that the enjoyment of the five *ms* involves the violation of all moral laws. They are the great temptations of ordinary men. Tantricism is designed as a spiritual homoeopathy: by the very poison of the snake the snakebite is cured. But the administering of this antidote must take place in a controlled way under an expert physician. The *pañca mā-kāras* have to be purified and are to be taken only under the guidance of a guru, lest they devour the unthinking.[16] The purification takes place by means of mantras whose meaning is clear only to the initiated. Before partaking of any of the *ms* the *sādhaka* has to recite the mantra—only then is the *mā-kāra* a sacrament and not a sin.

One of the most conspicuous elements of Tāntricism is the use of the *yantra* (see Figure 17.3). The *yantra* is the symbol of the Goddess and upon it are inscribed the letters of the alphabet, or short monosyllabic mantras, which constitute the mantra- or *śabda*-body of the Goddess.[17] The design as such is intended to focus on the center point, which is formed by the very essence of the Goddess, usually symbolized with a dot and the sign *śrī*. It is situated in a system of interlocking triangles, forming a polygonal (6 to 14) pattern. The upward pointing triangle stands for Śiva, identified with *puruṣa*, the downward pointing triangle for śakti or *prakṛti*. They are encircled by time. On lotus petals within the rims of concentric wheels are inscribed the letters of the alphabet and *bīja-mantras*, "seed-spells," identical with certain aspects of the divinity. The whole system is surrounded by two walls with four gates; one at each cardinal point. Again, the gates are connected with major manifestations of the Goddess, with seed mantras and *mudrās*, that is, gestures accompanying the recitation of mantras. The gates, as well as the corners of the walls, are fortified with the *siddhis*, miraculous yogic powers. The idea behind it all is that the devotee is supposed to choose one aspect of the Goddess as *Iṣṭā*: through this "door" one enters the wall that separates the profane world from

Figure 17.3. *Śrī Yantra*

the realm of worship, using as vehicle the appropriate *mudrā* and mantra and acquiring the super-sensory power through the signs on the lotus petals, as an expression of the deity, until one finally realizes the Goddess in her own nature as the inmost core of all beings. There one's attention remains fixed, because one's whole search has found its goal.[18]

The identification of śakti with *prakṛti*, with "matter" rather than with "spirit," has one further implication: the body is the seat of the divinity and that too expresses itself in the form of worship and meditation. The fifty letters of the alphabet constitute the body of the Goddess as well as that of the worshipper. Through *nyāsa* the worshipper places the letters upon different parts of the body, transforming it, limb by limb, into a divine one. In most forms of tantric worship the awakening of the Kuṇḍalinī *śakti* plays a great role—again demonstrating the close connection between physiology and metaphysics in Śāktism. Śakti is supposed to lie dormant, coiled up like a snake at the base of the spine: through Tantric yoga she is awakened and sent through the six *cakras* or nerve centres[19] up through the spinal cord into the lotus with the thousand petals, situated above the base of the nose, where śakti meets with Śiva. Their blissful union there is at the same time liberation and supreme joy for the devotee.

According to Tantric physiology the human body contains thirty-five million *nāḍīs*, conceived as fine tubular canals through which śakti is moving. Of these, fourteen are of primary importance. Three of these, *Idā*, *Piṅgalā* and *Suṣumnā*, constitute the central complex. *Suṣumnā* runs through the hollow of the spinal cord. Fire, sun, and moon are associated with it as its *guṇas*. On its sides lie *Idā* and *Piṅgalā*. *Ida* encircles *Suṣumnā* on the left and ends in the left nostril; *Piṅgalā* forms its right counterpart. *Idā* is of a bright hue and contains "the liquid of immortality"; *Piṅgalā* is red and contains "the liquid of death." The three main *nāḍīs* are also identified with the Ganges, the Yamunā, and the Sarasvatī, the three principal holy rivers of India identified with forms of Devī.

The *cakras* correspond to *yantras* in all their details. Thus *mūladhāra*, the first of the *cakras*, lying at the base of the spine, the root of *Suṣumnā* and the resting place of *Kuṇḍalini*, is depicted as a triangle encircled by an orb with four lotus petals, on which the syllables *vaṃ*, *śaṃ*, *ṣaṃ*, *saṃ* are written. In the center of the lotus lies the *śyaṃbhu liṁga* of a rust-brown color. There is *citra nāḍī*, a tube through which Devī descends and closes the *brahman* door. Inside the fiery red triangle that encloses the *linga* is *kaṇḍarpa vāyu*, the "wind of the love-god," and outside a yellow spot, called *pṛthvī maṇḍala*, the place of the *bīja-mantra laṃ*.

The next *cakra* is *svādhiṣṭhāna*, a six-petalled lotus at the base of the sexual organ; above it is *Maṇi-pura*, the jewel city, a ten-petalled golden lotus in the navel. In the region of the heart is *anāhaṭa cakra*, a deep-red lotus with twelve petals; above it, at the base of the throat, is *viśuddha cakra*, the dwelling place of the goddess of speech, a lotus with sixteen petals. Between the eyebrows we have *ājñā-cakra*, a two-petalled lotus, also called *paramakula* or *mukta-triveni*, because here the three main *nāḍīs* separate. This is the place of the *bīja-mantra* OM and the dwelling place of the three main *guṇas*. Here dwell Para-Śiva in the form of a swan and Kālī-śakti. Brahmā, Viṣṇu and Śiva are in the three corners of the triangle within the lotus. Above this is *manas-cakra* and *soma-cakra*, with sixteen petals. These are *kṛpā*, grace; *mṛdutā*, sweetness; *dhairya*, firmness; *vairāgya*, renunciation; *dhṛti*, constancy; *sampat*, wealth; *hasyā*, gaiety; *romañcā*, enthusiasm; *vinaya*, discipline; *dhyāna*, meditation; *susthiratā*, relaxation; *gaṃbhīrya*, seriousness; *udyamā*, effort; *akṣobhya*, imperturbability; *audārya*, generosity; and *ekāgratā*, one-pointedness. Above this *cakra* is the *Nirālaṃbanāpurī*, the city without support, wherein the yogis behold the radiant *Īśvara*. Above it is *praṇava*, luminous as a flame; above this is the white crescent of *nāda* and above this the dot *biṇḍu*, forming the altar for the *paramahaṃsa* who in turn provides the cushion for the guru's feet. The body of the swan is *jñāna-māyā*, knowledge-and-illusion, the wings are *āgama* and *nigama*, the scriptures, its feet are Śiva and śakti, the beak is *praṇava*, the eyes and the throat are *kāma-kāla*. The supreme *cakra* is the thousand-petalled lotus, which is the dwelling place of the First Cause, *Śiva-sthāna* for the Śaivas, *Devī-sthāna* for the Śāktas. Here shine the sun of illumination and the sun of darkness; each petal of the lotus contains all the letters of the alphabet and whatever appears in the world is represented here in its nonmanifest form.

While the Kuṇḍalinī śakti moves upward, it assumes all the deities and qualities inherent in the different *cakras*, thus becoming "everything." Devī is ultimately identical with *brahman*—*brahman* not conceived as supreme spirit but as supreme matter, or better, as life-force. Most of the Tantric literature, including the hymns, is written in *saṃdhyā-bhāṣā*, "twilight-style," which has a double meaning. Only the initiated are able to grasp the true, spiritual meaning.

## DEVĪ WORSHIP AND DEVĪ PHILOSOPHY

Devī-worship differs sharply in its two main branches, left-handed and right-handed Śāktism. The latter could be described as Devī *bhakti*, similar other forms of *bhakti*, except that instead of Viṣṇu or Śiva, the name of the Goddess is invoked. Left-hand practices are even today surrounded by secrecy: sexual mysteries and human sacrifices are associated with it—a combination that was not restricted to the barbaric gangs of the Thags, but also found its way into the holy books of Śāktism. The *Kālikā Purāṇa* describes in great detail the ritual of a human sacrifice, which was followed in some temples of Devī as a regular weekly rite.[20] Even now the Indian dailies report from time to time cases of both human sacrifice and self-immolation in honor of the Goddess.

In former times the Śāktas did not attribute any importance to pilgrimages, since the union of Śiva and Śakti was found in one's own body. But later on the fifty-one śakti *pīṭhas* came to be recognized as centers of pilgrimage; each has its own legends and promises of gain and merit in this world and the next.[21] Assam whose old name is Kāmarūpa has been the centre of Śaktism as far back as our knowledge of it goes. The most famous of the Assamese temples, Kāmākhyā near Guvahatī, is the most important of the *śakti-pithas*, being the place where the *yoni* of Devī fell down, which is worshipped in the form of a cleft rock under the title Kameśvarī. Reportedly even now both right-hand and left-hand rituals are performed in this temple, and animals are slaughtered at its altars.[22]

Devī worship intensifies in times of epidemics, which are seen as signs of her wrath for being neglected. She is then appeased by the sacrifice of buffaloes, pigeons, and goats. Devī is also invoked if someone has been bitten by a snake or otherwise shows signs of poisoning.[23]

Much of the philosophy of Śāktism forms an integral part of certain schools of Śaivism. Śiva and Pārvatī are considered to be "world parents": their

Photo 23. Kālī: Bengal [Heras Institute]

mutual dependence is so great that one cannot be without the other. In the figure of *Śiva ardhanārī*, Śiva and his consort are combined into one being manifesting a dual aspect. It is often only a matter of emphasis whether a certain philosophy is called Śaiva or Śākta. The roots of this thinking may be traced back to the sources of Vedic religion.[24] Fully developed Tantric philosophy is characterized by its acceptance of the material world as the basic reality and its emphasis on the real existence of *māyā*. Śakti is often called *ādya*, or *mūla-prakṛti*, primeval matter (associating *matter* as the Latin word does, with *mother*!) and *mahā-māyā*, the great illusion. An important Tantric text, the *Tripura Rahasya*, explicitly says:

> Do not conclude that there is no such thing as the world. Such thinking is imperfect and defective. Such a belief is impossible. One who tries to negate the whole world by the mere act of thought brings it into existence by that very act of negation. Just as a city reflected in a mirror is not a reality but exists as a reflection, so also this world is not a reality in itself but is consciousness all the same. This is self-evident. This is perfect knowledge.[25]

At the same time it is not possible to classify Śaktism proper under any of the other Vedāntic systems. The *Mahānirvāṇa Tantra* calls it *dvaitādvaita vivarjita*, freed from both dualism and monism. For Śāktism the fetters that bind humans are neither illusory, as the Advaitins claim, nor are they pure evil to be removed from the *ātman*, as the Dvaitins attempt to do. The imperfections are the very means to perfect freedom. The oneness of *bhukti* and *mukti*, of the enjoyment that binds to the world and the renunciation that frees, of *māyā* and *vidyā*, of illusion and knowledge, are characteristics of Śākta thought. Thus the *Tripurā Rahasya* declares: "There is no such thing as bondage or liberation. There is no such thing as the seeker and the means for seeking anything. Part-less, nondual conscious energy, *Tripurā* alone pervades everything. She is knowledge and ignorance, bondage and liberation too. She is also the means for liberation. This is all one has to know."[26]

The metaphysical principle behind this teaching is the realization that the body is not evil, but the incarnation and manifestation of Śiva-śakti, taking part in this divine play. In poison there are healing qualities, if rightly applied by a wise physician. In the body, seemingly the prison of the spirit, lies the coiled-up energy that enables a person to reach absolute freedom. The awakening of the Kuṇḍalinī śakti is only partly understandable through theory: it is primarily a practice, requiring the supervision of those already enlightened in order that no harm should come to the *sādhaka*. Certain stages are critical and more than once it has happened that novices have developed serious physical and psychic or mental illnesses as a result of practicing Kuṇḍalinī yoga without proper guidance. This is not due to any superstitious belief in a magical intervention of the Goddess, but simply and truly based on experience: the system of Kuṇḍalinī yoga as a psychophysical realization undoubtedly has repercussions on the nervous system, which can also be observed clinically.

## NEW DEVELOPMENTS IN ŚĀKTISM

Historically, the development of Śaktism as an organized form of religion with a theology of its own came after the development of Śaivism and Vaiṣṇavism. Today almost all schools of Hinduism have strong elements of Śāktism blended with their teaching. Rāmakṛṣṇa Paramahamsa, the great Bengalī saint whose name is connected with one of the most vigorous neo-Hindu movements, was the priest of Kālī at the Dakṣineśvara temple near Calcutta. He had frequent visions of the Divine Mother and spent countless hours in a trance before her image. Yet he did not accept the *vāmācāra* as a reputable way. Asked about certain groups of Śāktas he answered:

> Why should we hate them? Theirs is also a way to God, though it is unclean. A house may have many entrances—the main entrance, the back door, and the gate for the *bhaṅgi* who comes to sweep the unclean places of the house. These cults are like this door. It does not really matter by which door one enters; once inside the house, all reach the same place. Should one imitate these people or mix with them? Certainly not![27]

Today among the numerous Śāktas there are still followers of the left-hand way, who worship the cruel and horrible aspect of the Goddess. But there are also philosophers like Aurobindo Ghose who find in Śāktism the basis of a religion for our age, in which life and matter are accepted as reality and not shunned as illusion. As V. S. Agrawala writes:

> Mother Earth is the deity of the new age. The *kalpa* of Indra-Agni and Śiva-Viṣṇu are no more. The modern age offers its salutations to Mother Earth whom it adores as the super-goddess. The physical boundaries of the Mother Land stretch before our eyes but her real self is her cultural being which has taken shape in the course of centuries through the efforts of her people. Mother Earth is born of contemplation. Let the people devote themselves truthfully to the Mother Land whose legacy they have received from the ancients. Each one of us has to seek refuge with her. Mother Earth is the presiding deity of the age: let us worship her. Mother Earth lives by the achievements of her distinguished sons.[28]

Lately Western scholars have shown great interest in the various forms of Devī and her worship.[29] This is partly due to the development of feminist perspectives also in religion. It is no longer uncommon also for Westerners to speak of God as Mother rather than as Father and to address her in terms not unlike the prayers Hindus have uttered for centuries to Devī. In addition the importance of Devī in the practical political sphere of India has been highlighted. The universal name *śakti* given to each and every form of the Goddess had not only cosmological and theological overtones but also pragmatic political implications. The King required the sanction of the local temple of the Goddess, which embodied power. As Gupta and Gombrich express it: "while (*śakti*) *has* no authority, she *is* authority, concretized or personified as god's *ajñā*. . . . the sign of royal authority is the *mudrā* or seal which the king gives to his officers. *Śakti* is called *mudrā*. To have god's *mudrā* is thus to have his authority, to be empowered to act on his behalf. A person thus empowered is called *ajñādhāra*, 'bearer of authority,' 'wielder of the mandate'; the term is common to (Tantric) religion and politics."[30] The relation between *śakti* and political power does not belong to the past alone. Several Śāktas like Yogi Dhirendra Brahmacari were associated with top-ranking politicians of post-independence India and at one point a Tantrika priest was hired by members of an opposition party to perform a Tantric ritual with a view to killing then Prime Minister Indira Gandhi.[31]

CHAPTER EIGHTEEN

# Mudalvan, Murukan, Māl: The Great Gods of the Tamils

A, as its first of letters, every speech maintains; The Primal Deity is First through all the world's domains.

—*Tirukkuraḷ* I, 1, 1

The Sanskritization of Indian culture that took place gradually with the spread of Vedic religion from Northwestern India, brought about a certain measure of uniformity and universality of ritual and belief. As the Vedic *caturvarṇa* organization of society took hold of the entire country, so the celebration of Vedic *yajñas* became a status symbol all over India from North to South. The systematic expansion of *Āryavārta* through missionaries like Agastya, resulted in the all-India acceptance and use of Sanskrit for religious purposes.[1] Legend associates Ṛṣi Agastya with Śiva. The people from the south, who had gone in great numbers to witness Śiva's marriage to Pārvāti, asked for a sage. Śiva chose Agastya. He was very short but immensely powerful: in a fit of rage he once drank the whole ocean. Agastya, keen on familiarizing himself with his mission country asked Śiva to initiate him into Tamil language and literature. He settled in the Podhukai hills, in today's Tinnelvelly district, with his family and a group of northern farmers. Agastya is supposed to have written the *Āgastyam*, a large grammatical work on Tamil, which is lost except for a few fragments. Some—if not most—of the greatest works on Hindu philosophy and religion (such as Śaṅkara's, Rāmānuja's, and Madhva's numerous treatises on Vedānta, the *Bhāgavata Purāṇa*, and many others) originated in the South. Since Śaṅkara established the four strategic *maṭhas* in the four corners of India, South Indian priests serve in several of the temples of the Kedarnāth complex in the Himalayas. As F. W. Clothey observed: "At its apex between the eighth and fifteenth centuries, the Tamil region was the major center of Hindu civilization, and indeed, one of the major centers of civilization in the world."[2]

It was assumed by scholars for long that in the religion of the epics and Purāṇas the indigenous traditions and religions mingled and mixed with the Vedic-Aryan and that in the major heroes and heroines of these works non-Aryan deities—often with Sanskritized names—found entry into Hindu orthodoxy.

In the northern and central parts of India, where people speak Sanskrit-derived languages, it is difficult to identify pre-Sanskritic traditions and cults, except on a local level. In the South however, where Dravidian languages prevail, and with the renewed pride especially of Tamils in their distinct cultural heritage, an impressive case can be stated for the non-Aryan and pre-Sanskritic religions of the area.

Some Tamils have gone so far as to claim, for Tamil culture, superiority in age and sophistication over Sanskrit culture. Some of the literary documents connected with the so-called Saṅgam period have been assigned dates that would place them into pre-history.[3] While much research is still necessary to fix dates and establish a chronology of South Indian literary documents, it does seem certain that there was not only an Aryanization and Sanskritization of South-India but also a reverse penetration of Aryan Vedic religion and culture by Dravidian elements. Nirad Chaudhuri, who claims that "the South Indian languages are Dravidian only in syntax and the workaday part of the vocabulary," that "all the words which embody cultural notions are Sanskritic," and that "there is not a single element in the culture of any civilized group in South India which is not Aryan Brahmanic,"[4] has been refuted by the works of serious scholars such as T. Burrow, who points out that the *Ṛgveda* already contains at least twenty words of Dravidian origin and that later classical Sanskrit too borrowed a great many words from Tamil sources.[5]

Tamiḷnāḍu, the country of the Tamils, comprised in former times a much larger area than it does today and included roughly the areas where today Dravidian languages are prevalent: besides the present state of Tamiḷnāḍu, also the states of Andhra Pradesh, Karṇātaka, and Kerala, that is, the countries where Telugu, Tulu, and Malayalam are spoken.[6]

The Tamil country was continuously inhabited for at least three hundred thousand years and possesses some of the earliest remnants of late Stone Age flint industries, rock paintings, Neolithic sites, and megalithic monuments.[7] It is also dotted with a great number of temples and sanctuaries. Even the original (and still widely used) names of Śiva and Viṣṇu are different in the South, and the legends associated with them are either quite peculiarly Dravidian or have significant variations as compared to the North Indian versions. In addition, there are many local deities and customs that do not have equivalents in other parts of the country. The feasts too, that are celebrated there have their own distinctive trappings and rituals.[8]

Several lessons can be learned from a brief survey of the major deities of South India: First, they represent a local tradition within Hinduism that is largely intact and quite strong and thus exemplifies a situation that in other parts of India is no longer as clearly discernible, suggesting the composition of Hinduism from a mosaic of local cults and traditions. Second, they demonstrate the transformation ("Sanskritization") of a formerly independent tradition, the adaptation of a distinct mythological lore to the wider context of Hinduism. Third, they still exhibit elements of indigenous religious traditions that have resisted absorption into Hinduism as practiced in other parts of India.

Major South Indian temple complexes like the Mīnākṣī temple of Madurai or the Viṣṇu sanctuary of Śrīraṅgam, the sacred complex of Tanjore, or the expansive site of Cidāṃbaram, have nothing comparable in North India, or anywhere in the world, for that matter. Some of these magnificent places were developed after the North had come under Muslim rule. When Islam came to South India it had spent most of its iconoclastic fury and left most of the Hindu tradition intact. Nothing surpasses or even matches the splendor of the temple feasts of Kerala, Tamiḷnāḍu or Andhra, as they are celebrated every year by millions of Hindus.

## THE ARYANIZATION OF THE TAMIL GODS

Śiva is so powerfully present in Tamiḷnāḍu's artistic heritage and literature that one thinks of Tamiḷnāḍu predominantly as Śiva country and Śaivism as a South-Indian religion. In fact, the name Śiva occurs rather late in Tamil documents and by then, as a matter of fact, he is considered to be the same as the indigenous Mudalvan, who had a Tamil background and a history of his own.[9] A tradition peculiar to the Tamil country—in evidence to this day—is that of ritual dance in connection with the worship of Śiva. The Śiva Naṭarāja image is a creation of the South—admired all over the world, especially in the masterful bronzes from the Chola age.[10] While the *liṅga* is associated with Śiva worship throughout India, it seems to have been a tradition in the South long before the emergence of Śaivism as an organised religion. A South Indian representation of a *liṅga* with a bull crouching in front of it has been ascribed to the Neolithic age[11] and up to the Saṅgam age stumps of trees known as *kaṇḍu* were worshipped as *liṅgas*.[12] Many of the Śiva myths found, for example, in the *Śiva Purāṇa* have been incorporated into Śiva lore also in South India. It is significant, however, that major changes took place in the process of adaptation.[13]

Thus in the Tamil version of the Dakṣa saga—originally a North-Indian Śiva myth, dealing with the Śaivite conquest of the famous sub-Himālayan *tīrtha* of Kanakhala—Dakṣa, who in the original myth was a Vedic patriarch with Vaiṣṇavite leanings, is represented as a devotee of Śiva whose mind was temporarily clouded.[14] The association of Śiva with burning *ghaṭs* and death in general seem to represent a Śivaization of the pre-Dravidian *Suḍalai māḍan*.

Viṣṇu is known in South India as *Māl*, meaning "Great." Māl is often prefixed by the title *Tiru*, the equivalent of the Sanskrit Śrī, "Lord."[15] Kṛṣṇa worship seems also to have been prominent among the shepherds and cowherds of Tamiḷnādu, and many references to it are found in ancient Tamil literature. It is highly probable that the *Bhāgavata Purāṇa*, the major text of the Kṛṣṇa worshippers, received its final form in Tamiḷnādu. In Tamil he is called Kannan. Viṣṇu is also known as Māyōn, Māyān, or Māyavān[16]—references to the dark complexion of the God. It is hard to say how many of the myths now associated with Viṣṇu originated in Tamiḷnādu. There certainly are also peculiar local variants of otherwise commonly known Viṣṇu myths.

Balarāma or Baladeva, in North Indian mythology considered as the younger brother of Kṛṣṇa, figures in Tamiḷnādu as the elder brother of Viṣṇu under the name of Vāliyon.[17] Tirumāl and Vāliyon together are "the two great Gods." Vāliyon's features are entirely South Indian (in spite of his later association with Balarāma): he is described as of white complexion, resembling the combination of the conch shell and of milk. He has one earring and uses a ploughshare as a weapon. His emblem is the palmyra tree.[18]

It is interesting to note that in South India Indra retained and even gained prominence at a time when he was supplanted in North India by other deities. Lavish Indra festivals were celebrated by the Chola kings—the so-called *Indravīḷā* lasted a full moon-month with royal participation.[19]

## NON-ARYANIZED TAMIL GODS

Whereas the amalgamation of Mudalvan with Śiva and of Tirumāl with Viṣṇu became fairly complete in the course of time—the Tamilians adopting the Sanskrit names also in their own texts—the wholly Tamil deity Murukan largely resisted this process.[20] Attempts were made in later times to associate him with Śiva and his son and equate him with Skanda, the North Indian god of war, but these were neither fully successful nor did they dislocate Murukan from the prominence that he always had. K. K. Pillai states that "Murukan has been doubtless the preeminent God of the Tamils through the ages."[21] The name Murukan evokes associations with beauty, youth, and divine freedom. According to ancient Tamil texts Murukan was the lord of all Seven Worlds. He was the war god of the Tamils: the spear was his favorite weapon. Known also as Śey, Vēl, and Neṭuvēl (his priests were known as Veḷān) he is associated with both the blue-feathered peacock and the elephant. A frenzied form of sacred dance is associated with his cult, the so-called Veriyadāl: "It was the dance of the priest in a frenzy, when he was supposed to be under divine inspiration. It took place when the parents of a lovesick girl wanted to know the cause of and a remedy for her condition. After offering prayers and sacrificing a goat, the priest danced, as if possessed. Invariably under the influence of intoxicating liquor and consequently in a state of delirium, he used to proclaim his diagnosis, prescriptions, and predictions."[22]

The Tamils of old also knew a variety of war dances, which were performed by men and women at the beginning of an expedition. War, obviously, played a major role in the life and thought of Tamils.[23]

The common worship of Murukan consists of offering flowers, paddy, millet, and honey and usually ends with the sacrifice of a goat. During the Saṅgam era Murukan became Aryanized into Subrahmania and several North Indian legends became associated with him. Murukan's sanctuaries were primarily on hilltops. In Sangam works his name and place of worship is associated with six military camps, which have been largely identified with modern settlements. Two of these sites, now the places of Viṣṇu temples, may have seen transformation from Murukan to Viṣṇu worship.[24] Palani, the second most frequented pilgrimage site in Tamiḷnādu, is associated with Murukan. So are several other popular temples.[25] Besides Murukan, the god of war, the Tamils also worshipped Koṭṛavai, the goddess of war.[26] Being of early Dravidian (and possibly pre-Dravidian) origin, she was later associated with the Hindu deity Mahiṣāsuramārdiṇī. She is also called the younger sister of Māl. The all-Indian Lakṣmī, venerated in Tamiḷnādu under the name of Ilakkumi, is also known as Tiru (the exact equivalent of the Sanskrit Śrī, used today as an honorific in Tamiḷnādu, as Śrī is used in the rest of India).

Nature worship as a dimension of Hinduism is much more in evidence in Tamiḷnādu than in most other parts of India. Thus the sun and moon had—and have—a special place in Tamil worship. Also the worship of trees and of animals—especially the snake—is very prevalent.[27]

The local association of Hindu deities goes beyond the specific Tamil traditions associated with pan-Indian religions like Vaiṣṇavism, Śaivism, and Śāktism. Within the Tamil country itself separate regions were assigned to the major Tamil deities: thus Śeyon (or Murukan) was the favorite deity of Kuriñchi, Māyōn (or Māl, Viṣṇu) of Mullai, Vendan (or Indra) of Maridan, and Varuṇa of Neydal.[28]

As has happened in other countries and in the context of other religions as well, the Tamils, after having been converted to Vedism, became the staunchest and most conservative defenders of Vedic religion. The Tamil kings of the Saṅgam age performed enormously expensive Vedic sacrifices.[29] One of the Chola monarchs, Rajasuyam Vetta Perunarkilli, obtained his title through the performance of the extensive Vedic *rājasuya* sacrifice.[30] Also the Chera kings were renowned for their orthodox Vedic performances.[31] South Indian Brahmins even today are renowned for their tenacious traditionalism—and again, not uncharacteristically, Tamiḷnādu has also brought forth the most articulate organized anti-Brahmin movement.

The Madras Government's Hindu Religious and Charitable Endowments Administration Department, which goes back to the 1920s, oversees the administration of Tamiḷnādu's approximately thirty-two thousand public temples, which together own about half a million acres of land and have a yearly income of hundreds of millions of rupees. Most temples in Tamiḷnādu are today administered by government-appointed trustees. In the most important pilgrimage temples a resident executive officer controls the books and prepares the budgets. Several changes enacted recently have met with resistance from the priesthood.[32]

## THE TAMILIZATION OF THE VEDA

Nammāḷvār, also called Śatokopan, enjoys the greatest favor among the Hindus of Tamiḷnādu. His writings are considered the Dravida Veda and are paralleled in detail with the Sanskrit Veda of the North: the four *prabandhas*, named *Tiruviruttam, Tiruvasiriyam, Periya Tiruvantati,* and *Tiruvaimoli,* are equated with the four Vedas. The first three are called *Iyarpa* (not set to music), whereas the last one is compared to the *Sāmaveda* and set to music. The six *Vedāṅgas* have their Tamil counterparts in the six *Divya-prabandhas* of Tirumangai Āḷvār. The eight *Upāṅgas* of the Vedas have their equals in the works of the other Āḷvārs. The *Tiruvaimoli* is also compared to the *Chāndogya Upaniṣad,* which belongs to the *Sāmaveda.*

Not satisfied with the parallelism between Vedas and Tamil *Prabandhas,* the Tamils claim superiority of the Āḷvārs over against the Vedic *ṛṣis.* Whereas the *ṛṣis* gained their power through karma and *tapasya,* the Āḷvārs were blessed directly with *bhakti* by the Lord.

> With all their study and yoga, the vision of God of the *ṛṣis* remains unclear, and they stand tied by bounds of worldly desires. Not so with the Āḷvār: he sees clearly, aided by the power of the divine vision granted by Him, subtlest truths difficult of perception even for Brahmā and Śiva, and all his worldly ties drop. . . . While *ṛṣis* subsist on raw fruits, roots, leaves, air, and water, all that our Āḷvār eats as food, drinks as water, and chews as betel leaf is his chosen God.[33]

In a further parallel to the Veda tradition, the recitation of the *Tiruvaimoli* is chanted in all temples for ten nights, beginning with Vaikuṇṭha Ekādaśī before the *ārca* forms of Viṣṇu and Nammāḷvār. This is preceded by the recitation during ten nights of the Tamil *Vedāṅgas.*

The daily worship in temples and homes begins with the recital of hymns from the Tamil *prabandhas* and not from the Sanskrit collections. In a further attempt to not only parallel but surpass the Sanskrit tradition, well-known works in Maṇipravāla like *Śrī Vācana-bhuṣana, Ācārya Hṛdaya,* and *Rahasya-Traya-Sāra* are regarded as equal, if not superior to the *Brahmasūtras.* Commentaries on the *prabandhas* are considered the equal of the Sanskrit commentaries to the *Upaniṣads* and the *Brahmasūtras.*

## ANTI-BRAHMIN, ANTI-HINDU, ANTI-CASTE

From the beginning of the twentieth century there arose movements in South India that attempted to promote—simultaneously—the creation of an independent Dravidian state, the cultivation of a pure, de-Sanskritized Tamil, the abolition of caste, and the demotion of Brahmins from their leading positions. By 1912, the Brahmins, who formed about 3 percent of the population of the then Madras presidency, occupied about 60 percent of the government positions, and they dominated also the politics of the state. That same year a Dravidian association was formed that aimed at establishing a separate state under British supremacy with a government for and by non-Brahmins. In 1917 the famous "Non-Brahmin Manifesto" was issued that called on the non-Brahmins of South India to unite against the Brahmins. In its wake the Justice Party arose, which published a paper by the name *Justice*. In 1925 E. V. Ramaswami Naikker, later called "Periyar" (Great Man) founded the Self-Respect movement. He wanted to get rid of caste altogether and thereby break the influence of the Brahmins and of the Hindu religion. He denounced the epics and Purāṇas and called for a burning of the *Manusmṛti*. An early member of the movement was C. N. Annadurai, who was later to found the Dravida Munnetra Kazhagam (DMK, Dravidian Progress Movement). Several vernacular newspapers were founded to spread the anti-Brahmin and anti-Hindu sentiment. The Justice Party started an Anti-Hindī agitation in 1938 and pressed for the creation of a federal republic of Draviḍanādu, comprising the states of Tamiḷnādu, Kerala, Andhra Pradesh and Karṇātaka. Annadurai asked his followers to drop all caste suffixes and proper names, so as to transform Tamiḷnādu into a de facto casteless society. While the DMK eventually succeeded in taking over the government of Tamiḷnādu, it was not able to realize all its declared sociopolitical aims.

Constant splits in the Tamil movements and shifting alliances with outside parties have considerably toned down the radicalism of the erstwhile Dravida Kazhagam. The "All India Anna DMK," which formed a government in Madras in 1977, showed little of the former movement's anti-Hindu and anti-Brahmin stance. Its representatives visited temples and Anna himself, widely popular and revered by high and low, was buried in a *samādhi* on the shore of the Arabian Sea, which has become like a place of pilgrimage for thousands of devotees, who lay down flowers and fruits for him.[34]

## TAMIL FOLK-RELIGIONS

The typical religiosity of Tamiḷnādu also manifests itself on the level of folk beliefs and superstitions.[35] As in all such traditions fate, called *Ul* or *Ūḷ Vinai*, plays a major role. The Tamil classic *Tirukkuraḷ* devotes an entire chapter to it: "What powers so great as those of Destiny? Man's skill some other thing contrives; but fate's beforehand still."[36]

Also in line with other folk traditions, ghosts and demons play a major role in Tamiḷnādu. Ghosts were formerly associated especially with the battlefield—they were supposed to feed on corpses. It is still believed that mustard seed spread around a house and the burning of camphor and incense would keep them away from homes at night.[37] In order to protect children from the malicious actions of goblins mothers carry a twig of margosa leaves with them when leaving the house.[38] Margosa leaves are also tied to the entrances of houses during epidemics of smallpox. Infectious diseases, especially of children, and in particular smallpox, which ravaged India's countryside in previous times, brought on the cult of specific goddesses: Mariamma, associated with smallpox, received many offerings designed to placate her.[39] Belief in auspicious and inauspicious times and places is prevalent throughout Hindu-India. Tamils follow a calender of their own, according to which *rahukālam*, inauspicious time, is indicated during which major new ventures and business transactions are avoided.[40]

At some time, roughly from the second century BCE to the eighth century CE, Buddhism and Jainism were very strong in South India, dominating the cultural life of the country. Jains and Buddhists created major literary and scientific works and several of the influential rulers are said to have been active in promoting Jainism and Buddhism and persecuting Śaivas and Vaiṣṇavas.[41] The tables were turned during the time of the Āḷvārs and Nāyanmārs—roughly from the sixth century onward—when some quite sensational conversions of royalty to Śaivism took place and when Vaiṣṇavas gained majority status in some districts. Śaivite kings supposedly persecuted Jains.[42] There is a series of gruesome murals in the temple of Madurai, illustrating the killing of Jains by impaling and boiling in kettles. Śaivites also purportedly persecuted Vaiṣṇavas: Rāmānuja had to flee from his see in Śrīraṅgam because he refused to accept Śiva as his Lord and Kureśa, his faithful servant who impersonated Rāmānuja had his eyes put out. He got his eyesight miraculously restored through the grace of Viṣṇu when Rāmānuja wept over him.

## THE SAINTS OF TAMIḶNĀDU

Tamiḷnādu is the birthplace of a great many saints and religious scholars of all-India repute. In a volume entitled *Ten Saints of India*, T. M. P. Mahadevan[43], formerly Professor of Philosophy at the University of Madras, includes nine saints from Tamiḷnādu—the only "foreigner" is the Bengali Ramakrishna. Besides the Vedāntācāryas Śaṅkara and Rāmānuja, there are the Śaivite saints Tirujñāna Sambandhar, Tirunāvukkaraśu, Sundaramūrti and Manikkavācakar, the author of the famous *Tiru-vācakam*, the Vaiṣṇava saints Nammāḷvār and Āṇṭāl and the 20th century saint Ramaṇa Maharṣi. Śaṅkara and Rāmānuja wrote in Sanskrit and had already during their lifetime a large following outside Tamiḷnāḍu. Ramaṇa Maharṣi knew some English and composed his simple didactic verses in both Sanskrit and English (as well as in Tamil) and obtained international stature. The others knew only Tamil and are little known outside Tamiḷnādu, except by interested scholars. Their expressions of Śaivism and Vaiṣṇavism are quite peculiarly Tamil and are apt—even in translation—to convey something of the specific religiosity of Tamiḷnādu.

To underscore their importance within the major Hindu communities in Tamiḷnāḍu it must be mentioned that their Tamil devotional hymns did attain canonical status and form part of the officially sanctioned temple worship throughout Tamiḷnāḍu.

The legend and poetry of Tiru Jñāna Saṃbandamūrti Swāmi, who flourished in the seventh century CE is both typical and instructive.[44] It was a time when Buddhism and Jainism had all but eliminated Śaivism from the Tamil country. One of the few Śiva devotees remaining prayed to Śiva in the temple of his hometown Sīrkāḷī that a son should be born to him who would win his people back to Śiva. The child of such a prayer uttered his first hymn in praise of Śiva at the age of three, after he was fed milk by Śiva's spouse, from which event his name, "the man connected with divine wisdom," derives. When he grew up he went on pilgrimage to all the Śiva sanctuaries of South India. He was deeply worried by the conversion of the King of Madurai to Jainism. The queen's consort and her prime minister, however, had remained Śaivites and with their help Sambandar not only reconverted the king but also had him impale eight thousand Jains. In another part of Tamiḷnādu he converted a great number of Buddhists to Śaivism. Saṃbandar is an example of the formation of sectarian Hinduism in opposition to non-Hindu religions, a process that made Śaivism much more of a dogmatically defined "religion" than it had been through its earlier history. Still, Saṃbandar does articulate something of the *bhakti* that knows no boundaries, the generosity of heart and mind that makes Hinduism overall so attractive a faith. Thus does he sing:

For the Father in Ārur
Sprinkle ye the blooms of love;
In your heart will dawn true light,
Every bondage will remove.
Him the holy in Ārur
Ne'er forget to laud and praise;
Bonds of birth will severed be,
Left behind all worldly ways.
In Ārur, our loved one's gem,
Scatter golden blossoms fair.
Sorrow ye shall wipe away
Yours be bliss without compare.[45]

The Vaiṣṇavas were no less fervent in preaching devotion to Viṣṇu, whose sanctuary at Tirupati draws millions of pilgrims every year. Among the Āḷvārs, the god-intoxicated singers who were responsible for kindling Viṣṇu *bhakti* throughout India, there was a woman, Āṇṭāl (see Figure 18.1), whose fame has spread far and wide. Her birth was preceded and surrounded by a great many miraculous events as well as by prophecies. She was believed by her father to be the incarnation of *Bhū Devī*, one of the two consorts of Viṣṇu. Āṇṭāl considered herself the bride of Viṣṇu as he is worshipped in Śrīraṅgam.

Photo 24. Saṃbandamūrti (Tamilnadu) [Heras Institute]

Figure 18.1. Āṇṭāl

It is interesting that she began to imitate the ways of the *gopīs* of faraway Vṛndāvana and desired to marry the Kṛṣṇa of the *Bhāgavata Purāṇa*.[46]

The lyrics of these God-filled souls not only captured the hearts of the simple people in Tamiḷnādu, but they also shaped the theology of the major centers of Vaiṣṇavism and Śaivism and became part of the ornate worship that is continued up to this day: Statues of Āḷvārs and Nāyanmārs decorate homes and temples in Tamiḷnādu and receive homage.

Toward the end of the Indian Middle Ages, in the twelfth century, when large parts of India were already under Muslim rule, the Liṅgāyat movement arose in Karṇāṭaka.[47] The Liṅgāyat movement represents a monotheistic radicalization of Śaivism parallel to the radical monotheism of Islam. The Liṅgāyats, after initiation, have to wear a *liṅga* at all times and consider themselves the property of Śiva. On the other hand the Liṅgāyats are reformist: they abolish caste differences, they engage in public works for the benefit of the community, they no longer cremate their dead but bury them—again, perhaps, under the influence of Islam. Basavanna, the reputed twelfth century reformer of Liṅgāyatism sings:

> The rich will make temples for Śiva
> What shall I, a poor man do?
> My legs are pillars, the body the shrine,
> The head a cupola of gold.
> Listen, O lord of the meeting rivers,
> things standing shall fall,
> but the moving shall ever stay.[48]

## SCHOLARSHIP AND FOLK TRADITION

Tamiḷnādu has brought forth its share of philosophers and theologians in the past and in the present—such luminaries of modern India as S. Radhakrishnan, T. R. V. Murti, T. M. P. Mahadevan, and many well-known living representatives of Indian philosophy originated from Tamiḷnādu. On the other hand, the religion of Tamiḷnādu has always had, and still has, a quality of earthiness and joie de vivre. Nothing is better suited to prove this point than the celebration of Pongāl, the great national feast of Tamiḷnādu.[49] Cows and oxen, water buffaloes and goats are decorated, garlanded, and led in processions. Large amounts of rich and varied foods are consumed in daylong celebrations, punctuated with the singing of hymns, the exploding of fireworks, and joyous noises day and night. All the gods receive worship and are invoked for blessings—but the central focus of all is life and that which sustains it, the food grown in the fields and the faithful bovines, without whose help humans could not subsist.

# Part III

## The Structural Supports of Hinduism

Hinduism is a way of life and not only a religion or a system of philosophy in the more narrow sense of these words, and Hinduism is what it is because of the physical reality of India: the land and its people. Hinduism is intimately connected with the specific features of the landscape of India in which the Divine has revealed itself to its people. The mountains, the rivers, and the oceans of India are an essential ingredient of the Hindu tradition. The Divine is present in India also in the shape of images made of stone and wood, of metal and of paper.

Hinduism has created holy cities and was in turn profoundly shaped by them. Millions undertake pilgrimages each year to famous temples in the North and South, East and West. Hindus, finally, have an acute awareness of the qualitative differences embedded in time: of holy and ordinary days, of auspicious and inauspicious occasions. A great many professionals are constantly employed to interpret the signs of time since all rites have to be performed at specific auspicious times.

Sacred spaces, places, and times are connected with the physical reality of India and provide a sacred structure in its nature. The age-old *caturvarṇāśrama-dharma* provides a sacred structure to society and to history. By divine fiat society was divided into functional strata and the life of the individual was structured in such a manner to give room to the realization of all essential human values. It was the caste structure that provided Hinduism with a social and political basis strong enough to not only accommodate change and development but also to withstand attacks from outside.

The assignment of a specific function in society provided individuals with a purpose in their lives, ensured on the whole a noncompetitive kind of society, and also created a social security net for all its members. Its major failing did not concern those who belonged to it but those who did not: the outcastes. Either by expelling from its fold such members who did not conform to the caste regulations or by not accepting outsiders into it, Hinduism created a parallel society of people without social standing and without rights, considered good only for doing the most degrading work and treated worse than cattle.

Hinduism has always reserved the highest respect for those who made religion their profession. It expected the members of the upper castes to abandon toward the end of their lives all attachment to the world and to concentrate all efforts on *mokṣa*, spiritual liberation. *Saṃnyāsis* have been the spiritual backbone of Hinduism for many centuries, and they are so today as well. There are millions of them, belonging to hundreds of orders and associations. They include all types of men and women—attractive and repulsive, old and young, learned and illiterate, pious and fanatical, serene and excitable. In more than one way they provide the ultimate support to Hinduism. They are the living examples to the rest of the Hindus of a life dedicated to the activities and ideals that they only casually partake in or aspire to. As an ideal, *saṃnyāsa* has enormous attraction also for many a modern-educated Hindu, not to mention Westerners who have joined modern Hindu movements in fair numbers. One can safely predict that Hinduism will flourish as long as *saṃnyāsa* is followed by a significant number of Hindus. There can be no doubt that this is the case today.

In Hinduism, as in most religions, women play a very important role as transmitters and preservers of sacred stories and domestic rituals. While women had been legally deprived in the public arena since medieval times, they continued to command a major role in worship and character formation.

As important as the physical environment of India and the social structures are, it is the thought systems that hold the symbolic world of Hinduism together. Philosophical speculation and critical enquiry were characteristic for Hinduism throughout its long history. The Hindu mind excelled in both analytic and systematic thinking. The controversies that periodically erupted, leading to the formation of new schools of thought, sharpened concepts and logic to a degree probably not reached anywhere else. The assumption of the greatest exponents of Hinduism, that eternal happiness and release from rebirth depended on a specific kind of knowledge and that wrong notions about the nature of Self and Reality could cause misery and suffering not only in this life but in many lives to come, gave to philosophical debates an urgency that has hardly any parallel in history.

The *ṣaḍdarśanas* are often called the *six orthodox philosophical systems* of Hinduism. *Darśana* literally means "seeing" and provides a fairly exact equivalent to the original meaning of the Greek *theoría*. It is a "viewpoint," a simultaneous apprehension of all that is of importance. Each of the six *darśanas* has sufficiently different interests and methods to distinguish it from the others. Within specific *darśanas*, for example, those of *Mīmāṃsā* and *Vedānta*, further controversies led to the emergence of more schools of thought, that, while sharing many more presuppositions, also entered into sharp exchanges and mutual strife.

CHAPTER NINETEEN

# The Divine Presence in Space and Time

## *Mūrti, Tīrtha, Kāla*

> A Hindu is he . . . who above all addresses this land, this Sindhusthan, as his *punyabhū*, as his Holy Land—the land of his prophets and seers, of his godmen and gurus, the land of piety and pilgrimage.
>
> —Vir Savarkar, "Essentials of Hindutva"

That space and time are permeated and filled with the presence of the Supreme is not a mere theological idea with the Hindus: it is a tangible reality in India. Countless temples, quite many of impressive dimensions, many also of very recent origin, manifest the presence and power of Hinduism in all towns and villages. Numberless images—artistic creations in stone, metal, and wood and cheap prints on colored paper—reveal the intensity of devotion of the Hindus. A great number of centers of pilgrimage attract a continuous stream of pilgrims, and an unbroken string of festivals impress the foreign visitor as much as the indigenous worshipper with a sense of the sacredness of time.

It is doubtful whether the original Vedic tradition knew temples and images. In the Vedic texts the focus of worship was the *vedī*, the sacrificial altar, built according to precise specifications on a preselected site, which for the time of the sacrifice became the place where *devas* and *pitṛs* shared with humans the gifts offered for sacrifice. The constantly maintained fire in each home, too, was considered to be a divine presence—as were the more striking natural phenomena like thunderstorms and the celestial bodies. We do not know whether it was a deeper conviction that the divine could not be captured in finite forms, a lack of artistic expression, or sectarian rivalry that made some Vedic texts pour contempt on image worshippers and temple builders, who probably were present in India since times immemorial. Excavations of Sindhu-Sarasvatī Civilization sites include what have been interpreted as sacred tanks and sacrificial sites housed in buildings that may have been temples. Also *liṅgas* and goddess figurines were found that probably served as cult images.[1] If this early civilization was contemporary to, or even part of the ancient Vedic civilization, we will have to revise the notions of an aniconic Vedic religion, held in traditional scholarship.

In and around Mathurā, an ancient center of trade and religion, as well as in many other places, terra-cotta figurines of mother goddesses have been found, dated around 500 BCE. Figurative representation reached a first peak in the Indo-Greek art of the golden time of Buddhism.[2] Individual specimens of Hindu sculpture can be traced to the second century BCE.[3] The great theoretical development, according to which temples and figures had to be fashioned, belongs to the fifth century CE. In all probability there was an early Hindu art and architecture that used wood and other perishable materials.[4] Even now a number of temples and statues are fashioned of wood and several famous temples give the impression that they are copies in stone of more ancient wooden models.[5] With regard to the size and number of temples and images, Hindu India has no equal in the world; compared with temple cities like Śrīraṅgam, Madurai, Kāñcī, Khajurāho or Bhuvaneśvara, Western religious centers and even medieval cathedral cities look modest and poor. And we must not forget that what we admire in India today is largely that which the Muslim invaders either did not destroy or allowed to be rebuilt.[6] A great many temples also of considerable proportions are being constructed in our time—temples associated with modern Hindu movements as well as temples funded by pious individuals and families. Indeed, during the last fifty years, since India's independence, more temples have been built than in the five hundred years before!

## *MŪRTI*: THE EMBODIMENT OF THE DIVINE

For Hindus the most important of all the spatiotemporal manifestations of the Divine is the *mūrti*.[7] *Mūrti* means literally "embodiment"; technically it designates the images of the divinities, made of metal, stone, or wood but sometimes also of some perishable material for special purposes. Though the first impression is that of an infinite variety of figures and poses, a more thorough acquaintance with the subject reveals that each artist has to follow very definite rules with regard to proportions, positions, gestures.[8] The Purāṇas, the Āgamas, Saṃhitās, and Tantras contain many chapters detailing the way in which images to be used in worship have to be made; these rules are supposed to go back to divine revelation and must therefore not be violated if the image is to become an abode of the divine. These works do not constitute the source for the canons they prescribe; we have old Buddhist texts that specify the proportions of the Buddha images and also other Indian texts, not yet sectarian in their character, that provide guidelines for architects and sculptors.[9] One of the most important works is the *Vāstuśāstra*, ascribed to Viśvakarma, the architect and director of all arts of the *devas*, the patron of all the artists and artisans in India.[10] The various *vāstuśāstras* in existence manifest the variety of different artistic traditions in India. Though one can say that all images that are to be used as cult objects in temples and homes have to conform to definite rules, one cannot reduce these rules to one single canon. Different centers follow different canons of art.[11]

The image produced by the sculptor, according to the prescribed canons, is not yet an object of worship: it has to be consecrated in a formal ceremony of *pratiṣṭhāpana*, the solemn installation. Rituals vary according to the religious affiliation and locality, but the consecration of the *mūrti* is an essential requirement and usually marks the formal opening of a new temple. In older temples one finds quite often so-called *svayam-vyakta mūrtis*, images not fashioned by human hands but miraculously revealed: washed up on the seashore, carried to a particular place by a river, or found buried in a location revealed to someone in a dream. Local tradition often tells that a *ṛṣi* received the image of the temple directly from the deity. Depending on the material used and the rite employed, the consecration is limited to a certain time. The clay and paper images used, for instance, for *Durgā-pūjā* by the *Śāktas* at the time of the Dasserah festival, are consecrated only for the duration of the festivities; when the celebrations are over, the images, after the Goddess has left them, are thrown into the sea or a river.

A worshipper who has no other image may even use a paper image or an image drawn in sand and invoke the divine presence upon it for the time of his worship. Images made of stone or metal are usually given a *nitya-abhiṣeka* a permanent consecration, which is terminated only when the image suffers a major injury.[12]

The *Bṛhatsaṃhitā* of Viramitrodaya, one of the most important and interesting texts of early Hindu literature, a kind of early encyclopedia, describes this ceremony in the following way:

> To the south or east (of the new temple) a pavilion, furnished with four *toraṇas*, or arches, should be erected, decorated with garlands and banners. Inside, an earthen altar should be raised, sprinkled with sand and covered with *kuśa* grass upon which the image should be placed. The image should be bathed successively with various kinds of water; first a decoction of *plakṣa, aśvatha, uḍumbara, śirīṣa,* and *vaṭa* should be used; then the auspicious *sarvauṣadhi* water and next the water from *tīrthas*, in which earth raised by elephants and bulls, earth from mountains, anthills, confluences of rivers, lotus ponds and *pañca-gavya*, the five products of the cow[13] are mixed, should be poured. When the image has received this bath and is sprinkled with scented water in which gold and precious gems are put, it should be placed with its head toward the east; during this ceremony the *tūrya* trumpet should be blown and *puṇyāhā* (auspicious day!) and Vedic mantras should be uttered. The most respected of the Brahmans should then chant mantras connected

with Indra in the eastern and mantras connected with Agni in the south-eastern quarter; these Brahmans should be honored with handsome fees. The Brahman then should offer *homa* to the fire with the mantra peculiar to the enshrined deity. If during the performance of the *homa* the fire becomes full of smoke, or the flames turn from right to left or the burning faggots emit frequent sparks, then it is not auspicious, it is also inauspicious, if the priest forgets his mantras or the flames turn backward. After having bathed the image and decked it with new cloth and ornaments and worshipped it with flowers and sandal paste the priest should lay it down on a well-spread bed. When the image has rested for its full time it should be aroused from sleep with songs and dances and should be installed at a time fixed by the astrologers. Then, after worshipping the image with flowers, garments, sandal paste, and the sounds of the conch shell and trumpet, it should be carefully taken inside the sanctum from the pavilion, keeping the temple to the right. After making profuse offerings, and honoring the Brahmans and the assembly, a piece of gold should be put into the mortise hole of the base and the image fixed on it. One, who installs the image, honoring specifically the astrologer, the Brahmans, the assembly, the image maker and the architect, enjoys bliss in this world and heaven hereafter. The installation should take place in the bright fortnight in the period of the summer solstice and during certain particular positions of the planets and asterisms, on days other than *maṅgalavāra* (literally, auspicious day, our Tuesday) and in a time particularly auspicious to the donor of the image.[14]

Later texts describe much more elaborate ceremonies; the interested reader can consult more special works that provide all the details.[15] Whereas the main image of a Vaiṣṇava and Śākta temple is always a figurative image, the object of worship in the *garbha-gṛha*, the central shrine of a Śaiva temple, is the aniconic *liṅga*. The older centers boast of *svayambhū liṅgas*, *liṅgas* that have been revealed by Śiva himself and not fashioned by human hands; indeed quite many of them are natural objects and not artifacts. Some of them are oblong stones; the *liṅga* at Amarnāth in the Himālayas is formed by water dropping from the ceiling of the cave and congealing into a cone of ice. The *svayambhū liṅgas* are surrounded by legends, contained in the *Sthala-purāṇas*, the local chronicles of the temples. The legend connected with Kālahasti in Andhra Pradesh may serve as a typical example: the main *mūrti* of the temple consists of a natural oblong slab of stone; with some imagination one can find that it resembles the head of a two-tusked elephant on one side and the head of a five-hooded cobra on the other side, with a small marking that is reminiscent of a spider. Legend has it that these devout animals offered daily *pūjā* to the *liṅga*: the spider would weave a net to protect it from the sun's rays, the elephant sprayed it with water, and the snake shielded it with its hood. One day the snake, ignorant of the elephant's devotion, noticed that some leaves had fallen on the *liṅga* and this aroused her anger. When the elephant returned, the snake thought him to be the culprit and got hold of his trunk. The elephant, mad with pain, smashed his trunk against the stone, killing both snake and spider and also dying in the process. Śiva, pleased with the devotion that those animals had shown, granted *mukti* to all of them. This *liṅga* is also one of the *pañcabhūta liṅga*, connected with *vāyu*, the wind, because an oil lamp kept burning in front of the *liṅga* flickers continuously, although there is no visible opening anywhere.[16]

Though there is no uniformity as regards the theology of images in Hinduism and though one can hear Hindus nowadays in a liberal way explain the images as only symbolizing God, the average Hindu still sees in the images a real and physical presence of God and not only a symbolic one. Vaiṣṇavas connect the worship of the *mūrti* with their theory of the five different manifestations of Viṣṇu: the *ārcāvatāra* is the Lord himself present in an image. Thus the *Arthapañcaka* says: "Although omniscient, he appears unknowing; although pure spirit, he appears as a body; although himself the Lord, he appears to be at the mercy of men; although all-powerful, he appears to be without power; though perfectly free from wants, he seems to be in need; although the protector of all, he seems helpless; although invisible, he becomes visibly manifest; although unfathomable, he seems tangible."[17] Other Vaiṣṇava scriptures speak of the suffering that the Supreme takes upon himself becoming present in an image because of his love for humankind.

*Mūrti-pūjā*, worship of God who is present in the image, is one of the prominent features of contemporary Hinduism both in temples and homes. Rules for it vary greatly from place to place and from sect to sect; manuals are available that, in thousands of details, set out the form of worship obligatory in a temple or a *saṃpradāya*.[18] The *Bhāgavata Purāṇa* offers the following instructions:

> Having purified oneself and having gathered the materials of worship, the worshippers should sit on their seats of *darbha* grass facing east or north and conduct the worship with the image in front. They should then utter the mantras with proper *mudrās*, which render his different limbs duly charged with spiritual power.[19] They should then invoke with mantras and proper *mudrās* my presence in the image. They should keep before them a vessel of sanctified water and with that water sprinkle thrice the image, the materials of worship, themselves, and the vessels. When the worshippers' whole being has become pervaded by my form, which is the inner soul of all beings, they, having become completely immersed in myself, shall make my presence overflow into the image established in front of them and then, with all the paraphernalia, conduct my worship.
>
> They must first offer me a seat; my seat is made of nine elements: virtue, knowledge, dispassion, and mastery as the four feet, and the opposite of these as the enclosed plank upon which I sit, the other parts of my seat are the three sheets spread over it representing the three *guṇas* of which my *māyā* is composed; there are also to be established on the seat my nine *śaktis*.

> With clothes, sacred thread, jewels, garlands, and fragrant paste my devotees should decorate my form suitably and with love. With faith my worshippers should then offer me water to wash, sandal, flower, unbroken rice, incense, light, and food of different kinds; also attentions like anointing, massage, showing of mirror, etc., and entertainments like song and dance; these special entertainments may be done on festive days and even daily. They should engage in singing of me, praising me, dancing with my themes, imitating my exploits and acts, narrating my stories or listening to them. With manifold hymns of praise of me, taken from the Purāṇas, or from vernacular collections, the devotees should praise me and pray to me that I bless them, and they should prostrate before me. With hands and head at my feet, they should say: "My Lord, from the clutches of death save me who have taken refuge under you!" Having consecrated an image of me, one should build a firm temple for me and have beautiful flower gardens around for conducting daily worship and festivals. For the maintenance of my worship in special seasons as well as every day, one should bestow fields, bazaars, townships, and villages.[20]

## THE HINDU TEMPLE

True to the suggestion given in the previously quoted text, Hindus have over the centuries built "firm temples" for the God embodied in the *mūrti*. The Hindu temple is not primarily the assembly room of a congregation, like the synagogues and churches of the biblical religions, but the palace of the *mūrta bhagavān*, the embodied Lord. The more powerful the *mūrti* of a temple, the larger are the crowds that come for *darśana*, and the richer and bigger, usually, also the temple. Most temples used to be the hereditary property of individual families; quite a number of the larger temples are nowadays administered by temple trusts under the control of a government department.[21]

Indian temple architecture has lately attracted the interest of many Western scholars who have studied the ancient *vāstuśāstra* texts and gained an understanding of the symbolism expressed in it.[22] According to Kramrisch, the "structure [of the Hindu Temple] is rooted in Vedic tradition, and primeval modes of building have contributed their shapes. The principles are given in the sacred books of India and the structural rules in the treatises on architecture. They are carried out in the shrines which still stand throughout the country and which were built in many varieties and styles over 1,500 years from the fifth century."[23]

Indian architects worked under the supposition that their creation had to conform to, and be expressive of, the cosmic laws. The cosmos, as they saw it, was the combination of the perfect and the imperfect, the absolute *brahman* and the contingent *jīva*, of the eternal and of time. The eternal is symbolized in the square; the circle is the symbol of time. As the symbol model of the *vāstu-puruṣa* (Figure 19.1) reveals,[24] also in India "the human person is the

Photo 25. Gopura of Viṣṇu temple: Kāñcī (Tamilnadu)

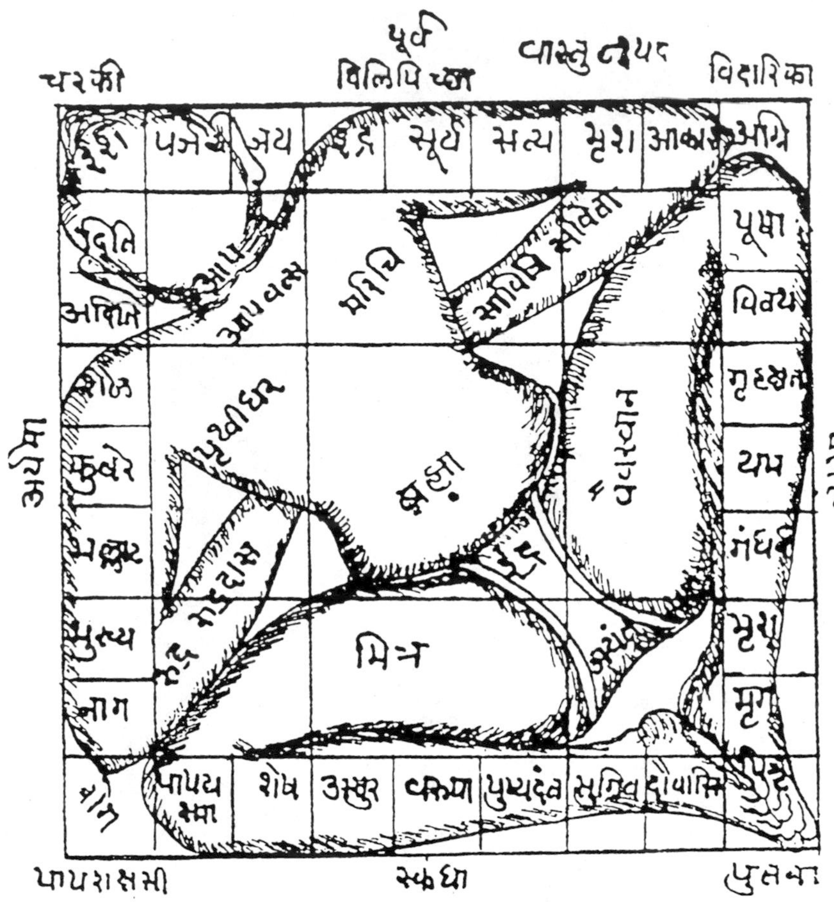


Figure 19.1. *Vāstu puruṣa maṇḍala*

measure of all things": the figure of a person enclosed by a square is the basic pattern from which all temple architecture develops: "The gods are settled on the *vāstu-puruṣa*. The fight between the demons and the gods is over, for it is won conjointly. Every building activity means a renewed conquest of disintegration and at the same time a restitution of integrity so that the gods once more are the limbs of a single 'being,' of Existence, at peace with itself."[25] The center square, equal to 3 × 3 small squares, is given to Brahmā who gave shape to the world (see Figure 19.2). The inner ring is occupied by the main gods, the outer ring by the thirty-two minor gods, representing at the same time the lunar mansions so that the *vāstu-puruṣa maṇḍala* becomes the instrument to determine both the spatial and also the temporal components of temple construction. The gods in the corners and in the middle of each side of the square

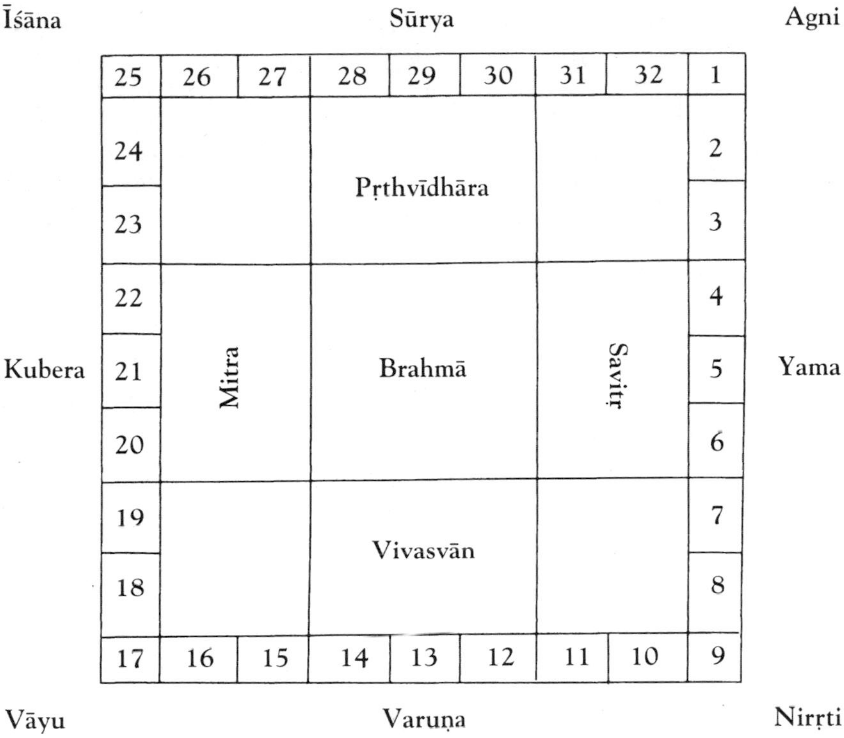


Figure 19.2. Ground pattern of temple-plan

are the *dig-pāla*, the guardians of the cardinal points, determining the spatial orientation of the *maṇḍala*.[26]

The *vāstu-puruṣa maṇḍala* serves the town planner as well as the temple builder: the whole town is ideally structured according to this cosmic model; within the town a certain area is reserved for the temple, which again is patterned according to the laws of the cosmos.[27] The dimensions and proportions of the temple to be built depend on an intricate system of calculations designed to bring the edifice within the framework determined by six prerequisites. Apart from achieving an aesthetically pleasing harmony of proportions between height, length, and width of the building, the actual dimensions must express the caste of the builder and the calculations must also determine the spatiotemporal position of the temple.[28] A good example of the application of this scheme is offered by the *Brahmeśvara* temple in Bhuvaneśvara.[29]

In South India a slightly different ground plan is followed. The *padmagarbha maṇḍala* of the *Bṛhadeśvara* temple at Tanjore (Figure 19.3) will illustrate these differences.

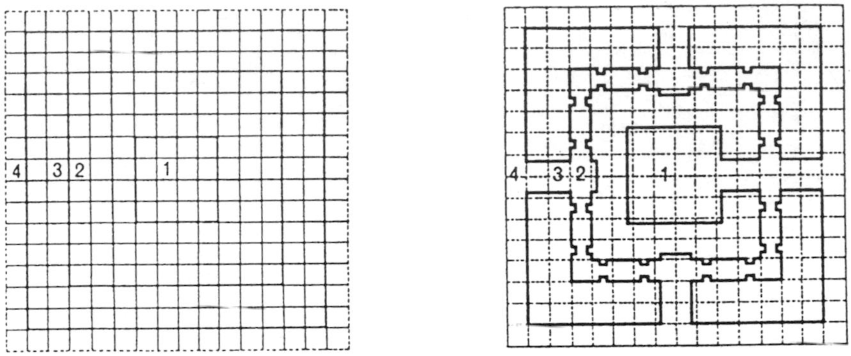


Figure 19.3. *Padmagarbha maṇḍala* of Bṛhadeśvara temple [Tanjore]

| | | |
|---|---|---|
| 1. | Brahmā | Sanctuary (*garbha-gṛha*) with interior *pradakṣiṇa-patha* |
| 2. | Spheres of the gods | Circumambulatory path (exterior *pradakṣiṇa-patha*) |
| 3. | Sphere of humans | Circuit wall |
| 4. | Sphere of demons | Terrace |

The center and essence of the cosmos is Brahmā, surrounded by an inner ring, the world of *devas*. Around these, another ring is formed by the world of humans. Still further removed, but within the realm of *jīvas*, and therefore of importance for all the other living beings, are the *asuras*. The *sthaṇḍila maṇḍala*, which forms the model for the temple at Tanjore, consists of 16 × 16 fields: 16 are occupied by the *Brahmā-sthāna*, identical with the *garbha-gṛha*, 84 by the world of the *devas*, identical with the *pradakṣiṇa patha*, 96 for the world of the humans, identical with the *prakāra*, the outer wall of the sanctuary. The ring of the *asuras*, occupying 60 fields, is situated outside the wall on the terrace that surrounds the temple. Later the *maṇḍapas* and other shrines within the temple compound have been added.

In a grandiose way the original South Indian *sthaṇḍila maṇḍala* has been realized in the temple city of Śrīraṅgam.[30] The central sanctuary of Viṣṇu is surrounded by seven concentric walls representing the outer spheres. Each wall is broken through at the four quarters: the pilgrims on their way to seeing the Supreme have to pass through seven gates, topped by mighty *gopuras*, before reaching the goal of their endeavors. Within the outer enclosures normal city life goes on: shops and coffee bars run along the huge walls. In the inner enclosures are *maṇḍapas*, places where the pilgrims can rest without being disturbed by worldly traffic. When passing through the last gate they first encounter the *Garuḍa-stambha*, the roosting place of Viṣṇu's *vahana*. Then only do they enter

Photo 26. Shore temple: Mahabalipuram (Tamilnadu)

the sanctuary where Viṣṇu's image, representing the Lord of the World resting on Śeṣa, is offering itself for worship.

Students of Indian temple architecture have created a number of classifications for describing the various styles that have developed over the centuries in various parts of India. Whereas the oldest extant temples show a basic pattern that is taken from profane or from Buddhist models, from the seventh century onward the development of two definite Hindu styles set in (modified later in various regions), the so-called *nāgara* or North Indian style and the so-called *draviḍa* or South Indian style.

One of the most interesting sights in India are the five *rathas* or monolithic temples at Mahabalipuram, not far from Chennai (the former Madras) on the seacoast. King Narasimhavarman apparently founded a school for architects and sculptors to develop models for temples that would then be built in full size in different parts of his kingdom.[31] Besides imitations of Buddhist Caitya halls and existing wooden structures, the spatial realization of the *yantra*, as shown in the Dharmarāja *ratha*, became the most successful model for the further development of the *draviḍa* style.[32] It can be seen in the famous *Vīrūpakṣa* temple at Paṭṭadakal, which in turn served as the model of the *Kailāsa* temple at Ellora, carved out from the mountain on a previously unheard of scale. The most magnificent specimen of the *draviḍa* model is, however, the aforementioned *Bṛhadeśvara* temple at Tanjore: its tower is more than 200 feet tall, topped by a block of granite weighing 80 tons.[33] Situated in flat country, it can be seen from miles away. The *garbhagṛha* houses the largest *liṅga* in any Indian temple.

The *nāgara* style seems to have developed from bamboo buildings, which gave to the towerlike *śikhara*, the most typical element of this style, its characteristic form (see Figure 19.4). Originally the *garbha-gṛha*, in the base of the *śikhara*, was the only structure of the North Indian temple; later a place was added for the worshippers to assemble, the so-called *jaga-mohan* or *mukha-śāla*, also topped by a towerlike structure. In several instances also a *naṭa-maṇḍira*, a dancing hall, and an *artha-maṇḍapa*, a place for the sacrificial offerings, were added.[34] Some of the best known examples of this style are the Brahmeśvara temple at Bhuvaneśvar,[35] the Khandārīya Mahādeva temple at Khajurāho,[36] and the Sun temple at Konārka,[37] all built between the ninth and the twelfth centuries CE. An interesting fusion of the *nāgara* and the *draviḍa* styles, called *vesara*, can be seen in the temples built in the thirteenth century by the later Cālukya rulers of Hoyśala in Belur, Halebid, and Somnāthpur.[38] Under Tantric influences circular temples, imitating the *cakra*, were constructed in several parts of India.[39] These models neither exhaust the basic types of temples found in Hindu India nor do they reflect even in a minor way, the extraordinary richness of Indian temple architecture in every detail of the temple structure.[40]

Although Hindus are quite often also truly appreciative of the beauty of the temple, the most important reason for going to the temple is the *darśana* of the *mūrti*: an audience with God.[41] Besides the chief image, installed in the *garbha-gṛha* of the main temple, the temples usually have a large number

Photo 27. Maṇḍapa of Śrī Raṅganātha temple: Vṛndāvana

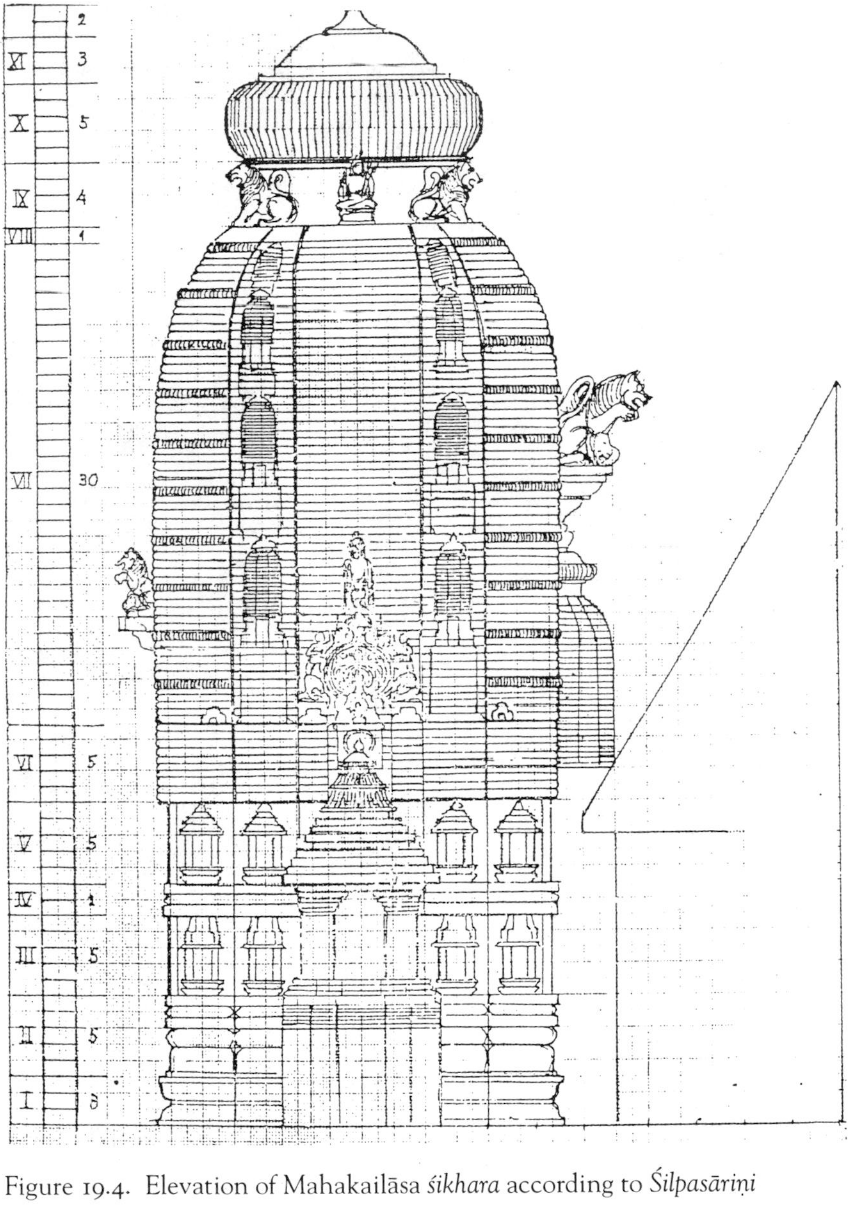


Figure 19.4. Elevation of Mahakailāsa *śikhara* according to *Śilpasāriṇi*

of minor images. The second most important is the processional image, the *utsava bera*, often a replica of the *mūla bera*, or fixed image. Though the ritual books prescribe the details of *mūrti pūjā* very strictly, the impression that an observer of Hindus worshipping the image gets is that of a rather informal and very personal style of cult: some people throw money into the small enclosure where the image is kept, hoping to get a wish fulfilled, others prostrate before it, uttering prayers in a murmur or quite audibly, others again practice meditation with *yoga-āsanas*, people ring the bell before the image to rouse its attention, they get *tilakas* painted on their forehead by the *pūjāris*, receive small morsels of sweets or fruit as *prasāda*, sip holy water; children play hide and seek, women chatter and giggle, letting their children touch the image; sick people lie around waiting for a cure, others again sit in a corner and read holy books. At least three times a day the priests offer worship according to the prescribed ritual, usually with a large crowd participating. Waving of lights, ringing of bells, and recitation of hymns and mantras are common ingredients of this worship. There is no formal obligation for Hindus to visit the temple, but there will hardly be any Hindu who would not go to the temple once in a while and many make it a point to honor the Lord through a daily visit and to receive *prasāda* as a kind of communion and a talisman against misfortune. Many of the larger temples have a fixed order of services, the timing of which can be learned from their notice boards. Temples built in our own time often resemble Christian churches in their attempts to create a large hall where people congregate for common worship and for regular religious instruction. In large cities, where the Sunday is kept as a public holiday, those temples have begun to conduct regular Sunday services with sermons. The Birla temples, built by one of the members of perhaps the richest Hindu industrial family, possess besides the *maṇḍira* also *dharmaśālas*, hostels for pilgrims, parks for recreation, and many other facilities. The number and size of temples recently built or under construction is very considerable—another sign of the vitality of Hinduism.

## HINDU FESTIVALS

All temples have their feasts that often attract huge crowds. It may be as impossible to describe a Hindu temple festival to someone who has not seen it as it is to describe a surrealist painting to a blind person. The basic structure of the festival is quite simple: usually it is a procession in which the *mūrti* is taken through town. But what makes it such an interesting experience is *how* this is done. When the feast of a famous *mūrti* is coming near, many thousands of people gather days ahead; they camp out on the roadside, squat together in picturesque groups, cook their curries and bake their *capāttis* on cow dung fires, roam the streets, loudly singing their religious songs—and wait for the great occasion. Usually, too, *sādhus* in the thousands, belonging to many *saṃpradāyas*, flock together. Yogis demonstrate their tricks; all sorts of crippled and deformed human beings and animals are exhibited; lepers come from far away, sitting in a row on the roads leading to the temple. The streets are lined with hawkers of devotional articles and with kitchen carts. Finally the great day has come. If it is a large temple and a big festival, the procession is repeated several times so as to give the chance to participate to all who want to do so. Often a *ratha*, a processional chariot, is used, several stories high. It is a temple on wheels with the *mūrti* as its center. Pulled with thick ropes, often by hundreds of men, it moves along, swaying and creaking, quite often stopped by means of wooden blocks thrown under its wheels by those whose task it is to keep it on its track. Richly caparisoned elephants, horses, and groups of *sādhus* in festive robes walk in front. Huge crowds move with the procession, throwing flowers, coins, and fruits into the chariot. A silver trumpet gives the sign to stop and to move on again. The *mūrti* is taken to a cooler place at the beginning of summer, or returned to its temple when the heat abates, or it is simply shown its realms: even legally the *mūrtis* of the big temples are the owners of the temple land, amounting very often to thousands of acres, besides possessing jewels and other valuables.

The determination of the dates of the great Hindu feasts is the task of professionals: the compilers of the *Pañcāṅgas*, the traditional calendars. All major festivals coincide with certain phases of the moon and the auspiciousness of a particular day depends on its constellations. The seven days of the week are connected with the planets and special *devatās* and each has its own peculiarity: *Ravi-vāra* is the day of the Sun, an auspicious day for beginning Vedic studies and journeys. *Soma-vāra*, the moon day, is consecrated to Śiva. It is auspicious for weddings and births, inauspicious for the purchase of clothing and for a journey eastward. *Maṅgala-vāra*, the day of Mars, is not auspicious for sowing, shaving, entering a new house, or for journeys northward. Whatever is done on *Budha-vāra*, Mercury day, brings double fruit; it is a good day for purchases and court cases. *Bṛhaspati-vāra* is named after the teacher of the *devas*, auspicious for the opening of schools, inauspicious for a journey southward. *Śukra-vāra* is sacred to Venus and a good day for buying land; inauspicious, however, for journeys westward. *Śani-vāra*, the day of Saturn, is inauspicious for practically everything.

Finding the right time is important for every undertaking; its determination is in the hands of the *jyotiṣi*, the astrologer. In India astrology is closely linked with scientific mathematics and calendar making. *Jyotiṣa* was cultivated as one of the *Vedāṅgas* from earliest times to determine the right time for sacrifices; time, *kāla*, also formed one of the most important topics of speculation in the Upaniṣads. As the *Maitrī Upaniṣad* says:

> From time are all creatures produced. Through time they grow, through time they fade. There are indeed two kinds of *brahman*: time and timelessness. That which is prior to the sun is timeless, that which begins with the sun is time having parts; the year is the form of time with parts. All beings are produced by the year, they grow by the year and fade by the year. Therefore the year is *Prajāpati*, time, nourishment, *brahma*'s dwelling and *ātman*. It is

Photo 28. Carvings on *śikhara*: Khajurāho

> said: "Time cooks all things in *paramātman*. He who knows in what time is cooked, he is the knower of the *Veda*."[42]

The need to find the right *kairós* is theologically supported by the Vaiṣṇava theory that Viṣṇu's grace waxes and wanes like the moon: he has times of *anugraha* or attraction, and of *nigraha* or rejection. One must seek him when he is full of grace.

As the divine becomes spatially available in the *mūrti*, according to its own will and decision, so it determines its temporal availability in the *utsava*, the feast celebrated at the auspicious and revealed time. Since Hinduism is still very much a cosmic religion, despite its superstructure of mythic history, the essence of time must be found in the interaction of all the cosmic bodies. The fixing of the right time for a religious action depends as little on human will as does the time for the ripening of a fruit, or the course of the year. Grace and merit are insolubly and divinely linked with time. Therefore it is essential to know about the auspicious time; the astrologer, conversant with the movement of the celestial bodies and their various influences, is indispensable for the average Hindu in every important situation. In many families the competent *paṇḍit* will set up a child's horoscope immediately after birth; and all the important occasions in the child's life will be determined according to it. There will be very few Hindu weddings for which the astrologer has not selected the *muhūrta*, the auspicious hour, when the marriage is being solemnized. The public festivals are also determined by the "right time," celebrated at such junctures as to ensure the full benefit of grace to those who participate in it.

It is meaningless to try to enumerate all the Hindu festivals.[43] Apart from the more or less universal ones, there are countless local feasts; catalogues count more than a thousand—enough to demonstrate that no Hindu can practice all of Hinduism.

*Kṛṣṇa-jayānti*, celebrated all over India, falls on the eighth *kṛṣṇa-pakṣa* of the month *Śravaṇa*: Kṛṣṇa's birth is celebrated at midnight, after a day of fasting, midnight being the exact hour in which he was born in the *bandha-gṛha*, the prison house, at Mathurā. Through his birth he manifested this hour to be the most auspicious—and so it is.[44]

*Rakhi bandhan*, on the full moon day of the same month, has a more social character: girls tie colored threads round their brothers' wrists and make them their protectors, receiving a small gift in return. According to a legend Indra was saved from the demon Bali through the magical armlet that his wife had tied for him. On this day Brahmins also usually renew their *janëus*.

*Gaṇeśa catūrthi* is celebrated on the fourth *śukla-pakṣa* of *Bhadra*; businessmen and students place their books before the image, artisans implore Gaṇeśa's blessing upon their tools.

*Dassera*, in the first half of *Aśvina*, is celebrated all over India as a holiday season.[45] It is a string of festivals during the most beautiful time of the year after the monsoon. The great heat of summer is broken by then and the sun sparkles in a radiantly blue sky. The first nine days, *nava-rātrī*, are also the time for *Durgā-pūjā*, the greatest festival of Bengal. The *pūjā* is not only limited to the Great Mother: taxi drivers decorate their cars, farmers their cows, and factory workers their machines and perform *pūjā* before them; all worship that by which they live. On the tenth day the victory of Rāma and his monkey allies over Ravaṇa is celebrated.

Another series of festivals is connected with *Divālī*, also called *Dipāvalī*, the feast of the lamps, in the second half of *Aśvina*. Countless little oil lamps on houses and temples and along the rivers and roads softly illuminate the darkness of the star-studded tropical sky, a sight which no one who has seen it could ever forget and which every Hindu living abroad remembers nostalgically every year.

Feasts like the commemoration of Prahlāda's rescue by Nṛsinha or *Vāmana dvadaśī* are celebrated only by small groups. *Nāga-pañcamī* is still quite popular especially in the south, where many people regularly feed the cobras in the house with milk, worshipping them as guardians.

At the time of the winter solstice, a kind of harvest festival is celebrated in the North Indian countryside. In February *Vasanta*, Spring, is greeted by women and children, wearing bright yellow dresses the color of *dāl* that flowers at this time.

*Śiva-rātrī*, on the thirteenth *kṛṣṇa-pakṣa* in *Magha*, is about as widespread as Kṛṣṇa's birthday. It is the principal feast of the Śaivas and also celebrated by Vaiṣṇavas for whom Śiva is Viṣṇu's first devotee and servant. The *liṅga* is decorated and painted for the occasion, bathed in honey and milk.[46]

*Holi*, in *śukla-pakṣa* of *Phalguṇa*, has much in common with the Western carnival. It is New Year's Day for many Hindus, celebrated with gaiety and abandon. According to temperament and upbringing the festivities are funny to rough. In better circles people are content to sprinkle each other with colored water and red powder; less civil big and small boys shout indecent words after people and throw dirt from the gutters on everyone. One legend explains the feast thus: Once upon a time there lived a female demon named Holikā who ate a child every day; the place where she had her dwelling had developed a system so that the burden was distributed evenly. One day the lot fell on a poor widow's only son. A good *sādhu*, seeing the woman's sorrow and despair gave her the advice to gather all the children of the place and receive Holikā with a cannonade of filthy abuse. The advice was followed and Holikā was sensitive enough to die of shame and anger.

These are just a few examples of Hindu festivals, which occupy such a prominent place in the life of the ordinary Hindu even today.

## THE IMPORTANCE OF PILGRIMAGE: *TĪRTHA*

As the Supreme becomes concretized in space and time through images and festivals, so his grace becomes localized at the *tīrthas* forever, intensified at certain times but always available to the pilgrim.[47] There are thousands of recognized *tīrthas* in India and millions of Hindus are constantly on pilgrimage. Numerous *samnyāsis* spend their whole life wandering from one *tīrtha* to another—the most meritorious way of utilizing one's time. Just as worldly globetrotters boast of the many countries and cities they have visited, so one can find *sādhus* competing with each other in enumerating the *tīrthas* visited by each. Places of pilgrimage are not made; they are found. They are what they are by divine manifestation, not by human arrangement. A complex set of rules surrounds the important undertaking of the pilgrimage: fasting, worship of Gaṇeśa, and continence are required before departure. For the pilgrimage itself a certain mode of clothing is prescribed, a copper ring and a brass vessel. Tonsure before or after pilgrimage is still quite common. Ideally the pilgrim should walk the whole distance; today most Hindus take public transport or private cars to come to the places of grace. Of importance is the *saṁkalpa*, the explicit declaration of intention to undertake a pilgrimage to a certain place. Pilgrimage by proxy is also possible; the *śāstras* lay down in detail what percentage of the merit accrues to the donor, to his parents, or his guru. The rivers are the great streams of grace in India; most of the famous *tīrthas*, literally fords, are situated on the banks of the rivers. All the *tīrthas* have *mahātmyās*, praises of their greatness, sometimes of book length, enumerating all the sacred spots and the merits attached to visits.[48]

Mother Gaṅgā is the first among India's holy rivers, sacred from where she flows through such famous *tīrthas* as Haridvāra, Prayāga, and Kāśī till she reaches the estuary in the Bay of Bengal. Gaṅgā is considered the supreme *tīrtha* in this *Kaliyuga*. Already the utterance of her name is supposed to cleanse the sinner, and a bath in the Gaṅgā or the drinking of her water (said not to putrefy) purifies the families seven generations back. As long as even a fraction of the bones of a person are lying in the Gaṅgā or touching Gaṅgā water, can they remain in heaven. Pilgrims carry small bottles of Ganges water home to use it on many occasions; even after years it is supposed to be fresh and unspoiled.[49]

The three main *tīrthas* on the Gaṅgā, called *tristhalī*, are considered to be superior to any other place in the world. They are: Prayāga, renamed Allāhābād by the Muslims, on the confluence of the Gaṅgā, Yamunā, and invisible Sarasvatī; Gāyā, sacred also to the Buddhists as Bodhgāyā, the place of enlightenment of Gautama; and Kāśī, also called Vārāṇasī (anglicized into Banares), for some time renamed Mohammadābād by the Muslim rulers. One of the maxims of pilgrims goes: "One should shave one's head in Prayāga, offer *piṇḍas* in Gāyā, give presents in Kurukṣetra and end one's life at Kāśī," continuing: "Why offer *piṇḍas* in Gāyā, why die in Kāśī when one has shaved one's head at Prayāga?"

A question much discussed in the ancient *śāstras* and among Hindu *sādhus* even today is that of religious suicide.[50] Quite a few famous *tīrthas* were for hundreds of years the final goal of many pilgrims who took their lives there in order to break out from the cycle of rebirths. Generally Hinduism considers suicide a crime leading to miserable rebirths. But at certain places it can become the supreme act of liberation. The *śāstras* mention several famous precedents, and the Purāṇas are definite that whosoever dies in Prayāga, be it naturally or through his own hand, is sure to obtain *mokṣa*. Four kinds of ending one's life were considered legitimate: burying oneself in a fire fed with dried cow dung; drowning oneself by hanging head downward in the Gaṅgā; disappearing in the waters where Gaṅgā and Yamunā meet; and cutting off one's flesh to feed the birds. Only a few years ago a popular Hindu magazine, in an appeal for the ban of cow slaughter wrote: "Starving oneself to death in a religious cause like the protection of cows is a sort of penance. In the *sanātana dharma* such fasts are recommended as *parāka* and *santapana*."[51]

The most famous of all holy cities in India is Kāśī. Although it is first and foremost the holy place of Śiva, who as Lord of Kāśī resides in the Golden Temple, all, including the Buddhists, consider it a place of pilgrimage. The city must be extremely old; archaeological excavations should reveal much more than has been known so far about this interesting place.[52] The praise showered upon Vārāṇasī surpasses everything that has been said about other Eternal Cities of the world. In the *Matsya Purāṇa* Śiva is saying: "Vārāṇasī is always my most secret place, the cause of liberation for all creatures. All sins, which one may have accumulated in thousands of previous lives, disappear as soon as one enters Avimukta. Brahmins, Kṣatriyas, Vaiśyas, and Śūdras, people of mixed castes, worms, *mlecchas* and other casteless people, insects, ants, birds, all mortal beings find bliss in my auspicious city." Even today many old people settle down in Vārāṇasi toward the end of their lives, others are taken there when dying: one funeral procession after another treks through the narrow lanes of this holy place, funeral pyres are burning constantly at the Maṇikarṇikā *ghaṭ*, which may mark the oldest site of an ancient settlement.

Vārāṇasī is filled with a peculiar atmosphere: death and life, piety and cynicism, asceticism and abandon, learning and superstition side by side; an illustration of the Lord of Kāśī who dispenses grace and terror.[53] Vārāṇasī suffered greatly under Muslim rule; its temples were destroyed repeatedly and what we see today has been rebuilt only after the eighteenth century. Before the Muslim invasion it must have been a splendid city with thousands of temples and sanctuaries. The *liṅga* of the Viśvanātha temple was saved from the invader's fury and reinstalled in its old place, which is now partly occupied by a mosque. Many miraculous cures are said to have happened to people who touched this embodiment of the Lord of the Universe. For many centuries Vārāṇasī has also been the seat of Hindu scholarship and even today almost every school has an establishment at Vārāṇasī. Vārāṇasī was chosen as the seat of the Hindu University, toward whose foundation the theosophist Madame Besant also contributed her own college. It is also the seat of the Sanskrit University, founded in 1791 by the British Resident Jonathan Duncan "primarily with a view to appease the restive citizens of Vārāṇasī after the siege of Chet

Photo 29. Houses on Ganges waterfront: Vārāṇasī (Uttar Pradesh)

Singh's fort and secondarily to collect ancient texts and carry out research on them and to produce *paṇḍits* who could be readily available to assist the English judges for the correct interpretations of the Hindu personal law."[54] A number of famous Indian and Western scholars taught at this institution, which even now conducts most of its classes in Sanskrit.

Vārāṇasī is not the only holy city, nor the only center of Hindu learning; there are thousands of *tīrthas* and dozens of places famous for scholarship. All of them convey the unique atmosphere of Hinduism, of the Supreme being present in different ways and forms in places, images, and temples, approachable at certain times and distributing grace to those who are watchful enough not to miss the occasion of its appearance and to recognize it under its manifold guises.[55]

When the Vedic *dharma* was carried into the south of India, attempts were made to duplicate the most sacred features of the *Āryavārta*, the Holy Land of the North in the south, and local rivers such as Kṛṣṇā and Kauverī were termed "Gaṅgā" and "Yamunā" of the South, Kāñcīpuram the "Vārāṇasī of the South," to create local *tīrthas* providing as much merit to pilgrims as a visit to the more distant places in the North. In the course of time the South overtook the North in wealth and splendor, and both the size of the holy cities and the number of people attending temple festivals are greater now in the South than anywhere else in India. There are veritable temple-cities associated with Śiva and Viṣṇu, with a large permanent population, where almost incessantly some festivity or the other is in progress. At particular occasions hundreds of thousands of pilgrims arrive to join in the celebrations and to augment the treasures of the temple. The arguably richest temple in the world is the Tirupati complex in Andhra Pradesh.[56] Situated in picturesque hill country, formerly reached only after days of arduous climbing, it consists of a great number of different temples to various manifestations of Viṣṇu, crowned by a chapel on the hilltop, surrounded by small dwellings where pilgrims can stay. Tens of thousands of pilgrims arrive every day by bus, car, and train, receive blessings from the temple priest, and leave some token of appreciation.

The former Kacheri Nammāḷvār temple within the Tirupati compound on the lower level has been transformed into the Śrī Venkateśvara Museum on Temple Art, the most complete of its kind, with a number of well-described exhibits explaining all aspects of temple worship, from the planning stage to the completion of the building, from the daily routine of *pūjās* to the musical instruments used.

The most famous Śiva centers in Tamiḷnādu are Cidāṃbaram, where Śiva according to legend first danced his cosmic *taṇḍava*, and Kāñcīpuram, the "Golden City," which boasts 124 temples.[57] The former capital of the Pallava rulers, it attracts hundreds of thousands of pilgrims each year. The most famous of its temples, Kailāsanātha-devaram, was built in the eighth century and is famous for its ancient paintings. Towering *gopuras* give the whole city the impression of a fortress of God.

The Mīnākṣī temple in Madurai[58]—another city of God in the Tamil country—although administered by Śaivite priests, propagates the glory of the Goddess, called "fish-eyed" here. The major celebrations at the Mīnākṣī temple are famous the world over and can even be viewed on various films and videocassettes.

The largest temple complex probably is Śrīraṅgam, situated on an island in the Kauverī River, not far from Tiruchirapalli. The seat of the Śrī-Vaiṣṇava pontiff, it is the goal of hundreds of thousands of Vaiṣṇava pilgrims from all over India.[59]

Murukan, the old Tamilian war god, has several popular centers of pilgrimage in Tamiḷnādu, which continue to attract large crowds: Tiruttanī, the birthplace of the former president-philosopher Sarvepalli Radhakrishnan may be the best known.[60]

The most famous Hindu place of pilgrimage in religiously mixed Kerala is Guruvayūr, a Kṛṣṇa sanctuary that has a unique wooden construction. It burnt down some years ago and was reconstructed in an identical fashion. Many miracles such as healing of incurably sick persons have been reported by pilgrims.[61] Guruvayūr is also famous for the recitation of the *Nārāyaṇīyam*, an artful short rendering of the *Bhāgavata Purāṇa* composed by the sixteenth-century Meppattur Nārāyaṇa Bhāṭṭatiripad, which is regularly recited at the temple.

Photo 30. Venkateśvara Temple Museum: Tirupati (Andhra Pradesh)

In all those places there is constant routine worship going on and thousands of *pūjāris* are busy performing rituals on behalf of, and for the benefit of, those who pay the sums specified for each particular form of worship. It is this uninterrupted and often quite noisy worship in thousands of sacred places all over India, the flow of millions of Hindus on pilgrimage across the country, and the mass celebration of countless local and regional feasts that lends to India, also in this age of secularization and Westernization, of motor cars and airplanes, the air of timeless religiosity and widespread concern for another kind of reality.

CHAPTER TWENTY

# The Hindu Social Order

## *Caturvarṇāśramadharma*

> In order to protect this universe He, the most resplendent One, assigned different occupations and duties to those who originated from his mouth, arms, thighs, and feet.
>
> —*Manusmṛti* I, 87

Caste has been seen as an essential institution of Hinduism from the very beginning—both by Hindus and by outsiders. A great many studies have been devoted to this phenomenon either in its entirety, or to particular aspects of it. L. Dumont observed:

> It has often been said that membership in Hinduism is essentially defined as the observance of caste rules and respect for the Brahman. T. Parsons, following Max Weber, states categorically: 'Hinduism as a religion is but an aspect of this social system, with no independent status apart from it' (*The Structure of Social Action*, 557). More subtle is the following judgment: 'in some regards, [Hinduism] is inseparable from philosophic speculation; in others, it is inseparable from social life' (L. Renou, *L'Hindouisme*, 28).[1]

The historic development and the theory of caste has been expertly described and analyzed in such classics as H. Hutton's *Caste in India*[2] and more recently in L. Dumont's *Homo Hierarchicus*.[3] It has been both defended as the best and most natural functional division of society, of model value for the whole world and also attacked as the root cause of all social evil and economic backwardness of India.

Whatever one's judgment may be, there is no doubt that caste has shaped Indian society throughout the last several thousands of years and that it is still of large practical significance. R. Inden rightly warns against isolating caste from the context of Indian civilization, "substantializing" it, and in general conceiving it as "India's essential institution . . . both the cause and effect of India's low level of political and economic 'development' and of its repeated failure to prevent its conquest by outsiders."[4] Caste in contemporary India has lost much of its economic importance, but it has gained immensely in political significance. In contrast to a centuries-long process of fission that produced more and more subcastes, who for one reason or another had separated from the major body, a process of fusion has recently been noticed: clusters of castes unite behind a political candidate, who in turn becomes their spokesman and representative.

These developments have enormous practical consequences, which we cannot fully explore in the context of this book. However, it should be clearly understood that the caste structure of Hinduism is much more flexible in many more ways than previously assumed and that the meaning of caste in India has changed, but its importance is not diminished.

## THE FOUR ORIGINAL DIVISIONS: *CATURVARṆA*

The word *caste*, derived from the Portuguese *casta*, is not really an adequate translation of the original Sanskrit term *varṇa* and is apt to generate wrong associations connected with the traditional Indian social structure. We have to keep this in mind when using it. In ancient Indian literary documents the origin of the traditional Indian social structure is associated with the creation of humankind: the *puruṣa-sūkta* of the *Ṛgveda*[5] dramatically explains the origin of humankind out of the sacrifice of the primeval *puruṣa* and his dismemberment; out of his mouth originated the *Brāhmaṇas*, from his chest came the *Kṣatriyas*, from his belly issued the *Vaiśyas*, and from his feet the *Śūdras*.

From as far back as we know the distinction of *varṇas*, and later the further division of *jātis*, based upon it, had multiple aspects. *Varṇa* originally means "color," not "caste." It was for a long time understood by Western scholars to refer to skin color, a differentiation between the supposedly fairer skinned "Aryan invaders" and the darker skinned earlier inhabitants of India. D. Bernstorff in a carefully argued study suggested that *varṇa* originally did not refer to skin color but designated the four directions identified by white, black, red, yellow according to which the participants were arranged during the Vedic *yajña*.[6]

As the Ordinances of Manu imply, the division was also occupational. The *Brāhmaṇas*, as custodians of ritual and the sacred word, were to be the teachers and advisors of society. The Kṣatriyas as defenders and warriors were to be the kings and administrators. The Vaiśyas comprised farmers and merchants, the backbone of the economy, the middle class, to introduce a modern term. The Śūdras were to be the large mass of virtually unpropertied laborers, a class of servants and menials.

The *caturvarṇa* system also embodied a religious hierarchy; combined with the universally accepted dogma of karma it implied a scale of merit. Brahmins were born into the highest caste on account of good karma accumulated over past lives. Lesser karma resulted in lesser births. The birth as a Śūdra was designed to atone for sins past. The three upper castes were eligible for initiation and the other *saṃskāras*. They had a degree of purity not to be attained by the Śūdras. Within the *dvi-jātis*, the twice-born, again a hierarchy obtained that was important in the regulation of intermarriage and commensality: on principle, the higher caste was the purer and the lower-caste member could accept food from a higher without incurring pollution.[7]

In practice the system is much more complicated and beset with what appears like contradictory regulations. The mere fact that in the end there were more than three thousand *jātis*, arranged hierarchically within the four *varṇas*, regionally following not always the same ranking and observing traditions not always in line with what would logically follow from the *caturvarṇa* scheme, should caution any observer not to draw conclusions too hastily from a superficial knowledge of the principle of how caste works. A number of detailed studies of caste ranking in specific villages or studies of *jātis* (subcastes) over a region are available to gain some understanding of the intricacies of caste in India.[8]

Every observer of Indian life will attest to the immense importance of caste and caste rules also in present, post-independence India. It is not true, as many outsiders believe, that the constitution of the Republic of India abolished caste or even intended to do so. It merely abolished the notion of "outcaste" and made it a punishable offense to disadvantage a person because of such a status.[9] Both within political parties, professional groups, municipalities, in social and economic life, in education and in government service caste has remained an important fact of life.

Though theoretically the position of one's caste is determined once and for all by birth—otherwise it would be meaningless of speak of *sva-dharma*, a certain upward mobility, besides the downgrading as result of certain offenses, can be found throughout history. Quite a number of *ādivāsis*, the aboriginals of India, were made Hindus by associating them with one of the three lower castes. According to an old Indian tradition Candragupta, the founder of the Maurya dynasty, was a Śūdra who rose to the rank of a Kṣatriya. Many Mahratta princes came from low castes and were helped by Brahmin experts to reconstruct their family tree in such a way as to show Kṣatriya ancestry, often claiming Rāma as their ancestor. In our own time quite a number of people from the lower castes have risen to prominence in administration and education. But the Brahmins defend their exclusivity: only those who are born Brahmins are Brahmins; nobody can become a Brahmin. There is a curious ancient tale about King Viśvamitra, a Kṣatriya who underwent extremely hard *tapasya* in order to compel Brahmā, the creator, to make him a Brahmin:[10] not even Brahmā was able to change someone born a non-Brahmin into a Brahmin. L. Dumont, adopting a structuralist interpretation of the institution of caste comes to the following conclusion:

First Hocart, and still more precisely than Hocart, Dumézil have shown that the hierarchical enumeration of the four *varṇas* was based on a series of oppositions, the principle of which was religious.[11] The first three classes, respectively priests, princes, and herdsmen-husbandmen, are taken together as twice-born or as those bestowing gifts, offering sacrifices, and studying (the Veda) as opposed to the fourth class, the Śūdra, who are devoid of any direct relation to religion, and whose sole task is to serve the former without envy (*Manu* I, 88–91). Among the three kinds of twice-born, the first two are opposed to the third, for to the latter the lord of creatures has made over only the cattle, to the former all creatures. It is worth noting that this particular opposition is the least frequent of all in the texts. On the contrary, the solidarity of the first two categories, priests and princes, vis-à-vis the rest, and at the same time their distinction and their relative hierarchy are abundantly documented from the *Brāhmaṇas* onward.[12]

## THE FOUR STAGES IN LIFE: *CATURĀŚRAMA*

Hindus possess an irresistible urge to classify and to organize everything into neat and logical patterns. The number four serves not only to classify the Veda (into four Saṃhitās and into four classes of books considered Veda in the wider sense) and to divide humanity into basic sections but also to structure the lives of individuals themselves. The successive life stages of a high-caste person, the *caturāśrama*, were correlated to another tetrad, the *caturvarga* or the "four aims of life" (*puruṣārtha*): *dharma* (moral law), *artha* (material goods), *kāma* (enjoyment), and *mokṣa* (liberation).[13] During studenthood (*brahmacarya*), the first stage in the life of (mostly) Brahmins, which would normally comprise about twelve years and which began after initiation (*upanayana*), the young Brahmin would, in the family of his preceptor, learn the sacred texts, acquire the necessary skills for the ritual function, get grounded in discipline, and receive his preparation for his future life. The classical writings from the Upaniṣads onward are full of descriptions of *āśramas*, training schools for Brahmins, and the routine followed there. The young novice was supposed to serve his teacher in many practical ways in return for what he was taught. Normally the stage of *brahmacarya* would terminate with the marriage of the student with which he entered the second stage of his life, *gārhastya*, the life of a householder, devoted to the enjoyment of life and to the duties associated with the care for a family: the acquisition of *artha*, material wealth. When his own children had become adults, or as one text describes it, when his temples started greying, the householder was supposed to hand over his worldly business to his sons and to lead a retired life, devoted to spiritual pursuits.

The term used is *vānaprasthya*—life in the forest. Older literature describes how the now elderly couple should set up house outside the village and its bustle and devote themselves to *mokṣa*, liberation in preparation for the end of life. Ideally, this stage should be followed by an even more radical renunciation—*samnyāsa*, the life of a homeless ascetic who possessed nothing and desired nothing but liberation from the body.[14]

While not all Hindus would follow this sequence of stages in their lives, the structure that the *caturāśrama* scheme suggests and the interests to be pursued according to the *caturvarga* scheme certainly have deeply influenced the personal and social history of Hindus and Hinduism. Its structure apparently so well reflects what Hindus understand to be the essentials of Hinduism that R. N. Dandekar chose it as the schema for his representation of Hinduism in the influential *Sources of Indian Tradition*.[15]

It also appeals to contemporary Hindus who believe it to have great practical value to provide orientation to today's India. As Dindayal Upadhyaya, a former General Secretary of the *Bhāratīya Jana Sangh*, wrote: "The ideal of the Hindu life on the basis of the four-fold *puruṣārthas*—*dharma*, *artha*, *kāma*, and *mokṣa*—can take us out of the morass. Hinduism and not socialism is the answer to the world's problems. It alone looks at life as a whole and not in bits."[16]

## THE CONTEST BETWEEN BRAHMINS AND KṢATRIYAS

In many civilizations we have the phenomenon that the holders of intellectual and spiritual power and those who wield economic and political dominance vie with each other for supremacy and that this contest—supported by historical and legal arguments on both sides—often breaks out in open rivalry. Hinduism is no exception.

Throughout the history of Hindu India there has been a contest of supremacy between Brahmins and Kṣatriyas, the religious and the secular powers.[17] Depending on the viewpoint, therefore, Hindu theories of society and state emphasize the one or the other as the sovereign power, arriving at quite different schemes of the ideal society.

In a somewhat simplified manner we may say that the *dharmaśāstra* tradition in classical Hindu literature represents the typical Brahmin view of society, whereas the Kṣatriya views are expressed in the *arthaśāstra* literature; the very terms express the direction of thought.

The *Manusmṛti*, a Brahmin text, takes for granted the division of society into the four *varṇas* and elevates the Brahmin to the position of the preserver and protector of the universe by means of the sacrifice:

> The very birth of a Brahmin is an eternal embodiment of *dharma*; for he is born to fulfill *dharma* and worthy to become Brahman. He is born as the highest on earth, the lord of all created beings, for the protection of the treasure of *dharma*. Whatever exists in this world is the property of the Brahmin; on account of the excellence of his origin the Brahmin is entitled to it all. The Brahmin eats but his own food, wears but his own apparel, bestows but his own in alms; other mortals subsist through the benevolence of the Brahmin.[18]

The duties of all the *varṇas* are spelled out in such a way as to strengthen the authority of the Brahmin. The Brahmins are to study and to teach the Veda, to offer sacrifices for themselves and for others, to give and to accept alms. The Kṣatriyas are to protect the people by means of their arms and to offer gifts to Brahmins. The Vaiśyas must tend cattle and devote themselves to agriculture and make gifts to the Brahmins, besides engaging in trade and money lending. The Śūdras are to serve the three upper classes. This Brahmin's view of society is also repeated in other works. In the *Mahābhārata* and the Purāṇas we find contemporary reflections and a contemplation of the evils of the present age, the *Kali-yuga*, whose corruption consists mainly in the abandonment of the duties of castes, as contained in the Brahminical codes. The need to fulfill *svadharma*, to stick to one's caste duties irrespective of the immediate consequences, for the sake of the world order, is also the central message of the *Bhagavadgītā*.[19]

From the time of Gautama Buddha to the contemporary *Dravida Kaẓhagam* and the *Dalit senās*, there have been anti-Brahmin movements, trying to undermine the claim of the Brahmins to leadership by exposing their theories of superiority as fallacious. Despite all these efforts the Brahmins have continued to enjoy the most respected positions in society, not only because people in India believe the Brahmin's version of religion, but also because of their overall intellectual and educational superiority.

Evidently quite a number of the ruling *Kṣatriyas* in ancient times considered themselves to be superior to the Brahmins; not only did they possess the actual political power, but they also had a theoretical framework that founded this superiority on the divine institution of kingship.[20] All the ancient accounts agree in describing the original political constitution of humankind as close to what we would call today democratic or republican. As the *Mahābhārata* has it:

> Neither kingship nor king was there in the beginning, neither scepter[21] nor the bearer of a scepter. All people protected each other by means of *dharma*. After some time they became lax in it[22] and were overcome by *moha*, a state of mind in which they lost their sense of righteousness. As a consequence of this, *lobha*, greed, developed and desire for each other's property. Then *kāma*, lust, overcame them, along with attachment to things that should be avoided and general moral decay set in. The *devas* in their distress approached Viṣṇu who brought forth from his mind Virajas who became the first king.[23]

According to this Kṣatriya version of the origin of kingship, the king does not need Brahmin sanction but is divinely appointed. According to the Brahmin's account he becomes king effectively only through the consecration. That Brahmins did exert considerable influence over the appointment of kings and also their eventual removal, if necessary by violent means, is amply born out by the facts of Indian history as known to us. The *Purāṇas* contain an account of a regicide perpetrated by Brahmins that could have a historical core: Veṇa, a mythical king, proclaimed himself supreme Lord and forbade sacrifices and donations to Brahmins.[24] The *ṛṣis* sent a delegation to him, which politely but strongly urged him to rescind his edict and to restore the rights of the Brahmins "for the preservation of your kingdom and your life and for the benefit of all your subjects." Veṇa refused to acknowledge anyone superior to him and maintained the thesis that the king, a Kṣatriya, is the embodiment of all divinities and therefore the Supreme Being. The first duty also of the Brahmins, he explained, is to obey the king. The text proceeds: "Then those pious men were filled with wrath and cried out to each other: 'Let us slay this wicked wretch! This impious man who has reviled the Lord of sacrifice is not fit to reign over the earth.' And they fell upon the king, and beat him with blades of holy grass, consecrated by mantras and slew him, who had first been destroyed by his impiety toward God." Down with the "wicked king" went also the firm hand needed to deal with the unruly, and universal chaos broke out, leaving the people at the mercy of large bands of marauders and robbers. Thus the Brahmins were forced to find another king. Apparently there were two contenders: according to the story they arose through the activity of the Brahmins who rubbed or drilled the right thigh and the right arm of the dead king; thus perhaps alluding to their castes. They rejected Niṣāda and chose Pṛthu, on whom they conferred universal dominion and who accepted and confirmed the Brahmins' demands and superiority. For the writers of this story the beginning of true kingship dates from Pṛthu, the Brahmin-appointed ruler, "a speaker of truth, bounteous, an observer of his promises, wise, benevolent, patient, valiant, and a terror to the wicked, knowing his duties, compassionate and with a kind voice, respecting the worthy, performing sacrifices, and worshipping Brahmins."[25] The prosperity of his rule is ascribed to his orthodoxy and his submission under the Brahmin's *dharma*—and, to drive the point of their story home to all, the very name of the earth, *pṛthvī*, is associated with this king, the first to be appointed by Brahmins and in their eyes the first who really and rightfully bore the title *rāja*.

In a different, and perhaps more historical context, the name of India, Bhārata, is associated with king Bharata, the son of Ṛṣabha, who is praised as virtuous and who in recognition of his merits was later reborn as a Brahmin—revealing again the Brahmin claim to superiority over the Kṣatriyas.

Throughout Indian history, state and religion lived in a symbiotic alliance, more or less happy according to the circumstances and persons involved. The Brahmins served as counsellors and advisors, developing a complex *rājadharma* designed to combine the exigencies of statecraft with Brahminic ideology.[26] In the Brahmins' view *dharma* was the central point and the source of political power and economic prosperity; in the Kṣatriyas' opinion *artha*, statecraft, political power, and economic strength were the basis of *dharma*.

The *arthaśāstra* works, therefore, are treatises recommending *Realpolitik*, utilizing, if necessary, religious beliefs and customs to strengthen the king's position. Most of these manuals are lost, and we know about them only from quotations. The *Kauṭilīya Arthaśāstra*, however, whose full text was recovered and published in 1905 by R. Shamasastry and translated into English ten years later, and which is, according to its testimony, a compendium of all its predecessors, gives a fairly typical picture of the style and contents of this type of literature. Ancient Indian tradition identifies Kauṭilya with Cāṇakya or Viṣṇugupta, the Minister of Candragupta Maurya.[27] (Some Western scholars have expressed doubts about this dating and would place the work around the fourth century CE.) Historically Kauṭilya's work is of great interest, as it gives us a fairly realistic idea of the life in ancient India, of the working of the Mauryan administration, and the economic and social conditions before Aśoka. Not content with wise maxims and theological principles, as are the authors of *dharmaśāstra*, Kauṭilya offers precise instructions of a very concrete nature concerning all aspects of government. The lip service that he pays to *dharma* in the introductory pages is completely overwhelmed by shrewd practical schemes designed to make the king an absolute monarch and the state he serves the most powerful one around. *Vārtā* and *daṇḍa*, economy and law enforcement, constitute the two pillars of the king's power.

However powerful the king's position may be in Kauṭilya's scheme, he is but one of the elements of the state; the real theme of the *Arthaśāstra* is the absolutism of the empire—the actual emperor can be exchanged as any other functionary. "The king, the ministers, the country, the fort, the treasury, the army, the friend and the enemy are the elements of sovereignty." These depend so much on each other that they can only stand or fall together, and the king should never make the fatal mistake of thinking of himself as being the state! Kauṭilya's ideal ruler is equally far removed from any type of altruistic dedication and world-saving fanaticism of a religious autocrat as he is far from the cynicism and power play of a modern self-made dictator.[28] Kauṭilya demands that the ruler be educated and really competent in the art of ruling a country. In many ways the *Arthaśāstra*'s approach may shock a modern democrat, but we must not forget that this book was not supposed to be read by the common man who is told to follow his traditional *dharma*. It is a royal art—the art of being master. Success in power politics, as history teaches us, does not depend on sensitivity and piety but on determined ruthlessness to acquire power, to keep it, and to increase it. That is *artha*.[29]

In a broader classification Kautilya describes his work as belonging to *rājanīti*. *Nīti* is often translated as "ethics"; the associations that most of us have with the term ethics would not necessarily coincide with what we have just described. *Nīti* is the art of surviving in a world of enemies, thriving on the folly of others, making the best out of a given situation.

## TRADITION VS. MODERNITY

The Muslim invasion and occupation, the British rule and modernity in general have made their inroads into Hindu society for better and for worse. The basic caste structure of the four *varṇas*, subdivided into some three thousand *jātis*,[30] is still remarkably strong in many areas of life. Though social reformers have attacked it for almost two centuries as the major cause of all social and economic ills in India, it has served to provide not only large sections of the population with a minimum of social security and status in society, but it also has deep emotional roots that cannot be severed easily without doing great harm.

Much has been written on "tradition and modernity in India" from the sociological viewpoint, and for everyone with even a cursory acquaintance with India it is clear that Indian society has enormous problems to contend with, problems arising largely out of India's history and not amenable to modern Western solutions (if there are such!). A. D. Moddie, himself a modern Indian businessman, has written a thoughtful book entitled *The Brahmanical Culture and Modernity*, in which he analyses the situation in quite an original way. Thus he writes: "If any country had the problem of two cultures in a bad way, with the leaden weight of dead history and an archaic society behind it, it is India. But here the split is not between anything as simple, as purely intellectual as the literary and the scientific. It is deep and sociological and historical: it is more than an intellectual gap between two quite different types of minds." He goes on to define the attributes of the Brahmanical culture as traditional, caste dominated, hierarchical, authoritarian, village and land based, status oriented, inherently averse to change, essentially undemocratic, accepting as law, life, and reality what is written in the *patra*, the authoritative book.

In contrast to this the modern, industrial culture is essentially international, not village or caste based in its social motivations, but scientific, rational, achievement oriented, with a mobile elite of intellect, skills and wealth, making material advancement its major objective.

Whereas Moddie quite frankly sides with modernity,[31] others, seeing the same dilemma facing Hindu society, try to return to pure Hinduism as the only hope for India's future. Mahātmā Gandhi's aversion to modern technology and scientific progress had at its source a concern for the masses, who would be left without work and without a frame of moral rules if industrialization and the impersonal, exclusively profit-oriented mentality that goes with it, were to take over in India. Deeper down, however, Gandhi also felt a concern for Hinduism as a way of life and a religion, which he saw threatened and which he treasured and wanted to see preserved.

## THE DARK SHADOW OF THE *CATURVARṆĀŚRAMA* IDEAL: THE OUTCASTES

Theoretical and theological the *caturvarṇāśrama* scheme may have been. But it also translated into Indian reality so that socially, and quite often also economically and physically, nobody could survive outside caste. The Brahmins did not articulate "human rights" but "caste rights," which had the side effect that in the course of time about one-fifth of the total population, as "outcastes," had virtually no rights. They were treated worse than cattle, which even in legal theory ranked above them.[32] People became casteless by violating the rules of their castes, either by marring contrary to the caste regulations, by following professions not allowed by caste rules, or by committing other acts that were punished by expulsion from the caste. Some books give them the appellation "fifth caste," but that may leave a wrong impression: they were cut off from all the rights and privileges that caste society extended to its members, ritually impure and ostensibly the product of bad karma coming to fruition.

A notorious example of the distance that Brahmins put between themselves and the outcastes was offered by the Nambūdiris of Kerala. Whenever a Nambūdiri left his house, a Nayar had to precede him to proclaim that the great Lord was about to come. All outcastes had to hide; the mere sight of them would make a Nambūdiri unclean. If by any accident the shadow of a *paria* fell upon a Nambūdiri, he had to undergo lengthy purification ceremonies. Though the Indian constitution has legally abolished untouchability, it is still an unpleasant reality in the lives and minds of many Hindus even today. In the villages the former untouchables still usually live in secluded quarters, do the dirtiest work, and are not allowed to use the village well and other common facilities.[33] The government tries to help them through privileges in schools and offices; but these are often eyed with jealousy and suspicion by the caste Hindus. When some time ago the Mandal Commission recommended reserving a percentage of placements at universities and positions in government service for members of the "scheduled castes," violent protests erupted, culminating in the public self-immolation of students from higher castes.

Mahātmā Gandhi fought for their rights, especially the right to enter Hindu temples (quite often they are still refused admission!) calling them *Harijan*, God's people. But even he wanted to maintain the caste structure and was extremely angry with Dr. Ambedkar, the leader of the outcastes, who severed all ties with caste society by turning Buddhist and drawing some three million of his followers with him.[34] The casteism of the outcastes, however, is highlighted by the fact that, despised and humiliated as they are, they have established among themselves a caste structure analogous to the *caturvarṇa* system and jealously observe their own ranking within it. They have begun organizing recently under the banner of a number of *Dalit* (oppressed) movements and have made modest progress, at least economically. Dalits have become a political force to reckon with. Their effectiveness, however, is impaired by the divisions that exist among them and the mutual hostilities of various groups that are often organized along religious or political party lines.[35]

CHAPTER TWENTY-ONE

# *Saṃnyāsa*

## *The Highest Hindu Aspiration*

> One who has cut off all desires with the sword of knowledge, boards this boat of Knowledge Supreme and crosses this ocean of relative existence, thereby attaining the Supreme Abode—this one indeed is blessed.
>
> —Śaṅkarācārya, *Vijñāna-nauka* 10

The Vedic system of *caturvarṇāśrama* singled out one of the four great sections of society for professionally practicing religion: studying and teaching the Veda, performing sacrifices for themselves and for others was defined as the foremost social duty of Brahmins.[1] In the course of their individual lives, too, a progressive spiritualization was provided for. After the period of *brahmacarya*, youth spent in studying with a guru, and after the time of *gārhastya*, family life devoted to fulfilling the duties enjoined by scriptures and offering sacrifices for the benefit of *devas, pitṛs*, and humans, the Brahmin was supposed to become a *vānaprastha*, a forest hermit practicing meditation of the Upaniṣadic type, and finally a *saṃnyāsi*, a renouncer without a fixed abode and without any possession or attachment, solely devoted to the realization of the absolute.

This ideal schema never corresponded in its entirety to the reality of Hindu life, but it institutionalizes a very strong current within Hinduism: the desire to make religion one's whole purpose in life rather than just one of the many things in life. Whereas the oldest law books explicitly state that *saṃnyāsa* is only for Brahmins who have passed through the other three stages of life,[2] Hindu practice, for as long as we know it, has been less strict. Many Brahmins chose to enter *saṃnyāsa* right after *brahmacarya* as its continuance and perfection, and many non-Brahmins took up this mode of life as well.

## VARIETIES OF HOLY MEN AND WOMEN

The terms used to identify the "religious" vary, and despite the quite precise definition of some of them, they are applied very loosely by the average Hindu. *Sādhu*, "holy man" or its feminine form, *sādhvī*, or *sant*, "saint," are common designations applied by most people to all categories of the religious. *Saṃnyāsi* (feminine: *saṃnyāsinī*), "renouncer," is a fairly common term, too, though sometimes it is restricted to the members of the order founded by Śaṅkarācārya, the Daśanāmis (who do not accept women ascetics). In contrast to these the Vaiṣṇava religious are called *vairāgis* (feminine: *vairāginī*), a word that has the same meaning, but is used in a more exclusive way. *Yogi* (feminine: *yoginī*) as a professional designation can also mean holy men or women in general, or it can designate members of particular groups. Quite often the designation of the *saṃpradāya* or specific order is used as a name particularly in those places where either one *saṃpradāya* is especially prominent or where so many *sādhus* and *sādhvīs* live that people are familiar with the more subtle distinctions among them. Not all the estimated eight to fifteen million religious, male and female, of today are formally members of a particular order; many are *svatantra sādhus*, people who without going through the formalities of initiation through a guru and membership in an order don the religious garb and follow a path within the general frame of Hindu religious life. Quite often English books speak of the *sādhus* as "ascetics" or "monks," terms with associations within the Western Christian religion, which do not really apply to Hinduism. The etymology of *sādhu* goes a long way toward clarifying its meaning. It is derived from the root *sādh-*, to accomplish, and describes someone who follows a certain *sādhana*, a definite way of life designed to accomplish realization of his ultimate ideal, be it the vision of a personal God or the merging with the impersonal *brahman*. As long as one has not yet reached the goal one is a *sādhaka*; the perfect one is called *siddha*, having achieved *sādhya*, the end to be reached.

The various groups of religious differ in their *sādhana*; differences that sometimes concern doctrinal and dogmatic issues, sometimes ways of life and behavior, sometimes rituals and practices. It is hardly possible even to list all the *saṃpradāyas*, numbering three hundred or more. Though there have been efforts on many occasions in the past to organize and classify them, all these attempts have been overtaken by the development of ever new groups and orders.[3] Especially in modern times there has been a proliferation of new religious orders, often with a reformist or activist character; almost every popular svāmi becomes the founder of a new *saṃpradāya*.

A very impressive demonstration of the variety and strength of Hindu religious orders is offered by the *Kumbhamelās*. Not only do the many thousands of *sādhus* and *sādhvinīs* assembled form an ordered procession in which a place is assigned to each group according to a strict canon of precedence, but they also hold their own *saṃpradāya* conferences there and settle disputes concerning teachings and practices.

The forerunners, and quite often still the ideals, of the *saṃnyāsis* of today are the Vedic *ṛṣis*, the sages of the Upaniṣads, the ancient *kavis* and saints. The history of Hindu *saṃnyāsa* thus goes back into the mythical past and appears to have been a well-established institution of long standing by the time of Jīna Mahāvīra and Gautama Buddha. Jain and Buddhist sources offer us a detailed account of many different orders.

The *Mahābhārata* enumerates what may have been the four original and oldest *saṃpradāyas*: *kuṭicakas*, who practiced religious life while living with their families; *bahūdakas*, who lived near settlements and begged their food from Brahmin families only; *haṃsas*, literally, "swans," wandering ascetics, still enjoying a minimum of comfort; *paramahaṃsas*, "supreme swans," homeless and divested of everything, including their begging bowl, their staff, and their clothes, "a condition that is divested of sorrow and happiness, auspicious and free from decrepitude and death, knowing no change."[4]

The *Mahābhārata* also described various *vratas* practiced by these people; they very often constitute what was later called *sādhana*. The *Paramahaṃsa Upaniṣad* describes the highest ideal as follows:

> The way of the *paramahaṃsa* is very difficult to find; truly such a one ever rests in pure *brahman*, he is *brahman* as proclaimed in the Vedas, for his spirit always rests in me and I in him. Having left his sons and friends, his wife and relatives behind and having cut off the *śikhā*,[5] put away the sacred thread, given up Vedic studies, all karma, and the entire world, he may possess only the *kaupina*, the staff and food enough to keep his body alive. He does not need anything beyond that. He experiences neither heat nor cold, neither joy nor sorrow, neither honor nor disdain. Having given up all deceit, untruth, jealousy, arrogance, pride, affection and disdain, lust and anger, selfishness and conceit, envy and avarice, he considers his own body like a corpse, getting altogether rid of the body idea. Forever liberated from the root of doubt, from false and unfounded knowledge, realizing *brahman*, he lives in the self and knows: "I myself am He, I am That which is ever calm, immutable, undivided, conscious of itself and blissful; this alone is my true nature!" This knowledge alone is his *śikhā*, his sacred thread, and his *saṃdhyā*. He who has renounced all desire and finds his supreme peace in the One, he who holds the staff of knowledge, he is the true *ekadaṇḍi*. The four quarters of heaven are his clothing, he prostrates before none, he no longer offers sacrifices, and he scolds none and praises none. The *saṃnyāsi* is always independent. For him there is no invocation, no ceremony, no mantra, no meditation, no worship; this phenomenal world does not exist for him, or the world beyond. He neither sees duality nor unity; he neither sees I nor Thou nor all this. The *saṃnyāsi* has no home. He will not accept gold or disciples, or any other gift. If asked, why not, he will reply: "Yes, it is harmful!"[6]

## THE *SAṂNYĀSI'S* PROGRESS

Very few at any given time have reached this ultimate freedom of the *paramahaṃsa*; for the rest there have been rules that regulate their lives and offer a certain framework within which they can develop. All *smṛtis* have special sections on the rights and duties of *saṃnyāsis* and later writers have brought these together into the *Yatidharma*, which leaves a certain freedom in quite a few matters, but also regulates the basic structure of the life of the religious.[7]

It begins by stating the *adhikāra*, the prerequisite qualification in aspirant and master: normally the birth as a Brahmin and the performance of the prescribed *saṃskāras* are insisted upon, together with certain physical qualities: a pleasing appearance, certain auspicious marks on hand and feet, unimpeded speech and absence of physical defects in the limbs. As the *Yatidharma* says: "A Brahmin after examining those worlds, which are reached through Vedic rituals, should become indifferent after seeing that these actions do not result in anything that is eternal. The learned teacher should correctly explain to the disciple, endowed with self-control and a tranquil mind, the knowledge of *brahman*, revealing to him the imperishable and eternal Being."[8] Moral purity, sincere thirst for ultimate reality, and trust in the guru are the basic requirements in practically all schools. Rāmānuja demands in addition a real calling from the side of Viṣṇu.[9] Śrīpati requires the *sādhaka* to wear a *liṅga* on his body as prerequisite for *sādhana* proper.

The surest sign of a religious vocation for the Hindu is the formal acceptance of the novice by the guru whom he approaches. Also the qualification of the spiritual master must be established. Very often the guru is well known as an authority and there is no need for further tests. An important factor is the *guru paraṃparā*, the succession of spiritual masters.[10] It is one of the first things each disciple learns and recites. According to Śaṅkara only a Brahmin can be a proper guru. The guru must be "endowed with the power of furnishing arguments pro and con, of understanding questions and remembering them; he must possess tranquillity, self-control, compassion; he must have a desire to help others, must be versed in the scriptures, be unattached to enjoyments, a knower of *brahman* and firmly established in *brahman*. He must never transgress the rules of good behavior, must be free from pride, deceit, cunning, jugglery, jealousy, falsehood, egotism. He must have as his sole aim the wish to help others and the desire to impart *brahmavidyā*.[11] To some extent the guru must be perfect; this is the more true in Vaiṣṇava *saṃpradāyas*, where the role of the guru becomes all-important as the representative of God on earth and the association of guru and disciple lasts for a lifetime.

After the disciple has been accepted by his guru there follows a period of training and probation, differing in length and depth from one group to the other. Conscientious gurus will see to it that the disciple has made genuine spiritual progress before *dīkṣā*, the official ordination, is imparted. Others, who pride themselves in having a large number of disciples, will undertake it almost without any instruction. Though they vary from one *saṃpradāya* to the other, some elements of initiation are common enough to be mentioned: the body of the novice is completely shaved, including the *śikhā*, nails on hands and feet are cut. The novice prepares a pyre and lays down on it for a short while. Then he gets up and lights it, thus performing his own cremation; from now on he is considered dead to the world. When he dies, he will be buried and not cremated. The candidate then immerses himself in the water of a nearby river or tank. He strips completely and takes a few steps naked, like a newborn, before his guru binds the *kaupina*, a piece of cloth, around his waist, and invests him with staff and water bowl. One of the common features is the imparting of the mantra, which is whispered into the ear, not to be revealed to anyone, except to one's own disciple. Śaṅkara Daśanāmis normally get a *śloka* from the Upaniṣads and Vaiṣṇavas a *śloka* from the *Bhāgavata Purāṇa* as their mantra.

Usually a final *upadeśa*, a lesson of religious instruction, is given. According to the classic tradition, maintained by the Daśanāmis, the newly ordained religious sets out for a year-long pilgrimage, traversing the length and breadth of India and visiting as many *tīrthas* as possible. Vaiṣṇavas continue to stay with their guru, quite frequently also in a *maṭha*, a kind of monastery, where a large number of monks may live together. Nowadays many Hindu religious change from one order to another, or return to family life, although in former times quite heavy penalties had been instituted for such circumstances.[12] The *saṃpradāya* may also expel members who are found to hold unorthodox views or who commit offenses against the rules. Without attempting to offer anything like a complete list of Hindu *saṃpradāyas*, we may give a few details, following the classification in an authoritative Hindu work.[13]

## *SAṂNYĀSI* ORDERS

Vedānta is basically nonsectarian and the main tradition built upon it calls itself *smārta*, claiming to represent the mainstream Vedic religion rather than particular later churches. Its *paraṃparā* includes all the great Vedāntins mentioned in the *Vedānta-sūtra*, beginning with Bādarī, Kārṣṇa, Atreya, Audulomi, and so on, to Śaṅkara[14] who reputedly founded the order of the Daśanāmi Saṃnyāsis, so called because they are divided into ten groups, each of which attaches one of the following names to its accepted religious name: Āraṇya, Āśrama, Bhāratī, Giri, Pārvata, Pūrī, Sarasvatī, Sāgara, Tīrtha, and Vāna.[15] The religious names proper usually end with *-ānanda*, bliss: Yogānanda finds his bliss in Yoga, Vivekānanda in discriminatory knowledge, Dāyānanda in mildness, and so forth.

Śaṅkara wanted his orders to become the vanguard of orthodoxy, the scourge of Buddhism, and the protagonists of the reform of Hinduism. In contrast to the Buddhists, who were somewhat decadent at this time, Śaṅkara insisted on rigorous discipline and intellectual activity. According to tradition, he founded bulwarks of Advaita in the four corners of India:[16] Vimalā Pīṭha at Jagannātha/Pūrī on the east coast, with which the Āraṇyas and Vānas are associated, having as their mantra: "*prajñānam brahman*"; Jyoti Maṭha near Badrinātha in the Himālayas, the center of the Giri, Pārvata, and Sāgara, with the mantra: "*ayam ātman brahman*"; Kalikā Pīṭha in Dvārakā on the west coast, with the Tīrthas and Āśramas, having as their mantra: "*tat tvam asi*"; and Śāradā Pīṭha in Śṛṅgerī in Kārṇāṭaka, the home base of the Bhāratis, Pūrīs, and Sarasvatīs, with the mantra: "*aham brahmāsmi*." The *ācārya* of the latter is considered to be the actual head of the entire order, addressed as *jagadguru*, spiritual master of the whole world.

The Daśanāmis are the most respected group of religious in India, usually well versed in Sanskrit learning and Vedānta philosophy, and often possessing a modern education. In former times they had to suffer the attacks of the Bauddhas and Vaiṣṇavas; being bound to *ahiṃsā*, they recruited armies of Daśanāmi *nāgas*, equipped with heavy iron tridents, who defended the *saṃnyāsis*. As late as the nineteenth century there were regular battles between these and the Vaiṣṇava *nāgas* in which hundreds were killed.[17] At present there are six *ākhāḍas*, centers of Daśanāmi *nāgas*, with several hundred members each. They are often illiterate and their religious program is limited to *haṭha yoga*, physical exercises, which are meant to make them insensitive to pain and endow them with supernatural powers.

The Śaṅkarācāryas of the four *maṭhas* trace their *guru paramparā* back through a number of illustrious Vedāntins like Padmapada, Maṇḍanamiśra, Vācaspatimiśra, Vidyāraṇya, Ānandagiri, Appaya Dīkṣita, Sadānanda, and others to Ādiśaṅkārācarya, the founder.

The living Śaṅkarācāryas "represent an institution and are themselves an institution in India's religious life."[18] They are not only fairly universally respected in India as successors to the great Śaṅkara, the restorer of Hinduism in the eighth century, but they exert a major influence through their educational institutions that they maintain. Each of the Śaṅkara *maṭhas* has a number of schools attached to it in which Sanskrit and the traditional subjects of Hindu learning are cultivated. These schools are a major employer of India's traditional Pandits and they produce most of today's traditionally trained Hindus. They use Sanskrit as a medium of instruction and the Śaṅkarācāryas propagate Sanskrit as not only the sacred language of India but also the lifeblood of Indian culture. These eminent leaders of Hinduism are wholly committed to their tradition—but most are not fanatics. They have their parallel in the institutionalized *saṃnyāsa* of other Hindu denominations, the heads of the Śrīraṅgam *maṭha*, of Uḍipī and other places. There is no doubt at all that in and through them *saṃnyāsa* proves to be an institutional support of Hinduism—perhaps the most important one. Their position has gained in strength in the past decades and is likely to increase more so in the future.

Śaṅkara, the great reformer of Hinduism in the eighth century, also redefined the idea and ideal of *saṃnyāsa*. Whatever its conception may have been before his time and whatever forms of religious life prevailed after him, the description of *saṃnyāsa* in terms of study and self-consciousness rather than yoga, devotional practices or self-mortification is due to him and his ideas of self-realization. In its intellectuality and its outward moderation, its emphasis on introspection and unperturbed serenity of mind it has created a prototype of universal appeal, free from sectarian fervor and masochistic self-torture.

Vaiṣṇava religious are usually known as *vairāgis*. A conference in the fourteenth century affiliated the numerous groups to four *saṃpradāyas* in a rather artificial way; the system has been broken up through many new developments.

The Śrīvaiṣṇavas are organized in the Rāmānuja *saṃpradāya*, whose head is the ruling *mahant* of the temple *maṭha* of Śrīrangam, endowed since Rāmānuja's time with infallibility in matters of doctrine and ritual.

The second is the *Brāhma saṃpradāya* founded by Madhva, also called Ānanda Tīrtha or Pūrna Prajñā. Madhvites are largely restricted to the south where they keep custody over the *maṭhas* established by the founder. In former times they must have been quite numerous. Among their peculiar customs is the adoption of a name of Viṣṇu and the branding of the body with a red-hot iron to imprint upon it forever the *cakra* of Viṣṇu.

The third *saṃpradāya* is associated with Nimbārka, a twelfth-century Vaiṣṇava. The *Nīmavats*, however, claim to owe their foundation to Viṣṇu himself in the form of the Haṃsa *avatāra*; they have several centers in the district of Mathurā, in Bengal and Rājasthān.

Vallabha, the founder of the Rudra *saṃpradāya*, was a married man; in his order the feasts honoring his two sons and seven grandsons are still celebrated as major events. He taught the *puṣṭimārga*, promising salvation to all who unconditionally follow the guru.

Caitanya's followers belong technically to the Madhva *saṃpradāya*, but are in fact a quite distinct branch by themselves. They are quite numerous in Bengal and northern India, augmented recently by numerous Westerners in the Hare Krishna movement.

One of the largest *saṃpradāyas* today is that founded by Rāmānanda, called Śrī *saṃpradāya*; its members worship Sītā and Rāma as their divine patrons. Rāmānanda, who was born around 1300 in Prayāga, accepted people from all castes, including women, into his order. His twelve best-known disciples founded subsects, known as *dvāras*. Their main center, called *bara sthāna*, is in Ayodhyā, the home town of Rāma. They have several hundred centers today in India, peopled by thousands of fervent, if uneducated, people. They are said to indulge quite frequently in kidnapping to provide new members for their order. As part of their initiation rites they burn the name of Rāma into their skins and usually suffix the word *dāsa*, slave, to their accepted names. Their formula of greeting is "*jay sītārāma*."

As some Kṛṣṇa worshippers take on the role of *gopīs*, thus there are also Rāmānandis who imagine themselves to be Sītā, dressing in women's clothing and walking around laden with jewelry. It is not unusual for Rāmānandis to run *Gośalās*, old age homes for cows.

Photo 31. Śiva Kānphaṭa (Maharashtra) [Heras Institute]

The counterpart to the Daśanāmi *nāgas*, the so-called *catursaṃpradāya nāgas*, are militant Vaiṣṇavas, organized into *ākhāḍas*. They are subdivided into two groups; one carries a banner with the image of Rādhā-Kṛṣṇa, the other one with Sītā-Rāma. Of one Vaiṣṇava *nāga* it is reliably told that he had taken a vow not to eat one mouthful before he had killed at least one Śaiva monk. A Śaiva in his turn had sworn never to eat his daily meal, unless he had first slain at least one Vaiṣṇava. Bloody clashes, frequent in former centuries, have become rare nowadays, but they are not unknown.[19]

Śiva is the *saṃnyāsi* par excellence; he is described as the great *tyāgi*, the one who renounced to such an extent that he even cut off his member with his own hand, living on burning *ghaṭs* and in mountain recesses. Sāiva *saṃnyāsis* claim to have the oldest tradition of all, and in fact they predate the writing of the *Mahābhārata*. Śaṅkara knew of several distinct Śaiva schools in his time; one can classify the numerous sects into those that follow the benevolent, or Śiva, aspect of the deity, and those that follow the terrible, or Rudra, aspect. Amongst the former figure prominently the *Vīra-śaivas*, mentioned before, and the *Pāśu-patas*, reputedly a foundation of Lakuliṣa, a Śiva *avatāra*. Among the latter, the most prominent are the *Kālamukhas* and the *Kāpālikas*, practicing rites and a mode of life that few educated people would associate with religion.[20] The Aghoris are closely associated with them, and are quite numerous even today, especially in Vārāṇasī. According to their rules they are not allowed to beg, nor are they allowed to refuse anything that is offered to them. All their rites are performed on cremation grounds from which they also get all their belongings. They are reputed to even eat meat from human corpses and spend entire nights dancing around them. They smear their bodies with the ashes from the cremation grounds and are also considered to be masters of the occult arts. They claim to owe their supernatural powers to the *pretas*, the spirits of the departed, whom they worship.

The *samādhi* of their founder, Bābā Kinarām,[21] is a famous place in Vārāṇasī: he is said to have worked many miracles during his lifetime, to have called dead animals back to life and to have restored the sight of the blind. An Indian journalist gave the following report:

> The Aghori leader who now presides over the Bābā Kinarām Ashram is Bābā Avadhūt Bhagvān Rām. He is, no doubt, a true representative of the Aghori Panth in all its *raudra* and *tamasa* aspects. But he is—what a paradox!—essentially a humanitarian. He has dedicated himself completely to the cause of providing relief for the lepers. He is the moving spirit of the Leper Asylum at Rajghat on the east bank of the Gaṅgā. Indeed, the Aghoris are as fond of the living as they are of the dead. Avadhūt Bhagvān Rām is a big burly man, full of cleverly concealed contempt for the so-called normal human being. "He bores me," he says with a sinister smile and lapses into silence. Suddenly, after a prolonged pause, he bursts out good-humouredly: "You see, I can't even eat him till he is dead."[22]

Yogis, the next major section, are also divided into numerous subsections, the largest and best known of which are the *Nāṭha-panthis*, followers of Gorakhnāṭha.[23] They have a male and a female branch and are subdivided into *Aughara* and *Kānphaṭa*. They wear red and yellow garments and carry a vessel without a handle for eating and drinking. This vessel used to be a human skull; nowadays it is usually the blackened half of a coconut shell. Round their neck they wear a thread made of black sheep's wool with a single *rudrākṣa* bead and a goat's horn on a cotton string. The goat's horn is blown before the meals. Often they carry a long pair of iron tongs with a ring. The name of the Kānphaṭis, hole-in-the-ear, derives from their initiation ceremony: the guru pierces the ear of the novice with a double-edged knife and inserts an iron ring. Though they also have their centers, most of them are constantly on the move. One of their peculiarities is the circumambulation of the river Narbadā. They begin their pilgrimage in Broach, on the Arabian Sea, go up to the source at Amarakaṇṭaka and return on the other bank. In their *maṭhas* they keep a fire burning and a bunch of peacock feathers near it.

A more recent foundation is that of the *Caraṇadāsis*, originating with Śukadeva (1760–1838), who wrote a number of books dealing with different aspects of Yoga. In former times the worshippers of Gaṇapati and Sūrya formed separate orders; little of these movements remain.[24] A considerable number of *saṃpradāyas*, however, have developed within Śāktism, divided mainly into right-hand Tāntrikas and left-hand Tāntrikas. Of their twelve *saṃpradāyas* (with subsections) the most important today are the *Lopāmudrā* and the *Manmathā*.[25]

There are numerous orders that cannot be classified under the above groups and Rāmdās Gaur characterizes them as *sudhāraka* or reformist. Taking their inspiration from the *Bhāgavata Purāṇa*, many poet-saints like Jñāneśvara, Nāmadeva, Nabhajī, and others, founded movements that can be loosely put together under the name of *Bhāgavata Saṃpradāya*. Tukārām, born 1665, one of the most popular saints of Mahārāṣṭra, did not really found a new *saṃpradāya*, but out of the groups that he led to the sanctuary of Viṭṭal in Pandharpur developed the order of the *Vārkarīs*, consisting mostly of householders who follow a certain mode of life.[26] Rāmadāsa Swāmi, born in 1865, became the founder of another popular order that attracted mainly low-caste people.[27] A somewhat less reputable order is the Dattā *saṃpradāya*, also called Mānabhāū, a Vaiṣṇava sect founded in the fourteenth century and proscribed by several rulers. There is also a Narasinha *saṃpradāya*, of unknown origin and date, a Rāmavata *saṃpradāya* quite close to the *Rāmadāsīs* mentioned previously. Kabīr, the Muslim weaver who became a Hindu saint, and whose hymns have become part of the Ādi Granth, the holy book of Sikhs, became the founder of the Kabīr Panth, which comes close to a nonsectarian religious brotherhood (if that is possible).[28] Popular are also the Dādū Panth and the Lāldāsī Panth. An interesting group are the Satya-nāmīs: claiming a very ancient history, they suffered persecution and near extinction at the hands of Aurangzeb. They were revived in the late eighteenth century by Jagjīvandās and are found today mainly in western India. The Vaiṣṇava suborders of the Śrī-rādhā-vallabhīs, the Śrī-haridāsī saṃpradāya, the Śrī-svāmi nārāyaṇī saṃpradāya, the Śrī-sātānī saṃpradāya, and the Pariṇāmi saṃpradāya are popular and quite numerous in certain localities.[29]

In our own time numerous new religious movements sprang up around famous living saints like Ānandamayī or Śrī Satya Sāī Bābā. The disciples of recently departed gurus like Śrī Aurobindo and Śivānanda—as well as numerous others—have begun to develop into independent quasi-*saṃpradāyas.*

## *SĀDHUS* AND THE MODERN AGE

Gulzarilal Nanda, Home Affairs Minister of the Central Government under Jawaharlal Nehru and a devout Hindu, established in 1962 the *Akhil Bhāratīya Sādhu Samāj*, the All-India Society for the *sādhus*, with the aim of organizing and controlling the rather confusing variety of movements and utilizing the moral authority of the *sādhus* for the general uplift of Indian society. A considerable number of criminals try to escape from the clutches of the police by donning the "holy robe" and numerous vagrants misuse the respect people still have for the *sādhus* to live a relatively easy life without having to work. Generally speaking the reputation of the *bābājīs*, as many people call them (not very respectfully), is rather low. The Home Affairs Minister wanted to enforce registration and issue identity cards for the genuine *sādhus*. He also tried to employ them in the anticorruption campaign started by the government. Only a few thousand enlisted with the *sārkarī sādhus*, the "Government Monks," as they were sarcastically called by the independent *sādhus*. The attempt to establish centers of training for the *sādhus*, with something like a standard theological education, has not produced many results to far.

Nowadays a number of *sādhus* are also politically active. In the eighteenth century they led the famous *saṃnyāsi* revolt in Bengal, aimed at overthrowing the British and reestablishing Hindu rule. The widespread discontent of the populace with the secular government, which has been unable to perform miracles, economic or otherwise, is utilized by many *sādhus* to promise utopia for all, if only they would work for the Kingdom of God by faithfully reverting to the observance of the *smṛtis*. Karpātrijī Mahārāj, a Vaiṣṇava *sādhu*, founded in the late 1940s the Rāma-Rājya-Pariṣad, the Kingdom-of-God Party, which advocated reactionary right-wing Hinduism. In this Kingdom of God there is no room for Christians or Muslims, Marxists or Democrats.[30] Another *sādhu*, Swāmi Dvijayanātha, was for many years general secretary of the *Hindū Mahāsabhā*, a radical right-wing party. Swāmi Rāmeśvarānanda, a Member of Parliament on a Jana Sangh ticket, was the instigator of the "black Monday," November 7, 1965, in Delhi, leading a "*sādhus*' war for cow protection" that came dangerously close to a coup d'état.[31] Swami Cinmayānanda, who established a huge enterprise in Bombay to train Hindu missionaries, acted as the first president of the Viśva Hindū Pariṣad, the Hindu World Fellowship, which was designed to actively propagate Hinduism in India and abroad. It was founded in 1964 to counteract the presumed Christian missionary efforts in connection with the Eucharistic Congress in Bombay.[32] In 1986 Swami Vāmadeva, a Daśanāmi *saṃnāysi*, founded the Akhil Bhāratīya Sant Samiti (All-India Saint's Association) designed to agitate for a restoration of Hindu political power in India. They had been in the forefront of the Ayodhyā agitation and the fight against secularism.[33] Among other things they demand that the name India be substituted by Bhārat also in English language documents, and that the present national anthem, which "carries the foul smell of slavery" (because it was sung at a ceremony welcoming King George V to India), be replaced by the "Bande Mātaram."[34]

Many Westerners have joined Hindu *saṃpradāyas* of all varieties: an Englishman, under the name Kṛṣṇa Prem, became a recognized guru of Gauḍīya Vaiṣṇavas; the Ramakrishna Movement has a number of Western disciples, and people like Mahesh Yogi Maharishi, the founder of the Transcendental Meditation Society, or Swami A. C. Bhaktivedānta, the founder of ISKCON, have emerged as major figures of the Western counterculture, initiating thousands of young Americans and Europeans. There may be a good deal of faddism in it, which will rub off after a few years, but for many it is more than a fad: it is the discovery of a lifestyle that is rooted in the ultimate by way of inner experience.

The frustrations of life, its disappointments and sorrows, which thousands of years ago prompted people in India to look for the unchanging and never disappointing Reality, are still with us—and that makes it possible to understand someone like Bhartṛhari, who in his *Vairāgya-śatakam* explains the deeper meaning of *saṃnyāsa* in poetical language:

> I have travelled to inaccessible and perilous places without becoming rich; I have sacrificed self-respect and dignity of birth and position to cater to the wealthy, in vain; like the crows have I fed myself in others' houses hoping for gain—but, you, desire, you prompter of evil deeds, you are not satisfied and keep growing. I have dug into the earth in quest of precious minerals, I have smelted metals from rocks, I crossed the ocean and I sought the favors of Kings, I have spent nights on cremation grounds with my mind occupied with mantras and *pūjās*—nothing have I got for it, oh desire! In our servile attendance on the filthy rich, their shabby manners and their silly talk we did not mind; suppressing the tears that welled up from our hearts we have smiled out of vacant minds; we have paid homage to idiots spoiled by too much wealth! What more folly would you have me suffer, you desire, never satisfied? We have forgiven, but not out of forgiveness; we have renounced the comforts of the home, but not because we were content; we have suffered heat and cold, but not because we wanted to undergo austerities; we have brooded day and night on money, and not on Śiva—we have done what

> the *munis* do, but we have deprived ourselves of their rewards! We have not enjoyed pleasures, they have eaten us up; we have not practiced asceticism, but we have been chastised; time is not gone, but we have lost it. Desire is not reduced, but we are now senile. With the hand as a cup, with food begged on pilgrimages, with the quarters of the sky as the garment and the earth as the bed—blessed are they, who have given up all connections with desire and self-contented with a heart fully matured through their acceptance of *saṃnyāsa* root out all karma. O earth, my mother; O wind, my father, O fire, my friend, O water, my good relation, O sky, my brother! Here is my last salutation to you! I have cast off illusion with its wonderful power through pure knowledge gained from my association with you, and now I merge into the *parabrahman*![35]

Not all of the many millions who are generically called *sādhus* by the populace are ideal persons—in fact the complaints against them are numerous: some of them commit criminal acts, others irritate their fellow citizens through their aggressive begging and their uncivilized behavior. However, even Hindus critical of some of practices of present-day *sādhus* would defend *saṃnyāsa* as something essential to Indian culture. Thus a writer in *Seminar*, a decidedly progressive and unquestionably secular monthly, after highlighting some of the more common complaints against *sādhus* goes on defending them against government regulations and public condemnations alike by stating that "the *sādhu* is in our blood and cannot be excised from the total Indian community. . . . So long as the Indian people wish to maintain their *sādhus* the *sādhu* will survive. And so long as India is an India with heart, *sādhus* will be maintained."[36]

More specifically he protects the *sādhus* from accusations of being useless and unproductive members of society by pointing out that "if [the *sādhu*] pays no taxes, he costs the government nothing. If he is not gainfully employed, he neither competes for employment nor seeks poor relief. In an overpopulated country he practices and preaches sexual abstinence. Where greed and corruption are rife the true *sādhu* demonstrates a life based on honesty, truthfulness, and self-restraint." All this and in addition the engagement of modern *sādhus* in works of charity and education seems, however, to be a rather superficial excuse for the radical challenge that *saṃnyāsa* is to the Hindu. Thus the writer concludes: "Above all, the people look to the man of the spirit to provide them with a meaningful interpretation of existence and from him draw courage to face the tribulations of their lives."

CHAPTER TWENTY-TWO

# *Strīdharma*

## *The Position of Women in Hinduism*

> We will have to produce women, pure, firm and self-controlled as Sītā, Damayantī and Draupadī. If we do produce them, such modern sisters will receive the same homage from Hindu society as is being paid to their prototype of yore. Their words will have the same authority as the *śāstras*.
>
> —M. K. Gandhi, from R. K. Prabhu and U. R. Rao, *The Mind of Mahatma Gandhi*

Recent incidents of *satī* and a rash of "dowry murders" have made headlines not only in India, but all around the world and have focused attention to women's issues in India, evoking all kinds of responses: from spokesmen for Hindu orthodoxy, from representatives of political parties, from vocal Indian women's movements, and from social scientists and observers of contemporary India. In the wake of the discussion it emerged that Indian women's problems are not only problems of Hindu women, or problems caused by traditional Hinduism. It also became clear that within the long history of Hinduism itself, the story has many plots and subplots, and the narrative takes us down many different avenues.

### WOMEN AS THE EQUALS OF MEN IN EARLY VEDIC RELIGION

Minoti Bhattacharyya, herself a Hindu woman, argues that in Vedic times women and men were equal as far as education and religion were concerned.[1] Women participated in the public sacrifices alongside with men. One text[2] mentions a female Ṛṣi Viśvarā. Some Vedic hymns[3] are attributed to women such as Apalā, the daughter of Atri, Ghoṣā, the daughter of Kakṣīvant, or Indrāṇī, the wife of Indra. Apparently in early Vedic times women also received the sacred thread and could study the Veda. The *Hārīta smṛti* mentions a class of women called *brahmavādinīs* who remained unmarried and spent their lives in study and ritual. Pāṇini's distinction between *ācāryā* (a lady teacher) and *ācāryānī* (a teacher's wife) and *upādhyāyā* (a woman preceptor) and *upādhyāyāni* (a preceptor's wife) indicates that women at that time could not only be students, but also teachers of sacred lore. He mentions the names of several noteworthy women scholars of the past such as Kathī, Kālapī, and Bahvricī. The Upaniṣads refer to women philosophers who disputed with their male colleagues, such as Vācaknavī who challenged Yājñavalkya.[4]

The *Ṛgveda* also refers to women engaged in warfare. One queen, Biṣpalā,[5] is mentioned, and even as late a witness as Megasthenes (fifth century BCE) mentions heavily armed women guards protecting Candragupta's palace.

The Vedic pantheon includes a substantial number of female goddesses. There are beautiful hymns to Uṣas, the dawn, imagined as an alluring young woman:

> Dawn on us with prosperity, O Uṣas, daughter of the sky,
> Dawn with great glory, goddess, lady of the light, dawn you with riches,
> bounteous one. . . .
> O Uṣas, graciously answer our songs of praise with bounty and with
> brilliant light . . . grant us a dwelling wide and free from foes . . .[6]

One of the most important of all Vedic hymns, the so-called *Devī-sūkta*, is addressed to Vāk (speech, revelation), a goddess described as the companion of all the other gods, as the instrument that makes ritual efficacious: "I am the queen, the gatherer-up of treasures . . . through me alone all eat the food that feeds them. . . . I make the man I love exceedingly mighty, make him a sage, a *ṛṣi* and a brahmin . . ."[7] It is not unimportant that Earth (*pṛthivī*) is considered female, the goddess who bears the mountains and brings forth vegetation.[8]

Some Vedic goddess worship may be an echo of goddess worship indigenous to India before the spread of Vedic religion; the Vedic hymns to the Goddess certainly made it easier in later centuries to legitimize Goddess worship as orthodox in the context of *bhakti* and *śākta* traditions, where Vedic and non-Vedic elements were blended.

## A GROWING NET OF RESTRICTIONS FOR WOMEN

With the expansion of Vedic religion in northern India and the growing specialization of Brahmanic ritual—possibly also under the impact of threats from the outside—a definition of the place of women in Vedic society took place, which amounted to increasing restrictions of their independence and a clear preponderance of patriarchal rule. Hindu law books contain specific and detailed sections on *strīdharma*,[9] the socioreligious law as applicable to women. One of the more comprehensive such texts is the eighteenth century

*Strīdharmapaddhatī*, by Tryambakayajvan (1665–1750), a minister to the Mahratta kings of Tanjore.[10] Much of this law, which was considered binding till recently (and would still be considered normative by orthodox Hindus today), restricts the rights of women considerably. It is largely based on the notion that the husband is "god" for the wife, the source of her salvation, the purpose of her life, in whom she realizes her *puruṣārthas*.[11] For Manu marriage is the sum total of a woman's *saṃskāras*, including the *upanayana*, *guruseva*, and *agnihotra* for males.[12] He also admonishes women to serve their husbands like a god and not to take vows, religious orders, or any other religious obligations without the husband's permission.[13]

Manu reflects popular opinion when describing women as fickle and unstable, and he voices what must have been already practice all along, namely never to give independence to a woman.[14] Hindu tradition did not as a rule impose the death penalty for adultery by women, but it did consider it a criminal act, which had to be atoned for by lengthy and arduous *prāyaścittas*.[15] Normally a woman would not get much of a chance to commit such a crime, since her life was regulated and supervised from many sides. The Hindu family functioned as a joint family, where not only the husband, but also the in-laws and other relations would keep an eye on a young wife. Public opinion would connect a woman's independent leaving her house, her associating with strangers, and her indulging in drinking liquor with adulterous behavior.[16] A woman's duty would be so exhausting that she would have hardly any inclination to seek for adventure outside the home. As one text[17] details: "The housewife is to be the first to get up in the morning; she then has to clean the house, light the fire, and prepare the early morning meal. She has to work throughout the day to provide food for the family, serve everybody's needs. She must not indulge in games and plays. At mealtime she had to serve everyone first and had to eat what was left over, all by herself."

The metaphors that Vyāsa employs are telling: a wife has to follow her husband everywhere like a shadow, she has to support him like a companion, has to execute his orders like a servant or slave. Such good behavior, the *śāstras* say, will be rewarded in this life by well-being and after this life by heaven; contrary behavior will be punished by lengthy sojourns in hell and a bad rebirth.

All law books devote sections to the "impurity caused by the menses." Women were supposed to completely withdraw from the family for three days to an outhouse, to keep silence, not to wear any ornaments, to sleep on the floor, not to show themselves to anyone. According to one *smṛti* text[18] the menstruating woman is on the first day impure like a *caṇḍāla* (outcaste; traditional sweepers and removers of refuse), on the second like a Brahmin murderess, on the third like a washerwoman. After a bath on the fourth day she is considered "pure" again.[19]

While from a modern perspective traditional Hindu law certainly severely restricted the freedom of women in many ways, it also created for them "a room of their own," an area of competence and a sphere of authority that guaranteed her considerable power in domestic concerns. Somehow reversing what Vyāsa had said, the *Dakṣa-smṛti* calls the wife and mother of the house the "pillar of domestic well-being" and considers her the source of *artha*, *dharma*, and *kāma* for her husband. Through her friendliness and good disposition she can transform the home into a heaven; she can also turn it into a hell for all, if she is disagreeable and badly treated.[20]

What has been described so far as "Vedic law for women" was largely the tradition followed in North India: the *Āryavārta*, the Hindu heartland. South India, and to some extent also Bengal and Assam, too, preserved elements of pre-Vedic matriarchy. In certain South Indian castes the line of inheritance is from mother to (eldest) daughter, and marriage is a "visiting" relationship. Naturally, the role of a wife and mother in such a context will be quite different as compared to the "servant of the god-husband" described previously, and women were much more independent and free in every respect.

## THE LIBERATION OF WOMEN IN THE PURĀṆAS

If originally the Purāṇas were meant to entertain the nonactive participants at the great public Vedic sacrifices through the long stretches of Brahmanical Veda recitation, they became, from the fifth century CE onward, the main source of popular Hindu religion, and were considered scriptures containing everything required for finding salvation. One of their major innovations consisted in granting to women equal access to the means of grace, and to promise to them liberation independent of their role as wives and mothers. While on the whole conservative in social matters, religiously the Purāṇas were progressive by describing practices accessible to everyone, irrespective of gender or caste.

In all Purāṇas goddesses play a major role as consorts of gods like Viṣṇu and Śiva; they often persuade their spouses to reward the offerings of the faithful and they serve as channels of their grace. There are also Purāṇas in which the Goddess herself is equated with the Supreme Being, and where the whole religion centers on Goddess worship. One such text is the famous *Devī-bhāgavata Purāṇa*, a huge work with many goddess myths and long litanies and prayers to the Goddess. In the Goddess tradition to which the *Devī-bhāgavata* belongs, women not only had an equal chance of salvation but even became the preferred gurus to initiate also male devotees to religion. Throughout the past several centuries there were women heads of *āśramas*, who provided guidance to a mixed following of women and men. Some were considered already during their lifetime *avatāras* of the Goddess, and were themselves elevated to the rank of a goddess after their death.

Śāktism and Tāntrism are fairly integral elements of today's popular religion in India, regardless of sectarian affiliation. In some parts of the country like Bengal and Assam the worship of Devī, especially in the form of Durgā, is hugely popular. Bengal's most famous modern saint, Paramahamsa

Ramakrishna, was a devotee of the Goddess, often falling in a trance before her image and seeing her in visions. Not all of Tāntricism is a religion for and by women, but it certainly shows the importance attributed to the female aspect of the deity, and the power associated with the Goddess.

## DRAUPADĪ AND SĪTĀ: HEROIC WOMEN OF THE EPIC TRADITION

The *Mahābhārata* is certainly dominated by male characters on both sides of the warring factions, but some women stand out playing a not insignificant role. The most important of these is Draupadī, the wife of the five Pāṇḍava brothers. Polyandry was practiced in some parts of India in ancient times and is still in existence in some areas of the Tehrī-Garhvāl region in the Himālayas. Draupadī accompanied the Pāṇḍavas on their journeys during their long years of exile. She became the focus of contention, when, after a lost game of dice, with nothing else to lose, the Pāṇḍavas gambled Draupadī away, and the Kauravas humiliated her publicly. The hatred that this action evoked in the hearts of the Pāṇḍavas, together with their feeling of shame, because of their helplessness and ignominy, was one of the leading causes for the subsequent Great War.

More than Draupadī, who remained a more remote figure in Indian popular imagination, Sītā, the heroine of the *Rāmāyaṇa*, has captured the minds and hearts of the Indian population. The *Rāmāyaṇa*, through re-creations in several Indian vernaculars and through frequent theatrical performances, remained alive throughout the centuries and today is better known in the whole of India than any other literature. In its reworkings in regional languages the figure of Sītā has undergone quite typical transformations as well. Because of her fame and because of frequent references to her as a role model, Sītā has become the focus of feminist resentment against traditional Indian notions of womanhood. Sītā in Vālmīki's *Rāmāyaṇa* is not really a representative of Vedic *strīdharma*. To begin with, she is choosing her own husband in a competitive *svayamvara*: only the strongest and the smartest prince will do.[21] Again, after Kaikeyī's intervention, when Rāma goes into forest exile, she insists on accompanying him. She is not an obedient servant to a godlike husband; she has a will of her own and her relationship to Rāma is governed by love for him, rather than by obedience to his orders. She shows her determination and independence throughout the years in the forest; her insistence that Rāma get the gold-spotted deer and her command that Lakṣmaṇa come to his rescue eventually leads to her abduction by Rāvaṇa. It is in the context of this "dwelling in another man's house" that Vedic regulations for women are invoked and popular sentiment demands an ordeal to prove her purity.

The romantic elements in Vālmīki's *Rāmāyaṇa* are heightened in Tulasīdāsa's *Rāmacaritamānasa*, the late medieval Hindī re-creation of the epic, and Sītā is appearing both as more contradictory and more goddesslike. The very fact that Rāma and Sītā are always mentioned in one breath endows Sītā with equality: whatever status Rāma occupies will also be Sītā's. If he is king, she will be queen; if he is god, she will become goddess. However, she is queen and goddess out of her own merit, not because of Rāma's grace.

Tulasīdāsa's Sītā shows many features of the ideal wife that the average Hindu male was dreaming of: submission to elders and persons of respect, loyalty in adversity and courage in the face of danger, beauty and sweetness, total devotion to husband and children. Those old-fashioned virtues have made her the target of modern Indian feminists. It could be argued that, while Tulasīdāsa draws a quite differentiated picture of Sītā, endowing her with lifelike, often contradictory qualities, in the present-day polemics the figure of Sītā becomes stereotyped into something quite artificial. Also, the perspective is getting skewed in the process. While Tulasīdāsa, following the Hindu tradition of epic writing, depicted a religious ideal, giving a transcendental rationalization of the characters, the contemporary debate proceeds as if Sītā and Rāma had been a typical Indian middle-class couple. The average modern Indian woman, emancipated or not, is certainly not expected to accompany her husband on a twelve-year jungle tour; nor is the average Indian male likely to become king of Ayodhyā and one of Viṣṇu's *avatāras*.

## RĀDHĀ-KṚṢṆA

The "down-to-earth" interpretation adopted by many contemporaries does a disservice also to another one of India's great female characters and goddess representations: Rādhā. The Rādhā-Kṛṣṇa dalliance, as described in some of the more colorful Vaiṣṇava writings, such as Jayadeva's *Gītāgovinda* or Rūpa Gosvāmi's *Ujjvala Nīlāmaṇī*, was found offensive by some Hindu contemporaries, who felt that their authors had gone too far in their transcendental realism. However, when the figures of Kṛṣṇa and Rādhā are completely divested of their divine character, and the love they are demonstrating becomes reduced to mere sexuality, the figure of Rādhā turns into something rather bizarre, and her relationship with Kṛṣṇa becomes rather perverse.

Rādhā, as visualized by the fervent followers of Caitanya in the sixteenth century, was not a historical but an emotional reality. As A. K. Majumdar has observed:

> It is not possible, nor indeed is it necessary, to establish her identity on an empirical basis. She is the idealized form of an ontological conception, nevertheless real, because she is ethereal. The pious Goswāmis of Vrindābana have gone into great details in describing her; it is in their language that Rādhā takes a definite form, a human form, and the *līlā* of Rādhā-Kṛṣṇa adds a human dimension to subtle theological and philosophical discussions. The vivid description of Rādhā and of her union with Kṛṣṇa are related in everyday human terms, but still, it is a *līlā*, a sport, but a divine sport, for

> no ordinary human being can take part in it or perceive it. . . . Rādhā is the realization of the principal emotion . . . the dance of duality ends in ultimate unity.[22]

To reduce Rādhā to a commonplace adulteress and to speak of the Rādhā-Kṛṣṇa *līlā* as expressing "coitus fantasies," as Nirad Chaudhuri does,[23] is certainly doing injustice to the Vaiṣṇava poets and completely misses their point.

Figures like Sītā or Rādhā live in a multidimensional universe. Contemporary intellectual fashion reduces all reality to one dimension: the grossly material and pragmatic. That kind of "realism" knows no categories to deal adequately with figures like Sītā and Rādhā, whose ideal is not held up for imitation but for contemplation and worship. The imagination that concretized such ideas into humanlike figures does not agree with a one-to-one translation of its religious vocabulary into present-day sociological or feminist notions. The "divine couple" Sītā-Rāma cannot be used as a model for working out budget problems in a modern family, be it in India or anywhere else. And the Rādhā-Kṛṣṇa *līlā* is not a valid subject matter for Freudian psychoanalysis, whether performed by professionals or amateurs.

## WOMEN POET-SAINTS IN SOUTH AND NORTH

The *bhakti* movement, which initiated the religious liberation of women, was largely promoted and supported by women devotees. Among the many popular poet-saints whose compositions are heard throughout India (and beyond), there were a fair number of women. Only two of these—Āṇṭāl from South India and Mīrābāī from the North—will be highlighted here, while recognizing that there are numerous others who deserve to be known and written about.

In the Tamil country the name of Āṇṭāl is as fresh today as it had been for the past one thousand or more years, and her songs, too, are sung every day in temples during worship.[24] According to traditional accounts, Kōṭai (Āṇṭāl's original name) grew up in the shadow of the temple of Śrīvilliputtūr—now boasting the tallest *gopura* of the whole of India, built in honor of Āṇṭāl—where her father Viṣṇucitta served as priest. Without her father's knowledge Koṭai would take up the garland of flowers prepared for the evening *pūjā*, put it around her neck and admire herself in a mirror, playing God's bride. Ordinarily this would be considered sacrilegious; one cannot offer a garland to the deity that has been worn by anyone else before. When Viṣṇucitta discovered one day Koṭai's playful secret, he was very disturbed and conducted the evening service without offering the already used garland to the image. That night Viṣṇu appeared to him in a dream and told him that a garland, which Āṇṭāl had worn before, was even dearer to him than any other and so Viṣṇucitta realized that his daughter Koṭai was a very special person in the eyes of the Lord.

Confirmed in her devotion to Viṣṇu, Āṇṭāl spent her days in contemplation, composing a series of hymns in praise of Viṣṇu and refusing all suggestions of marrying: she would not accept any man but Viṣṇu as her husband. Viṣṇucitta, worried about Āṇṭāl's state of mind, was comforted again by Viṣṇu in a dream, telling him that Āṇṭāl would indeed be his bride. Legend has it that Viṣṇu miraculously organized a marriage party with musicians and dancers to accompany Āṇṭāl from Śrīvilliputtūr to Śrī Raṅgam. When Āṇṭāl left the palanquin and stepped up to the reclining Viṣṇu image, she mysteriously vanished into the image. Viṣṇu appeared again to Viṣṇucitta, accepting him as his father-in-law and requesting him to continue serving him at Śrīvilliputtūr. There, a shrine was built in honor of Āṇṭāl within the compound of the Viṣṇu temple containing her richly adorned bronze statue and a long inscription, phrased as a love letter from Viṣṇu to Āṇṭāl. Her hymns are sung daily in Śrīvilliputtūr and other shrines in Tamiḻnādu.[25]

Mīrābāī is a household name all over northern India; her songs are still sung at countless gatherings, and people look up to her as one of the perfect devotees who were granted the privilege of not dying but being absorbed into one of the *mūrtis* of Viṣṇu in Vṛndāvana.[26] She was born at Mārwāḍ in 1547, and from early childhood on loved and worshipped an image of Kṛṣṇa as her future bridegroom. She used to adorn it, to bathe it, to sleep with it, to sing to it, to dance around it, and she imagined herself to be wedded to it. When she grew up, she was betrothed to Bhojrāj, the Prince of Chitor, a fiercely independent Rājput ruler, who would never accept Muslim rule, whatever the cost. The ruling family of Chitor worshipped Śakti, the Goddess. Mīrā, invited by her mother-in-law to join in the worship of the Goddess, refused, saying that she had given her heart and her head to Kṛṣṇa. She used to spend entire nights in a small Kṛṣṇa temple, conversing with the idol, singing her own songs to it, and dancing in front of it. According to tradition, her sisters-in-law reported her to her husband, accusing her of secretly meeting at night with a paramour, while refusing to join her husband. Enraged, Bhojrāj threatened to kill her. But when he burst into the room from which Mīrā's love songs and whispered conversations had come, he found her alone, sitting in raptures before a Kṛṣṇa image. Declaring her crazed, he left her alone, till another incident infuriated him even more. Having heard about Mīrā's beautiful *bhajans* and unable to invite her to the court, Emperor Akbar and his court musician Tansen traveled incognito to Chitor to listen to the famous *bhaktā*. They were overwhelmed by the fervor and ardor of Mīrā's devotion, and the emperor pressured her into accepting a necklace on behalf of Kṛṣṇa. When the identity of the mysterious visitors was revealed, Bhojrāj, for whom the Mogul rulers were archenemies, forced Mīrā to leave his kingdom. He advised her to drown herself by way of atonement for the shame she had brought upon him. About to do so, she was rescued by Kṛṣṇa himself and told to turn toward Vṛndāvana and to serve him in his holy city.

Everybody in Vṛndāvana treated her as someone special; her fame spread throughout northern India, and she began to believe that in a previous incarnation she had been Rādhā herself. One day the unexpected happened: her husband, going to Vṛndāvana disguised as a pilgrim, asked for her forgiveness and requested her to come back with him to Chitor, free to pursue her Kṛṣṇa worship as she liked. She did so, but after the death of her husband she had to suffer much under the persecution by the new Rānī. Several miracles reportedly saved her life: under her touch a snake, meant to kill her with a deadly bite, turned into an image of Kṛṣṇa; a cup of poison became a draught of nectar; a board full of nails was transformed into a bed of roses. She returned to Vṛndāvana completely immersed in her love for Kṛṣṇa, who eventually absorbed her into his image.

Mīrābāī and Āṇṭāl, although thousands of miles and more than half a millennium apart, share many features: both were devotees of Viṣṇu-Kṛṣṇa, whose brides they considered themselves. Both were gifted poet-singers, totally devoted to the praise of their Lord. Both were accorded the ultimate honor of not dying but of being bodily united with the object of their devotion—an event reported of only a few other devotees throughout the centuries. Women and men alike honor them as embodiments of the purest *bhakti* and the most ardent emotion. The memory of both is alive in today's India and their songs inspire contemporary devotees as much as they did those of past centuries.

## THE "MOTHERS"

An interesting phenomenon of twentieth century Hinduism is the emergence of *Mās*, "Mothers," with a large following of male and female devotees, who are acting as gurus and spiritual advisers on a large scale. Aurobindo Ghose, after fleeing to Pondichéry to escape from possible British retribution, dedicated himself completely to the task of preparing for the *śakti-nipāta*, the divine empowerment that would turn him into the *avatāra* of the twentieth century. He was soon joined by M. and Mme. Richards, who increasingly took over the burden of looking after the worldly needs of the sage. After her husband's departure, Mira Richards, of mixed Egyptian-French descent, became the key organizer of the growing ashram and, sharing Aurobindo's spiritual aspirations, she also became the channel for his teaching and ministrations. For the twenty or so years before Aurobindo's *samādhi*, it was "The Mother" who guided the outer and inner affairs of the Aurobindo Ashram. Ordinarily she would convey visitors' requests to Aurobindo, and he would respond through her, insisting that her mind was the same as his and that she fully participated in his consciousness. After her death in 1982 a group of devotees started to worship her as the embodiment of the Goddess. Her memory is kept alive in Auroville and her devotees claim to receive evidence of her continued presence and power.

Ānandamayī Mā, like many other god-intoxicated individuals, was considered mentally unstable, till someone recognized and appreciated her quite unique status. Without the aid of a male guru, she initiated herself, acquired a reputation for spiritual power and insight, and began attracting a varied congregation. Over the decades her fame spread in India and abroad. She established a number of ashrams in major places of pilgrimage, which in addition to maintaining temples, also began to produce literature by and about her.[27]

A few more Mā's will be mentioned in the chapter on Hindu Reformers (chapter 30) without claiming to exhaust the issue.

## GANDHI AND WOMEN

Throughout his life Mahātmā Gandhi not only defended the dignity and rights of women but found them valuable fellow fighters in his struggle for India's freedom. In his autobiography he described his own maturing process as a thirteen-year-old husband with a child wife. While much of his experimenting with different lifestyles at home was done at the expense of his wife's freedom and self-determination, he eventually arrived at a stage where he could acknowledge the strength and wisdom not only of his wife, but womanhood in general. He was aware of the injustices that the Hindu and other legal systems had done to women, and he believed that a reform could be brought about without totally abandoning the Hindu tradition. As he said: "Of all the evils for which man had made himself responsible, none is so degrading, so shocking, or so brutal as his abuse of the better half of humanity to me, the female sex, not the weaker sex. It is the nobler of the two, for it is even today the embodiment of sacrifice, silent suffering, humility, faith and knowledge."[28]

Gandhi early on insisted on equality of women, on women's education, and on women taking their rightful place also in public life. He also argued for an abolition of the dowry system, of *purdah*, and for remarriage of widows. Time and again he came back to the classical ideals of woman as depicted in the great epics and he rejected the criticism of those who believed that Sītā represented a wrong idea of womanhood. At several occasions he stated: "My ideal of wife is Sītā and of a husband Rāma. But Sītā was no slave to Rāma. Nor each was slave to the other. Rāma is ever considerate to Sītā."[29] Gandhi believed that women were by nature more predisposed towards practicing *ahiṃsā* and that they had a special role to fulfill in India's Independence struggle. Some of his fellow workers like Sarojini Naidu rose to prominence in post-Independent India and made major contributions to the country's progress.

## FROM *SATĪ* TO DOWRY MURDERS

Even small local papers in North America found the report about an eighteen-year-old, otherwise unknown woman, who on September 4, 1987, became a *satī* in Deorala, a small village in Rājasthān, "newsworthy." A large audience, notified in advance, watched the young widow, married for only eight months, mount the pyre of her twenty-four-year-old deceased husband, and die in the flames. Police, which were alerted, were kept off by armed relations of the bridegroom. The bride's parents honored the voluntary self-immolation of their daughter by participating thirteen days later in a *satī* ceremony. Soon

Photo 32. Satī memorial: Vṛndāvana

afterward a shrine was built at the site—a *satī* shrine, as so many others, which have become the centers of popular pilgrimages and fairs.

*Satī*, the ritual burning alive of a spouse together with her deceased husband, has a long history in India.[30] While not restricted to India in antiquity, the custom has attracted much attention from people visiting or describing India. The word *satī* means a wife who is faithful, true to her vows, loyal, joining her deceased husband in death as the supreme proof of such faithfulness. *Satī* is also the name of one of the daughters of Dakṣa, the Vedic patriarch. Satī married Śiva against the will of her father. When Dakṣa arranged a great Vedic *yajña* and failed to invite Śiva, Satī, humiliated and despairing, took her own life. Thus in the worship of a *satī*—and *satī* memorials can be found all over India—the memory of a heroic faithful woman and Satī, the wife of Śiva, are combined. It is interesting to see also emancipated Indian women, who abhor such a practice, point with pride to *satī* memorials in their villages.[31]

The eighteenth-century British traveler and painter William Hodges was one of the few Westerners to actually observe and describe a *satī*. Normally, foreigners would be kept away.[32] The ceremony of *satī* resembled the marriage rites. The widow had to indicate her willingness to become a *satī*. Dressed like a bride, she was taken in procession to the cremation site. Before mounting the pyre she distributed her ornaments and was believed to possess at that moment supernatural powers. The pyre itself was compared to the marriage bed on which she joined her husband for their wedding in heaven.[33]

The rationalization of *satī* was complex. A wife whose husband died young was supposed to have been guilty of husband murder in one of her previous incarnations. She could atone for that crime by self-immolation. Also, widows were not allowed to remarry. Since after marriage they belonged to the family of their husbands, they were often perceived as an economic burden. Rules governing the lives of widows were so severe that many may have considered voluntary death preferable to the miserable life they could look forward to, especially since all kinds of celestial blessings were promised to those who became *satīs*.

While the practice of *satī* was common throughout northern India, the actual numbers apparently were not very large. They were certainly much smaller than the numbers of dowry murders in today's India. Whereas economic motives were probably part of the background to *satī*, they are unquestioningly the *only* reason for dowry murders. Like *satī*, the giving of dowry was originally only a high-class practice, first introduced by Kṣatriyas, and associated with high status. In the course of time it seeped down into lower strata of society and was believed to confer status on those who practice it, till it became the thing to do for everyone.

Initially, dowry was meant to provide some kind of security to a daughter who married into a stranger's household. If things went wrong, if her husband deserted or divorced her, she could fall back on what was her own property, given to her by her father. Today dowry is a gift of the bride's family to the bridegroom's family, often specified exactly in rupee figures and never quite finalized. The bridegroom's family, after the first and initial payment, often tries to extort more and more, by threatening or even abusing the young wife so as to intimidate her and her family to provide more dowry. If the young wife does not relay the messages to her father or if the father is unwilling or unable to pay up, attempts are made on her life. Dorothy Stein, in an article entitled "Burning Widows, Burning Brides," mentions that in Delhi alone, between 1979 and 1988, 2,055 young wives, aged eighteen to twenty-five, died in presumably prearranged kerosene stove burning accidents, victims of "dowry murder." A large number of such deaths are also reported from all over the country. The veritable epidemic of such deaths has provoked protest marches from women's groups demanding that no dowry should be given or taken.[34] Ironically India has, since 1961, a Dowry Prohibition Act, passed by Parliament subsequent to a number of Dowry Restraining Acts. The act intends to suppress a custom that, even when not leading to dowry murders, often ruins the brides' families financially, especially if they have more daughters than sons.

## INDIAN FEMINISM AND HINDU TRADITION

Modern feminism everywhere had to struggle against political and religious establishments, which generally tended to be conservative, male dominated, and patriarchal. The story is no different in India. In spite of the worship of Śakti and the important role that the "mother" plays in the extended family, the struggle for more adequate legal protection of women generally, and for their acceptance in public life, had to be waged against traditional religious prejudice, which stereotyped women as submissive wives and devoted mothers, with no rights to a development of their own. The large number of successful Indian businesswomen, women politicians, lawyers, professors, and other high-profile professionals is certainly proof of some success of feminism in India. Indian feminists are not satisfied with what has been accomplished so far; overall, Indian women are still disadvantaged, undereducated, overworked, and exploited. Like other patriarchal religions, Hinduism has its blind spots when it comes to questions of social justice, equality, and women's rights. Not surprisingly, prominent orthodox representatives of Hinduism have resisted every improvement of the lot of women, be it the abolition of *satī*, the ability to file for divorce, the freedom to choose their own careers, or the right to receive an education equal to that of men. As the examples of recent *satī* and dowry deaths demonstrate, there is a great risk in keeping the outer shell of a tradition that has lost its social substance. Traditional *satī* may have been a barbaric custom, but it was part of a functioning social system, with safeguards of its own. Contemporary *satī* is lacking these. Reportedly, most of the post-Independence *satīs* were pregnant women who would have been forbidden under the traditional rules from electing *satī*. Hindu tradition would unqualifiedly forbid the killing of a wife for the sake of material profit, as is done in the dowry murder.

While one might respect someone who, out of a sense of honor or motivated by a strong transcendent faith, sacrifices his or her life in the hope of winning a better existence, one feels nothing but horror and contempt for those who drive others into death for filthy lucre and have no regard even for elementary rights of their fellow humans.

Traditional Hinduism is still strongly supported by women; women form the largest portion of temple-goers and festival attendants, and women keep traditional domestic rituals alive and pass the familiar stories of gods and goddesses on to their children. One can only hope that the representatives of traditional Hinduism reciprocate this faithfulness by developing within Hinduism regard for contemporary women's concerns and support the endeavors of those who are working toward full equality. There is much in the various strands of the Hindu tradition that lends itself to a timely defense of women's rights and to the development of a contemporary *strīdharma* anchored in genuine spirituality and flexibility to accommodate the changing concerns of today's society. The well-being of women should not only be the concern of feminists but of the whole society. Violence against Indian women and deprivation of their rights is a cause for shame for all. Population increase and the diminishing of resources will, in the next few decades, put great pressure on Indian society and it is to be feared that women and children, as traditionally the most vulnerable sectors, will bear the brunt of it.

A surprising development in the context of Indian feminism is the newly awakened interest in asceticism: not only are there a number of well-known women gurus, but also political activists like Umā Bhāratī parade their feminism in the ochre robe of traditional *saṃnyāsa*.[35]

Recently also training schools for women priests have been established: since many male priests perform their rituals often rather perfunctorily and routinely, women priests who personally engage themselves and carefully enact the ceremonies are preferred by many people.

The *Times of India* found it noteworthy to report the recent ordination of an American woman as a Mahant Mahāmaṇḍaleśvarī—a Hindu High priestess—in Vārāṇasi; certainly a first in many ways![36] Under her new name and title Lakxmi Devi Chalanda Saravanandamayi Ma she formally initated her American, Australian, and European disciples into Hinduism and gave them Hindu names. The ceremony was performed by leading *sādhus* on the Maṇikarṇikā Ghaṭ and was presided over by Mahāmaṇḍaleśvara Viṣṇuswāmi Yamunācārya, head of Satua Baba Ashram.

CHAPTER TWENTY-THREE

# Hindu Structures of Thought

## *The* Ṣaḍdarśanas

> There are many different opinions, partly based on sound arguments and scripture, partly based on fallacious arguments and scriptural texts misunderstood. Those who embrace some of these opinions without previous examination will bar themselves from the highest beatitude and incur grievous loss.
>
> —Śaṅkara, *Brahmasūtrabhāṣya* I, 1

All cultures—as the languages associated with them reveal—have made attempts to transform their life experiences into abstract concepts and connect these into coherent mental world pictures. Indian culture has done so more than most others: coining words, translating reality into thought, elaborating systems of explanation on the basis of universal principles are some of the most prominent features of Indian civilization. The sheer mass of writing that we possess—probably only a fraction of what once existed—is eloquent testimony to this.

In the enormous Indian religious literature one cluster of words and ideas stands out: words and ideas designating mind, consciousness, thought: terms like *cit, caitanya, jñāna, vijñāna, buddhi, bodha.* Indian religions have been consciousness conscious from a very early date on. Not all are going as far as the "consciousness-only" school of *Vijñāna-vāda* Buddhism or the "absolute-consciousness-alone" teaching of *Advaita Vedānta.* But the awareness of mind as irreducible reality, radically different from nature and society, was a very important factor in the history of Hinduism as a whole.

To consider the physical structures of the Hindus' holy land as a support of Hinduism will be quite easily acceptable. After all, Hindus live and die in this sacred geography. To see in the specific societal arrangements that

Hinduism created a structural support of Hinduism will equally appear quite plausible. All Hindus are, in very important ways, affected by *varṇāśrama-dharma* that structures their lives in many ways. It may need some arguing, however, to prove that the *ṣaḍ darśanas* are structural supports of Hinduism of equal importance.

## HINDUISM: A TRADITION OF LEARNING

Hindu tradition has always shown great respect for scholarship. It rested upon a book, the Veda, that was memorized, studied, surrounded by other books that were designed to protect it, explain it, and apply it. Not only had a Brahmin according to traditional Hindu law to devote the first part of his life to study, *svādhyāya*, study on his own, was one of the permanent duties imposed upon him for his whole life. Although the injunction to devote the first part of his day to study may not always have been literally followed by all Brahmins, study as a habit certainly characterized them throughout and formed the whole class. Study, according to Manu, was enjoined by the creator himself "in order to protect the universe" and it was also the most effective means to subdue sensual desires and obtain self-control. Manu quotes an ancient verse: "Sacred Learning approached a Brāhmaṇa and said to him: 'I am your treasure, preserve me, deliver me not to a scorner; so preserved I shall become extremely strong."[1]

The learning that a Brahmin acquires is his only claim to eminence: "A man is not considered venerable because his head is grey; him who, though young, has learned the Vedas, the gods consider to be venerable."[2] Veda study, Manu says, has been declared the highest form of *tapas* (austerity, self-mortification) of a Brahmin.

Correspondingly the role of the teacher has always been important. "They call the teacher 'father' because he gives the Veda: for nobody can perform a sacred rite before the investiture with the girdle of *muñja* grass."[3]

The teacher was compared to God—even placed above God: because he could not only convey the sacred knowledge but could also intercede on behalf of his pupils in case of their wrongdoing. The king, according to Kauṭilya, had the duty to see to it that no student and no teacher in his realm would be lacking the essentials.

The prominence of the Brahmins, whose "natural" function was to learn and to teach, is a further indicator of the central place that study occupied in Vedic society. The true centers of Hinduism were always centers of study: be it the *āśramas* of classical India or the *patha-śālas* of later times, the private libraries of individual scholars or the large universitylike centers of major denominations.[4]

To the extent to which Brahmanic ideas shaped the outlook of Hindu society—and they did so with great effectiveness—scholarship and study occupied a prominent place in it.[5] While much of the Brahmanic learning consisted in memorizing the sacred texts and acquiring the skills to perform the rituals, reflection and critical examination of the content of the tradition is also in evidence from very early times. The Upaniṣads contain accounts of debates between learned sages and indicate that certain lines of thought had already crystallized into schools associated with prominent names.[6]

The emergence of Buddhism and Jainism (and a host of other movements within Brahmanism critical of certain aspects of it) shows that by the fifth century BCE complete systems of thought had formed, challenged by rival systems, and that the notion had arisen that it was important to have a clear and correct idea of the intellectual supports of practical life.[7] The fierce polemics carried on between representatives of different schools of thought—polemics not restricted to books and academic retreats, but carried out in public with the participation of large numbers of people—is a further fact that corroborates the importance given to thinking and system building. The fully developed Hindu systems of early medieval India leave no doubt that they consider it of the highest importance to have correct notions of the key concepts of religion: a person's ultimate felicity depends on it, as Śaṅkara explains.[8]

Contrary to the West, where philosophical and theological discussion, with very few exceptions, was traditionally a concern for professional philosophers and theologians only, in India this debate always interested all levels of the population. While not everybody in India is capable of arguing the finer points of *śāstrāic* controversies, nearly everyone even today knows about the controversy between the followers of Śaṅkara and Rāmānuja, can discuss the points where Buddhism differs from Hinduism, or is able to marshal arguments for or against *saguṇa* and *nirguṇa brahman*, and so on. Many of the most popular *bhajans*, religious lyrics sung at popular gatherings, contain an amazing amount of such highly philosophical thought.[9]

Intellectual penetration of reality, enlightenment, knowledge, insight are absolutely central in Hinduism. The classical systems are part of the structure of Hinduism as much as anything else. As in the case of the other supports there is a corresponding level of reality. Hindu *darśanas* have provided real insight, have helped people to acquire real knowledge, have been found reliable guides in the search for Truth. It is that element of truth realized, freedom gained, and transcendence experienced that has prevented Hinduism from becoming an ideology in the service of a power structure, an escape for dreamers, or a merely romantic worldview.

The close proximity of religious theory and social practice in India through the ages brought with it strong repercussions in "real" life of changes in philosophical-theological orientation. Thus acceptance of Buddhism or Jainism brought about a loss of caste—with enormous consequences for those concerned. It also deprived a person of the experience of bliss after death. In the context of the practice of *śrāddha*, which was supposed to secure a blessed afterlife for the ancestors, this had repercussions not only with regard to one's own fate but with regard to one's entire lineage as well. Although Hinduism throughout its history has shown a great fondness for speculation and system building, the need to remain within the sociocultic context of the Vedic tradition brought up the question of how far one could go with critical thinking. Vedic tradition did not consider itself the result of human thought: it related its content to a revelation received by seers and sages in meditation and trance, it aimed at maintaining and duplicating these states of mind through yogic practices, it exempted Vedic teaching from criticism by declaring its origin *apauruṣeya*, not man-made, but eternally present. Thus the Veda was taken to be the foundation of all thinking, and not its object, to be analyzed or discussed. No tradition is founded on analytical and critical thought alone—a society needs more than speculative philosophy to flourish and to provide for the needs of its members.

Wide ranging and deep searching as Indian philosophy may be, it also had to respect the boundaries that practical life had set. Wanting to go beyond these boundaries meant placing oneself outside society. The *nāstikas*, those who did not accept the Veda as authority, did just that.[10] The *āstikas*, those who wished to remain inside tradition, had to stay inside a framework of questions defined by the Veda. The limit of permitted questions and answers was not always easy to ascertain. The various *āstika* systems carried on fierce polemics among each other from the seventh century onward. Kumārila Bhaṭṭa, a great authority in *Mīmāṃsā* and a staunch defender of *sanātana dharma* against Buddhism, considers *Sāṁkhya*, *Yoga*, *Pāñcarātra*, and *Pasúpata* philosophies as *nāstika*.[11] Some of the followers of Madhva would classify Śaṅkara's Advaita Vedānta as *pracanna-bauddha*, crypto-Buddhist, and thus unorthodox. This is a position taken even at the present not only by the Caitanyites and their modern Western exponents but also by some scholarly philosophers.[12] Śaṅkara himself condemns *Sāṁkhya* as non-Vedic and the teaching of *pradhāna* as heretical.[13] S. Radhakrishnan, quite clearly placing himself within the orthodox tradition, explains the rationale for this attitude thus: "If the unassisted reason of man cannot attain any hold on reality by means of mere speculation, help may be sought from the great writings of the seers who claim to have attained spiritual certainty. Thus strenuous attempts were made to justify by reason what faith implicitly accepts. This is not an irrational attitude, since philosophy is only an endeavor to interpret the widening experience of humanity. . . . If we cannot establish through logic the truth of anything, so much the worse for logic."[14] And: "The acceptance of the Veda is a practical admission that spiritual experience is a greater light in these matters than intellectual reason. . . . The philosophical character of the systems is not much compromised by the acceptance of the Veda."[15] The options that the Veda leaves are indeed quite liberal. It did not demand a creed or a declaration of faith in this or that God.

Vedic tradition embodied the principle of pluralism insofar as a number of family traditions (*śākhas*) were considered as equally authoritative and it also recognized a variety of valid local traditions. Even the *nāstikas* developed the pluralistic spirit in orthodoxy: it was faced with alternative viewpoints and had to engage in rational argumentation, admitting in the process that many questions had to remain open, questions that permitted a plurality of answers.

Hindu intellectual tradition has dealt in various ways with this pluralistic situation. Some have accepted it as a matter of fact and simply pursued their own path without looking left or right. Others have taken a defensive stance and polemicized in order to vindicate the truth—often absolute, final, *siddhānta*—of their own school of thought. Others again have made a scholarly study of the whole of it, seeing some sort of complementarity of viewpoints. Among the classical writers belonging to this genre, Vācaspati Miśra deserves mentioning: he wrote scholarly commentaries on most of the *darśanas*, entering, as it were into the spirit of each and clarifying their teachings. Among modern Hindu philosophers S. Radhakrishnan comes to mind, whose catholicity of thought was able to see the essential unity of Hindu thought behind the diversity of systems.[16]

## HINDU PHILOSOPHY OR HINDU THEOLOGY?

Neither *philosophy* nor *theology*—whatever these terms may mean today—are adequate translations for the Indian term *darśana*.[17] *Darśanas* contain psychology and physics, exegesis of Vedic texts and speculation about language, psychophysical practices as well as meditation and much more. They demonstrate another type of intellectual approach to the world, variations not only to the answers given but alternatives to the very questions asked by the Western tradition. We are only slowly beginning to appreciate and to understand these. Without exception they claim to lead to an ultimate existential "religious" aim and to represent the cumulative reflection of Hinduism through the ages.

A common characteristic of all *darśanas* is that at some time their basic teachings were condensed into *sūtras*, "leading threads," that helped to express precisely the content of the systems in a technical terminology and also served as texts for students to memorize. Instruction would largely consist of commenting upon the pithy sutras and expanding on the meaning of the terms used in them, pointing out differences between one's own system and others and providing proof for the truth of the sutra. Since many of the sutras are virtually unintelligible without commentary and explanation, often the commentary (*bhāṣya*) has become the most important exposition of a system. These *bhāṣyas* in turn have become the object of further subcommentaries (*vṛttis*), commentaries on these (*ṭīkas*), and further glosses (*ṭippaṇīs*), which constitute the material that an expert in a particular branch of learning has to study. Hindu scholars have invented most peculiar names for their subcommentaries and glosses.[18] The sutras that we possess today are not always the oldest texts of the schools, and they are not always the work of the authors to whom they are ascribed. But they can be relied upon as containing the gist of the teaching of the systems and providing the technical terminology for each.

And here we encounter another peculiarity. The basic scholarly vocabulary is shared by virtually all six *darśanas*. But the meaning given to the technical terms and the place value accorded to each are very different. This situation has lead to the necessity of specializing in one specific *darśana* rather than calling oneself a philosopher or a theologian of Hinduism. Each *darśana* possesses a highly technical terminology—often new terms are coined or very specific meanings are given to terms used otherwise—a terminology that one does not pick up by learning classical Sanskrit and reading courtly Sanskrit literature. Traditional Indian scholars who specialize in a *darśana* indicate in their academic title their specialization[19] and they would not consider themselves competent to instruct in other fields. Reading into a text of a specific *darśana* resembles in many ways the learning of a new language: familiar as the sounds of the words may be, their meaning has to be learned anew and must not be confused with that of other systems.

Representations of Indian philosophy in English often restrict themselves to describing those elements from the Hindu *darśanas* that have a parallel in contemporary Western philosophy and leave out the rest.[20] This not only gives a slanted impression of Hindu thought, it often deprives the student of the most valuable lessons to be learned from such a study, the really original and specific contributions to human thought that India has made. Indian writers have no longer to fight for the recognition that they, too, possess a philosophical tradition; they can concentrate on its technicalities and proper contents. While restrictions of space and considerations of accessibility do not allow us to go into much technical detail of the Hindu *darśanas* in the following chapters, the description attempts to convey the idea that Hindu *darśanas* offer not only parallels to Western thought but contain also novel elements for which there are no parallels. Translations of many of the major texts as well as specialized studies are nowadays abundantly available for a more detailed investigation.[21]

The enumeration and combination of the *darśanas* follows the traditional schema that has been accepted for at least the past one thousand years. In works like Mādhava's *Sarva-darśana-saṁgraha* many other *darśanas* are mentioned that do not find a place among the six described here.[22] Also the designation of the classical *darśanas* has not always been the same in Indian history. Thus *Nyāya* was used in former times to designate the system today called *Mīmāṃsā*, *Yoga* was used as a name for *Vaiśeṣika*, *Anvīkṣikī* designated our *Nyāya* and so on.[23] Information like this may not appear of great significance for a reader who is looking for basic information on the Hindu systems but it will be of importance for those who consult sources and wish to learn more about the history of each *darśana*. Doing so they will discover that the description offered here focuses on what might be called the "classical phase" of each *darśana*. Much of the origin and early development has yet to be uncovered, conflicting views found in older sources have to be reconciled. More recent developments often go off in many different directions and have become much too intricate to permit a nontechnical summary.

This enumeration does not represent an evaluation. Each of the following systems considers itself the best suited to achieving its aim. India's intellectual history over the past millennium (and before) consists of sustained debates between the *āstika* and *nāstika darśanas* as well as between the adherents of the *ṣaḍdarśanas*, and between rival schools of one and the same *darśana*. Even texts that are not explicitly polemical—and many are!—contain innumerable references to and attacks against other systems. Precision in expression and incisiveness of thought were qualities aimed at by all professional Hindu thinkers. The English translation of texts does not do full justice to this aspect of Indian systematic since it has to fill in many words and circumscribe many terms in order to provide an intelligible text for readers not steeped in the subtleties of an intellectual tradition that enjoyed prestige and renown already at a time when Greek thought was only beginning to form and crystallize.

It is not without significance that in our age Western scientists of repute like H. Weyl, E. Schrödinger, C. F. von Weizsäcker, D. Bohm, A. Wheeler, and many others have discovered parallels between modern scientific thinking and some of the Hindu *darśanas*. Some contemporary Western logicians and linguistic philosophers avidly dig into the intricacies of *Mīmāṃsā* and *Nyāya*. Yoga, too, is now widely studied and practiced all over the world. If we can learn from India it is certainly from the *ṣaḍdarśanas* that can teach us some valuable lessons both in areas in which we feel competent and in areas unknown to us and so far unmapped.

The very notion of philosophy, which has acquired in the West the meaning of independent systematic and critical thought, of coherent reflection and sustained argumentation, has to be used with qualifications when applied to "Indian philosophy." As the student of the major histories of Indian philosophy such as S. N. Dasgupta's, S. Radhakrishnan's, or M. Hiriyanna's scholarly accounts will discover soon, Indian philosophy as a whole is not separate from Indian theology: systematic thought in India has been throughout pursued with the aim to find salvation. The specializations within Indian philosophy—physics and logic, anthropology and metaphysics, and so on—again do not correspond to the Western notions employed.

Using technical terms coined by the Western cultural tradition to describe the thinking and systematizing of Indian traditions is at one and the same time unavoidable and misleading. Unavoidable, because these are the terms which we know and understand. Risky, because they have connotations that are not wholly appropriate. Thus, writing on "Logic in the West and in India," Kuppuswamy Sastri remarks: "Those who are familiar with Western logic and desirous of studying Indian logic from a historical and comparative point of view will do well to bear in mind the fact that, while one may find striking parallels in the Indian and Western systems of logic, one would not be misled by such parallels and lose sight of the fundamental differences in respect of scope and method, which Indian logic discloses in its rise and development, as compared with Western logic."[24] The six "orthodox" systems have been grouped in three pairs from early times. The reason for doing this is in most cases quite clear—they complement each other in various ways. However it should not be overlooked that each of them was developed as a quite independent system, capable of achieving its aims by its own methods.

## THE *ṢAḌDARŚANAS* AND MODERN WESTERN PHILOSOPHY

There still is a large number of traditional Indian scholars, usually called *paṇḍits* or *śāstris*, who, mainly through the medium of Sanskrit, keep the knowledge of the *ṣaḍdarśanas* alive and whose contributions to the translation and interpretation of Sanskrit texts is indispensable, as most Indologists would readily admit. Usually they are attached to vernacular schools of traditional learning, *āśramas* and *pathaśālas*, but also modern Indian universities usually employ some in their departments of philosophy or Sanskrit. Their knowledge of detail of the particular specialty in which they hold their degrees is unsurpassed. They usually begin their training at age four and by the time they get their degrees they have memorized hundreds of substantial philosophical texts that they can recall instantly. They are able to identify implicit references in texts without referring to any written source and can reproduce quotes with incredible speed and accuracy. They have their own gatherings, the *śāstrārthas*, to debate problems that arise in the understanding of certain points of traditional doctrine. But until recently most of them kept away from contacts with exponents of non-Indian systems of thought.

In this context it was a bold and innovative step that M. P. Rege from the University of Pune took by arranging a *saṃvāda*, a dialogue between Western-trained Indian professors of philosophy and traditional Indian *paṇḍits* of Nyāya in Pune, followed by similar conferences in Tirupati on Mīmāṃsā, and in Śrīnagar on Kashmir Śaivism.[25] To everybody's surprise and delight the traditional *paṇḍits* not only agreed to participate in such ventures but made original and meaningful contributions to this philosophical dialogue. While for the past several centuries the major preoccupation of Indian traditional scholars had been to preserve the tradition and to appropriate the past, there is now an endeavor to take up the challenge and to further develop the tradition for the future. India's philosophical tradition has developed over the centuries such a richness of approaches and has dealt with so many issues that time and again one discovers not only uncanny parallels to modern Western thought but also a great many novel ideas and insights that lead to fruitful new areas of enquiry.

CHAPTER TWENTY-FOUR

# Hindu Logic and Physics

## *Nyāya-Vaiśeṣika*

> The Supreme Good results from the knowledge, produced by a particular *dharma*, of the essence of the categories: substance, attribute, action, genus, species, and combination, by means of their resemblances and differences.
>
> —*Vaiśeṣika Sūtra* I,1,4

The *Vaiśeṣika Sūtras*, ascribed to Kaṇāda, are, in the words of S. N. Dasgupta, "probably the oldest that we have and in all probability are pre-Buddhistic."[1] That does not entitle us, however, to make any statement about the age of the system itself, which is known particularly for its interesting early atomistic theory and its classification of categories. Vaiśeṣika may initially have been a school of Vedic thought, as its emphasis on *dharma* and its traditional opinion on *adṛṣṭa* as its fruit would suggest.[2] The work, which besides the sutras contains the most complete representation of the system, the *Daśapadārtha Śāstra*, is no older than the sixth century CE.[3]

Several recent works deal with Nyāya-Vaiśeṣika as if it were one single system.[4] Though they have much in common and supplement each other in many areas, they began as separate systems with quite different aims. Professor Kuppuswamy Sastri has this to say on the conjunction of Nyāya-Vaiśeṣika: "That Indian logic is usually described as the Nyāya-Vaiśeṣika system is not because it is the result of the syncretism of the two opposing systems, Nyāya realism and atomistic pluralism; rather it is so described because at a very early stage in the history of Indian logic, the Vaiśeṣika stress on the inductive phase of inference came to be synthesized with its deductive phase in the Nyāya theory of syllogistic reasoning."[5]

Recent Western philosophical preoccupation with logic, especially under the influence of the Anglo-American school of linguistic analysis, brought about an extensive and intensive study of Nyāya texts during the last few decades. Much of it is far too technical and too difficult to summarize to find a place in this survey. The interested reader is asked to consult the more specialized books available.[6]

The beginnings of the Nyāya systems may go back to the disputations of Vedic scholars; already in the times of the Upaniṣads debating was cultivated as an art, following certain rules in which the basic elements of logical proofs were contained.[7] The *Nyāya Sūtras*, ascribed to Gautama, the main text of the school, have received very important commentaries. It cannot be assigned to a definite date. All scholars agree that a considerable part of the sutras consists of additions to an original work, additions that suggest early Buddhist interpolations and later Hindu insertions to invalidate the Buddhist arguments. From the probable identification of *nyāya* with the *anvīkṣikī* in Kauṭilīya's *Arthaśāstra*[8] we may assume that the Nyāya system already existed in some form in the fourth century BCE. Professor Kuppuswamy Sastri mentions some more references that prove that "these two schools should have appeared in a fairly definite form with their characteristic methods of reasoning and metaphysics by the middle of the fourth century BCE, though the chief doctrines of these schools came to be systematized and redacted in their basic sutras at a relatively later date."[9] Followers of the Nyāya system have produced a large amount of important works, and of all the Hindu systems Nyāya enjoys the greatest respect on the part of Western philosophers, who are coming to discover the enormous subtleties and intricacies of Indian logic.

## A BRIEF SUMMARY OF VAIŚEṢIKA

"Now an explanation of *dharma*," begins the Kaṇāda Sutra. "The means to prosperity and salvation is *dharma*." The attainment of salvation is the result of the cognition of the six categories of substance, quality, action, class concept, particularity, and inherence.[10] The substances are: earth, water, fire, air, ether, time, space, *ātman*, and mind. The qualities are: taste, color, odor, touch, number, measure, separation, contact, disjoining, prior and posterior, understanding, pleasure and pain, desire and aversion, and volitions.

Action (karma) is explained as upward movement, downward movement, contraction, expansion, and horizontal movement. The feature common to substance, quality, and action is that they are existent, non-eternal, and substantive; they effect, cause, and possess generality and particularity. A major part of the sutra consists in a further elucidation of the various terms just mentioned, much in the same way in which the early Greek philosophers of nature analyzed and described the elements, their qualities, and the interrelations. In the third book the sutra deals with the inference of the existence of the *ātman*, which is impervious to sense perception, from the fact that there must be some substance in which knowledge, produced by the contact of the senses and their objects, inheres. Thus the *ātman*'s existence may be inferred from inhalation and exhalation, from the twinkling of the eyes, from life, from movements of the mind, from sense affections, from pleasure and pain, will, antipathy, and effort. It can be proved that it is a substance and eternal. Eternal (*nitya*) is that which exists but has no cause for its existence. The non-eternal is *avidyā*, ignorance.

In the seventh book we are told that *dṛṣṭa*, insight based on observation and rationality, is able to explain even natural phenomena only up to a certain point. All the special phenomena of nature are caused by *adṛṣṭa*, an unknown invisible cause. *Adṛṣṭa* is also said to be the cause of the union of body and soul, of rebirth and of liberation. This "invisible fruit," which is the cause of ultimate happiness, is produced by ablutions, fasting, continence, life in the guru's family, life in the forest, sacrifice, gifts and alms, observation of the cosmic cycle and the following of the rules of *dharma*. Thus *Vaiśeṣika* places itself quite explicitly in the tradition of Vedic orthodoxy. The sutra also discusses at some length the means and instruments of valid knowledge, topics that are dealt with more thoroughly in the sister system of Nyāya. The *Vaiśeṣika Sūtras* do not contain any polemics against the Buddhists, although these are opposed to some of their quite fundamental tenets: Buddhism denies the "thing in itself" and explains all phenomena merely as a chain of conditions that ultimately can be reduced to nonexistence; the *Vaiśeṣikas*, on the contrary, hold fast to the real existence of things.

Later works of the school, the commentaries on the sutra by Śaṅkara Miśra and Candrakānta, the *Padārtha-dharma-saṅgraha* by Praśastapāda and the *Daśa-padārthī* by Maticandra (preserved only in a Chinese version), also give a more detailed explanation of Indian atomism. What we hear, feel, see, and so forth are not *continua* but *discreta* (*quanta* we would say today), and these again are not units but compounds of infinitely small indivisible parts (*aṇu*) that clearly differ from one another. Things are products, therefore, and not eternal.

The primordial elements, earth, water, fire, and air, are partly eternal, partly temporal. Only ether is completely eternal. The first four elements have mass, number, weight, fluidity, viscosity, velocity, characteristic potential color, taste, smell, or touch. *Ākāśa*, space or ether, is absolutely inert and without structure, being only the substratum of *śabda* or sound, which is thought to travel like a wave in the medium of air. Atomic combinations are possible only with the four basic elements. Both in dissolution and before creation, the atoms exist singly; in creation they are always present in combination. Two atoms combine to form a *dvyaṇuka*, a molecule. Also *tryaṇukas*, *caturaṇukas*, that is, aggregates consisting of three or more molecules, are possible. Atoms are possessed of an inherent, incessant vibratory motion; but they are also under the influence of the *adṛṣṭa*, the will of *īśvara*, who arranges them into a harmonic universe. Changes in substances, which are limited within the frame of possible atom combinations, are brought about by heat. Under the impact of heat corpuscles a molecule may disintegrate, and the specific qualities of the atoms composing it may change. The heat particles, which continue to impinge on the individually changed atoms, also cause them to reunite in different forms so that definite changes are effected through heat. In many details the *Vaiśeṣikas* reveal a keen observation of nature and describe in their books a great number of phenomena that they try to explain with the help of their atom theory. Similar to modern physicists, the ancient *Vaiśeṣikas* explained heat and light rays as consisting of indefinitely small particles that dart forth or radiate in all directions rectilinearly with inconceivable velocity. Heat also penetrates the inter-atomic space or impinges on the atoms and rebounds, thus explaining the conducting and reflecting of heat. All the *paramāṇus* are thought to be spherical. Attempts have been made to link the atomism of the *Vaiśeṣika darśana* with Democritus—so far without any positive evidence.

Leaving out most of the technicalities of the system, a brief explanation of *viśeṣa*—the term that gave the name to the whole system—may give an idea of the specific approach taken by this school of classical Indian philosophy.[11] Praśastapāda writes:

> *Viśeṣas* are the ultimate principles of specification or differentiation of their substrates. They reside in such beginningless and indestructible eternal substances as the atoms, *ākāśa*, time, space, *ātman*, and *manas*—inhering in their entirety in each of these, and serving as the basis of absolute differentiation of specification. Just as we have with regard to the bull as distinguished from the horse, certain distinct cognitions—such, for instance as (a) that is a "bull," which is a cognition based upon its having the shape of other bulls, (b) that it is "white," which is based upon a quality, (c) that it is "running swiftly," which is based upon action, (d) that it has a "fat hump," which is based upon "constituent parts" and (e) that it carries a "large bell," which is based upon conjunction; so have the Yogis, who are possessed of powers that we do not possess, distinct cognitions based upon similar shapes, similar qualities, and similar actions—with regard to the eternal atoms, the liberated selves and minds; and as in this case no other cause is possible, those causes by reason whereof they have such distinct cognitions—as that "this is a peculiar substance," "that a peculiar self," and so forth—and which also lead to the recognition of one atom as being the same that was perceived at a different time and place—are what we call the *viśeṣas*.[12]

According to the teaching of the *Vaiśeṣikas*, there are many different *ātmans* distinguished by their relative and specific *viśeṣas*. The common man, however, is able to recognize their diversity only on account of externally perceptible actions, qualities, and so on. Only the Yogi has the "insight into the essence of the soul itself and thus into the real cause of their diversity." The *ātman* is eternal and not bound to space and time. But the actions of *ātman*—thought, will, emotions—are limited to the physical organism with which it is united at a given time. *Jñāna*, knowledge, is according to the *Vaiśeṣikas* only an accident of *ātman*, not his nature as such, since in dreamless sleep there is no cognition. Emotions and will are, likewise, mere accidents. The "spiritual" is not substantial but accidental. *Manas*, the mind given to every *ātman*, is merely its instrument and does not produce anything of itself. On the other hand, the cooperation of *manas* is necessary.

The state of *mokṣa* or freedom "is neither a state of pure knowledge nor of bliss, but a state of perfect absence of any quality, in which the self remains in itself in its own purity. It is the negative state of absolute painlessness."[13] Concerning the way to reach it we read in the *Daśa-padārtha Śāstra*:

> One who seeks eternal emancipation ought to devote himself to *śīla* or morality, *dāna* or liberality, *tapas* or austerities, and *yoga*. From these comes supreme merit, which leads to the attainment of emancipation and *tattva-jñāna* or knowledge of ultimate truth. "Prosperity" is enjoyment of pleasure in *svarga* or heaven. Knowledge of ultimate truth brings *mokṣa* or permanent liberation, when merit and demerit have been completely destroyed and *ātman* and *manas* no longer come in contact with each other, i.e. when the nine things are no longer produced.[14]

*Dharma* and *adharma* together form *adṛṣṭa*, which supports the cycle of *saṃsāra*, of attraction and aversion, and continuously drives the *ātman* back into bodily existence. The activity, which is guided by the feeling of the particular existence, depends on *avidyā*; when a person realizes that things as such are only varying combinations of atoms of the particular elements, all affection and aversion ceases. If the right knowledge of the self is achieved, egotism and all selfish activity cease. When *adṛṣṭa* is no longer produced, the cycle of transmigration comes to an end. On the other hand, *ātman* is never completely without *adṛṣṭa*, because the series of births is without beginning. When the soul has rid itself of its gross body, it still is and remains attached to the subtle body, even in *pralaya*, the dissolution of the universe. Time, place, and circumstances of birth, family and duration of life are all determined by *adṛṣṭa* and it is not possible ever to destroy it completely.

Kaṇāda's sutras do not require the idea of an *īśvara*. The substances are eternal; movement is due to the impersonal, eternal principle of *adṛṣṭa*. Later authors introduce an eternal, omniscient, and omnipresent *Īśvara* who is responsible for the universal order of atoms and their movements. This *Vaiśeṣika* God, however, resembles very much the *deus otiosus* of deism. *Ātman* and the *aṇu* do not owe their existence to a creator: they are eternal and independent. *Īśvara* differs from the *ātman* only insofar as he is never entangled in *saṃsāra*. He gives laws to the world but never interferes with it subsequently. He winds up the clockwork and lets it run its course.

## NYĀYA AND NAVYA-NYĀYA

Nyāya was, even in ancient times, composed of two parts: *adhyātma-vidyā*, or metaphysics, and *tarka-śāstra*, or rules of debate, often simply called logic. Thus the *Nyāya Sūtra*, famous for its acute analysis of discursive thought as such, also has substantial sections on suffering, soul, and salvation. It begins with the following aphorism: "It is the knowledge of the true character of the following sixteen categories that leads to the attainment of the highest good: (1) The Means of Right Cognition; (2) The Objects of Right Cognition; (3) Doubt; (4) Motive; (5) Example; (6) Theory; (7) Factors of Inference; (8) Cogitation; (9) Demonstrated Truth; (10) Discussion; (11) Disputation; (12) Wrangling; (13) Fallacious Reason; (14) Casuistry; (15) Futile Rejoinder; and 16) Clinchers."

Logic is practiced for the sake of salvation. That gives greater weight to the *Nyāya Sūtra* within Hinduism than a book on logic would normally have within a religious tradition. Logic as a way to truth is a means of liberation: "Suffering, birth, activity, mistaken notions, folly—if these factors are cancelled out in reverse order, there will be *mokṣa*."[15]

S. K. Sarma makes an important point when he states: "Nyāya is not logic in the strict sense of the word. It is a system of philosophy. It is true that it lays stress on inference or reasoning as a means to correct knowledge, but it is not formal. It is not a mere device for correct thinking, but a well-thought-out and complete metaphysical thesis."[16]

A definite break in the development of Nyāya took place in the twelfth century, which marks the rise of *Navya-Nyāya* or the New Logic. Whereas the earlier works had been concentrating on the elucidation of the categories, as enumerated in the *Nyāya Sūtra*, the *Tattva-cintāmaṇi* by Gaṅgeśa, the major work of the new school, emphasized the *pramāṇas*, the means of valid cognition, devoting one chapter each to perception (*pratyakṣa*), inference (*anumāna*), analogy (*upamāna*), and verbal testimony (*śabda*).

In spite of the intention to keep the description nontechnical it may be remarked that *Navya-Nyāya* not only developed a highly complex epistemology but also created a technical language with the help of newly coined terms and thus initiated a quite peculiar style of philosophical writing in India that stands out for its brevity and precision. The development of *Navya-Nyāya* and the focusing upon *pramāṇas* instead on the categories of the *Nyāya Sūtra* did not prevent the continued production of works of the "old school" alongside the flourishing "new logic." Works in both branches keep appearing even in our day.

The special field of *Navya-Nyāya* is epistemology. It acknowledges four legitimate means of finding truth: *pratyakṣa* or sense perception, *anumāna* or inference, *upamāna* or analogy, and *śabda* or scriptural authority. *Pratyakṣa* is the perception that results from the contact of one of the senses with its proper object: it is definite, uncontradicted, and unassociated with names. *Anumāna* is of three kinds: *pūrvavat* or from cause to effect, *śeṣavat* or from effect to cause, and *sāmānyato dṛṣṭa* or from common characteristics. *Upamāna* is the knowing of anything by similarity with any well-known thing. *Śabda* is defined as the testimony of reliable authority, which may also transcend one's own experience.

The objects of knowledge are: *ātman*, the body, senses, sense objects, *buddhi* or understanding, *manas* or mind, *pravṛtti* or endeavor, rebirths, enjoyment of pleasure and suffering of pain, sorrow and liberation. Desire, aversion, effort, pleasure and pain, as well as knowledge, indicate the existence of the *ātman*. Whereas the classical Aristotelian syllogism has three members—major, minor, and conclusion—the Nyāya syllogism has five:

1. *pratijñā*, or the stating of the point to be proved;
2. *hetu*, or the reason that establishes the proof;
3. *udahāraṇa*, or illustrative example;
4. *upanaya*, or corroboration by the instance;
5. *nigamana*, or inference, identical with the initial assertion.

The standard example of Indian logic for many centuries has been the following:

The mountain there in the distance is ablaze (1);

Because it is wreathed in smoke (2);

Whatever is wreathed in smoke is on fire, as in a stove (3);

The mountain there is wreathed in smoke in such manner (4);

Therefore: the mountain there in the distance is ablaze (5).

The discussion of fallacies and doubt demonstrates the lucidity and sharpness of the Naiyāyikas' intellects. All kinds of fallacies are analyzed and the causes of doubt are explained, but the general scepticism of the Buddhists, who maintained that nothing can be known with certainty, is refuted. The polemics against Buddhism, especially the *Śūnyavādis*, plays a large part in Nyāya literature. Naiyāyikas dissolve the extreme scepticism of the Buddhists with their critical realism and take the wind out of the Buddhists' sails by disproving their teaching of emptiness and the impossibility of true cognition with the very arguments that the Buddhists have used. The Naiyāyikas seek to demonstrate that real liberation is possible through true cognition of reality. They largely agree with the Vaiśeṣika metaphysics when they define *mokṣa* only in negative terms as "absolute freedom from pain."[17] It is a "condition of immortality, free from fear, imperishable," to be attained only after bodily death—there can be no *jīvan-mukta*.[18]

Quite unique in Indian philosophy are the arguments for the existence of *Īśvara*, which we find in *Nyāya* works.[19] The *Nyāya Kusumañjalī* states that the experience of contingency, eternity, diversity, activity, and individual existence requires an *adṛṣṭa*, an unseen cause, responsible ultimately for the joys and sorrows of human life. Above the *adṛṣṭa* of the *Vaiśeṣikas* the Naiyāyikas postulate a Lord as the cause of right knowledge, of creation and destruction.

"From effects, combination, support, etc. and traditional arts, authority, *śruti* and so on, an everlasting omniscient being must be assumed." The commentary on this text explains:

> The earth and other objects must have had a maker, because they have the nature of effects like a jar; by a thing's having a maker we mean that it is produced by some agent who possesses the wish to make, and has also a perceptive knowledge of the material cause out of which it is to be made. "Combination" is an action, and therefore the action, which produced the conjunction of two atoms, initiating the *dvyaṇuka* at the beginning of a creation, must have been accompanied by the volition of an intelligent being, because it has the nature of an action like the actions of bodies such as ours. "Support" etc.: the world depends upon some being who possesses a volition that hinders it from falling, because it has the nature of being supported. . . . By traditional arts etc.: The traditional arts now current, such as that of making cloth, must have been originated by an independent being, from the very fact that they are traditional usages like the tradition of modern modes of writing. "From authority": The knowledge produced by the Vedas is produced by a virtue residing in its cause, because it is right knowledge, just as in the case in the right knowledge produced by perception. "From *śruti*": The Veda must have been produced by a person: having the nature of a Veda like the *Āyur Veda*. . . . At the beginning of creation there must be the number of duality abiding in the atoms, which is the cause of the measure of the *dvyaṇuka*, but this number cannot be produced at that time by the distinguishing perception of beings like us. Therefore we can only assume this distinguishing faculty as then existing in *Īśvara*.[20]

The Lord is qualified by absence of *adharma*, of *mithyā-jñāna*, or false knowledge, and of *pramāda*, or error, and the positive presence of *dharma*, right knowledge and equanimity. He is omnipotent, though influenced in his actions by the acts of his creatures. He acts only for the good of his creatures and acts toward them like a father toward his children.[21] The Naiyāyikas also develop a theory of grace: "*Īśvara* indeed supports the efforts of people, i.e., if a person tries to attain something special, it is *Īśvara* who attains it; if *Īśvara* does not act, the activity of people is fruitless."

Much of Nyāya is so technical that it taxes the understanding even of a specialist in Western logic, not to speak of the general reader. Much of it is of interest mainly against the background of inter Indian disputes, especially with the Buddhist logicians. It is, however, important to note that India, too, has its schools of critical logicians, and that, despite the popular opinion of Indian philosophy being merely opaque mysticism, there is also the disciplined reasoning of logic.

*Tarka-śāstra*, the study of formal logic, is a difficult business and no more popular in India than anywhere else. Keśava Miśra of the fourteenth century, the author of a concise textbook that is still widely used, starts off his course in the following gruff manner: "I am writing this 'Exposition of Reasoning' consisting, as it does, of short and easy explanations of arguments, for the sake of the dull youth who wishes to have to learn as little as possible for the purpose of entering the portals of the Nyāya *darśana*."[22]

*Nyāya-vaiśeṣika* has remained a living philosophical tradition even in our age. The more it is studied, the more respect it commands for its incisiveness and brilliance of definition. It could also possibly make a substantial contribution to the contemporary philosophy of science, anticipating, often by many centuries, problems that we are only now discovering.

CHAPTER TWENTY-FIVE

# Hindu Metaphysics and Psychology

## *Sāṁkhya-Yoga*

Absolute freedom comes when the *guṇas*, becoming devoid of the object of the *puruṣa*, become latent; or the power of consciousness becomes established in its own nature.

—Patañjali, *Yoga Sūtra* IV, 34

*Yoga* is one of the most popular and most ambiguous words in Indian literature, a word with which everybody seems to be familiar, as the advertisements of numerous Yoga schools suggest. Etymologically the word is derived from the root *yuj-*, to join, to unite. Pāṇini, the grammarian, explains the meaning of *yoga* as virtually identical with that of our word *religion*, union with the Supreme. Patañjali, in his *Yoga Sūtra*, defines *yoga* as "cessation of all fluctuations in consciousness." According to the Vedāntins *yoga* means the return of the *jīvātman*, the individual being, to its union with the *paramātman*, the Supreme Self. In a more general sense Hindu scriptures use the word *yoga* as a synonym to *mārga*, denoting any system of religion or philosophy, speaking of *karma-yoga*, *bhakti-yoga*, *jñāna-yoga*.

We propose here only to deal with *yoga* in its technical and classical sense, with the Yoga system as explained by Patañjali. The system is called Rāja Yoga, the "royal way," in contrast to Haṭha Yoga, the tour de force[1] of most Western Yoga schools, or the Kuṇḍalinī Yoga of the Śāktas, mentioned before. It is also called Sāṁkhya-Yoga, because of its intimate connection with the *darśana* known as *Sāṁkhya*.[2]

### A BRIEF HISTORICAL SURVEY

*Sāṁkhya-Yoga* has become, in one form or another, part and parcel of most major religions of India: thus we find *Sāṁkhya-Yoga* combined with Vaiṣṇavism,

Śaivism, and Śāktism, and most of the Purāṇas contain numerous chapters on *Sāṁkhya-Yoga* as a path to salvation.[3] It fell into disfavor at a later time, when Vedānta became the predominant theology of Hinduism. The reasons for this development are twofold: *Sāṁkhya* does not base its statements on scripture; it even explicitly rates *śruti* no higher than reasoning. And it does not recognize a Supreme Lord above *Puruṣa* and *Prakṛti*, an idea that was crucial to the theistic systems of medieval Hinduism.

Some seals from the Sindhu-Sarasvatī civilization show figures that were interpreted as depicting yoga postures. The basic idea of *Sāṁkhya* philosophy, the male-female polarity as the source of all development, does not need a specific "inventor"; it can easily be considered a "natural system." In some of the earlier Upaniṣads we find allusions to doctrines that could be termed *Sāṁkhya*, leaving open the question whether the Upaniṣads made use of an already developed philosophical system or whether the system developed out of the elements provided in the Upaniṣads. In order to explain the name *Sāṁkhya*—in modern Indian languages the word means "number"—some scholars have resorted to the hypothesis of an original *Sāṁkhya* that, like the school of Pythagoras, was concerned with numbers and conceived of the world as being constructed from harmonious proportions.[4] S. N. Dasgupta sees, moreover, a close inner relationship between *Sāṁkhya-Yoga* and Buddhism. He writes: "*Sāṁkhya* and the Yoga, like the Buddhists, hold that experience is sorrowful. *Tamas* represents the pain-substance. As *tamas* must be present in some degree in all combinations, all intellectual operations are fraught with some degree of painful feeling."[5]

The original meaning of *Sāṁkhya* must have been very general: understanding, reflection, discussion, so that the name simply came to connote *philosophy* or *system*. Kapila, its mythical founder, figures in the Indian tradition quite often as the father of philosophy as such. Vedāntins who assume a different position on many basic issues, especially with regard to the place that *prakṛti* holds, quite frequently attack the *Sāṁkhya* system, but there is hardly a book that does not deal with it or that would not betray its influence by using *Sāṁkhya* terminology.

The basic ideas of *Sāṁkhya* may be found already in the cosmogonic hymns of the *Ṛgveda*, in sections of the *Atharvaveda*, in the notion of the evolution of all things from one principle, dividing itself, in the Upaniṣads and also in the Upaniṣadic attempts to classify all phenomena under a limited number of categories. The *Mahābhārata* has sections explaining the full *Sāṁkhya* system, though with significant differences as compared to the classical *Sāṁkhya*. The great epic makes Kapila the son of Brahmā; according to the *Bhāgavata Purāṇa* he is an *avatāra* of Viṣṇu who teaches *Sāṁkhya* as a system of liberation through which his mother reaches instant release.[6] There is not much historical evidence for the opinion, found in some works on Indian philosophy that as a historical person, Kapila belongs to the sixth century BCE. The oldest traditional textbook of the school, the *Sāṁkhya-kārikā* of Īśvara Kṛṣṇa was probably composed in the third century CE. This work, which has received numerous important commentaries in later centuries, claims to be the complete summary of the entire *Śaṣṭi-tantra*, perhaps an older work. The *Sāṁkhya-kārikā* is a short treatise, containing only seventy aphorisms.[7] The *Sāṁkhya-sūtra*, ascribed to Kapila himself, has been found to be a later work, much longer than the *Kārikā* and going into more detail.[8]

Yoga as a system is already dealt with quite extensively in some of the later Upaniṣads, which in fact are sometimes brief compendia of Yoga.[9] The *Tejobindu Upaniṣad* gives a rather detailed description of *rāja-yoga*. Many of the teachings found in it can be discovered word for word in Patañjali's *Yoga Sūtra*, which has become the classical textbook, commented upon by great scholars like Vyāsa and Bhoja.[10] This Upaniṣad suggests to the Yogi, who is intent on realization, to repeat constantly: "I am Brahman." He is advised sometimes to affirm and sometimes to negate the identity of all things with *brahman*. "Renouncing all the various activities, think thus: 'I am Brahman—I am of the nature of *sat-cit-ānanda*.' And then renounce even this!"[11]

Most Indian schools, be they followers of the *Sāṁkhya* or of the Vedānta philosophy, accept Patañjali Yoga as a practical and indispensable means for purification and concentration. In 1952 a commentary to the Patañjali *Yoga Sūtra*, ascribed to Śaṅkara, was published from a manuscript in Madras. Many scholars assume it to be genuine, in spite of the polemic against *Sāṁkhya* Yoga in Śaṅkara's *Brahmasūtrabhāyṣa*.[12]

## THE BASIC PHILOSOPHY OF *SĀṀKHYA*

The *Sāṁkhya-kārikā* begins with the aphorism: "From torment by threefold misery the inquiry into the means of terminating it."[13] Our frustrations and pains, caused by *devas* and *asuras*, fellowmen, beasts, and inanimate objects, as well as by oneself,[14] are the stimulus for the quest for freedom from misery: *Sāṁkhya* offers the solution. *Sāṁkhya* neither denies the reality of experience nor the reality of pain accompanying every experience, but it offers a possibility of terminating this pain of experience. Rejecting all other means, the *Kārikās* establish the thesis that "the discriminative knowledge of the evolved, the unevolved, and the knower is the means of surpassing all sorrow.[15]

*Sāṁkhya* defends, or rather presupposes, a dualistic realism. There are two beginningless realities: *prakṛti* and *puruṣa*, the female and the male principle, matter and spirit. Ideally, before the development of concrete existences, they exist separately in polarity. In actual existence they are combined and interacting. *Puruṣa*, in himself pure consciousness, experiences the changes that *prakṛti*, on account of her three *guṇas*, is undergoing, as if these were his own. *Puruṣas* are originally many; *prakṛti* is originally one. The association with a *puruṣa* makes *prakṛti*, as the evolved being, manifold and makes *puruṣa* interact with it. Under the influence of *puruṣa*, out of the unevolved primordial *prakṛti*, develop macrocosm and microcosm according to a fixed pattern. Each part of it is characterized in a different measure by the presence of the three *guṇas*. Originally the three *guṇas*—*sattva* or lightness, *rajas* or passion, and *tamas* or darkness—had been in equilibrium in *prakṛti*. Under *puruṣa*'s influence the equilibrium is disturbed and evolution begins. The first product of this evolutionary process, which simply takes its course without needing a creator or a world soul, is *mahat*, the Great One, also called *buddhi*, the intellect: from *mahat* issues *ahaṁkāra*, the principle of individuation. Having the *tri-guṇa* structure, it communicates it to the further evolutes: the senses and the elements that form their object. The enumeration of the twenty-four basic elements is intended also to provide a physically correct description of the universe and to prepare the ground for the way back to the source. Against those who assume that there is only one spirit in the universe, the *Kārikās* establish the following argument: "The plurality of *puruṣas* follows from the fact of individual death and individual birth, and from the fact that the organs of cognition and action are individual; moreover not all people are active at the same time and the relationship of the three *guṇas* varies from person to person."[16]

In *devas* and saintly people *sattva* dominates, in ordinary people *rajas*, and in animals *tamas* prevails. To dispel the objection that *prakṛti* is mere fiction because she cannot be seen, heard, touched, and so forth, the *Kārikās* state: "The nonperception is due to its subtlety, not to its nonexistence, since it is cognized from its effects."[17]

Knowing *prakṛti* as *prakṛti* means to become free from her: for *prakṛti* is not only the means to bind *puruṣa* but also the means to free him. A person who is able to analyze experience in such a way as to differentiate *puruṣa* from *prakṛti* in consciousness, seeing in *prakṛti* the reason for the contingence of all things and the basis for all change and multiplicity, is free. Though *puruṣa* is free by nature, he is incapable of acting and thus unable to free himself when united with *prakṛti*: "Certainly no *puruṣa* is in bondage and none is liberated nor has he to undergo any changes; it is *prakṛti*, dwelling in many forms, who is bound, freed, and subject to change. *Prakṛti* binds herself sevenfold and through one form she causes liberation for the benefit of *puruṣa*."[18]

The *Kārikās* compare the relationship between *puruṣa* and *prakṛti* with that of a seeing lame person being carried by a blind able-bodied person: it is the seeing lame one that directs the blind walking one and realizes her own purpose. In another simile the *puruṣa* is compared to a spectator observing a dancer. After the dancer has shown all her skills, she cannot but repeat her performance over and over again. When the onlooker becomes aware of the repeat performance, interest is waning. And the dancer, seeing that the spectator pays no more attention to her, ceases to dance. Although the union still persists, nothing more is produced from it. "*Puruṣa*, because of former impressions, remains united with the body, just like the potter's wheel continues to rotate for a while without being impelled again, due to the impulse received before."[19]

When the separation from the body finally takes place and the aim has been fulfilled, *prakṛti* ceases to be active and *puruṣa* reaches *kaivalya*, aloneness, and perfect freedom. By doing away with objective sense perception, by tracing back egoism and discursive reasoning to *prakṛti*, by coming to know the true nature of *prakṛti*, *puruṣa* becomes emancipated. Spirit, having been restless in connection with matter, realizes matter to be the cause of his restlessness. By realizing the nature of *prakṛti* as contrary to his own nature and recognizing all objective reality as but evolutes of *prakṛti*, the spirit becomes self-satisfied and self-reliant. The very dissociation of *puruṣa* from *prakṛti* is ultimate liberation.

## THE THEORY AND PRACTICE OF YOGA

The practical process of discriminative knowledge leading to the actual achievement of the "isolation" of the *puruṣa* is proposed in Patañjali's *Yoga Sūtra*. Yoga is not mere theoretical knowledge but it also implies physical training, exertion of willpower, and acts of decision, because it intends to deal with the complete human situation and provide real freedom, not just a theory of liberation.

The *Yoga Sūtra* itself—a short work of but 194 aphorisms—is clearly structured into four *pādas*, with the subject titles *samādhi*, *sādhana*, *vibhuti*, and *kaivalya*. The first sutra, defining the aim and meaning of Yoga as *citta-vṛtti-nirodha*, the cessation of all fluctuations of consciousness, goes to the very core of *Sāṁkhya* metaphysics. *Citta* is the same as the *mahat* of the *Sāṁkhya*, the first evolved, whose changes ultimately cause all suffering. For *citta* the cessation of all changes means merging into *prakṛti*. *Prakṛti* then becomes again undifferentiated and dissociated from *puruṣa*: the *puruṣa* achieves *ekāgratā*, one-pointedness, *kaivalya*, aloneness, being-with-oneself-only, being nothing but consciousness. The changes that may affect *citta* are enumerated as fivefold: perception, delusion, imagination, deep sleep, and memory.[20] The means to do away with them is *abhyāsa* and *vairāgya*, the dialectic interaction of positive effort and renunciation. The *Yoga Sūtra* introduces *Īśvara*, the Lord, as one of the supports of concentration. *Īśvara* is defined as a *puruṣa*, untouched by suffering, activity, and karma, the teacher of the ancients, denoted by the sign OM, whose constant repetition is recommended to the Yogi to attain *kaivalya*.[21] The Lord is also a helper in removing the obstacles that hinder self-realization: sickness, suffering, indecision, carelessness, sloth, sensuality, false views, and inconstancy, which cause distraction. In the company of these distractions come pain, despair, tremor, hard and irregular breathing. For the purification of the mind the *Yoga Sūtra* recommends truthfulness, friendliness, compassion, and contentment together with indifference toward happiness and unhappiness, virtue and vice. Breath control, too, is recommended.

The second part of the *Yoga Sūtra* dealing with *sādhana*, the means to liberation, begins with the aphorism: "The yoga of action is constituted by *tapas* or austerities, *svādhyāya* or scriptural study, and *īśvara praṇidhāna* or meditation with the Lord as object." Its goal is to attain *samādhi*, which may be translated as blissful inner peace, and to terminate the *kleśas*, the frustrations and afflictions. The root cause and source of all suffering is identified as *avidyā*, lack of insight and wisdom. It manifests itself in four principal forms, namely as *āsmitā* or egoism, *rāga* or attachment, *dveṣa* or aversion, and *abhiniveṣa* or love of physical life. *Avidyā* is further explained as mistaking the non-eternal for the eternal, the impure for the pure, the painful for the pleasurable, and the not-self for the Self.[22] To combat these afflictions the *Yoga Sūtra* commends *dhyāna* or meditation. The actual vehicle of liberation is *viveka*, discrimination, implying understanding of the Self as the only true and worthwhile being and the rest as illusory. This knowledge arises only after the impurities of the mind have been destroyed through the practice of the eight *yogāṅgas*, limbs of Yoga. These are *yama* and *niyama*, ethical commands and prohibitions, *āsana* or certain bodily postures, *prāṇayama* or breath control, *pratyāhāra* or withdrawal of the senses, *dhāraṇa* or concentration exercises, *dhyāna* or meditation, and *samādhi* or inner composure.

The *Yoga Sūtra* reasons that the cause of all sin lies in *lobha*, *moha*, and *krodha*—greed, delusion, and anger—whereas the practice of the virtues produces many side effects that are helpful either for the Yogis' own realization or for their fellow beings. Thus when *ahimṣā*, nonviolence, is firmly established, others too will give up their enmity and violence in the presence of the Yogi; not only people but also animals will live peacefully with each other. When *satya*, the love of truth, is perfected it enables a person to perform great deeds. When *asteya*, abstention from misappropriation is practiced, the treasures from which the Yogi runs away will spontaneously materialize. When *brahmacārya*, perfect continence, is practiced, great strength will come to the Yogi. The practice of *aparigraha*, of generosity in the widest sense, brings with it the knowledge of the round of births. *Śauca*, or disgust with one's own body brings to an end the desire to have bodily contact with others. Purity also helps to attain physical well-being, control over one's senses and concentration. *Santoṣa*, or contentment, brings inner peace and happiness to the Yogi. *Tapasya*, practice of austerities, purifies from sins and makes the Yogi acquire *siddhis* or supernatural faculties. Through *svādhyāya*, or scriptural study, one can reach the *Iṣṭadevatā*. *Īśvara praṇidhāna*, surrender to the Lord, brings about *samādhi*, inner illumination.

*Āsana*, posture, a way of sitting that is agreeable, enables the practitioner to sit motionless for a long while without falling asleep or straining. It is intended to overcome the distraction caused by the *dvandvas*, the pairs of opposites like heat and cold, hunger and thirst, comfort and discomfort. While Hatha Yoga manuals develop a veritable science of the *āsanas*, enumerating altogether eighty-four often extremely difficult bodily postures for curing or preventing diseases or attaining certain other results, Patañjali is of the opinion that any position will serve, provided that it allows a person to practice continued concentration and meditation: the aim is neither self-mortification for it own sake, nor the cure of bodily ailments, but spiritual realization.[23]

In the third *pāda* Patañjali speaks about the extraordinary or miraculous faculties of the Yogi, *siddhis* or *vibhutis*, which appear as side effects of Yoga. Despite Patañjali's warning that they should not be cultivated because they detract from the principal aim of Yoga as spiritual realization, a number of Yogis at all times have practiced Yoga for the sake of those *siddhis*—becoming invisible, reducing one's size to that of a grain of sand or increasing it to the volume of a mountain, adopting a radiant body, or leaving the body and reentering it at will.

Patañjali stresses the moral aspects of the preparation for *kaivalya*. If evil desires and intentions are not completely purged, there is the danger that the increased power that a Yogi wins through his mental concentration may be used for evil purposes, rather than for realization of the highest aim.

Dietetic rules are rather prominent in many books on Yoga; whatever is sour, salty, or pungent should be avoided. Nonstimulating food will allow the body to come to rest; milk alone is the ideal food for Yogis.

## THE CORE OF YOGA

One of the most important topics in the *Yoga Sūtra* is *prāṇayama*. The great significance of *prāṇa*, or life breath, in philosophical speculation was mentioned earlier. *Prāṇayama* is one of the most widely practiced disciplines and one of the most ancient methods of purification. Perfect breath control can be carried so far that to all appearances a person does not breathe anymore and the heartbeat becomes imperceptible. Thus we hear quite frequently about Yogis who get themselves buried for days or weeks and let themselves be admired on coming out from their graves. According to all indications there is neither fraud nor miracle involved. The secret lies in the consciously controlled reduction of the body's metabolism to the minimum required for keeping the life processes going and in the overcoming of fear through concentration; for fear would increase the need for oxygen. The *Yoga Sūtra* ends the explanations on *prāṇayama* with the statement: "The mind's ability for concentration." Breath control is the basis of body control and of mental realization.

*Pratyāhāra*, withdrawal of the senses, is dealt with immediately afterward: "When the senses do not have any contact with their objects and follow, as it were, the nature of the mind."[24] The senses, in this condition, not only no longer hinder the intellect, but the power invested in them actively helps it.

The next section is probably the most crucial one: it deals with three stages of realization. They are briefly explained as follows: "*Dhāraṇa* is the fixation of the intellect on one topic. *Dhyāna* is the one-pointedness in this effort. *Samādhi* is the same (concentration) when the object itself alone appears devoid of form, as it were."[25] The commentaries explain the first stage as a concentration of the mind on certain areas in the body: the navel, the heart, the forehead, the tip of the nose or the tip of the tongue. In the second stage all objects are consciously eliminated and the union with the absolute is contemplated. In its perfection it glides over into the third and last stage. Here the identification has gone so far that there is no longer a process of contemplation of an object by a subject, but an absolute identity between the knower, that which is known, and the process of knowing. Subject-object polarity disappears in a pure "is-ness," a cessation of the particular in an absolute self-awareness.

The three stages together are called *samyama*. They are understood not as something that incidentally happens to someone but as a practice that can be learned and acquired and then exercised at will. It is the specific schooling of the Yogi to acquire those tools with which one masters the world. Though we must omit the details here, suffice it to say that as with the mastery of any science, so Yoga requires a certain talent, hard work, and progress through many small steps, avoiding numerous pitfalls on the way, before one can competently use the instruments. If the training is applied to the various objects and the various levels of reality, the Yogi can win knowledge of the future and the past, obtain a knowledge of all languages and the sounds of all living beings, understand the language of the animals, know about former births, read other people's thought, become invisible, foresee the exact time of death, become full of goodwill toward all creatures, gain the strength of an elephant, have knowledge of what is subtle, distant, and hidden; know the regions of the firmament, the stars and their orbits, and the whole anatomy of the human body; suppress completely hunger and thirst, see the *devas*, have foreknowledge of all that is going to happen, receive extrasensory sight, hearing, and taste; acquire the ability to enter other bodies mentally at will, walk freely on water without even touching it, walk across thorny and muddy ground without getting hurt or dirty, acquire a body that is bright and weightless, leave the body and act without it, become master of all material elements, obtain a body that is beautiful, strong, and as hard as a diamond; have direct knowledge of the *pradhāna*, the ground from which all beings come, and mastery over all conditions of being as well as omniscience.[26]

More than anything else those *vibhutis* have been described and dreamed about in literature about Indian Yogis. Biographies and autobiographies of Yogis are full of reports about achievements following the line of the *Yoga Sūtra*. In actual Indian life one hardly ever encounters any miracles of this sort. Living for two years in a place where thousands of holy men and women dwelled and where countless rumors about such things circulated, the author never witnessed a single incident corresponding to this idea of the miraculous. Not too many years ago a Yogi called a press conference in Bombay and announced that he would demonstrate walking on water without wetting even his feet, against a reward of one million rupees. The bargain was agreed upon and a tank was built and filled with water. The Yogi could choose the auspicious time for his performance. When the hour had come, scores of journalists and hundreds of curious onlookers were present to watch the Yogi win his million. He lost it, being unable even to swim like an ordinary mortal. Later "unfavorable circumstances" were blamed for the Yogi's failure and another attempt was announced for an undisclosed future date.

According to Patañjali the purpose of many of these *vibhutis* is fulfilled if the Yogi experiences in trance those miraculous happenings as if they were real. In the overall context of *rāja-yoga* the *siddhis* are an obstacle on the way to *samādhi*.

The fourth and last *pāda* of the *Yoga Sūtra* deals with *kaivalya*, the goal of Yoga. The introductory aphorism states that the aforementioned *siddhis* are brought about either by imprints left in the psyche from previous births, by drugs, by mantras, or by *samādhi*. The proper thrust of *samādhi*, however, is not backward into the world of objects, from which it is freeing the spirit, but forward into the discrimination of *puruṣa* from the *guṇas* that belong to *prakṛti*. *Viveka*, discriminatory knowledge, means freedom from the influence of the *guṇas*: they return to their source as soon as their task is fulfilled. *Prakṛti* withdraws as soon as *puruṣa* has seen her as *prakṛti*. When the *guṇas* cease to be effective, activity and passivity, action and suffering also cease: "*Kaivalya* is realized when the *guṇas*, annihilated in the objectives of a person, cease to exert influence, or when *citta-śakti*, the power of consciousness, is established in her own proper nature."[27]

Yoga is the reversal of the evolutionary process demonstrated in the *Sāṁkhya* system; it is the entering into the origins. It is not, however, simply an annihilation of creation. *Sāṁkhya* does not work in terms of the model of the genetic method of modern science, but it uses a phenomenological method. *Prakṛti*, "matter," is not an object of physics but of metaphysics. Her eternity is not the nondestructibility of a concrete object but the everlastingness of potentiality.[28] When *puruṣa* combines with her, there is no need for any additional cause from outside to set evolution going. It is an unfolding of primeval matter that until then had existed as mere potency, but that is always there. Yoga comes close to what we today would call *psycho-science*, a detailed observation of human nature, paired however with a deep conviction of an ultimate that is missing in much of contemporary psychology.

CHAPTER TWENTY-SIX

# Hindu Theology, Old and New

## *Mīmāṃsā and Vedānta*

*Dharma* is that which is indicated by means of the Veda as conducive to the highest good.

—*Mīmāṃsā Sūtra* I, 1, 2

*Brahman* is that from which the origin, subsistence, and dissolution of this world proceeds.

—*Brahma Sūtra* I, 1, 2

*Mīmāṃsā*, "enquiry," is the name of two very different systems of Hindu theology, which have, however, one thing in common: based on selected statements of *śruti*, they develop complete and coherent systems of theology.

Pūrva-Mīmāṃsā (often simply called Mīmāṃsā), the "earlier enquiry" has *dharma* as its proper subject and the *karma-kāṇḍa* of the Vedas as its scriptural source. *Uttara-Mīmāṃsā*, the "latter enquiry," better known as Vedānta, has *brahman* knowledge as its subject and the *jñāna-kāṇḍa* of the Veda as its scriptural basis. Though historically there was considerable friction between the two systems, they are also in many ways complementary and are considered to be the two most orthodox of the six systems. Certainly they are the two *darśanas* that come closest to the idea of systematic theology as developed in the West.

### THE OLD THEOLOGY

Mīmāṃsā, the "old theology," uses as its basic textbook the *Mīmāṃsā Sūtras*, ascribed to Jaimini, dated around 200 BCE. The terse sūtras have received ample commentaries by various writers; the most extensive and famous of these is the *Śābarabhāṣya*, written probably in the first century BCE.[1] The "old theology" has also produced brilliant philosophers like Prabhākara and Kumārila Bhaṭṭa; the latter is supposed to have been an older contemporary of the great "new theologian," Śaṅkara.[2] Though a good deal of the specific theology of Mīmāṃsā, dealing with the Vedic sacrificial ritual, has ceased to command the leading role and has been replaced by the more speculative approach of the Vedāntins, the Old Theology is still of unquestionably great importance. As S. N. Dasgupta writes: "Not only are all Vedic duties to be performed according to its maxims, but even the *smṛti* literatures, which regulate the daily duties, ceremonials and rituals of the Hindus even to the present day are all guided and explained by them. The legal side of the *smṛtis*, which guide Hindu civil life . . . is explained according to Mīmāṃsā maxims."[3] The principles of Vedic exegesis developed by the Mīmāṃsakas, as well as their epistemology, are accepted by the Vedāntins, too, who otherwise disagree with some of their fundamental tenets.[4]

*Athāto dharma-jijñāsā*, "Now, then, an enquiry into *dharma*," is the first aphorism of the *Jaimini Sūtras*. The text goes on to explain: "*Dharma* is that which is indicated by Vedic injunctions for the attainment of the good."[5] The Mīmāṃsakas took it for granted that the performance of sacrifices was the means to attain everything and that the Veda was intended to serve this end alone. Despite their insistence that the Veda was *a-pauruṣeya*, not human-made and infallible revelation, they were prepared to drop all those parts of the Veda as nonessential that had nothing directly to do with sacrificial ritual. "The purpose of the Veda lying in the enjoining of actions, those parts of the Veda that do not serve that purpose are useless; in these therefore the Veda is declared to be non-eternal."[6]

Classical Mīmāṃsā does not admit the existence of any *īśvara* as the creator and destroyer of the universe. Mīmāṃsakas even formulate arguments that positively disprove the existence of God.[7] The world, in their view, has always been in existence and the only real agent of a permanent nature was the sacrifice, or rather its unseen essence, the *apūrva*. Sacrifice, therefore, is the only topic that really interests the Mīmāṃsakas. The texts treat of the eternity of the Veda, of the means to its correct understanding and of the validity of human knowledge as preliminaries to this question.[8]

Many times we read in the *Brāhmaṇas*, "Desiring heaven, one should perform sacrifice." Consequently the Mīmāṃsakas emphasize that "desire for heaven" is the basic presupposition for performing a sacrifice. Besides animals, *devas*, and the Vedic *ṛṣis*, women and *śūdras* are categorically excluded from the performance of sacrifices. So are those who lack sufficient wealth or suffer from a physical disability.[9] The theory of *apūrva* is intended to explain the infallible effect of a sacrifice. The Mīmāṃsakas say that the *apūrva* is related to the verb of the Vedic injunction because this expresses something as yet to be accomplished. More subtly, Mīmāṃsā distinguishes between principal and secondary *apūrva*.[10]

The *Mīmāṃsā Sūtra* is very brief in its description of the state to be achieved through sacrifice, namely *svarga* or heaven. Mīmāṃsakas are probably convinced that one cannot know much about it. By the very principles that they established they must come to the conclusion that those passages in the Vedas that describe heaven, not enjoining certain acts, cannot be taken as authoritative. One sutra says: "That one result would be heaven, as that is equally desirable for all."[11] To which the commentator adds: "Why so? Because heaven is happiness and everyone seeks for happiness." The *Mīmāṃsā Sūtra* does not mention the term *mokṣa* at all. Śabara declared that the statements concerning heaven found in the *Mahābhārata* and the Purāṇas can be neglected (because these books were composed by mere humans) and also that Vedic descriptions of heaven were mere *arthavāda*, that is, without authority.[12] Later Mīmāṃsakas, perhaps influenced by Vedānta, introduce the term *mokṣa* into their vocabulary and describe it as not having to assume a body after death.[13] They also offer a description of the way to liberation: First of all people become disgusted with the troubles that they have to undergo during their life on earth; finding the pleasures of the world to be invariably accompanied by some sort of pain, they come to lose all interest in, and longing for, pleasures. They thereupon turn their attention toward liberation, cease to perform such acts that are prohibited and lead to misfortune, as well as those that are prescribed only to lead to some sort of happiness here or hereafter; they attenuate all previously acquired merit and demerit by undergoing the experiences resulting from them; they destroy the sole receptacle or abode of his experiences by the knowledge of the soul and are aided by such qualities as contentment, self-control, and so forth, all of which are laid down in the scriptures as helping to prevent the further return of the soul into this world. It is only when all this has come about that the souls become free: *muktas*.[14]

With their interest in language and analysis the Mīmāṃsakas are often close to the Grammarians, who developed a philosophical school of their own. Quite important epistemological observations are to be found already in the *Śabarabhāṣya*, observations that have prompted contemporary scholars to undertake interesting investigations.[15] The first major commentary on Pāṇini's sutras, the *Mahā-bhāṣya* by Patañjali (second century BCE) contains questions concerning the nature and function of words. The unquestionably most famous name in Indian linguistic philosophy, however, is Bhartṛhari (ca. 500 CE), whose *Vākya-padīya* has been studied with great interest by Western scholars in recent years. His system is also called *sphoṭa-vāda* after its most characteristic teaching, which compares the sudden appearance of meaning at the enunciation of a word with the process of the sudden ejection of liquid from a boil.[16]

## THE NEW THEOLOGY

*Athāto brahma-jijñāsā*, "Now, then, an enquiry into *brahman*," begins the *Vedānta Sūtra*, also called *Brahma Sūtra*, which is ascribed to Bādarāyaṇa and forms the basic text of Vedānta *darśana*. The 555 sutras, purporting to summarize the teaching of the Upaniṣads, are mostly so short—often consisting of not more than one or two words—that without a commentary they remain incomprehensible. In all probability there had been a living tradition of Vedāntins in which the meaning of the *Vedānta Sūtra* was passed on from one generation to the next. As the Upaniṣads themselves took great care to maintain the *guru paramparā*, the succession of authorized teachers of the *vidyā* contained in them, so also the systematized aphoristic sutra text and its meaning was preserved in a carefully guarded tradition whose beginning we are unable to identify.

According to an old Indian tradition there had been other *Brahma Sūtras* before the one composed by Bādarāyaṇa. The most famous of these predecessors seems to have been an Ācarya Bādarī, who is credited with having written both a *Mīmāṃsā Sūtra* and a *Vedānta Sūtra*.[17] Other *ācāryas*, whose names are found in ancient texts as forerunner to Bādarāyaṇa include Kārṣṇājini, Atreya, Audulomi, Asmarāthya, Kāśakṛtsna, Kaśyapa, Vedavyāsa—all mentioned in the extant *Brahma Sūtra*—whose works have not been preserved. In all probability Bādarāyaṇa's sutra impressed his contemporaries as being superior so that in the course of time it completely replaced the others.[18] The *bhāṣyas*, or commentaries to the *Brahma Sūtra*, have gained an authoritative position in the various branches of Vedānta, combining a textual exegesis with other living traditions, as we saw earlier when dealing with Vaiṣṇavism and Śaivism.[19] The oldest of the extant complete commentaries is that by Śaṅkarācārya. We know that there had been earlier commentaries associated with names like Bhartṛ-prapañca, Bhartṛmitra, Bhartṛhari, Upavarṣa, Bodhāyana (whose authority is several times invoked by Rāmānuja against Śaṅkara), Brahmānaṇḍi, Taṅka, Brahmadatta, Bhāruci, Sundarapāṇḍya, Gauḍa-pāda and Govinda Bhagavatpāda, the guru of Śaṅkarācārya.[20]

As the commentators expounding the most diverse theological views demonstrate, the original *Brahma Sūtra* is merely a kind of general frame for the further development of ideas that are left fairly vague and undetermined. Looking at the bare sutras without a commentary one can only give a general idea of their structure without discussing their import.

The *Vedānta Sūtra* is divided into four *adhyāyas*, chapters, each subdivided into four *pādas*, literally, "feet" or parts, which again are made up of a varying number of sutras or aphorisms.

The entire first *adhyāya* is devoted to a discussion on *brahman*: *brahman* is the sole and supreme cause of all things. Systems that teach otherwise are rejected as heretical. The detailed polemics against the Sāṁkhya system is continued into the second *adhyāya*, which also refutes Vaiśeṣika theories. Toward the end of the second *pāda* the *Bhāgavata* system is mentioned. The comments on this part of the text (II, 2,42–48) are a classic example of the wide diversity that exists in the commentaries. Śaṅkara understands the sutra to say that the *Bhāgavata* system is untenable; Rāmānuja sees in it a recognition and justification for the *Bhāgavata* system. The next two *pādas* show the origin of the various phenomena that go into the making of the universe. The third *adhyāya* discusses the *jīvātman*, the individual living being. The condition and circumstances of the soul after death and the various states of dream, dreamless sleep, and so forth are inquired into. A long series of sutras deals with meditation and the types of *brahman* knowledge. The fourth *adhyāya* takes up again the topic of meditation and ends with a description of the *brahman*-knower's fate after death.

## SCHOOLS OF VEDĀNTA

As it is not possible to expatiate on all the questions broached here, and since complete texts and translations of the most important *bhāṣyas* are available to those who are interested in Vedānta, this exposition will limit itself to a few essential points and illustrate them with excerpts from the writings of Śaṅkara, the great Advaitin, from Rāmānuja, the famous exponent of *Viśiṣṭādaita*, and from Madhva, the illustrious defender of Dvaita—thus covering the most important sections of the spectrum of the Vedānta *darśana*.

The specifying terms given to the different systems within Vedānta have as their point of reference the relationship between the absolute supreme *brahman* and the individual *ātman*: thus *Advaita*, literally, "non-duality," implies ultimate identity of *brahman* and *jīvātman*. *Viśiṣṭādvaita*, literally, "qualified non-duality," maintains a crucial differentiation as well as a fundamental identity. *Dvaita*, literally, "duality," opposes *Advaita* on almost all points and maintains an ultimate diversity of *brahman* and *jīvātman*.[21] Translations that one can sometimes find in books explaining Advaita as monism and Dvaita as dualism are misleading, because these Western philosophical terms have quite different frames of reference and therefore quite different implications that are not applicable to the Indian systems.

The commentaries to the *Vedānta Sūtra* have become the main works of the Vedāntācāryas, whose very recognition as such depends on this as well as the commentaries on the *Upaniṣads* and the *Bhagavadgītā*, constituting the *prasthāna-trayī*. The last one to have done this is Dr. S. Rādhākrishnan, a former President of India, one of the foremost twentieth-century Indian thinkers.

## ADVAITA VEDĀNTA

Śaṅkarācārya (see Figure 26.1), in the opinion of many the greatest Vedāntin and perhaps the greatest of India's philosophers, born, according to tradition, in 788 CE near Kālādi in today's Kerala, became a *saṃnyāsi* at a very young age.[22] He vanquished all his opponents in debate, established four headquarters in the south, east, north, and west of India for the missionaries of his doctrine, the Daśanāmi saṃnyāsis, wrote numerous books, and died at the age of thirty-two.[23] He built his Advaita Vedānta upon principles set forth by Gauḍapada

Figure 26.1. Ādiśaṅkarācārya

in the *Kārikās* to the *Māṇḍukya Upaniṣad.*[24] Gauḍapada is held to be Śaṅkara's *prācārya*, that is, his guru's guru. Śaṅkara's commentary on these *Kārikās* may be the earliest and most concise statement of his philosophy, which he then expands in the *Śārīraka-bhāṣya*, his famous commentary to the *Brahma Sūtra*.

As all Indian philosophical theologians do, Śaṅkara also clarifies his epistemological position in the introduction to his main work. He offers his own critique of human knowledge and states that all subject-object knowledge is distorted by *adhyāsa*, superimposition, which falsifies knowledge in such a way that the subject is unable to find objective truth. Quoting the familiar example of the traveler mistaking a piece of rope on the road for a snake (or vice versa), he proceeds to call all sense perception into question as possibly misleading due to preconceived, superimposed ideas. But though all object-cognition can be doubted, the existence of the doubter remains a fact. Every perception, be it true, doubtful, or mistaken, presupposes a subject, a perceiver. Even if there were no objective perception at all, there would still be a subject. It cannot be proved, nor does it have to be, because it precedes every proof as its inherent condition. It is distinct from all objects and independent. *Ātman* is pure consciousness, which remains even after *manas*, rational thought, has passed away. *Ātman* is ultimately *sat-cit-ānanda*: the unity of being, consciousness, and bliss. Śaṅkara does not regard the world of things as "pure illusion" (as is sometimes said of him): the world is neither *abhāva*, nonexistence, nor, as Buddhist idealism has it, *śūnyatā*, emptiness. For Śaṅkara, the Buddhists are the arch-antagonists of *brahman* knowledge; using Buddhist patterns of thought (which later earned him the title "Crypto-Buddhist" by zealous Vaiṣṇavas) he set out to reestablish Brahmanism. Sense objects, in his view, are different from fiction, but they also differ from reality in the ultimate sense. In order to understand Śaṅkara's statements, one must always place them in the frame of reference in which they are made: all his assertions are explicit or implicit comparisons with absolute reality that alone is of interest to him. The "natural" person does not know how to distinguish between relative and absolute being, between "things" and "being," between *ātman* and non-*ātman*. This is congenital *avidyā*, the basic not-knowing that one is not even aware of. It is this ignorance that keeps a person in *saṃsāra*. *Ātman* is *brahman*—that is good Upaniṣadic doctrine; the self of a person is identical with the ground of all being. *Brahman*, however, is invisible, impervious to any sense or mind perception: *brahman* is not identical with any one particular thing. Some Upaniṣadic passages speak of a "lower" and a "higher" *brahman*,[25] they speak of the immutable supreme *brahman* and also of the *īśvara* who is creator, Lord, and ruler of the world. Śaṅkara takes those passages as the occasion to introduce his most controversial distinction between *brahman saguṇa* and *brahman nirguṇa*, the Supreme with attributes and the Supreme without attributes, the *īśvara* of religious tradition, and the absolute and unqualified reality, a no-thing. According to Śaṅkara *īśvara* is only a temporal manifestation of *brahman*, creator for as long as creation lasts. Śaṅkara is credited with numerous beautiful hymns to the traditional Lords of religion, to Viṣṇu, Śiva and Devī.[26] Devotion is one of the stages that one has to go through, but not a goal to remain at: the ultimate aim is deliverance also from God, a complete identification with the Reality that neither develops nor acts, neither loves nor hates but just *is*. The process of achieving this complete liberation is a cleansing process that separates the *ātman* from all untruth, unreality, and temporality. The doing away with *avidyā*, obscuring ignorance, is in itself already *vidyā*, knowledge that is identical with being. In this *vidyā* the self experiences its identity with *brahman nirguṇa*, the pure and immutable reality. Commenting on the first sutra of the *Vedānta Sūtra*, Śaṅkara writes:

> The special question with regard to the enquiry into *brahman* is whether it presupposes the understanding of *dharma*. To this question we reply: No! Because for a person who has read the Vedānta it is possible to begin the inquiry into the nature of *brahman* before having studied the *dharma*. The study of *dharma* results in transitory heaven and this depends on the performance of rituals. The inquiry into the nature of *brahman*, however, results in *mokṣa*, lasting liberation. It does not depend upon the performance of ceremonies. A few presuppositions preceding the inquiry into the nature of *brahman* will have to be mentioned. These are:
>
> 1. Discrimination between the eternal and the non-eternal reality;
> 2. Giving up the desire to enjoy the fruit of one's actions both here and hereafter;
> 3. The practice of the recognized virtues like peacefulness, self-restraint, and so on;
> 4. The strong desire for liberation.
>
> If these conditions are fulfilled, then a person may inquire into *brahman* whether before or after the *dharma* inquiry; but not if these conditions are not fulfilled. The object of desire is the knowledge of *brahman* and complete understanding of it. Knowledge is therefore the means to perfect *brahman* cognition. The complete knowledge of *brahman* is the supreme human goal, because it destroys the root of all evil, namely *avidyā*, which is the seed of *saṃsāra*. One may now ask: is *brahman* known or unknown? If *brahman* is known then there is no need for further inquiry; if *brahman* is unknown we cannot begin an inquiry. We answer: *brahman* is known. *Brahman*, omniscient and omnipotent, whose essential nature is eternal purity, consciousness, and freedom, exists. For if we contemplate the derivation of the word *brahman* from the root *bṛh-*, to be great, we understand at once that it is eternal purity, etc. More than that: the existence of *brahman* is known because it is the *ātman*, the self of everyone. For everyone is conscious of the "self" and no one thinks: I am not. *Ātman* is *brahman*. If the existence of the self was not known each one would think: I am not. But if *ātman* is generally known as *brahman*, one does not have to start an inquiry. Our answer is: No. Because there is a diversity of opinions regarding its nature. Uneducated people

> and the Lokāyatas are of the opinion that the body itself, having *caitanya*, consciousness, as an attribute, is the *ātman*. Others believe that the sense organs, endowed with the potency to experience, are the *ātman*. Others again believe that *cetana*, reasoning, or *manas*, mind, is the *ātman*. Others again believe the self to be simply a momentary idea, or that it is *śūnya*, emptiness. Some others explain that there is besides the body some supernatural being, responsible for the transmigrations, acting, and enjoying; others teach that this being enjoys only but does not act. Some believe that besides these there exists an omniscient, omnipotent *īśvara* and others finally declare that the *ātman* is that enjoyer.
>
> Thus there are various opinions, partly founded on reasonable arguments and texts from scripture. If these opinions were accepted without thorough prior investigation and inquiry, one would exclude oneself from liberation and suffer deplorable loss. The sutra, therefore, presents a discussion of the Vedānta texts with the motto: "Inquiry into *brahman*," which proceeds with appropriate arguments and aims at supreme bliss.[27]

Already his direct disciples and immediate successors considered Śaṅkara a superhuman teacher, the embodiment of divine wisdom, and his words were treated on a par with the words of revelation.[28] Extreme care was taken not only to preserve his written works but also to ensure the succession in the *maṭhas* founded by him.[29]

## VIŚIṢṬĀDVAITA VEDĀNTA

Rāmānuja (Figure 26.2), who, after an eventful life of ecclesiastical glory but also some sectarian persecution, died according to traditional accounts in 1137, aged 120, as the resident head of the great temple monastery of Śrīraṅgam in South India, is the greatest among the Vaiṣṇava Vedāntins, offering a theistic interpretation of the *Brahma Sūtra*.[30] For Rāmānuja, too, reality is ultimately one, but reality is tiered. It is composed of three components: the world of material things, the multiplicity of *jīvātmas*, individual living beings, and *brahman*, who is identical with *īśvara*, who is none other than Viṣṇu. Creation is the body of *brahman* but not without qualification.[31]

At the time of Rāmānuja Hinduism was firmly established. Buddhism had all but disappeared from India and Jainism was concentrated in relatively small areas of western India. The inter-Hindu controversy was taken up again and Rāmānuja's main opponents were Śaivites, as far as religion was concerned, and Advaitins in the area of philosophy. Rāmānuja's *Śrī-bhāṣya* contains many pages of polemics against Śaṅkara, finding fault with Śaṅkara's distinction between *nirguṇa* and *saguṇa brahman* and his presupposition of *adhyāsa*.[32] *Īśvara*, as the creator and lord of *prakṛti* and the *jīvas*, has an infinite number of supreme and auspicious qualities; this makes him ipso facto *brahman saguṇa*, above whom there is none. He has a most perfect body that is eternal and

Figure 26.2. Rāmānuja

immutable. He is radiant, full of beauty and youth and strength. With his body full of *satva*, devoid of *rajas* and *tamas*, he is omnipresent; he is the *antaryāmin*, the inner ruler of all. For Rāmānuja the process of salvation is not just a process of isolation, the elimination of *avidyā*, the disengagement from nonreality, but it is the product of divine grace and human self-surrender. His *viśiṣṭa* theory enables him to incorporate into the philosophical system of Vedānta all the traditional Hindu notions of the *bhagavān* from the epic-Purāṇic-Āgamic tradition. Rāmānuja himself established a detailed code of ceremonial worship at the *maṭha* of Melkote, where he spent the twelve years of his exile and where, according to tradition, the *Draviḍa Prabandha* was recited at his deathbed together with the Vedas and the Upaniṣads. Those passages in the Upaniṣads that speak of a *nirguṇa brahman* are interpreted by Rāmānuja as meaning "absence of inauspicious qualities" rather than absolute absence of qualities. *Jīvas*, individual souls, are of three kinds: *nitya-muktas*, who are always free, *muktas*, those that have become free in time, and *baddhas*, who are still bound. For these the "way" is essential. Despite the prevalent opinion, also held by many Western scholars, that Śaṅkara represents Vedānta in its purest form, we must say that it is probably Rāmānuja who can claim to have the majority of Hindu tradition on his side and that his interpretation of the Upaniṣads may on the whole be fairer than Śaṅkara's. This is also the opinion of S. N. Dasgupta, who writes: "The theistic Vedānta is the dominant view of the Purāṇas in general and represents the general Hindu view of life and religion. Compared with this general current of Hindu thought, which flows through the Purāṇas and the *Smṛtis* and has been the main source from which the Hindu life has drawn its inspiration, the extreme Sāṁkhya, the extreme Vedānta of Śaṅkara, the extreme Nyāya, and the extreme dualism of Madhva may be regarded as metaphysical formalisms of conventional philosophy."[33]

In his commentary on the first aphorism of the *Brahma Sūtras*, Rāmānuja emphasizes his difference from Śaṅkara's position wherever possible. He adds to the explanation of the four words of the sutra an exposé of his own theology, covering more than one hundred pages in print.

> The word *athā*, now, expresses direct sequence; the word *ata*, then, intimates that what has taken place before (namely the study of *dharma*), which forms the basis (for the *brahman* inquiry). For it is a fact that the desire to know *brahman*—the fruit of which is infinite and lasting—follows immediately when someone who has read the Veda and *Vedāṅgas* realizes that the fruit of rituals is limited and temporary and thus wishes for final release. . . . The word *brahman* means *puruṣottama*, who is by his very essence free from imperfections and possesses an unlimited number of auspicious qualities of unsurpassable excellence. The term *brahman* applies to all things possessing greatness, but primarily it denotes that which possesses greatness essentially and in unlimited fullness; and such is only the Lord of all. Hence the word *brahman* primarily denotes him alone and in a secondary sense only those things that

> possess a small amount of the Lord's qualities. . . . The term is analogous with the term *bhagavat*. It is the Lord alone who is sought for the sake of immortality by all those who are afflicted by the threefold misery. Hence the All-Lord (*sarveśvara*) is that *brahman*, which according to the sutra constitutes the object of enquiry. . . . The *Pūrva-Mīmāṃsā* and the *Uttara Mīmāṃsā* differ only in the material they teach as the two halves of the *Pūrvamīmāṃsā Sūtras* differ. The entire *Mīmāṃsā-śāstra*, beginning with the sutra: *Athāto dharma-jijñāsa* and ending with the sutra: *an-āvṛttis-śabdāt*[34] has, due to the special character of its contents, a definite order of internal succession.

At this juncture Rāmānuja takes the Advaitins to task, whose main arguments he summarizes in his own words as follows: "Eternal and absolutely immutable consciousness, whose nature is pure undifferentiated reason, shows itself—owing to an error—illusorily as divided into multifarious distinct beings: knower, object of knowledge, and acts of knowledge. The discussion of the Vedānta texts aims at completely destroying *avidyā*, which is the root cause of this error, in order to attain a firm knowledge of the unity of *brahman*, whose nature is pure consciousness—free, without stain and eternal." Then Rāmānuja introduces his hundred-page counter-argument, the *mahā-siddhānta*, or great final statement, as follows:

> This entire theory (of the Advaitins) rests on a fictitious foundation of altogether hollow and vicious arguments, incapable of being stated in definite logical alternatives, and devised by men who are destitute of those particular qualities which cause individuals to be chosen by the *puruṣottama* revealed in the Upaniṣads, whose intellects are darkened by the impression of beginningless evil, and who thus have no insight into the meaning of words and sentences, into the real purport conveyed by them, and into the procedure of sound argumentation, with all its methods depending on perception and the other instruments of right knowledge. The theory therefore must need be rejected by all those who, through texts, perception and the other means of knowledge, assisted by sound reasoning—have an insight into the true nature of things.

In a massive offensive, in the course of which countless passages from the Upaniṣads, the *Smṛtis*, and the Purāṇas are quoted. Rāmānuja then proceeds against the main views of Śaṅkara. There is, he says, no proof for the acceptance of undifferentiated being; on the contrary, all arguments speak for a differentiation: the use of language, sense perception, and inference. Sense perception does not show us a being in its undifferentiated absoluteness but a being endowed with attributes. The multiplicity of things is not unreal; being and consciousness without an object and consciousness can undergo changes. Consciousness is a quality of a conscious self and it is preposterous to assume that the conscious subject is something unreal. The subject exists even when there is no actual consciousness, as in dreamless sleep. And the conscious subject continues to exist also in the state of perfect liberation. Rāmānuja quite boldly states that no *śruti* text teaches an undifferentiated *brahman* and that also Smṛtis and Purāṇas were against it. The *avidyā* theory cannot be proved, because all knowledge relates to what is real. Again, no scripture teaches it. Nor does *śruti* support the teaching that *mokṣa* is realized by the cognition of an unqualified *brahman*. Moreover, ignorance does not simply cease if one understands *brahman* as the universal *ātman*. In this connection Rāmānuja explains the *mahā-vākya* "*tat tvam asi*," one of the core texts of the Advaitins, in his own way:

> In texts such as *tat tvam asi*, the coordination of the constituent parts is not meant to convey the idea of the absolute unity of a nondifferentiated substance: on the contrary, the words *tat* and *tvam* denote a *brahman* distinguished by difference. The word *tat* refers to the omniscient etc. *brahman*. . . . The word *tvam*, which stands in coordination to *tat*, conveys the idea of *brahman*, which has for its body the *jīvātmas* connected with *prakṛti*. If such duality of form were given up there could be no difference of aspects giving rise to the application of different terms, and the entire principle of coordination would thus be given up. And it would further follow that the two words coordinated would have to be taken in an implied sense. There is, however no need to assume *lakṣaṇā* or implication in sentences such as "this person is Devadatta." . . . Moreover, if the text *tat tvam asi* were meant to express absolute oneness, it would conflict with a previous statement in the same section, namely *tadaikṣata bahu syām*, that is, it thought, "may I be many."[35]

We cannot decide here whether Rāmānuja has always been fair to Śaṅkara and whether he does justice to his rather subtle thinking, but it is very clear that he wished to distinguish his position as sharply as possible from that of the Advaitins.

## DVAITA VEDĀNTA

Madhva (Figure 26.3), the representative of the Dvaita Vedānta, lived from 1238 to 1317 CE. The son of one of his disciples wrote a biography, considered authentic.[36] Madhva was born into a humble Brahmin family in a village not far from Uḍipī, now in the state of Karṇātaka. When he was sixteen he entered the *Ekadaṇḍi* order of the *Ekānti Vaiṣṇavas* and was given the name *Pūrṇaprajñā*, fullness of wisdom. He quite frequently disagreed with the Advaita interpretation of Vedānta given by his teacher, a fact that did not hinder the guru from installing Madhva under the name of *Ānandatīrtha* as the head of his own *maṭha*. He then went on a missionary tour, engaging Jains, Buddhists, and Advaitins in discussions and defeating them all. According to tradition he wrote his *Brahma Sūtra-bhāṣya* after a pilgrimage to the Vyāsa Āśrama in the Himālayas. The image of Kṛṣṇa that Madhva installed at his Uḍipī *maṭha* is still an important focus of pilgrimage and the rotation of the headship of the

Figure 26.3. Madhva

*maṭha*, taking place every two years, is also a major social occasion about which newspapers report. Madhva was the most prolific of all the great Vedāntins; he left more than thirty major works as well as a number of minor ones. In addition to the traditional commentaries on the Gita, the Upaniṣads, and the *Brahma Sūtra*, he wrote partial commentaries on the *Bhāgavata Purāṇa* and the *Ṛgveda* and a digest of the *Mahābhārata*, along with several philosophical monographs, the most famous of which is the *Aṇuvyākhyāna*, a masterful exposition of the *Brahma Sūtra* in verses.[37]

In his arguments he uses not only traditional *śruti*, but also quotes from the Viṣṇu and *Bhāgavata Purāṇa*, from *Pāñcarātra saṃhitās*, and other sectarian writings. All Śaiva literature is taboo for him. He is closer to Rāmānuja than to Śaṅkara, but he goes a decisive step further toward uncompromising Dvaita. He develops his whole system upon the presupposition of the *pañca bheda*, the five differences between *īśvara* and *jīvātman*, between *prakṛti* and *īśvara*, between *prakṛti* and the *jīvas*, between the individual *jīvas*, and between the various inanimate objects. *Īśvara*, who is Viṣṇu, is absolute: he has an infinite number of excellent qualities and a spiritual body wherewith he shows himself at will in the *vyūhas* and *avatāras*. The world is made through his *līlā*, the free play of his disinterested will; everything depends on his will: "All knowledge is to be ascribed to the action of Hari, the ties of the world and the release there from, rebirth and the unfolding of all things. Hari permeates everything, even the souls, and he lives there as the inner witness, the *sākṣi*; in nature he lives as the *antaryāmi*, the inner ruler. *Prakṛti* is the opposite of Hari, insofar as she is pure dependency, total contingency. It is true, she exists from eternity, but in the hand of Hari she is a mere instrument."[38]

The *jīvas* have, individually, a spiritual self-consciousness. They are of the nature of *sac-cit-añanda*, even if for the duration of bodily life this is obscured. The *ātman*, therefore, is a mirror image of God. It is completely dependent on God in all its actions. The way to liberation is perfect self-surrender to Viṣṇu through an active love that centers on ritual worship of the image. Vāyu as mediator between Viṣṇu and the *jīvas* plays an important role. It is important to note that Madhva considered himself an *avatāra* of Vāyu. Madhva begins his commentary on the first sutra of the text thus:

> The basis for the inquiry into *brahman* is the grace of the Lord Viṣṇu. Since greater grace can be gained from him only through appropriate cognition, *brahman* inquiry is indispensable as a source of *brahman* knowledge in order to gain his attention. Inquiry into *brahman* itself is to be ascribed to the grace of the Great Lord, for he alone is the mover of our minds. There are three grades of preparedness for the study of Vedānta: an eager person who is devoted to Lord Viṣṇu is in the third grade; a person who has the sixfold moral qualification of self-discipline, etc., is in the second grade; and the person who is attached to none but the Lord, who considers the whole world as transitory and is therefore completely indifferent, is in the first grade. The following of the Vedic injunctions can merely give us a claim to the lower grace of the Lord; the listening to the texts of scripture provides us with a somewhat higher grace; but the supreme grace of the Lord, which leads to *mukti*, can be secured only through knowledge. Right knowledge can be acquired only through *śravaṇa*, the listening to scripture, *manana*, meditation, *nidhi-dhyāsana*, contemplation, and *bhakti*, devotion; nobody can attain right *jñāna* without these. The term *brahman* designates primarily Viṣṇu, of whom some Vedic texts say: "He who dwells in the ocean and is known only

to the sages, he who surpasses understanding, who is eternal, who rules all things, from whom issue the great mother of the universe and who brings the *jīvas* into the world, bound to life by their actions and prisoners of the five elements." And another passage: "He is the embodiment of pure wisdom, he is consciously active and is, according to the sages, the one Lord of the universe."[39] From the following sentence: "And may therefore Viṣṇu inspire us" it is clear that only Viṣṇu is meant in the preceding passages. All the Vedas speak of him only; in the Vedas, in the *Rāmāyaṇa*, in the *Mahābhārata* and in the Purāṇas, in the beginning, in the middle and in the end—everywhere only Viṣṇu is sung of.[40]

## TEXTS AND COMMENTARIES

These short extracts from the commentaries to the first four words of the *Vedānta Sūtra* illustrate the great amount of diversity within the Vedānta *darśana* and also provide a glimpse into the very rich and subtle philosophical tradition drawn upon. Since these *bhāṣyas*—very often subcommented upon in *ṭīkās* (subcommentaries) and further explained in *ṭippaṇīs* (glosses) by the disciples and followers in later ages—are both difficult and lengthy, the great masters themselves composed smaller manuals for the laity in which they provided the gist of their teaching in an abbreviated form, without compromising the essentials. Quite popular are valuable little works, ascribed to Śaṅkarācārya himself, expounding Advaita Vedānta in a straightforward manner such as *Ātma-bodha*, "The Self-Cognition," *Upadeśa-sahasrī*, "The Thousand Teachings," and *Vivekacudāmaṇi*, "The Crest Jewel of Discernment."[41] The most widely used and easiest introduction, however, may be Sādānanda's *Vedānta-sāra*, a small literary work offering a clear and full explanation of the major terms of Śaṅkara's thought.[42] The most famous among the post-Śaṇkara Advaita treatises is the celebrated *Pañcadaśī*, "Fifteen (Chapters)," of Vidyāraṇya, one of the greatest Hindu scholars of the fourteenth century.[43] The *Vedānta-paribhāṣa*, providing concise definitions of Vedantic key terms, written by the seventeenth-century Advaitin Dharmarāja, is still widely used in Indian universities.[44]

The Viśiṣṭādvaitins also possess short compendia of their teachings. The most famous and most beautifully written is Rāmānuja's own *Vedārtha-saṅgraha*, "A concise summary of the true meaning of the Veda," with ample quotations from scriptures, despite its brevity.[45] For beginners the most suitable book may be Śrīnivāsadāsa's *Yatīndra-mata-dīpikā*, "The Lamp of the King of the Renouncers," which offers a systematic teaching of the school according to key subjects.[46] Easy to understand and accessible in an English translation is Bucci Venkatācārya's *Vedānta-kārikāvalī*, "A Short Collection of Vedānta Verses."[47] Vedānta Deśika, considered second in importance only to Rāmānuja, wrote a large number of works that have become very popular among Śrīvaiṣṇavas, such as the *Rahasya-traya-sāra*,[48] "The Gist of the Three Mysteries."

In addition to the minor works of Madhva himself, the manual by Jayatīrtha called *Vādā-valī*, "Discussion Companion," written in the fourteenth century, may offer the most systematic introduction to the thought of Dvaita Vedānta.[49]

Vedānta does not belong to the past only, but is also the most important contemporary expression of Indian philosophy and theology. An unbroken tradition of scholars and saints leads from the great *ācāryas* into our time; all their major institutions are still centers of living Vedānta. Vedānta is not only speculative, abstract thought, but also mysticism, realization, and the way to ultimate freedom. The basic types of this spiritual life-thought, as they are represented by the great *ācāryas* whom we have briefly dealt with, may be representative of basic types of mysticism, for which we also have parallels in the Western tradition. They are alive in India in numerous gurus, who express their own experiences and convictions in the terminology of Śaṅkara, Rāmānuja, and Madhva, thereby acknowledging the timeless greatness of these thinkers of the absolute.[50]

# Part IV

## Hinduism Encountering the "Other"

During its early history many movements arose in India that broke away from mainstream Brahmanism—such as Jainism and Buddhism—movements that developed into major independent traditions. For many centuries Hindu thinkers were busily working out arguments against Jains and Buddhists, whom they considered ritually heretical and philosophically mistaken. In the course of the last two thousand years India has also become the home of many religions that originated outside India. When the Roman Emperors began persecuting Jews, many fled to India, where some of the oldest synagogues in the world can be found. The Bene Israel became citizens of India, intermarried, and preserved their Jewish faith. When the Arab Muslims overran Persia, a large number of Zoroastrians received asylum in India, whose Parsi community has become one of the wealthiest segments of Indian society. India also has a Christian population of some thirty million, divided into numerous churches. For over five hundred years India was under Muslim rule. In spite massive efforts to turn it into a Muslim country, India did remain, in its majority, Hindu. Even after the separation of Pakistan and Bangladesh, the Republic of India is also a country with one of the largest Muslim populations in the world.

While Hindus have made their peace with Jains and Buddhists, which after some periods of confrontation became accepted as sharing the same culture, and while Parsis never were a problem for Hindus, because they kept to themselves and did not try to convert Hindus to their faith, relations between Hindus and Muslims and Hindus and Christians have been problematic for a long time. Both religions claim uniqueness and exclusivity and both are aiming at winning the whole world for their faith.

In this part an attempt is made to show that Hinduism not only developed a dynamic and a mission of its own, but also that it did not remain isolated from other religions. Its interaction with these is a vital part of its history as well as of its present agenda. In order not to expand this section over duly, full chapters have been devoted only to the relation between Hinduism and Buddhism, Islam and Christianity in India. Only major episodes of this fascinating story can be offered here—by necessity much important and interesting detail had to be left out.

The encounter with modern Europe, in the guise of the European colonial powers that from the sixteenth century onward played an increasingly large role in India, provoked a many sided reaction among Indians. Early on many Hindus resented the presence and influence of these foreign powers and resisted attempts to Europeanize and to Christianize them. Others took up the challenge of the criticism leveled against the Hinduism of the time and began reforming and remodeling their traditions.

The freedom struggle against the British Raj in the late nineteenth and early twentieth centuries took on religious overtones that found their purest expression in Mahātmā Gandhi and their worst consequence in the partition of the British Indian Empire along religious lines.

While India is on the way to becoming an economic and military superpower, it has not ceased to be a country in which religion exerts great influence on the public and private lives of its citizens. While more often than not the frequent Hindu-Muslim riots dominate the news about India and the ideological battles between "secularists" and the proponents of "Hindutva" find commentators in Western papers, a great revival and consolidation of Hinduism is taking place in India and among the expatriate Indian communities. Hindus are proud again of being Hindus and prove it by building temples and forming associations that preserve and enhance the Hindu heritage in India and outside.

CHAPTER TWENTY-SEVEN

# Hinduism and Buddhism

> Hinduism cannot live without Buddhism and Buddhism not without Hinduism . . . the Buddhists cannot stay without the brain and philosophy of the Brahmins, nor the Brahmin without the heart of the Buddhist, let us then join the wonderful intellect of the Brahmin with the heart, the noble soul, the wonderful humanizing power of the Great master.
>
> —Swami Vivekananda, *Selections from the Works of Swami Vivekananda*

Gautama Siddhārtha, the founder of Buddhism, grew up in a Hindu aristocratic family.[1] Having recognized the transience of beauty, enjoyment, and earthly life, he decided to become a *saṃnyāsi*, as thousands before him had done, in order to search for the eternal. The quest took him to some of the most famous masters and philosophers of his time, whose meditation practices he learned and whose systems he recognized as unsatisfactory. *Bodhi*, enlightenment, happened one night, after many years of false starts and wrong turns. The Buddha had to be persuaded by Brahmā himself, the highest of the Hindu gods, to forgo the bliss of his meditation and to communicate to the world that he had found what all Hindu seekers had been looking for: freedom from death!

The Buddha's first impulse was to return to his former teachers and tell them what he had found. Being shown in a vision that they had died, he searched for his former companions in asceticism, who had abandoned him because they believed he had lapsed from the *saṃnyāsi* ideal. They became his first followers. They did not consider themselves "Buddhists," followers of a new religion, but disciples of one who had realized the Truth they were all searching for.

In all his sermons Gautama the Buddha kept emphasizing that he had not learned his teaching from some other master but that he had come by it himself and that he owed nothing to any other teacher. It was a new beginning—but also the continuation of an old tradition. The Buddha himself compared his way with the clearing of an overgrown jungle path that had been used by former generations but had been forgotten and was overgrown with vegetation. Clearly, much of Buddhism owes its language as well as its worldview to the old *sanātana dharma*, especially to the Upaniṣads, whose wisdom tradition it largely follows. The Pali canon contains debates of the Buddha with Brahmins, many of whom accepted his teachings and became followers. They did not feel that thereby they relinquished their ancient tradition but that they interiorized it at a higher level. Whereas the old tradition had honored nobility by birth, the Buddha declared only those to be Brahmins who followed high ethical standards. And whereas formerly rituals and sacrifices were deemed central to religion, interiority and virtuous life were now prized above everything else.

The Buddha disagreed with traditional Brahmanism on the necessity and efficacy of rituals in connection with an afterlife and the importance of the hereditary priestly role of the Brahmins. The Upaniṣads—recognized in Hinduism as *śruti*, revealed truth—had said the same thing, but it had not become the religion of the ordinary people. The Upaniṣads had remained an esoteric teaching for an elite—its insights and practices were the preserve of those who had retired from active life in society. The Buddha taught in the vernacular of the day and place and addressed everyone alike: in the centuries to come, Buddhism became the majority religion of the people of India as well as of their rulers.

Conservative Brahmanism was not dead, it received a considerable boost by the Guptas from the fourth century CE onward: the revival of Hinduism expressed itself in the Purāṇas, the new popular Bibles that summarized popular Hinduism. "The Purāṇas," said P. V. Kane, one of the greatest authorities on Hindu *dharmaśāstra*, "played a substantial role in bringing about the decline and disappearance of Buddhism, by emphasizing and assimilating some of the doctrines of the Buddha, such as *ahiṃsā*, by accepting Buddha himself as an *avatāra* of Viṣṇu, by adopting vegetarianism as a high form of austerity, by making use of monasteries and asceticism as stated in such *smṛtis* as those of Manu and Yājñavalkya."[2] The *Viṣṇu Purāṇa*, one of the oldest and most authoritative of such texts, devotes considerable space to Buddha and Buddhism: as we have seen in chapter 2, it presents the Buddha as a heretic and a seducer of people, one of many forms of the *māyā-moha* (delusive power) of Viṣṇu[3] and recommends complete shunning of Buddhists in order to prevent pollution and punishment.

In all probability it was the orthodox Mīmāṃsakas who were the originators of these teachings in the Purāṇas. In their more technical writings they carry on extensive polemics with Buddhists. Kumārila Bhaṭṭa, one of the most famous defenders of Hindu orthodoxy in the eighth century CE, faults the Buddhists for their rejection of the authority of the Veda.[4] He also finds the claim absurd that the Buddha had been omniscient. He slights the followers of the Buddha as being composed only of outcasts, foreigners, and tribals.

Kumārila Bhaṭṭa shows considerable detailed knowledge of Buddhism, which by then—after a development of over a thousand years—had given rise to several philosophical schools. According to an old Indian tradition, the famous Buddhist philosopher Dharmakīrti had lived in disguise with Kumārila in order to learn about Hinduism. He then used his knowledge to defeat Hindu scholars in open debate and to win them over to Buddhism. Kumārila, too, was thus defeated and became one of Dharmakīrti's disciples. After having studied Buddhism thoroughly, Kumārila challenged and defeated Buddhist scholars, including his teacher Dharmakīrti. According to Hindu *dharma* this was a great sin, and Kumārila proceeded to perform the prescribed *prāyaścitta*: he went to Prayāga to end his life at the Trivenī in a slow-burning cow dung fire in expiation for the supposed crime. Legend has it that Śaṅkara, the famous champion of Advaita Vedānta, met him there and held a last discussion with him.

## MEDIEVAL HINDU-BUDDHIST POLEMICS

Kumārila Bhaṭṭa in his *Śloka-vārttika*, a thoroughly systematic work, attacked Buddhism methodically. It provoked the Buddhist scholar Śāntarakṣita to counterattack Hinduism in great detail in his magnum opus *Tattva-saṅgraha*.[5] Quoting extensively from the *Śloka-vārttika*, Śāntarakṣita demolishes the Hindu positions with great ingenuity and a certain sense of humor. This polemical exchange between Hindus and Buddhists was continued on both sides for centuries. It became customary for Hindu scholars to refute rival Buddhist schools in their writings before expounding their own teachings.

The *Vedānta-sūtras* contain several aphorisms that have traditionally been understood as directed against the Buddhists.[6] They show considerable familiarity with the major philosophical schools of Buddhism that were more concerned with metaphysics than with discipline or ethics. Śaṅkara deals in this context with three different schools of Buddhism, which in his opinion mutually contradict each other: Sarvāsti-vādis, Vijñāna-vādis, and Śūnya-vādis.[7] He offers separate arguments against each of them and sees them agreeing on one point: *kṣanikatvam*, the momentariness of everything. Against this "nihilism" Śaṅkara sets the existence of the eternal *ātman*. He accuses Buddhism of an overall lack of consistency and of teaching doctrines that lead to perdition:

> From whatever points of view the Bauddha system is tested with reference to its probability, it gives way on all sides, like the walls of a well dug in sand. It has, in fact, no foundation whatever to rest upon and hence the attempt to use it as a guide in the practical concerns of life are mere folly. Moreover Buddha, by propounding the three mutually contradictory systems, teaching respectively the reality of the external world, the reality of ideas only and general nothingness, has himself made it clear that he was a man given to make incoherent assertions or else hatred of all beings induced

> him to propound absurd doctrines by accepting which one would become thoroughly confused. . . . Buddha's doctrine has to be entirely disregarded by all those who have a regard for their own happiness."[8]

Virtually all the later commentators of the *Vedānta-sūtras* include anti-Buddhist polemics in their works, although Buddhism itself began to lose hold on India and flourished more in the neighboring countries. Some Hindus, considered saints by their followers, such as Manikkavācakar (ca. 650–715), reportedly used the power of secular rulers to punish and destroy Buddhists. *Bauddha*, Buddhist, becomes an invective in later Hindu literature, and the followers of Madhva considered it the ultimate condemnation of Śaṅkara to have unmasked him as *pracanna-bauddha*, a Buddhist in disguise.

Although Buddhism had almost disappeared from India by the twelfth century, after Hindu theologians and rulers had brought about a Hindu renaissance and after the Muslims had destroyed the great Buddhist universities of Nālandā and Mithilā, anti-Buddhist polemic continued in Hindu scholarly literature and became a standard part of the Hindu scholastic curriculum, though hardly any encounters with Buddhism had taken place.

## A NEW BEGINNING

In some remote areas of Bengal close to Tibet, where a large number of Indian Buddhist *bhikṣus* had taken refuge from the Muslim onslaught in the twelfth century, some Buddhist communities had survived over the centuries. In the second half of the nineteenth century Bhikkhu Saṅgharāja, belonging to the Hīnayāna Theravāda tradition, the spiritual preceptor of the King of Burma (now Myanmar), established contact with the Buddhist Tantrik master Tilopa in Paṇḍita Vihāra, Chittagong district (now in Bangladesh). Young novices from Chittagong were educated in Burma in the Pāli scriptures, establishing at their return new Buddhist communities. The Bengali scholars Rajendra Lal Mitra and Hara Prasad Sastri began cataloguing Buddhist manuscripts in neighboring Nepal. Sarat Chandra Das traveled through Tibet and brought back numerous manuscripts from the ancient libraries of Lhasa. He edited several volumes of Buddhist Sanskrit literature for the newly founded *Bibliotheca Indica*. The Buddhist Text Society, founded in Calcutta in 1892, invited Buddhists from abroad to teach Buddhism in India again and succeeded in establishing a department of Buddhist Studies at the Government Sanskrit College in Calcutta. Satis Chandra Vidyabhusana, a great Hindu scholar, was the first Indian to obtain an MA degree in Pāli from Calcutta University in 1901. He traveled to Ceylon (now Śrī Laṇkā) for further studies before becoming principal of Government Sanskrit College in Calcutta, which has remained a center of Buddhism scholarship.

Dharmanand Kosambi (1871–1947) played a major role in the revitalization of Buddhist studies in India. Though a Mahratta, who are among the staunchest defenders of Hindu traditions, he not only studied Buddhist scriptures but he became a Buddhist and devoted much of his lifetime to the propagation of Buddhism in India. His travels took him to Ceylon and Burma as well as to the United States, where he completed the Pāli edition of Buddhaghoṣa's masterpiece, *Visuddhimagga*, which H. Warren had left unfinished. The work is one of the most systematic and celebrated fifth-century CE summaries of Theravāda Buddhism, still used as a manual of instruction in Buddhist monasteries in Śrī Laṅkā. Kosambi considered his own Devanāgarī edition of the Pāli *Visuddhimagga* the crowning of his life's work in the service of Buddhism. His example had repercussions: three young Hindu intellectuals, members of the Ārya Samāj, joined the Mahābodhi Society. They collected, edited, and translated a great number of Pāli texts and helped the Mahābodhi Society gain scholarly prestige in India. Though they left the society again in later years, they remained faithful to their chosen task of promoting the Buddha dharma in India. One of them, Jagdish Kashyap from Bihar, won the distinction of serving as general editor of the Devanāgarī edition of the entire Pāli canon, published in 1956 by the Government of Bihar as a contribution to the celebrations of the great Buddha jubilee commemorating the 2500th anniversary of Gautama Buddha's entry into *parinirvāṇa*.

With Buddhism being appreciated by famous European scholars like Rhys Davids, Indian scholars, too, began to feel proud again of Gautama the Buddha and his religion: they edited Buddhist works and restored Buddhist monuments, which were the destination of Buddhists from all over the world. There remained, however, a certain ambivalence among Hindus vis-à-vis Buddhism, created by centuries of anti-Buddhist polemics. Thus Svāmi Vivekānanda emphasized in one of his lectures the complementary nature of Hinduism and Buddhism, while in another one he blamed Buddhism for much of India's degeneration. Said he: "Hinduism cannot live without Buddhism and Buddhism not without Hinduism. . . . The Buddhists cannot stay without the brain and philosophy of the Brahmins, nor the Brahmins without the heart of the Buddhists. . . . Let us then join the wonderful intellect of the Brahmin with the heart, the noble soul, the wonderful humanizing power of the Great Master."[9] And: "In spite of its wonderful moral strength, Buddhism was extremely iconoclastic and much of its force being spent in merely negative attempts, it had to die out in the land of its birth and what remained of it became full of superstitions and ceremonials, a hundred times cruder than those it was intended to suppress."[10]

## "INDIA'S GREATEST SON"

Modern Hindus took pride in "Bhagvān Buddha" being a son of India, and they also claimed that Buddhists had misunderstood the Buddha: Hinduism had absorbed the essentials of Buddha's teachings and Buddhist thought was replaced by Vedānta, the synthesis of all religions. Thus Mahātmā Gandhi declared: "It is my deliberate opinion that the essential part of the teachings of the Buddha now forms an integral part of Hinduism. It is impossible for Hindu India today to retrace her steps and go behind the great reformation that Gautama effected in Hinduism. . . . What Hinduism did not assimilate of what passes as Buddhism today was not an essential part of the Buddha's life and his teachings."[11] And even more: "It is my fixed opinion that the teachings of the Buddha found its full fruition in India and it could not be otherwise, for Gautama was himself a Hindu of Hindus. He was saturated with the best that was in Hinduism and he gave life to some of the teachings that were buried in the Vedas and which were overgrown with weeds." In Gandhi's opinion "the Buddha never rejected Hinduism, but he broadened its base. He gave it a new life and a new interpretation."[12]

Morning and evening prayer services in Gandhi's ashram in Wardha began with "Homage to all Buddhas," followed by two minutes of silent meditation. For Gandhi the Buddha was not so much the intellectual genius who had understood the chain of conditionings that caused rebirth, but in his opinion "Buddhism is one long prayer."[13]

The Māhatmā claimed the Buddha not only as a Hindu among Hindus, but also as an associate in the campaign for *ahiṃsā* and against untouchability. "Great as the Buddha's contribution to humanity was in restoring God to His eternal place, in my opinion greater still was his contribution to humanity in his exacting regard for all life, be it ever so low." And: "Gautama taught the world to treat even the lowest creatures as equal to himself. He held the life of even the crawling things of the earth to be as precious as his own." He anticipated contemporary ecological concerns and animal rights advocates' arguments when declaring: "It is an arrogant assumption to say that the human beings are lords and masters of the lower creation. On the contrary, being endowed with greater things in life, they are trustees of the lower animal kingdom. And the Great Sage lived that truth in his own life."[14]

Jawaharlal Nehru, India's first prime minister (1947–1964), came from a Hindu background, but even his father, Motilal, had already adopted a modern, Western outlook that determined the atmosphere in which his children grew up. As a student in England, Jawaharlal Nehru established close ties with the Fabians and declared himself a Socialist. Back in India, entering politics like his father, he found traditional Hinduism one of the major obstacles on the way to a prosperous, democratic India. While admiring Gandhi's political acumen and his hold on the masses, he freely admitted that he found Gandhi's Hinduism disturbing. Nehru quite openly distanced himself from all religions and declared that for him the problems of this world offered enough challenge not to bother about those of a world beyond.

In his *Discovery of India*, written in 1941 in Ahmednagar Fort during one of his lengthy spells of imprisonment, Nehru devoted much room to the description of the rise of Buddhism, its teachings, and its impact on Hinduism. He was fascinated by the Buddha's "ideal of righteousness and discipline,"[15] his experiential approach to truth, and his rejection of the pieties of Hinduism in favor of intellectual search and moral practice. He confessed that "the Buddha story attracted me even in early boyhood" and that Edwin Arnold's *Light of Asia*, a poetic rendering of the life of Gautama Buddha, "became one of my favorite books." He took more interest in visiting the places connected with the Buddha's life than in Hindu places of pilgrimage. When he later traveled to Buddhist countries, he tried to find out "what Buddhism had done to the people: how had it influenced them, what impress had it left on their minds and on their faces, how did they react to modern life?" He had to realize that Buddhists through the centuries had done many things that the Buddha would have abhorred: "Despite Buddha's warning, they had deified him, and his huge images, in the temples and elsewhere, looked down upon me and I wondered what he would have thought." But he had to admit: "I also saw much that I liked. There was an atmosphere of peaceful study and contemplation in some of the monasteries and the schools attached to them. There was a look of peace and calm on the faces of many of the monks, a dignity, a gentleness, an air of detachment and freedom from the cares of the world."[16] In spite of all that he decided that Buddhism was not for him: "The pessimism of Buddhism did not fit in with my approach to life nor did the tendency to walk away from life and its problems."

Fourteen years after he had written those words, Jawaharlal Nehru, together with President Sarvepalli Radhakrishnan, presided over the celebrations of the Buddha *Jayantī*, the 2500th anniversary of Buddha's entry into the *parinirvāṇa* according to the tradition of Śrī Laṅkā. Under his government the places connected with Gautama Buddha's life were restored, and Buddha celebrations were held all over the country. Addressing a seminar in New Delhi he said:

> I believe it is essentially through the message of the Buddha that we can look at our problems in the right perspective and draw back from conflict, and from competing with one another in the realm of violence and hatred. Every action has certain consequences. An evil action has evil consequences. That I believe is as good a law of nature as any physical or chemical law. If that is so, hatred, which is evil, must have evil consequences. Violence, which is evil, must have evil consequences, and indeed it leads to the growth of violence. How then are we to escape from this vicious circle? I hope and believe that this year of the *parinirvāṇa* of the Buddha has lead people to look deeper into those problems, and made them realize that they have to search for some kind of union between their day-to-day political, scientific, technological and other activities and a certain measure of spirituality.[17]

Later in life Nehru quite openly said that he found Buddhism more appealing than other philosophies and that he believed it to have the potential to bring about real changes in life. His biographer, Marie Seton, mentions that Nehru kept a number of Buddhist statues, presented to him by the Dalai Lama, on the mantle piece of his New Delhi home, and that his living room was decorated with three large photographs of Buddha images, which he apparently loved.[18]

## BUDDHISM AS RELIGION OF HOPE FOR THE OUTCASTES

While Mahātmā Gandhi tried throughout his life to reintegrate the Harijans into mainstream Hindu society, Dr. Bhimrao Ramji Ambedkar, himself a Māhār, a member of an untouchable caste in Mahārāṣṭra who had risen to high positions in the Congress Party, wanted to separate all ties between the Untouchables and Hinduism. At a meeting of the Depressed Classes Conference in Nasik on October 13, 1935, he invited the eight hundred delegates to a performance of the "last rites of Hinduism" by publicly burning a copy of the *Manusmṛti* and other *śāstras* that sanctioned caste and untouchability. Ambedkar did extensive research into the history of untouchability and came to the conclusion that the Untouchables of India were in their majority the remnants of Buddhists who had refused to rejoin Hinduism after the Guptas supported a Hindu renaissance in the fourth century CE.[19] He saw in Buddhism and not in Brahmanism the true tradition of India. Ambedkar became a Buddhist not because he was convinced that *nirvāṇa* was his true ultimate aim or that the Four Noble Truths revealed the deepest insight into reality, but for the more practical reason that Buddhists did not observe caste rules. He had considered Christianity and Islam as alternatives and was pressed by a high-ranking representative of the Sikhs to join their community. He decided for Buddhism because it was an Indian tradition. His adoption of Buddhism was accompanied by the declaration: "I renounce Hinduism."[20] When Hindu missionary Masurkar Maharaj asked him to desist from his conversion to Buddhism, Ambedkar declared that he would be willing to postpone his decision under the following condition: an untouchable should be made Śaṅkarācārya and a hundred Citpavan Brahmins should every day bow down before him.[21]

Ambedkar made an extensive study of all major religions before opting for Buddhism. What appealed to him was that Gautama Buddha, in contrast to Jesus, Mohammed, and the Hindu *avatāras* never claimed to be anything but a human being, not a savior but only a *mārga-dātā*, a guide on the way. Buddha did not claim infallibility for his teachings either and placed emphasis on ethics: "What God is to other religions, morality is to Buddha."[22] According to Ambedkar the Buddha "taught as part of his religion social freedom, intellectual freedom, economic freedom, and political freedom. He taught equality not only between man and man, but also between men and women."[23]

Ambedkar worked for many years on a book that would present Buddhism in an understandable idiom to his followers. When *Buddha and His Dhamma* finally appeared it was severely criticized by Bhikkhu Jovaka from the Mahabodhi Society in Calcutta. The Buddhist missionary found fault with Ambedkar's refutation of the notion of karma, his views on *ahiṃsā*, and his reducing *dhamma* to a sociopolitical system, leaving out spiritual enlightenment. He also resented Ambedkar's expectations of Buddhist *bhikkhus* to become social workers instead of being meditators. He concluded his review by stating: "The title should be changed from the misleading one, as *The Buddha and His Dhamma* to *Ambedkar and His Dhamma* for he preaches *non-dharma* as *Dharma* for motives of political ambition and social reform."[24]

Ambedkar had visions of India turning into a Buddhist country again and if the growth of Buddhism had continued at the pace that it reached between the census of 1951 and 1961—a growth of more than 1,500%—it would have come about within one generation. But growth stopped and membership in Dr. Ambedkar's Neo-Buddhism is fairly restricted to the Untouchables of Mahārāṣṭra and has remained stable at around three million.

While politicians like Gandhi and philosophers like Radhakrishnan embraced Buddhism as part of the Hindu tradition and expressed pride in "India's greatest son," there were others who continued polemics and viewed Buddha as an archenemy of Hinduism. In sectarian manuals one still finds the old arguments against Buddhist nihilism and atheism—even the disciples of Prabhupāda Bhaktivedānta, who probably never encountered a live Buddhist, repeat what medieval Hindu theologians had found wrong with Buddhism.

Vir Savarkar, for much of his life the main theoretician of the Hindū Mahāsabhā, maintained that Buddhism was the cause for the downfall of India. The fall of Buddhism, he maintains, could not be explained by either the philosophical reaction that it provoked, nor by the prevalence of "a loose and promiscuous crowd of men and women who lived on others and spent what was not theirs on disreputable pursuits in life,"[25] but by its unconcern for the political integrity of its domain. He sees the whole of Buddhism mirrored in an incident reported in the life of the Buddha: after the Buddha had left his home country, it was overrun by invaders and annexed by a neighboring power. Buddha did not show any concern. Also his gathering of a large number of fellow Śakhyans into the *saṅgha* is viewed by Savarkar as depriving his home country "of its bravest and its best," making it easy prey for warlike aggressors. When the whole of India had become Buddhist its fate was likewise sealed: it was raided and overrun by the Lichis and the Huns "whose barbarous violence could ill be soothed by the mealymouthed formulas of *ahiṃsā* and spiritual brotherhood, and whose steel could ill be blunted by the soft palm leaves and rhymed charms."[26] According to Savarkar, Buddhist idealism, its attempt to lay the foundations of the Kingdom of Righteousness through nonviolence and meditation, was in political and military terms one big mistake. "Nobly did [Buddhist India] try to kill killing by getting killed—and at last found out that palm leaves at times are too fragile for steel! As long as the whole world was red in tooth and claw and the national and racial distinction so strong as to make man brutal, so long, if India had to live at all a life whether spiritual or political according to the right of her soul, she must not lose the strength born of national and racial cohesion."[27] Savarkar's main objection in the end is

Buddhism's universalism, contrasted with Hindu nationalism. Buddhists where people without a national identity: "Buddhism had its geographical center of gravity nowhere."

## HINDU-BUDDHIST MUTUALITY FOREVER

The interaction between Hinduism and Buddhism has influenced and shaped the intellectual and religious, the social and political history of India to a degree perhaps not yet fully appreciated. The very rise of Buddhism from Brahmanism, its survival and growth in the face of the decline and disappearance of scores of rival movements, its inability to either completely separate from or identify with Hinduism reveals something of the inner polarities and dialectics of the Indian tradition as a whole.

Three areas of conflict stand out: the religious issue of Buddhist atheism, the philosophical issue of the Buddhist denial of the self, and the social issue of the Buddhist rejection of caste as a necessary and natural structure of society. Buddhism apparently needed the cultural basis that it shared with Brahmanism: the belief in karma, in rebirth, in a transcendental meaning of human life. Even in its protest against *īśvara*, *ātman*, and *caturvarṇa* it depended on the existence of a community that maintained those beliefs. The determination with which religious Hinduism fought Buddhism on the issue of Supreme Being, philosophical Hinduism on the issue of momentariness, and practical Hinduism on the issue of caste and ritual reveals the self-understanding of Hinduism. However, Hinduism, the religion of the historic concretization of the absolute, needs Buddhism as much as Buddhism needs Hinduism to exist. By pointing out the finitude of what was taken to be the infinite it keeps the search for the absolute going. Buddhism touched the very core of Hinduism and articulated the most profound level of its inner contradictions.

CHAPTER TWENTY-EIGHT

# Hinduism and Christianity in India

> I may say that I have never been interested in a historical Jesus. I should not care if it was proved by someone that the man called Jesus never lived, and that what was narrated in the Gospels was a figment of the writer's imagination. The Sermon on the Mount would still be true for me.
>
> —Mahātmā Gandhi, *Young India*

News of the burning of an Australian Christian missionary and his young sons near an Indian village made headlines the world over in January 1999 and led to many commentaries on the relations between Christians and Hindus in India. As there are centuries-old hatreds between Hindus and Muslims, there are centuries-old suspicions between Hindus and Christians. Ashok Chowgule, a leading figure of the Hindū Viśva Pariṣad, in his *Christianity in India: The Hindutva Perspective*, writes about "the Christian challenge" and quotes with approval from an article by G. M. Soares-Prabhu, an Indian Catholic priest: "In their 'spiritual and temporal' conquest of the East and the West [the Christians] unleashed a reign of violence and destruction unparalleled in human history. Religion fuelled their violence. It fed their racial arrogance, legitimised their insatiable greed, and added to their depredations a ruthless ferocity which only religious fanaticism can give."[1] India, the author proudly states, was one of the few countries that resisted the Christian onslaught: five centuries of Christian missions have not made much of an impact on the country. Only 2.4 percent of India's population are Christians, many of them tracing their roots back to a time long before the colonial missionary expansion of Western Christendom.

## A SHORT HISTORY OF CHRISTIANITY IN INDIA

According to an old Christian tradition the Apostle Thomas brought the Gospel to India and founded the first Christian communities there—centuries before most of Europe was Christianized. The Acts of St. Thomas mention the conversion of a king named Gondophares in northern India. Thomas then established churches along the Malabar and the Coromandel coasts in South India. At Mount Thomas near Chennai (Madras) the apostle achieved martyrdom: it has become a popular place of pilgrimage with an ancient chapel that originally contained his grave.[2] His remains were later transferred to the Cathedral Church in San Thome. While the Christian communities in North India seem to have disappeared in the Muslim onslaught without a trace,[3] the Thomas Christians in South India maintain that they are the descendants of the communities founded by the apostle. They follow an Eastern Christian rite and use Syriac as their liturgical language. Apart from the legendary violent death suffered by Thomas himself, no conflicts between Hindus and Thomas Christians are known: the Christian communities remained within the Indian cultural context and were treated as one of many castes with their own usages and customs.

Another version of the beginnings of Christianity in India has it that a Syrian Christian merchant by the name of Thomas settled in the fifth century CE at Travancore and established a Christian community there. An argument in favor of this story is the fact that the Thomas Christians till very recently kept connections with the See of Edessa in Syria, from where all of their bishops came.

With the spread of Islam in the countries of West and South Asia, information about India in Europe was reduced to legendary stories like that of "Prester John" and to reports by individual adventurers like Marco Polo, "Il Millione," who found little acceptance. The situation changed dramatically with the opening up of the sea route to Asia via the Cape: Indian pilots guided Vasco da Gama from Madagascar to the Malabar Coast. He landed in 1498 and was received by the local Zamorin, who was used to dealing with Arab traders. The Portuguese, however had not just come to load their vessels with the spices of South India and depart with them to their homeland: they soon occupied and claimed as theirs a piece of land that they named Goa. It was the policy among the Catholic nations of Europe to not only claim foreign lands for their sovereigns but also to win the souls of their inhabitants for Christ. It was mostly the members of the orders of Franciscans, Dominicans, and Jesuits who went overseas to convert the natives to Christianity.

While the story of Christian missions in India is not as stained with blood and crimes as the Conquista of the New World, it is not a happy one either. The Portuguese insisted that in the territories that they had occupied the natives either become Christian or leave the place. Many accepted baptism and received instead of their Indian names, usually connected to Hindu gods, those of their Portuguese sponsors. Many left. The Hindu temples were destroyed and their property confiscated for the benefit of the Church. The sacred books of the Hindus were burned, and the converts were forbidden to possess or read any of them. The Holy Inquisition also opened up a branch in Goa, which soon acquired the reputation of being one of the most severe.

Photo 33. Eighteenth-century Portuguese Church in Bandra/Mumbai

The sixteenth-century Christian missionaries in India were astonished to find inland large communities of Christians who worshipped in their own churches according to an unknown rite. Since these Indian Christians neither knew of nor acknowledged the supreme authority of the Roman Pope, they were considered heretics who also had to be converted to Roman Catholicism. Some joined the Roman Church, the majority remained associated with the Syriac Mar Thoma Church.

Franciscans and Jesuits also began missions along the west coast, encouraging the locals—mostly low-caste Parava fishermen—to destroy their temples and to smash their idols. Francis Xavier (1506–1552), perhaps the most famous of all Christian missionaries and the patron saint of Roman Catholic missions, proudly described his mission method in one of his letters that he sent to his superior Ignatius:

> I would gather all the boys of the village and go to the place where they had made and worshipped the idols; and then the dishonour heaped on the devil was greater than the honour paid to him by the parents and relations of the boys at the time when they made and venerated the idols. For the boys would take the idols and break them to tiny pieces, and then they would spit on them and trample them under foot and do other things which perhaps it is better not to record in detail, thus showing their contempt for the one who had the impertinence to demand the veneration of their fathers.[4]

In spite of the wondrous tales about Xavier's command of a great number of Asian languages, we must assume that he did not know enough of the local Indian languages to base his low opinion of the Brahmins on impressions gained from personal encounters, when he characterized them as "the most perverse people in the world," averting that "they never tell the truth, but think of nothing but how to tell subtle lies and to deceive the simple and ignorant people, telling them that the idols demand certain offerings and these are simply things the Brahmans themselves invent and of which they stand in need in order to maintain their wives and children and houses." He probably was right, although for the wrong reasons, when complaining: "If there were no Brahmins in the area, all the Hindus would accept conversion to our faith."[5]

Roberto de Nobili (1577–1656), a Jesuit of the next generation who undoubtedly knew Tamil and Sanskrit, adopted the lifestyle of the Brahmins and was able to converse with them and apparently also adopted some of the qualities ascribed to them by Xavier: he used "subtle lies," like his being an Italian-born Brahmin, and tricks like darkening his skin with some tincture. He apparently also tried to "deceive the simple and ignorant people" by pretending that he had found an unknown Vedic scripture, the *Ezourvedam*, that taught the truths of Christianity. Controversies within his own order as well as opposition from local Hindus made his mission to the Brahmins a short-lived experiment with no future.[6]

Catholic missions in India began when the Roman Church in Europe was challenged by various Protestant movements and when entire countries severed their connection with Rome. For almost two centuries after its beginnings Protestantism did not show any missionary interest outside Europe.[7] It saw its major task in reforming the Church and in theologically working out its positions. The Thirty Years War (1618–1648) that devastated much of Central Europe and its aftermath absorbed all the energies and resources that the fledgling Protestant Churches possessed. However, when Protestant countries of Europe began acquiring overseas colonies, Protestant rulers were put under pressure to Christianize these countries according to their own faith, following the example of the Catholic powers.

The Indian situation was peculiar insofar as the first contacts from the side of Protestant countries were made by trading companies rather than by emissaries of governments.[8] These initially did not want Christian missionaries from their homelands to work in their colonial territories. They feared it would interfere with their trade and their lifestyle. The British East India Company had contracted to respect the religious customs of the country and even paid the salaries of Hindu priests and paṇḍits in important centers. Although it allowed from 1660 on Anglican chaplains to serve its English employees, it did not permit missionaries to work among the Indian population until 1813. King Frederick IV of Denmark, unable to find qualified Danish volunteers to go to the Danish trade post in Tranquebar, in 1705 sent two German Pietists, Bartholomäus Ziegenbalg (1683–1719) and Heinrich Plütschau, members of the Lutheran Halle mission, in order to minister to the resident Dutch traders, who also initially resented their presence. Ziegenbalg, interested in learning Tamil[9] and curious about the culture of the country, collected a great amount of information about Hinduism. The manuscript *Das malabarische Heidentum* (Malabar Heathenism) that he sent to his superiors at Halle contained, in their opinion, too positive a picture of the indigenous tradition: it remained unpublished for over two centuries.[10] The secretary of the Halle mission, A. H. Francke, let Ziegenbalg know that "the missionaries were sent out to exterminate heathenism in India, not to spread heathen nonsense all over Europe."[11] Ziegenbalg had written in a 1710 letter that he did "not reject everything [the Hindus] teach, rather rejoice[d] that for the heathen long ago a small light of the Gospel began to shine." In the foreword to his work, which gives a fair description of South Indian Śaivism, he wrote that the Indians "know by the light of nature that God exists, a truth which they do not have to be taught by Christianity." He continued: "One will find here and there such teachings and passages in their writings which are not only according to human reason but also according to God's Word."[12]

Tranquebar and the Danish king also paved the way for the work of William Carey, a British Methodist who established himself in the Danish settlement of Serampore.[13] He was determined to translate the Christian scriptures into as many Indian languages as possible.[14] He set up a press that became famous for its large variety of fonts for Asian languages and its skill in producing high-quality books in these. Carey employed a large number of Hindu paṇḍits who assisted him in creating a Christian theological vocabulary. Among those who came into contact with him was Ram Mohan Roy, the "Father of Modern India," who was to found the Brahmo-Samāj, intended as a synthesis of the best that Hinduism and Christianity had to offer to humankind. Carey, together with his colleague Marshman, also edited and translated parts of the *Rāmāyaṇa* into English.

Colonel Bie had suggested to Carey to open schools for the local population, both in order to spread education and to secure a source of income. By 1800 Carey had started a Bengali medium school for boys that was open to all, regardless of caste. In 1818 he opened a school for Bengali girls, a pioneering enterprise that soon flourished. Carey was known for his skills in the use of Bengali. Another English missionary, Alexander Duff, received permission in 1830 to open an English medium school in Calcutta. Schools, usually with English as the medium of instruction, became a major tool for spreading Christianity, as well as the modern Western ideas that were perceived intrinsically linked.

## HINDU CHRISTIANS

On December 28, 1800, Carey received the first Hindu, Krishna Pal, into his church. With the presence of Hindu converts a new situation arose. On the one hand one could expect a certain amount of disaffection of neophytes toward their "old faith." On the other hand they had a much more detailed and intimate knowledge of Hindu scriptures and practices than the foreign missionaries. They were less inclined to condemn Hinduism wholesale and remained emotionally attached to the culture that was shaped by the old traditions.

Nilakantha Sastri (1825–1895), a Chitpavan Brahman from Mahārāṣṭra who became known in Christian circles as Nehemiah Goreh, had grown up in the Śaivite tradition. He became a Christian in 1848, but throughout his life retained "doubts about the truth of Christianity itself, doubt about the divinity of Christ, doubt about the mode of baptism."[15] In 1860 he published (in Hindī) *Ṣaḍdarśana Darpaṇa*, a critique of the six orthodox Hindu systems, which appeared in English in 1862 under the title *A Rational Refutation of the Hindu Philosophical Systems*. While critical of many aspects of the six systems, he acknowledged many points of agreement, like the theistic basis of *Nyāya* and *Vaiśeṣika*. As Robin Boyd states: "He loved his Hindu fellow-countrymen, felt at home in their society, and was convinced that in some unknown way God had been preparing their hearts and minds to receive the Christian revelation."[16] Specifically he believed that the Hindu teachings of *ananyabhakti*, undivided love of God; *vairāgya*, renunciation; *namratā*, humility; and *kṣamā*, forgiveness "enabled them to appreciate the precepts of Christianity."

One of the most interesting and intriguing figures was Bhavani Charan Banerji (1861–1907), a Bengali Brahmin better known under the name he assumed after becoming a Christian, Brahmabandhab Upadhyāya. Through personal friendship with two Anglican missionaries he was gradually drawn toward Christianity and was baptized in 1891. He made it clear, however, that he did not wish to become a member of the Church of England. He later became a Catholic, but he developed his Hindu-Christian theology in a quite original and independent manner. He encouraged his students to participate in Sarasvatī worship and defended Kṛṣṇa as *avatāra*. He even underwent a *prāyaścitta* to purify himself from the defilement incurred by associating with foreigners and crossing the sea. His theological writings are profound, and some of his Sanskrit hymns are widely used in Christian churches in today's India. For him *Sat-cit-ānanda* remained the name for the highest reality—Hindu and Christian.

*Samnyāsa* undoubtedly exerted a fascination also for Christians who recognized it as a parallel to the Christian monastic and ascetical tradition that initially may have well developed under Indian influences in the first Christian centuries. Consequently a Christian ashram movement developed within the Christian Church in India—virtually all of the ashrams were ecumenical[17]—and several individuals adopted the lifestyle of Hindu *samnyāsis*, albeit often in a less rigorous way than most Hindu ascetics. One of the best known of the latter is Sadhu Sundar Singh (1889–1929). Although his family was Sikh, his mother introduced him, as is not unusual among Sikhs, into the Vaiṣṇava *bhakti* tradition and made him memorize the *Bhagavadgītā* as a small child.

The first contact with Christianity in a mission school aroused his antipathy against the Bible, which he burnt. A vision of Jesus on December 18, 1904, changed all that. He received baptism a year later and became, at age sixteen, a Christian *sādhu*. He wandered all over India and Tibet and was invited to give lectures in Europe, America, and Australia.[18] He insisted that he considered himself a disciple of Christ but not a member of any Christian Church.

One of the most remarkable instances of Hindu-Christian friendship was offered by Mahātmā Gandhi and C. F. Andrews, an English scholar and Anglican missionary. Andrews had befriended Mahātmā Gandhi in South Africa, where both joined in the fight for the rights of non-Whites. He followed him to India and, during the struggle for independence, became one of his most important allies and counselors. There is no doubt that Gandhi's respect for the teachings of the New Testament and his love for Jesus had much to do with his relationship to C. F. Andrews, who, in his turn, expressed his sympathy and acceptance of many of the features of Hinduism ideally represented in Mahātmā Gandhi.[19] C. F. Andrews was also a friend and supporter of Yisu Das Tiwari, a convert to Christianity from a Brahmin family in Agra. Tiwari tried to keep independent from the organized Christian Churches, although he taught at several seminaries such as Serampore and Bishops College, Calcutta, and accepted ordination into the Baptist Church. He worked at a revision of the Hindī translation of the Bible and began formulating an Indian theology.[20]

By the early twentieth century India had become the largest mission field for Protestant missionaries from the United Kingdom. Many of these made sympathetic studies of various aspects and expressions of Hinduism whose value has been recognized as recent reprints of these works show.[21] Thus it is not surprising that Hinduism figured quite prominently on the agenda of the World Missionary Conference held at Edinburgh in June 1910.[22] There were moving testimonies by missionaries about their experience of Hindus possessing "as deep, genuine, and spiritual a religious life as is found amongst most Christians."[23] Generally, missionaries were advised to gain a solid knowledge of Hinduism and entertain a sympathetic attitude toward it. Naturally, there were missionary undertones. As one participant said: "It is a reasonable demand to any man who tries to tackle so difficult a problem as that of changing other men's faith that he should know what he is talking about, not only his own religion, but also that which he desires to lead the people away from."[24]

The openness toward Hinduism and the appreciation of its spiritual riches that the Edinburgh conference exhibited was not maintained for long. Neoorthodox theologians, notably Karl Barth, became influential in Protestantism, and at a meeting of the International Missionary Council at Tambaram near Cennai in December 1938, a prominent missiologist, Hendrik Kraemer, asserted that a Christian's interest in a non-Christian ought to be purely evangelical. All religions, considered mere human contraptions, fabricated under the influence of the evil one, had to be razed to make place for the Gospel, which was supposed to be of a different order altogether.[25] It took Protestant mission theorists a long time to overcome this stance, and it is the merit mainly of two Indian Christian lay theologians to have brought about a change of mind and heart: Pandipeddi Chenchiah (1886–1959) and Vengal Chakkarai Chetti (1880–1958).

Chenchiah, a lawyer and for a time chief judge at Pudukkottai State, became known for his 1938 book *Rethinking Christianity in India*, intended to be an Indian answer to Hendrik Kraemer's *The Christian Message in a Non-Christian World*, the basic discussion document of Tambaram. Chenchiah distanced himself from much of Western Christian theology and church practice. Basing his thought on the New Testament, on the teachings of Śrī Aurobindo Ghose and the ideas of "Master C. V. V.," he developed a quite novel interpretation of Christian doctrine. He had great respect for the Hindu tradition as possibly the highest expression of the human ideal: "Hinduism makes the perfect man, Christianity the new man" and "Hinduism harnesses the Mahāśakti of nature and man, Christianity brings into evolution the new Śakti of the Holy Spirit. Jesus is the first fruits of a new creation, Hinduism the final fruits of the old creation."[26]

Chakkarai was related to Chenchiah as his brother-in-law and became his admirer and collaborator. Throughout he uses traditional Hindu terminology to expound his Christian theology. For him "it is the same *paramātman*, the Supreme, that was in the *rishis* of old and by whom they spoke at different times and degrees, who is the secret of the Christian consciousness."[27]

Dr. William Miller, a greatly respected principal of Madras Christian College, played a major role in attracting Chenchiah and Chakkarai to Christianity and in encouraging them to rethink it in the Indian context. Principal Miller's memory is kept alive through the annual endowment lectureship in his name sponsored by the University of Madras. His successor A. G. Hogg became a major influence for Sarvepalli Radhakrishnan. Hogg took a great interest in Hinduism, writing, among others, *Gītā and Gospel* and *Karma and Redemption* in order to create a better understanding for Hinduism. He maintained that Hinduism was "a finding as well as a seeking" and that it also contained revealed truth.[28]

One of the most extensive and most appealing attempts to integrate Christianity and Hinduism can be seen in the work of Bishop Appasamy (b. 1891). Appasamy's father had been a convert from Śaivism to Christianity, largely through the influence of the Christian poet Krishna Pillai, who remained a close friend of the family. His best-known book is *Christianity as Bhaktimārga* in which an attempt is made to express Christian theology in the terminology of Rāmānuja's Śrīvaiṣṇavism. The closeness of Vaiṣṇavism and Christianity has been noted before, of course, sometimes suggesting mutual dependence or borrowing.[29] Appasamy thoroughly studied the major systems of Vedānta and adopted the methodology of the Vedāntins to articulate an Indian Christian theology.[30]

J. N. Farquhar (1861–1929) was a progressive missionary who found much to admire in Hinduism. His *Outline of the Religious Literature of India* is a comprehensive, sympathetic, and widely acknowledged survey of Hindu texts.[31] In *The Crown of Hinduism*, he explains the relationship between Christianity and Hinduism in terms of fulfillment, a view that was widely adopted by other Christian writers.[32]

Farquhar's son-in-law Paul Devanandan can rightly be called the father of Hindu-Christian dialogue in India. He became the founder of a circle in which ideas of interreligious dialogue were developed long before the Churches began endorsing it. After earning a doctorate from Yale University with a thesis on the concept of Māyā, he became the first director of the Christian Institute for the Study of Religion and Society (CISRS)in Bangalore, which did pioneering work in the area of Hindu-Christian dialogue. Its quarterly journal *Religion and Society* contains numerous contributions to this theme.[33] CISRS also initiated organized Hindu-Christian dialogue not only in India but worldwide. One of its former members, Stanley S. Samartha, after being invited to join the staff of the World Council of Churches headquarters in Geneva, developed a subsection for dialogue. In the 1960s and 1970s he organized a number of international interreligious dialogue conferences throughout the world in which representatives also of various Hindu traditions invariably participated.[34] In his own major theological study *The Hindu Response to the Unbound Christ*[35] he offers a reinterpretation of Christianity in terms of Advaita Vedānta. Worldwide nobody has done more than Samartha to promote Hindu-Christian dialogue on the highest level.

Another former director of the Christian Institute for the Study of Religion and Society in Bangalore, M. M. Thomas, while stressing the pragmatic and secular message of Christianity, co-organized and cochaired a major Hindu-Christian dialogue meeting held in Bombay in 1969.[36] His *The Acknowleged Christ of the Indian Renaissance* is a careful and sympathetic study of the thought of Ram Mohan Roy, Keshub Chander Sen, Vivekananda, Radhakrishnan, and Mahātmā Gandhi, all of whom had shown great respect for Jesus and his teachings.

Dhanjibhai Fakirbhai (1895–1967), loosely connected with the CISRS after his retirement, used Hindu terminology and literary genres to express Christian ideas in his *Khristopaniṣad* and *Hṛidaya-Gītā*. Having grown up a Hindu and joining the Christian Church as a young man, he found it completely natural to intertwine the two traditions that had given him everything he cherished. Developing what he termed *Khristadvaita*, he strove to deepen the Christians' understanding of their faith and to show to Hindus a depth dimension of Christianity that rarely appeared in the Church's routine. His thinking is close to that of Mark Sunder Rao's *Ananyatā*.

In this connection Rudolf Otto (1869–1937), one of the great names in *Religionswissenschaft*, deserves mention. As translator (into German) of substantial texts from the Vaiṣṇava tradition[37] and as sensitive interpreter of

"India's Religion of Grace" he introduced theistic Hinduism to a wider public in the West.

Following the success of Hindu movements in the West, such as ISKCON, old confrontational attitudes were revived among Protestant Christians. The Dialogue Center in Aarhus (Denmark), founded and directed by Rev. Johann Aargaard, later affiliated with the Spiritual Counterfeits Project in the United States (now Hong Kong) specializes in polemics against the new religious movements. Its bulletin, *New Religious Movements Update*, not only attacks the new movements but also pours ridicule on traditional Hinduism by focusing on some of its more bizarre representatives and some outlandish expressions. The Center has established a branch in Delhi and made a film that was meant to show to people in the West the negative side of Hinduism in India. Others warn parents of children who had joined ISKCON against "this futile path to an illusory salvation"[38] and advise them to "rescue their children from the clutches of a false, non-scriptural religion." Gary Lean, a Baptist, criticized the "exaggerated asceticism" of the movement.[39]

Over against these misguided zealots one has to highlight the positive evaluations of modern Hindu movements by leading Protestant theologians, like Robert Boyd, who defended ISKCON when it was threatened by legislation in Australia, or Harvey Cox, who praised the "simplicity and plainness of living" of its members and recognized the importance of their message in the modern West.[40]

Also in Catholic circles a "rethinking" took place. In the 1920s a small group of Jesuits working in Calcutta began publishing a series, Through Vedānta to Christ, in which they undertook sympathetic reviews of the main schools of Vedānta, highlighting their teachings that appeared to them compatible with Catholic teaching. This was in contrast to another school of Jesuits that believed that a tabula rasa had to be created in India before Christianity could take hold. Fathers Fallon and Antoine also actively supported the study of Sanskrit and classical Hindu literature.

Pioneering work was done by Norvin Hein whose thesis *The Miracle Plays of Mathurā* shows not only scholarly competence but also extraordinary religious sensitivity toward Kṛṣṇaism. Similarly, J. B. Carman's *The Theology of Rāmānuja* has been recognized as groundbreaking not only in Rāmānuja scholarship but also in theological understanding. Diana Eck in her popular *City of Light* provides a very open-minded and sympathetic sketch of Hinduism as lived and practiced in Vārāṇasī.

On the existential level, it is fair to say that virtually all Christians who came into contact with genuine Hindus welcome the many spiritual gifts that Hinduism so generously offers to the world. Thus Murray Rogers, an Anglican priest, the founder of Jyotiniketan Ashram in Kareli (Uttar Pradesh), movingly expressed the importance that Hindu worship and spiritual practice has for him and his Christian life practice: "How I wish that I could convey through a few strokes of the brush or a few notes on a pipe the gift that the Hindu revelation has been to me, a Christian in my spiritual life and experience." He was able to merge Hindu and Christian forms of worship and adopt a lifestyle that was to express both Hindu and Christian values. "We Christians have much to learn," he commented.[41]

For some time during the 1960s the Cuttat-Group was active in Hindu-Christian dialogue in India. It took its name from the then Swiss Ambassador to India, Dr. Jacques Albert Cuttat, a well-known philosopher, who undertook to invite Christians interested in interreligious dialogue to regular meetings. Participants included Swami Abhishiktananda, Raimon Panikkar, Bede Griffiths, and others who became known in dialogue circles.

The Society for Hindu Christian Studies, a scholarly association of Hindus and Christians of all denominations established in 1994, aims at providing a framework for fostering dialogue between Christians and Hindus on a worldwide basis. The organizational lead had been provided by Harold Coward, who in 1988 took the initiative to organize an international, interdenominational conference on Hindu-Christian Dialogue at the University of Calgary[42] and subsequently launched a *Hindu-Christian Studies Bulletin*.[43] It contains articles by authorities in the field and also provides information on current events relating to Hindu-Christian dialogue.

## THE INDIGENIZATION OF INDIAN CHRISTIANITY

The newly established government of independent India demanded from the Christian Churches that they appoint Indians as senior administrators and hand over to them the governance of their establishments. To a large extent that was done fairly quickly, but it took longer to convince them that also an indigenization of the Christian message was required. The Christian communities in the cities were largely Westernized, they had given up their Indian traditions and had received in Christian schools a training that was purely European. They were forbidden to read Hindu religious literature, visit Hindu temples, or participate in Hindu festivities. It was one of the main charges against Christian missionaries from the side of Hindus that they "denationalized" their converts. Those who tried to recover the ancestral Indian heritage faced unexpected problems. There were Christian doctrines that clearly opposed traditional Hindu beliefs, such as karma and rebirth, the existence of a plurality of gods, the worship of images, and so forth. And Hindus increasingly protest against the use of their symbols and practices as part of Christian worship. Thus Sita Ram Goel, once a supporter of Hindu-Christian dialogue, accused those Christians who took up *saṃnyāsa* as a Christian way of life of being swindlers rather than genuine *saṃnyāsis*.[44]

Focusing particularly on the "Tannirpalli Trinity" [Jules Monchanin, Henri le Saux, and Bede Griffith] he not only resented their illegitimate use of the *saṃnyāsi* garb, but was particularly infuriated by their superimposition of the sacred Hindu *praṇava* (OM) on the Christian cross as it appeared over the entrance to the chapel of Saccidānanda Ashram. "Nailing the Om to the Cross" he perceived as one of the worst sins against the Hindu spirit. Hindus today resent the appropriation of their culture for alien purposes, as they resent the interpretation of their tradition from alien and often distorting perspectives.

When multinational pharmaceutical concerns began patenting Indian indigenous medicinal plants for commercial exploitation, demands were voiced to protect India's natural and cultural heritage for the benefit of the people of India. This has relevance also for the Hindu religious heritage. Hindus object to subsuming their symbols and traditions under some alien label. Some Hindus, well read in Christian theology, traditional as well as contemporary, have begun to submit Christianity to a substantial critique. Christian theologians, not only in India, will have to answer searching questions from Hindus, who find Christian teachings unconvincing and Christian practices, past and present, often unacceptably "un-Christian." Old issues like the devastation of the Americas by some of the most Christian nations of Europe and the way the Portuguese treated Hindus in their Indian territories are being raised again. Hindus are not convinced that a conversion from Hinduism to Christianity would benefit them or their country spiritually or otherwise.

India—and with it Hinduism—has undergone a dramatic change in the last two decades, affecting also the relationship between Hindus and followers of other religions. No longer are Hindus eager, as Sarvepalli Radhakrishnan had been, to present Hinduism as universal spirituality, utterly other-worldly, without organization or dogma, accommodating virtually anything and everybody with a religious leaning. Hinduism is mutating from an open-air, self-serve bazaar from which all could pick up whatever they liked and put it to whatever use, into an increasingly tightly controlled organization that is establishing its own rules of business. Hindus have become self-conscious and have begun to define Hinduism in such a way as to exclude all religions that have not originated in India and that do not share the Indian cultural heritage. If Paul Hacker could in the 1960s describe *Inclusivism* as one of the characteristics of Hinduism, this is no longer true. There exist now powerful and influential Hindu organizations that speak and act exclusively for large numbers of Hindus. Although not all Hindus may identify with the Viśva Hindū Pariṣad and its affiliates, it has the sympathies of many and acts worldwide as a watchdog for Hindu interests, critically looking at everything that is spoken and written about Hinduism anywhere in the world, including the way Hinduism is being taught at American universities.[45] It also has revived the Dharma-parishad of earlier ages, attempting a Hindu *aggiornamento*.

A dialogue with this new Hinduism will be different from the dialogue that had been attempted under Christian auspices in the past.[46] This time it is the Hindus who lay down the rules of the game. Indian Christians will have to establish a dialogue with this new Hinduism, too, if only for the sake of survival. They are dealing now with Hindus who often know more about the history and reality of the Church than many Christians themselves. They will have to accept critique and instead of flaunting their difference in lifestyle and worldview—an attitude that earned them the doubtful distinction of a "Christian superiority complex"—they will have to demonstrate solidarity with their fellow Indians and largely reappropriate the culture of their forefathers. When adopting Hindu religious practices and symbols they will have to follow Hindu conventions and get the Hindus' agreement, demonstrating respect for their spirit.[47] The main issue and the principal stone of offense for Hindus is conversion: Hindus want to have it stopped altogether whereas Christians insist on it as their right and duty.

CHAPTER TWENTY-NINE

# Hindus and Muslims in India

> Rāma, Khudā, Śakti, Śiva are one and the same. To whom, then do the prayers go? The Vedas, the Purāṇas and the Quran are just different kinds of books. Neither Hindu nor Muslim, neither Jain nor Yogi knows the true secret.
>
> —Kabīr, *Bījak*, Śabda 28

On February 27, 2002, a group of about two thousand agitated people stopped the Sabarmati Express outside the station of Godhra, Gujarat. After exchanging abuses with those inside, they began to throw bottles filled with gasoline into compartments of the first four carriages. Soon the train was engulfed in flames. Fifty-eight people on the train perished in the fire. The attackers were Muslims—the victims were Hindus, most of them kārsevaks returning from Ayodhyā, the disputed temple/mosque complex that Hindus believe to have been Rāma's birthplace.

The incident on the train sparked off months-long Hindu-Muslim rioting involving over a million people leaving thousands dead and maimed and whole neighborhoods all over Gujarat in ruins.[1]

Both the attack by Muslims on Hindus and the following retaliation by Hindus followed an advance plan—far from being a spontaneous outburst, it was the unfolding of a scenario all too familiar in India: a confrontation between Muslims and Hindus who have been hating each other for centuries, have engaged in hundreds of similar riots, and still have to live with each other.

## MUSLIM INDIA

Over the centuries Hindu India had absorbed the cultures of many foreign invaders: Greeks, Parthians, Kuśānas, Hunas, and it accommodated followers of many different religions: Jews found refuge from the persecutions by Roman Emperors, Syrian Christians could freely establish their own communities, Zoroastrians fleeing from Muslims found asylum—Hindus were famous for their religious diversity, their tolerance, and their openness for newcomers.

Islam came to India as the religion of conquerors who saw it their mission to eradicate its native religion and to transform the country into a *Dār-al-Islām*.[2] In 711 CE—less than a century after the Prophet's death—Muhammed ibn al Qasim invaded some towns in the Indus valley, making Multan his headquarters and establishing the rule of the Quran in parts of Sindh. Between 1005 and 1030 CE Mahmud of Ghazni undertook seventeen raids into northwestern India, killing thousands of Hindus, looting temple treasures, and destroying one of the greatest Hindu sanctuaries, the Somanātha temple in Kathiawaḍ. His chroniclers waxed enthusiastic about the large number of infidels killed and the rich booty carried away from their temples. From then on Islamic forces systematically attacked and invaded India. By 1211 CE Iltutmish had established himself as the first Sultan in Delhi—the beginning of Muslim rule over large parts of India that terminated only in 1857! Muslim rulers in Delhi were ousted by other Muslim rulers, Turks were driven out by Mongols, but Hindus remained suppressed and were treated as *kafirs* who had the choice to either convert to Islam or to pay the *jizya*, the tax imposed on nonbelievers. There were exceptional Muslim rulers like Akbar the Great (1542–1605), who appreciated Hindu culture and religion, but most, like his own grandson Aurangzeb (1618–1707), fanatically tried to eradicate everything Hindu, destroying thousands of temples and dissolving their places of learning. No wonder that Hindus welcomed the British in Bengal, hoping to find in them allies against the Muslim rulers. While the British did bring an end to Muslim rule, at least at the center, they did not do much to strengthen the position of the Hindus, and the 1856 uprising, called "Mutiny" by the British and "First War of Independence" by the Indians, was undertaken by Hindus and Muslims conjointly who both resented foreign domination.

While the Islamic rulers of India strove for Muslim hegemony and kept a sharp diving line between Islam and Hinduism, individual Muslim scholars and mystics entered into a dialogue with Hinduism, integrating features of Hindu religious practice into their own and showing considerable respect for the accomplishments of the Hindus. Thus al-Bīrūnī, born 973 in Central Asia, who made a career as an Iranian scholar-diplomat, spent many years in (Hindu) India, collecting information about Hindu religion and science, customs and practices. His *Kitāb al-Hind* is the first major scholarly report about Hindu scriptures and Hindu beliefs, astonishingly objective and free from intrusive prejudice. He learned Sanskrit, translated the *Yoga Sūtras* into Persian, held discussions with Hindu scholars, and was criticized by fellow Muslims for exposing Hindu religion without refuting it. Al-Bīrūnī was realistic enough to realize that due to the havoc that Mahmud had created in India "the Hindus cherished the most inveterate aversion towards all Muslims."[3]

Photo 34. Mosque: Vṛndāvaṇa

Although the often brutal and reckless conquest of India by Muslim invaders has been in the foreground of Hindu-Muslim relations, there was also a peaceful penetration of Hindu India by Islam, carried out by teachers and preachers. Large numbers of outcasts, who had suffered under the disabilities imposed on them by the Hindu caste system, were attracted by the Islamic promise of an egalitarian society and became Muslims. Whether they were much better off now in their new religion is another question.

Sufis initiated a Muslim-Hindu dialogue in depth: they absorbed Buddhist and Hindu elements into their mystical practices. Riffat Hassan holds that "it was Muslim Sufis, not Muslim soldiers who converted masses of Hindus to Islam."[4] The first Sufi to have done so seems to have been Abū Yazīd Biṣṭāmī (d. 874), believed to have had an Indian teacher by the name of Abū Alī Sindh. His ideas of sameness of human self and Supreme Being and the notion that the ego has to disappear before the union with God can take place betray Hindu influence. Possibly the most famous of all Sufis, Ibn Manṣūr al-Ḥallāj (d. 922) visited Sindh in order to study "Indian magic." He not only accepted Hindu ideas of cosmogony and of divine descent, but he also seems to have believed in transmigration. Clearly his enemies considered him an apostate from Islam. His Vedānta-inspired "I am the Truth" was enough of a provocation to the orthodox to condemn him to death.

The Sufi centers served also as meeting places between Muslims and Hindus: in turn, both Muslims and Hindus became devotees of Sufi masters. One feature of Sufi spirituality was the musical performance that brought Muslims and Hindus together—the cradle for the later (classical) Hindustani music.

Besides the Sufis that were attached to a center, there were wandering Muslim mendicants, such as the Qalandāras and the Madārīs whose style of life very much resembled that of the Hindu *saṃnyāsis*. Under the influence of Hindu Yogis some Sufi orders such as the Chistiyas became vegetarians and practiced breath control (*prāṇa-yoga*) and Hatha Yoga. One Rukn-ud dīn Samarqandi translated the *Amṛtakuṇḍa*, a manual of Hatha Yoga around 1215 into Persian after receiving initiation through a Hindu *siddha*: the book became popular among Sufis in Bengal. Sayyid Murtazā (1590–1662) attempted in his *Yoga Qalandār* to demonstrate the compatibility of Yoga with Islamic theology. Yoga seems to have exerted a great attraction on Sufis and it was at the same time a link between Muslim and Hindu ascetics.

Similarly, poetry acted as a link between Sufis and Hindus: in much of the Sufi poetry of the sixteenth century Hindu ideas are expressed as there was a great closeness in ideas between the Hindu *bhakti* movement and Sufism. In both traditions the repetition of divine names, *nāma-japa*, played a great role. Muslims, who had a tradition of reciting the "ninety-nine beautiful names of Allah," began adding Hindu names such as Nirjan, Kratār, Vidhāta, Prameśa, among others to their own litany—a practice that orthodox maulvis found objectionable. Both Hindus and Muslims considered the divine names of (Hindu) Rāma and (Muslim) Rahman as identical—one God was the father of all. If Vaiṣṇavism was the main Hindu expression with which Muslims came into contact and which they found congenial—it taught devotion to one God and insisted on a life of selfless love and service—in Kashmir the Sufis also encountered and accepted Śaivism: the mystic poetess Lallā Yogīśvarī, a Śaiva, met repeatedly with Mīr Seyyed Hamadānī. Her influence shows especially in the poems of Shaikh Nurudin Rishi (b. 1378) the founder of the Rishi order of Sufis.

Theologically some Muslims went quite far to accommodate Hinduism: Pīr Sadruddin of Ucch in the early fifteenth century adopted the *Daśāvatāra* schema of Vaiṣṇavas and declared that Alī was the tenth *avatāra* of Viṣṇu. Sadruddin's great-grandson identified the Prophet's wife Aiṣa as Savitrī, her daughter as Lakṣmī, Adam as Īśvara. Seyyed Sultan declared Muhammed an *avatāra* of Viṣṇu. Some Sufis compiled dictionaries where they gave Muslim interpretations to Hindu religious terms. Others adopted Hindī as the linguistic medium for their compositions and used Hindu mythological themes and images.

## KABĪR

Among the many mystics and poets who downplayed the differences between Hinduism and Islam and insisted instead on interiority and a virtuous life, Kabīr takes the most eminent place.[5] Muhammed Hedayetullah calls him "The Apostle of Hindu-Muslim Unity."[6] He holds that "the Bhakti Movement—a religion of devotion—is a combination of the efforts of Hindu and Muslim mystics who, in their highest spirituality, transcended all distinctions between man and man religiously as well as socially."[7]

Kabīr is indeed a key figure in Muslim-Hindu relations at the grassroots: by caste and profession a weaver, it still is a point of debate whether he was born a Muslim or a Hindu. He probably did not care to decide that question. By using the common dialect of his birthplace, by freely mixing Hindu and Muslim sacred names, and by pointing out the narrowness and petty-mindedness of both Hindu and Muslim professional religious he acquired already during his lifetime a large following of Muslims and Hindus. Knowing that the followers of both religions ardently claimed him as theirs, when he was about to die—so the legend goes—he withdrew into a closed chamber all by himself. When his followers opened the room to take away his body, they only found a heap of flower petals. This was divided equally between Hindus and Muslims who cremated and buried their shares.

While the story certainly commends the broad-mindedness of Kabīr and his ability to bridge the gap that divided Hindus and Muslims religiously, it also underscores the pertinacity of religious sectarianism: although united in their veneration for the teacher Kabīr, Hindus and Muslims continued being divided over the claim on his communal affiliation—for the Hindus he remained a

Hindu, for the Muslims a Muslim. They could not conceive of a saint without a sectarian label!

Later the Sikhs claimed Kabīr as one of their prophets, and when Gurū Arjun compiled the Gurū Granth Sahīb, the sacred scriptures of the Sikhs, he included a large number of Kabīr's poems in it. Like Kabīr, Gurū Nānak, the founder of the "Community of Disciples," wanted to bridge the gap between Hindus and Muslims. That did not prevent, however, later Mogul rulers from persecuting Sikhs and cruelly executing some of their leaders.

## FROM AKBAR TO AURANGZEB

With the accession of Akbar, later called "the great," to the Mogul throne in Delhi, a new chapter of Muslim-Hindu relations opened. He married Hindu princesses, employed Hindu officials and generals, and showed great interest in the culture of India, including its native religions. He gave court appointments to a large number of paṇḍits who were to assist Muslim scholars in translating Hindu scriptures into Persian. Abū-al Fazl, his court historian, wrote an introduction to the Persian translation of the *Mahābhārata*, explaining the reason why Akbar had commissioned it: "Having observed the fanatical hatred between the Hindus and the Muslims and being convinced that it arose only from mutual ignorance, that enlightened monarch wished to dispel the same by rendering the books of the former accessible to the latter. He selected in the first instance the Mahābhārata as the most comprehensive and that which enjoyed the highest authority and ordered it to be translated by competent and impartial men of both nations."[8]

Akbar's religious liberalism and his love for Hindu culture had made it possible for Muslims and Hindus to work together constructively and to relegate religious disputes to theologians without affecting the daily lives of the people. His immediate successors, Jehangir and Shāh Jahān, followed his example. After Shāh Jahān's death a contest for succession broke out between Dārā Shikūḥ, the eldest son and rightful successor, and Aurangzeb, the younger son, who had Muslim orthodoxy on his side.

Dārā Shikūḥ, inspired by his grandfather Akbar, began studying Hindu scriptures. In 1653 he met Bābā Lāl Dās Bairāgi, a Vaiṣṇava *saṃnyāsi*, who became a major influence on him. He produced a work, *Majma'-al bahrayn*, "Mingling of the Two Oceans," in which he attempted to find Muslim parallels and synonyms to Hindu theological and philosophical concepts. With the assistance of Hindu paṇḍits he translated in Vārāṇasī fifty-two Upaniṣads from Sanskrit into Persian under the title *Sirr-I-Akbar*, "The Great Secret," finding numerous parallels between the Quran and the Upaniṣads, which he considered the expression of the highest insight into the Unity of the Divine. These two works were condemned by a fatwa from the Muslim legal scholars, whom Aurangzeb, his brother and rival for the throne, had employed. They testified that "he had apostatized from the *Shariā't* and having vilified the Religion

Photo 35. Moti Masjid: Agra Fort (Uttar Pradesh)

of God, had allied himself with heresy."[9] Subsequently he was tried and executed—making the way free to Aurangzeb's fanatical Islamic restoration.

Aurangzeb ordered Hindu temples to be razed—as well as those that his predecessors had allowed to be rebuilt—images to be destroyed, and Hindu schools to be closed. Muslim orthodoxy in all its fierceness established itself again—only to suffer its fatal defeat with the death of Aurangzeb in 1707: a new power had established itself on the subcontinent eroding the reign of the Moguls as well as of Islam. The last outburst of intolerant Islam in India brought about its downfall. The Mahratta Śivajī challenged Aurangzeb in the Mogul heartland and established a rival Hindu kingdom, reviving the Hindu traditions of the holy cities of Mathurā and Vārāṇasī.

## THE MUSLIMS IN BRITISH INDIA

In 1680 the Mogul Emperor Aurangzeb had issued a *firmān* to the English East India Company containing far-reaching concessions with regard to trade and the establishing of company posts, especially in Bengal. Six years later he was engaged in a bloody war against the English. He lost and had to sign a humiliating list of conditions. When he died in 1707 his three sons began murderous wars of succession that, together with raids like those of Nadīr Shāh of Persia (1732) and the increasing presence of European powers, hastened the decline and eventual demise of Muslim rule in India.

Photo 36. The Presence of Islam in Kṛṣṇa's Holy City: Mathurā

In 1806 the British openly took control of Delhi and treated the ruling Mogul Shāh Alām II virtually as their prisoner. When he died under mysterious circumstances, he was succeeded by Akbar II, who was asked by Lord Hastings of the East India Company "to give up all ceremonial, implying supremacy over the Company's dominions."[10] The last Mogul, Bahādūr Shāh, accused of having sympathized with the 1857 uprising, was officially deposed and sent into exile to Burma. Before he left he was forced to witness the execution of his two sons—an ignoble end to half a millennium of Muslim rule in India!

It was not easy for the former Muslim ruling class to decide what to do: the domination of the British, of infidels and foreigners, was certainly not desirable. A withdrawal of the British, on the other hand, would mean Hindu domination, which was even less desirable in view of the potential backlash for centuries of suppression and persecution. Upper-class Hindus like Rām Mohan Roy, found it easier to accommodate to the new culture than Muslims, whose education was far more tradition bound. Fear of Hindu resurgence as well as resentment against the British made Muslims form associations that were the beginning of the kind of communalism that has so bedeviled Indian history in the last century and eventually lead to a division of the country along religious communal lines.

## FROM SAYYID AḤMAD KHAN TO MUHAMMED ALĪ KHAN

Sayyid Aḥmad Khan (1817–1898) "is hailed and assailed as the founder of Muslim separatism on the subcontinent. He is blamed and praised as a modernizer of Islam."[11] Whether friend or foe, all are agreed that he was a key figure in giving directions to Indian Muslims in the difficult period of transition from Mogul to British rule. Born into a noble family in Delhi, with some ties to the already powerless Mogul Emperor Akbar Shāh, he received the customary Muslim education and lived a fairly carefree life. He received appointments as a junior judge in various towns of northern India. During the 1857 Uprising, posted at Bijnor, he courageously led the Magistrate, Mr. Shakespear, his family, and a group of other Englishmen to safety: a feat which earned him the lifelong gratitude of the British government. He was offered a choice of positions, given a medal, and knighted for his loyalty.

Observing the daily worsening situation of his community, he advised a radical change in attitude: Muslims had to open up to the new time and had to take their chance in reestablishing themselves in the changed circumstances. He told his fellow Muslims not to consider the land under British rule as *Dār-al-Harb* (Land of Infidels) but as *Dār-al-Islām* (Land of Islam), because Muslims were completely free to exercise their religion. He also advised the Muslim theologians to give up traditions and beliefs that had become harmful and to follow the laws of nature instead of human law. And finally, the system of education had to change. Instead of continuing the traditional learning of the

Madrasas, Muslims had to be introduced to the natural sciences and to modern education. In 1858 he founded an English medium school in Morādābad and later one in Ghazipur. In 1864 he established a Scientific and Literary Society and supported the translation of English works into Urdū for the benefit of those who did not read English.

When his son was awarded a scholarship to Cambridge, he decided to accompany him and then lived for seventeen months in England (1869–1870). He studied the educational system, spending time in Oxford as well as in Cambridge. Impressed by what he saw, and undeterred by opposition, he founded with a number of like-minded Muslims the Muhammedan Anglo-Oriental College in Alīgarh in 1875, on land donated by the government and with generous support from high-ranking British officials. The language of instruction was English—Sayyid Aḥmad Khan even recommended to the British government in India to prohibit all vernacular instruction! The Alīgarh College, which became Alīgarh Muslim University in 1920, developed into the most influential Muslim institution of higher learning in India with an international reputation.

While choosing deliberately the name "Muhammedan" for his college in order to express solidarity with his community, Sayyid Ahmad kept it open for Hindu students and teachers and appointed a number of Englishmen to responsible positions. One of them, Theodore Beck, a Cambridge graduate whom Mahmud Ahmad had persuaded to come to Alīgarh, became as college principal a very important figure, more Muslim communal minded than Sir Ahmad himself. It is believed that Beck was instrumental in creating in 1883 the Muhammedan Defense Association, conceived as counterweight to the Indian National Congress, which Sir Ahmad had totally rejected. Prior to the founding of the Muhammedan Defense Association there were Hindu-Muslim riots in Bombay and the demand of Hindu revivalist movements for a total ban on cow slaughter.

Sayyid Aḥmad has been called the first Muslim communalist because of his refusal to join the Congress and to cooperate with Hindus for a democratic free India. He openly declared the India of his time unfit for self-rule and accepted the British Rāj as divinely ordained. But he also saw that the fate of Muslims and Hindus in India was intertwined: while apprehensive of Hindu rule—Hindus outnumbered Muslims then four to one—he insisted: "India is a beautiful bride and Hindus and Muslims are her two eyes. . . . If one of them is lost, this beautiful bride will have become ugly."[12]

Sayyid Aḥmad exemplifies and articulates the existential dilemma in which Indian Muslims found themselves: while attached to India and a personal friend of many Hindus, the absoluteness of Islamic faith and the sociopolitical order it envisages make it impossible to meet Hinduism on equal terms. While prepared to recognize the affinity of Hindu *bhakti* and Muslim devotion, the Islamic *sharīa* and the Hindu *dharma* are irreconcilable. The desire to live in peace together in one country is constantly undermined by the attempt to shape private and public life by the *sharīa*. If Sayyid Aḥmad is, rightly or wrongly, said to be the first advocate of Pakistan, he also shows how the partition of India along religious, communal lines happened as the result of events not controlled by anyone in particular, rather than through the deliberate action of those who became its executors. This is becoming clearer the closer we get to that fateful event.

Muhammed Alī (1878–1931), one of the architects of the All-India Muslim League, founded in 1906 in Dacca an organization that lobbied for the reservation of a disproportionate number of Muslim representative seats. He was torn between his feelings for an India inhabited by members of all religions and an Islamic state. He became a major influence on Mohammed Alī Jinnāḥ (1876–1948) a brilliant lawyer and erstwhile leading member of the Indian Congress:

> He seemed on the way to leading India; he founded Pakistan instead. For much of his life he championed Hindu-Muslim unity; later he demanded, obtained, and, for a year, ran a separate Muslim homeland. Neither Sunni nor mainstream Shiite, his family belonged to the small Khoja or Ismaili community, lead by the Aga Khan, yet Muhammed Alī Jinnāḥ was in the end the leader of India's Muslims. Anglicized and aloof in manner, incapable of oratory in an Indian tongue, keeping his distance from mosques, opposed to the mixing of religion and politics, he became inseparable, in that final phase, from the cry Islam in danger.[13]

Jinnāḥ's career is symptomatic for the events that lead to the creation of Pakistan: it had nothing to do with religion, either Muslim or Hindu, and everything with communalism, the instrumentalizing of religion for sociopolitical and economic purposes. Muslim leaders had threatened on and off to lobby for a separate Muslim state should England give independence to India. Most of these hints were taken as mere tactical moves to pressure the Hindu majority in Congress to make special concessions. When, however, after the end of World War II the Muslim-Hindu tensions and riots increased and the Labor Government in England was pushing for a speedy dissolution of the Empire, even Gandhi and Nehru agreed to Jinnāḥ's demand to divide India, to separate the majority Muslim provinces from the rest of India and to create two successor nations to British India: Pakistan[14] and the Republic of India or Bhārat. The inhabitants of former British India should be free to choose which of the two states they wanted to live in, and mass migrations involving tens of millions of people began. Nobody had foreseen that the mass migration would soon turn into a mass slaughter: millions perished in probably the worst communal conflict that India had ever seen. If the politicians had believed that the Muslim problem in India could be solved in that way, they found themselves soon badly mistaken. Many Muslims stayed on in Bhārat, where they had been born, and continued to be a thorn in the side of Hindu nationalists. In the three wars that Bhārat fought with Pakistan—the second of which ended in the dismembering of Pakistan and the creation of an independent Bangladesh—Bhārat always proved stronger.

Kashmir, which Bhārat claimed its own because it was ruled by a traditional Hindu royal family in spite of its Muslim majority, has remained a bone of contention between Bhārat and Pakistan for the last half century. Pakistan-supported militants occupied almost half the state and almost daily incidents are reported of bombs detonated in markets and bus stations and attacks by guerillas.

If anything, Hindu-Muslim confrontations in India have intensified in the last few years—Godhra and its aftermath is just one of many examples. Hindu minorities in Pakistan and Bangladesh either fled or found themselves exposed to harassment—partition has neither worked for the Muslims nor for the Hindus. Whether the reunification advocated by some Hindu parties would work is another question. In over fifty years of separate statehood, Pakistan and India have developed different cultures that may no longer be compatible.

## MUSLIM-HINDU DIALOGUE

There is no doubt that many prominent as well as ordinary Hindus and Muslims have throughout the past centuries attempted to reach out to each other and to cooperate rather than separate. Muslims and Hindus, especially those with higher education, normally mixed freely and worked together without emphasizing religious differences. If mutual antipathies often prevailed, if India was divided along Hindu-Muslim lines, and if frequent Muslim-Hindu riots disrupt the lives of millions that only shows how difficult a task Hindu-Muslim dialogue is.

Mahātmā Gandhi, who had worked throughout his life for a reconciliation between Hindus and Muslims, was murdered by a Hindu fanatic who believed that "Mohammed Gandhi" had unduly favored the Muslims. Gandhi went to great length to demonstrate his sincere belief in Hindu-Muslim dialogue. He read the Quran, he inserted Muslim prayers in his *Āśram Bhajanāvalī*, and even joined the Khilāfat Movement in the belief that Indian Muslims would recognize his sympathies for their cause. He undertook a fast to the death to stop Hindu-Muslim riots in Calcutta, and he did everything in his power to care for Muslim refugees after partition. In the volume *To the Hindus and Muslims*[15] Anand Hingorani has collected hundred of texts in which Gandhi implores both Hindus and Muslims to overcome their differences peacefully on the basis of their religion. Unfortunately, the voices of hatred prevailed. One of the Mahātmā's grandsons, Rajmohan Gandhi, entitled his study of eight Muslim leaders *Eight Lives: A Study of the Hindu-Muslim Encounter*, maintaining the hope that eventually Muslims and Hindus in India will come together.

Some other attempts in that direction should be mentioned without claiming to exhaust them. Z. Haq in *Prophet Mohammed in Hindu Scriptures* quotes the Quran to prove that Hindu-India also had its real prophets and that it, too, was part of Allah's covenant with humankind. He identifies Brahmā with Abraham, Sarasvatī with Sarah, and Manu with Noah. "Muslim historians of India hold the opinion that the graves of the prophets Shees and Ayub (Job) are in Ayodhyā, Uttar Pradesh."[16] It is especially the *Bhaviśya Purāṇa* that served as a key text to the claim that Hindu prophets gave witness of Prophet Mohammed's coming. Haq uses a series of fanciful etymological explanations of Indian words to demonstrate the presence of Islamic traditions in Hindu India.

More promising for Muslim-Hindu dialogue in depth seems Bikrama Jit Hasrat's detailed study of Dārā Shikūḥ[17]. Hasrat shows great sympathy for the enterprise this Mogul prince was engaged in and also exhibits considerable knowledge of Hinduism.[18] He quotes at length Dārā Shikūḥ's appreciative statements of Hindu thought and practice and shows throughout a personal interest in Hindu-Muslim harmony and understanding. There is no doubt that Dārā Shikūḥ had come closest to a Muslim religious appreciation and assimilation of Hinduism and that nobody since that time has come even near to the kind of inner and outer dialogue that he initiated. The fact that he was condemned as an apostate from Islam may have prevented Muslim scholars from taking up his agenda. Aurangzeb, however, is no longer in charge and the new environment of independent India should provide sufficient motivation, as well as the necessary intellectual freedom within the Indian Muslim community, to carry on the Hindu-Muslim dialogue in the spirit of Dārā Shikūḥ.

A comparative approach is taken by Azad Faruqi, who in his *Sufism and Bhakti* draws sympathetic parallel portraits of Jalāl-al-dīn Rūmī (d. 1273) and Paramahamsa Ramakrishna (1834–1886). He takes care to distance *bhakti* with its "emphasis on the devotional approach towards the deity and the monotheistic concept of the object of worship" from "the *Ṛgveda* or Brahmanical tradition which conceived of the highest objects of religion in the form of many gods and goddesses and attempted to reach them though sacrifices or *yajña*."[19] After a fairly detailed description of the major Vaiṣṇava *sampradāyas* the author draws parallels between Muslim *ishq* and Hindu *bhakti* as exemplified by Rūmī and by Ramakrishna. He concludes that with all their differences of approach and style there is no doubt that "Mawlana Rūmī and Śrī Ramakrishna were personalities of the highest spiritual order. Divine love was for them the one passion that inspired their whole lives, and we think that from this study it would not be wrong to infer that love is that strong current that, barring ethnic and societal differences, reveals the essential unity of all mankind and the unity of its true object of veneration."[20]

While Hindus often pride themselves of their religious tolerance there is little serious Hindu theological literature that engages Islam. At a time when Islam was already a powerful presence in India, including Islamic schools and Sufi orders, Hindus continued writing polemical literature against a nonexistent Buddhism as well as against a marginal Jainism and rival Hindu schools, not even mentioning Islam. Dāyānanda Sarasvatī, the 19th century Hindu reformer, in his *Satyārtha Prakāśa* devotes an entire chapter to Islam: he does not go much beyond heaping abuses on the Prophet and the Quran, initiating an anti-Muslim campaign especially in the Punjab. Rāmakrishna Paramahamsa claimed to have bodily seen the Prophet in a vision and generally assumed all religions to be the same, but there are no specific utterances that reveal that he knew much about Islam and its teachings.

The horrors that accompanied and followed the partition of India and the numerous murderous Muslim-Hindu confrontations of the last fifty years have generated more hatred than sympathy for Islam among Hindus, and Hindu extremists do not hesitate to broadcast: "Revenge on Islam must become the sole aim of life of every Hindu today. Islam has been shedding Hindu blood for centuries. This is something we should neither forget nor forgive . . . the day will come when Hinduism obliterates this cruel excuse of a religion off the face of India."[21]

Another website[22] has published a list of hundreds of Hindu temples that had been destroyed by Muslims, furnishing each entry with texts taken from Muslim historians or inscriptions on mosques that "glorify and justify the acts of the barbaric Muslim invaders by invoking Allah and the Koran. Thus this leads to the conclusion that Islam openly supports the criminal acts of loot, plunder, rape, murder, torment, torture and destruction."

Hindus have enduring memories, and the reminders of this rape of their culture are still all around them. No wonder that some demand the destruction of some of the most notorious Muslim monuments and the reconstruction of such famous sanctuaries as the Viśvanātha temple at Vārāṇasī and the great temple at Kṛṣṇa's birthplace in Mathurā.

## MUSLIMS AND SECULAR INDIA

Whereas Pakistan was founded explicitly as an Islamic state, Bhārat, the Republic of India, defined itself under Jawaharlal Nehru's guidance as a "socialist secular state," guaranteeing to all its citizens the freedom to practice their religion of choice and making none of them a state religion. Hindu parties like the Hindū Mahāsabhā and Hindu organizations like the Rāṣṭrīya Svayamsevak Saṅgh (RSS) kept pushing for a reunification of divided India under Hindu auspices and for the establishment of a *Hindū rāṣṭra* in Bhārat. The struggle between "secularists" and "Hindutvavādis" is still going on and is affecting not only Indian Muslims.

In the upper echelons of government, Bhārat has always preserved its secular and democratic ideals: Muslims rose to the highest office in the Republic of India. Zakir Husain (1897–1969), a staunch member of the Indian Congress under Mahātmā Gandhi's and Jawaharlal Nehru's leadership, an internationally recognized scholar and educator—he had been vice chancellor of Alīgarh Muslim University from 1948–1962—served as president of India from 1967–1969, after having been vice president under Sarvepalli Radhakrishnan from

Photo 37. Tāj Mahal: Agra

1962–1965. Even the BJP-dominated Bajpāī government asked in 2002 the internationally recognized Muslim scientist Abdul Kalam to become president of Bhārat—perhaps the clearest indication of its intention of keeping India multicultural and multireligious, as it had been since Independence.

If, as Svāmi Vivekānanda had said, the fate of Buddhism and Hinduism are historically and intellectually inextricably intertwined, the same is true of Islam and Hinduism in India. The massive presence of Islam in India and India's thousand-years-long Islamic past cannot be negated or eradicated. At the level of spirituality Hindus and Muslims have much in common and there are spiritual teachers who draw from both traditions and whose burial sites have become places of pilgrimage for both Hindus and Muslims. Muslims have famous academic institutions of world renown in India: besides the Alīgarh Muslim University there is its offspring, the Jamia Millia College in Delhi and the Great Muslim Seminary in Deoband. The scholars and leaders of these schools should play a key role in developing a constructive dialogue with secular as well as with Hindu India. The greatest hindrance to such a dialogue is communalism: the exploitation of the fears of Muslims for political ends by party politicians. Muslims must come to appreciate that they can live in freedom in a predominantly and originally Hindu country. Hindus on their side have to be generous, let the past be past and also appreciate the positive contributions that Muslims have made to Indian culture: India today would be unthinkable without the Tāj Mahal and the Red Fort, without the Jamī Masjid and Akbar's tomb, or without the treasures of miniature painting and of the musical culture that were introduced by Muslim rulers in India. All nations on earth have experienced in their histories bitterness and injustice inflicted by insiders and outsiders and it is important for their own survival and prosperity that the living should not continue the quarrels of the dead. There is nothing in the nature of either Islam or Hinduism that would prevent people from understanding each other and from cooperating for the sake of building a new great nation called India.

CHAPTER THIRTY

# Hindu Reforms and Reformers

> Religion must establish itself as a rational way of living. If ever the spirit is to be at home in this world and not merely a prisoner or a fugitive, secular foundations must be laid deeply and preserved worthily. Religion must express itself in reasonable thought, fruitful actions and right social institutions.
>
> —S. Radhakrishnan, *My Search for Truth*

The history of Hinduism consists of a series of challenges and responses to challenges, reforms and efforts to resist change, struggle between those who tenaciously cling to tradition and those who wish to go with the times. It took centuries before Hinduism responded as a body to the challenge that Buddhism and Jainism had posed—it needed a Maṇḍana Miśra and a Śaṅkara to consolidate and reform Hinduism and to return the initiative to it. While much of this response was creative—advancing the theory and practice of Hindus over against the times of Buddha and Mahāvīra, the reaction to the challenge posed by Islam was totally negative and defensive. Except for a few movements, which became more or less independent from mainstream Hinduism,[1] the Hindu reaction to Islam was one of withdrawing, letting the shutters down, hardening customs and beliefs, not admitting any change. That did not prevent Hinduism from decaying and corrupting. The picture that eighteenth-century visitors to India draw is not only one of a Mogul rule no longer really in control, but also of a Hinduism—still the majority religion—beset by cruel customs, superstition, and abysmal ignorance.

Foreign visitors considered Hinduism a hopeless case and expected it to die of degeneration within a century. To quote but one example, here is a page from a book that appeared in its second edition in Madras in 1900, published by the Christian Literature Society for India, entitled *India Hindu and India Christian or, What Hinduism Has Done for India and What Christianity Would*

*Do for It: An Appeal to Thoughtful Hindus.* It enumerates as the fruits of Hinduism: Ill-health or shortness of life, poverty, national ignorance, intellectual weakness, despotism and religious intolerance, polytheism, animal worship, idolatry, pantheism, the sanction of robbery, murder and human sacrifices and promises to India under Christian rule better health and longer life, increase of wealth, diffusion of true knowledge, intellectual strength, national greatness, the brotherhood of man. There is—for us a century later—some irony in the following remark:

> England is now one of the richest countries in the world. One great cause of this is her commerce. Every sea is traversed by her ships; her merchants are to be found in every land where wealth can be gained. The Parsis have copied their example and have similarly benefited. Hinduism teaches the people of India to regard all foreigners as impure *mlecchas*. "In their country the twice-born must not even temporarily dwell." The folly of this is now acknowledged by enlightened men; but the above is the doctrine of Hinduism."[2]

Hindus have changed. So has England. History has not been kinder to the following assertion made in the same book under the title: "Hinduism Incapable of Reform."

> All intelligent Hindus admit that great reforms are needed to purify Hinduism. Many think that this is all that is necessary to render it worthy of retention. Some even affirm that it would then occupy one of the highest places among the religions of the world.
>
> Let the changes necessary to reform Hinduism up to the light of the nineteenth century be considered:
>
> 1. Reformed Hinduism should be neither polytheistic nor pantheistic, but monotheistic. All intelligent men now believe in the existence of only one true God. There are no such beings as Viṣṇu, Śiva, Sarasvatī, Durgā, or the thirty three crores of the Hindu Pantheon. The Viṣṇu *bhakti*, the Śiva *bhakti*, etc., would all come to an end. No sectarian marks would be worn. The blasphemous assertion *aham Brahmāsmi*, I am Brahma, would no longer be made.
> 2. All idols would be destroyed, and no longer worshipped as giving false and degrading ideas of God. The indecent images on some temples would be broken down. There would no longer be Vaiṣṇava nor Śaiva temples.
> 3. The Vedas, the Code of Manu, the *Rāmāyaṇa*, *Mahābhārata*, the Purāṇas, etc., as teaching polytheism, pantheism, containing debasing representations of God, unjust laws, false history, false science, false morals, would no longer be considered sacred books.
> 4. Hindu worship in temples would cease. Festivals would no longer be celebrated. Pilgrimages to supposed holy places would come to an end. *Pūjā* to idols would not be observed in private families.

5. As Hindu temples contain only small shrines for idols, buildings like churches would require to be erected, in which people might assemble for public worship, and receive instruction in the duties of life.
6. Caste would no longer be recognised, and the brotherhood of man would be acknowledged; all caste distinctions would cease.

Every one of the above changes is necessary to meet the view of enlightened men.

Take away sweetness from sugar, and it is no longer sugar; deprive a man of reason, and he is no longer a human being. Hinduism without its gods, its sacred books, its temples, its worship, its caste, would be no longer Hinduism, but an entirely different religion, like the Sadhārana Brahmo Samāj. It would be simply Theistic."[3]

This was not only the opinion of prejudiced Christian missionaries but was also shared by the highly regarded Professor Friedrich Max Müller whose first edition of the *Ṛgveda* with Sāyaṇa's commentary had made him famous in the world of Indology. "Brahminism as a religion," he wrote, "cannot stand the light of the day. The worship of Śiva or Viṣṇu and all other popular deities is of the same, nay, in many cases of a more degraded and savage character than the worship of Jupiter, Apollo and Minerva; it belongs to a stratum of thought which is long buried beneath our feet, it may live on, like the lion and tiger, but the mere advance of free thought and civilised light will extinguish it."[4]

Although he had never visited India, he denounced in strong terms the popular religiosity of Hindus that he knew only from biased accounts of foreigners:

> It is true that there are millions of men, women and children in India, who fall down before the stone images of Viṣṇu with his four arms, riding on a creature half-bird half-man, or sleeping on a serpent; worship Śiva, a monster with three eyes, riding naked on a bull, with a necklace of skulls for his ornaments. There are human beings who still believe in a god of war, Kartikeya, with six faces, riding on a peacock and holding bow and arrows in his hands; and who invoke a god of success, Gaṇeśa, with four hands and an elephant's head, sitting on a rat. Nay it is true, that in the broad daylight of the nineteenth century, the figure of the goddess Kālī is carried though the streets of her own city, Calcutta, her wild dishevelled hair reaching to her feet. With a necklace of human heads, her tongue protruded from her mouth, her girdle stained with blood. . . . How long this living dead of national religion in India may last, who can tell?[5]

Hinduism, as we well know now, has been capable of reform. It has not given up its belief in Viṣṇu, Śiva, or Durgā, it has not abandoned its images, has not ceased to worship in temples. Pilgrimages are as popular as ever, *pūjā* continues to be offered in homes.

Contrary to all predictions Hinduism not only survived but recovered and in many ways may be today stronger than ever. The revival and regeneration of Hinduism is largely the achievement of Hindu reformers who for the past two centuries tirelessly worked for the betterment of their country on the basis of religion. There have been too many of them to mention them individually. The issues they concerned themselves with and the institutions they founded to address these concerns are too numerous again to find place within such a short survey.[6] Briefly one can say that they tried first to rid Hinduism from practices that were perceived to be inhuman and cruel, like the burning of widows and female infanticide. Some felt that the strictures of caste should go, especially the disrespect shown to people who were considered to be outside the caste system altogether. Improving the social standing and the education of women became a major issue too. While it may be admitted that these reforms were effected under the impact of a new social consciousness that was sharpened by the contact with representatives of Christianity and often in response to accusations by Western missionaries, the religious reform properly speaking, the intensification of devotion, the purification of ritual, and the new seriousness shown in the study of the religious classics were Hindu inspired phenomena that in the end turned out to be more important for Hinduism.

Reforms and reformers brought new tension to Hindu society: the tension between the secular and the religious, which in that form was unknown to traditional Hinduism. Western secular civilization became both a fascination and a terror to Hindus. Some found it so attractive that they were able to envision India as a secular society with Hinduism as the private mystical religion of those who had a taste for it, mere interiority and piety. Other considered the onrush of secularism a challenge to recapture the *dharma-kṣetra*, to re-hinduise the public life of India.

Svāmi Vivekānanda, himself one of the foremost of Hindu reformers, expressed it well when he said:

> There are two great obstacles on our path in India: the Scylla of old orthodoxy and the Charybdis of modern European civilization. Of these two I vote for the old orthodoxy and not for the Europeanized system, for, the old orthodox man may be ignorant, he may be crude, but he is a man, he has a faith, while the Europeanized man has no backbone, he is a mass of heterogeneous ideas picked up at random from every source—and these ideas are unassimilated, undigested, unharmonized. . . .[7]
>
> This is my objection against the reformers. The orthodox have more faith and more strength in themselves, in spite of their crudeness. But the reformers simply play into the hands of the Europeans and pander to their vanity. Our masses are gods as compared with those of other countries. This is the only country where poverty is not a crime.[8]

## A NINETEENTH-CENTURY HINDU RENAISSANCE

The momentum of Hindu reforms, especially in the area of social customs, gained considerable strength in the early nineteenth century, when several European powers had established themselves in India, welcomed by many Hindus as liberators from the corrupt Muslim rule and admired for their technical achievements. There is an extensive literature in English on these so-called Hindu Renaissance movements; since many of the modern Hindu reformers wrote and spoke English, it is the most easily accessible area of Hinduism for people without knowledge of Indian languages. The sheer bulk of books available in this area and the captivating attribute *modern* has led many people in the West to believe that these modern Hindu reform movements are identical with contemporary Hinduism, except perhaps for a few remnants of "unreformed" Hinduism that one need not take seriously. Quite on the contrary, these modern Hindu movements, despite their appeal to Westerners and Westernized Hindus, represent only a small fraction of actual Hinduism, which is still much more rooted in its ancient and medieval traditions than inclined toward the modern movements.

The real Hindu Renaissance took place in traditional Hinduism: the traditional *saṃpradāyas* consolidated their influence; generous donations made it possible to restore hundreds of old and build thousands of new temples; grassroots religious organizations gave new life to the religious observations and festivities. This cautionary remark seems necessary for gaining a correct perspective when we now go on to consider a number of reformers and their work.

The first of the really significant modern Hindu reformers was Ram Mohan Roy (1772–1833), who was called the "Father of Modern India" by his admirers; a genial and many-sided personality.[9] His father was a Vaiṣṇava, his mother came from a Śākta family, and as a boy he was sent to Patna to study at the Muslim University, learning Arabic, Persian, and becoming interested in Sufism. This turned him against image-worship, an issue over which he fell out with his father. He left for Tibet. His father, however, gave in under the condition that he spend twelve years at Vārāṇasī, the center of Hindu learning, before returning to his home in Bengal. Ram Mohan Roy engaged in the study of Sanskrit and Hindu scriptures; but he also studied English and entered the service of the East India Company at Calcutta. In 1814 he left its service and devoted himself fully to religious propaganda and reform. He tried to purify Hinduism by returning to the Upaniṣads and translated several books. He sought connection with the English missionaries, who had opened a college at Serampore (modern Śrīrāmpur), not far from Calcutta. He studied Greek and Hebrew in order to translate the Bible into Bengalī. The publication of a little pamphlet, *The Precepts of Jesus: The Guide to Peace and Happiness*, estranged him from both his Hindu friends and the missionaries. The former accused him of canvassing for Christianity, the latter objected to his Hinduizing of

Christianity. In the course of quite bitter polemics Ram Mohan Roy accused the missionaries of having misinterpreted the words of Jesus; a reproach that has been leveled against Christian missions ever since. Ram Mohan Roy won a triumph in his battle against the practice of *satī*, the (not always voluntary) burning of women together with their deceased husbands. As a boy he had witnessed the forced *satī* of a much-liked sister-in-law that had stirred him so profoundly that he vowed to devote his life to the abolition of this cruel custom, allowed by the British officials as part of their policy of noninterference with local religions. Ram Mohan Roy succeeded in convincing the government that *satī* did not form part of the original and pure Hindu *dharma* and thus, against violent opposition, the anti-*satī* law was passed.[10] Interestingly, a number of prominent Englishmen, among them the famous Sanskrit scholar H. H. Wilson, supported Hindu orthodoxy against Ram Mohan Roy, arguing that *satī* was part of the Hindu religious tradition and that England's policy of not interfering with religious practices should also apply there.[11] It is an ominous sign of the times that more than a century after the abolition of *satī* and the prohibition of infanticide by the British Government of India, instances are dramatically on the rise where young women are burnt to death by their husbands or their husbands' relations in order to obtain (officially abolished!) dowry and that thousands of cases of poisoning of female babies have recently been reported among just one group in South India.[12]

Several times Ram Mohan Roy tried to organize a group of people to begin a new religious movement, embodying his ideas of religion. He finally succeeded five years before his death with the *Brahmo Samāj*, somehow combining Hinduism and Christianity. Ram Mohan Roy kept his sacred thread and wanted to remain a faithful Hindu. Hindu orthodoxy, however, excommunicated him. Ram Mohan Roy also became instrumental in establishing English schools in Calcutta, emphasizing the value of modern, scientific education. In its heyday many Europeans thought the *Brahmo Samāj* would become the future religion of India; subsequent history has proved the traditional streams of Hinduism stronger than this courageous new attempt.[13]

Ram Mohan Roy's successor was Debendranath Tagore, called Maharṣi, the father of the more famous Nobel Prize winner for literature, Rabindranath Tagore. Maharṣi founded a Bengalī paper and a school for Brahmo missionaries with the explicit purpose of checking the spread of Christian missions. He also openly broke with orthodox Hinduism by declaring the Vedas as neither free from error nor inspired. His book *Brahmo Dharma*, an anthology from the Upaniṣads and *Smṛtis*, became the official catechism of the movement.[14] With the entrance of Keshub Chandra Sen (1838–1884), some explosive issues were brought into the Brahmo Samāj. Since Keshub was not a Brahmin, several members left in protest. The development of peculiar rituals to replace Hindu *saṃskāras* and Keshub's close connections with Christians led to a split within the Samāj: Debendranath Tagore remained with the Ādi Samāj, whereas Keshub became the leader of the Brahmo Samāj of India, which due to his extravagance suffered another split in later years. Keshub developed tremendous social activity, collecting funds for victims of famines and floods, founding schools for boys and girls, a workers' association, agitating for literacy and for a civil marriage legislation against the widespread Indian custom of child marriage, pleading for inter-caste marriage and widow remarriage. Ironically, he married his own daughter off while she was still a child—an incident that estranged quite many of his followers. In his youth he lectured enthusiastically on Christ; later he considered himself a superman and expected to be worshipped as such. He preached the *New Dispensation*, to replace the Old and the New Testaments. While he was becoming increasingly engrossed in ideas like these, the social activities of the *Brahmo Samāj* declined.[15]

Whereas the largely idealistic *Brahmo Samāj* is all but defunct as an organized movement, its more radical and often fanatical sister foundation, the *Ārya Samāj*, not only continues to attract members to its local centers but has also spawned a number of notable organizations exerting considerable influence on India's present-day politics.

Svāmi Dāyānanda Sarasvatī (1824–1883) from Morvi in Gujarat, describes how he lost faith in Śiva and image worship while keeping night vigil on *Śivarātrī*, compelled to do so by his father. He saw rats climbing onto the image that was powerless to defend itself. Meanwhile his pious father was solidly asleep. At the age of twenty-four, just before he was to enter a marriage arranged by his parents, he fled from home in search of the means to overcome death. After twelve years of wandering from one guru to the other, dissatisfied with all, he met Svāmi Virājānanda Sarasvatī of Mathurā. A temperamental man, the blind old svami succeeded in completely subduing the restless spirit of Dāyānanda and prophesized that he would become the restorer of Hinduism of his age. His was a strictly orthodox Vedic religion, rejecting the religion of the epics and the Purāṇas, the *Saṃhitās* and the *Āgamas*, as corrupt and untrue. In his *Satyārtha Prakāśa* Dāyānanda lays down the principles of his *sanātana dharma*, quoting Vedas, Upaniṣads, the *Manusmṛti*, and some *Dharmasūtras*. The last two chapters are devoted to a refutation of Islam and Christianity. A quotation from the Bible induces the *samīkṣaka*, literally, "inquisitor," to ask for its meaning. The Īsāī, representing Christianity, gives an unsatisfactory answer. A dialogue ensues in which the Ārya Samājist proves his superiority over the man of the Bible. He closes by saying that the Bible is a bunch of lies and that only the Vedas teach truth. In practice the Ārya Samāj, founded in 1875 in Bombay, went further, using persuasion or even moral and physical violence to reconvert Muslim and Christians. The Ārya Samāj also established traditional *gurukulas*, training institutions, in which children from the age of four are brought up strictly along Vedic lines.

After initial successes in Punjab, Dāyānanda Sarasvatī shifted his headquarters to Lahore and plunged into numerous social and religious activities. After his death the *Ārya Samāj* split into a conservative branch that had its center in the Kangrī Gurukula, now DAV University, and the progressives who kept their headquarters in the DAV College, Lahore. The Mahātmā Party became more and more aggressive, and its leader, Śraddhānanda, was shot dead by a Muslim in 1925. They founded many schools all over India and started many activities with the aim of spreading Vedic culture. They tried to counteract Christian missions by means both fair and foul and performed the *śuddhi* ceremony on thousands of converts.[16]

In a very real sense one can also include Mahātmā Gandhi among the great Hindu reformers of the Indian Renaissance whose work had considerable impact on the West.[17] He never left any doubt about his Hindu identity. Thus he declared early on in his Indian career:[18]

> I call myself a *sanātani* Hindu because
>
> 1. I believe in the Vedas, the Upaniṣads, the Purāṇas and all that goes by the name of Hindu Scriptures, and therefore in *avatārs* and rebirth.
> 2. I believe in the *varṇāśrama dharma* in a sense, in my opinion, strictly Vedic, but not in its present popular and crude sense.
> 3. I believe in the protection of the cow in its much larger sense than the popular.
> 4. I do not disbelieve in idol worship.

He qualified and explained all these points in a lengthy commentary: "I have purposely refrained from using the words 'divine origin' in reference to the Vedas or any other scriptures: For I do not believe in the exclusive divinity in the Vedas. I believe the Bible, the Koran and the Zend Avesta to be as much divinely inspired as the Vedas. My belief in the Hindu scriptures does not require me to accept every word and every verse as divinely inspired. . . . I do most emphatically repudiate the claim (if they advance any such) of the present Shankaracharyas and Shastris to give a correct interpretation of the Hindu scriptures."[19]

The great merit of Gandhi and of his disciples was their tolerance and a genuinely religious spirit that comprises both love of God and service to humanity. Many Gandhians were engaged in activities designed to overcome the hostility and exclusivity of the various religions, most notably the "Gandhian Patriarch" Kaka Kalelkar, who started a *Viśva Samanvaya Saṅgha*, working toward a "familyhood of religions."[20]

## HINDUISM REACHING OUT FOR THE WHOLE WORLD

The best known of all the Hindu reform movements is the Ramakrishna Mission, founded by Svāmi Vivekānanda (1863–1902), a disciple of Paramahaṃsa Rāmakrishna (1836–1886). Rāmakrishna (Figure 30.1), a temple priest at Dakṣineśvar and a mystical devotee of Kālī, became a source of religious renewal for a large number of Bengalis who met him during his lifetime.[21] Totally withdrawn and averse to any organization or reformist activity, after his death

Figure 30.1. Ramakrishna Paramahamsa

he nevertheless became the central figure in the world movement initiated by his favorite disciple after the latter's appearance at the world Parliament of Religions in Chicago in 1893. Touring America and Europe, Svāmi Vivekānanda brought home to India a new self-consciousness of Hinduism and a sense of social mission that induced him to work restlessly for the improvement of his countrymen through relief organizations, schools, hospitals, and innumerable other activities. Basically an Advaitin, he was open to the other *mārgas* and also to religions other than Hinduism, though he considered them inferior and spiritually underdeveloped. The Rāmakrishna Mission is a well-organized community today, with some seven hundred permanent members and a large number of associated workers, maintaining several colleges, high schools, hostels, hospitals and publishing an impressive amount of religious literature. It also established, with grants from the Indian Government and the Ford Foundation, the well-known Institute of Culture in Calcutta. Svāmi Vivekānanda inspired Hindu India with immense pride and a sense of mission. He articulated the rationale for the new Hindu religious movements in the West in the following manner:

> We Hindus have now been placed, under God's providence, in a very critical and responsible position. The nations of the West are coming to us for spiritual help. A great moral obligation rests on the sons of India to fully equip themselves for the work of enlightening the world on the problems of human existence.[22]

> Once more the world must be conquered by India. This is the dream of my life. I am anxiously waiting for the day when mighty minds will arise, gigantic spiritual minds who will be ready to go forth from India to the ends of the world to teach spirituality and renunciation, those ideas which come from the forests of India and belong to Indian soil only. Up India, and conquer the world with your spirituality. . . . Ours is a religion of which Buddhism, with all its greatness, is a rebel child and of which Christianity is a very patchy imitation.[23]

The Rāmakrishna Mission, as is well known, not only promotes a nonsectarian (neo-) Hinduism but also a kind of religious universalism. Rāmakrishna is the source of the widely accepted "all-religions-are-the-same" theory. Accordingly, the Rāmakrishna Mission does not only spread Hinduism in the West but also invites representatives of other religions to its temples and centers in India to speak about their own traditions.

Svāmi Vivekānanda inspired many young people in India not only to join his mission and devote themselves to the causes of reform and uplift but also to continue his rearticulation of Hinduism and its application to the modern world as well as its reaching out to the West.

Aurobindo Ghose, beginning as a nationalist firebrand, became one of the foremost spiritual leaders, not only of India but beyond, from his exile in Pondichéry. His followers are not organized in an order, but their sense of mission is strong and active, as can be seen in the development of Auroville, a city, which tries to realize and put into practice the principles of Aurobindo's spirituality.[24]

In the eyes of educated Westerners the most impressive figure of twentieth-century neo-Hinduism was probably Dr. Sarvepalli Rādhākrishnan. Educated in Protestant mission schools in South India, well read in Eastern and Western philosophical and religious literature, a successful diplomat and politician, a prolific writer and an excellent speaker, he seemed to embody what all were looking for: purified, spiritualized, nonsectarian Hinduism, the "religion of the spirit" and "the world religion of the future," a valid and final answer to all the great questions of our time. As president of India he served, in an eminent way, as the "conscience of the nation" and wherever he spoke he stressed the importance of spirituality, regardless of his audience. More than any other representative of the Indian intelligentsia, Dr. Radhakrishnan took up also the concrete problems of India, attempting to contribute a religious dimension to their solution.[25]

Universalism and worldwide validity of its principles is a claim that many exponents of Hinduism make—both at home and abroad. Few however, would go as far as M. S. Golwalkar, the former leader of the RSS, who wrote: "The mission of reorganizing the Hindu people on the lines of their unique national genius which the Sangh has taken up is not only a process of true national regeneration of Bhārat but also the inevitable precondition to realize the dream of world unity and human welfare . . . it is the grand world-unifying thought of Hindus alone that can supply the abiding basis for human brotherhood. This knowledge is in the safe custody of the Hindus alone. It is a divine trust, we may say, given to the charge of the Hindus by destiny."[26]

A great many well-known, respected, and popular representatives of Hinduism of the more charismatic type, who have their major audience in India, have attracted Western followers who very often establish centers in their own countries, propagating the words and works of their masters.

Ramaṇa Maharṣi (1879–1950) has been among the greatest and deepest spiritual influences coming from India in recent years. He was not educated in the traditional sense, but he intuited Advaita Vedānta and became something like a Socrates among the Indian yogis. He relentlessly questioned his visitors: "Who are You?" till they lapsed into silence, arriving finally at some intimation of their true self. Even after his death the place where he lived is somehow charged with spiritual power and has become a center of pilgrimage for his devotees.[27]

Svāmi Śivānanda (d. 1964), the founder of the Divine Life Society with headquarters at Śivānandāśram in Rishikesh, began as a physician before he turned *saṃnyāsi*. His interest, however, continued to be devoted to body and soul. At Rishikesh his followers collect herbs to produce Āyurvedic medicines, and disciples from many countries are living a religious life that intends to synthesize the great world religions.[28]

Photo 38. Ramaṇa Maharṣi [Ramana Ashram Annamalai]

Speaking of Hindu reform Movements one cannot leave out the *Theosophical Society*, although it was initiated by non-Indians and still has a largely cosmopolitan membership with an agenda that is global. Founded by the Russian-born Helena Blavatsky and the American Colonel Henry Olcott in New York in 1875, it moved its headquarters in 1905 to Adyar, then a suburb of Madras (now Chennai). One of the most active early members was Annie Besant (1847–1933). As an Irish woman she joined in defiance of the British Indian Administration the Indian National Congress, who elected her in 1917 as President of the Annual Meeting in Calcutta. In her book *Hindu Ideals* she admonished Hindus: "And if Hindus do not maintain Hinduism, who shall save it? India alone can save India, and India and Hinduism are one. Without Hinduism India has no future." She also challenged Hindus to spread the message of the 'spiritual East' to the 'soulless, materialistic West.' Together with an early member of the Theosophical Society, Bhagvan Das, she produced *An Advanced Textbook of Hindu Religion and Ethics*. Today, the Theosophical Society has a worldwide presence. At the headquarters in Adyar an important Oriental research center with a large collection of manuscripts has been established that also publishes several series of studies and text editions and a reputable scholarly journal *Bhahmavidyā*.

J. Krishnamurti, groomed to be the *avatāra* of the twentieth century by Annie Besant, developed into quite an independent man, denouncing his mother-in-God and theosophy. He became known in his own right as a lecturer and writer on spiritual topics.[29]

Among the better-known women saints of our time was Mā Ānandamayī, with establishments in Vārāṇasī, Vṛṇdāvana, and Mumbāī and quite a considerable following who consider her a living deity.[30]

Paramahamsa Yogānanda, author of the *Autobiography of a Yogi* and founder of the Yoga Fellowship of California,[31] is far better known in the United States than in India.

Mahesh Yogi Maharishi, became the founder guru of the International Transcendental Meditation Society.[32]

Svāmi Bhaktivedānta, at a very advanced age established the Krishna Consciousness Movement in the United States.[33]

Svāmi Taposwāmi Mahārāj, quite well known in his own right,[34] has become more famous through his world-touring disciple Svāmi Cinmayānanda, who not only gave well-advertised Gītā lectures in big Indian cities but has also founded Sandeepany Sadhanalaya, a training institution for Hindu missionaries in Bombay.[35] He was assisted by Subramuniaswami, an American convert to Śaivism, to found a center in California.

One of the most colorful of the contemporary saints is easily Śrī Sathya Sāī Bābā, (b. 1924) sporting a bright red silk robe and an Afro hairdo. As a boy of fourteen he declared that he had no more time for such mundane things as going to school, announcing that he was Sāī Bābā and that his devotees

Photo 39. Headquarters of the Theosophical Society: Adyār/Chennai

were calling for him. The Sāī Bābā he was referring to was a well-known saint, living during the first decades of the twentieth century in Śīrdī (Mahārāṣṭra) and who is credited with many miracles, even now appearing to people in their dreams and initiating them.[36] The first miracle of the now living Sāī Bābā, who was eighty in 2004, was to create sweets for his playmates and flowers for the villagers of Puthaparthi his home village, at which he later established his impressive headquarters, Prasanthi Nilayam. The sacred ashes that he now creates (following the lead of the old Sāī Bābā, on whose images often a curious ashlike substance is forming) is said to have miraculous properties to effect cures in sickness and to accord mental relief. Modern as he is, he also creates photographs of his own holy person out of nowhere and distributes them, still damp, to his followers. His healing powers are said to be phenomenal and people come from far and wide so that he may help their bodies and their souls. He is said to be able to read thoughts and to have the gift of prophecy and of multilocation. Thus he speaks: "Trust always in me and lay your burden upon me; I shall do the rest; It is my task to prepare you for the grace of Bhagvān, when you receive it, everything else will be simple." He does not demand any special exercises, only trust: "Sāī is mother and father. Come to him without fear, doubt or hesitation. I am in your heart."[37] Sāī Bābā meanwhile has many congregations of followers in India and also in Western countries. There is a Śrī Sathya Sāī Trust that administers a number of educational, medical, and charitable institutions in India and abroad, a Radio Sāī and numerous websites that bring updated information on Sāī Bābā and the many activities of his devotees. Born in 1924, he predicted that he would live to an age of 95 and would reincarnate thereafter for a last time for the benefit of humankind.

One of the most notable living woman saints today is Mātā Amritānandamayī, who celebrated her fifty-third birthday in 2006. Her headquarters is the Amritapuri Ashram in Kollam (Kerala) where every day she meets hundreds of admirers and people who expect help in mundane needs. She is the founder of the Amrita Ayurveda Medical College at Vallikavu as well as of other hospitals in the area. She is conducting regularly mass marriages for her followers. Besides other charities—such as centers for the distribution of food and clothing—she has established the Amrita Nidhi pension program for destitute women.

## INDIAN SECULARIST CRITIQUE OF HINDUISM

The difference between orthodox and reformist Hinduism, so pronounced in the nineteenth century, is no longer easy to make out. Some of the reformist movements have settled into orthodoxies of their own, and some of the staunchest defenders of orthodoxy advocate quite radical reform. K. M. Munshi, a great literary and political figure and the mastermind behind the establishment of the influential Bhāratīya Vidyā Bhavan in Mumbāī, certainly as articulate a defender of Hinduism in our century as any, declared that the *varṇāśrama-dharma* was now obsolete and that "exercises in faith must be satisfying to the modern mind, ceremonies and rituals must be uplifting and religious symbols inspiring. Temples must be clean, set in a sanctified atmosphere, the music, accompanying prayers, must be soulful and the officiating priests must be men of learning and faith."[38]

The Śaṅkarācārya of Purī, Swāmi Niranjan Dev, considered the most conservative of the traditional defenders of *sanātana dharma*, is also quoted as having pleaded for the abolition of caste and class differences.

The difference between religious and secularists, however, has become more pronounced and is quite an issue in present-day India. Secularism in India emerged as an ideology with Hindu reform in the nineteenth century. Foreign-educated Indians, impressed by what they had seen in the "secular West" and impatient with the obscurantism of traditional religion, the interminable clashes between the religious communities and their obvious inability to agree on essentials of matters important for Indian society, pressed for a secular India. Thus, in spite of his close association with the devout Hindu Mahātmā Gandhi, the first premier of India, Jawaharlal Nehru, pushed through his concept of the Indian Republic as a "Secular Democracy" in contrast to the simultaneous emerging of Pakistan as an "Islamic theocracy." A whole generation of modern educated and highly placed Hindus distanced themselves from religion and went to work to transform India into a modern state with a secular outlook. While antireligious movements as such were few, pro-secular statements by intellectuals are quite pronounced. M. N. Roy's "Radical Humanism" is perhaps the best-known formulation of it.[39] Another Bengali philosopher, P. C. Chatterji came recently out with a spirited defense of *Secular Values for Secular India*. He goes into the recent history of communal rioting in India, identifying the narrow factionalism of the representatives of religious communities and pleading for a science-based secularism as the basis of Indian society.[40]

The urban modern educated class, more interested in careers and living standards than in traditional loyalties and pieties, is voicing often quite articulate critique of religious Hinduism. An important Indian weekly some years ago invited some prominent Indians to express their ideas on "the role of religion in our lives." One Hindu reader had the following to say:

> The influence of religion on our lives has been detrimental. The dependence on religion and religious gurus has reduced us to a state of helplessness and we are always tempted to look out for an invisible, higher power, which is supposed to solve all our problems. The common people are unable to understand the philosophy of religion and therefore they content themselves with ridiculous ceremonies, making a mockery of everything that is sublime and holy. The impossibility of practicing the lofty commands of religion,

> the lack of a synthesis between these high values and the daily demands of secular life and the endeavor of every Indian to pretend to live according to these ideals have made us the most hypocritical amongst all the peoples on earth. This hypocrisy pervades every aspect of our life. Also the false emphasis on the "other world" while we are engaged in securing an existence for ourselves here on this earth has made us the most corrupt of all nations—a people which shirks work and is always hoping that something will come, making fate responsible for its misfortune. If our religion, instead of teaching us renunciation, could give us guidance in our life and work to make this world a better place to live in, then we Indians, with all our masses of men and our economic potential could be one of the leading nations of the world. In short—our religion has taught us, instead of "elevating us to the state of spiritual ecstasy," to be hypocrites and like Triśaṅku we have lost touch with both heaven and earth. We have remained behind in the race for a higher living standard because of the queer belief that we could live in the twentieth century according to ideals that had been proclaimed long, long ago. The result is a hopeless stagnation in our spiritual values.[41]

Another modern Hindu, writing on "Our Changing Values"[42] called the present intellectual situation in India "A World of Make-Believe," deploring the aspects of hypocrisy and falseness that pervaded everything.

> A half-hearted mysticism justifying India's failure to face life squarely leads the Indian intellectual to a sphere where the individual human being loses his significance in the mumbo-jumbo of a sham-mysticism. A deep-rooted apathy towards change and development—born out of frustration and the certificates that the pseudo-intellectuals get from their fellow-travellers in the West have jointly created a world of make-believe. . . . To rub out the rugged edges of their spiritual bankruptcy many Indian intellectuals entertain some make-believe picture of India and use it as a sort of spiritual sandpaper. . . . Power has become the cornerstone of goodness. . . . The ordinary Indian bestows respect on the powerful. Even a cursory survey of the causes for the reverence of the Babas and Mas and astrologers will convince us that the average Indian does not respect them for any spiritual upliftment. He respects them for very mundane reasons—for getting promotions in his job, for being successful in business, for curing his diseases etc. Today he is finding that he can be more benefited by the politically powerful and that is why he has developed reverence for them.[43]

A major source of friction between the Hindu reformers and the secularizers are laws that affect Indian society as a whole. A case in point is the Hindu Marriage Act of 1956 that, with amendments of 1978, became signed into law in 1992 by the president of India. While still basically respecting the rights of the religious communities to follow their own traditions, the

Indian government drastically secularized Hindu marriage laws and legislated changes that go quite manifestly against the letter and the spirit of the traditional Hindu law.[44] Other points of conflict are the Hindu demand to ban cow slaughter all over India,[45] to prohibit the consumption of alcohol, the government control of Temple Boards, and the support of schools maintained by various religious communities.

Modern India's intellectuals were supposed to be the principal support of secularism, believed to be the only ideology capable of promoting harmony among the followers of the great diversity of religions in India. According to V. K. Sinha, "the major responsibility of accelerating the secularization of Indian society will rest on nongovernmental associations and groups. It is the press, the universities, the intellectuals and the artists who will have to take the initiative in promoting secularism in India."[46]

However, some leading intellectuals seem to have had second thoughts. Thus T. N. Madan, the director of the Institute of Economic Growth in Delhi, an internationally known social scientist, declared secularism as "the dream of a minority, which wants to impose its will upon history but lacks the power to do so under a democratically organised polity."[47] The great majority of Indians, Madan holds, are still guided by their religious traditions. These traditions are "totalizing," that is, they encompass the whole of life and do not permit a distinction between a "secular state" and a "private religion," typical for Western countries.[48]

That Hinduism, after having been abandoned and shrugged off as a relic from the past by the progressive, Westernized, modern educated Indians, is making a comeback is evident in all big cities in India. Among the more popular swāmis attracting large crowds also of young people are many with a modern scientific education, which they use to advantage in explaining the Vedas or the *Bhagavadgītā*. In many affluent, modern neighborhoods new temples are being built, *bhajan* groups are forming, and committees are established to support religious causes.

In the wake of the Ayodhyā agitation it became quite clear that while the by now fairly large modern educated Indian middle class may not be in favor of rioting and violence, it is basically sympathetic to the ideology of the Hindu movements.[49] Secularism as the West understood it has no chance in today's India. The best one could hope for is tolerance on a religious basis, the kind of Hinduism advocated by S. Radhakrishnan or Mahātmā Gandhi.[50]

Hindus can be very critical of their tradition too, but that should not mislead us into thinking that they are waiting for Westerners to solve their problems. Self-righteous as many Westerners still are, the social, psychological, and spiritual problems of the West are of such a magnitude that we should think twice before offering our precious advice to India. Even the most critical Indians admit at the end of their devastating self-criticism that they believe in the self-regenerating power of their culture and people and that—if they see any hope—they expect the solution of their difficulties to come from within their own culture rather than from without. Two world wars, racial and political tensions, flagrant greed and materialism have disillusioned India about the West's savior role, which it assumed in earlier centuries. The best we can do is to try to become partners in a worldwide community that comprises a great variety of cultures and ideologies coexisting side by side and interacting for the benefit of all.

CHAPTER THIRTY-ONE

# Mahātmā Gandhi

## *A Twentieth-Century* Karmayogi

> A leader of his people, unsupported by any outward authority: a politician whose success rests not upon craft nor the mastery of technical devices, but simply on the convincing power of his personality; a victorious fighter who has always scorned the use of force; a man of wisdom and humility, armed with resolve and inflexible consistency, who has devoted all his strength to the uplifting of his people and the betterment of their lot. . . . Generations to come, it may be, will scarce believe that such a one as this ever in flesh and blood walked upon this earth.
>
> —Albert Einstein, in *Ideas and Opinions*

*Gandhi*, the film, was, in many ways, a surprising success both outside India and inside. No doubt the acting of Ben Kingsley, the photography of Sir Richard Attenborough, and the dramatic mass scenes filmed in India did much to make it so attractive to so many. However, it surely also succeeded in getting something of Gandhi's own life and thought across, and Gandhi himself proved to be the main attraction.[1]

The fact that it was a Hindu who shot Gandhi, one of the extremists who believed that in the communal conflict Gandhi took the side of the Muslims, reveals the whole dilemma when highlighting Mahātmā Gandhi in a survey of Hinduism. Fully aware of the hostility against Gandhi from the politically right-wing Hindus, as well as of the disdain for him from many "secularists" and progressives, he may—with all his contradictions—serve as a live example of a modern Hindu and, at the same time, offer the opportunity to discuss substantive issues that have become worldwide concerns, issues that Gandhi farsightedly addressed already in his life and time. Gandhi's secretary Mahadev Desai issued in 1936 what came to be known as Gandhi's *Autobiography*.[2] Urged on and helped by his close collaborator, Rev. Andrews, Gandhi reported under the title "My Experiments with Truth" his inner development up to the year 1924. Then, he believed, he had reached the point in his life from where events could be interpreted on the basis of his by now mature convictions. The book has become a classic of twentieth-century spirituality and provides insight into the growth of possibly the greatest human being that the twentieth century has seen in the sphere of public life.

## AN AVERAGE INDIAN CHILDHOOD

Mohandas Karamchand Gandhi was born on October 2, 1869, in Porbandar, Gujarat. The Gandhis belonged to the Bania (traders) caste, although both his father and his paternal grandfather were premiers in princely states in Kāthiawār. Gandhi's mother was a devout Vaiṣṇava who used to pay daily visits to the temple and who kept many *vratas*. She imbued little Mohandas with her religious mind. Mohandas went to elementary school in Porbandar. Reports describe him as friendly, conscientious, and of average intelligence. His third engagement took place when he was seven (two earlier brides had died by then), followed by marriage at age thirteen. By then Gandhi had moved to Rajkot High School. He was a good student, but he did not read anything besides his textbooks. He preferred to be by himself and did not join the school sports. A somewhat older fellow student attempted to draw the overly introverted Mohandas out from his shell. He induced him to eat meat, to drink liquor, to smoke cigarettes, even to visit a brothel, from which he ran away, frightened. The crisis was getting serious. Gandhi called himself an atheist and planned to commit suicide in a temple. The performance of a religious drama effected a kind of conversion in him. He confessed all his wrongdoings to his father, asked for a penance, and never relapsed. The *Rāmacaritamānasa* of Tulasīdāsa, which he began to read and to love, was preparing him for a personal relationship with his God. After graduation from high school Gandhi entered Samaldas College in Bhavnagar in order to study law. He found his studies too demanding and returned home without quite knowing what to do with himself. A friend suggested he go to England. For an orthodox Hindu that was something unheard of. His mother categorically refused to give her permission. Later she relented under the condition that Mohandas would assure her by way of an oath not to eat meat, not to drink liquor, and not to touch any woman. Mohandas first thought of becoming a medical doctor. Here, again, Hindu taboos interfered. His brother made it clear to him that as a Vaiṣṇava he was not to have anything to do with corpses. His caste declared him impure and outcaste because of his "travels across the dark ocean." Mohandas kept his vows and realized his plans. Difficult as life in England was, he completed his law studies with honors and there came in touch with many persons who influenced his thinking decisively. He was introduced to Madame Blavatsky and Mrs. Annie Besant, the founder-leaders of the Theosophical Society. He read, for the first time, the

*Bhagavadgītā*, in a translation by Edwin Arnold. His roommate, Dr. Josia Oldfield, a vegetarian like Gandhi, wanted to convert him to Christianity and took him to Sunday sermons at the major churches. During a strike of longshoremen in 1899 together with a friend he visited Cardinal Mannings to express his appreciation for the help he had given to the strikers. Gandhi became fond of England and the English, and later in life he would say that his sojourn in London taught him to make a distinction between the British colonial government, which he detested, and the English people, whom he loved.[3]

## YEARS OF DECISION

After his exams at the Bar, Gandhi did not waste one day before returning to India. He was not interested in traveling through Europe, as did most of his compatriots, who had absolved their studies in England. Arriving in Rajkot in 1891 he underwent the purification ceremony prescribed by his caste-*pañcāyat*, paid his penance, and was fully accepted again. In his own home he began "reforming": he introduced oatmeal and cocoa for breakfast and insisted on European-style dress. He made the acquaintance of a young Jain, whose religiosity deeply impressed him. His debut as a lawyer was not very encouraging. When asked to defend a client in a minor legal matter, he lost his nerve and asked his client to look for another lawyer. He applied for a position as a high school teacher but did not possess the required papers. He finally earned a living by preparing resumes and petitions for other people. In 1893 he signed a contract with Abdullah and Company to represent the firm in a major case in South Africa.

For the first time Gandhi was facing racial discrimination. He was a "coolie lawyer," not accepted by the white ruling class. A minor episode turned into a major personal event. Gandhi was on the way from Durban to Pretoria. A white man entered the first-class compartment and demanded that the "colored" copassenger leave. The conductor asked Gandhi to move into a second-class compartment. Gandhi refused. He rather preferred to spend the night in an uncomfortable waiting room than to forgo the right to a first-class compartment for which he had a valid ticket. "My active nonviolence dates from this point in time" Gandhi later commented.[4]

Gandhi's interest in religion led him to make the acquaintance of Dr. Baker, who maintained a private chapel and supplied him with Christian literature. Gandhi also read the Quran. But the most profound impression was made by reading Tolstoj's *The Kingdom of God Is Within You*. Tolstoj's way of interpreting the Bible became Gandhi's own and Gandhi henceforth considered Tolstoj his guru.

Originally Gandhi had planned to stay only for a few months in South Africa. It turned out to be almost seventeen years. Interest in Abdullah and Company's legal affairs receded more and more into the background. Gandhi became involved in the concerns of his fellow Indians, who as a colored minority were exposed to a great deal of oppression and injustice. He was opening a legal practice in Pretoria and soon became the moral leader of the Indian community in South Africa. A short visit to India enabled him to participate in the 1901 All-India Congress in Bombay and to travel throughout India. His utterances about conditions in South Africa angered South African politicians.

A telling incident in his private life took place that same year. His son Manilal fell severely ill. The physician prescribed a diet of eggs and bullion. Gandhi did not allow this. His vegetarianism had become part of his religion. He rather risked the life of his son than break his own principles.[5]

After returning to South Africa in late 1902, he had to face the anger of the white population, which felt slighted by Gandhi's remarks in India. He read books by Vivekānanda and Tagore and memorized the *Bhagavadgītā*. He considered adopting the Gītā notions of *aparigraha* and *samābhāva*. He let his life insurance run out and told his brother that henceforth he would not send any more money to India, but would distribute all his surplus income to the Indian community in South Africa. He began simplifying his own life and experimenting with all kinds of diets and nature cures.

Ruskin's *Unto This Last* became the second "key book" of his life. He drew three conclusions from it. First, that the well-being of the individual was contained in the well-being of all. Second, that the work of a lawyer had the same value as that of a barber, insofar as all have the same right to earn their living through their work. Third, that the life of manual labor, that is, the life of peasants and craftsmen, was the most desirable life.[6]

Moving from theory to praxis he established the Phoenix Settlement to which he transferred the editorial offices of his recently founded *Indian Opinion*.[7] An international group of ideal socialists began work in the desert-like wastelands. Every settler received a hut and an acre of land. Gandhi was against the use of machines. Self-sufficiency was to be reached by an utmost restriction of wants. All had to work in the fields, all had to collaborate in producing the *Indian Opinion*. Gandhi continued his legal practice and had a large clientele: his honesty and conscientiousness were widely appreciated. To the poor he gave free legal advice.

In his home he continued to reform. At 6:30 A.M. all male members of the household had to get up in order to grind wheat. Bread was made in the home. Gandhi walked to his office, a distance of six miles. On the way to and from the office his children had to accompany him: he taught them Gujarati. He did not send them to school. He edited a "health guide," incorporating elements of his philosophy of life and began to contemplate taking vows of voluntary poverty and chastity, as preparation for unconditional service of India.[8]

## THE BEGINNING OF *SATYĀGRAHA*

When the South African government passed a law demanding that all Indians be registered and have their fingerprints taken, Gandhi called for passive resistance. It was the occasion when the term *satyāgraha* was coined, which would circumscribe Gandhi's entire future life. *Satyāgraha*, Gandhi explained, was the strength that was born of truth, love, and nonviolence.[9] *Satyāgraha* was more than passive resistance, it was action in the awareness of having truth on one's side, and the belief that truth will prevail in the end. When the government arrested 155 *satyāgrahis* on January 29, 1908, Gandhi exhorted all strictly to follow the prison regulations: they were not law breakers but truth defenders. He used his time in prison to study religious scriptures. Mornings he was reading the Gītā, afternoons the Quran, in the evenings he instructed a Chinese fellow inmate in the Bible.

Gandhi's second spell in prison followed his appeal to the Indians to burn their registration papers. Prison became his "university": he began an extensive reading program in religion, political science, economics, and sociology. He was not dejected at all; on the contrary he praised his time in prison and thought that it was the greatest blessing to be in prison for the sake of the well-being of his country and his religion.

In London in 1909 he met with the radical youth wing of the congress. They celebrated Dinghra who shortly before had killed a British official like a national hero. Gandhi condemned the act and advised nonviolence. He studied Britain's India policy and wrote his famous *Hind Swarāj*, containing some of his basic principles.[10] He believed in a real meeting of East and West, but he wholeheartedly condemned modern civilization and technology. Modern medicine was particularly abhorrent to him. He admonished India to unlearn everything she had learned from the West. He referred to the ancient sages as the true teachers of life for India and stated categorically that a mere exchange of government would not be an improvement of the situation.

Gandhi began to become known in India. Gokhale, the great old man of the congress movement, praised Gandhi on his visit to South Africa.[11] When Dr. Hermann Kallenbach, a German architect, offered Gandhi his extensive ranch for the *satyāgraha* movement in 1910, Gandhi accepted and began his large-scale experiment of communal living with his "Tolstoj-Farm." The ideological basis was a kind of idealistic naturalistic communism. The daily routine was structured along the prison regulations of Pretoria. The needs of everyone were reduced to the essentials. The aim was total self-sufficiency. Things that could not be produced locally were supposed not to be required. All worked in the fields and all attended the religious devotions of all religions represented on the farm. Only nature cures were allowed. All had to practice some handicraft. Kallenbach had learned sandalmaking in a German Trappist monastery: he taught this art to Gandhi and Gandhi handed it on.

Gandhi developed his own system of education for the children on the farm. Mornings they had to work in the fields, afternoons they had to study. There were no textbooks. Gandhi's endeavor was to transmit education of the heart and mind. He personally taught religion. In 1912 he published *Nīti Dharma or Ethical Religion*. In 1910 Gandhi closed his legal practice and moved with his whole family to Tolstoy Farm. In 1912 he took a vow renouncing all private property. At the outbreak of World War I Gandhi traveled with his family to England. He volunteered for the medical corps, but his physical condition made him ineligible.

January 9, 1915, Gandhi returned to India for good. He received a hero's welcome, but Gokhale asked him to observe a year of silence: he should travel throughout India and familiarize himself with the situation before appearing in public. Gandhi agreed.

The same year he founded his Satyagraha Ashram in Wardha, not far from Ahmedabad in Gujarat. It was to be the place to educate perfect servants for the *satyāgraha* movement on a national level. He divided the ashram population into managers, candidates, and students. All managers had to work in the fields out of solidarity with the Indian country people. Indian languages were taught. Children were admitted at age four and had to undergo ten years of schooling in religion, agriculture, weaving, literature, Sanskrit, Hindī, and a Dravidian language. Dress and food were Spartan. There was no holiday and no vacation. For three months each year the students had to walk throughout India.

The first serious ashram crisis happened when a family of Untouchables asked for membership. The donors who had so far supported the ashram withdrew their financial help. Gandhi indicated that he was willing to move the whole ashram into the Untouchable quarters of Ahmedabad. Other supporters emerged, and the Satyagraha Ashram became the focus of Gandhi's activities in the next few years.

## RULES FOR AN IDEAL INDIAN LIFE

In his *Ashram Rules* Gandhi expressed the entire program of his life, the fruits of his "experiments with truth." Throughout his further life he strove to realize what he had put down in that small booklet. The *Ashram Observances in Action*[12] contain eleven observances, seven activities, and some remarks about the acceptance of applicants. "The first and foremost vow is that of truth." Truth was the cornerstone of Gandhi's religion; he was proud to have reversed the statement "God is Truth" into "Truth is God." Truthfulness was to be the basis on which independent India was to be built. Devotees of truth are not supposed to deviate from truth, not even for the sake of a seeming advantage for the country. Throughout his life Gandhi called himself a seeker after truth, never claiming to have found it, but insisting that he had found a way to truth on which he was determined to go.[13] One of the preconditions for finding truth was self-effacement: Gandhi called it "making oneself a zero," or "drown[ing] oneself in the infinite ocean of life."[14] This notion of truth excludes an escape from social and political responsibilities. Gandhi could not find his *mokṣa* in a Himālayan hermitage—he had to engage in ceaseless work, as Kṛṣṇa in the *Bhagavadgītā* had told Arjuna. No wonder that the Gītā played such a central role in his thought—a gospel of action, a doctrine of *niṣkāma karma*, cooperation with the process of world deliverance. Gandhi called his life "experiments with truth," and in the light of what was said before we can call it experiments with God. He felt "like an earthen vessel in the hands of his creator"; for him even the smallest act gained immense importance as a stage to God-realization. For him the independence of India was part of the Truth for which he was willing to give his life. "Only a free India can worship the true God."

The second principle upon which Gandhi founded his life and his institution was *ahiṃsā*, nonviolence. It is complementary to truth, the only way to truth. *Ahiṃsā*, Gandhi explains, is not only non-killing; it means active love, a love that extends to all living things from the smallest insect to the greatest human. Someone who follows that law cannot be angry with even the most evil of persons, but must love her, wish her well and serve her. While loving the evildoer, one must hate the evil done. *Ahiṃsā* is the only means to reach self-realization. Nonviolence in the negative sense, as practiced in noncooperation and civil disobedience, became the most powerful weapon in the freedom struggle. It is the weapon of truth. In the last analysis, *ahiṃsā*, like *satya*, is not our doing, but it is God's activity in a human, it is the elimination of the egotistical violent element in human nature. *Ahiṃsā*, Gandhi repeats, is not cowardice, it presupposes the ability to fight and constitutes a conscious renunciation of violence. "*Ahiṃsā* without fearlessness is impossible."[15] Gandhi proved his point throughout his life. He walked into dangerous situations—consciously and knowingly—that others would have run away from. He was not deterred by threats of death in situations of communal rioting and did not break his routine of his evening prayer meetings in Delhi's Birla House, even after the first attempts on his life had been made and he had premonitions of death.

The third vow Gandhi took and wanted his followers to adopt was that of *brahmacarya*, sexual continence. Gandhi believed that *satya* and *ahimṣā* could only be observed by people who lived a celibate life in thought, word, and action, as the ancient Indian ideal had suggested. Similarly, his fellow workers had to abstain from all intoxicating drinks, from tobacco, drugs, and everything that was designed to stimulate the senses. He considered his own practice of fasting the culmination of this vow of abstention.[16]

Gandhi's dramatic public "fasts to death" became legendary in his own time and made him, possibly, better known in the West than anything else he did or said. Gandhi used fasting both as a weapon against colonialism and as a means to self-purification. He claimed to have undertaken his big fasts in response to a call from God. For him, fasting was an essential part of religion.[17] Fasting, of course, is an integral part of the Vaiṣṇava tradition in which he had grown up. Gandhi goes much further both in the extent of fasting and in the importance attributed to it. Fasting presupposes unlimited faith in God. When his first public *Swadeshi* ("Own Country") movement in 1921 led to severe rioting in Bombay by Hindus against Muslims, Christians, and Parsis, Gandhi decided to fast "in order to obtain further credit from God."[18] He was prepared to die in his fast, if that was to be God's will. Or to be transformed into a more suitable instrument of God's will. His last fast was undertaken in January 1948, shortly before his death, in response to the large-scale Hindu-Muslim communal rioting following the partition of India. He believed in the redeeming and transforming effects of self-imposed suffering; fasting unto death was the most perfect form of *ahiṃsā*.

Although Gandhi personalized and modernized the "vows" of *satya*, *ahiṃsā*, and *brahmacarya*, they are easily recognizable as part of the age-old *yama-niyama* ethics of Hinduism. Gandhi adopted the rest of it, too, in his vows of *asteya*, nonstealing, and *aparigraha*, nonpossession, and added bodily labor as his own precept for the India of his time. On his extensive travels through India, Gandhi saw not only the abject poverty in which a great majority of his countrymen lived in the villages, but he also noticed their—often enforced—idleness throughout much of the year. He insisted on "bread labor": all should contribute, through their own manual work, to their physical upkeep, and nobody should exploit others. He insisted on reducing wants to a minimum and to asking oneself with regard to any material possession, whether it was really necessary. He understood bodily work as a means to realize *asteya* and *aparigraha*. In India, where most housework was done by servants and menial employees and manual work was considered degrading by the socially higher classes, Gandhi's message of manual labor certainly sounded revolutionary. The universal obligation of bread labor found a uniquely Gandhian expression in the *carkhā*, the spinning wheel, which for some time was even used as an emblem in the Indian flag. When pondering possibilities of providing additional work and income to the largely underemployed rural population, Gandhi struck upon the spinning wheel. Hand spinning and weaving had been widespread activities in India's villages before the import of cheap, machine-made cloth from England had ruined these indigenous industries. Gandhi not only led agitations against imports of foreign cloth—he held large bonfires of such fabrics in major cities—he also offered a workable substitute. Almost a hundred years of interruption of the local textile manufacture had made it difficult to reactivate it on a large scale. By chance someone brought Gandhi an old handmade spinning wheel, which, with some improvement, was distributed throughout the villages. Handlooms were repaired and brought back into production. Gandhi insisted that all members of congress had to devote at least half an hour each day to spinning and they had to wear only handspun and handwoven cloth (*khādī*). The "Gandhi cap" has remained a symbol of congress membership to this very day. Many from the upper classes protested against Gandhi's "primitivism" but he insisted that India's leadership had not only to lead by words, but had also to demonstrate solidarity with the concerns of the masses in a visible way. From the early 1930s on, Gandhi would rarely be seen without his spinning wheel, which he praised as his "wish-fulfilling tree" and as the instrument of salvation for India.[19] In his spinning wheel Gandhi saw the confluence of *ahiṃsā*, bread labor, and *swarāj*, independence. It also symbolized God, who, as Gandhi said, can appear to a hungry person only in the form of bread. Independence was meaningless for the masses, if it did not also bring with it increased employment and income.

## ADDRESSING UNTOUCHABILITY

Untouchability, which seemed inextricably connected with Hinduism, Gandhi maintained, was wholly irreligious.[20] He demanded that his fellow workers take a vow to eradicate untouchability. In order to show his respect for the *asp*ṛ*hyas*, the Untouchables, Gandhi called them *Harijan*, "People of God." He gave equal status to the Untouchables in his ashram and thereby created a dilemma for many orthodox Hindus. Paradoxically, Gandhi did not attempt to abolish caste, as some nineteenth-century reformers had done. He believed in the importance of the *varṇāśramadharma*. In his opinion this was an occupational, not a personal division of society and as such beneficial to humanity. Untouchability he rejected as being against *ahiṃsā*; as far as the distinctions of *āśramas* were concerned, all his fellow ashramites who had taken the vows were deemed to be *saṃnyāsis*.

Gandhi undertook fasts in order to achieve the opening of temples to the Untouchables, but he also defended Hinduism. When Dr. Ambedkar, himself an outcaste and the leader of the Depressed Classes Conference, recommended in 1935 that all Untouchables leave Hinduism and adopt another religion, Gandhi was quite upset. He commented that *varṇāśramadharma* was a natural law, and that Dr. Ambedkar had unfairly attacked the very essence of Hinduism. Religion, Gandhi argued, is not like a piece of garment that one can change at will. Religion is an essential part of our selves, more essential even than the body.[21]

Gandhi acquainted himself early on with the scriptures and doctrines of various major religious traditions and intended to develop his Satyāgraha Ashram into a multireligious community. Through his study and contact with believers from different backgrounds he had come to the conviction that all major religions of the world were revelations of truth—fragmentary, human, imperfect, but to be respected for what they offered. he admonished his coworkers to show equal respect to all religions—there was no need to proselytize, but also no reason to reject any religion. Religions, he said, are different paths that converge on one point; it does not matter which way we go as long as we reach the goal. There are as many religions as there are individuals.[22] This position also allowed him to profess his loyalty to the Hindu tradition while criticizing certain historic expressions of it.

He loved the Hindu tradition in spite of its flaws, being connected with it through his whole existence. In spite of his admiration for the Sermon on the Mount, the *Bhagavadgītā* and Tulasīdāsa's *Rāmacaritamānasa* inspired him most. Time and again he affirmed his belief in *karma*, in rebirth, his faith in the *avatāras*, and the *guru-paraṃparā*. It was from a deep understanding of, and sympathy for, Hinduism that he condemned untouchability and other inhumane practices historically connected with Hinduism. While faithfully undergoing religious rites he chastised the greed of the *paṇḍas* and the sloth of *pūjāris*.

## RELIGION-INSPIRED ECONOMICS AND ECOLOGY

Gandhi was a thoroughgoing pragmatist, in spite of his otherworldly idealism. He knew that the cornerstone of India's independence was its economy. In prison he studied economists and drew his own conclusions from their writings. While he advocated limitation of wants and self-limitation in the use of material goods, he never glorified abject poverty or destitution. Traveling third-class by railway through India, walking to remote villages, and sharing shelter with ordinary people, he learned firsthand about India's economic problems. The spinning wheel was one response—a response that he considered important and effective. As a member of congress and its sometime president, he also developed more elaborate plans, such as the Constructive Program of 1945, which he wanted to be accepted as the basic document for India's economic development after independence. He believed that the ideal society was the village community. He envisaged an India consisting of five hundred thousand self-sufficient villages, grounded in *satya* and *ahiṃsā*, supportive of each other and of the whole. He spoke of an "oceanic circle,"[23] over against the commonly used pyramid of power. The whole country should be structured in concentric circles, with the individual as the center. The individual, however, would be willing to sacrifice itself for the sake of the village, the village for the sake of the village cluster, the village cluster for the sake of the country. The larger unit would not use its power to oppress the smaller unit, and the smaller unit would not take undue advantage of the larger.

Gandhi knew about the utopian character of his model, but he argued that it had incomparable value as an idea, similar to the Euclidean point that has no physical existence but is crucially important for all geometry. His ideal future India would be a community of economically equal citizens. Appalled by the gulf that separated the very rich from the masses of the very poor, he implored the former to lower their living standard for the sake of the latter. He feared that a bloody revolution might bring about later what the elite was unwilling to do now.[24] Gandhi advocated the idea of trusteeship: it might be difficult to put into practice, but, he said "that is true of nonviolence as a whole." As far as material needs were concerned he pleaded to "give to everyone according to his needs." When told that Karl Marx had used the same formula he remarked that he would not mind calling himself a *socialist* or a *communist* and accused those who called themselves *Communists* and *Socialists* of not knowing the true meaning of these terms. For Gandhi socialism meant "the incarnation of *satya* and *ahiṃsā*"[25] and communism was "to reduce oneself to the level of the poorest of all." And that, he said, he had tried for half a century; so he could call himself a model communist. He never refused help from the "capitalists" and defended them against unjust attacks. The bottom line of his economics was: All land belongs to God and has been given to humans in trusteeship. All should have what they need—nobody should own more.

From early on Gandhi showed an almost irrational aversion against machines. The most important reason for this attitude was that with machines a subhuman element invades human life. For Gandhi, manual work that machines were invented to make easier was not an unpleasant necessity but a religious duty, the fulfillment of a divine command, and the principal means to find truth. His economics was not based on maximizing productivity and profit, but on full employment (in the literal sense of the word), even at the cost of a decline in productivity. He had no sympathy for the leisure time society of the Socialists, and Soviet Russia rather repelled him. He called it a madness to produce labor-saving machines and then to throw millions out of work. The highest consideration must be the human person, and a machine should not lead to a stunting of humanity.[26] Gandhi refused to define the aim of economics as "achievement of the highest possible good for the highest possible number": it had to be the highest good for all. He demonstrated what he meant through his life: he identified with the poorest by not possessing more or using more than what the poorest have. In his famous "Talisman"[27] he recommended to all politicians to visualize the face of the poorest and weakest human being they had seen in their life and then to ask themselves whether the intended action was of any use for this person. As he saw it, industrial mass production was the reason for worldwide economic crises. Industrial mass production is based in principle on the exploitation of the weaker members of society. Gandhi wanted to replace it through a production by the masses. Every one should equally participate in the growth of national wealth.

Gandhi saw enough of the reality of Indian villages to be aware of the need to improve them. He did not hesitate to call the average North Indian village a "dung heap" and scolded his compatriots for their lack of sense of cleanliness and hygiene.[28] He emphasized the need for sanitation and wanted to see *bhaṅgis* (waste removers) and *dhobis* (washer people), traditionally the lowest of castes, elevated to the highest rank because of the importance of their work for the well-being of society. He insisted that in his ashram everybody take turns to clean the latrines and to do all the work required to keep the place neat.

## MAHĀTMĀ—THE GREAT SOUL

Gandhi certainly was a practically minded person, a skillful politician, a man concerned with the well-being of his fellow humans, and constantly responding to challenges of a very down-to-earth kind. Nevertheless, all his restless activity was motivated by his religion and its ultimate aim was not the welfare state but Rām Rājya, the Kingdom of God.[29] For Gandhi Rām Rājya was not the quasi-totalitarian rule of a right-wing political party, but "the rule of justice" and the "realization of God." He never separated the personal aim of reaching the vision of God from his public activities of transforming India into a truly humane society. At several occasions he said that "*satyāgraha* is a religious movement, a process of progressive purification and penance."

The India that Gandhi visualized was a holy land that had purified itself through suffering and made itself acceptable to God. One of his most mature maxims, uttered only months before his assassination, engulfed by a sea of tragedy after the partition, reveals his heart best: "By my fetters I can fly, by my worries I can love, by my tears I can walk and by my cross I can enter the heart of humanity. Let me praise my cross, O God."[30]

CHAPTER THIRTY-TWO

# *Hindūtva*—Hinduism—Hindu *Dharma*

> Since politics is a main part of Hindu Dharma, Dharmacharyas should in their religious discourses give top priority on the impact of present-day politics on their Dharma and their survival.
>
> —"What Hindus Should Do," http://www.hinduunity.org, November 2, 2002

The whole world watched with fascination and horror the televised demolition of the Babri Masjid on December 6, 1992, by thousands of Hindu political activists and the subsequent large-scale rioting, burning, and looting in dozens of India's major cities. While for decades the West used to stare at the growth of Communism in India as the greatest threat to democracy, it finally awoke to the reality of a far more serious challenge from the right, that of Hindu extremism, by now well organized and powerful and well within reach of success. The "Militant Revivalism" of Hinduism has been coming for quite long. It was not taken seriously by most Westernized Indians and all but ignored by most foreign observers.[1]

Traditional Hinduism, consisting of a great number of quite independent and more often than not conflicting religions and philosophies, cannot possibly provide an ideology for Hindu party politics. The nineteenth-century Hindu Renaissance, too, has spawned all kinds of new understandings of Hinduism, from a humanistic, universalistic, tolerant, and generous religiosity to exclusivist, sectarian, and narrow-minded fundamentalisms. The political Hinduism of our age requires a unified, denominational understanding of Hinduism—something that so far has not existed but that is obviously taking shape in our time.

Traditional Hinduism had always a political dimension, too, a consequence of its holistic nature, which did not divide life into a religious and a secular sphere. *Dharma* comprises all aspects of life. In the nineteenth century, under the influence of European nationalism, Hindus turned nationalist, too.

Terms like Holy Mother India were not meaningless rhetoric for Hindus but signified a living reality that every Hindu was called upon to defend, protect, and foster. Bankim Chandra Chatterjee, the great Bengali novelist, whose *Ānandamaṭha* depicted the 1770 *saṃnyāsi* uprising as a national war of liberation from foreign rule, made his patriotic ascetics sing a hymn to Mother India that for some time became the national anthem of the freedom movement and that Hindu activists today want to reintroduce, the "Bande Mātaram," Mother, I bow to thee, in which India is identified with the Goddess:

> With many strengths who are mighty and stored,
> To thee I call, Mother and Lord!
> Thou who savest, arise and save! . . .
> Thou art wisdom, thou art law,
> Thou our heart, our soul, our breath,
> Thou the love divine, the awe
> In our hearts that conquers death.
> Thine the strength that nerves the arm,
> Thine the beauty, thine the charm.
> Every image made divine
> In our temples is but thine.
> Thou art Durgā, Lady and Queen,
> With her hands that strike and her swords of sheen,
> Thou art Lakshmī Lotus-throned,
> And the Muse a hundred-toned.
> Pure and Perfect without peer,
> Mother, lend thine ear.[2]

Another Bengali, Śrī Aurobindo Ghose, who first fought for India's political independence in a terrorist band, had according to his own testimony, a vision of Kṛṣṇa through which he was made to understand that his lifework was to be for the restoration of the true *dharma*, that is, Hinduism. Bāl Gaṅgādhar Tilak and many others undertook their political agitation against the British *rāj* as duty imposed on them by their religion; their aim was the restoration of Hindu India on the sociopolitical level.[3] The most radical advocates of the restoration of Hindu *dharma* on the sociopolitical level today are the many groups and parties that developed out of the Ārya Samāj, the Aryan Society of Svāmi Dāyānanda Saraswatī briefly described in Chapter 30.

## RADICAL HINDU POLITICAL MOVEMENTS ON A NATIONAL LEVEL

In 1909 Pandit Mohan Malaviya, who became later the first vice chancellor of Banares Hindu-University, founded together with other leading Ārya-Samājists the Hindū Mahāsabhā, which soon developed into a right-wing militant Hindu political party. It has remained one of the national parties based on a narrow definition of Hindu nationhood. Their election manifesto read:

> Hindustan is the land of the Hindus from time immemorial. The Hindū Mahāsabhā believes that Hindus have a right to live in peace as Hindus, to legislate, to rule, to govern themselves in accordance with Hindu genius and ideals and establish by all lawful and legal means a Hindu state based on Hindu Culture and Tradition, so that Hindu ideology and way of life should have a homeland of its own. The cardinal creed of the Hindū Mahāsabhā is:
>
> 1. Loyalty to the unity and integrity of Hindustan.
> 2. The Hindū Mahāsabhā reiterates once again that it is pledged to the reestablishment of Akhand Bhārat by all legitimate means.
> 3. The Hindū Mahāsabhā again reiterates its clarion call, as given by Vīr Savarkar as far back as 1938: "Hinduize Politics and Militarize Hinduism."[4]

The referred to Vīr Savarkar (1883–1966), the greatest theoretician of the Hindū Mahāsabhā, fought in countless speeches and publications for a violent liberation of India under the Hindu banner from everything foreign and a complete restoration of Hindu ideas and Hindu society. India's independence from British rule in 1947 was not enough for him, he bitterly opposed Nehru's secular state concept and continued agitating for the total Hinduization of India (which earned him long spells of house arrest in his Bombay-Matunga home). In his essay "Hindutva" he developed the outlines of the new Hindu India. He distinguished between *Hindu-dharma*, Hinduism as a religion, which is divided into countless *saṃpradāyas*, and *Hindutva*, Hindudom, as the unifying sociocultural background of all Hindus.[5]

One of the members of the Hindū Mahāsabhā, K. V. Hedgewar (1890–1940), a medical doctor who never practiced medicine, founded in 1925 the Rāṣṭrīya Svayam-sevak Saṅgh (RSS), the National Volunteer Organization. He was afraid of Muslim influence over the Indian National Congress. The RSS, strictly organized from the very beginning, is the most powerful and most controversial Hindu organization of today: it claims to be a cultural organization and is not registered as a political party.

Nathuram Godse, Gandhi's murderer, was a member of the RSS, which also had been held responsible for a great deal of the communal slaughter around the time of partition.[6] Nehru's reaction to Godse's crime was swift and decisive: he banned the RSS and jailed tens of thousands of its members. About a year later the ban was lifted and the leaders were freed. Apparently the movement had friends in high places, and so it was declared that no direct involvement of the RSS in Gandhi's death could be proved.

The events connected with partition that had brought great suffering to many millions of Indians were perceived by the Hindus in India as inflicting more than an equal share of sacrifice on the Hindus. Differences over

Muslim-Hindu policies brought about several breakaways from the monolithic congress party from 1948 onward.

Events in East Bengal in early 1950 led to the formation of the Jana Sangh Party, which had a clearly pro-Hindu and anti-Muslim orientation.[7] Millions of Hindus had fled from Pakistani East Bengal to Indian West Bengal telling about forcible eviction, Muslim brutalities, and large-scale repression. The conciliatory talks between Nehru and Liaquat Ali were considered inadequate by a number of politicians in West Bengal and at the Center. The major figures involved were Dr. Shyamaprasad Mookerjea (minister for industries and supplies), Mr. John Mathai (finance minister), and Mr. K. C. Neogy, who resigned from the Nehru Union cabinet. They proposed their own set of conditions for Pakistan to agree to and while ostensibly promoting the cause of the Hindus in Pakistan articulated also an alternative approach to Indian internal and external politics.

The new party called itself Bhāratīya Jana Sangh, and in Bengal it first appeared under its English name People's Party of India. While its origins were connected with dissatisfaction with the existing Nehru congress government's policies, the founders of the Jana Sangh pointed out—correctly—that it did not just constitute a breakaway congress faction. As Deendayal Upadhyāya wrote:

> The Jana Sangh was founded as an all-India party on 21 October 1951. It was not a disgruntled, dissident or discredited group of Congressmen who formed the nucleus of the party, as is the case with all other political parties. . . . Its inspiration came from those who basically differed from the Congress outlook and policies. It was an expression of the nascent nationalism. It was felt that the ruling party had failed to harness the enthusiasm created by freedom to the task of realization of the great potentialities of the country. It was because of their anxiety to make Bhārat a carbon-copy of the West, that they have ignored and neglected the best in Bhāratīya life and ideals. The Jana Saṅgh predicted that the Abhāratīya and unrealistic approach to the national problems by the party in power would create more complications than solve any. Its forebodings have come true.[8]

The leading light in the early years was Dr. Shyamprasad Mookerjea. A man with a distinguished academic record and an early involvement in Bengal politics, he joined the Hindū Mahāsabhā in 1937. In 1946 Nehru offered him a cabinet position. Mookerjea was one of five non-congress members of the fourteen member cabinet. Dr. Mookerjea disagreed with the Hindū Mahāsabhā on many issues and demanded, after the assassination of Mahātmā Gandhi, that it either withdraw from political activities altogether or shed its communal Hindu character. The Hindū Mahāsabhā had not been very successful in the 1946 elections anyhow. Eventually Dr. Mookerjea left the Hindū Mahāsabhā and also resigned from the Nehru cabinet in 1950 over the Bengal issue. He established links with the RSS leaders Vasantrao Oak and Balraj Madhok.

He tried to persuade the RSS to become a political party. The RSS leadership had rejected such an idea since its foundation: the RSS had wider aims. The Jana Saṅgh won considerable support in some state elections and became powerful enough on the national level to attract the attention and vituperation of both congress and leftist parties as being "fascist," "totalitarian," and so forth. Apart from its overall view to Indianize/Hinduize Indian politics it kept pleading for a reunification of India, the introduction of Hindī as the national language, the recognition of Israel, and the ban of cow slaughter.[9] It merged with a number of other parties (among others the anti-Indira Gandhi wing of the congress party) to form the Janatā Party, which after the resignation of Indira Gandhi in 1977 won elections in a landslide victory.

The coalition that was Janatā was shaky from the very beginning. Its lack of initiative and its increasing internal quarrels—largely about the relations of former Jana Saṅgh members with the RSS—created widespread disappointment. Eventually a split of the party occurred and this brought about the downfall of the Janatā government with a return to power of Indira Gandhi's congress. A further split occurred in March 80 and again in April 80 when the former Jana Saṅgh group formed a new party called the Bhāratīya Janatā Party. The leadership was taken over (again) by Mr. A. B. Bajpai, who had been external affairs minister under the Janatā government. In a speech on April 6, 1980, he had declared: "We are proud of our association with the RSS." Lately he was quoted as saying he is disillusioned with the new party as well.[10] With L. K. Advani's popular rhetoric and organizational skills, the BJP became a nationalist movement attracting worldwide attention through such highly visible events as the *Rām-śila-yātra*, a "pilgrimage" through India to collect bricks for a new Rāma temple in Ayodhyā in 1991, an *Ektā-yātra*, a "unity pilgrimage," terminating in Śrīnagar/Kashmir in early 1992 at the height of the state's crisis, and finally the destruction of the Babri Masjid in December 1992. The BJP with its allies took over the leadership of the country in 1996 at the union level.[11]

Deen Dayal Upadhyāya, Atal Bihari Bajpāī, Lal Krishna Advani, Nanaji Deshmukh, Balraj Madhok, Lal Hansraj Gupta, men who shaped national politics in the 1960s and 1970s, were all prominent activists of the RSS. The RSS spawned a great number of other front organizations like the *Bhāratīya Mazdūr Sabhā*, a trade union, the *Akhil Bhāratīya Vidyārthi Pariṣad*, a students' union, and the *Viśva Hindū Pariṣad* (VHP), "World Hindu Association," a religiocultural organization (founded in 1964) that attempted to articulate a kind of universal Hinduism that would embrace the different sects and at the same time possess a basic common creed and common practice.[12]

It is not always clear where the borderline between RSS and VHP passes, if there is one, to begin with. Both organizations boast thousands of centers all over India, millions of members, and both are extremely active on behalf of *Hindū Jāgaran* (Hindu Awakening).[13] They organize processions, meetings, festivities and they work toward a bridging of the differences between different

Hindu denominations in the interest of a united and politically strong Hinduism. Membership figures mentioned are impressive, as are the number of violent confrontations. One of the immediate aims of the *Viśva Hindū Pariṣad* after the Ayodhyā victory is to repossess the areas of the Kṛṣṇa Janmabhūmī temple in Mathurā and of the Viśvanātha temple in Vārāṇasī—two of the holiest places of Hinduism, which were (partially) occupied and desecrated by the Muslims in the Middle Ages.

Partly cooperating and partly competing with these organizations are others, devoted to the same goal of Hindu awakening and Hindu political power: the *Virāt Hindū Sammelan*, the *Hindū Samājotsav*, *Bajraṅg Dāl*, and others.

There cannot be any doubt that the major role in the Hindu revival has been played for quite some time by the RSS. The training of the RSS members is rigorous and purposeful: bodily exercises and indoctrination sessions have to be attended by all members daily for at least an hour. The leaders are usually unmarried and unsalaried and devote all their time and their energy to the movement.[14]

M. S. Golwalkar, the successor to K. V. Hedgewar (d. 1973), published early in his career his *Bunch of Thoughts*, in which he systematically and openly laid out the ideology and the policies of the RSS. He quite frankly declared Muslims, Christians, and Communists (in that order) the major enemies of India and promised that they would not be citizens of a Hindu India shaped according to RSS principles. According to Golwalkar the Hindu nation has been given the divine mandate to spiritualize the world and this mandate has fallen on the RSS in our time. With genuinely religious fervor Golwalkar exhorted his followers to do their utmost for the reestablishment of this Hindu order not only in India but worldwide. Thus he wrote: "The RSS has resolved to fulfil that age-old national mission by forging, as the first step, the present-day scattered elements of the Hindu Society into an organized and invincible force both on the plane of the Spirit and on the plane of material life. Verily this is the one real practical world-mission if ever there was one."[15] After Golwalkar's death Madhukar Dattatreya, known as Balasaheb Deoras—also a bachelor and a member of the RSS since his twelfth year—became *Sarsaṅghachalak*, the supreme leader of the RSS. He echoes Savarkar when stating: "We do believe in the one-culture and one-nation Hindu *rāṣṭra*. But our definition of Hindu is not limited to any particular kind of faith. Our definition of Hindu includes those who believe in the one-culture and one-nation theory of this country. They can all form part of the *Hindu-rāṣṭra*. So by Hindu we do not mean any particular type of faith. We use the word Hindu in a broader sense."[16]

Many Indians who subscribe to the idea of a secular democratic state with equal rights for all its members, regardless of race, creed, and sex, consider the RSS to be a threat to this state—the biggest and most serious threat considering its membership (upward of five million) and the caliber of its organization. While the RSS and its front organizations may be the most visible manifestation of extremist and radical political Hinduism on the national level, it is not the only one. Thus, Swāmi Karpartriji Maharaj founded in the late forties the *Rām Rājya Pariṣad* (Kingdom-of-God-Party), which also contended in national elections, objecting to Nehru's secular democracy.[17] It is not very powerful but it has attracted also a number of swāmis who campaign on its behalf for seats in the *Lok Sabhā*, the Indian Lower House.

## REGIONAL HINDU POLITICAL MOVEMENTS

In the 1960s numerous regional organizations developed in India with the aim to either establish language- or religion-based separate states or to protect the natives of a particular state from the competition of out-of-state immigrants. Regional interests and Hindu interests very often overlap. They are meanwhile too numerous to be dealt with in the context of this book.[18] The example of one, the earliest, most active and exclusive Hindu organization of this type may suffice to make the point.[19]

The Shiv Sena (Shivaji's Army) was founded in 1966 in Bombay by Bal Thakkeray, a former cartoonist for a local paper. It was to protect the rights and jobs of Maharastrians, especially in Bombay, a metropolis with large contingents of Indians from all parts of the country. Thakkeray demanded, among other things, that 80 percent of government jobs be reserved for native Maharastrians. By 1969 it had become powerful enough to organize a general strike in Bombay, paralyzing the entire huge city for three days, burning buses and trains, and terrorizing non-Maharastrians. Many South Indian coffee shops were burned down, many non-Maharastrian businesses were vandalized. Not long afterward the Shiv Sena won the majority of seats in Bombay's municipal election and became a major factor in Maharastrian state politics.[20] It succeeded in officially renaming Bombay into Mumbāī—changing a Portuguese "good harbor" into a "city of Muṃbā Devī." Hindu interests and regional interests overlap in the Shiv Sena: while the organization is purely Hindu, it demonstrated hostility to all non-Maharastrians, Hindu as well as non-Hindu. During the past few years the Shiv Sena has expanded to other Indian states, especially to Uttar Pradesh and Punjab. It claims to have hundreds of thousands of followers there.

While the Shiv Sena may have arisen as a rightist Hindu movement counterbalancing leftist forces, its rise has occasioned the emergence of a great number of regional communal "defense organizations." A Muslim Sena and a Christian Sena emerged with the aim to protect the interests of these minorities. It is often difficult to arrange the *senas* within the Indian political spectrum (Kaṇāda Sena, Gopāla Sena, Tamiḷ Army, Lachit Sena, Bhīm Sena, among others). While many of them may not have a significant following and may not have more than local importance, they certainly have helped to polarize the Indian political scene and to weaken whatever sense of unity on the basis of a common Indianness had developed over the years. While not all of them are Hindu, several of them are increasingly becoming the instruments of politically active and often extreme Hinduism that throughout history has considered regional loyalties of greater importance than all-Indian interests.

## HINDU COMMUNALISM

In its sixty years of independence India has so far successfully upheld its ideal of a secular democracy on the national level. This did not prevent extremist political Hindu groups from putting pressure on non-Hindu minorities in a number of states like Madhya Pradesh, Uttar Pradesh, Bihar, and Orissa. While documents such as the Niyogi report purport to attack only foreign Christian missionaries, the Indian Christians rightly interpreted it as an attack on Christianity in India. Again, while it was India that was at war with Pakistan, and not Hindus with Muslims in the several armed conflicts that eventually lead to the establishment of Bangladesh, Muslims did experience during these wars harassment from the side of fanaticized Hindus as "enemies of India." The potential for violence that political Hinduism possesses translated at numerous occasions in the past six decades into provocations of Muslims and subsequent large-scale rioting along communal lines.[21]

*Communalism* is, of course, not only a Hindu problem.[22] It is a vast and complex phenomenon with which many social and political scientists have dealt and which seems to develop ever new forms, although its basic structure remains the same. Moin Shakir, an Indian political scientist calls communalism "the most intractable problem of the Indian polity and society." His view is that "under the mask of religion, culture, and tradition the communal leaders have been aiming at protecting the interests of the lower middle class and urban intelligentsia."[23]

All are agreed that religious identities are a major factor in communalism and that it constitutes a misapplication of religious principles. For several decades it appeared as if communalism was largely a Hindu-Muslim problem. In the 1990s Sikh communalists raised their voices and the regional chauvinisms that find expression in the various *senas* described previously are not only promoting intrareligious but also intraregional hatred.

The parallels that the advocates *Hindutva* try to evoke between their ideas of a Hindu *rāṣṭra* and the rule of *dharma* under the rulers of the Indian classical past, and the arguments used to convince the populace of the need for a Hindu India are, however, flawed. The kind of symbiosis that existed in classical India between traditional monarchies and traditional Hinduism was of a different kind than today's intertwining of party politics and an ideologized Hinduism. The responsibility of the traditional Indian king extended to all his subjects, and he was held responsible for their well-being regardless of sectarian affiliation. Likewise traditional Hinduism took a rather liberal view of doctrinal and ritual matters and was primarily focused on ethical concerns. Political parties as well as denominational religions have partisan concerns. The mix of modern party politics and denominational religions can lead to rather fatal consequences, as one could observe repeatedly in our century in several countries. Almost invariably the outcome is a dictatorial, intolerant, narrow-minded, and highly arbitrary kind of regime. In and through it both government and religion will become corrupted. Government, instead of focusing on the needs of the people, will concentrate on matters of ideology and party discipline. Religion, instead of acting as the repository of the moral conscience of the people, will become part and parcel of the oppressive system itself and will sell its soul for the sake of power.

## A PRELIMINARY ASSESSMENT

A long history of foreign invasions and occupations has given an extra edge to political Hinduism: it almost always contains an element of rejection of foreign institutions, customs, and authorities. Considering the high sophistication of traditional Indian thought also in the area of government—the detailed provisions made for the bearers of political authority from the ancient *smṛtis* onward—it is understandable that traditional Hindus want to see these provisions once more in place. Such a suggestion gains even more weight when one compares a glorified Indian past with an often disenchanting and problematic Indian present.

Political Hinduism is not a homogenous "movement." It is the result of a reinterpretation of Hinduism along many different lines. Neither are all Hindus agreed that Hinduism or its professional representatives ought to be involved in power politics at all. The traditional *yatidharma*, as explained before, forbids involvement of *saṃnyāsis* in political or economic affairs. There are many voices in today's India who demand a separation of religion and state and many view the influence of Hindu authorities on party politics with disapproval. While *Hinduism Today*[24] proudly presented "The Holy Men in India's New Parliament" and expects them to "reestablish the supremacy of moral values in both politics and society and work for the betterment of the lot of the poor and the downtrodden in the country,"[25] others resent the substitution of spirituality by party politics and influence pandering. As a visitor to Rishikesh expressed it: "You come here for getting as close to *nirvana* as you can and end up being lectured on today's petty politics."[26]

Political Hinduism is right-wing. Its major support comes from landowners and industrialists, shop owners, high school and college teachers, students, and small entrepreneurs. The potential power of the Hindu political parties, however, does not only lie in the as yet pervasive traditionalism and obscurantism of the large masses (especially in rural and small town India) but also in the correct perception of a widespread lack of social, ethical, and personal values in Western-style party politics. Indians, who have become aware of the value vacuum of the formal democratic process frequently fall back on Hinduism (often somewhat modernized, desectarianized, and enlightened in Sarvepalli Radhakrishnan's way) as the only acceptable basis: Hinduism, after all, is indigenous, it has shaped Indian society and mentality for thousands of years, it is flexible and—in the opinion of most Hindus—far superior in its philosophy to any other religion or philosophy.

The standard Western sociological and economic investigation that leads to the compilation of statistics of election results, distribution of incomes, family size, and so forth leaves out important factors. It seems to tacitly presuppose U.S. society and politics as the standard model that contains all the relevant parameters. It also seems to presuppose that developments can go only in one direction—namely the direction of what the West calls *modernity*. One indication that things are still different in India is the widespread and frequent large-scale defections from parties, the "crossing over" of large groups of elected representatives from one party to another, the splitting of existing parties, and the formation of new ones. Personal loyalties have priority over party tradition, personal rifts override party discipline. Matters of conviction and principle (however questionable and shallow) very easily win out over against an economic or voting calculus.

Contrary to the commonly held belief that ideological parties are obsolete and that modern politics boils down to a distribution of shares in the economy of a given county, we are clearly in for a new wave of ideological politics on all levels.[27] Issues with highly emotional content become anew the focus of world and national politics. The peace issue is one of them, reunification of divided nations is another. Language issues, too, become a source of political ferment. In the process the structures of political parties, built upon the rationalization of societal needs seem to become irrelevant. Grassroots movements, cutting across the classical political spectrum, mobilizing people, who would never join an existing political party, arise, and become decisive. Grassroots movements are usually not wholly spontaneous; they develop out of issues that had been for a long time neglected by the official parties but were cultivated by interest groups.

All these elements are present in political Hinduism. By declaring its contempt for the institution of Western style political parties it attracts all those who find the spectacle of party bickering and horse trading distasteful. By promoting Akhaṇḍ Bhārat—undivided India—it appeals not only to those who have suffered directly under the partition and its continued aftereffects but also to all those for whom Mother India is a reality.[28] And they are many. By its emphasis on Indianization it again appeals to vast numbers who feel that the present elite is much too Western oriented and forgetful of India's own cultural and spiritual heritage. And, last but not least, by emphasising Hindudom, it speaks to many shades of religiosity and nationalism alive in present-day India.[29]

The majority of Indian political scientists and sociologists are Marxist oriented. They try to find emerging "classes" in India as the major political agents and class struggle (of sorts) as the key to political dynamics. This may be too simple a solution—and too Western a view, too. Of course there are "new classes," of course there is "class struggle" (there always was), but the Indian sociopolitical scene has other dimensions, too, not covered by these categories.

The Indian Freedom Movement was not a class struggle; the Hindu *jāgaran* is not a matter of class either, although some of the above interpreters try to make it out as a reactionary middle-class movement designed to reinforce Brahmin dominance. The age-old fascination with renunciation, selfless service, worship of an absolute incarnate in a person, a place, a tradition is still alive. It was alive enough to attract hundreds of dedicated coworkers to Gandhi, who had renounced all property, title, and class affiliation. It is alive in the RSS, which demands from its leaders rigorous self-control, renunciation of private property, pleasure, and status and not only insists on classlessness but also on castelessness.

Hindu *jāgaran* cannot be understood by applying either a Western party democratic gauge or a Marxist socialist pattern. Its potential has much to do with the temper of Hinduism, which was able throughout the ages to rally people around causes that were perceived to be of transcendent importance and in whose pursuit ordinary human values and considerations had to be abandoned. Whether one considers this good or bad will depend on one's standpoint. The fact remains, however, and a student of Indian politics will be able to ignore this only to his or her own detriment.

## HINDUISM AS WORLD RELIGION

India has been for thousands of years not only the cradle of many religions and philosophies, but it also became the source of spiritual and cultural inspiration to many other countries. The question whether the high cultures of ancient Mesoamerica had been influenced by Indian immigrants from 500 BCE onward is still an open one[30]—the similarity between Mexican and Indian temple architecture is certainly striking! But there is no doubt about the colonial and cultural expansion of India in Southeast Asia from the first to the eighth or ninth centuries CE—Indonesia, Burma, Thailand, Laos, Cambodia, Vietnam—all have magnificent Indian temple ruins and all of their languages show the influence of Indian tongues. Vernacular versions of the *Rāmāyaṇa* and the *Mahābhārata* became popular in Indonesia and Sanskrit inscriptions have been found as far away as the Philippines.[31] Hindus founded kingdoms in these countries and introduced Hindu customs and rituals that have survived the centuries of Muslim and Western rule. Throughout South Asia one can find sculptures of Hindu deities and reliefs depicting Hindu myths. Khmer, Cham, and other Southeast Asian dynasties justified their rule by claiming descent from Śiva, Viṣṇu, or Brahmā and invoking the guardianship of these deities to maintain their rule. One of the world-famous temple sites in Cambodia, Angkor Wat, was dedicated to Viṣṇu by the twelfth-century Khmer king Suryavarman II. Bali, now part of Indonesia, has preserved its Hindu heritage into our own time and has become one of the major tourist attractions of Southeast Asia.[32]

One of the results of the aggressive Christian missionary activity in India from the late nineteenth century on was the awakening of Hindus to their own rich religious traditions and a Hindu countermission in the West. The pioneering activities of Svāmi Vivekānanda and of "Prabhupāda" Svāmi Bhaktivedānta have been mentioned before. They have been joined by numerous others who established Hindu centers in the West, such as Satya Sāī Bābā, Svāmi Chinmayānanda, and others.

The Chinmaya Mission West was set up in 1975 in San Jose, California, with the assistance of Satguru Sivaya Subrahmuniyaswāmi (1927–2001), an American convert to Śaiva Siddhānta, who not only had founded a Hindu monastery in Kauai, Hawaii, but also had built in 1957 a Hindu temple in San Francisco, the first in North America. He started a monthly, *Hinduism Today*, whose agenda were described as follows:

1. To foster Hindu solidarity as a "unity in diversity" among all sects and lineages;
2. To inform and inspire Hindus worldwide and people interested in Hinduisṃ;
3. To dispel myths, illusions and misinformation about Hinduism;
4. To protect, preserve and promote the sacred Vedas and the Hindu religion, especially the Nadinatha Sampradāya;
5. To nurture a truly spiritual Hindu renaissance
6. To publish a resource for Hindu leaders and educators who promote Sanatana dharma.

His Himalayan Academy trains Indian and Western Hindu priests and monks and his Hindu heritage endowment provides a source of income especially for priests belonging to the Śaiva Siddhānta *saṃpradāya* worldwide. In his various books he depicts a Hinduism that is modernized and appealing to modern Westerners. Subramuniya was honored and recognized by Hindu leaders in India and abroad. His successor, whom he named before his death, Satguru Bodhinatha Veylanswāmi, is carrying on with the mission.

India has brought forth in the modern era not only a Dāyānanda and a Tilak, but also a Gandhi and a Sarvepalli Radhakrishnan, an Aurobindo Ghose and a Krishnamurti, true citizens of the world and prophets of a universal religion. What we see happening with Hinduism today may be the formation of a truly new world religion. Hinduism, of course, always was a world religion on account of the large number of its adherents. But its strong ties to the geographic entity India and to traditional social structure had prevented it from reaching out into the world at large. Its intense sectarianism, too, was a hindrance for many to join it.

All this is changing. Hinduism has produced high profile exponents in our century who downplayed sectarianism, emphasized the common foundations of all its branches, and modernized and revitalized Hinduism. Hinduism has proved much more open than any other religion to new ideas, to scientific thought, and to social experimentation. Many beliefs, basic to Hinduism and initially strange to the West, like reincarnation, poly-devatism, meditation, and guruship have found worldwide acceptance. Also Hinduism's traditional fuzziness with regard to doctrinal boundaries is becoming a fairly universal feature of religion worldwide. Its living tradition of Yoga and of methods of interiorization give it an edge over other traditional religions that stress the absolute authority of an official or the ultimate truth of a scripture.

Hinduism is organizing itself, it is articulating its own essentials, it is modernizing, and it is carried by a great many people with strong faith. It would not be surprising to find Hinduism the dominant religion of the twenty-first century. It would be a religion that doctrinally is less clear-cut than mainstream Christianity, politically less determined than Islam, ethically less heroic than Buddhism, but it would offer something to everybody, it would delight by its richness and depth, it would address people at a depth level that has not been reached for a long time by other religions or by the prevailing ideologies. It will appear idealistic to those who look for idealism, pragmatic to the pragmatists, spiritual to the seekers, sensual to the here-and-now generation. Hinduism, by virtue of its lack of an overall ideology and its relying on intuition, will appear to be much more plausible than those religions whose doctrinal positions have petrified a thousand years ago or whose social structures remain governed by tribal mores.

That is how an open-minded scholarly Hindu like A. S. Altekar sees it, too: "Hindu religion, philosophy and social structure are nothing but the records of a glorious and instructive struggle of the human mind to free itself from limitations that become meaningless in the course of time, and to attain to more and more glorious heights that are revealed by man's ever expanding vision. There is no doubt that Hinduism will become once more a great world force, the moment this consciousness becomes a part and parcel of the modern Hindu mind and begins to mould and influence its activities in the different spheres of life."[33]

Hinduism will spread not so much through the gurus and swāmis, who attracted a certain number of people looking for a new commitment and a quasi-monastic lifestyle, but it will spread mainly through the work of intellectuals and writers who have found certain Hindu ideas convincing and who identify with them as their personal beliefs. A fair number of leading physicists and biologists have found parallels between modern science and Hindu ideas. An increasing number of creative scientists will come from a Hindu background and will consciously and unconsciously blend their scientific and their religious ideas. All of us may be already much more Hindu than we think. Various strands of Hinduism have provided much of the substance of the New Age thinking, and Hinduism may take up New Age ideas much more readily than any other historic tradition.

While initially, for the sake of avoiding a customary misidentification, the difference between Hinduism and what is called *religion* in the West had to be stressed, we now have to virtually reverse that position. Many people in the West realize more and more that organized denominational Christianity (called *Churchianity* by Hindus) does not really represent the spirit of Christianity, let alone that of religion in the most general sense. A new, broader, and looser understanding of religion is emerging that comes closer to the Hindu notion of *dharma*.[34] It recognizes on the one hand the impossibility of dogmatizing what is beyond human grasp and understanding, and it realizes, on the other hand, that "religion," to be genuine, must inform all aspects of life and not only consist of a worship routine.

Hinduism, both in the past and in the present, had and has its shortcomings. Nobody can overlook these. But it also had always enough vitality and genuine spiritual substance to outweigh its deficiencies. Its openness to reality, its experimental and experiential character, its genuine insights, and its authentic sages are a guarantee for its continued growth and relevance.

# Part V

## Miscellany

There were some issues that did not fit into the framework of the earlier four parts, but were deemed sufficiently important to be included in this *Survey of Hinduism*. They do not form a coherent unit by themselves and are simply juxtaposed.

"India and the West," deals with the history of the relationship between India and Europe and America, especially with the beginning of Indian studies in European and American universities.

"Hinduism and Science" provides background information on a topic that has become quite prominent in Indian studies in recent years.

Similarly, "Hinduism and Ecology" addresses an issue that has become a worldwide concern.

"Hindu Measures of Time" should prove useful for readers wanting to compare Indian and Western calendars and also summarizes information on world-cycles that play a great role in Hinduism.

"Indian Chronology" provides a summary of the Pre-and Proto-history of India and supplies, to the extent possible, dates for historical persons and events mentioned in the text, including reconstructions of the early history of India to which the Epics and the Purāṇas refer.

CHAPTER THIRTY-THREE

# India and the West

Since the beginning of recorded history, the West has been fascinated by India.[1] From classical antiquity onward, countless fanciful tales and amusing fables circulated throughout Europe about the peoples of India, its strange animals, and stranger plants, its scorching sun and torrential rains, its sky-high mountains and raging rivers. While most medieval books about the wonderland India were nothing but fancy, accurate descriptions of certain parts of India were available in the writings of some ancient authors who had either accompanied Western adventurers or who had traveled there for trade or out of sheer curiosity.

## EARLY CONTACTS BETWEEN EAST AND WEST

The greatest single impetus in this direction in antiquity was the Indian campaign of Alexander the Great in 327–326 BCE. In his company traveled writers like Aristobulos and Ptolemy, who described the battles Alexander fought, the rivers he crossed and the cities he conquered, the allies he won, and the kings he defeated. The Greeks suffered under the heat of the Indian plains and were awed by the great numbers of war elephants. They marveled at the enormous size of the population and the strangeness of their customs and manners. Even then, the wisdom of Indian holy men was proverbial. One of the first things Alexander did on entering India was to call upon and converse with some of these gymnosophists, in spite of the fact that they were instrumental in encouraging Indian resistance against the Macedonian invasion.[2] The Greeks seem to have admired the brusque and incisive manner of these men, and eventually Alexander asked one of them (whom the Greeks called Kálanos) to succeed his preceptor, Aristotle, as his constant companion and counselor. This "naked wise man" probably was a Jain *muni* of the Digambara sect: he was to end his life voluntarily on a pyre after having discovered that he was suffering from an incurable disease.[3]

The early medieval fiction *Alexander Romance* contains an exchange of letters between Alexander and an Indian king called Dindimus in which Alexander asks for, and receives, information about the Brahmins. "We Brahmins," the king writes, "lead a pure and simple life; we commit no sins; we do not want to have more than what is reasonable. We suffer and sustain everything." In short, the Brahmins lead an ideal life, they can teach wisdom and renunciation. In his reply to Dindimus Alexander recognizes that "only the Brahmins are good people."[4] This high opinion of Brahmins is still noticeable in the eighteenth century, when the German poet Lessing in his *Nathan* proclaims that only at the Ganges one can find morally perfect people.

For several centuries a lively commerce developed between the ancient Mediterranean world and India, particularly the ports on the western coast. The most famous of these ports was Sopāra, not far from modern Mumbāī. Coins and other objects found on several places suggest maritime contacts between Rome and India till the sixth century. Present-day Cranganore in Kerala, identified with the ancient Muziris, claims to have had trade contacts with ancient Egypt under Queen Hatsheput, who sent five ships to obtain spices, as well as with ancient Israel during King Solomon's reign. Apparently the contact did not break off after Egypt was conquered by Greece and later by Rome. According to I. K. K. Menon, "there is evidence of a temple of Augustus near Muziris and a force of 1200 Roman soldiers stationed in the town for the protection of Roman commerce."[5] Large hoards of Roman coins were found also on the east coast, near today's Mahabalipuram; a sign of commerce with Roman traders who must have rounded the southern tip of India to reach that place. Taprobane, identified with today's Śrī Laṅkā, plays a major role in ancient accounts of India—an island described to be even more wonderful and exotic than India herself. The kings of Magadha and Malwa exchanged ambassadors with Greece. A Maurya ruler invited one of the Greek Sophists to join his court, and one of the greatest of the Indo-Greek kings became famous as the dialogue partner of the great Buddhist sage Nāgasena,[6] while in the opposite direction, Buddhist missionaries are known to have settled in Alexandria and other cities of the ancient West.[7] These early contacts were not limited to the exchange of pleasantries; one Greek ambassador went so far as to erect a Garuḍa column in honor of Vāsudeva, while Greek epic poetry was translated into Indian languages and heard with appreciation in the court of Broach. The celebrated collection of Indian animal fables, the *Pañcatantra*, found its way into the West in a variety of translations and adaptations. So did a version of the life of Buddha, which resulted in the creation of the legend of Saint Josaphat.[8]

It is evident, then, that Indian thought was present in the fashionable intellectual circuit of ancient Athens, and there is every reason to suppose that Indian religious and philosophical ideas exercised some influence on early and classical Greek philosophy.[9]

Interest in India increased considerably during the time of the Roman emperors. Between the reign of Augustus (63 BCE–14 CE) and that of Caracalla (188–217 CE), East-West commerce flourished. A colony of Indian merchants is known to have existed in Alexandria, and under Augustus, Claudius, and Antoninus Pius Indian embassies visited Rome. At least one celebrated Greek philosopher, the neo-Pythagorean Apollonius of Tyana (first century CE), is reputed to have visited India in order to converse with learned Brahmins.

Both Greeks and Romans habitually tried to understand the religions of India by trying to fit them as far as possible into Greco-Roman categories. Deities in particular were spoken of, not in Indian, but in Greek terms and called by Greek names. Thus Śiva was identified as Dionysos, Kṛṣṇa (or perhaps Indra) as Heracles. The great Indian epics were compared to those of Homer. Doctrinally, the Indian concept of transmigration had its counterpart in the metempsychosis taught by Pythagoras and Plato; nor was Indian asceticism altogether foreign to a people who remembered Diogenes and his followers.[10] According to one persistent legend, Jesus spent the time between the twelfth and thirtieth years, a period of his life about which the Gospels are silent, in India, studying with Buddhist *bhikkus* and Vedānta *ācāryas*.[11]

Toward the end of the second century CE Tertullian, a Christian writer, defended his fellow believers from the accusation that they were "useless and should therefore be exterminated" by stating that the Christians were "neither Brahmins, nor Indian gymnosophists, forest-dwellers or withdrawn from life," but that they participated fully in the public and economic activities of Rome.[12] Some centuries later, the writer of the treatise *De moribus Brachmanorum* (originally thought to have been written by Ambrose of Milan, now considered to be the work of Prosper of Aquitania) has high praise for the Brahmins who could serve, he says, as exemplars to Christians.[13]

With the victory of Christianity in the West and the simultaneous decline of the Roman Empire, and still more with the Arab conquest of the Near and Middle East, the West lost contact with India; all that remained were faint and often distorted memories of India as a land of fabulous riches, of exotic creatures and a fantastic religion. However, the Arab conquest of India once more intensified exchange between India and the West, a West over which Arab influence was also now becoming more deeply felt.[14] Alberuni, a Muslim traveler who visited India between 1017 and 1030 CE, gave an admirably comprehensive account of many aspects of India's culture, including a fairly detailed summary of some important works of religious literature, unknown to the West until then.[15] It was through the Arabs that Indian learning reached the West, particularly in the fields of medicine, mathematics, and astrology. Indeed, the Indian decimal system and its symbols became known in the West as "Arabic numerals."

The great merchant-adventurer Marco Polo (1254–1324 CE) visited and described a number of places in India that he had seen, but his accounts were not usually taken seriously by his contemporaries, who considered him to be something of a storyteller rather than a serious topographer.[16] It was the search for India that led Cristoforo Colombo to the discovery of America in 1493. To this very day we call the original inhabitants of America Indians and find it often awkward to specify whether we mean American Indians or East Indians. The West's contact with India intensified after Vasco da Gama's historic voyage around the Cape of Good Hope in 1498, which led to an increased interest in India by the European powers. Together with the generals and the merchants came Christian missionaries. Some of them became interested in India's local religions and, though frequently showing a heavy apologetic bias, the works produced by some seventeenth- and eighteenth-century missionaries provided much useful material about India.[17] Of particular interest—both to their contemporaries and to us today—is the work of some artists of the eighteenth century who traveled through India and left vivid sketches and paintings of life and country. Thus William Hodges[18] spent three years in India between 1780 and 1784, most of them in Vārāṇasī, which offered vast scope to his pen and brush. He was one of the few white men to ever see a *satī* performed,[19] leaving a moving description. Between 1785 and 1788 he published *Select Views in India*, a collection of historically very interesting drawings of Indian monuments and landscapes. His slightly younger contemporaries, Thomas and William Daniell, famous for their paintings of Indian landscapes, traveled in India between 1786 and 1793 and inspired an Indian fashion in architecture in Britain.

## BEGINNING SCHOLARLY INTEREST IN INDIA

By the middle of the eighteenth century, European scholars were starting to get interested in India's literature. They were initially severely handicapped because of the Brahmin's reluctance to teach Sanskrit to *mlecchas* (impure foreigners) or to allow them to read their scriptures. The German philosopher Arthur Schopenhauer (1788–1860), whose enthusiastic praises of the Upaniṣads are frequently cited, had to rely on a Latin translation made by Anquetil du Perron from a Persian version made by Prince Dārā Shikūḥ (1615–1659 CE) of the original Sanskrit text!

During the first half of the eighteenth century J. E. Hanxleden wrote the first Sanskrit grammar under the title *Grammatica Granthamia seu Samscrdumica*.[20] It was never printed, but was put to use by J. Ph. Wessdin (Fra Paolino de St. Bartolomeo), who published two Sanskrit grammars and some quite informative works on India toward the end of the eighteenth century.[21] The greatest incentive to the scholarly study of India's history and culture was, however, provided by scholars affiliated with the British administration.[22] Typically, the first Sanskrit works to be translated into English were the Hindu law codes that the British officials needed to know. The British East India Company commissioned a group of Indian paṇḍits to compile a compendium of current Hindu law from the numerous original sources. The resulting work, named *Vivādarṇavasetu*, had first to be translated into Persian before an English translation could be made by an Englishman: it was published in 1776 by the East India Company under the title *A Code of Gentoo Law*.

The first Englishman to have a good knowledge of Sanskrit was Charles Wilkins, whom Warren Hastings (then governor general of Bengal) had encouraged to study with the Brahmins in Banares. In 1785 he published an English translation of the *Bhagavadgītā*, followed two years later by a translation of the *Hitopadeśa*. His Sanskrit grammar, which appeared in 1808, became the basis for all later work.

One of the most important figures in European Indology was Sir William Jones (1746–1794) who had acquired a good command of Persian and Arabic before coming to India in 1783, where he immediately took up the study of Sanskrit. One year later he founded the *Asiatick Society of Bengal*, which was soon to become the leading center for the publication of text editions and translations of important Hindu sources. Jones translated the *Manusmṛti* and published it in 1794 under the title *Institutes of Hindu Law, or the Ordinances of Manu*.[23] After Jones's untimely death Thomas Colebrook continued the work; he also edited and translated numerous Sanskrit works. As Professor of Sanskrit at Fort William College Calcutta he published in 1798 a four-volume series entitled *A Digest of Hindu Law on Contracts and Successions*, which consisted of translations of legal materials collected by a group of Indian pandits. Less interested in literature and poetry than in more scholarly Hindu works on law, arithmetic, astronomy, grammar, philosophy, and religion, he was the first Western scholar to provide correct and precise information about the Veda in his paper "On the Vedas, or Sacred Writings of the Hindus."[24]

Another Englishman, Alexander Hamilton, who had studied Sanskrit in India and was detained in Paris on his way back to England on account of Anglo-French hostilities, became instructor to the first generation of French and German Sanskritists for whom university chairs were established in the first half of the nineteenth century. While thus far those in Continental Europe who wished to study Indian culture had had to rely on French and German translations of English versions and monographs, they now could draw upon the resources of their own scholars who began to produce text editions and original versions. August Wilhelm von Schlegel, the brother of the poet Friedrich Schlegel, became the first professor of Sanskrit at the newly established University of Bonn in 1818. A. L. Chézy, the first French Sanskrit scholar, held the chair at the Collége de France in Paris.[25] Franz Bopp, a fellow student of Schlegel's at Paris, became the founder of comparative philology and linguistics.[26]

Though the East India Company did not allow Christian missionaries into its territories and maintained a policy of religious noninterference, Western Christians considered India as a mission field and tried to employ Indian studies for this purpose. Missionary activities on East India Company territory began in 1813, although William Carey had been at work in Serampore

(Śrīrampur), a Danish settlement near Calcutta, since 1800. A further important step was taken in 1830 with the opening of the Scottish missionary Alexander Duff's school in Calcutta. In the same year the famous Sanskritist H. H. Wilson became the first holder of the Boden Professorship in Oxford, founded in order "to promote the translation of the Scriptures into Sanskrit, so as to enable his countrymen to proceed in the conversion of the natives of India to the Christian religion." Both H. H. Wilson (1832–1860) and his successor to the chair, M. Monier-Williams (1860–1888), engaged in lexicographic work in order to lay the foundations for Bible translations that were soon made into the main languages of India.[27]

Following the historical trend that dominated in European scholarship in the nineteenth century, French and German scholars concentrated on studying the Vedas, the oldest document of Indian religious literature. Some of the students taught by Eugéne Burnouf at the Collége de France later attained lasting eminence as Vedic scholars. One of these was Rudolph Roth, who together with Otto Böthlingk edited the seven-volume *St. Petersburg Wörterbuch* (1852–1875), which has remained unsurpassed.[28]

Friedrich Max Müller became the most famous of them all. The son of the poet Wilhelm Müller, he earned fame through his monumental edition of the *Ṛgveda with Sāyaṇa's Commentary* (1849–1874). Of even greater significance than his Indological work is the fact that due to his wide general education and interests he became the founder of Comparative Religion as a scholarly discipline. Perhaps the crowning achievement of his life's work was his editorship of the fifty volumes of the *Sacred Books of the East* (1876–1904).[29] Müller did not find in his native Germany the support for his studies offered by England, which subsequently became the main center of Indian studies and libraries.

An astonishingly large number of brilliant scholars devoted themselves in the decades that followed to the study of India's past. Indology became a respected discipline at most major European universities, and scholars published a steady stream of critical text editions and translations, monographs, and dictionaries.[30] They even impressed traditional Indian pandits by their learning, and soon the first Hindu scholars arrived to study in European departments of Sanskrit in order to familiarize themselves with the scholarly methods developed in the West. Recognized Indian scholars, especially those proficient in English, were invited on lecture tours through the West and were thus given opportunity to explain authentically the traditions of India to an attentive but often misinformed audience.[31]

In the United States the popular philosophers Ralph Waldo Emerson (1803–1882) and Henry David Thoreau (1817–1862) were the first to show some serious interest in Indian thought, especially in Vedānta. The first to teach courses in Sanskrit was Isaac Nordheimer, who offered a course at the City University of New York as early as 1836. Edward Eldridge Salisbury introduced Sanskrit at Yale in 1841, where also the prestigious American Oriental Society was founded in 1842. Though Indologists make up only part of its membership, its journal and its monograph series are the major organ for classical Indian studies in the United States. Since the latter half of the nineteenth century several outstanding Sanskritists have taught and worked in the United States: Charles Rockwell Lanman (1850–1941), one of Rudolph Roth's students, became the founder-editor of the Harvard Oriental Series. His *Sanskrit Reader*, first published in 1883, is still in use. J. H. Wood's (1864–1935) translation of the major commentaries and glosses to Patañjali's *Yoga Sūtra* is still widely referred to. Maurice Bloomfield (1885–1928) emerged as one of the major Vedic scholars of his time; his *Vedic Concordance*, a monumental work, has been recently reprinted. Edward Washburn Hopkins's (1857–1932) books on the *Mahābhārata* are still authoritative on many points. Robert Ernest Hume (1877–1948) has deservedly gained fame for his translation of the *Thirteen Principal Upaniṣads*, which has seen many reprints. Franklin Edgerton's (1885–1963) *Bhagavadgītā* has been acknowledged as the most scholarly translation to date.[32]

Today all Western countries have university departments and research institutes in which advanced studies in Indology, including religious and philosophical Hinduism, are being undertaken. An impressive percentage of scholars referred to in this book are native Indians who enjoy the added advantage of working with materials from their own traditions. It almost goes without saying that India is today once more the leading country in Indian studies, both in the traditional way of learning as represented by the paṇḍit schools and in the modern methods, as initiated by Western scholars and continued and refined by Indian academicians. Indian universities publish numerous scholarly journals in English and in this way contribute to the West's understanding of Indian traditions.

## SCHOLARLY AND EXISTENTIAL INTERESTS

Early Western interest in Indian studies was kindled on the one hand by the practical requirements of the British administration in India to familiarize itself with its traditional law, and on the other by the predominantly historical and philological interests of Western scholars, trained in their own classical Greek and Latin traditions. More recently the accent has shifted to the contents of Indian philosophical and religious literature. The attitude of classical Western Indology had been that of strictly objective scholarly research; the professionals often frowned upon people who tried to identify themselves with certain positions of the Indian tradition on which they worked. The great works of this period, like Christian Lassen's monumental *Indische Altertumskunde* or Georg Bühler's *Grundriss der indoarischen Philologie und Altertumskunde* dealt with India as the established classical scholars had dealt with Ancient Greece and Rome. For all their enthusiasm in their professional studies (which centered on India's classical past) these scholars did not give up their typically Western way of thinking. By their own choice they remained outsiders, fulfilling their calling as scholars according to the Western ideal, sometimes even refusing, as Max Müller did, when invited, to pay a visit to India, in order not to upset their own image of the culture they studied.

The social, political, economical, and spiritual convulsions of our time, beginning with the First World War, together with the renewed self-consciousness of the generation that had experienced the Indian Renaissance, have made many of our contemporaries more ready to listen to what India has (and always had) to say. There was a remarkable growth of interest in Buddhism in the early twenties of the last century that had been rekindled lately by the visits of the Dalai Lama to many Western countries. On a more scholarly level, a great stimulus for Indian studies was provided by the First East-West Philosophers' Conference organized by Charles A. Moore (1901–1967) in Honolulu in 1939. Subsequent meetings have been attended also by a considerable number of eminent scholars from India.[33] A similar incentive came from the World Parliament of Religions, which decided to meet every four years after the centenary celebrations of the first meeting in Chicago in 1993. At the yearly gatherings of the American Academy of Religion, at which thousands of scholars meet, substantial sections are devoted to Indian traditions.

The contemporary West no longer has a unifying worldview, a commonly accepted religion or philosophy of life as a basis for the solution of its social or psychological problems and as sustenance in times of crisis. The experiences of the last century have undermined the naive optimism based on a faith in unlimited technological progress. Having witnessed a complete breakdown of much that was taken for granted in former times, we are now faced with a deep-rooted insecurity and also probably the irreparable loss of the authority of those institutions that for centuries had provided Westerners with a firm frame for their life and thought. An increasing number of people are opening to the suggestion that they might replace some traditional Western values and attitudes, which have proved short-lived and self-destructive, with Eastern modes of thought that have nourished cultures that have endured for thousands of years.[34] Slowly, however, the realization is also dawning that a mere replacement of one set of ideas and values by another would help us as little as did the timid or arrogant aloofness of former times.

Patterns of partnership prevail in international relations, partnerships that should include dialogue on all levels, allowing differences—even of a basic nature—to coexist without interrupting communication. A similar pattern also ought to determine the relationships between the major religions of the world. Much of what we find in Hinduism has no counterpart in the West. Hindu thinkers often have anticipated ideas and developed theories in many areas that have only recently begun to be explored in the West. In the analysis of language, in the technicalities of hermeneutics, in the methods of psychosomatic activation, and, last but not least, in philosophical and religious speculation and spiritual training, Hindu India is far ahead of the West. Western thinkers, through their study of Indian philosophics and religions have "discovered a new technical philosophy of undreamed-of complexity and ingenuity," and this contact has "expanded the imagination, increased the number of categories, made possible new studies in the history of logic, revealed new sensations and has driven the mind back to its origin and out to its possibilities."[35]

## INTERPRETING HINDUISM IN WESTERN TERMS

Early Western Indologists were all-round experts: they used to deal with everything that concerned India. Meanwhile the field has grown to such an extent that specialization has become necessary both for the sake of the integrity of research and for the sake of students interested in Indian studies. Even within the specialized field of the study of Hindu religions one has to narrow down one's enquiry either to a particular school of thought, a period, or even a single personality. However, in order to locate one's particular research within the larger framework of Hindu culture, one needs to reach out and familiarize oneself with other aspects and the history of the total phenomenon.

There is a certain temptation for Western students of Hindu traditions to follow through vaguely familiar thoughts and to complete them according to their own habitual thought models. We must, however, take seriously the historicity of each tradition, not only in the vaguely idealistic (and ultimately unhistorical) Hegelian sense but in its own historical factuality. Hinduism is what it is today because it has developed that way through its own history and through its specific worldview. Typically Western approaches to reality, the compartmentalization of knowledge into such categories as science and arts, philosophy and theology, sociology and psychology do not coincide with Indian approaches and their specific avenues of enquiry.[36] Despite two hundred years of diligent work by an increasing number of devoted Western scholars of Indian culture, on many essential points we have not yet reached a verbal understanding. Western languages have no adequate translations for many of the key terms in philosophical and religious Sanskrit texts. It is still true, what Ananda Coomaraswamy stated more than half a century ago: "Asiatic thought has hardly been, can hardly be presented in European phraseology without distortion, and what is called the appreciation of Asiatic art is mainly based on categorical misinterpretations."[37] Misunderstandings are bound to happen even with the best of intentions, which cannot always be taken for granted. To try to avoid some misunderstandings, this representation of Hinduism uses original terms wherever practicable.

Indian and Western traditions do not differ so much in the answers they give to similar problems but in the problems that they consider relevant, the questions they ask. Problems that never occur to the Westerner may be of the utmost significance for the Hindu. Take reincarnation and the ways to escape from it. Indian traditions are not just a variant of Western religions; their very structure is different. Scholars like Betty Heimann,[38] Heinrich Zimmer,[39] Maryla Falk,[40] Rene Guénon,[41] Stella Kramrisch,[42] and Wilhelm Halbfass,[43]

Westerners well grounded in their own traditions, have made structural studies of Hinduism that presuppose not only specialized Indological expertise but also a comprehensive general knowledge and a great deal of empathy. We must not expect everything we find in Hinduism to fit into the frame of our present knowledge. As modern science cannot be adequately explained in the terminology of medieval philosophy of nature, so Indian philosophical and religious thought cannot be satisfactorily reproduced using our current Western idiom. Translations of authoritative Hindu literature are always interpretations, for better or for worse, according to the insight of the translator. This is true for the translations of Western scholars with an insufficient philosophical background, not to mention those "translators" who, ignorant of the original languages, simply restyle an existing translation in the fashion and idiom of the day. It applies still more to some Indian translators who are unfamiliar with the deeper meaning of the Western philosophical terminology they frequently use. Occasionally a translation can be more tendentious than an original work, if it is meant to support the particular viewpoint of a particular proselytizer. In those points that are really crucial the meaning of a text cannot be found without a thorough study of the sources in the original languages within their original context. The literary sources of Indian philosophy and religion, moreover, are quite frequently written in such a peculiarly concise style that a student cannot even understand them grammatically without oral instruction and commentary. Furthermore, the same terms are given different meanings in different systems. The texts often contain indirect quotations from, and references to, writings with which the Indian expert is familiar but which a Western reader without a competent guide would overlook.[44] Only from contact with learned Hindus can a Western student of Hinduism learn how to read and to understand Hindu sources: the premises they work with, the axioms they take for granted, the problems they consider relevant, the theoretical presuppositions in the interpretation of texts.

While India and the West quite obviously and visibly differ from each other in many ways, one ought to beware of dichotomizing East and West along the lines of spiritual versus materialistic, or collective versus individualistic, or archaic versus modern. There are idealists and materialists in India and in the West. Indians have made some major contributions to contemporary modern science and technology. Western scholars have been recognized by their Indian colleagues as specialists in Sanskrit studies and others have been commended for their genuine understanding of Hindu culture.

CHAPTER THIRTY-FOUR

# Hinduism and Science

The word *Hindu* designates not just a particular religion in the narrow modern sense, but it stands for a cultural tradition that developed over thousands of years on the South Asian subcontinent, embracing also different religions, such as Vaiṣṇavism, Śaivism, Śāktism, and others. The Hindu tradition comprises, besides religious rituals and festivities and detailed ethical regulations for individuals and communities, also the "arts and sciences." Hinduism never knew the Western antagonism between philosophy and theology, nor does it have a "history of warfare between science and religion." It was the highest aim of Hindus to find *satya*, truth/reality, which could be approached in many ways and appear in many forms.

The well-organized, publicly as well as privately sponsored ancient Indian universities—the most famous were Taxila in the northwest and Nālandā and Mithilā in the east, considered venerable institutions already at the time of Gautama the Buddha, with thousands of teachers and tens of thousands of students, taught not only the Veda and the *Vedāṅgas* but also the "eighteen sciences," later supplemented by the "sixty-four arts." The basic curriculum included *śabda-vidyā* (linguistics), *śilpasthāna-vidyā* (arts and crafts), *cikitsa-vidyā* (medicine), *hetu-vidyā* (logic and dialectics), and *adhyātma-vidyā* (spirituality).[1] Religion, while suffusing all life and activity, was not isolated from other subjects or given exclusive attention. The Brahmins, the custodians of the sacred texts, were also the leading intellectuals who studied and taught secular subjects.

The Hindus called their most ancient and most venerated scripture *Veda* (from the verbal root *vid-*, to know). *Vidyā*, from the same root, designated knowledge acquired in any subject (a medical doctor was called a *vaidya*), particularly that of the highest reality/truth taught by the Upaniṣads. The term *śāstra* (from the root *śās-*, to order) became the most general designation for "science" (in the sense of French *science* or Italian *scienza*): authoritative, systematic teaching, ranging from *Dharma-śāstra*, the exposition of traditional law,[2] and *Artha-śāstra*, the teaching of statecraft and administration,[3] to *Śilpa-śāstra*, the instruction in art and architecture,[4] and *Kṛṣī-śāstra*, the theory and practice of agriculture.[5] A learned person carried the title of *Śāstri*, respected by the community regardless of the subject of his learning. Graduation was a "third birth": members of the three higher castes became *dvījati* (twice-born) through *upanayana* (initiation); the *śāstri* degree made them *trijati* (thrice born).

High ethical standards were expected both from students and teachers. Students not only had to pass stringent examinations to prove their aptitude for the subject of study, but also had to live an austere life according to traditional ideals of higher learning. Medical students, for instance, had to take an oath of initiation and a professional oath at the end of their training period, expressing their resolve to follow the code of ethics of their calling.[6]

Traditional Indian thought is characterized by a holistic vision. Instead of breaking experience and reality up into isolated and unrelated fragments, the Indian thinkers looked at the whole and reconciled tensions and seeming contradictions within overarching categories.[7] Thus the poets of the *Ṛgveda* speak of *viśva-jyoti*, cosmic light, as the principle and source of everything and of *Ṛta*, the universal cosmic order connecting and directing all particular phenomena and events. As Betty Heimann emphasizes: "*Ṛta* is the functional balance of already existent single phenomena of which each in its proper place functions in its own law of activity and all of them collectively balance each other in mutually retarding or accelerating, limiting or expanding rhythm."[8]

The Upaniṣads organize the world by relating everything to the *pañcabhūtas* (five elements: earth, water, light, wind, ether) and strive to gain knowledge of *brahman*, the all-embracing reality principle. As the *Taittirīya Upaniṣad* has it:

> Fire, air, sun, moon. and stars.
> Water, plants, trees, ether, and the body.
> Thus with regard to material existence.
> Now with regard to the self.
> *Prāṇa, vyāṇa, apāṇa, udāṇa*, and *samāṇa*
> Sight, hearing, mind, speech, touch
> Skin, flesh, muscle, bone, marrow.

"Having ordained in this manner, the sage said: Fivefold, verily, is this all. With the fivefold, indeed, does one win the fivefold."[9]

The name of the major deity of later Hinduism is *Viṣṇu*, the "all-pervading," whose body is the universe.[10] Nature (*prakṛti*) was never seen as mere object, but always as productive agent.

The Hindu view of life found expression in the four *puruṣārthas*: one was to acquire wealth (*artha*), enjoy life (*kāma*), practice morality and religion (*dharma*), and seek final emancipation (*mokṣa*) in appropriate balance. Religion was a natural part of the universally accepted order of things. Texts dealing with medicine or agriculture contain religious regulations, and philosophical/theological treatises also frequently refer to worldly matters. The study of Nyāya (logic and epistemology) was undertaken to achieve *mokṣa* (spiritual emancipation). The notion of *ātman* (conscious self) was applied to humans, animals, and plants. Many Indian scientists show an interest in religious issues, and Hindu spiritual leaders frequently appeal to the sciences to illustrate their instructions. They would never relegate science to pure "reason" or religion to pure "faith" and treat them as natural enemies, as is often done in the West.

According to the Vedas only one-fourth of Reality is accessible to the senses (which also include *manas*, instrumental reason). Supersensual reality revealed itself to the *ṛṣis*, the composers of the Vedic *sūktas*. The Upaniṣads know an ascending correlation of subject/consciousness and object/reality: only the lowest of four stages (*jāgarita*) concerns sense perception of material objects. The three higher levels of reality are intuited through meditative introspection, which culminates in the insight *ātman* is *brahman*: Spirit-Self is Supreme Reality.[11]

The central ritual of Vedic culture, the *yajña* was offered on altars built with specifically produced bricks arranged in a prescribed geometric pattern, performed at astronomically fixed times. The altar was conceived as a symbol of the human body as well as of the universe: one text relates the 360 bricks of an altar to the 360 days of the year and the 360 bones in the human body. The building of altars of different configurations, and more so their change in shape and volume, as required in certain rituals, involved a sophisticated geometry. *Śūlva-sūtras* (part of *Kalpa-sūtras*, ritual texts) provided the rules for constructing a variety of shapes of altars and their permutations. As Abraham Seidenberg has found out, they exhibit an algebraic geometry, older and more advanced than early Egyptian, Babylonian, or Greek geometry. The exact timing of the performance of the sacrifices was done by people conversant with the movement of the stars. *Jyotiṣa*, one of the six early *Vedāṅgas* (auxiliary sciences of the Veda), reveals a good deal of astronomical knowledge.

Study was mandatory for Brahmins, whose profession was to recite the Veda and officiate at the public and private rituals. They had to devote the first part of their lives up to age twenty-four to systematic training under the supervision of a guru. Later they had to practice *svādhyāya*, "study on their own." While the study of the Vedas and the *Vedāṅgas* was reserved for Brahmins, the study of the *Upavedas* was open to all (higher) castes.[12] These comprise *Āyur-veda* ("life science," medicine), *Dhanur-veda* ("bow science," martial arts), *Gandharva-veda* ("art science," music and dancing), and *Stāpathya-veda* ("building science," architecture, sculpture, and painting). The universities where these subjects were taught attracted a large body of students from all over Asia. Reports from fourth- and sixth-century Chinese guest students praise the physical amenities as well as the high standard of learning. In the eleventh century, after the Muslim invaders had already destroyed much of India's cultural infrastructure, the Muslim scholar-diplomat Al-Bīrūnī spent a decade in India researching and documenting many aspects of traditional Indian science in his *Al-Hind*.[13]

Research in the history of Indian science is still at an early stage, and much work remains to be done. Even so, the information offered in some of the available histories of science in India is already quite substantial. Much of it has not yet reached Western students of the history of science and has not been incorporated into the standard Western treatises on science and religion. New material is regularly published in the well-established *Indian Journal for the History of Science*, the newly founded quarterly *Vedic Science*, and other periodicals dealing with Indian history or Indian thought in general.

## THE PRACTICAL SCIENCES OF HINDU INDIA

### Astronomy

Astronomical knowledge of a fairly high order was required to determine the right time for the performance of Vedic *yajñas*. One of the *Vedāṅgas*, the *Jyotiṣa*, explains how to determine the positions of sun and moon at solstices and of the new and full moon in the circle of the twenty-seven *nakṣatras*. The basis of the calculations was a five-year cycle called *yuga*: it began with the coming together of sun, moon, and Dhanistha *nakṣatra* on the first *tithi* of the bright fortnight of Māgha, at the autumn solstice. The solar year of 366 days and the lunar year of twelve months of thirty days each were harmonized by adding two intercalary months at the end of the third and the fifth year, when the cycle of sixty-two full moons and sixty-two new moons was completed, comprising 124 complete *parvaṇs*. The *Jyotiṣa Vedāṅga* embodies the teaching of Lagadha and has been dated by internal evidence to 1200 BCE. Earlier mentioned markers of the vernal equinox suggest astronomical observations made in 4500 BCE, recorded in the *Ṛgveda*, and in 2500 BCE, recorded in the *Śatapatha Brāhmaṇa*.[14] In addition, according to Subhash Kak, the structure of the *Ṛgveda* text and of the Vedic altars contain an "astronomical code," embodying fairly accurate information about distances and revolutions of planets and more general astronomical data. When the more recent Siddhānta calendar was adopted that divided the zodiac into twelve *rāśis*, the older division into twenty-seven *nakṣatras* became obsolete. The most famous of the numerous works called *siddhāntas* is the *Sūrya-siddhānta* (fourth century CE).

The ancient Indians operated with various cycles of lunar and solar years and calculated cosmic cycles of 10,800 and 432,000 years: the duration of one *kalpa*—a cycle of the universe during which all the heavenly bodies return to their original positions—was reckoned to be 4,320,000,000 years.

Several Purāṇas contain cosmogonic and cosmological sections utilizing astronomy, describing periodic creations and destructions of the universe, and also suggesting the existence of parallel universes. While the main purpose of the Purāṇas is to recommend a specific path of salvation, this is always set into a cosmic context. Many popular *stotras* (hymns, prayers) recited at religious gatherings allude to cosmic events as well. One of the most interesting figures among Indian astronomers is Varāhamihira (fifth/sixth century CE), the author of the celebrated *Pañca-siddhāntika* and of the *Bṛhat-Saṃhitā* that besides astronomical information teaches astrology and all kinds of occult arts.

Astrology was an integral part of the later *Jyotiṣa* and is widely regarded by Hindus as one of the traditional sciences. There is a department of *Jyotiṣa* at Banares Hindu University that publishes a yearly *Pañcāṅga*, an almanac with astronomical information required to settle the exact dates of most of the major Hindu festivals (nationally and regionally) and fortnightly charts used by Hindu astrologers for establishing birth horoscopes still fairly universal in India, that are consulted before every important event of a person's life. Also the *Rashtriya Panchang*, published by the Indian government every year for the Śaka Era, contains together with astronomical detail all pertinent astronomical information for every day of the year.

## Mathematics

Like geometry, mentioned before, other fields of Indian mathematics developed out of the requirements for the Vedic *yajña*. The *Yajurveda Saṃhitā* knows terms for numbers up to $10^8$—by comparison the highest number named by the Greeks was *myriad* ($10^4$). The *Pañcavimśa Brāhmaṇa* has terms for 1 (*eka*), 10 (*daśa*), 100 (*śata*), 1000 (*sahasra*), 10,000 (*ayuta*), 100,000 (*niyuta*), 1,000,000 (*prayuta*), 10,000,000 (*arbuda*), 100,000,000 (*nyarbuda*), 1,000,000,000 (*samudra*), 10,000,000,000 (*madhya*), 100,000,000,000 (*anta*), and 1,000,000,000,000 (*parārdha*). Later on the Indians coined terms for numbers up to $10^{23}$ and $10^{52}$. Algebra, in spite of its Arabic name, is an Indian invention, and so are the Zero and the decimal system, including the "Arabic" numerals. We know the names of some great Indian mathematicians and some particulars of their accomplishments. Thus Āryabhata I (fifth century CE), a link in a long chain of unknown earlier master mathematicians, knew the rules for extracting square and cubic roots. He determined the value of $\pi$ to four decimals and developed an alphabetical system for expressing numbers on the decimal place value model. His *Āryabhatīya* was translated into Latin (from an Arabic translation) by a thirteenth-century Italian mathematician. Brahmagupta (seventh century CE) formulated a thousand years before the great European mathematician Euler (1707–1783) a theorem based on indeterminate equations. Bhāskara II (twelfth century) is the author of the *Siddhānta-śiromaṇī*, a widely used text on algebra and geometry. Hindus have continued to show great aptitude for mathematics. Recently the South Indian mathematician Ramanujan (1887–1920), practically untutored, developed the most astounding mathematical theorems. The astounding role that India plays today in the area of computer and information technology is rooted in the Hindu tradition of mathematics.

## Medicine

The *Atharva-veda* (by some considered the oldest among the four Vedas) contains invocations relating to bodily and mental diseases. Its *Upa-veda*, the *Āyur-veda*, "life science," was cultivated systematically from early on. It was mainly oriented toward preventing diseases and healing through herbal remedies, but it also later developed other medical specialties. Good health was not only considered generally desirable, but also prized as a precondition for reaching spiritual fulfillment. Medicine as a "charity" was widely recommended and supported by the rulers. Two Indian medical handbooks, the result of centuries of development, became famous in the ancient world far beyond India: the *Cāraka-saṃhitā* and the *Suśruta-saṃhitā*.[15] They were later translated and utilized by the invading Muslims. *Cāraka* deals mainly with general medicine and identifies hundreds of medical conditions for which (mainly) plant pharmaca are prescribed. *Suśruta* focuses on surgery, which by that time was already highly developed, with an array of specific surgical instruments. Indian surgeons were famous in the ancient world—their skills were especially appreciated by the wounded in the frequent wars. Hindus also called upon the divine physician of the gods, Dhanvantari, "the one who removes arrows." The theory of *Āyur-veda* was based on the *tri-dośa* theory, which is older than the similar Greek three-humors teaching, used for diagnosis as well as in the treatment of diseases. While the healthy body has a perfect balance of *vata*, *pitta*, and *kapha*, disease is a disturbance of that harmony, to be cured by reestablishing the right proportion.

*Āyur-veda* was also applied to animals and plants. There is an ancient *Vṛksāyur-veda*, a handbook for professional gardeners and a *Gavāyur-veda* for veterinarians of cattle. Other texts deal with veterinary medicine relating to horses and elephants. Ancient India also had hospitals as well as animal clinics. *Gośālās*, places in which elderly cattle are provided for, are still popular in some parts of India. *Āyur-veda* was the source of much of ancient Greek and Roman as well as medieval Arabic medical knowledge. The scientific value of Ayurvedic pharmacology is being recognized today by major Western pharmaceutical companies who apply to get worldwide patents on medicinal plants discovered and described by the ancient Indian *vaidyas*.

## Architecture

The ancient Sindhu-Sarasvatī civilization exhibits a high degree of architectural achievement. The well laid out cities, the carefully built brick houses, the systems of drainage, and the large water tanks reveal the work of professional town planners and builders. This tradition was continued[16] and enhanced in later centuries especially in connection with the building of temples to provide abodes for the deity. No village or town was deemed fit for human habitation if it did not possess a temple. Careful selection and preparation of the ground preceded the building activity proper. The edifice had to be constructed according to an elaborate set of rules that took into account not only structural engineering and quality of materials, but also circumstances of caste and religious affiliation. The *Upaveda* of *Sthāpatya-vidyā* was expanded into a professional *Vāstu-śāstra* and *Śilpa-śastra*. Elaborate handbooks like the *Manasāra* and the *Mayamata* provide detailed artistic and religious canons for the building of temples and the making of images. Temples and images of deities were consecrated only if they conformed to the standards established. The temple (*maṇḍira*) was a visible symbol of the universe, showing the entire range of entities from the highest to the lowest. The image (*mūrti*) was the very body of God, who descended into it for the purpose of receiving worship. Thousands of large and beautiful temples dot the landscape of India and millions of images adorn *maṇḍiras* and homes.

## Music and Dance

Traditional India eagerly cultivated the *Gandharva-veda*: music (vocal and instrumental) and dance. Both were intimately connected with the temple and temple worship.[17] Classical Indian music developed out of Vedic chanting, which had as much of a scientific basis as Vedic astronomy or mathematics. The subtle laws of sound worked out by Indian musicians, the long and systematic training the students had to undergo, the care they had to exercise in performing their art makes it an equal to the training that a scientist undertakes. The field, however, is too large and too complex to be dealt with in a paragraph in this context. Fortunately, it is one of the areas that has been explored quite thoroughly also by Western musician scholars who have undergone training under Indian masters and have studied the underlying theory.[18]

## Linguistics

While India's medical doctors, its architects, metallurgists, mathematicians, astronomers, and others were appreciated for their knowledge and skills in their fields, the pride of place in the world of brahmanic knowledge always belonged to the study of the Word (*vāk*), which from early on was seen as imbued with divine power. The Brahmins who preserved and investigated the Word occupied the highest social rank. Sanskrit, the (refined) language of the Veda and of higher learning, was considered a gift of the gods. The *Vedāṅgas* of *Śīkṣā* (Phonetics) and of *Nirukta* (Etymology) as well as of *Vyākaraṇa* (Grammar) and *Chaṇḍas* (Metrics) relate to the study of language, followed by a large number of later works that go into intricate detail of linguistic problems.

The Sanskrit alphabet, in contrast to the chaotic alphabets used in Western languages, is based on a scientific system: all vowels are arranged in an orderly fashion according to acoustic principles. The consonants are organized in five classes (guttural, palatal, cerebral, dental, labial), and in each of these five varieties were distinguished (hard, hard-aspirate, soft, soft-aspirate, nasal). This system shows great ingenuity and a keen sense of observation and it proved conducive to formulating general grammatical and phonetic laws. It was in place already by 1000 BCE. By 600 BCE, Pāṇini, a linguistic genius of the first order, systematized Sanskrit in his *Aṣṭādhyāyī*, deriving verbs and nouns from about eight hundred roots and formulating four thousand interconnected grammatical rules—an achievement unparalleled in any other language until now. Pāṇini was followed by a long line of commentators who continued his work: the best known is Patañjali, the author of the *Mahā-bhāṣya*. Traditional Indian scholarship was based on memorizing enormous amounts of literature and transmitting it orally over thousands of years. In the process Indians developed very sophisticated mnemo-technical devices.[19]

## Ancient Indian Theoretical Sciences

Among the *ṣaḍ-darśanas*, the traditional "six orthodox philosophical systems" of Hinduism, *Sāṁkhya* stands out as possibly the oldest and certainly the most interesting in the religion and science context. It offers a general theory of evolution based on the interactive polarity of nature/matter (*prakṛti*) and spirit/soul (*puruṣa*). All reality is subsumed under five times five principles (*tattvas*) originating from one substratum (*pradhāna*), covering all possible physical, biological, and psychological categories.

*Sāṁkhya* shows the interconnections between the various components of our world, in order to unravel the evolutionary process (seen as the cause of all unhappiness and misery) and to return to the changeless bliss of spirit existence. The twenty-five categories to which *Sāṁkhya* reduces the manifold world became widely accepted in Hindu thought. The Yoga system of Patañjali is wholly based on it. The Purāṇas also accept it as their philosophical basis, with one amendment: *prakṛti* and *puruṣa* are overarched by *īśvara*, a personal creator-maintainer-savior God.

*Vaiśeṣika*, another one of the six orthodox *darśanas*, offers a theory of atomism more ancient than that of Democritus, and a detailed analysis of *viśeṣas*, qualities, differences, after which the system is called. The *Vaiśeṣika-sūtra* describes the formation of physical bodies from atoms (*aṇu*) through dyads (*dvyaṇuka*) and triads (*tryaṇuka*) in a strict cause-effect series. The positioning of the atoms determines the qualities of a body. *Vaiśeṣika* also developed the notion of impetus—a concept that appeared in Western science only in the fourteenth century. In *Vaiśeṣika* the relation of science to religion is less clear than in the case of *Sāṁkhya*. However, the other *darśana* with which it has been paired, *Nyāya*, concerned with epistemology and logic, declares that such analysis is neceessary for obtaining spiritual liberation.

## The Spiritual Sciences

Among the prescribed subjects of the ancient Indian university curriculum we find *adhyātma-vidyā*: the science relating to spirit. As the most important level of Reality, *brahman* was the subject of the highest science, employing personal experience (*anubhāva*), a coherent epistemology (*yukti*), and the exegesis of revealed utterances (*śruti* or *śabda*). The Upaniṣads mention thirty-two *vidyās*, paths leading to the goal of all science. The knowledge aimed at through these was of a particular kind, involving a transformation of the student: "One who knows *brahman* becomes *brahman*."

The ideas of the Upaniṣads were further developed into the systematics of Vedānta philosophy laid down mainly in commentaries (*bhāṣyas*) on the *Brahma-sūtras* ascribed to Bādarāyaṇa (second century BCE). Beginning with Śaṅkara (eighth century CE), through Rāmānuja (eleventh century), to Madhva (thirteenth century), the greatest minds of India have endeavored to cultivate that science that concerns itself with the eternal reality of the spirit. Yoga, too, in the form in which it was systematized by Patañjali (*Rāja-yoga*) is proceeding "scientifically" by analyzing the world of experience in terms suitable to spiritual enlightenment and describing experiential steps to be taken to find enlightenment.

India's spiritual fame in the West is of long standing: Alexander was intrigued by the proverbial wisdom of the Brahmins. Six centuries later Plotinus joined the expedition of Emperor Gordian in order to touch base with the famed Indian sages. No less a modern Western scientist than the Nobel Prize-winning physicist Erwin Schrödinger has paid tribute to that "other" science: "The subject of every science is always the spirit and there is only that much true science in every endeavor as it contains spirit." Consciousness is being treated as the last frontier in today's science: the nature of the knowledge exhibited in quantum theory demands an engagement of the subject and leads to a kind of secular *adhyātma-vidyā*.[20]

## INDIA AND SCIENTIFIC TECHNOLOGICAL PROGRESS

Glazed pottery appeared in Mohenjo Daro fifteen hundred years earlier than in Greece. Indian steel was so famous three thousand years ago that the ancient Persians were eager to obtain swords from India. Indian silk and cotton fabrics were among the most prized imports of ancient Rome. The famous Iron Pillar in Delhi, almost eight meters high and weighing more than six tons, has weathered more than fifteen hundred monsoons without showing a trace of rust. Amazing engineering feats were displayed in the construction of numerous temples of huge dimensions. The capstone of the Bṛhadīśvara temple of Tanjavur, weighing eighty tons, was moved up to a height of sixty-five meters in the eleventh century! The skills of ancient Indian craftsmen who created innumerable tools and works of art from ivory, wood, metal, and stone show a broad-based technical culture that had few equals in its time. Many of the intellectual or practical achievements later ascribed to the Babylonians, the Greeks, or the Arabs had originated in India.[21] India was the envy and the marvel of the ancient world before it fell victim to Muslim invaders, who massively disrupted its cultural, scientific and religious traditions. The British who succeeded the Muslims encountered a weak, backward, fragmented, and demoralized India. Together with machine-made fabric, British-India imported

Western education and with this a hitherto unknown tension between culture and religion. Modern science and technology were touted as an accomplishment of Christian Europe and seen as the most effective instruments in overcoming superstitious Hinduism. Ram Mohan Roy, an early Hindu reformer, believed in the possibility of harmonizing Hinduism with modern Western science (and the teachings of Christ). He founded English-language schools in which modern Western scientific knowledge was taught. Swāmi Dāyānanda Sarasvatī asserted that the ancient Hindus had known the principles of Western science long ago, had anticipated some of the technological marvels like steam engines and airplanes, and did not need a new religion. He founded a traditional *gurukula* with Sanskrit as medium of in studies and only traditional Indian subjects. Today there are thousands of Indian scientists with a Hindu background. Most do not see a conflict between their religion and their science, but some do notice a difference in orientation. Some have been lead to astounding discoveries through the application of ancient Hindu insights to new fields of enquiry. Thus Nobel Prize-winner Sir Jagdish Chandra Bose used the Upaniṣadic idea of the universal *ātman* to conduct groundbreaking research in plant physiology. The traditional Hindu holistic and personalistic orientation could serve as a necessary corrective to mainstream Western science with its Cartesian legacy of an impersonal mechanistic worldview and its Baconian utilitarian emphasis on the employment of the sciences primarily for the exploitation of nature. Traditional Indian solutions in many practical areas such as home building and field irrigation often have proven superior to modern (foreign) high-tech approaches.

CHAPTER THIRTY-FIVE

# Hinduism and Ecology

India's ecology is in deep trouble. Its rivers are extremely polluted. Yamunā, the daughter of Yama, the god of death, is today a river that lives up to its name.[1] The Gaṅgā is no better. Indeed, no river, once it hits the plains, remains clean. . . . The air in most Indian cities is becoming literally unbreathable. . . . Tens of thousands of people die prematurely in Delhi each year due to environmentally induced causes."

—Anil Agarwal, "*Can Hindu Beliefs and Values Help India Meet Its Ecological Crisis?*"

The ecological crisis that exercises so many people in the Western world has also reached India, one of the most densely populated countries of the world with one of the fasted growing economies. In order to alleviate mass poverty, governments since the time of Jawaharlal Nehru have pushed ahead with industrialization and agricultural development—the "Green Revolution" has transformed India, in spite of an enormous increase in population, from a food import dependent country in the 1960s to a major grain-exporting nation in the 2000s. India's industrial capacity is impressive and the "outsourcing" of many information technology related jobs from North America and Europe has brought affluence to a large number of well-trained Indian workers. The "collateral damage" caused by industrial progress to the environment has been enormous, and Indian ecological activists are getting alarmed. India has ample legislation to protect the environment, but most people care little for it.

Anil Agarwal, an engineer turned journalist and ecological activist, blames Hinduism for this sorry state of affairs. "Hinduism," he writes "is a highly individualistic religion. It looks into the self, emphasizing the *ātman* as the key to spiritual ascent. *Dharma* focuses first on oneself, emphasizing one's own behavior. The consequences of one's behavior on others play a secondary role. The primary concern is to do one's *dharma* for the sake of one's own well-being. . . . Under the onslaught of modern-day secularism this has brought out the worst type of individualism in Hinduism."[2] He mentions instances of pollution and sanitary neglect, which no visitors to India fail to see as soon they leave the airports: heaps of garbage in public places, roadsides used as public latrines, untreated sewage flowing into waterways, and so forth. He also points out aspects of ecological degradation that are not so obvious:

> Groundwater is being overexploited across the country and in urban industrial areas is becoming irreversibly polluted. Nearly one third of the country's land lies bare, due to abuse and mismanagement. Biomass shortages are acute and women can spend eight to ten hours just collecting basic necessities like firewood, fodder and water. . . . The air quality of New Delhi rivals that of Mexico City as the most polluted in the world."[3]

Veer Bhadra Mishra, a retired hydrological engineer and head of the "Swatcha Ganga Foundation" in Vāraṇasī as well as the guru of a religious association who made it his life's mission to clean up the Ganges, maintains that Hinduism is an essential part of the ecological salvation of India. Pointing out to his fellow Hindus the horrendous pollution of "Mother Gaṅgā" in a place like Vārāṇasi, the most holy of India's holy cities, he asks them: Would you consciously throw garbage at your mother and defile her thus? In an apt simile he compares the two banks of the Gaṅgā to science/technology and religion/tradition and explains: for the river to be able to flow properly, both banks must stand firmly. He seems to be encouraged by what he has been able to do so far with his initiative of the Ganges cleanup.[4]

In a country that has been so much shaped by its religious traditions and in which so many people actively participate in its rituals and festivities, religion must be a major partner in the restoration of the ecology. Traditional Hinduism offers indeed many insights into nature and many incentives for preserving it and contemporary Hindu scholars and gurus make use of Hindu mythology and philosophy to awaken an ecological consciousness in their audience.[5]

## NATURE AS SPIRITUAL GUIDE AND TEACHER

The epic and dramatic literature of India contains numerous vivid and loving descriptions of nature. The beauty of the forest through which Rāmā and Sītā proceeded, the peace and tranquility of the famous hermitages visited by the Pāṇdavas, the majesty of the Himālayas and the awesomeness of the Vindhyas are immortalized in beautifully articulated language. Students of comparative literature have remarked on the richness of the vocabulary employed in these descriptions of nature, the astonishingly great number of species of fauna and flora identified by name and described in detail.[6] Surely, Indian writers have not been unaware of the beauty and greatness of nature, a nature so luxuriant in many parts of the country as to be almost without comparison. This variegated nature serves in the epics as background for the development of human drama and as scaffolding for divine intervention in history.

Over and above this, nature is seen as spiritual guide, as described in an intriguing episode in the *Bhāgavata Purāṇa*.[7] A young ascetic—identified in another passage as Dattātreya[8]—relates how he had adopted nature as a guide to wisdom and to liberating knowledge. The account of the teachings of the "twenty-four gurus" is prefaced by words put into the mouth of the Lord: "The investigators of the true nature of the world are uplifted by their own efforts in this world. The self is the infallible guide of the self: through direct perception and through analogy one can work out one's salvation."[9]

It is suggested that "true knowledge of nature" leads to "true knowledge of self and God." The twenty-four gurus from nature, that Dattātreya has chosen to follow, induce him to adopt practices and rules for his life that reaffirm his ideal of *saṃnyāsa* and contribute to his liberation. Nature acts precisely as a human guru does: proposing through words and by example a path leading to insight and realization. The qualitative, humanistic science of nature thus communicated could well serve as the starting point of an alternative science that is humanly meaningful, and in turn, beneficial instead of harmful to nature. The text itself is fairly lengthy and the treatment of the individual teachers is quite uneven. A sampling will suffice to make the point.

Earth has taught Dattātreya steadfastness and the wisdom to realize that all things, while pursuing their own activities, do nothing but follow the divine laws, which are universally established. Furthermore, earth has taught him that existence in a body is a being-for-others (*parārtha*) to be lived out in humility and forbearance. Wind has taught Dattātreya that he ought to be content with the bare necessities of existence: enough to keep the intellect active, not to pamper the senses. Moreover, wind has shown him the importance of remaining unattached and moving around freely. The sky's teaching consists in pointing out the affinity between the soul and the infinite, its own being the same everywhere, untouched by the elements which it overarches. Water offers itself as a teacher possessing close affinity to the *saṃnyāsi* with regard to being transparent, soft by nature, sweet. The parallelism extends to the water's being the seat and source of purity, making people clean by sight, touch, and utterance of its mere name. Fire, too, is an excellent teacher and an example for the ascetic, being "full of splendor and made brighter by the glow of *tapas* . . . not sullied by what is consumed . . . sometimes hidden, sometimes visible, assuming the shape of the fuel that it consumes, burning up past and future sin." (xi, 7, 45) The deep sea teaches the student of nature to be calm and quiet, grave and inscrutable, dominated by none. The great sea is unaffected by the modalities of space and time, unperturbed by likes and dislikes, neither made greater by the rivers that empty into it nor made less by the water taken out from it.

If the teaching provided by the elements could be called a kind of spiritual physics, the teaching imparted by the animals is its biological counterpart. A brief summary should suffice to indicate the thrust.

The honeybee teaches the student to go out and collect the essence from all scriptures. It also provides a negative lesson: do not hoard any food. To substantiate this part of the bee's teaching, the text recounts a popular story about a bee that perished together with its stored-up supply of food. The spider serves as model for the activity of the Lord Himself: "Just as the spider projecting the web from its heart through its mouth sports with it and then swallows it again so does the Supreme Lord create, preserve, and destroy the universe." (xi, 10, 21) The larva of the wasp provides another basic insight: "On whatever the embodied being deliberately centers its mind in its entirety, through love, hatred, or fear, that very form it attains. The larva, confined by the wasp in a hole in the wall and contemplating the wasp, transforms itself into the latter without discarding its former body." (v.23)

Added to the spiritual physics and biology is a spiritual anthropology that has helped Dattātreya in his own search. A child at play taught him that happiness lies in freedom from cares. From a maiden, who broke all her bangles except one, so as not to be heard when pounding rice, he learns the value of being all by himself: "Where many dwell together, quarrel will ensue; even between two persons there is talk. Therefore one should dwell all alone like the single bangle on the wrist of the maiden." (xi, 9, 10) Piṅgalā, a courtesan, realizing how foolish it was to expect happiness from anyone but from the Lord, teaches surrender to God and to be content with whatever He may send. Finally Dattātreya learns the most decisive lesson from his own body: "This body, subject to birth and death, and a constant source of affliction, is my guru as it prompts me to renunciation and discernment. Though it helps me to contemplate, it really belongs to others. Realizing this I am going forth, renouncing all." (xi, 10, 25)

Thus Dattātreya has reached through physics, biology, anthropology and psychology, a stage of wisdom, which makes him aware of the true nature of things and delivers him from the need to transform nature into consumer goods.

In all this there is no diminishing of the stature of humans and no denying their very special destiny. The Creator, we are told in the beginning, was not satisfied with having created a great variety of other beings: "He rejoiced only when he had created the human body endowed with reason and capable of realizing the Supreme Deity. Having after many births in this world acquired the rare human body, however frail, which is the means of attaining the object of life, a wise person should speedily strive to attain liberation, before this perishable body is destroyed. The enjoyment of sense pleasures can be had in all species."[10]

## NATURE AS HELPMATE OF THE SPIRIT

Sāṁkhya stands out among the classical Indian *darśanas* as the one most concerned with nature and the evolution of matter. Many scholars consider it to be the oldest system. It does not refer to scriptural authority; however, many of its basic tenets have been assimilated into mainstream Hindu philosophy and religion: Sāṁkhya has supplied the terminology of *puruṣa* (spirit) and *prakṛti* (matter), of the three *guṇas* (constituent principles of matter), the classification of elements and senses. Its overriding concern, as it declares quite explicitly, is the liberation of the spirit.[11] This, in turn, may be one of the attractive features of the system for us today.

It has been noted by all scholars who have worked on Sāṁkhya that on the one hand we have abundant references to Sāṁkhya (and Yoga) in the *Mahābhārata* and in the major Purāṇas, where quite often Sāṁkhya is used as a generic name for speculative wisdom and systematic thought and Kapila, its founder, appears as the teacher of salvation, while on the other hand the classical texts (mainly the *Sāṁkhya-sūtras* and the *Sāṁkhya-kārikās* with their commentaries) offer disappointingly little evidence for the greatness of this *darśana*.[12] Especially in the crucial area of linking the liberation effort with the detailed analysis of nature, they exhaust themselves in a few general cryptic remarks. Also Yoga, as expounded by Patañjali, does not give us much of a clue. The widespread opinion that Yoga offers the practice based on Sāṁkhya theory is mistaken: while Yoga has adopted (as have most Indian *darśanas*) a certain amount of technical terminology from Sāṁkhya, the Sāṁkhya as represented in the classical texts could not possibly have been its theoretical basis.[13] Moreover, the epic and Purāṇic texts make it quite clear that Sāṁkhya was a path to the liberation of the spirit by itself and not just in conjunction with Yoga.[14]

Thus in the following an attempt has been made to utilize Sāṁkhya passages from the *Mahābhārata* and the *Bhāgavata Purāṇa* to supply details that are not found in the existing *Kārikās* and *Sūtras*.

The *Sāṁkhya-kārikās* are fairly cryptic in their account of how the knowledge of nature can become the way to the liberation of the spirit. It contains the remark that "the evolution from *mahat* (primary matter) down to specific elements . . . is for the sake of the liberation of each mind . . . in spite of its apparently being for the sake of nature herself."[15] Thus a certain self-transcendence is assumed built into nature. The subjectivity of nature is linked up with the subjectivity of the human person in constituting the purpose of the evolution of the universe. This aspect of nature ceases to play a role for humans if and when it has fulfilled its purpose.

The *Bhāgavata Purāṇa* offers a detailed version of this process: it is a double reflection that leads the spirit back into its own interiority—nature being the medium in which the reflection of the spirit is broken: "Just as a reflection of the sun in water is discovered with the help of a reflection of that reflection on the wall of the house, and the sun in the heavens can be seen with the help of its own reflection in water, even so the threefold ego is revealed through its reflections on the body, the senses, and the mind; and through the ego that contains a reflection of the Spirit is seen God, who is possessed of true wisdom, is absolutely free from egotism and keeps awake even when the subtle elements get merged in the Un-manifest on account of sleep."[16]

In reply to the question of how the mind, which is inexorably intertwined with nature, could ever become free from the dominance of the *guṇas*, the text replies that as consequence of spiritual practice "*prakṛti*, which binds the soul gradually withdraws even as a stick, used to kindle fire, is consumed by the very fire which it produces."

Although Indian *darśanas* do distinguish between *dharma* and *dharmin*, between *viṣaya* and *viṣayin*, subject and object, this epistemological distinction never translated into an ontological dichotomy of the Cartesian type: "India has never made any clear-cut distinction between spirit and matter. This opposition is peculiar to the Occident and has been the cause of a respectable number of major catastrophes. . . . Spirit and matter are each aspects of a totality."[17] While Indian traditions are quite insistent that the "ego" which can be objectified and identified in terms of physical bodies and sensations is different from the "self," which cannot be so identified and objectified, they recognize the same situation also applying to all entities outside the individual: nature, to the extent to which it possesses reality, has objectivity as well as subjectivity intertwined in the "real" human person. The total reality of nature comprises objectivity and subjectivity: a true knowledge of nature cannot exhaust itself in objectivity alone.

This observation is of some importance in the context of the history of Western thought. The beginning of modern science is associated with the complete and successful objectivation of nature, which evoked as its counterpart the complete subjectivation of the human person in idealistic philosophy. Marxist thinkers, while addressing humans as "subject-object" of the evolution of matter still insist (to the extent to which it becomes a theme of their thought) on the exclusive "objectivity" of nature (external nature, matter) as the object of science.

The view, that both "external" nature and humans possess subjective as well as objective aspects, will make us accept the findings of "objective" science as true observations of genuine aspects of reality and also necessitate the development of an approach to apprehend the subjectivity of nature as the foundation of an ecology that is more than just a patching up of the mistakes of the past so as to enable technology to exploit "objective" nature more thoroughly than ever before.

Sāṁkhya, which devotes so much space to the enquiry into the nature of nature, does not aim at appropriating nature through the senses, or their extension in technology, and it does not cultivate instrumental reason, the tool of such appropriation. The proper attitude for this science of nature is, the texts suggest, detachment from the sense appetites, so as to let the subjectivity of nature appear as it is, before it has been distorted by human interference—it aims at a knowledge of nature, not at its use.

In its most generic sense nature, understood as *prakṛti*, is not seen as a substance to which certain qualities are added, but it is defined as "equilibrium of the three *guṇas*" without particular name or form. The very choice of the "qualities" universally identified with nature and their applicability to human nature seems to be further proof for the view that Sāṁkhya deals with the subjectivity of nature rather than its objectivity.

The similarity between Sāṁkhya and Pythagorean teachings has been noted before. Out of the Pythagorean fascination with numbers, regular geometric figures, proportions and correspondences grew—via Plato and the Neoplatonists—our mathematics-based modern natural science. The most obvious parallelism between Sāṁkhya and Pythagoras the central role played by the number five. While the thoroughgoing fascination with numbers (as Gerald Larson has well shown)[18] in general has surely something to do with the effort to accommodate the variety of phenomena in a grid composed of five-times-five principles, it also hints at a preoccupation (very obvious in Pythagoras) with the Golden Section (Fibonacci Numbers etc.) so crucial and central in nature.[19] Mathematics provides us with an instrument to envision unity behind the diversity of the phenomena. The liberation of the spirit does come from the contemplation of nature as a whole, as Oneness. That is the very point of a system, or a theory, that must be intuited as a whole, and not studied piece by piece only.

Why did no "modern-type science" develop from Sāṁkhya (or the Pythagorean school)? One of the possible answers to this is that the interest of Sāṁkhya was quite different: over against the exploitation of nature, the domination of nature and the dissecting of nature (terms found in Francis Bacon's *Novum Organon* characterising science), Sāṁkhya aimed at the liberation of the spirit by leading to the experience of the subjectivity of nature, actualizing nature's own "best side," its *sattva* quality, and not interfering with it. This the Sāṁkhya system accomplished so well that what it provided by way of insight into the nature of nature was perceived to be sufficient.

## NATURE AS IMAGE OF THE SPIRIT

What distinguishes the modern scientific enquiry into the nature of nature from Vedānta is a different orientation in thinking, a different interest. While Vedānta was interested in finding out the ontological status of nature in relation to consciousness, modern science wants to find out how it works. It was as clear to the medieval Indian Vedāntins as it is to modern Western scientists that "to perform activities the world need not be thought real."[20] Vedānta combines instrumental and reflective analysis of nature. From the question, what do you see? the questioner leads to the problem, where does it come from? and what is it? From an examination of what appears to be part of the external world, the question leads to an investigation of the self.

Can we still make the transition from physics to metaphysics, which the *Chāndogya Upaniṣad* suggests, to explain the no longer visible as the source of the visible, to identify the invisible with the All and this with the Self? The path of liberation through knowledge of nature that Mādhavācārya has laid it out in his *Pañcadaśī*[21] is still quite intriguing.

He connects his argument with the Upaniṣadic "experiments," however, and provides additional support for the transcending of objective nature. He did so in response to an antimetaphysical position, which by then was thoroughly worked out.[22] In Mādhava's view, the naturalistic ("scientific") position falls short of a total explanation of the world in terms of causality operating on physical realities. While we have today an immense body of scientific knowledge concerning details of the working of organisms, we do not have a satisfactory answer to Vidyāraṇya's question: "Tell us, if you can, how the body and the senses came out of the seed, or how consciousness was born in the fetus?"[23] The fourteenth-century Indian naturalist's answer, "It is the nature of the seed to evolve into a body with its sense organs and so forth," which Vidyāraṇya found unsatisfactory, has not been essentially improved upon. Vidyāraṇya's rejoinder is still valid: "What is the basis of your belief? In the end you will have to say: I do not know!" Vidyāraṇya employs the term *indrajala*, "Indra's net," as descriptive of the nature of the physical world.[24] It is a far from naive observation (and a question far from being answered by modern biology, genetics, etc.) that follows: "What can be more magical (*indrajalamaparam*) than the fact that the seed in the uterus becomes a conscious individual, that it develops head, hands, feet, and other organs, that it passes through the states of childhood, youth, and old age, and that it perceives, eats, smells, hears, comes, and goes?"[25]

Among those who believed that they had all the answers were the medieval Indian logicians. Vidyāraṇya says that while they themselves may be satisfied with their logical explanation, he is not. The nature of the world is not accessible to the rational mind: being unthinkable (*acintya*), it cannot fall under the canons of logic.[26] Logic, he has said somewhere else, is secondary with regard to experience: Logic can at best examine the description of an experience. It cannot create or replace experience as the basic mode of intellectual awareness.

The "seed" (*bīja*) of the world that is thus found to be neither accessible to natural science nor to logic is termed *māyā*. This *māyā* (a term that is used already in some later Upaniṣadic texts)[27] is circumscribed by Vidyāraṇya on the basis of a depth insight: the apparently contradictory statements that are being made preempt the notion that *māyā* could ever be used either for a naturalistic or a logical explanation of the world.

In deep sleep (*suṣupti*), he claims, we are experiencing *māyā-bīja*. Deep sleep is the "implicate" form of waking and dreaming, as the seed is the "implicate" form of the tree. *Māyā* contains the *vāsanas* ("impressions," potential developments, natural laws?) of the entire universe.[28] Consciousness actively reflects in the states of waking and dreaming the mental imprints (*buddhi-vāsana*).

In association with this reflection, that seed emerges in the form of intellect (*dhi*). In the mind (*buddhau*) the consciousness reflection (*cidabhāsa*) is unclearly reflected. This view of nature as being grounded and contained in an entity, that is neither scientifically nor logically ascertainable and manageable, should not create the impression that we are talking about an "illusion" in the everyday world. Vidyāraṇya is as aware as any of us that "nobody has the power to alter the world of waking and dream states."[29] Individual persons as well as the Lord (God) himself are "reflections" (*abhāsa*) of *ātman* in *māyā*. Its reality obviously is accessible only through a third path, a sensibility not employed in either science or logic. Between *Īśvara* and *māyā* there is a kind of mutuality (both being ultimately *acintya*, that is, inaccessible to reason): *Īśvara* is the *māyā* reflection of consciousness and at the same time its inner ruler (*antaryāmin*), omniscient (*sarvajñā*) and womb of the world (*jagadyoni*).[30]

The Lord as the "bliss-sheath" is the carrier of all *vāsanas* (information potentials) of all living beings,[31] that is, his "omniscience." As all-pervading he is also all-supporting (*sarvopadāna*, material cause of the universe).[32]

He is detectable as "Inner Ruler" through an analysis of the fine structure of the universe: "Where the progress from the subtle to the subtler stops, there do we confront the Inner Ruler. . . . Being minuter than the minute of the second and third degree, the inmost being is not subject to perception, but by logical argument and scriptural texts his existence is ascertained."[33]

This Lord is the source of the universe, insofar as both the manifestation and concealment of the world are due to Him. "The universe remains 'implicate' in the Lord. He creates it according to the karmas of living beings."[34]

As waking and sleeping complement each other, cancel each other out, but presuppose, each in different ways, someone who is awake or asleep, so also the creation and the destruction of the universe are complementary and related to an overarching ground.

Obviously Vidyāraṇya is not interested in *māyā* for the sake of *māyā*. Liberation is the theme and "liberation can only be reached through knowledge of the reality of *brahman*. One's dreaming does not come to an end without one's waking up." (210) This juxtaposition is quite crucial: we cannot dream a dream to its end. Awaking, the only possible end of a dream, is a different condition of being. The dream metaphor is expanded when we are told that: "This entire world—God, individual persons, animate and inanimate objects—is a dream in the nondual brahman-reality."[35] In a further specification the whole world is described as a projection of *māyā* brought forth by God and human individuals projected back onto *māyā*. The range of God-projections reaches from the desire to create up to the entering into his creation. The range of the human projections reaches from waking to release. The obvious paradox is probably intended: the seeming contradiction of externalizing oneself in a visible effect and interiorizing the effect by entering it as it were from outside.

Vidyāraṇya (with the mainstream Advaita tradition) is not declaring that the insight into the ultimate nonduality of nature translates into a transcending of the natural laws as far as the body is concerned. He also does not suggest that we have to reverse our entire thinking: both duality and nonduality are partially known[36] and we experience daily that the nature of the world is mysterious, impervious to rational thought.[37] While consciousness (the goal) is mysterious too, it is eternal over against momentary *māyā*. Also, ontologically the experience of nonduality precedes duality.

The instrument to liberation/enlightenment is *viveka*, "discriminative insight," a kind of rationality, which the materialists and the logicians are lacking. It is a metaphysical sensibility that cuts, as it were, at a right angle into the infinite plane of *māyā*-derived "reality." It is, finally, nature, which as mirror image of *brahman* provides all the crucial insights: through the discovery of the *acintya*-aspect of *māyā* a person realizes the insufficiency of linear logic and a materialistic explanation of reality. The realization of the ultimate oneness of *māyā* directs human awareness to that crucial insight that Reality is One and undivided. The perception of different levels of depth in the phenomenal world leads the mind to the decisive understanding of degrees of consciousness. It is, finally the mirror-image quality of nature which in a dialectic makes the spirit find its own reality in itself.

To realize that the true vocation and destiny of humanity is spiritual liberation, Self-realization, and not amassing of wealth and power, exploitation of nature and humanity, would certainly have also an "ecological" impact!

## NATURE AS BODY OF GOD

The *Ṛgveda*, the most ancient document of the Hindus, refers to the *puruṣa*, the primeval cosmic being, as the source and origin not only of the physical universe but also of religion and the social order. Quite clearly everything in this world was perceived as bodily related to the divine source, the Body of God: "The moon was born from his spirit, from his eye was born the sun . . . from his navel arose the sky and from his head originated heaven."[38] So evident must have been this conception of the universe as the Body of God that based on it a convincing case could be made for the overriding importance of the institutional sacrifice and the division of society into the four *varṇas*.

The Brāhmaṇas elaborated this vision and invested it with rich symbolism: the sacrifice as the symbolic reenactment of the creation of the world reflects the Body of God in its varied detail. The Upaniṣads greatly exploited this idea and developed the parallelism of macrocosm-microcosm into a path of ultimate liberation.

The *Bhagavadgītā* restates and summarizes a great deal of the Upaniṣadic teaching. It presupposes as well known the idea that the deity dwells in the universe as the soul dwells in the body. Over and above the expression of this by now traditional insight it offers in its famous eleventh chapter the grandiose vision of the *viśvarūpa* of Kṛṣṇa-Viṣṇu. Arjuna has received the oral instruction of Kṛṣṇa concerning his immanence-cum-transcendence and he has mentally understood it. What he now desires is to *see* with his own eyes the divine form of the Cosmos-Creator. Kṛṣṇa promises that he would "see here today the whole universe summed up in [his] body."[39]

Seeing the divine form, and by implication seeing the world as God's body, requires a "supernatural eye": the ordinary eye cannot truly see reality, it perceives only the surface. With supernatural vision, a gift of the very same Deity whom he beholds, Arjuna can see the supreme and divine form of God exhibiting itself as "the whole universe, with its manifold divisions gathered together in one, in the body of the God of Gods." (xi, 13)

In a powerful hymn Arjuna describes the body of God, which evokes feelings of awe and of terror in him. Like the splendor of a thousand suns He shines forth—it is time, world-destroying. Arjuna praises Kṛṣṇa as "the one who pervades the entire universe." Arjuna is shaking with fear—he cannot stand to see the true nature of the God whose body is the universe.

For his sake Kṛṣṇa assumes again the guise of the human being. What the Gītā adds to the Vedic-Vedāntic image of the body of God is an illumination of the meaning of history: the body of God is not merely a static presence and unchanging support for physical existence, it is also a historic agent. History, too, is an aspect of the body of God—the successive manifestation of the concrete deity. This haunting vision of Viṣṇu *viśvarūpa* has influenced a great deal of Hindu theology through the ages. It is a statement about the nature of the world as much as about the nature of God; it explains the importance of worshipping the material image of God through a variety of material substances, and it lays out nature and history as ways to God.

Hindu theologians, while commenting on such texts, have developed a systematic philosophy of the body of God. Thus, Rāmānuja writes in his commentary on the *Bhagavadgītā*: "God has two *prakṛtis*: a lower and a higher one. The former is constituted by the physical world, the latter by the souls of living beings. All spiritual and nonspiritual things, whether effects of causes, constitute God's body and depend on God who is their soul."[40]

Rāmānuja is fond of the Upaniṣadic image where the creation of the world is compared to the activity of the spider, who emits from his body the thread that he uses to build his web and then reabsorbs it. The universe, then, is God's body also in the sense that it owes its existence—materially as well as causally—entirely to Him: "These entities . . . depend on God, whose body they constitute. God himself, however, does not depend on them."[41]

Rāmānuja wishes to make it clear that the analogy between the relationship of the human body and the human soul cannot be pushed too far without distorting the meaning of the world as body of God: "The relation of God to his body is not the same as that of the individual souls to their bodies. With the latter the bodies, though depending on the souls, serve some purpose for the sustenance of the souls within them. To God his body serves no purpose at all: it serves to nothing but his sport."[42]

In addition to this twofold nature, which forms the body of God, God himself has his own supernatural body, constituted by "auspicious qualities peculiar to him" on account of which the qualities of material nature (viz, *sattva*, *rajas*, *tamas*) do not affect him.[43] Thus it can be explained that in spite of His eternity and His omnipresence, He is not known to the world, "for the world is perplexed by the entities consisting of (material) qualities (*guṇas*), however small and transient they may be, which are the material objects to be experienced by means of body and senses in accordance with their previous karma."[44]

The paradox of humans not knowing a God whose very body they constitute and who is their creator and their support is explained by Rāmānuja with a reference to "God's *māyā*, which consists of *guṇas* and which, being created by the sporting God, [which] is difficult for anyone to know. This real *māyā* obscures the proper form of God and lets one's own being be thought of as the only fit object of experience. Perplexed by God's *māyā* the whole world is ignorant of God whose real being is boundless bliss. Only those who resort to God relinquish *māyā* and worship Him alone."[45] Only those who have this true knowledge of God can perceive the world as a multitude of independent objects in a fragmented and fragmentary vision.

Pāñcarātra as adopted by Śrivaiṣṇavism speaks of five different levels of God's presence: in His highest form as *parabrahman* He is all but unknowable by humans and inaccessible to them directly. In His four *vyūhas* He creates vehicles of mediation, further particularized and concretized in the *vibhavas*, commonly known as *avatāras*, "descents" of the deity into an organism of either animal or human form. The deity descends even further into the heart of each human being as its *antaryāmi* or Inner Ruler, and eventually into a material image as the *arcā-avatāra*.[46] This progressive self-diffusion of the divine essence takes place for the sake of gathering in again all things unto the Godhead. The statement that nature is the body (lower *prakṛti*) of God need not be understood as a contradiction to the Advaitin's notion of *māyā*: it does distinguish, after all, between a soul, which can be "rationalized," and a body, remaining somehow outside rationalization, but with its own kind of reality.

Śaṅkara and Rāmānuja, in spite of their diametrically opposed statements in the introductory passages of their commentaries, adopt literally the same definition of the world as the mysterious product of a transcendent agent.[47]

## HINDU ECOLOGICAL HEROES AND MOVEMENTS

Anil Agarwal, with whose graphic description of India's ecological sins the chapter was introduced, complains that while India has brought forth ecological heroes, it has not been able to generate institutions that would effectively protect the environment. Nevertheless, some of these heroes deserve to be mentioned in the context of Hinduism and ecology.

The Bishnois, a small Vaiṣṇava community in Rājasthān, trace their tradition back to the fifteenth-century Guru Mahārāj Jambajī, who disapproved of the cutting of branches from trees in order to feed the goats and sheep in times of drought, as was common practice. Among his twenty-nine regulations he included the prohibition to cut green trees and to kill animals. The community, who followed his rules, flourished and in the otherwise desertlike Rājasthān a lush forest developed. This became the target of the king of Jhodpur, when he was looking for timber to build a new palace. The Bishnois, in an attempt to prevent their trees from being cut down, encircled their trees and chained themselves to the trunks. The Mahārāja's servants began killing the Bishnois in order to cut down the trees. When the king was told about this, he ordered his workers back and gave protection to the Bishnois.

The Bishnois became an inspiration for the better-known Chipko Movement, which started in a remote mountain area of Uttar Pradesh in 1973. Its beginning had economical, rather than ecological or religious reasons: an out-of-town manufacturer of sports goods for export had been awarded the right to the cutting of a number of ash trees, which a local manufacturer of agricultural tools had applied for and was refused permission. To prevent the trees from being removed, the local population of Gopeshwar formed a human chain, encircling the trees and thus kept the work crews from entering the forest. A year later, the women of the village of Reni, in the Himālayas, protected the local forest by hugging the trees—the origin of the name *Chipko*. The same strategy was then adopted also by other villagers in similar circumstances and helped both the local economy and its ecology. Chipko became a byword for active resistance to "development."

A rather more complex and less clear-cut case of ecological self-help arose out of the various protest movements against the Narmadā dam project: one of the largest and longest rivers of Western India, the Narmadā overflows its banks during the monsoon season and is almost dry for the rest of the year. In the 1970s already far-reaching plans were developed, with support from the World Bank, to both collect the water for irrigation purposes year-round and to harness the stream for the generation of electricity. Hundreds of dams at various stages were planned, and one large reservoir—the Sardar Sarovar—was to be created by one of the highest dams in the world. When completed, it would flood dozens of villages and submerge thousands of hectares of land, largely tribal areas. Massive protests were launched. Complaints about the ecological unsoundness of the project resulted in the World Bank's withdrawal of its support. The government of Gujarat, however, decided to continue building the dam on its own.

Reasons brought forward by those who opposed the Narmadā project were not only economical-ecological but also religious: circumambulating the Narmadā has been one of the most cherished religious exercises for Hindu ascetics, and both banks of the river are dotted with sacred places and memories of saints and heroes, most of which would be submerged under the waters. Gandhi was posthumously brought into the picture, too: everywhere one can see Gandhi figures and pictures that are supposed to transform the multifaceted anti-dam protests as a form of *satyāgraha*.[48]

Some initiatives, such as the Vṛndāvana and the Annamalai reforestation projects are clearly religiously inspired: they attempt to restore these holy places to the condition described in the sacred literature associated with these places. Another initiative, carried by the Braj Rakshak Dal, tries to save the hills of sacred Braj that are blasted and carted away wholesale by building entrepreneurs. Locally and regionally many initiatives have sprung up that are motivated partly by practical economics and partly by religious considerations, demonstrating visibly at the grassroots level the ecological dimension of Hinduism. Traditional Hinduism encouraged frugality and a restriction of one's wants rather than luxury and overconsumption. As Mahātmā Gandhi expressed it: There is enough for everyone's need but not for everyone's greed.

CHAPTER THIRTY-SIX

# Hindu Measures of Time

## THE HINDU CALENDAR (*PAÑCĀṄGAM*)

The traditional Hindu calendar is lunar-solar (Figure 36.1). While the months (*māsa*) are defined by the moon cycles, the beginning of the year (*varṣa*) is fixed by either the solar spring or fall equinox. The difference between the year of twelve lunar months and the solar year (amounting to roughly 10.87 days every year) is made up by inserting an intercalary month every third year: the so-called *adhika māsa* (additional month).

At the time of India's independence in 1947, about thirty different calendars were in use in India. In order to eliminate the confusion caused by the great variety of traditional calendars and to correlate the Indian calendar with the Gregorian, the government of India established in 1952 a Calendar Commission that recommended the introduction of a reformed Indian calendar, valid for the whole of India for official purposes. It became effective with the spring equinox on March 22, 1957, which became New Year's Day: Chaitra 1, 1879 Śaka era. The reformed Indian calendar unlinks the Indian months (whose old names have been preserved) from the moon phases and approximates the length of each month to those of the Gregorian calendar.[1]

The traditional Indian calendar, called *Pañcāṅgam* (Five Limbs) consists of five parts: *tithi* (lunar day), *vāra* (solar day), *nakṣatra* (asterism), *yoga* (planetary conjunctions), and *kāraṇam* (influences of stars). Each *tithi* is subdivided into two *kāraṇas*, which are either *cara* (changing) or *sthira* (fixed). Each of these has a presiding deity, whose influence determines the auspicious or inauspicious character of the time span designated. The reformed Indian calendar issued by the government in New Delhi also contains basic information on all of these items, but does not offer all the minutiae required for religious and astrological purposes, for which the numerous regional *pañcāṅgas*, which are published every year from many places, have to be consulted.[2]

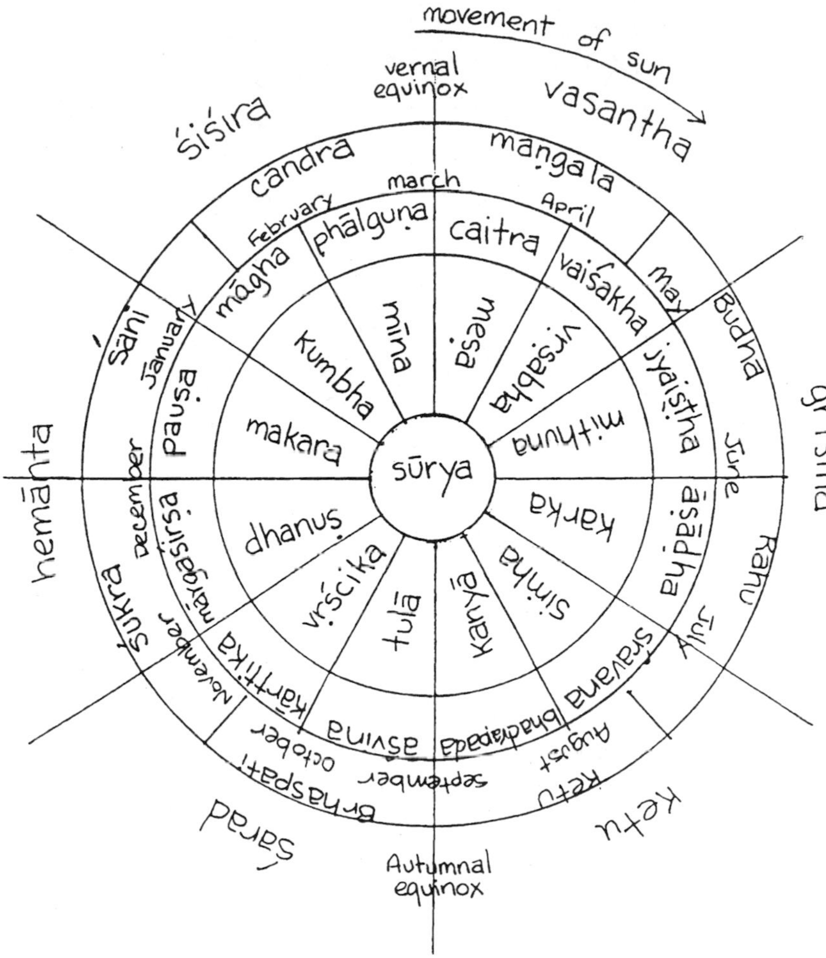


Figure 36.1. The Hindu calendar

Inner circle: signs of the zodiac (solar)

Second circle: names of the months (lunar-solar)

Third circle: corresponding months of Julian Calendar; Planets

Outer circle: names of seasons

NB: The coincidence of the vernal equinox and the beginning of the month *caitra meṣa*, upon which the calendar has been based in the sixth century C.E., has since moved, due to an inexact calculation.

## Correlation of Reformed Indian Calendar with Gregorian (Western) Calendar

The months of the reformed Indian calendar begin on these dates of the Gregorian calendar:

| | |
|---|---|
| Caitra (30 days; 31 in leap year) | March 22 (21 in leap year) |
| Vaiśakha (31 days) | April 21 |
| Jyeṣṭha (31 days) | May 22 |
| Āsāḍha (31 days) | June 22 |
| Śravana (31 days) | July 23 |
| Bhādrapada (31 days) | August 23 |
| Aśvina (30 days) | September 23 |
| Kārtika (30 days) | October 23 |
| Mārgaśirṣa (30 days) | November 22 |
| Pauṣa (30 days) | December 22 |
| Māgha (30 days) | January 21 |
| Phālguṇa (30 days) | February 20 |

The Indian calendar knows six seasons [*ritu*]:

1. Vasantha (Spring): comprising Phalguṇa and Caitra
2. Grīṣma (Summer): comprising Vaiśakha and Jyeṣṭha
3. Varṣa (Rainy Season): comprising Āṣāḍha and Śravana
4. Śarada (Autumn): comprising Bhādrapada and Aśvina
5. Hemānta (Late Fall): comprising Kārtika and Mārgaśirṣa
6. Śiśira (Winter): comprising Pauṣa and Māgha

(The Ṛgveda mentions only five seasons, leaving out Śiśira, but later texts have six.)

The days of the week (*vāra*) are:

| | | |
|---|---|---|
| *ravivāra* | = | Day of the Sun |
| *somavāra* | = | Day of the Moon |
| *maṅgalavāra* | = | Day of Mars |
| *budhavāra* | = | Day of Mercury |
| *guruvāra* | = | Day of Jupiter |
| *śukravāra* | = | Day of Venus |
| *śanivāra* | = | Day of Saturn |

(There is some evidence that in Vedic times there was a six-day week.)

The times for religious festivals are still set according to lunar months. Since in some areas of India, such as Punjab and Orissa, the beginning of the (moon-) month is reckoned from the end of the bright fortnight (*śuklānta*), in others from the end of the dark (*kṛṣṇānta*), there is no India-wide agreement concerning the beginning of a feast day, and thus many problems arise in connection of the setting of popular feasts. The Rāṣṭrīya Pañcāṅga (Indian Reformed Calendar) provides alternate dates for various regions. Regional Pañcāṅgas decide the case for each locality.[3]

Each lunar month is divided into two *pakṣas*: *śukla pakṣa* (bright half) and *kṛṣṇa pakṣa* (dark half). Each *pakṣa* is subdivided into 15 *tithis* (moon days). Dates of festivals are given in the form: *māsa/pakṣa/tithi*. For example: Kṛṣṇa's birthday is always celebrated on Śravana [*māsa*] Kṛṣṇa [*pakṣa*] Aṣṭamī [*tithi*]. According to the Reformed Calendar Kṛṣṇa's birthday is a movable feast, whose commencement is calculated differently in various parts of India according to the system locally used to determine the commencement of a *tithi*.

The names of the 15 moon days (*tithis*) in each half-month (*pakṣa*):

| | |
|---|---|
| 1. *pratipad* | 9. *navamī* |
| 2. *dvitīya* | 10. *daśamī* |
| 3. *tṛtīya* | 11. *ekādaśī* |
| 4. *caturthī* | 12. *dvadaśī* |
| 5. *pañcamī* | 13. *trayodaśī* |
| 6. *ṣaṣṭhī* | 14. *caturdaśī* |
| 7. *saptamī* | 15. *pañcadaśī* |
| 8. *aṣṭamī* | a. in *kṛṣṇapakṣa*: *amāvāsyā* (new moon) |
| | b. in *śuklapakṣa*: *pūrṇimā* (full moon) |

Each *tithi* is divided into 30 *muhūrtas* (hours), each *muhūrta* into 60 *nimeṣas* (minutes), each *nimeṣa* into 60 *kṣaṇas* (moments, wink-of-the-eyes).

For astrological purposes it is important to find the right *tithi* (and *kāraṇa*) as well as the appropriate *muhūrta* for every activity: there are auspicious and inauspicious times for everything and no important enterprise is to be undertaken without ensuring the auspiciousness of the day and hour. Many Hindus even today follow a timetable called *Rahu-kāla*, which identifies auspicious/inauspicious times for every day of the week.

The *Jyotiṣa* Department of Banaras Hindu University (like many other places in India connected with traditional centers of learning) issues a yearly (traditional) *Pañcāṅga* following the prereformed Indian calendar.[4] Its charts for every lunar *pakṣa* with traditional astronomical/astrological information are widely used by astrologers in India. The central government's *Rāṣṭrīya Pañcāṅga* follows the Reformed Indian Calendar. It, too, offers additional information on lunar *tithis*, *nakṣatras*, *yogas*, *kāraṇas*, and *rāśis*, which can be also used for astrological purposes. It contains a comparative table showing the beginnings of years in other eras used in some parts of India such as Vikram, Bengali San, Kollam, Kali, Buddha Nirvāṇa, Mahāvīra Nirvāṇa and Hejra. The year 2006 Common Era corresponds to Śaka 1927/28; Vikram Samvat 2063/64; Bengali San 1413/14; Kollam 1182/83; Kali Yuga 5108/09; Buddha Nirvāṇa 2550/51; Mahavīra Nirvāṇa 2533/34; Hijra 1426/27.

## YUGA

The term *yuga* (literally, "yoke") has many meanings. It is sometimes used for the number four and as designation of various periods of time. In early Indian astronomy it designated a five-year cycle (beginning with the conjunction of sun and moon in the Dhaniṣṭa *nakṣatra* on the first *tithi* of *śuklapakṣa* of Māgha, the autumnal equinox). In that period of five years the solar year of 366 days and the lunar year of 360 days were "yoked" together by adding two intercalary months at the end of the third and the fifth year when the cycle of sixty-two full moons and sixty-two new moons was completed. The more popular use of the term *yuga*, however, occurs in connection with the later "world-ages" (*kalpas*) made up of four *yugas*. Traditional accounts do not agree on their length. According to the *Manusmṛti*[5] each *kalpa* begins with a *Kṛta-yuga*, lasting four thousand years, followed by a *Tretā-yuga*, lasting three thousand years, a *Dvāpara-yuga* of two thousand years, and finally a *Kali-yuga*, lasting one thousand years. Each of these *yugas* is preceded and followed by a *sandhyā* (twilight) lasting six hundred, four hundred, and two hundred years respectively. The four (human) *yugas* together comprise twelve thousand human years: this span of time is called a *yuga* of the *devas* (*divya-yuga*). One thousand of these *divya-yugas* constitute one Day of Brahmā—the same duration is allotted to one Night of Brahmā. Seventy-one combinations of twelve thousand *divya-yugas* constitute one *Manvantara*. In the Purāṇas we find variant accounts of *yugas*: all are connected with huge numbers. According to the *Viṣṇu Purāṇa*[6] each Mahā-yuga (= Day of Brahmā) consists of a Kṛta- or Satya-yuga lasting 1,728,000 human years, a Tretā-yuga, lasting 1,296,000 years, a Dvāpara-yuga, lasting 864,000 years, and a Kali-yuga, lasting 432,000 years. According to the Purāṇa the condition of the world is constantly deteriorating and living conditions for humans worsen from the Kṛta-yuga (also called the Golden Age) down to the Kali-yuga (also called the Iron Age).

In the Kṛta-yuga *dharma* was four-footed and complete—and so was truth—and no gain accrued to humans by unrighteousness. In the other three *yugas* the *dharma* was successively deprived of one foot and through theft, falsehood, and fraud merit was diminished by one-fourth. People were free from disease in the Kṛta age; they accomplished all their aims and lived four hundred years. In the succeeding ages life was lessened by one-quarter each. In the Kṛta-yuga austerity was the chief virtue, in the Tretā-yuga wisdom, in

Dvāpara-yuga the performance of rituals, in the Kali-yuga *dāna* (giving, charity) is the means to find salvation. The Purāṇas describe the present age as close to universal chaos and final destruction. According to the *Viṣṇu Purāṇa* the Kali-yuga will end with the apparition of Viṣṇu's *Kalki-avatāra*, who will defeat the wicked, liberate the virtuous, and initiate a new Kṛta-yuga.

## MANVANTARA

There is no unanimity in Hindu literature with regard to the length allotted to a *manvantara* nor with regard to their number. According to *Manusmṛti* I, 63 a *manvantara* comprises one-fourteenth of a Day of Brahmā or 4,320,000 human years. Fourteen *manvantaras* constitute one full Day of Brahmā. Each of the fourteen periods is presided over by its own Manu. We are presently living in the seventh *manvantara* with seven more to come before the end of the current Day of Brahmā. The first Manu was Manu Svāyambhuva, who produced the ten Prajāpatis (progenitors of famous human races). He is also the author of the *Manusmṛti*, arguably the most important Hindu code of laws. The present Manu, born from the sun, is the creator of the now living race of human beings. He was saved from the great flood by Viṣṇu in the form of a fish (*Matsya-avatāra*). He is also the founder of the solar race of kings who ruled over Ayodhyā. The names of the fourteen Manus are not identical in all sources. The most widely accepted list reads: (1) Svayāmbhuva, (2) Svārociṣa, (3) Auttami, (4) Tāmasa, (5) Raivata, (6) Cākṣuṣa, (7) Vaivasvata, (8) Sāvarṇi, (9) Dakṣasāvarṇi, (10) Brahmasāvarṇi, (11) Dharmasāvarṇi, (12) Rudrasāvarṇi, (13) Raucya-daivasāvarṇi and (14) Indrasāvarṇi. The first six Manus belong to the past—the last seven to the future.

## DAY AND NIGHT OF BRAHMĀ [*BRAHMĀHORĀTRA*]

In accordance with the differences in Hindu sources concerning the length of *yugas*, there are proportionate differences in the reckonings of the length of a Day and Night of Brahmā.

According to the *Manusmṛti* a Day of Brahmā consists of 1,000 *divya-yugas*, of which each lasts 12,000 human years. However, according to the *Viṣṇu Purāṇa* a Day of Brahmā equals one *kalpa* (4,320,000,000 human years) consisting of 14 *manvantaras* (Ages of Manu) and 15 *sandhyās* (periods of twilight). Each *manvantara* (and each *sandhyā*) consists of 71 *mahā-yugas* totaling 306,720,000 years. Each *mahā-yuga* (4,320,000 years) consists of four *yugas*: Kṛta- or Satya-yuga (1,728,000 years), Tretā-yuga (1,296,000 years), Dvāpara-yuga (864,000 years), and Kali-yuga (432,000 years). After each Kali-yuga a *pralaya* (dissolution) follows equal in length to a *mahā-yuga*. Similarly after the completion of a *manvantara*, a period of *sandhyā* (calculated to be of the length of a satya-yuga) follows, during which no manifest creation exists. A Year of Brahmā is equal to 3,110,400,000,000 human years. The Life of Brahmā is made up of 100 years of 360 days each (and an equal number of nights of the same duration) of Brahmā, lasting 311,040,000,000,000 human years. According to some authorities the Life of Brahmā lasts 108 years, of which 50 have already elapsed. With the completion of a Life of Brahmā the universe disappears together with Brahmā and a new universe with a new Brahmā appears after a hiatus of equal length. According to the *Viṣṇu Purāṇa* one Life of Brahmā equals one Day of Viṣṇu. Assuming again a Life of Viṣṇu to last 100 or 108 years of 360 days each, the resulting figure expressed in human years is nearly impossible to imagine: 3,110,400,000,000,000 years!

## *PRALAYA*: DISSOLUTION (OF THE WORLD) ALSO *PRASAṀJARA, PRATISARGA*

Traditional Hindu cosmology presupposes an endless cycle of periodic creations and dissolutions of the universe. *Viṣṇu Purāṇa* VI, 2 ff. speaks of three kinds of *pralaya*: the first one is called *naimittika pralaya* (occasional) and occurs at the end of a *kalpa*, coinciding with a Night of Brahmā, to be followed by a new Day of Brahmā. The second is called *prākṛitika pralaya* (material) and occurs at the end of a Life of Brahmā, after two Parārdhas (2 times 10 years to the 17th!), ending one Day of Viṣṇu. The third is called *atyāntika pralaya* (final): terminating all notions of time and individual existence. The text describes in great detail the processes involved in each of these. In *naimittika pralaya* all the worlds are burned up and absorbed by Viṣṇu, who then reposes for a thousand *kalpas* (= One Night of Brahmā) on *śeṣa* (the world snake) in the midst of the original ocean. "Awaking, at the end of his night, the unborn Viṣṇu, in the form of Brahmā, creates the universe anew." In *prākritika pralaya*, after the dissolution of all entities, the elements (*bhūtas*) are absorbing each other till unformed *prakṛti* (primary matter) alone remains. This *pralaya* also involves the Egg of Brahmā (*brahmāṇḍa*) and eventually *prakṛti* itself is dissolved in Puruṣottama. The Life of Brahmā is equal to a Day of Viṣṇu, who after an equally long Night begins to issue Brahmā again to begin another world cycle. *Atyāntika pralaya* results in the complete and final absorption of *jīvas* (living souls) into Viṣṇu. In addition to these three, the *Agni Purāṇa* mentions a fourth, *nitya pralaya*: the constant death of those that were born in this world, the end of their individual bodily existence.

CHAPTER THIRTY-SEVEN

# Indian Chronology

In 2005 a team of French archaeologists, led by Laurent Marivaux of the University of Montpellier, found in the Pakistani province of Baluchistan, in the Indus River basin, fossils of primate teeth belonging to the Oligocene (ca. 34–23 million BCE), fueling renewed speculation about an Asian origin of primates and of hominids over against the long-held opinion about an African origin.[1]

A. K. Sharma,[2] of the Archaeological Survey of India, had earlier unearthed remains of a Paleolithic settlement in northern India, described as "extending over 400 square km, dated 1.2 million years ago or even earlier." The oldest Paleolithic sites in Tamilnāḍu and Punjab are dated at ca. 470000 BCE. The so-called Soan culture (with different phases)[3] flourished between 400000 and 200000 BCE. Excavations in Mehrgarh in 1974 uncovered remains of a Neolithic culture dating back to the eighth millennium BCE. The area was continuously inhabited for several thousands of years. Other settlements representing early phases of the Sindhu-Sarasvatī civilization date back to ca. 5500 BCE.[4] The Sindhu-Sarasvatī civilization reached its peak between 2700–1700 BCE. It did not die suddenly, but slowly faded out and elements of it entered later riverine cultures along the Ganges and Nārbada.

It is becoming ever more evident that there is no single-track prehistoric or protohistoric development in South Asia but a variety of different cultures coexisted in this large area and developed at different paces and in different directions. Thus cultural developments in the Indus region were paralleled by developments in Gujarat (Dvārakā: Kṛṣṇa dynasty), Delhi[5] (Pāṇḍava/Kaurava clans), eastern India[6] (Ayodhyā: Rāma dynasty). The "parallel histories" of these different populations show some common elements but even more distinctive features. It was only at a relatively late period that a systematic attempt was made to extend the northern Vedic culture through most of India;[7] even then leaving out large areas in the interior, inhabited by a number of populous tribes. The formerly widely held notion that the invasion of the Aryans, the Vedic Indians, brought a sudden and violent end to the Indus civilization has been all but abandoned: "Harappan culture did *not* fall, die, or come to a more or less abrupt end . . . many, but not all Indus settlements were abandoned, not destroyed."[8]

India's traditional chronology, supported by astronomical calculations,[9] provides precise dates also for prehistoric events. Thus the creation of the present world is dated at 1972947101 BCE and the beginning of the Kali-yuga at 3102 BCE, thirty-five years after the end of the Bhārata War according to one school. Scholars accepting the historicity of the Purāṇic materials[10] take this also to be the date of Manu. According to another school, Rāmacandra is said to have flourished around 1950 BCE and Kṛṣṇa around 1400 BCE. That would then also be the date for the Bhārata War.

According to P. C. Sengupta,[11] July 25, 3928 BCE is the date of the earliest solar eclipse mentioned in the *Ṛgveda*. He set Kṛṣṇa's birth date on July 21, 2501 BCE and the date of the Bhārata War at 2449 BCE. Using astronomical data provided in the *Bhīṣma Parvan* of the *Mahābhārata*, Anand Mohan Sharan, who teaches engineering at Memorial University Newfoundland (Canada) set the date for the Mahābhārata War in 2156 BCE.[12] S. B. Roy, using astronomical observations recorded in the *Ṛgveda* and working with the list of Purāṇic kings and *ṛṣis* as established by Pargiter arrived at a fairly precise dating of most of the major events of early Indian history.[13] By cross-referencing Indian events and names with exactly dated events and names of Babylonia and Persia, he appears to provide a fairly good foundation for his dates. Roy held that Max Müller—whom most earlier Western scholars followed in dating Vedic literature and events of early Indian history—had based his calculations only "on the ghost story of *Kathāsaritasāgara* composed in about 1200 AD, i.e., nearly three thousand five hundred years after the event." Max Müller, in fact, based his conjectures on the by then believed to be established dates of the life of Buddha. Assuming that the Upaniṣads were pre-Buddhist and conjecturing that it would take about two centuries for each of the four parts of the Veda to develop, he arrived at 1200 BCE as the date of the completion of the composition of the Ṛgveda. No archaeological evidence was then available, but even without it, some younger contemporary scholars like M. Winternitz, C. Bloomfield, and others challenged these dates and gave a much greater age to the *Ṛgveda*, as did most Indian scholars. Max Müller's conjecture was also predicated on the suppositions that the Indians and Iranians had once formed one single people, inhabiting the area of northern Iran or southern Russia, and that they split up around 1500 BCE. Indologists of that time had to be careful not to challenge the presumed higher age established for the Biblical Patriarchs.

S. B. Roy also assumed that certain events mentioned in the *Ṛgveda* took place in Iran where the Vedic Indians had lived before the then widely believed invasion of India. He provides a list of basic dates according to "high chronology" (h.c.) and "low chronology" (l.c.).

Manu Vaivāsvata, the first of the kings in the Purāṇic list, was born in 3167 BCE according to the high chronology (h.c.) and in 2851 BCE according to the low chronology (l.c.) On the assumption that Bhārata (no. 44 in the Purāṇic list) was a contemporary of Ṣargon of Accad, his birth date would either be 2393 BCE (h.c.) or 2077 BCE (l.c.). The major portion of the Vedic hymns was composed at the time of Viśvamitra I (2609 BCE h.c., 2293 BCE l.c.) whereas the invasion of India took place under the Divodāsa dynasty (2051–1961 BCE h.c., 1735–1645 BCE l. c.). The Aryans then spread throughout northern India in the next five centuries. The Bhārata battle took place in 1424 BCE (h.c.) or 1088 BCE (l.c.). The early Upaniṣads were composed between 1450–1350 BCE (h.c.) or 1100–1000 BCE (l.c.). *Vedāṅga* and *Sūtra* literature is assumed to be of similar age. The *Aṣṭādhyāyī* of Pāṇini was composed in 1320 BCE (h.c.) or 1000 BCE (l.c.). By the end of the eighth century BCE Sanskrit ceased as a spoken tongue.

Many of these dates appear surprisingly high compared to the dates found in most Indological literature. While it may be premature to endorse S. B. Roy's chronology without further study, it should be kept in mind that the chronology suggested by Max Müller is based on very shaky ground indeed and lately has been seriously questioned.

Geological evidence suggests that the Sarasvatī (Ghaggar-Hakra river system) dried out around 1900 BCE, well within the period established beyond doubt for the flourishing of the Indus civilization.[14] Since the majority of settlements mentioned in the *Ṛgveda*, as well as a great many sites connected with the Indus civilization, are situated on the banks of the Sarasvatī,[15] the conclusion appears plausible that the "Vedic Indians" were in the Indian heartlands by the second millennium BCE and that they did not invade and destroy the Indus civilization in 1500 BCE as has been assumed by the defenders of an Aryan invasion theory.

S. C. Kak estimates that the population of North India was around twenty-four million at that time, and he rightly points out that it is not imaginable that such a vast number of people could have migrated into northern India in one major wave or that they would have accepted the language and religion of a comparatively small band of "Aryan" invaders.

As regards the date of composition of the Vedic Saṃhitās there is as yet a wide difference of opinion among modern scholars. Leaving aside Dāyānanda Saraswatī's claims of a prehistoric antiquity for the Vedas, there still remains a wide divergence among scholars: P. V. Kane assumes that the bulk of the Saṃhitās, Brāhmaṇas and Upaniṣads were composed between 4000 and 1000 BCE and thinks that some hymns of the *Ṛgveda* and *Atharvaveda*, parts of the *Taittirīya Saṃhitā* and *Brāhmaṇa*, go back to the time before 4000 BCE. B. G. Tilak arrives at 4500 BCE as the date of the Vedas, M. Winternitz at 2500 BCE, and C. Bloomfield at 2000 BCE. Indian chronology reaches comparatively firmer ground with the life of Gautama Buddha, whose traditional dates and the dates as established by Western scholarship differ by only about half a century.[16] From then on numerous dated inscriptions and monuments ensure a fairly commonly accepted chronology.

Indians who do not use the Western (Gregorian) calendar have several other systems of dating. The most common are *saṃvat* (beginning 57 BCE) and *śaka* (beginning 78 CE).[17]

On the basis of the more recent research, based on archaeology and astronomy, the following chronology can be tentatively established:

| | |
|---|---|
| ca. 6500 BCE | Mergarh: first city cultures in northwest South Asia, coexisting with earlier (8000 BCE) village cultures. Multiethnic pattern of settlement. |
| ca. 4000 BCE | Some of the groups settled in northwest South Asia compose and collect hymns, embodying their knowledge of the universe (Veda). Some others practice early forms of Yoga, akin to Shamanism. Some continue ancestral Himalayan traditions of Śiva worship. Others develop early forms of asceticism, later to be known as Jainism. |
| ca. 3500 BCE | Early Harappan civilization. Cities with multiethnic populations. Maritime trade with Mesopotamia, possibly also with Egypt. |
| ca. 3100 BCE | Traditional dates for the Great Flood and Manu Vaivāsvata. |
| ca. 3000–2750 BCE | Traditional date for Yayāti period. |
| ca. 2750–2550 BCE | Traditional date for Mandhātri period. |
| ca. 2700–1500 BCE | Mature Sindhu-Sarasvatī civilization. |
| ca. 2350–1950 BCE | Traditional date for Rāmacandra period. |
| ca. 1900 BCE | Drying out of Sarasvatī. Major tectonic changes, causing large migrations toward the east and desertion of Indus Valley by the majority of its inhabitants. Age of *Rāmāyaṇa*. |
| ca. 1500–500 BCE | Major Upaniṣads, development of early Sāṁkhya, early Pūrva Mīmāṃsā. |
| ca. 1400 BCE | Great Bhārata War—Age of Kṛṣṇa. Early version of *Mahābhārata*. |
| ca. 1200 BCE | Early *Sūtra* literature. Consolidation of Vedic civilization: *Manusmṛti*. |
| 624–544 BCE | Life of Gautama Buddha according to traditional Śrī Laṅkā reckoning (563–483 according to most Western scholars). |

| | |
|---|---|
| 527 BCE | End of Mahāvīra's earthly life according to Jain tradition. |
| 518 BCE | Persian invasion under Skylax and conquest of the Indian satrapy for Darius I. |
| ca. 500 BCE–500 CE | Composition of *Śrauta Sūtras*, *Gṛyha Sūtras*, *Dharma Sūtras*, *Vedāṅgas*; the basis of the orthodox systems; composition of the epics and the original Purāṇas. |
| ca. 500–200 BCE | Composition of the *Bhagavadgītā* (according to P. V. Kane; others date it ca. 100 BCE–100 CE). |
| ca. 500–200 BCE | Bādarāyaṇa's *Vedānta Sūtra* (according to P. V. Kane). |
| ca. 490–458 BCE | Reign of Ajātaśatru, king of Magadha. |
| ca. 400 BCE | Pāṇini's *Aṣṭādhyāyī* (Grammar). |
| ca. 400–200 BCE | Jaimini's *Pūrvamīmāṃsā Sūtra*. |
| 327–325 BCE | Alexander of Macedonia's expedition to India. |
| ca. 322–298 BCE | Reign of Candragupta of Magadha. |
| ca. 300 BCE | Megasthenes, Greek Ambassador to Magadha. |
| ca. 300 BCE | Kauṭilīya's *Arthaśāstra* (according to some scholars: 100 CE). Gautama's *Nyāya Sūtra* and Kaṇāda's *Vaiśeṣika Sūtra*. |
| ca. 273–237 BCE | Reign of Aśoka. |
| ca. 200 BCE–100 CE | *Manusmṛti*. |
| ca. 200 BCE–100 CE | Invasions of Śūṅgas, Iranians, Śākas and Kuśānas, who founded kingdoms in India. |
| ca. 200 BCE–200 CE | Peak period of Buddhist and Jain influence. |
| ca. 150 BCE–100 CE | Patañjali *Mahābhāṣya*. |
| ca. 115 BCE | Besnāgar inscription of Heliodorus with a mention of Kṛṣṇa worship. |
| ca. 100 BCE–500 CE | Patañjali's *Yoga Sūtra*. |
| ca. 100 BCE–100 CE | Upavarṣa commentary to *Pūrvamīmāṃsā Sūtra* and *Vedānta Sutra* (according to P. V. Kane). |
| ca. 100 BCE–400 CE | *Śābara-bhāṣya* on Jaimini *Sūtras*. |
| ca. 100 BCE–800 CE | Composition of *Tirukkural*. |
| ca. 100 BCE | Early Mathurā sculpture; images of gods in temples. |

| | |
|---|---|
| ca. 25 BCE | Indian Embassy to Emperor Augustus of Rome. |
| ca. 50 CE | First documentation of images of gods with several pairs of arms. |
| ca. 10 | Indian Embassy to Emperor Trajan of Rome. |
| ca. 100–500 | Expansion of Hinduism in Southeast Asia. |
| ca. 100–200 | *Yājñavalkyasmṛti.* |
| ca. 100–300 | *Viṣṇudharma Sūtra.* |
| ca. 100–400 | *Nāradasmṛti.* |
| ca. 200–500 | Composition of *Viṣṇu Purāṇa.* |
| ca. 250–325 | *Sāṁkhya Kārikā* of Īśvarakṛṣṇa. |
| ca. 300–600 | Composition of some of the older Purāṇas in their present form. |
| ca. 300–888 | Pallava rulers in South India (Kāñcīpuram). |
| ca. 319–415 | Gupta Empire of Mathurā. |
| ca. 400–500 | Vātsyāyana's *Kāma Sūtra.* |
| ca. 400 | Composition of *Harivamṣa Purāṇa, Ahirbudhnya Saṃhitā.* Age of Kalidāsa, the greatest Indian dramatist. Spread of Vaiṣṇavism, especially Kṛṣṇa cult. Beginning of Tantricism. |
| ca. 400–500 | Vyāsa's *Yoga-bhāṣya.* |
| ca. 450–500 | Hūṇa invasions. |
| ca. 500 | *Devī-māhātmya* (in *Mārkaṇḍeya Purāṇa*). Spread of Śāktism into larger areas. |
| ca. 500–800 | Composition of *Kūrma Purāṇa.* |
| 547 | Kosmas Indikopleustes travels to India. |
| ca. 600–650 | Poet Bāṇa, author of *Kādāṃbarī* and *Harṣacarita.* |
| ca. 600–800 | Peak of Pāñcarātra Vaiṣṇavism. |
| ca. 600–900 | Late (metrical) *smṛtis*; composition of *Agni Purāṇa* and *Garuḍa Purāṇa.* |
| after 600 | Strong development of Vedānta. |
| ca. 600–800 | Brahmanical renaissance; successful fight against strongly Tāntric Buddhism. |

| | |
|---|---|
| ca. 640 | King Harṣa of Kanauj sends embassy to China. |
| ca. 650–1200 | Several independent kingdoms in Western, Central, East, and South India. |
| ca. 650–700 | Life of Kumārilabhaṭṭa and Maṇikavācakar. |
| since ca. 700 | Prevalence of *bhakti* religions. |
| ca. 700–750 | Gauḍapada, author of a *kārikā* on the *Māṇḍukya Upaniṣad* and Paramaguru of Śaṅkarācārya. |
| since ca. 700 | Flourishing of Kāśmīr Śaivism. |
| ca. 788–820 | Life of Śaṅkarācārya. |
| ca. 800–900 | Composition of the *Bhāgavata Purāna* in its present form; *Śukra-nīti-sāra*. |
| ca. 800–1250 | Chola dynasty in Tamiḷnāḍu. |
| ca. 825–900 | Medāthiti, writer of a commentary on *Manusmṛti*. |
| ca. 900 | Udāyana's *Nyāyakusumañjalī*. |
| ca. 900–1100 | *Śiva Purāṇa*; Śaivite Tantricism in Indonesia. |
| ca. 900–1100 | Composition of *Yogavāsiṣṭharāmāyaṇa* and *Bhaktisūtra*. |
| 999–1026 | Mahmud of Ghazni repeatedly raids India. |
| 1026 | Muslim raiders loot temple of Somnāth. |
| 1025–1137 | Life of Rāmānuja. |
| ca. 1100 | Buddhism virtually extinct in India; Life of Abhinavagupta; Composition of Hindu Tantras. |
| ca. 1100–1400 | Composition of *Śākta Upaniṣads*; rise of Vīraśaivism in South India. |
| ca. 1150–1160 | Composition of Kalhana's *Rājataraṅginī*, recording the history of Kāśmīr. |
| ca. 1150 | *Śrīkaṇṭha-bhāṣya*; building of Jagannātha temple at Pūrī. |
| 1238–1317 | Life of Madhva. |
| ca. 1250 | Beginning of *Śaiva-siddhānta*; building of Sun temple in Koṇārka. |
| 1211–1236 | Reign of Iltutmish, first Sulṭān of Delhi; beginning of Muslim rule over large parts of India. |

| | |
|---|---|
| ca. 1216–1327 | Rule of Pāṇḍyas at Madurai; foundation of the Mīnākṣī and Śiva temple of Madurai. |
| ca. 1275–1675 | Jñaneśvara of Mahārāṣṭra and other *bhakti* mystics. |
| 1288 | Marco Polo at Kalyan. |
| ca. 1300–1386 | Life of Śāyaṇa, famous commentator of the Vedic Saṃhitās and Brāhmaṇas. |
| 1327 | Muslim soldiers loot temple at Śrīraṅgam. |
| ca. 1333 | Ibn Battuta's travels in India. |
| ca. 1340 | Life of Mādhava. |
| 1336–1565 | Kingdom of Vijāyanāgara, last Hindu empire in India extending as far as Malaysia, Indonesia, and the Philippines. |
| ca. 1350–1610 | Vīraśaivism as the state religion of Mysore. |
| ca. 1350–1650 | Composition of many works of the Pūrvamīmāṃsakas. |
| ca. 1360 | Life of Vedāntadeśika. |
| ca. 1400–1470 | Life of Rāmānanda. |
| ca. 1420 | Life of Mīrābāī. |
| 1440–1518 | Life of Kabīr. |
| ca. 1449–1568 | Life of Śaṅkaradeva, great Vaiṣṇava preacher in Assam. |
| ca. 1475–1531 | Life of Vallabha. |
| ca. 1469 | Birth of Gurū Nānak, founder of Sikhism. |
| ca. 1485–1533 | Life of Caitanya. |
| 1498 | Vasco da Gama, after having rounded the Cape of Good Hope, lands on the Malabar coast. |
| ca. 1500 | Composition of *Adhyātma Rāmāyaṇa* and of Sadānanda's *Vedānta-sāra*. |
| ca. 1500–1800 | Peak of Durgā worship in Bengal. |
| ca. 1500–1600 | Life of Sūrdās of Agra. |
| ca. 1550 | Life of Brahmānanda Giri, author of a famous commentary on Śaṅkara's *Śārīraka-bhāṣya*. |
| 1510 | Portuguese occupy Goa. |

| | |
|---|---|
| ca. 1526–1757 | Moghul rule in India, destruction of most Hindu temples in North and Central India. |
| ca. 1532–1623 | Life of Tulasīdāsa. |
| ca. 1542 | Jesuit missionary Francis Xavier in Goa. |
| ca. 1548–1598 | Life of Ekanātha. |
| 1580 | Akbar the Great invites some Jesuit missionaries from Goa to his court for religious discussions. |
| ca. 1585 | Life of Harivaṃśa, founder of the Rādhā-Vallabhis. |
| 1608–1649 | Life of Tukārāma. |
| 1608–1681 | Life of Rāmdās. |
| 1610–1640 | Composition of Mitramiśra's *Viramitrodaya*, famous digests of the *dharma-śāstras*. |
| ca. 1630 | Śrīnivāsadāsa's *Yatīndramatadīpikā*. |
| 1631 | Death of Mumtaz, in whose honor Shah Jahan built the famous Tāj Mahal of Agra. |
| 1651 | The East India Company opens first factory on the Hugli (Bengal). |
| 1657 | Dārā Shukūḥ translates the Upaniṣads into Persian. |
| 1661 | Bombay becomes a British possession. |
| 1664 | Śivajī declares himself king of Mahārāṣṭra. |
| 1675 | Foundation of the French colony of Pondichéry. |
| ca. 1670–1750 | Life of Nagojībhaṭṭa, author of numerous works on grammar, *dharma-śāstra*, yoga, and so forth. |
| 1690 | Foundation of Calcutta through East India Company (Fort St. George). |
| ca. 1700–1800 | Life of Baladeva, author of *Govinda-bhāṣya*. |
| ca. 1750 | Composition of the (reformist) *Mahānirvāṇa-tantra*. |
| 1757 | Battle of Plassey; Clive is master of India. |
| 1784 | Asiatic Society founded in Calcutta by Sir William Jones. |
| 1818 | Defeat of the last Maratha Peshwa. |
| 1828 | Ram Mohan Roy founds Brahmo Samāj. |

| | |
|---|---|
| 1829 | Law against *satī*. |
| 1829–1837 | Suppression of the *thags*. |
| 1834–1886 | Life of Rāmakrishna Paramahaṃsa. |
| 1835 | Introduction of English school system in India. |
| 1842–1901 | M. D. Ranade, great social reformer. |
| 1857 | "Mutiny"/"First Indian War of Independence." |
| 1858 | The British Crown takes over the administration of India from the East India Company. |
| 1875 | Foundation of *Ārya Samāj* by Swāmi Dāyānanda Sarasvatī. |
| 1885 | Foundation of Indian National Congress in Bombay. |
| 1913 | Nobel Prize in literature for Rabindranath Tagore. |
| 1920 | Mahātmā Gandhi begins first All-India Civil Disobedience Movement. |
| 1926 | Foundation of Rāṣṭrīya Svayamsevak Sangh. |
| 1947 | Partition of India and creation of the Indian Union (Bhārat) and Pakistan as independent nations. |
| 1948 | Assassination of Mahātmā Gandhi; foundation of Rām Rājya Pariṣad; Pandit Nehru prime minister of the Indian Union; Śrī Cakravarti Rajagopalacari appointed governor general. |
| 1950 | India declared a republic within the commonwealth. Dr. Rajendra Prasad appointed first president of India; acceptance of the Constitution; death of Śrī Aurobindo Ghose and Ramaṇa Maharṣi. |
| 1951 | Beginning of the first Five Year Plan; inauguration of the Bhūdān movement; foundation of the Bhāratīya Jana Sangh. |
| 1955 | Hindu Marriage Act passed in parliament; reorganization of states (provinces) according to linguistic principles; inauguration of the second Five Year Plan. |
| 1961 | Goa, Damao, and Diu, Portuguese colonies in India, liberated in a military action. |
| 1962 | Dr. Rajendra Prasad the first president of Bhārat dies. Dr. Sarvepalli Radhakrishnan, vice president, succeeds him; Chinese attack on India. |

| | |
|---|---|
| 1964 | Death of Jawaharlal Nehru; Lal Bahādūr Sastri succeeds as prime minister. |
| 1965 | Armed conflict with Pakistan (West). |
| 1966 | Tashkent Conference; death of Lal Bahādūr Sastri; Indira Gandhi succeeds as prime minister. |
| 1967 | Unprecedented droughts precipitate severe crisis. |
| 1971 | India again at war with Pakistan; Bangladesh (East Pakistan) becomes independent. |
| 1975 | "National Emergency": suspension of many civil rights. |
| 1977 | Morarji Desai heads government as prime minister and minister for foreign affairs. |
| 1979 | Resignation of Morarji Desai; Indira Gandhi reelected. |
| 1984 | Sikh agitation for an independent Khalistān; central government troops storm Golden Temple in Amritsar; Indira Gandhi assassinated by two of her Sikh guards. |
| 1985 | Rajiv Gandhi, Indira's oldest son, becomes prime minister. |
| 1991 | Rajiv Gandhi assassinated by Tamil extremist. |
| 1992 | Hindu agitation on behalf of temple on Rāma's presumed birthplace in Ayodhyā culminating in destruction of Babri-Masjid and major communal riots in many Indian cities. |
| 1997 | General elections: Coalition under leadership of the Bhāratīya Janatā Party (BJP) establishes minority government. New elections: BJP-led coalition forms majority government under Atal Bihari Vajpayi as prime minister. |
| 2003 | Abdul Kamal (Muslim) is elected President of India. |
| 2004 | General elections: a Congress Party-led coalition wins majority; Manmohan Singh, a Sikh, is appointed prime minister; an estimated thirty million people attend the Kumbhamelā at Ujjain. |

# Maps

Map of India showing present state boundaries

Map of India showing major ancient and holy places

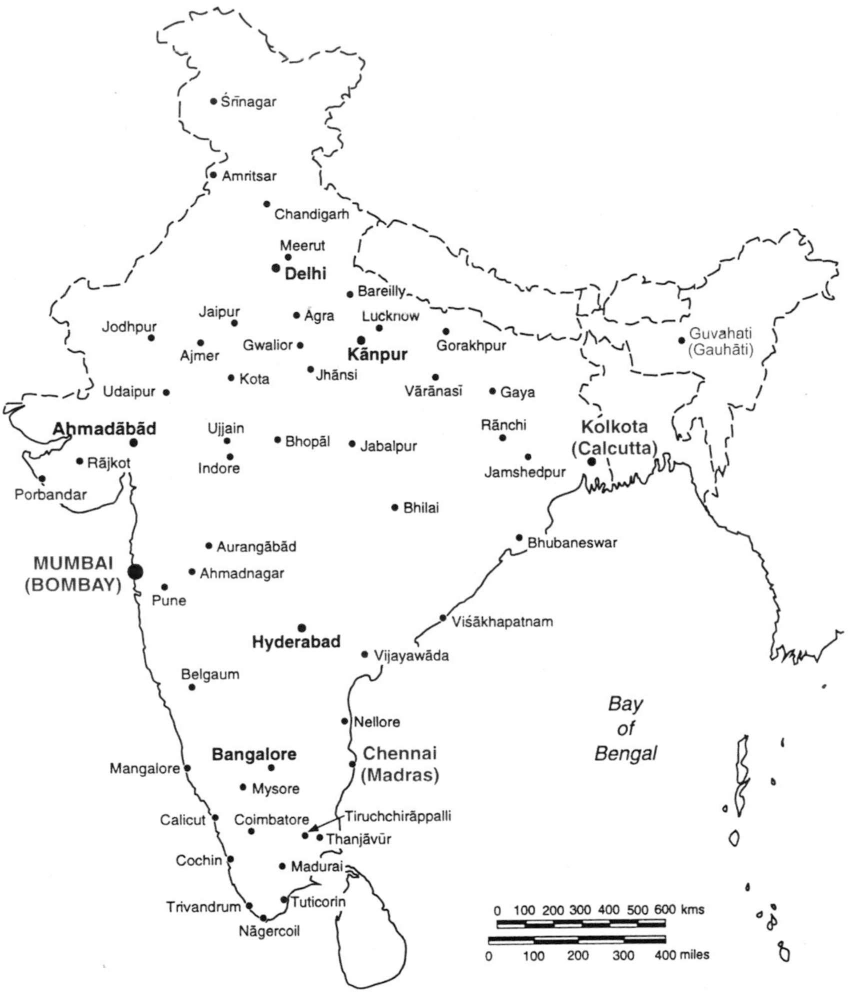


Map of India showing major modern urban centers

# Notes

## INTRODUCTION

1. According to the 2001 census of India, India's population on March 1, 2001 was 1,027,015,247 persons. The growth rate between 1991 and 2001 was 21.34 percent. Annual growth is estimated at ca. twenty million. In 2001 35 percent of India's population was under fifteen years old.

2. There is a website that lists and describes all Hindu temples in North America with impressive detail: www.garamchai.com/temples.htm.

3. Francis C. Assisi, "The Hinduization of America."

4. "De-anglicizing Asian Academia."

5. Recently Oxford University Press was forced to withdraw a book authored by Professor P. B. Courtright of Emory University, giving a Freudian interpretation of Gaṇeśa that was not only found offensive by Hindus but also is untenable from a scholarly standpoint, although it fits into the postmodernist paradigm. On the wider context see Alan Roland, "The Uses (and Misuses) of Psychoanalysis in South Asian Studies: Mysticism and Child Development."

6. See W. Halbfass, "Indien und die Geschichtsschreibung der Philosophie."

7. L. Dumont, "A Fundamental Problem."

8. Among "Western scholars" are also included Indian scholars who have adopted the presuppositions of contemporary Western scholarship, and among "Indian scholars," non-Indians have been included who have accepted traditional principles of Indian scholarship. A very detailed and well-documented analysis of this situation has been presented by Y. G. Rosser in "The Groan: Loss of Scholarship and High Drama in 'South Asian' Studies."

9. Malati J. Shendge, an Indian scholar who also had studied in the West, made a strong plea for "The Interdisciplinary Approach to Indian Studies."

10. Agehananda Bharati, (alias Leopold Fischer) a Western scholar who spent years in India, noted in a paper entitled "Psychological Approaches to Indian Studies: More Cons than Pros": "I strongly believe that psychological models are infertile and quite inadequate for Indian studies, particularly for antiquarian research."

11. L. Dumont, "A Fundamental Problem," 161. The emphases are L. Dumont's.

12. In 1991 the University of California at Berkeley established its first chair for Tamil as part of its Indian Studies program. *Hinduism Today* (November 1991): 28. Philip Lutgendorf, in an essay on "Mediaeval Devotional Traditions: An Annotated Survey of Recent Scholarship," in A. Sharma (ed.), *The Study of Hinduism*, 200–60, has documented a great number of translations from diverse Indian languages.

13. The usual way the name is written on local road signs is Vrindaban. The correct transliteration would be Vṛndāvana, "Vṛnda Forest." One can also find Brindaban, Brindabon, and Brindavan.

14. K. Klostermaier, *In the Paradise of Krishna* and "Remembering Vrindaban."

15. K. Klostermaier, "Hinduism in Bombay."

16. According to the 2001 Indian census, Hindus form 82 percent of India's population, Muslims 12.12 percent, Christians 2.34 percent, Sikhs 1.94 percent, Buddhists 0.76 percent, and Jains 0.40 percent.

17. See Alexandra George, *Social Ferment in India*, chapter 9, "The Tribes of India," 233–55. Also: Nirmal Minz, "Anthropology and the Deprived."

18. George, ibid., "The Scheduled Castes," 202–32. An interesting document shedding light on the life of an untouchable community is the so-called *Kahar Chronicle* by Tarashankar Banerjea. See Raja Kanta Ray, "The Kahar Chronicle."

19. R. Inden, "Orientalist Constructions of India."

## 1. THE BEGINNINGS OF HINDUISM

1. It would be wrong, however, to accuse the English as beings the "inventors of Hinduism," as Hadwa Dom, a Dalit activist does, in a recent internet article *The English Invention of Hinduism* "The Myth of One Hindu Religion Exploded."

2. The latest and most detailed exposition of the views and arguments of the two hostile camps is provided in the lengthy articles that have appeared in the *Journal of Indo-European Studies* (JIES) under the title "Indo-Aryan Migration Debate." Vol. 30/3&4 (Fall/Winter 2002) and Vol. 31/1&2 (Spring/Summer 2003). The controversy is brought to a sharp focus by the lead article of N. Kazanas, "Indigenous Indo-Aryans and the *Rigveda*," M. Witzel's response "Ein Fremdling im Ṛgveda," and N. Kazanas "Final Reply." In these articles the whole phalanx of pro- and anti-invasionist arguments is arrayed, and sharp taunts and missiles are exchanged reminiscent of religious wars of the past. Vishal Agarwal published on the Internet "A Reply to Michael Witzel's 'Ein Fremdling im *Ṛgveda*'" refuting not only Witzel's arguments but also highlighting the uncivil and offensive tone of his writings. It is telling that Witzel used the popular Indian Marxist fortnightly *Frontline* for his uncalled for attacks on all scholars who did not agree with him on the Aryan invasion theory.

3. One of the prominent Indian scholars who quite early rejected the Aryan invasion theory was Aurobindo Ghose. In *The Secret of the Veda*, written between 1914 and 1916, he points out that the text of the Veda has no reference to any such invasion.

4. Edition used: third edition, Oxford, Clarendon Press 1906 (reprint 1959).

5. In 1767 James Parsons had published a long work, entitled *The Remains of Japhet, Being Historical Enquiries into the Affinity and Origins of the European Languages*, using samples from over a dozen languages extending from Irish to Bengalī.

6. Ibid., 101.

7. The argument was entirely linguistic speculative, and wildly contradictory assertions were made from the same linguistic basis by various authors. Among them there was neither agreement on methodology nor on the interpretation of "linguistic facts."

8. M. Müller, *The Six Systems*, 35.

9. See Vishal Agarwal, "The Aryan Migration Theory."

10. G. Feuerstein, S. Kak, D. Frawley, *In Search of the Cradle of Civilization*.

11. S. Kalyanaraman has devoted a large part of his life to the search for the River Sarasvatī and the study of the settlements in its basin. As a result of his research, he published in 2003 seven volumes that provide an enormous amount of detail relating to the Sarasvatī civilization. Due to his efforts, the government of India is taking up several projects to bring the Sarasvatī back to life and to interlink the north Indian river systems.

12. Whereas Harappa and Mohenjo Daro occupy an area of approximately two hundred acres each, Lakhmirwala and Rakhigari cover almost five hundred acres and several others also situated in the former Sarasvatī basin either exceed or come close to the largest Indus valley settlements.

13. A. Seidenberg, "The Geometry of the Vedic Rituals." Traditional North Indian builders still use the same standard of measurements that had been used by the builders of Harappa and Mohenjo Daro.

14. "The Purāṇic Tradition of Historiography in India."

15. Philip von Zabern (ed.), *Vergessene Städte am Indus: Frühe Kulturen in Pakistan vom 8. bis zum 2. Jahrtausend v. Chr.*

16. The most complete representation and summary of research is found in E. Neumayer, *Prehistoric Indian Rock Paintings*. Attempts at interpretation are made by Kapila Vatsyayan in an essay entitled "Prehistoric Paintings."

17. E. Mayr, *Toward a New Philosophy of Biology*: "The time would seem to have come for the translators and interpreters of Aristotle to use a language appropriate to his thinking, that is the language of biology, and not that of sixteenth-century humanists" (56).

18. As Walter S. Fairservis has said: "One of the most complex, important and indeed vexing problems confronting South Asian archaeologists today is the relationship of early Vedic culture(s), as described in the *Ṛgveda*, to archaeological remains." "The Harappan Civilization and the Ṛgveda," in M. Witzel (ed.), *Inside the Texts—Beyond the Texts*. At the end of his article, Fairservis lists a number of cultural traits attested in the *Ṛgveda* and paralleled in Harappan cultural remains. He also insists that "rather than there being a gap between the later 3rd Millennium remains and those of the 2nd Millennium, suggestive of the demise of the earlier and the sudden appearance of the later, in fact some artifactual material is contemporaneous and thus a continuity existed" (61).

19. The most extensive work relating to this is Asko Parpola's *Deciphering the Indus Script*, a marvel of scholarship and a treasury of information about early Indian history, but far from offering a convincing decipherment of these signs.

20. Subhash Kak, *The Astronomical Code of the Ṛgveda.*

21. *In Search of the Cradle of Civilization.*

22. French scientists recently discovered in Baluchistan, close to the Indus valley, a great many fossil remnants of hominids from the Oligocene.

## 2. HINDU *DHARMA*: ORTHODOXY AND HERESY IN HINDUISM

1. "The word *dharm* in Hindī has an almost totally identical application to that of the English word 'religion' which has, of course, an enormous semantic spread, and it would seem highly probable that the English word and concept is the major determinant factor in the Hindī usage." S. Weightman and S. M. Pandey, "*Dharm* and *Kartavy* in Modern Hindī" in W. D. O'Flaherty and J. D. M. Derret (eds.), *The Concept of Duty in Southeast Asia*, 223. The same authors also point out that the word *mat* (literally "thought," "doctrine") is equally common and used like the word *dharm*: *Hindūdharm* = *Hindūmat.*

2. In Gautama's *Nyāya-Sūtra*, *dharma* is "a specific property of an object."

3. Pandit Dinanath Sarma, "Sanātana dharma," *Kalyāṇa.*

4. *HDhS*, vol. 1, 1.

5. *Manusmṛti* II, 6; cf. also *Yājñavalkyasmṛti* I, 7.

6. *Manusmṛti* II, 9.

7. Ibid., 11.

8. J. C. Heesterman, "On the Origin of the Nāstika."

9. *Manusmṛti* II, 17–24.

10. *Manusmṛti* I, 111–18.

11. "Sanātana dharma hi sarvabhauma dharma yā mānava dharma hai," *Dharmāṅka* (*Kalyāna*) [Hindī], my own translation.

12. *Bhagavadgītā* III, 35.

13. *Manusmṛti* VIII, 15.

14. W. D. O'Flaherty in her introduction to *The Concept of Duty in Southeast Asia*, xiii ff., comments on the essentially indefinable character of *dharma* and the clash between existing definitions. She also points out that *dharma* and *adharma* are correlative, that *devas* only appear where there are demons, and that "*dharma* is a problem rather than a concept, vague, indeterminable . . . an ambiguous concept."

15. P. V. Kane in his monumental *History of Dharmaśāstra* refers to over two thousand books!

16. The informative essay on "Use and Misuse of the Dharma," by A. Kunst, in W. D. O'Flaherty and J. D. M. Derret (eds.), *The Concept of Duty in Southeast Asia*, 3–17, shows some of the development.

17. "The Concept of Duty in Ancient Indian Jurisprudence: The Problem of Ascertainment," in *The Concept of Duty in Southeast Asia*, 18–65.

18. From *Gautama's Nyāyasūtras with Vātsyāyana Bhāṣya*, ed. and trans. Ganganatha Jha, I, 18.

19. *Yogasūtras* II, 30–32.

20. Vaikunthavāsi Śrī Bābu Sādhucaranprasād, *Dharmaśāstrasaṇgraha*, a digest of Hindu law for practical use, with selections from forty-six *smṛtis* according to topics, gives a good idea of the range of *dharmaśāstra*.

21. The best-known and best-documented case is that of Raja Ram Mohan Roy, who successfully fought for the abolition of *satī*.

22. "Hinduism, A Static Structure or a Dynamic Force?" in *Nehru Abhinandan Granth*, 421–25. The author was formerly head of the Department of Ancient Indian History and Culture, Banares Hindu University.

23. "Moral Foundations of Indian Society," ibid., 464–69. The author was the editor of the multivolume *Dharmakośá* (Wāī: Dharmakośa Maṇḍala, 1937–1961) and one of the most outstanding pandits of contemporary India.

24. Apart from the countless instances that one encounters in daily life in India itself, Indian dailies quite frequently carry letters to the editor with massive complaints like the following from *Times of India* (8 March 1968):

> At the national integration conference held at Delhi in September last a code of conduct was prescribed to be observed by political leaders. The code required them not to exploit communal and caste feelings for political purposes. Hardly six months later, during the recent general elections, one saw in Poona the sorry spectacle of the code of conduct being flagrantly violated by the political leaders in general and the Congress leaders in particular. In each of the six constituencies in Poona the Congress candidate nominated was of the same caste that was in overwhelming majority in that particular constituency. The election speeches of the leaders conveyed the impression that they were totally unaware of the existence of the code of conduct. Every candidate openly preached caste hatred and exhorted the electorate to vote for him as he belonged to their caste. Perhaps never before were caste and communal feelings so deeply aroused as they were during the recent general elections in Poona. (V. D. Mahajan).

Another reader complained that: "even after twenty years of freedom untouchability in the villages is still as virulent as ever. The social justice said to have been one to the Scheduled Castes and Tribes has just not been adequate" (Raja Sekhara Rao).

25. "Sādhana," *RS* 16, 2 (1969): 36–50.

26. The most complete and systematic description is to be found in: Ramdas Gaur, *Hindutva* [Hindī]. H. H. Wilson's *Religious Sects of the Hindus* (originally published in 1861; reprint 1958) is incomplete, unsystematic, and in quite a few instances incorrect.

27. G. S. Ghurye, *Indian Sādhus*, 110 ff. and 177 ff.

28. *Liṅgapurāṇa* I, 107, 41 ff.

29. We have to interpret some of these as a reaction against persecution on the part of non-Vaiṣṇavas such as Citrasena, who at the instigation of Śaiva monks prohibited the worship of Viṣṇu in his realm, ordered his officers to persecute the Vaiṣṇavas, and had the images of Viṣṇu thrown into the ocean. Cf. R. C. Hazra, *Studies in the Upapurāṇas*, vol. 2, 362 f.

30. W. O'Flaherty, "The Origin of Heresy in Hindu Mythology"; S. N. Dasgupta, *HIPh*, vol. 3, 19. See *Kūrma Purāṇa*, chapter 15.

31. For a more extensive treatment of this topic, see K. Klostermaier, "Hindu Views of Buddhism."

32. Cf. *HCIP*, R. C. Majumdar, general ed., vol. 3, 437; S. N. Dasgupta, *HIPh*, vol. 5, 45; M. Winternitz, *Geschichte der Indischen Literatur*, vol. 3, 426 ff.; Alkondavilli Govindacharya, *The Divine Wisdom of the Dravida Saints*, 78 ff.

33. *Viṣṇupurāṇa* III, 18, 15 ff. My translation.

34. P. V. Kane, *HDhS*, vol. 2, part 2, 716 ff.

35. Nārāyaṇa Bhaṭṭa's *Maṇimañjarī* as summarized by S. N. Dasgupta, HIPh, vol. 4, 52.

36. The English translation by E. B. Cowell and A. E. Gough is incomplete, it leaves out the last chapter on Advaita Vedānta. See K. Klostermaier, "Śaṁkaradarśanam."

37. *Brahma Sūtra Bhāṣya* I, 1, 2: Thibaut's translation, Part I, 15.

38. W. Ruben, "Materialismus im Leben des Alten Indien"; Dale Riepe describes himself in *The Philosophy of India and Its Impact on American Thought* as "interested in the naturalistic and materialistic philosophy in India," mentioning his dissertation on *The Naturalistic Tradition in Indian Thought*. In India M. N. Roy (*Materialism*, written in 1934, published 1940; reprint Calcutta: Renaissance Publishers 1951), on his way toward Radical Humanism via Marxism-Leninism, drew attention to the often underplayed materialistic stream of the Indian tradition.

39. II, 4, 12.

40. *Sarvadarśanasaṁgraha* I.

41. This has been proposed, for example, by Raymond Panikkar in *Kerygma und Indien*, 84 ff.

42. They also claim quite often personal infallibility!

43. See "Holy War in India."

44. "No Hold Barred Battle."

45. *India Today* (15 April 1993): 36.

## 3. THE VEDA: REVELATION AND SCRIPTURE IN HINDUISM

1. Most details mentioned in "Procedure of Reciting *Śrīmad Bhāgavata*," 6–8 apply (with appropriate modifications) to the recitation of other Hindu scriptures too.

2. Almost all the important popular scriptures have been supplied with a *Māhātmya*, a praise of the greatness of the work, containing also profuse promises attached to the reading of the scripture.

3. See, e.g., K. Sivaraman, "The Word as a Category of Revelation," in H. Coward and K. Sivaraman (eds.), *Revelation in Indian Thought, A Festschrift in Honor of Professor T. R. V. Murti*. 45–64.

4. Some interesting details are mentioned by A. Esteller in "The Quest for the Original *Ṛgveda*" and "The *Ṛgveda Saṃhitā* as a 'Palimpsest'."

5. The *guru-paraṃparā*, the succession of teachers, had to be memorized by each student as legitimation of his knowledge. In *Bṛhadāraṇyaka Upaniṣad* IV, 6, sixty links of this chain of tradition are mentioned, going back through mythical figures to Brahmā, the creator himself, who revealed it.

6. P. V. Kane, *HDhS*, vol. 1 (1930): 70–75.

7. See G. Srinivasa Murti's introduction to *Śrī Pāñcarātra Rakṣa of Śrī Vedānta Deśika*, ixx–xii.

8. The most exhaustive account is given in J. Gonda, *Vedic Literature (Saṃhitās and Brāhmaṇas)*. On the Vedic schools, see L. Renou, *Les écoles védiques et la formation du Veda*. See also S. W. Jamison and M. Witzel, "Vedic Hinduism," in A. Sharma (ed.) *The Study of Hinduism*, 65–113.

9. For annotated text, see T. Aufrecht, *Die Hymnen des Ṛgveda* and *Ṛgveda with the commentary of Sāyaṇa*, M. Müller (ed.). The best complete translation is H. F. Geldner's *Ṛgveda deutsch*. For a complete metric English translation see R. T. H. Griffith, *The Hymns of the Ṛgveda*.

10. For text, see Ram Sarma Acarya, *Sāmaveda*, the metric translation by T. R. H. Griffith, *The Hymns of the Sāmaveda*.

11. For text, see A. Weber, *Yajurveda Vājasaneyīsaṃhitā*, 2 vols., the metric translation by T. R. H. Griffith, *The Hymns of the Yajurveda*.

12. For text, see R. Roth and W. D. Whitney, *Atharvaveda Saṃhitā*, the translation by W. D. Whitney, *Atharvaveda Saṃhitā*.

13. L. Renou, *Vedic India*.

14. Ramdas Gaur, *Hindutva*, 81 ff.

15. Text: Pandurang Jawaji, *Śīkṣādivedaṣadaṅgāni*.

16. In later times, all these auxiliary sciences developed into independent scholarly disciplines, each with a voluminous literature of its own.

17. Max Müller edited and translated *Śaunaka's Ṛgvedapratiśākhya* (Leipzig 1856).

18. Gonda, *Vedic Literature*, 43.

19. I, 6, 3, 10: The story and the fatal formula are often repeated in the epics and Purāṇas.

20. For details, see J. Gonda, *Vedic Literature*, chapter 8: "The Brāhmaṇas."

21. As, for instance, in the *Bṛhadāraṇyaka Upaniṣad*. On *Āraṇyakas*: J. Gonda, *Vedic Literature*, chapter 9.

22. Text: W. C. Sastri Pannikar (ed.), *One Hundred and Eight Upaniṣads*. Most of these have been translated in the Adyar Library Series. English translation of the major early Upaniṣads with Sanskrit text and notes: S. Radhakrishnan, *The Principal Upaniṣads*.

23. Thus a *Ramakrishna Upaniṣad* has been published by the Ramakrishna Mission. Dhanjibhai Fakirbhai, an Indian Christian, composed a *Khristopaniṣad.*

24. For details consult L. Renou, *Vedic India,* 50 ff.

25. One of the most important Vaiṣṇava Saṃhitās is the *Ahirbhudhnyasaṃhitā.* No translation in any Western language exists so far. An important Śaivite Āgama is the *Ajitāgama:* No translation is available in any Western language. An important Śākta Tantra is the *Tripurārahasyam,* Swami Sanatanadevaji Maharaja, ed. [*Jñānakhanda* only]. English translation by A. U. Vasaveda.

26. F. O. Schrader, *Introduction to the Pāñcarātra and the Ahirbudhnya Saṃhitā.* For a useful, brief introduction, see Jean Filliozat, "Les Āgamas Çivaites," in N. R. Bhatt (ed.), *Rauravāgama.* Lately F. H. Daniel Smith has done extensive research in the literature (largely still in manuscript) of Vaiṣṇava Āgamas.

27. *Śrī Pāñcarātra Rakṣa of Śrī Vedānta Deśika,* Introduction, VI & IX.

28. "Purāṇas and Their Authority in Religious Matters," *Kalyāṇa Kalpatāru,* 5 ff.

29. For details consult L. Renou, *Vedic India,* 41 ff. Texts and translations are too numerous to be mentioned here; this type of literature has been extensively studied by nineteenth-century European Indologists. For a fairly representative selection of translated texts, see *Sacred Books of the East* (*SBE*), vols. 29 and 30. The most complete treatment is found in Jan Gonda, *The Ritual Sūtras.*

30. The unquestioned authority in this field was P. V. Kane: his seven-volume *History of Dharmaśāstra* offers an unrivaled wealth of details about works, their authors, and materials pertaining to *smṛti.* The major Western authorities in this field are Duncan M. Derrett, formerly Professor of Oriental Law at the School of African and Oriental Studies in London, and Ludo Rocher, Professor of Indian Studies at the University of Pennsylvania.

31. Text: J. Jolly, *Mānava Dharmaśāstra,* English translation: G. Bühler, *The Laws of Manu, SBE,* vol. 25. There are many editions with commentaries available now.

32. For a brief discussion of historical problems related to the *Manusmṛti* see Kane, *HDhS,* vol. 1, 79–85, as well as G. Bühler's introduction to his translation.

33. See Kane, *HDhS,* vol. 1, 60–70.

34. Ramdas Gaur, *Hindutva,* 755.

35. A great authority on Purāṇas, R. C. Hazra, wrote numerous books and papers on Purāṇas and *Upapurāṇas.* Two contributions of his on Purāṇas and *Upapurāṇas* in *CHI,* vol. 2, 240–86. The latest comprehensive work on the subject is L. Rocher, *The Purāṇas.*

36. Kane, *HDhS,* vol. 5, 973–80, with ample references to original sources.

37. See A. D. Pusalker, "Purānic Studies."

38. Its main texts are the *Nyāya-sūtras* by Gautama. More about it in chapter 24.

39. In H. G. Coward, ed., *Studies in Indian Thought: Collected Papers of Prof. T. R. V. Murti,* 357–76. See also "Revelation and Reason" in the same volume, 57–71.

40. Ibid., viii.

41. Ganganatha Jha, *Pūrva-Mīmāṃsā in Its Sources,* 146. A recent study of this issue is Othmar Gächter, *Hermeneutics and Language in Pūrvamīmāṃsā: A Study in Śābara Bhāṣya.*

42. Mādhava, *Sarvadarśanasaṁgraha*, XIII, 6. An excellent introduction to this school: H. G. Coward in *Sphoṭa Theory of Language*. See also H. G. Coward *Bhartṛhari*.

43. Mādhava, *Sarvadarśanasaṁgraha*, XIII, 13.

44. There are numerous editions, e.g., by Devaprakasa Patanjala Sastri. A complete English translation (with text and notes) was done by Srisa Chandra Vasu, 2 vols.

45. V. S. Agrawala, *India as Known to Pāṇini*, 3: "Pāṇini, unlike Sakatāyana did not carry to extremes the theory of treating all nouns as verbal derivatives, but also recognized the formation of fortuitous words in the languages for which no certain derivation could be vouchsafed."

46. A complete edition of Patañjali's *Mahābhāṣya* with Kayyata's and several other glosses is published in ten volumes by Haryana Sahitya Samsthan, Gurukul Jhajjar (Rohtak), 1961. Parts have been translated into various European languages. For details see: H. G. Coward and K. Kunjunni Raja (eds.), *The Philosophy of the Grammarians*, vol. 5 of *Encyclopedia of Indian Philosophies*.

47. K. A. Nilakanta Sastri, *The Culture and History of the Tamils* 10.

48. *(Deva)nāgarī* is the name of the characters in which Sanskrit is usually written, though in various parts of the country, other characters have been used as well.

49. J. Gonda, *Vedic Literature*, 57.

50. According to Jan Gonda (*Vedic Literature*, 61), Langlois and Wilson, early translators of the entire Ṛgveda, "suffered under the defect that they were based on the (not always correctly understood) commentary of Sāyaṇa." Ludwig's translation is called "stiff and abrupt," and Grassman's a "wholly inadequate Germanization." Griffith's translation is defective too—he apparently put too much reliance on Sāyaṇa. Geldner "missed the exact meaning of many words." Renou "had to leave his translation unfinished." Roth and Kaegi had vainly attempted an unambiguous uniform translation.

51. J. Gonda, *Vedic Literature*, 62.

52. R. N. Dandekar, *Some Aspects of the History of Hinduism*, 136.

53. Madhav M. Deshpande, "Changing Conceptions of the Veda: From Speech-Acts to Magical Sounds," 4.

54. Ibid., 8.

55. *RV* III.55.

56. *RV* X.71.5.

57. *RV* VIII.100.11.

58. S. Kak, *The Astronomical Code of the Ṛgveda*, 18.

59. Deshpande, "Changing Conceptions of the Veda," 38. The texts of the Veda are still the object of intense study by Hindu scholars: numerous publications on the Vedas appear every year in Indian vernaculars from research institutions such as the Jhajhar Gurukul in Rohtak or the Vaidik Samṣodan Samsthan in Pune. Also much of Western Indological scholarship is still focused on Vedic studies. An "International Foundation for Vedic Education" has been recently founded in the United States, which held an International Veda Conference attended by top researchers in the field.

An Atharva Veda Conference was held in 1993 in New York. The great temple at Tirupati established in 2006 the Śrī Venkateśvara Vedic University, devoted exclusively to Vedic studies, "to preserve, foster and promote oral traditions of Vedic and related literature, with focus on the right intonations, to bring out the depth of rational approach and the scientific temper present in the Vedas." *India Today Online*, August 12, 2006.

60. See the famous *Vāk-Sūkta* in *Ṛgveda* X, 125.

61. J. Woodroffe, *Introduction to Tantra Śāstra.*

62. II, 23, 3.

63. *Taittirīya Upaniṣad* I, 8.

64. *Māṇḍūkya Upaniṣad.*

65. *Skandapurāṇa*, Viṣṇukhaṇḍa XVI, 30 ff.

66. *Times of India*, 9 October 1963.

67. See also H. G. Coward and W. Goa, *Mantra.*

68. S. K. Belvalkar, *Shree Gopal Basu Malik Lectures on Vedānta Philosophy.* The individual *śākhas* try to expurgate the contradictions in their literatures. The existing *Brahmasūtra* is essentially a (Sāmavedi) *Chāndogyasūtra* with later revisions and additions.

## 4. *ITHĀSA-PURĀṆA*: THE HEART OF HINDUISM

1. For general orientation, see M. Winternitz, "The Popular Epics and the Purānas," *A History of Indian Literature*, vol. 1, part 2. Among modern Western studies of the *Mahābhārata* the following stand out: B. A. van Nooten, *The Mahābhārata* and A. Hiltebeitel, *Ritual of Battle: Krishna in the Mahābhārata.* Among older studies: E. W. Hopkins, *The Great Epic of India*, H. Oldenberg, *Das Mahābhārata*, and H. Jacobi, *Das Rāmāyaṇa.* The most recent survey of literature on epics and Purāṇas is offered by A. Hiltebeitel, "India's Epics," in A. Sharma (ed.), *The Study of Hinduism*, 114–38 and G. Bailey "The Purāṇas," Ibid., 139–68.

2. For details, consult P. J. Chinmulgund and V. V. Mirashi (eds.), *Review of Indological Research in the Last 75 Years*, 670 ff., as well as V. S. Sukhtankar, "Introduction," in *Critical Edition, Mahābhārata, Ādiparvan*, i–cx, and G. H. Bhatt, "Introduction," in *Rāmāyaṇa, Critical Edition*, Bālakāṇḍa, xiii–xxxv, i–xviii. See also S. M. Katre, *Introduction to Textual Criticism*, with an appendix by P. K. Gode.

3. Vishnu S. Sukthankar writes in his "Prolegomena to the Critical edition of the *Mahābhārata*," in vol. 1, (*Ādiparvan*): "Next to the Vedas [the *Mahābhārata*] is the most valuable product of the entire literature of ancient India, so rich in notable works. Venerable for its very antiquity, it is one of the most inspiring monuments of the world and an inexhaustible mine for the investigation of the religion, mythology, legend, philosophy, law, custom, and political and social institutions of ancient India" (iii).

4. N. Sen, "The Influence of the Epics on Indian Life and Literature." For details of the immense influence on drama, poetry, and the fine arts in India and in the whole of Southeast Asia, see the above article and B. R. Chatterjee, "The *Rāmāyaṇa* and the *Mahābhārata* in Southeast Asia."

5. H. Raychaudhuri, "The *Mahābhārata*: Some Aspects of Its Culture." See also J. L. Fitzgerald, "The Great Epic of India as Religious Rhetoric: A Fresh Look at the *Mahābhārata*."

6. The names connected with the former theory are Larssen, Sørenson, Winternitz, and Meyer; with the latter, especially J. Dahlmann. About the theories and their criticism, see A. D. Pusalker, "The *Mahābhārata*: Its History and Character." See also Fitzgerald, "The Great Epic of India."

7. *Mahābhārata, Critical Edition*. Several vulgate editions are available, e.g., one in four volumes from the Gītāpress, Gorakhpur.

8. I, 1, 50. See also M. Mehta, "The Problem of the Double Introduction to the *Mahābhārata*."

9. The Bhandarkar Oriental Research Institute has published a critical edition in two volumes. A vulgate edition is available from several publishers, amongst others from Gītāpress Gorakhpur (no date) with Hindī translation. (The same publisher has also brought out a vulgate edition of the entire *Mahābhārata* in four volumes with a *Nāmānukramāṇikā*).

10. *Yad ihāsti tad anyatrā yad nehāsti na tat kva cit.*

11. *Mahābhāratātparyanirṇaya*. Ch2: Engl. transl. by A. D. Pusalkar, "The Mahābhārata: Its History and Character," 68.

12. V. S. Sukthankar, *On the Meaning of the Mahābhārata*, 128 ff.

13. A complete English translation of the *Mahābhārata* was published by Pratap Chandra Roy toward the end of the last century; reprinted in twelve volumes by Oriental Publishing Co., Calcutta in the late fifties. A new English translation, following the critical edition, was begun by A. van Buitenen (Chicago: University of Chicago Press, 1973–1978), continued by J. L. Fitzgerald: vol. 12, *The Book of Peace*, part I, appeared in 2004. C. Rajagopalachari has published a one-volume rendering of important stories of the *Mahābhārata*, which has become very popular.

14. Pāṇḍu had been suffering under a curse that prevented him from having children of his own. So he arranged for his wives to conceive sons from gods: Kuntī begot Yudhiṣṭhira from Yama, Bhīma from Vāyu, and Arjuna from Indra. Madrī had twin sons, Sahadeva and Nakula, from the Aśvins.

15. *Āraṇyakaparvan*, chapters 295–98, condensed.

16. The present introduction contains the story of Vālmīki, who according to legend started out as a brigand, was converted into a Rāmabhakta, and did penance for his sins in a forest by keeping seated in meditation even while ants began building up an anthill (Sanskrit: *vālmīka*) around his body.

17. *Jātaka*, 461; about *Rāmāyaṇa* criticism, see A. D. Pusalker, "The Rāmāyaṇa" and C. Bulcke, *Rāmakathā* [Hindī].

18. See G. H. Bhatt's introduction to *Mahābhārata, Critical Edition*.

19. In the *Hindustan Times* (29 July 1972), a note appeared saying that the original manuscript of the *Rāmacaritamānasa* had been found in the house of a Pathan landlord in Malihabad, Uttar Pradesh, near Lucknow. There are countless editions of this work in India. The Gītāpress brought out the full text with an English translation in 1968.

20. See A. D. Pusalker, *Studies in Epics and Purāṇas of India*, 174 ff.

21. The Oriental Institute Baroda has published the *Rāmāyaṇa, Critical Edition*, in seven volumes (1960–1975). Vulgate editions are numerous and easily available from e.g., the Gītāpress.

22. Pusalker, "The *Rāmāyaṇa*," in *CHI*, 27 ff.

23. R. T. H. Griffith has brought out a metrical English translation of the *Rāmāyaṇa*. A prose translation, together with the Sanskrit text, appeared from Gītāpress Gorakhpur, *Kalyāṇa Kalpatāru*, 1960–1974. C. Rajagopalachari has summarized the stories of the *Rāmāyaṇa* in one volume, which also has become very popular. A new English prose translation, based on the critical edition, under the general editorship of R. Goldman, was published by Princeton University Press, 1984–1997. The introduction to the first volume (*Bālakāṇḍa*) by R. Goldman (3–59) deals both with the history of the *Rāmāyaṇa* text and the literature connected with it.

24. *Bālakāṇḍa*, chapter 67.

25. Laṅkā is often identified with Śrī Laṅkā; scholars are in disagreement, however, about its identity: many are inclined to look for it not far from eastern central India, where the rest of the Rāma story takes place.

26. *Uttarakāṇḍa*, 111, 21 ff.

27. See A. P. Karmarkar, "Religion and Philosophy of the Epics."

28. According to Swāmi Dāyānanda Sarasvatī, the founder of the *Ārya Samāj*.

29. Ludo Rocher, as part of the multivolume *History of Indian Literature*, edited by Jan Gonda, published a monograph on the Purāṇas that goes into the history of Purāṇa studies, the question of the number of Purāṇas, the controversies surrounding the division between *Mahāpurāṇas* and *Upapurāṇas*, the debate about the "*Ur-purāṇa*," and eventually lists all Purāṇas, giving short summaries of contents, indicating text editions, translations, and studies. See also G. Bailey, "The Purāṇas," in A. Sharma (ed.) *The Study of Hinduism*, 139–68.

30. R. C. Hazra, "The Purāṇas."

31. *Atharva Veda* XI, 7, 24. *Bṛhadāraṇyaka Upaniṣad* IV, 5, 11.

32. R. C. Hazra, op. cit.

33. Sixth century CE.

34. See F. E. Pargiter, *Ancient Indian Historial Tradition*.

35. See the preface in Ibid. Criticized by P. V. Kane, *HDhS*, vol. 5, part 2, 850 ff.

36. M. A. Mehendale, "Purāṇas," in *HCIP*, vol. 3, 296.

37. Thus the *Devībhāgavata Purāṇa* of the Śāktas claims to be the real *Bhāgavata Purāṇa* and is accepted as such by the Śāktas. See C. Mackenzie Brown, "The Origin and Transmission of the Two *Bhāgavata Purāṇas*: A Canonical and Theological Dilemma."

38. So does the *Bhaviṣya Purāṇa*, which claims to be an ancient prophetical book about the future (*bhaviṣyam*).

39. All *Mahāpurāṇas* have been printed, most of them by several publishers; Motilal Banarsidasś series, *Ancient Indian Tradition and Mythology* aims at providing a

complete translation of all the *Mahāpurāṇas*. Older translations are available of the *Mārkaṇḍeya*, the *Bhāgavata*, *Matsya*, the *Viṣṇu*, the *Agni*, and the *Garuḍa Purāṇas*. For the *Upapuraṇas* consult R. C. Hazra, *Studies in the Upapurāṇas*, two volumes, and L. Rocher, *The Purāṇas*.

40. *Viṣṇu Purāṇa* VI, 8, 40 ff.

41. *Skanda Purāṇa*, Viṣṇukhaṇḍa Margaśirṣamāhātmya XVI, 30 ff.

42. *Newsweek* (21 September 1987): 74 ff. reviewed a performance of Peter Brook's *The Mahābhārata*, a nine-hour long recreation of the Indian epic. He and his coworkers had been preparing this modern dramatization for twelve years. *India Today* (15 February 1987): 84, reported: "Britain's most influential body—the Inner London Education Authority—is to stage a 100,000 Pound spectacular based on the *Rāmāyaṇa* to be performed by school children in London's Battersea Park in June this year." *India Today* (30 April 1987), under the title "Ramayan: Divine Sensation," reported the unexpected success of a current TV dramatization of the *Rāmāyaṇa* in India. The TV version of the *Rāmāyaṇa*, circulating also in the Hindu diaspora, had the consequence that a great many Hindus living in the West were requesting a Hindī-cum-English version of the *Rāmacaritamānasa*. Motilal Banarsidass brought out a sumptuous edition, which found wide acceptance abroad. *SEMINAR* devoted its January 1989 (353) issue to analyzing "The Rāmāyaṇa Syndrome."

43. The "International Rāmāyaṇa Institute" organized in June 2005 a two-day International Rāmāyaṇa Conference at Northern Illinois University.

## 5. THE *BHAGAVADGĪTĀ*

1. E. J. Sharpe, *The Universal Gītā: Western Images of the Bhagavadgītā, A Bicentenary Survey*. R. Minor (ed.), *Modern Indian Interpretation of the Bhagavadgītā*. Arvind Sharma, author of *The Hindu Gītā: Ancient and Classical Interpretations of the Bhagavadgītā* is also the founder/editor of the *Journal of Bhagavadgītā Studies*. Much information on recent literature is also found in the bibliographical essay by M. Eder, "The Bhagavadgītā and Classical Hinduism: A Sketch," in A. Sharma (ed.), *The Study of Hinduism*, 169–99.

2. The *Mahābhārata* contains also an *Anugītā* and many of the Purāṇas have Gītās, summarizing in a popular form their main ideas.

3. A Kashmirian text of the Gītā with quite considerable variants was discovered about sixty years ago. *The Mahābhārata, Critical Edition*, vol. 7, *Bhīṣmaparvan*, 114–18, with the critical notes (769–786) contains a wealth of information about the text and the commentaries as well as major studies on the *Bhagavadgītā*.

4. Bombay: Bhāratīya Vidyā Bhavan, 1965.

5. Ibid., 83 ff.

6. *Die Bhagavadgītā*, 32.

7. N. C. Chaudhuri, *Hinduism*, however, accepts the Gītā's dependence on Christian ideas.

8. S. Buddhiraja, *The Bhagavadgītā: A Study*.

9. English translation, in two volumes.

10. Mahadev Desai, *The Gītā According to Gandhi.*

11. Sri Aurobindo, *Essays on the Gītā.*

12. S. Radhakrishnan, *The Bhagavadgītā.*

13. S. K. Belvalkar, "Vedānta in the *Bhagavadgītā,*" *Lectures on Vedānta Philosophy.*

14. Ibid., 118 ff., slightly revised.

15. Quoted in M. Winternitz, *A History of Indian Literature*, vol. 1, part 2, 375.

16. W. M. Callewaert and S. Hemraj, *Bhagavadgītānuvāda: A Study in Transcultural Translation.*

17. The term is *adhikāra*, qualification or prerequisite.

18. Despite the often-advocated spirit of tolerance in the Gītā the teaching is solidly Kṛṣṇaitic and would not admit that practicing any other religion would yield the same results.

19. *Bhagavadgītā* (BG) IX, 4–8.

20. Ibid., 16–19.

21. Ibid., 26–34, condensed.

22. The titles given at the end of the chapters are not found in many manuscripts and, in those in which they are found, they are not uniform; the critical edition leaves them out.

23. BG XI, 3.

24. BG XVIII, 51–55.

25. BG XVIII, 64–66; the term is *pāpa*, the Vedic technical word for "sin," not evil in the general sense as Rādhākrishnan translates.

26. Thomas McCarthy in the introduction (xxv) to his translation of Jürgen Habermas, *The Theory of Communicative Action*, vol. l., *Reason and the Rationalization of Society* (Boston: Beacon Press, 1984), 4: "Sociology became the science of crisis par excellence; it concerned itself above all with the anomic aspects of the dissolution of traditional social systems and the development of modern ones."

27. See the lengthy article by James A. Hijiya, professor of history at the University of Massachusetts Dartmouth, "The Gita of J. Robert Oppenheimer."

28. Heinar Kipphardt, *In the Matter of Robert J. Oppenheimer*, 74–5. [My own translation from the German original].

29. Published in Indian and Foreign Review, 1 March 1981, 27.

## 6. THE WORLD OF THE HINDU

1. A. A. Macdonell's *Vedic Mythology* originally published in 1897 in the *Encyclopedia of Indo-Aryan Research*, G. Bühler (ed.), vol. 3, part 1a, (reprinted 1963) is still the standard work. See also R. N. Dandekar, "Vṛtrahā Indra." On creation myths in general, see D. Maclagan, *Creation Myths: Man's Introduction to the World.* See also F. B. J. Kuiper, *Ancient Indian Cosmogony.*

2. *Ṛgveda* I, 185.

3. S. Kramrisch, "The Triple Structure of Creation in the *Ṛgveda*," 141.

4. *Ṛgveda* X, 82.

5. Ibid., verses 2, 3, 7.

6. *Ṛgveda* X, 90.

7. Ibid., verse 16.

8. *Ṛgveda* X, 129.

9. Kramrisch, "The Triple Structure," 147.

10. *Bṛhadāraṇyaka Upaniṣad* I, 1, 4.

11. *Kaṭha Upaniṣad* 3, 10 ff.; *Ṛgveda* X, 121, 1; *Manusmṛti* I, 9.

12. *Manas* cannot be exactly translated; the nearest Western concept is the medieval *sensus communis*, the coordinating faculty of the senses, not intellect itself.

13. *Ahaṁkāra* is sometimes translated "egoism" (G. Bühler, in M. Eliade, *From Primitives to Zen*, 112), which gives a wrong idea.

14. *Manusmṛti* I, 1 ff.

15. Ibid., I, 64 ff.

16. Ibid., 65–74.

17. Ibid., 81–86.

18. S. M. Ali, *The Geography of the Purāṇas*, offers not only exhaustive references to the sources, but also many serious suggestions concerning the identity of ancient names with contemporary geography. See also maps on "Purāṇic India."

19. Ali, *The Geography of the Purāṇas*, 32 and Figure 62.

20. *Viṣṇu Purāṇa* II, 4, and many parallels in other Purāṇas.

21. One *yojana* is approximately nine miles.

22. *Viṣṇu Purāṇa* II, 2, and parallels.

23. Ibid. 3, and parallels.

24. Ibid. 3, 24–26.

25. The account is taken from a Vaiṣṇava scripture.

26. *Viṣṇu Purāṇa* II, 4, 87.

27. Ibid., verse 98.

28. Ibid., 5–8.

29. Ibid., 5, 5.

30. Ibid., verses 13 ff.

31. Ibid., 7, 11.

32. Ibid., verses 15 ff.

33. Ibid. II, 7, 22 ff.

34. See the discussion of this date in P. V. Kane, *HDhS*, vol. 5, part 1, 648 ff.

35. A. D. Pusalker, "Historical Traditions," *HCIP*, vol. 1, 271–333.

36. According to Purāṇic accounts the Creator produced before the present creation several kinds of creatures, who, because they were produced from Brahmā's mind

in meditation, did not multiply themselves. He created "mind-born sons, like Himself," the nine Brahmārṣis, celebrated in Indian mythology, all absorbed in meditation and without desire of progeny. Brahmā's anger produced Rudra, half male and half female, who began multiplying into various beings. Finally he created Manu Svayambhuva "born of, and identical with his original self," and the female part of himself he constituted as *Śatarūpā* (*Viṣṇu Purāṇa* I, 7).

37. *Viṣṇu Purāṇa* I, 13, and parallels.

38. *Śatapatha Brāhmaṇa* I, 8, 1, 1–6 seems to be the oldest account. Also: *Bhāgavata Purāṇa* VIII, 24 ff.

39. To forestall a popular confusion: *Kali-yuga* comes from *kali*, "strife, fight," and has nothing to do with *Kālī*, "The Black One," the name of Devī, the Goddess in her terrible form.

40. Cf. *Viṣṇu Purāṇa* IV, 21 ff., and parallels.

41. Ibid., 20.

42. Ibid., 24, 128 ff.

43. Ibid., verses 121 ff.

44. The representatives of the Ārya Samāj have been most prominent in this regard.

45. Address given on December 10, 1965.

46. For details of this notion, see P. Hacker, *Vivārta: Studien zur Geschichte der illusionistischen Kosmologie und Erkenntnistheorie der Inder.*

47. B. A. Armadio, "The World Made of Sound: Whitehead and Pythagorean Harmonics in the Context of Veda and the Science of Mantra."

## 7. THE MANY GODS AND THE ONE GOD OF HINDUISM

1. See entry *God* in Sir M. Monier-Williams, *Dictionary, English and Sanskrit.*

2. E.g., A. A. Macdonell, *Vedic Mythology.*

3. K. Bhattacharya, *Studies in Philosophy*, vol. 1, 35, connects the *devatās* with Plato's *ideas* and the concept of *universalia ante rem*. Through *upāsana* (worship) one ascends from the concrete individual things to their *adhyātma* (spiritual) and *adibhūta* (primeval) aspect, their absoluteness. *Devatā* would correspond to the *noumenon* of Kant.

4. R. N. Dandekar, "God in Hindu Thought," lecture held at Bharatiya Vidya Bhavan, 13 January 1968.

5. See A. Esteller, "The Quest for the Original *Ṛgveda*."

6. R. N. Dandekar, "Vṛtrahā Indra." The etymology of Indra is not clear as yet. A. A. Macdonell derives it from *indu*, "drop" (*A History of Sanskrit Literature*, 44); J. Gonda from *intoi*, "pushing" (*Die Religionen Indiens*, vol. 1, 60); R. N. Dandekar from *indu*, bringing it in connection with "virile power" ("Vṛtraha Indra"); S. S. Sastri connects it with *in*, *inva*, "to rule," and *ina*, "sun," "lord" ("Vṛṣakapi," 159). A very thorough and insightful study of Indra is provided by Hertha Krick, "Der Vaniṣṭusava und Indras Offenbarung."

7. R. N. Dandekar, "Vṛtrahā Indra."

8. It is important to note that the Vedic *devas* are in constant conflict with the *asuras*, the demons, and that their high position is due precisely to their power to subjugate the hostile forces. In this context see H. von Stietencron's essay, "Dämonen und Gegengötter: Überlegungen zur Typologie von Antagonismen."

9. The exact number is 1,028 (divided into ten *maṇḍalas*), from which eleven Vālakhilya hymns are usually subtracted, because neither the great Sāyaṇa (fourteenth century) had commented upon them nor were they mentioned in the list, considered authoritative, ascribed to Śaunaka.

10. *Ṛgveda* I, 164, 46.

11. *Ṛgveda* II, 12. Translation (modified): R. H. T. Griffith, *Hymns of the Ṛgveda*.

12. There are still remnants of Indra worship in some parts of India. See, e.g., G. C. Tripathi, "Das Indradhvaja Fest in Orissa: Die Überreste der Indra-Verehrung in Ostindien."

13. *Ṛgveda* I, 1.

14. *Ṛgveda* I, 35.

15. E.g., *Ṛgveda* VII, 86.

16. Vol. 1: *Varuṇa und die Wasser*; vol. 2: *Varuṇa und das Ṛta*.

17. *Bṛhadāraṇyaka Upaniṣad* III, IX, 1, 9.

18. *Viṣṇu Purāṇa* I, 2, 66 ff. "The only God, *Janardana* takes the designation Brahmā, Viṣṇu, and Śiva accordingly as he creates, preserves, or destroys. Viṣṇu as creator creates himself, as preserver preserves himself, as destroyer, destroys himself at the end of all things."

19. E.g., the celebrated Maheśa (Śiva) *mūrti* in the main cave of Gharapurī (Elephanta). See S. Kramrisch, "The Image of Mahādeva in the Cave Temple on Elephanta Island."

20. According to this legend Viṣṇu and Brahmā had been disputing about their supremacy when a huge fiery column appeared before them. To find out about its nature Viṣṇu in the form of a boar dived down to find its lower end, and Brahmā in the form of a swan flew up to discover its upper extremity. After some time they met again. While Viṣṇu admitted that he had not found an end to it, Brahmā asserted that he had found the upper end and was hence greater than Viṣṇu and therefore the universal Lord. Just then the sides of the column opened and out stepped Śiva, the infinite, praising Viṣṇu for his truthfulness and establishing him second to Himself, severely chiding Brahmā for his lie and condemning him to remain without worship henceforth.

21. *Ṛgveda* III, 62, 10.

22. *Kūrma Purāṇa*, 20.

23. R. C. Hazra, *Studies in the Upapurāṇas*, vol. 1, 29 ff. H. von Stietencron has assembled much interesting information on sun worship in India and its possible connection with Iran in his monograph on Sūrya, *Indische Sonnenpriester: Sāmba und die Śākasdiśpīya Brāhmaṇa*.

24. The myth is told in both the epics and in most Purāṇas. The oldest version is probably in: *Vāyu Purāṇa* I, 30.

25. Cf. V. Paranjoti, *Śaiva Siddhānta*, 54 ff.

26. Cf. Ananda Coomaraswamy, *The Dance of Śiva*, 83.

27. *Śiva Purāṇa Śatarudrasaṃhitā*, 3.

28. Ibid., *Umāsaṃhitā*.

29. Ibid., *Rudrasaṃhitā Sātikhaṇḍa*, 38, 34.

30. A whole *Liṅga Purāṇa* is devoted to this.

31. A collection of hymns with English translation: F. Kingsbury and G. E. Phillips, trans., *Hymns of the Tamil Śaivite Saints*.

32. *Śatapathu Brāhmaṇa* I, 1, 2, 13; I, 9, 3, 9; III, 6, 3, 3.

33. S. K. Chatterji, "Race Movements and Prehistoric Culture," 165.

34. Cf. A. D. Pusalker, "Historicity of Kṛṣṇa."

35. The *Viṣnusahasranāma* is found in the *Mahābhārata* and in all Vaiṣṇava Purāṇas and has been printed separately many times. It has also been commented upon by several authorities.

36. Cf. N. Macnicol, *Psalms of the Maratha Saints*. There are countless collections of such hymns in Indian vernaculars, most of them as yet not translated.

37. E. Neuman, *An Analysis of the Archetype The Great Mother*, 120 ff.

38. R. C. Hazra, *Studies in the Upapurāṇas*, vol. 2, 16.

39. H. Whitehead, *The Village Gods of South India*, 11.

40. *Mahābhārata, Sauptikaparvan*, 8, 64 ff., describes a vision of "Death-Night in her embodied form" just before the Great War begins!

41. A. P. Karmarkar, *The Religions of India*, 99.

42. H. von Stietencron, *Gaṅgā und Yamunā*.

43. Examples: in A. Daniélou, *Hindu Polytheism*, 350 ff.

44. Ibid., 291 ff.

45. *Viṣṇu Purāṇa* I, 8 ff.; *Śiva Purāṇa: Rudrasaṃhitā* III, etc.

46. See J. Gonda, "The Historical Background of the Name 'Satya' Assigned to the Highest Being."

47. On this whole issue, see K. Klostermaier, *Mythologies and Philosophies of Salvation in the* Theistic Traditions of India.

## 8. THE PATH OF WORKS: *KARMAMĀRGA*

1. A brief analysis is given by L. A. Ravi Varma, "Rituals of Worship."

2. This is done with reference to *Manusmṛti* VI, 35 ff.

3. *Ṛgveda* X, 90.

4. A. A. Macdonell, "Vedic Religion."

5. About the technical aspects of the *yajña*, see P. V. Kane, *HDhS*, vol. 2, part 2, 983 ff.

6. *Taittirīya Saṃhitā* I, 8, 4, 1.

7. See the informative article by N. Wyatt "*Aśvamedha* and *Puruṣamedha* in Ancient India."

8. See F. M. Smith, "Financing the Vedic Ritual: The *Mūlādhyayāpariśiṣṭa of Kātyāyana*."

9. In the same report we read: "In the West, people talk of peace; they hold an atom bomb in one hand and a peace dove in the other. Thus peace was destroyed. But in the East the guiding principle is *pañca śila*, which has its deep roots in the moral and spiritual tradition of the East. This is the true way to peace."

10. *Blitz* (11 April 1970) reported that the Brahmin who was hired to perform the sacrifice died through electrocution while performing the *yajña*.

11. F. Staal, *Agni: The Vedic Ritual of the Fire Altar.*

12. F. Staal has dealt with Vedic ritual by itself and in a comparative fashion in many other important publications, e.g., *The Science of Ritual*; "The Meaninglessness of Ritual," "The Sound of Religion." See also his "Exchange with a Reviewer of *Agni*."

13. *Chāndogya Upaniṣad* V, 3–10 contains the *pañcāgni vidyā*.

14. See G. M. Carstairs, *The Twice-Born*, which describes in meticulous detail the rituals performed by a Brahmin family in Poona.

15. From *Śaiva Upaniṣads*, T. R. Srinivasa Ayyangar and G. Srinivasa Murti (trans.), 165 ff.

16. Ibid., 203 ff.

17. Quite typically, even former leader of the Communist Party in Kerala N. Nambudiripad belonged to the Brahmin caste. In Tamiḷnāḍu the Draviḍa Munnetra Kazhagam (DMK) staged a kind of anti-Brahmin revolt.

18. *Manu* II, 176 prescribes already daily *tarpaṇa*.

19. *Caṇḍālas* were the offspring of a Brahmin father and a *śūdra* mother and were considered the lowest in the social hierarchy.

20. In the *Kaṭha Upaniṣad* Yama, the god of death himself, apologizes to Naciketas, a Brahmin youth who has come to him for not having served him.

21. *Taittirīya Upaniṣad* II, 2, 1.

22. *Chāndogya Upaniṣad* VII, 26, 2.

23. Details may be found under the heading *bhojana*, in Kane, *HDhS*, vol. 2, part 2, 757–800.

24. Vedic ritual has been a major preoccupation of Western Indology for more than a hundred years. Part of the fascination that this type of study held for Western scholars may have to do with the age of the texts concerned—the quest for origins was a widely shared concern of nineteenth-century scholarship—as well as with the formalism of the texts themselves: rituals are designed to bring order into the cosmos, and ritual literature is characterized by the meticulousness with which it regulates every movement and every sound. In that respect it resembles scholarship: it leaves nothing unexplained, leaves nothing to chance, or to the layman's inexpert handling of things.

Modern scholarship dealing with Vedic sacrifice ranges from early comprehensive reconstructions from texts like J. Schwab's *Das indische Tieropfer* and Sylvain

Lévi's still often referred to *La doctrine du sacrifice dans le Brahmanas*, to specialized studies like those of F. Staal (see note 12), J. Gonda's *Vedic Ritual: The Non-solemn Rites*, J. C. Heesterman's *The Inner Conflict of Tradition: Essays in Indian Ritual, Kingship and Society*. In addition to these the following works are of interest: W. Caland and V. Henry, *L'Agnistoma: Description compléte de la forme normals du sacrifice de Soma dans le culte védique*, 2 vols.; C. G. Diehl, *Instrument and Purpose: Studies on Rites and Rituals in South India*; L. Dumont, *Homo hierarchicus: Essai sur le systéme des castes*; L. Renou, *The Destiny of the Veda in India*; M. Strickmann, ed., *Classical Asian Rituals and the Theory of Ritual*; and R. Kloppenborg, ed., *Selected Studies on Ritual in the Indian Religions: Essays to D. J. Hoens*. How detailed this kind of study can become is shown in the most recent work of the doyen of European Indology, J. Gonda, *The Ritual Functions and Significance of Grasses in the Religion of the Veda*, with thousands of textual references.

25. Interesting economic details are supplied by D. D. Kosambi, *An Introduction to the Study of Indian History*, 94 ff.

26. A. Weber, "Über das Menschenopfer bei den Indern der vedischen Zeit," collected all Vedic evidence concerning human sacrifice. See *Aitareya Brāhmaṇa* VII, 13–18; II, 8; VI, 8; *Śatapatha Brāhmaṇa* I, 2, 3, 6; VI, 2, 2, 18, and so forth.

27. *Bhāgavata Purāṇa* IX, 7, 20 describes a human sacrifice according to a Vedic ritual.

28. See P. E. Dumont, *L'Aśvamedha*.

29. The last seems to have been performed in the eighteenth century, as described in P. K. Gode's interesting article "The Aśvamedha Performed by Sevai Jayasingh of Amber 1699–1744 AD."

30. *Aitareya Brāhmaṇa* II, 18. According to the same text, the *medha* went from the goat into the earth and from the earth into rice. "All those animals from which the *medha* had gone [e.g., camel, ass, mule] are unfit to be sacrificed." See also *Śatapatha Brāhmaṇa* I, 2, 3, 6.

31. R. Gordon Wasson, "The Soma of the *Rig Veda*: What Was It?"

32. *Ṛgveda* VIII, 48, 3.

33. *Bhagavadgītā* IX, 26ff.

34. The ritual is minutely described in the *kriyā-pāda* of the Āgamas, Saṃhitās, and Tantras, the most elaborate of the four traditional parts of each of those scriptures.

35. The ritual of the famous Viṣṇu temple at Śrīraṅgam, as detailed in the *Parameśvara Saṃhitā*, is said to have been revealed to Yamunācārya by Lord Viṣṇu himself. Similarly the ritual of South Indian Śaivite temples, as outlined in the *Somaśaṃbhupaddhatī*, is associated with a Śiva revelation to its author.

36. A good example is R. V. Joshi, *Le rituel de la dévotion Kṛṣṇaite*.

37. The most famous is that of Ajamila, as reported in the *Bhāgavata Purāṇa*.

38. See M. Strickman, *Classical Asian Rituals*. See also A. J. Blasi, "Ritual as a Form of the Religious Mentality."

39. See note 9; also J. F. Staal, "Language and Ritual."

## 9. PURITY AND MERIT: THE TWIN CONCERNS OF *KARMAMĀRGA*

1. W. Cenkner, *A Tradition of Teachers: Śaṅkara and the Jagadgurus Today*, 150.

2. The importance of such activities in contemporary India cannot only be gauged from the increasing crowds at such events like the Kumbhamelā, with an attendance of up to thirty million pilgrims at the last in Ujjain, but also by the attention given it even in Western TV programs and news magazines.

3. P. V. Kane's aforementioned *History of Dharmaśāstra* is an inexhaustible source of information on all aspects of dharma.

4. A good account of it is given in S. K. Maitra, *The Ethics of the Hindus*, 81 ff.

5. Ibid., 83: "Thus for the Nyāya-Vaiśeṣikas righteousness is a quality of the *Ātman* or Self, i.e., is a subjective category to be distinguished from the objective act (*karma*) as well as from any impersonal transcendental category (*apūrva*) which may be generated by it. Nor is it any objective quality of an act which has any such super-sensuous category in its aid or support (*apūrvaprakṛtikarmaguṇa*)."

6. Ibid., 117 ff.

7. Ibid., 119.

8. S. N. Dasgupta, *HIPh*, vol. 5, 134.

9. *Bhagavadgītā* III, 47. *Niṣkāma Karma*, special volume of *Kalyāṇa* 54 (1980), contains over one hundred articles (in Hindī) on this topic.

10. *Bhagavadgītā* XVI, 21.

11. Jayanta uses the triad *moha* (delusion), *rāga* (attraction), and *dveṣa* (aversion), which materially is exactly the same; he utilizes *lobha* and *krodha* as derivations of *rāga* and *dveṣa*.

12. This is a typical Vaiṣṇava injunction.

13. *Viṣṇu Purāṇa* III, 12.

14. *Caraka Saṃhitā*, 45–51, *Sūtrasthānam* 8.

15. *Tirukkuṛaḷ*, nos. 72, 101, 156, 160, 203.

16. For detail, see Sadhucarana Prasad, *Dharmaśāstrasaṅgraha*. *Prāyaścittas* form chapter 21, the longest of all.

17. The *Manusmṛti*, as well as other *dharmaśāstras*, are quite up to date as regards protection of the environment: they punish by loss of caste the injuring of living plants, cutting down green trees for firewood, mining and all mechanical engineering that does damage to the environment, etc. See *Manusmṛti* XI, 64 ff.

18. Ibid., 53. In XII, 54 ff. (perhaps a later addition) Manu points out the various animal rebirths persons have to go through in consequence of their sins: "Those who committed *mahāpātakas*, having passed during large numbers of years through dreadful hells, obtain after that the following births: the slayer of a Brahmin enters the womb of a dog, a pig, an ass, a camel, a cow, a goat, a sheep, a deer, a bird, a Caṇḍāla, a Pukkasa; a Brahmin who drinks *sūra* shall enter the bodies of small and large insects, of moths, of birds feeding on ordure . . . the violator of the guru's bed enters a hundred times grasses, shrubs, and creepers."

19. See *Devībhāgavata Purāṇa* VIII, 22 ff.

20. *Manusmṛti* XI, 45 ff.

21. Ibid., 73–87. Note, however, that this applies only to a Brahmin; a man from a lower caste who kills a Brahmin has no such means available.

22. Ibid., 228–31.

23. Ibid., 31–33.

24. Thus in Viśvanātha Cakravarttin, *Bhaktirasāmṛtasindhubindu*. For Śaivite rules regarding violation of worship cf. *Somaśambhupaddhatī*, vol. I, 102 ff. For the means of expiation, see *Śaiva-upaniṣads*, nos. 142 and 149, where *bhasma* (sacred ashes) is praised as the great remover of sins: "This *bhasma* alone is possessed of the special virtue of bestowing the knowledge of Hari and Śaṅkara, of destroying the most heinous sins resulting from the murder of a *brahmana* and the like and of bestowing great power and glory."

## 10. *SAṂSKĀRAS*: THE HINDU SACRAMENTS

1. On *saṃskāras* in general the most exhaustive source is P. V. Kane, *HDhS*, vol. 2, part 1. See also R. B. Pandey, *Hindu Saṃskāras*: Socio-religious Study of the Hindu Sacraments.

2. *Manusmṛti* II, 26.

3. *Dvi-jāti*, twice-born, is the designation of the upper three castes, *Brahmins*, *Kṣatriyas*, and *Vaiśyas*, whose initiation is considered to be a second, spiritual birth.

4. *Manusmṛti* II, 27ff.

5. The child gets a "secret name" immediately after birth that is known only to the parents. *Manusmṛti* II, 30, says that the official name giving should take place "on the tenth or twelfth on a lucky *tithi*, in an auspicious *muhūrta* under an auspicious constellation."

6. *Viṣṇu Purāṇa* III, 10.

7. *Manusmṛti* II, 33.

8. Hindus calculate their years of life from the day of conception, not from the day of birth. A good study of the implication of *upanayana* is provided by B. K. Smith, "Ritual, Knowledge and Being: Initiation and Veda Study in Ancient India."

9. *Viṣṇu Purāṇa* III, 10, says: "If he does not propose to enter into the married state, he may remain as a student with his teacher, first making a vow to that effect, and employ himself in the service of his guru and the guru's descendants; or he may become at once a hermit or adopt the order of the religious mendicant according to his original determination."

10. *Manusmṛti* III, 20–42, mentions *brahmā*, *daiva*, *ārṣa*, *prājānatya*, *āsura*, *gāndharva*, *rākṣasa*, and *paiśāca* forms of marriage. He explains them and says that some of these are "ignoble," though valid, as, e.g., forcible abduction of the bride (*rākṣasa*), seduction (*paiśāca*), love marriage (*gāndharva*), or bride buying (*āsura*).

11. J. D. M. Derret, *The Death of a Marriage Law: Epitaph for the Rishis*. Derret has written extensively on Hindu law and taught for many years Oriental law at the

London School of Oriental and African Studies. Among his well-known publications are *Hindu Law, Past and Present*; *Introduction to Modern Hindu Law*; *Critique of Modern Hindu Law*; *History of Indian Law (Dharmaśāstra)*; *Essays in Classical and Modern Hindu Law*, 4 vols.

12. *Viṣṇu Purāṇa* III, 10; *Garuḍa Purāṇa* 62 ff.

13. The most complete source for all details and variations of ritual is again Kane's *HDhS*, vol. 2, part 1.

14. *Ṛgveda* X, 85, 36.

15. Manu has, however, also a verse that would weaken this argument, when he says: "Many thousands of *brahmanas* who were chaste from their youth have gone to heaven without continuing their race" (V, 159).

16. Manusmṛti III, 56.

17. Ibid. 58 ff.

18. Ibid. VIII, 68.

19. Ibid. V, 154.

20. Ibid., 150.

21. *Ṛgveda* X, 14–18.

22. E.g., *Viṣṇu Purāṇa* III, 13.

23. The *Pretakalpa* of the *Garuḍapurāṇa* contains a wealth of information on beliefs concerning the afterlife.

## 11. THE PATH OF KNOWLEDGE: *JÑĀNAMĀRGA*

1. *Muktika Upaniṣad* I, 30, 39, gives the list of the acknowledged 108 Upaniṣads and their classification with regard to the four Vedas.

2. The Saṃskṛti Samsthān Bareli (Uttar Pradesh) brought out in 1967 a complete edition of the 108 Upaniṣads (with Hindī paraphrase) divided into three volumes entitled *Jñāna Khaṇḍa*, *Sādhana Khaṇḍa*, and *Brahma Vidyā Khaṇḍa*.

3. A survey of work done in the early twentieth century in this area is given in P. J. Chinmulgund and V. V. Mirashi, eds., *Review of Indological Research in the Last 75 Years*, 40 ff. See also the bibliography to the chapter "Vedic Hinduism" by S. W. Jamison and M. Witzel in A. Sharma (ed.), *The Study of Hinduism*, 65–113.

4. This is the chronology given by R. D. Ranade in his excellent and comprehensive study, *A Constructive Survey of Upaniṣadic Philosophy: Being an Introduction to the Thought of the Upaniṣads*.

5. Cf. R. D. Ranade, *A Constructive Survey*, 30–40.

6. *Muṇḍaka* II, 1, 1 ff.

7. *Chāndogya* III, 19.

8. *Praśna* IV, 1.

9. *Chāndogya* III, 14.

10. *Bṛhadāraṇyaka* II.

11. *Chāndogya* VII, 17 ff.

12. Ellison Banks Findly, "Gārgī at the King's Court: Women and Philosophic Innovation in Ancient India."

13. E.g., *Śvetāśvatara* IX.

14. E.g., the *Māṇḍukya*, which reduces everything to OM.

15. *Bṛhadāraṇyaka* IV, 5, 15.

16. E.g., *Chāndogya* VIII, 9 ff.

17. *Taittirīya* I, 7.

18. Thus Meister Eckhart in one of his sermons: "Why does my eye recognize the sky, and why do not my feet recognize it? Because my eye is more akin to heaven than my feet. Therefore my soul must be divine if it is to recognize God!" It is the Platonic and the later Stoic philosophy with its idea of cosmic harmony and correspondences between humans and the universe that has kept those ideas alive in the West.

19. *Chāndogya* II.

20. *Bṛhadāraṇyaka* I, 2.

21. Ibid. III, 7.

22. *Māṇḍukya* I, 3 ff.

23. *Muṇḍaka* I, 1, 4 ff.

24. Neoplatonism, possibly under Indian influence, is the one Western intellectual tradition that comes closest to Vedānta. Plotinus, Proclus, Jamblichus, and others, too, speak of stages of ascent of the soul, of the need to turn inward and to dissociate consciousness from the senses.

25. *Īśa* 9.

26. End of *Chāndogya*.

## 12. *ĀTMAN* AND *BRAHMAN*: SELF AND ALL

1. *Bṛhadāraṇyaka* III, 8.

2. Ibid., 9, 1, 9.

3. *Taittirīya* II, 1 ff.

4. *Chāndogya* VI, 8 ff.

5. Ibid. VIII, 7.

6. *Muṇḍaka* II, 2, 10 ff.

7. *Bṛhadāraṇyaka* I, 4.

8. *Chāndogya* VI, 8, 7.

9. *Bṛhadāraṇyaka* II, 5, 19.

10. *Aitareya* III, 1, 3.

11. *Kaṭha* I, 2, 23.

## 13. *KARMA, VIDYĀ, MOKṢA*: LIBERATION FROM REBIRTH

1. *Bṛhadāraṇyaka* IV, 4, 1–7.

2. *Ibid.* I, 2, 7; III, 2, 10, ff. It should be emphasized that the frightening factor is not so much rebirth but the repeated painful experience of death!

3. *Kaṭha*. I, 2, 23.

4. *Muṇḍaka* III, 1, 10.

5. *Kaṭha* I, 5 ff.

6. This is a reference to the *pañcāgni vidyā*, treated immediately before this passage.

7. *Bṛhadāraṇyaka* VI, 2, 15; cf. also *Chāndogya* V, 10, 5.

8. A comprehensive coverage of the understanding of karma in various schools is given in W. D. O'Flaherty (ed.), *Karma and Rebirth in Classical Indian Traditions* and in R. Neufeldt (ed.), *Karma and Rebirth: Post-classical Developments*, See also the chapter "Karma," by H. W. Tull in *The Hindu World*, 309–31.

9. There are other expressions in Sanskrit for *fate*, such as *daiva*, *bhagya*, *niyati* etc.

10. *Muṇḍaka* I, 2, 7 ff.

11. *Chāndogya* IV, 11, 3.

12. *Muṇḍaka* II, 2, 9.

13. One of the varieties of the Śiva *naṭarāja* image, in which Śiva is shown with his right leg thrown high up, is interpreted as showing how Śiva accepts into himself all the karma of his devotees so as to offer them instant liberation.

14. The term *mukti* occurs only once in the principal Upaniṣads, namely in *Bṛhadāraṇyaka* III, 1, 3. The term *mokṣa* is used several times in *Maitrī* VI, 30.

15. S. N. Dasgupta, *HIPh*, vol. 1, 48.

16. *Muṇḍaka* III, 2, 6.

17. *Praśna* IV, 11.

18. *Muṇḍaka* III, 3, 8 ff.

19. *Bṛhadāraṇyaka* III, 8.

20. *Kaṭha* II, 3, 8 ff.

21. *Taittirīya* II, 9.

22. *Ibid.* I, 2, 1 ff.

23. *Muṇḍaka* III, 2, 8.

## 14. THE PATH OF LOVING DEVOTION: *BHAKTIMĀRGA*

1. *Śabdakalpadruma* III, 463b ff. offers the following etymology under the entry *bhakti*: *Vibhāga* [division, separation] *sevā* [worship, service] and refers to the two roots *bhañj-* [to split, to disappoint] and *bha-* [to serve, to honor].

2. S. N. Dasgupta, *HIPh*, vol. 4, 351

3. That they were not considered as of equal importance even within *bhakta* circles is demonstrated by the fact that they have not been commented upon as extensively as the *Brahmasūtras*. The real textbooks of *bhakti* are the Purāṇas, especially the Bhāgavatam and the special compendia of the various *saṃpradāyas*: Saṃhitās, Āgamas, and Tantras.

4. *Bhaktidarśaṇa*, 23 ff.

5. Swami Tyagisananda (ed. and trans.), *Aphorisms on the Gospel of Divine Love or Nārada Bhaktisūtras*. The notes offer numerous other definitions and descriptions of *bhakti*.

6. *Bhagavadgītā* XII, 6 ff.

7. P. V. Kane, *HDhS*, vol. V, part 2, 950 ff.

8. *Kaṭha* II, 22; Muṇḍaka III, 2, 3.

9. Another striking instance is offered by the *puruṣa-sūkta*, which contains the Vaiṣṇava cosmogony *in nucleo*: everything owes its existence to a transformation of a part of the body of the *puruṣottama*.

10. A good survey of literature in English on *bhakti* (up to 1975) is provided by Eleanor Zelliot, "The Mediaeval Bhakti Movement in History: An Essay on the Literature in English." More recent literature is mentioned in Philip Lutgendorf, "Mediaeval Devotional Traditions: An Annotated Survey of Recent Scholarship," in A. Sharma (ed.), *The Study of Hinduism*, 200–60.

11. Besides the work referred to in the next note, see D. Gold, *The Lord as Guru: Hindu Sants in the Northern Indian Traditions* and J. S. Hawley, *Sants and Virtues*.

12. Charlotte Vaudeville, "*Sant mat*: Santism as the Universal Path to Sanctity," in K. Schour and W. H. McLeod, *(eds.)*, *The Sants: Studies in a Devotional Tradition of India*.

13. *Sad-nām* is the key term in this religion, meaning the most profound revelation of God.

14. Vaudeville, "*Sant mat*," 31.

15. A famous collection is the *Bṛhatstotraratnakara* (Bombay: Sri Venkatesvar Press), containing 224 hymns, in many editions with old woodcuts. The Rāmakrishna Mission has also brought out small collections of hymns together with translations.

16. *Bhāgavata Purāṇa*.

17. Ibid. VI, 2, 14; XII, 12, 46.

18. 1 crore = 10 million.

19. *Kalyāṇa Kalpatāru* 18, 1 (August 1952): 3 ff.

20. Cf. Swāmi Rūpa Gosvāmi, *Bhaktirasāmṛtasindhu*, V. Snataka (ed.), I, 2, 90 ff.

21. *Varāha Purāṇa*, chapter 68.

22. *Padma Purāṇa* IV, 263.

23. *Bhagavadgītā* VII, 15.

24. Tyagisananda, ed., *Nārada Bhaktisūtras*, 82 ff.

25. *Bhāgavata Purāṇa* VII, 5, 23 ff.

26. *Rāmānuja's Vedārthasaṁgraha.*

27. Cf. *Sarvadarśaṇasaṁgraha of* Mādhava, chapter 5, the Pūrṇaprajñā system.

28. An important reference work is S. K. De, *Early History of the Vaiṣṇava Faith and Movement in Bengal.* Recently, possibly under the influence of *bhakti* missions in the West, much scholarly literature devoted to the study of *bhakti* literature has come out. Jayadeva's *Gītāgovinda* received a large amount of attention. Cf. B. Stoler-Miller, *Love Song of the Dark Lord*; G. Kuppuswami and M. Harihara (eds.), *Jayadeva and Gītāgovinda: A Study*, with a contribution by B. Stoler-Miller, "Rādhā: Consort of Kṛṣṇa's Vernal Passion"; L. Siegel, *Sacred and Profane Dimensions of Love in Indian Traditions as Exemplified in the Gītāgovinda of Jayadeva.* See also Basanti Choudhury, "Love Sentiment and Its Spiritual Implications in Gauḍīya Vaiṣṇavism."

29. Cf. Krishna Chaitanya, *Sanskrit Poetics.* P. V. Kane, *History of Sanskrit Poetics*, 355 ff.; "The Rasa School": "*Rasa* primarily means 'taste' or 'flavor' or 'savor' or 'relish' but metaphorically it means 'emotional experience of beauty in poetry and drama.'" By contrast Swami Bon Maharaj, *Bhaktirasāmṛtasindhu*, vol. 1, n. 2: "There is no English equivalent for *rasa*. It is a purely spiritual expression that may be explained like this. When the heart is perfectly purified of all the possible dirts of the three *guṇas* or attributes of *Māyā*, the Deluding Energy of the Godhead, viz. *rajas*, *tamas* and *sattva*, and when the unalloyed soul as distinct from the physical body of flesh and blood and the subtle body of mind-intelligence-ego far transcends the realm of imagination and mental thought-world, the fourfold ingredients called *Vibhāva*, *Anu-bhāva*, *Sāttvika-bhāva*, and *Sañcari-bhāva* of mellow-sweetness of the sentiment of the innate normal nature of the *cit*-soul combine with *Sthayī-bhāva* or permanent and eternal as also unconditional relation that exists between God and the individual soul, in manifold shades and forms, it gives rise to an inexplicably wondrous flow of charm, which is *Rasa*."

30. Cf. Viśvanātha Cakravartti, *Bhaktirasamṛtasindhubindu.*

31. Kṛṣṇadāsa Goswāmi, *Caitanyacaritāmṛta*, Mādhyalīlā XIX and XXII.

32. *Vedāntaratnamañjuṣa* VI.

33. *Sarvadarśanasaṁgraha of* Mādhava, chapter 7, "The Pāśupata System." An example of what Hindus call the *pāgala* (mad-type) of *bhakti* is available in Anne Feldhaus (trans. and ann.), *The Deeds of God in Ṛddhipur*, with introductory essays by Anne Feldhaus and E. Zelliot.

34. V. A. Devasenapathi, *Śaiva Siddhānta as Expounded in the Śivajñāna Siddhiar and Its Six Commentaries*, 250 ff. On Śiva *bhakti* in South India, Carl A. Keller, "Aspiration collective et experience individuelle dans la bhakti shivaite de l'Inde du sud."

35. Translation from E. J. Thompson and A. M. Spencer, *Bengali Religious Lyrics, Śākta*, 60. Cf. also M. Lupsa, *Chants á Kālī de Rāmprasād.*

36. *Words of Godrealization*, 415.

37. *Paramārtha Sopāna.*

38. Tyagisananda (ed.), *Nārada Bhaktisūtras*, 5 ff.

## 15. LORD VIṢṆU AND HIS DEVOTEES

1. *Viṣṇu Purāṇa* I, 19, 64 ff.

2. See his article "Vaiṣṇavism: An Overview."

3. The most complete survey is offered in Ramdas Gaur, *Hindutva*, chapter 17: "*Bhāgavata yā vaiṣṇava mata*." The doctrinal side is well covered in S. N. Dasgupta, *HIPh*, vols. 3 and 4. Much detail on individual branches of Vaiṣṇavism is offered in entries on Vaiṣṇavism by R. N. Dandekar and G. R. Welbon in *ER*, vol. 15, 168–81.

4. *Ṛgveda* I, 22; I, 154; VII, 100.

5. *Ṛgveda* X, 90.

6. "Śāntiparvan," *Mahābhārata* (critical ed.), vol. 16, chapters 321 ff.

7. *Bhagavadgītā* IV, 7 ff. One of the most extensive studies was done by Brajendranath Seal, in 1899, under the title *Comparative Studies in Vaishnavism and Christianity with an Examination of the Mahābhārata Legend about Nārada's Pilgrimage to Śvetadvīpa and an Introduction on the Historico-Comparative Method*. In articles in the *Journal of the Royal Asiatic Society of Bengal* in 1907 J. Kennedy tried to prove Christian influence on the development of Viṣṇu *bhakti*. His claims were refuted by B. D. Basu (translator) *Balarāma Vedāntasūtrabhāṣya*, in *SBH*, vol. 5, appendix I: "The Origin of the Bhakti Doctrine." N. Chaudhuri in his *Hinduism*, 256 ff., again suggests Christian influence on the development of Kṛṣṇa *bhakti*.

8. The most comprehensive discussion of the theory of *avatāra*-hood may be R. Seemann's article "Versuch zu einer Theorie des Avatāra . . ."

9. D. C. Sirkar, "Viṣṇu."

10. For details consult, e.g., A. Daniélou, *Hindu Polytheism*.

11. More about these in K. Klostermaier, *Mythologies*.

12. Ibid., 73 ff.

13. *Bhāgavata Purāṇa* VI, 8.

14. A. George, in *Social Ferment in India*, advances the theory that the "Rāma tradition probably goes much further back into remote layers of pre-Aryan folklore from the days of tribal struggles between Austric groups in the Gangetic valley. The word *Gaṅgā* itself has been identified linguistically with a non-Aryan Austric word signifying merely a "river." All this may account for the seeming paradox whereby the suffix "Rām," which ought to denote a blue-blooded Kshatriya prince, tends in modern India to be that of the lower castes" (236).

15. *Bālakāṇḍa* I, 1, of the *Adhyātma Rāmāyaṇa*, written probably in the fifteenth century. Of great importance is the *Yogavāsiṣtha Rāmāyaṇa*, pertaining to the ninth to twelfth centuries, in which the Rāma story serves as frame for the exposition of Advaita Vedānta. The most popular of all books on Rāma, however, is the Hindī *Rāmacaritamānasa* by Tulāsidāsa, praised by Mahātmā Gandhi as "the greatest religious book in the world." See the critical study by C. Bulcke, *Rāmakathā* (in Hindī).

16. *India Today* published on December 31, 1992, a special issue under the title "Nation's Shame," detailing the events leading up to, and following, December 6. A court order prevented construction of a temple on the site. Archeological excavations brought to light an ancient Hindu temple structure.

17. Literature on Kṛṣṇa by Indian authors fills bibliographies. Critical-historical writing by Western scholars is growing steadily. Most of it is devoted to studying certain aspects of the Kṛṣṇa tradition. Cf. John Stratton Hawley, *Kṛṣṇa the Butter Thief*. Many books on Indian art, especially on Indian painting, deal with Kṛṣṇa as well. E.g., W. G. Archer, *The Loves of Krishna*.

18. For more detail, see K. Klostermaier, Mythologies. Also V. Schneider, "Kṛṣṇa's postumer Aufstieg."

19. See Charles S. J. White, "Kṛṣṇa as Divine Child."

20. See Norvin Hein, "A Revolution in Kṛṣṇaism: The Cult of Gopāla."

21. The most thorough attempt to establish the historicity of Kṛṣṇa has been made by A. D. Pusalker. See his "Historicity of Kṛṣṇa" in *Epics and Purāṇas of India*, 49–81, and "Traditional History from the Earliest Time to the Accession of Parikshit" in *The Vedic Age*, vol. I of *HCIP*, 271–322. Pusalker places the "Kṛṣṇa Period" ca. 1950–1400 BCE. Recent archaeological excavations in Dvārakā, the reputed capital city of Kṛṣṇa, are supposed to have confirmed these assumptions. R. N. Iyengar, "Some celestial observations associated with Kṛṣṇa-lore" in *IJHSc* 41.1 (2006):1-13 argues that based on astronomical observations mentioned in *Mahābhārata*, *Viṣṇu Purāṇa*, *Skanda Purāṇa*, and *Bhāgavata Purāṇa*, the lifetime of Kṛṣṇa can be set between 1543 and 1443 BCE.

22. The most complete Kṛṣṇa scripture is the *Bhāgavata Purāṇa*.

23. See K. Klostermaier, *In the Paradise of Kṛṣṇa*.

24. Several recent theses have devoted substantial attention to the position of Śrī. Thus E. T. Hardy, *Emotional Kṛṣṇa Bhakti*; V. Rajagopalan, "The Śrī Vaiṣṇava Understanding of *Bhakti* and *Prapatti*"; and M. R. Paramesvaran, *Studies in Śrīvaiṣṇavism*.

25. See J. A. B. van Buitenen, "The Name Pāñcarātra," for numerous references to other literature.

26. *Yatīndramatadīpikā of Śrīnivāsadāsa*.

27. *Bhāgavata Purāṇa* III, 26, 12.

28. J. B. Carman in *The Theology of Rāmānuja: An Essay in Interreligious Understanding* deals only with some aspects of Rāmānuja's theology but provides extensive background and full information on the sources of Śrīvaiṣṇavism. A systematic exposition of the thought of Rāmānuja is given in Krishna Datta Bharadwaj, *The Philosophy of Rāmānuja*. The most recent systematic work is J. Lipner, *The Face of Truth*.

29. *Vedārthasaṁgraha*, S. S. Raghavachar (ed. and trans.).

30. *Śrībhāṣya* II, 1, 3.

31. *Ibid.* II, 3, 41.

32. *Vedārthasaṁgraha*, 126: a slightly condensed rendering.

33. *Śrībhāṣya* I, 1, 4.

34. The three *rahasyas* are:

a. The Tirumantra: Om nāmo Nārāyaṇāya.

b. The Dvayam: Śrīmān Nārāyaṇa caraṇauśāraṇam prapadye/Śrīmate Nārāyaṇāya namaḥ.

c. The Carama *śloka* (*Bhagavadgītā* 18, 66): Sarvadharmān parityajya māmekam śaraṇam vraja/Aham tva sarvapāpebhyo mokṣayiśyāmi mā sucaḥ.

35. A good comparison of the main points of difference is given in Narasinha Iyengar, *Mumukṣupadī of Lokācārya*, introduction.

36. The most extensive study in English is Satyavrata Singh, *Vedānta Deśika: His Life Works and Philosophy*.

37. B. N. K. Sharma, *Madhva's Teaching in His Own Words*. Also: I. Puthiadan *Viṣṇu the Ever Free: A Study of the Madhva Concept of God*. See also literature on Madhva mentioned in Chapter 27.

38. Roma Chaudhuri, "The Niṃbārka School of Vedānta."

39. "Life of Vallabha," in: S. N. Dasgupta, *HIPh*, vol. 4, 3711–72. See also R. Barz, *The Bhakti Sect of Vallabhācārya*; M. C. Parekh, *Śrī Vallabhācārya: Life, Teachings and Movement*; M. V. Joshi, "The Concept of Brahman in Vallabha Vedānta"; and, with a polemical twist, B. S. Yadav, "Vaiṣṇavism on Hans Küng: A Hindu Theology of Religious Pluralism."

40. M. I. Marfatia, *The Philosophy of Vallabhācārya* 70–76, "*Puṣṭi* or the Doctrine of Grace."

41. An extensive summary is given in the article "Vallabha" by D. Mackichan in *ERE*, vol. 12, and in *ER*, vol. 15 by R. K. Barz. See also J. Gonda, *Die Religionen Indiens*, vol. 2, 163. Also: D. L. Habermann, "On Trial: The Love of Sixteen Thousand Gopees."

42. *History of the Sect of the Mahārājas or Vallabhācāryas in Western India*.

43. A good survey of recent English and Hindī literature on Vallabha is provided in J. R. Timm's article "Vallabha, Vaiṣṇavism and the Western Hegemony of Indian Thought."

44. An extensive list of authors and works is given in Dasgupta, *HIPh*, vol. 4, 373–81. Marfatia, *The Philosophy of Vallabha*, provides extensive summaries of many of these works, 91–314.

45. G. H. Bhatt, "The School of Vallabha," Vallabha also wrote a short commentary on the *Brahmasūtras* with the title of *Aṇubhāṣya*, published by S. T. Pathak in the *Bombay Sanskrit and Prakrit Series*, 1921–26.

46. Bhatt, "The School of Vallabha," 348. Vallabha calls his system *Śuddhādvaita*, "Pure Non-Dualism." In 1992 an English translation by Kanti Chattopadhyay appeared (Brill) of Ramapada Chattopadhyay's commentary on the *Brahmasūtras* based on the *Bhāgavata Purāṇa* under the title *A Vaiṣṇava Interpretation of the Brahmasūtras*.

47. Bhatt, "The School of Vallabha," 356.

48. Dasgupta, *HIPh*, vol. 4, 355.

49. Bhatt, "The School of Vallabha," 357: "One may be constantly angry with the Lord and still get *sāyujya*."

50. Bhatt, quoted in Ibid., 354–55.

51. Dasgupta, *HIPh*, vol. 4, 349.

52. According to Vallabha, *bhakti* develops in the following seven stages: 1. *bhāva*; 2. *premā*; 3. *prāṇaya*; 4. *sneha*; 5. *rāga*; 6. *anurāga*; 7. *vyasana*.

53. Dasgupta, *HIPh*, vol. 4, 356.

54. The best work with substantial translations from sources is W. Eidlitz, *Kṛṣṇa-Caitanya, Sein Leben und Seine Lehre*. A good historical survey is offered by A. K. Majumdar, *Caitanya: His Life and Doctrine*. See also J. T. O'Connell, "Historicity in the Biographies of Caitanya."

55. The "*Śīkṣāṣṭaka*" in *Caitanya Caritāmṛtam* III, 20, 3–45, is considered to be his own formulation of the essence of Vaiṣṇavism.

56. See K. Klostermaier, trans., Viśvanātha Cakravarti's compendium of Rūpa Goswāmi's opus magnum, *Bhakti-rasāmṛta-sindhu-bindu*, including some background to the author and his works. See also K. Klostermaier "A Universe of Feelings" and "Eine indische Wissenschaft der Gefühle," explaining Rūpa's main ideas of *premā* and drawing some parallels. See also: N. Delmonico, "Rūpa Goswāmi: His Life, Family and Early Vraja Commentators."

57. The *Vedāntasūtras of Bādarāyaṇa with the Commentary of Bāladeva*. See also: M. Wright and N. Wright, "Bāladeva Vidyābhuṣana: The Gauḍīya Vedāntist." For post-Caitanya developments in Gauḍīya Vaiṣṇavism, see J. K. Brzezinski, "Prabodhānanda Saraswatī: From Banares to Braj" and "Prabodhānanda, Hita Harivaṃśa and the *Rādhārasasudhānidhī*."

58. See also E. Zelliot, "The Medieval Bhakti Movement in History: An Essay on the Literature in English."

59. For details consult K. Sharma, *Bhakti and the Bhakti Movements*.

60. Among Indian scholars writing in English on this subject the names of R. D. Ranade (*Pathway to God in Hindī Literature*; *Pathway to God in Marathī Literature*; *Pathway to God in Kaṇṇaḍa Literature)* and Bankey Bihari (*Sufis, Mystics and Yogis of India*, *Bhakta Mīrā*) deserve special mention. Also: V. Raghavan, *The Great Integrators: The Saint Singers of India*, offers a good selection of medieval religious poetry in translation. Among Western writers, Charlotte Vaudeville deserves special credit for her scholarly monographs and translations (in French and English) dealing with Kabīr, Tulasīdāsa, and others. See also: M. Neog, *Early History of the Vaiṣṇava Faith and Movement in Assam: Śaṅkaradeva and His Time*.

61. J. S. Hawley has brought out a very attractive monograph on Sūrdās with beautifully translated texts: *Sūrdās: Poet, Singer, Saint*. In a further article in the *JVS*, Hawley examines the question of "Why Sūrdās Went Blind," arriving at the conclusion that it is a spiritual blindness that Sūrdās attributes to himself and not a physical blindness.

62. See J. S. Hawley, "Author and Authority in the Bhakti Poetry of North India."

63. My own translation: following the text in R.D. Ranade's *Paramārtha Sopāna*: Sourcebook of Pathway to God in Hindī Literature. (Part I, Chapter I, No. 1).

64. A good contemporary example is Swami Ramdas, *God-Experience*.

65. Bankey Bihari, *Bhaktā Mīrā*, 109; more on Mīrābāī in chapter 22.

## 16. ŚIVA: THE GRACE AND THE TERROR OF GOD

1. *Stotra* 53 in *Bṛhatstotraratnākara* (96 ff.), ascribed to Vyāsa.

2. Sir Mortimer Wheeler, *The Indus Civilization*. Doris Srinivasan in "Unhinging Śiva from the Indus Civilization," tries to prove that the *liṅgas* found in remnants of the Indus civilization do not present a case for an origin of Śaivism in that civilization. The tribal/prehistoric origin of *liṅga* worship is widely accepted today.

3. B. K. Ghosh, "The Āryan Problem," 207. In the oldest ritual texts care is taken not to mention the name of this "terrible god" directly.

4. Cf. *Mahābhārata Śāntiparvan* 274; *Droṇaparvan* 201, 64–82; *Sauptikaparvan* 18; *Vāyu Purāṇa* I, 30; *Śiva Purāṇa*, *Vayavīyasaṃhitā* I, 23, and numerous other places.

5. I have developed the argument more fully in "The Original Dakṣa Saga."

6. T. M. P. Mahadevan, "Śaivism," 454.

7. Thus the idea of the Śiva *avatāras*, which never gained an importance in actual Śiva worship. Among the Vaiṣṇava Purāṇas the *Vāmana Purāṇa* has also Śaivite materials and the Viṣṇu Purāṇa explains the origin of the eight Rudras in I, 8.

8. Kumara Gupta (415–455 CE) was a Śaiva king. The Huna king Mihirakula seems to have been Śaiva, as were many of his contemporary rulers in Bengal and the Deccan. Mahendra Varman I (600–630 CE), a convert from Jainism, made his capital, Kāñcīpuram, into a stronghold of Śaivism, embellishing it with temples and statues of Śiva.

9. T. M. P. Mahadevan, in *HCIP*, vol. 4, 300ff.

10. *Ṛgveda* I, 114; II, 33; VII, 46.

11. Doris M. Srinivasan, "Vedic Rudra-Śiva," 544.

12. *Ṛgveda* I.114.4.

13. *Ṛgveda* IV.3.1.

14. D. M. Srinivasan gives interesting specific details concerning Rudra's role in some of these sacrifices and the ritual connected with it.

15. It forms chapter 16 of the *Yajurveda* according to the *Vajasaneyasaṃhitā*. English translations in *Śatapathabrāhmaṇa*, 150 ff. and in R. T .H. Griffith, *The Texts of the White Yajurveda*, 168.

16. It forms chapter 15 of the *Atharvaveda*; W. D. Whitney, trans., introduction, 769 ff. See also J. W. Hauer, *Der Vrātya: Untersuchungen über die nichtbrahmanische Religion Altindiens*.

17. *Atharvaveda* XV, 5, 1 ff.

18. *Aitareya Brāhmaṇa* I, 3, 9 ff.

19. Text and translation in S. Radhakrishnan, *The Principal Upaniṣads*, 707—50. As for content and structure, see T. Oberlies, "Die Svetāśvatara Upaniṣad: Eine Studie ihrer Gotteslehre."

20. *Svetāśvatara Upaniṣad* VI, 11.

21. *Anuśāsanaparvan*, 135.

22. The oldest among the Śaiva Purāṇas is probably the *Vāyu Purāṇa*, which was written before the second century CE according to R. C. Hazra, "The Purāṇas." The

Śiva Purāṇa, a very important source for many features of later Śaivism, belongs to the class of *Upapurāṇas*. For more detailed information consult L. Rocher, *The Purāṇas*.

23. Śiva Purāṇa, *Rudrasaṃhitā Sātīkhaṇḍa* 38, 34 ff.

24. V. Paranjoti, *Śaiva Siddhānta*, 53 ff.: "The importance attached to the dance of Śiva is due to the fact that it symbolizes in graphic, concrete, and dynamic form the religion and philosophy of Śaiva Siddhānta. Hence the dance cannot be understood without the philosophy, which it adumbrates in its movements. Love is the motif of the dance; the dance is love in practical form." On Śaiva Siddhānta see also V. A. Devasenapathi, *Śaiva Siddhānta as Expounded in the Śivajñāna-Siddhiyar and Its Six Commentaries*, and K. Sivaraman, *Śaivism in Philosophical Perspective*.

25. Śiva Purāṇa, *Śatarudrasaṃhitā*, 1 ff, and *Vāyavīyasaṃhitā* II, 9.

26. Śiva Purāṇa, *Kotirudrasaṃhitā*, 38 ff.

27. Several Āgamas have been published recently by the Institute Français d'Indologie at Pondichery, containing the *pādas* on *kriyā* (ritual) and *cārya* (mode of life). E.g. *Rauravāgama* (with an important introduction by J. Filliozat, "Les Āgamas çivaites," in vol. 1), *Mṛgendrāgama*, *Ajitāgama*, *Mataṅgaparameśvarāgama*, all edited by N. R. Bhatt.

28. Much information has been collected in the articles on Śaivism in *ER*, vol. 13, 6–20 by D. N. Lorenzen and others as well as in the chapter "Śaiva," by G. Flood, in *The Hindu World*, 119–39.

29. Mādhava, *Sarvadarśanasaṃgraha*, chapter 6, quoting from the *Gaṇakarikā*, an ancient *Paśupata* textbook.

30. Cf. V. A. Devasenapathi, *Śaiva Siddhānta*.

31. Ibid., 192.

32. Ibid., 175.

33. Ibid., 257.

34. Śrīkaṇṭha, *Brahmasūtrabhāṣya* IV, 4, 22. English translation by Roma Chaudhuri, 2 vols.

35. Jayadeva Singh in his edition and translation of the *Pratyabhijñāhṛdayam* mentions his guru, Laksman Joo, as "practically the sole surviving exponent of this system in Kashmir." Recently, however, Gopi Krsna, a layman who describes his own realization more or less according to classical Kashmīr Śaivism has brought out a number of publications that might gain more adherents and students to the system. A brief biography of Swami Laksman Joo appeared in *Hinduism Today*, 17, 7 (July 1991); 1 and 25: "Last Bhairav Master Will Teach Until Year 2006." Laksman Joo claims to have sixty thousand disciples. He named a small boy as his successor.

36. Śiva Purāṇa, *Kailāsasaṃhitā*, 17–19.

37. Mādhava, *Sarvadarśanasaṁgraha*, chapter 8.

38. Quoted by Jaideva Singh, *Pratyabhijñāhṛdayam* p. 21.

39. S. C. Nandimath, *A Handbook of Vīraśaivism*. A very attractive introduction to Vīraśaivism is provided by A. K. Ramanujan in *Speaking of Śiva*. Besides artistic renderings in English of numerous *vacanas* (lyrics by Liṅgāyat poet-saints) the book

also contains valuable introductions by A. K. Ramunjan and an essay on "Liṅgāyat Culture" by William McCormack.

40. Hayavadana Rao (ed.). Not all *Vīraśaivas*, however, accept Śrīpati's interpretation.

41. Sri Kumaraswamiji, "*Vīraśaivism*," 101.

42. Ibid.

43. Cf. S. Satchidanandam Pillai, "The Śaiva Saints of South India." Also: C. V. Narayana Ayyar, *Origin and Early History of Śaivism in South India*.

44. *Tiruvācakam* VI, 50, Ratna Navaratnam, trans., 126. The most celebrated complete translation of the *Tiruvācakam* was made by Rev. G. V. Pope in 1903, reprinted in 1970 by the University of Madras in a Jubilee edition.

45. *Tiruvācakam* XXV, 8–10; Ibid., 181.

46. T. M. P. Mahadevan, "Śaivism."

47. R. C. Majumdar, "Kāpāla and Kālāmukha Sects," 459 quoting R. G. Bhandarkar, *Vaiṣṇavism*. § 97.

48. Biographical sketch of S. Kramrisch by B. Stoler-Miller in *Exploring India's Sacred Art*, 3–33.

49. Besides her widely known monograph *Asceticism and Eroticism in the Mythology of Śiva*, Wendy Doniger O'Flaherty has written a number of scholarly articles on Śiva symbols and myths.

50. *Dancing with Śiva: a Hindu Catechism* and *Living with Śiva: Hinduism's Nandināthan Sūtra*.

51. Besides the numerous books by Gopi Krishna expounding Kuṇḍalinī Yoga, the remarkable coproduction of C. F. v. Weizsäcker and Gopi Krishna, *Biologische Basis religiöser Erfahrung*, deserves mention.

## 17. DEVĪ: THE DIVINE MOTHER

1. *Devīmāhātmya* I, 75 ff. (from *Mārkaṇḍeya Purāṇa*, chapter 81).

2. John Woodroff, who, under the pen name of Arthur Avalon, did much to make the Tantras known in the West, brought out a translation of the *Mahānirvāṇa tantra: The Great Liberation*. For Tantric doctrines in general his *Principles of Tantra*, a translation of the *Tantratattva* of Sivacandra Vidyaranya, may be recommended. His *Introduction to Tantra Śāstra* provides the explanation of the technical terms. More recent scholarly writing on Tantra includes H. V. Günther, *Yuganādha: The Tantric View of Life*, and A. Bharati, *The Tantric Tradition*. See also the richly illustrated volume by Ajit Mookerjee and Madhu Kanna, *The Tantric Way: Art, Science, Ritual*, with bibliography. The most recent succinct presentation is offered by K. M. Endl in the chapter "Śākta" of *The Hindu World*, 140–61.

3. Sanskrit edition Kāśī: Paṇḍit Pustakālaya, samvat 2016; English translation by Swāmi Vijñānanda, *SBH*. For a fuller treatment consult R. C. Hazra, *Studies in the Upapurāṇas*, vol. 2: *The Śākta Upapurāṇas*, 1–361.

4. For more details on Devī mythology, Śākta systems, and iconography of the Goddess see K. Klostermaier, *Mythologies*, part IV.

5. R. C. Hazra, *Studies in the Upapurāṇas*, 19 ff.: "The story of Devī's killing of the demon Mahiṣa in a previous *kalpa* and the tradition that whenever Devī kills the demons she has a lion as her mount seem to be based on the aboriginal concept of Devī as a spirit controlling wild beasts. The bell which is said to be carried by Devī might have been originally meant for scaring away wild beasts." Cf. also H. Whitehead, *The Village Gods of South India.*

6. See H. v. Stietencron, "Die Göttin Durgā Mahiṣāsuramārdiṇī: Mythos, Darstellung und geschichtliche Rolle bei der Hinduisierung Indiens."

7. *Devīmāhātmya* X, 1 ff.

8. See P. V. Kane, *HDhS*, vol. 5, part 1, 154 ff.

9. Devī Purāṇa, 38.

10. *Devī Bhāgavata; Śiva Purāna Umāsaṃhitā*, 28–45.

11. *Kālikā Purāṇa*, 15.

12. Śiva without the *i* is Śava, a corpse.

13. The five *ms* are: *mamsa* (meat), *matsya* (fish), *mudrā* (fried rice), *mada* (intoxicants), and *maithuna* (intercourse).

14. H. D. Bhattacharya, "Tantrik Religion," 320.

15. Ibid., 321.

16. *Mahānirvāṇa tantra* XVIII, 154 ff.

17. Cf. D. N. Bose, *Tantras: Their Philosophy and Occult Secrets*, chapter 10, "Tantric Symbols and Practices," explains a number of basic *yantras*.

18. For details see R. Fonseca, "Constructive Geometry and the Śrī-Cakra Diagram." A very professional study of Devī iconography is Om Prakash Misra's *Mother Goddess in Central India*.

19. Cf. John Woodroff, *Introduction to Tantra Śāstra*, 42 ff.

20. *Kālikā Purāṇa* chapter 14 is called the *rudhirādhyāya* or "blood chapter." A. P. Karmarkar, in *The Religions of India* cites many historical instances of human sacrifices in honor of Kālī. Volunteers were offered every Friday at the Kālī temple in Tanjore up to the nineteenth century. The head of the victim was placed on a golden plate before Kālī, the lungs were cooked and eaten by Tantra Yogis, the royal family ate rice cooked in the blood of the victim.

21. N. Sirkar, *Śaktipīṭhas*, rev. ed.

22. See the recent report on Kāmākhyā and its legends offered by Patricia Dold in "The Mahāvidyās at Kāmarūpa: Dynamics of Transformation in Hinduism," confirming the continued occurrence of animal and even human sacrifices.

23. Beni Kanta Kakati, *The Mother Goddess Kāmākhyā*. The snake-goddess Manasā is widely worshipped, especially in South India.

24. Cf. Maryla Falk, *Nāma-Rūpa and Dharma-Rūpa: Origin and Aspects of an Ancient Indian Conception*, 2 ff.

25. *Tripurā Rahasya, Jñānakaṇḍa*, A. U. Vasavada, (trans.), 156 ff.

26. Ibid.

27. A description of *Vāmācārī* practices is given in H. Wilson, *The Religious Sects of the Hindus*, 142 ff. The work also contains a translation of the *Śakti Sudhāna*.

28. V. S. Agrawala, "Mother Earth," in: *Nehru Abhinandan Granth* 490 ff.

29. D. R. Kinsley, *The Sword and the Flute: Kālī and Kṛṣṇa, Dark Visions of the Terrible and the Sublime in Hindu Mythology*; C. M. Brown, *God as Mother: A Feminine Theology in India*; D. Jacobsen and S. Wadley, eds., *Women in India: Two Perspectives*; J. S. Hawley and D. M. Wulff (eds.), *The Divine Consort: Rādhā and the Goddesses of India*; L. E. Gatwood, *Devī and the Spouse Goddess: Women, Sexuality and Marriage in India*. F. X. Clooney, S. J., in his recent work *Divine Mother Blessed Mother: Hindu Goddesses and the Virgin Mary* offers translations of Hindu and Christian hymns and an intriguing comparison and parallelism between these traditions.

30. Sanjukta Gupta and Richard Gombrich, "Kings, Power and the Goddess."

31. *BLITZ*, title page on April 11, 1970: "Tantrik priest dies half-way through *havan* to kill Indira."

## 18. MUDALVAN, MURUKAN, MĀL: THE GREAT GODS OF THE TAMILS

1. On Agastya see the entry in John Dowson, *A Classical Dictionary of Hindu Mythology*, 4 ff., which provides the major references for Agastya in *Ṛgveda*, *Mahābhārata*, and *Rāmāyaṇa* and specifically says: "The name of Agastya holds a great place in Tamil literature, and he is venerated in the south as the first teacher of science and literature to the primitive Dravidian tribes." The authority of Dr. Caldwell is cited, who thinks that "we shall not greatly err in placing the era of Agastya in the seventh or at least in the sixth century BC." See also information on the Agastya tradition in *HCIP*, vol. 2, 290 ff.

2. "Tamil Religion," 260b.

3. On dates concerning the *Saṅgam* (*Cankam*) see *HCIP*, vol. 2, 291 ff. and K. A. Nilakanta Sastri, *The Culture and History of the Tamils*, 127 ff. See also C. Jesudason and H. Jesudason, *A History of Tamil Literature*. A comprehensive history of Tamil literature is found in K. V. Zvelebil, *The Smile of Murukan*.

4. N. Chaudhuri, *Hinduism*, 64 ff.

5. T. Burrows, *The Sanskrit Language*.

6. Together, these areas comprise today about two hundred million people.

7. For details, see K. K. Pillai, *A Social History of the Tamils*, vol. 1, chapter 3, "Pre-History," and F. W. Clothey, *The Many Faces of Murukan*. See also maps of prehistoric sites in South India in *HASA*, plates II, 1 and 2.

8. See the instructive article by F. W. Clothey, "Tamil Religion."

9. K. K. Pillai, *A Social History of the Tamils*, 480 ff.

10. C. Sivaramamurti, *South Indian Bronzes*.

11. K. K. Pillai, *A Social History of the Tamils*, 476: referring to Bruce Foote.

12. Ibid., 477.

13. D. D. Shulman, *Tamil Temple Myths*. See also: B. Oguibenine, "Cosmic Tree in Vedic and Tamil Mythology: Contrastive Analysis"; G. Kuppuswamy and M. Hariharan, "Bhajana Tradition in South India." Significant differences between northern and southern interpretations of common religious symbols exist also in other areas.

14. K. Klostermaier, "The Original Dakṣa Saga."

15. K. K. Pillai, *A Social History of the Tamils*, 488 ff.

16. Ibid., 489.

17. Ibid., 492 (with references to Tamil sources).

18. Ibid.

19. K. Zvelebil, *Tiru Murukan*.

20. K. K. Pillai, *A Social History of the Tamils*, 484.

21. Ibid.

22. Ibid., 485. See also: D. Handelman, "Myths of Murukan: Asymmetry and Hierarchy in a South Indian Purāṇic Cosmology."

23. Ibid.

24. Ibid., 487 ff.

25. See also F. W. Clothey, "Murukan."

26. K. K. Pillai, *A Social History of the Tamils*, 497.

27. Peculiar features of Tamiḷnāḍu are the *Nāḍukal* (memorial stones) and *Vīrakal* (hero stones), which were erected with religious solemnities to commemorate warriors who had died in battle.

28. This division goes back to the *Tolkappiam*, an ancient Tamil grammar and reputedly the oldest document of Tamil literature, ascribed to the second century BCE.

29. See K. K. Pillai, *A Social History of the Tamils*, 504 ff.

30. Ibid., with references to Tamil sources.

31. Ibid. Pillai emphasizes that during these sacrifices live animals were sacrificed, a practice that continues to this day in certain forms of Śiva worship.

32. See also F. A. Presler, "The Structure and Consequences of Temple Policy in Tamiḷnāḍu, 1967–81." See also "Priestly Protest," reporting on an agitation in Andhra Pradesh against the abolition of hereditary priesthood and the demand for training of temple priests.

33. J. Parthasarathi, "The Dravida Veda-Vedāṅga—A Revolutionary Cultural Crosscurrent," 57.

34. See K. K. Pillai, "The Non-Brahmin Movement in South India." See also C. A. Ryerson, "Meaning and Modernization in Tamil Nadu: Tamil Nationalism and Religious Culture."

35. See also K. V. Zvelebil, "Some Tamil Folklore Texts."

36. *Tirukkural*, chapter 38, 9 (380): G. U. Pope's translation.

37. K. K. Pillai, *A Social History of the Tamils*, 524 ff.

38. Ibid., 426.

39. H. Whitehead, *The Village Gods of South India*, with illustrations.

40. The author once obtained a *rahu kālam* chart from his Madras landlord who was not only a modern-educated, successful industrialist, but also a staunch believer in *rahu kālam*, during which time he refused to conduct any business.

41. N. K. Sastri, *The Culture and History of the Tamils*, 108 ff., believes that many of the accounts of religious persecution in Tamiḷnāḍu are exaggerated. But there is no doubt that violence did occur and that the various religious communities denounced each other.

42. N. K. Sastri reports that "even now Madurai conducts an annual festival in the temple commemorating the incredible impalement of eight thousand Jainas at the instance of the gentle boy saint." Ibid., 110.

43. See also F. W. Clothey, "Tamil Religions."

44. Cf. F. Kingsbury and G. E. Philips, trans., *Hymns of the Tamil Śaivite Saints*, 30–33.

45. Ibid., 25.

46. Bankey Bihari, *Minstrels of God*, part I, 118–27. More on Āṇṭāl in chapter 23.

47. See literature mentioned in chapter 15 (notes 35–37) and A. K. Ramanujan, *Speaking of Śiva*.

48. A. K. Ramanujan, *Speaking of Śiva*, 88 (Basavanna No. 820).

49. Personal observations. See also P. V. Jagadisa Ayyar, *South Indian Festivities*, for other Tamil festivals such as Bhopi Pandigai, Sankrānti, and others.

## 19. THE DIVINE PRESENCE IN SPACE AND TIME: *MŪRTI, TĪRTHA, KĀLA*

1. See *HASA*, 264–65.

2. For details see J. N. Banerjea, *The Development of Hindu Iconography*, chapters 1–6.

3. See Nihan Ranjan Ray, "Sculpture."

4. See H. Zimmer, *The Art of Indian Asia*, vol. 1, 259 ff; plates on 268 ff.

5. E.g., the famous group of temples at Belur, Mysore.

6. Lively accounts are found in Elliot and Dowson (eds.), *The History of India as Told by Its Own Historians: The Muhammadan Period*. Some doubt has been expressed as to the truth of these reports, whose writers evidently wanted to impress their (Muslim) readers.

7. J. P. Waghorne and N. Cutler (eds.), *Gods of Flesh/Gods of Stone: The Embodiment of Divinity in India*.

8. A concise and comprehensive description of the technicalities of *mūrtis* can be found in the article "Ikonographie des Hinduismus" in V. Möller, *Götter und Mythen des indischen Subkontinents*, vol. 5 of H. W. Haussig (ed.), *Wörterbuch der Mythologie*, 86–112, with bibliography of primary and secondary sources.

9. Cf. J. N. Banerjea, *Hindu Iconography*, chapter 8. A seminal work is S. Kramrisch, *Indian Sculpture*. Also of great interest is H. Zimmer, *Kunstform und Yoga im indischen Kultbild*.

10. K. Vasudeva Sastri and N. B. Gadre (eds.), Tanjore Sarasvati Mahal Series No. 85 (1958). Two complete manuals of Hindu architecture are available in Western language translations: *Mānasāra*, P. K. Acharya, trans., and *Mayamata*, 3 ed. and trans. B. Dagens.

11. For details see T. Bhattacharya, *The Canons of Indian Art*, chapters 14 to 20.

12. There are special works giving rules for restoration of images and special rites for the re-consecration.

13. That is milk, curds, butter, dung, and urine.

14. *Bṛhatsaṃhitā* of Varāhamihira, published with a Hindī translation by Pandit Acutyananda Jha Sarmana, Chaukhambha Vidyābhavan Sanskṛt Granthamālā No. 49 , chapter 60, slightly condensed. An English translation by M. R. Bhat has recently been published in two volumes by Motilal Banarsidass.

15. The ritual of Viṣṇu worship as followed at Śrīraṅgam is described in *Śrī Parameśvara Saṃhitā*. A very detailed study, with illustrations, of Kṛṣṇa worship in the Caitanyite tradition, relying mainly on the *Haribhaktivilāsa* by Gopāla Bhaṭṭa, the authoritative work for it, is R. V. Joshi, *Le rituel de la dévotion Kṛṣṇaite*.

16. Cf. N. Ramesan, *Temples and Legends of Andhra Pradesh*, 70 ff.

17. *Arthapañcakam* of Pillai Lokācārya, no. 19.

18. One such complete manual detailing the daily ritual in South Indian Śiva temples is available in a French translation: H. Brunner-Lachaux (ed. and trans.), *Somaśambhupaddhatī*.

19. The technical expression for this is *nyāsa*: see R. V. Joshi, *Le ritual. . . .* 87 ff.

20. *Bhāgavata Purāṇa* XI, 27, 20 ff.

21. One of the earliest such government-appointed board was established to regulate the affairs of possibly the most famous and richest temple in India, the Tirupati Devasthānam in Andhra Pradesh.

22. Stella Kramrisch in the early 1920s made the first attempt to study Hindu temples with the aid of ancient manuscripts on architecture, resulting in her opus magnum, *The Hindu Temple*. Barbara Stoler-Miller edited essays by Kramrisch covering a span of almost fifty years and touching upon virtually all aspects of Hindu art under the title *Exploring India's Sacred Art*. It also contains a brief biography of Kramrisch and a full bibliography. Much recent work has been done by the Indologist-architect M. W. Meister, editor of the *Encylopedia of Indian Temple Architecture* and author of several important articles in scholarly journals, such as "Maṇḍala and Practice in Nāgara Architecture in North India" and "Measurement and Proportion in Hindu Architecture." See also his article "Hindu Temples" in *ER*, vol. 14, 368–73.

23. S. Kramrisch, *The Hindu Temple*, vol. 1, 97.

24. For an interpretation, see A. Volwahsen, *Living Architecture: Indian*, 43 ff.

25. S. Kramrisch, *The Hindu Temple*, vol. 1, 97.

26. A very informative article dealing with this issue is R. Kulkarni's "Vāstupāda-maṇḍala" with many diagrams and tables.

27. The most perfect application of this scheme can be seen in the city of Jaipur. On city planning in general the *Viśvakarman Vāstuśāstra*, an authoritative work, can be consulted. The most systematic modern Western work on the subject is D. Schlingloff, *Die altindische Stadt*.

28. The details of the calculation are given in A. Volwahsen, *Living Architecture*, 50–55.

29. Ibid., 51.

30. Cf. O. Fischer, *Die Kunst Indiens*, plates 253 ff.

31. B. Rowland, *The Art and Architecture of India*, plate 112.

32. Ibid., plates 101 and 118.

33. The placing of the capstone on top of such a tall structure was a marvelous engineering feat of the time. According to tradition a four-mile-long ramp was built upon which it was inched up. A different theory is held by some Western authors. See A. Volwahsen, *Living Architecture*, 180 ff. and B. Rowland, *The Art and Architecture of India*, plate 121b.

34. Cf. A. Volwahsen, *Living Architecture*, 145.

35. Cf. B. Rowland, *The Art and Architecture of India*, plate 103a.

36. Ibid., plate 106.

37. Ibid., plate 104.

38. Ibid., plate 124.

39. Ibid., plate 120a.

40. Ibid., chapters 15–17. Also J. C. Harle, *The Art and Architecture of the Indian Subcontinent*. Much fascinating detail on the technicalities of temple building, the tools used, and the organization of the trades employed can be gathered from A. Boner, S. R. Sarma, R. P. Das, *New Light on the Sun Temple of Konārka: Four Unpublished Manuscripts Relating to Construction History and Ritual of This Temple*. The work also contains reproductions of the late-medieval palm leaf manuscripts with the complete "blueprint" of the temple and appropriate annotations.

41. D. L. Eck, *Darśan: Seeing the Divine Image in India*.

42. *Maitrī Upaniṣad*, VI, 14 ff.

43. P. V. Kane, *HDhS*, vol. 5, part 1, 253–462, offers a list of *vratas* containing more than a thousand individual feasts and observances.

44. *Dharmayuga* brought out an issue dedicated to this feast on August 30, 1964; Also P. V. Kane, *HDhS*, vol. 5, part 1, 124 ff.

45. For details see P. V. Kane, Ibid., 154–87.

46. For details see Kane, Ibid., 227 ff. *The Illustrated Weekly of India* brought out a special *Mahāśivarātrī* issue 87, no. 8 (February 20, 1966). See also the very detailed and interesting study by J. B. Long, "Festival of Repentance: A Study of Mahāśivarātrī."

47. The Gītāpress brought out a special volume *Tīrthāṅka* [in Hindī] in 1956 describing, on more than seven hundred pages with numerous illustrations, thousands of *tīrthas*. See also M. Jha (ed.), *Dimensions of Pilgrimage*; R. Salomon (ed. and trans.), *The Bridge to the Three Holy Cities, the Samāyāna-Praghaṭṭaka of Nārāyaṇa Bhaṭṭa's Triṣṭhalīsetu*; E. A. Morinis, *Pilgrimage in the Hindu Tradition: A Case Study of West Bengal.*

48. The *Padma Purāṇa* contains a great number of *tīrtha māhātmyas*, as does the *Matsya* and *Agni*. The *Padma Purāṇa* has a long *khaṇḍa* in honor of Kāśī, which is perhaps the *sthala purāṇa* itself.

49. An interesting essay about a trip from the source of the Ganges to her entering the sea is J. J. Putnam and R. Singh, "The Ganges—River of Faith."

50. See H. von Stietencron, "Suicide as a Religious Institution."

51. *Kalyāṇa Kalpatāru*, 39, 12 (March 1966).

52. L. B. Havell, *Vārāṇasī, the Sacred City: Sketches of Hindu Life and Religion.* Also Diana Eck, *Vārāṇasī, the City of Light*. Valuable information also in P. V. Kane, *HDhS*, vol. 4, 618–42.

53. Quite instructive are the two special issues "Homage to Varanasi" brought out by the *Illustrated Weekly of India* 85, nos. 6 and 7 (9 and 16 February 1984) with numerous illustrations.

54. *Vārāṇasī at a Glance*, 17.

55. Cf. the section "Tīrthayātra" in Kane, *HDhS*, vol. 4, 552–827 including a list of *tīrthas* over one hundred pages long, with thousands of names and indications of further information. A visit to a *Kumbhamelā*, which is held in turn every three years in Allahābad (Prayāga), Hardwar, Ujjain, and Nasik gives a good impression of the fervor with which also today millions of Hindus engage in *tīrthayātra* and the observance of holy times. See also the report on the *Kumbhamelā* in Hardwar in 1986 in *India Today* (May 15, 1986), 74–85. According to press reports, thirty million pilgrims participated in the 2004 Kumbhamelā at Ujjain.

56. Good information on the history of Tirupati (and other major centers) in N. Ramesan, *Temples and Legends of Andhra Pradesh*, 56–69. At a pilgrimage to Tirupati in 1996 the author picked up a booklet, "Balajī Śrī Venkateśwara: Collected Myths, Legends, Chronicles," retold by Sri Muniswami, published by Chukkala Singaiah Chetty, Tirupathi (n.d.).

57. A great amount of detail on the architecture of these places can be found in M. W. Meister (ed.), *Encyclopedia of Indian Temple Architecture*, vol. 1, South India.

58. C. J. Fuller, *Servants of the Goddess: The Priests of a South Indian Temple*; W. P. Harman, *The Sacred Marriage of a Hindu Goddess*; S. Padmanabhan, *Temples of South India*; D. D. Shulman, *Tamil Temple Myths: Sacrifice and Divine Marriage in the South Indian Tradition.*

59. V. N. Hari Rao not only published a monograph on *The Śrīraṅgam Temple: Art and Architecture* but also translated *Koil Olugu: The Chronicle of the Śrīraṅgam Temple*, which provides insight into the vicissitudes of this famous place of pilgrimage.

60. For more details see F. W. Clothey, "Pilgrimage Centers in the Tamil Culture of Murukan."

61. For more details see K. R. Vaidyanathan, *Sri Krishna, the Lord of Guruvayūr.*

## 20. THE HINDU SOCIAL ORDER: *CATURVARṆĀŚRAMADHARMA*

1. L. Dumont, *Religion/Politics and History in India: Collected Papers in Indian Sociology*, 38 n. 10.

2. J. H. Hutton, *Caste in India: Its Nature, Function and Origins.*

3. *Homo Hierarchicus*, English translation. A very useful work is P. H. Prabhu's *Hindu Social Organization: A Study in Socio-Psychological and Ideological Foundations.* Also recommended is the work of the anthropologist Irawati Karve, *Hindu Society: An Interpretation*, highlighting especially the great diversity of Indian society and its customs in the various parts of India.

4. In "Orientalist Constructions of India" Inden writes: "Indological discourse, I argue, holds (or simply assumes) that the essence of Indian civilization is just the opposite of the West's. It is the irrational (but rationalizable) institution of 'caste' and the Indological religion that accompanies it, Hinduism. Human agency in India is displaced by Indological discourse not onto a reified State or Market but onto a substantialized caste" (402). However, caste *is* essential for Hindu society and has been understood as such not only by Indologists but by Indians themselves, high and low.

5. *Ṛgveda* X, 190.

6. Dagmar Gräfin Bernstorff, "Das Kastensystem im Wandel."

7. An important issue became the question of intercaste marriages and the position of the "mixed castes." See *Manusmṛti* X, 6–73.

8. Apart from encyclopedic works like E. Thurston and K. Rangachari's, *Tribes and Castes of South India* and parallels in other parts of India, village or regional studies like M. N. Srinivas, *Religion and Society among the Coorgs of South India*, and books inspired by this seminal work give a good idea of the actual working of caste.

9. *Article 17*: "Untouchability is abolished and its practice in any form is forbidden. The enforcement of any disability arising out of Untouchability shall be an offense punishable in accordance with law."

10. The story is told in the *Anuśāsanaparvan* of the *Mahābhārata*. Comments of the editor of the critical edition, vol. 18, lviii. Orthodox Hindus expressed resentment against Svāmi Bhaktvedānta's claiming Brahmin status for the members of ISKCON.

11. Dumont refers to G. Dumezil's *Mitra-Varuna* and A. M. Hocart's *Les Castes.*

12. "The Conception of Kingship in Ancient India," in *Religion/Politics*, 62 ff.

13. Arvind Sharma, *The Puruṣārthas: A Study in Hindu Axiology.* Also C. Malamoud, "On the Rhetoric and Semantics of *Puruṣārtha.*" See also the essays on *dharma* (B. Holdrege), *artha* (H. Scharfe), *kāma* (D. Killingley) and *mokṣa* (K. Klostermaier) in S. Mittal and G. Thursby (eds.), *The Hindu World.*

14. A rich source of information on these matters is P. V. Kane, *HDhS*, vol. 2, part 2.

15. *Hinduism* in Wm. Theodore de Bary (general ed.), *Sources of Indian Tradition*, vol. 1, p. 200–361.

16. "Another Path," 41.

17. For an overall view see U. N. Ghosal, *A History of Indian Political Ideas: The Ancient Period and the Period of Transition to the Middle Ages*. For the question of Brahmanic vs. Kṣatriya views see R. M. Dandekar, "Ancient Indian Polity."

18. *Manusmṛti* I, 98–101.

19. See especially *Bhagavadgītā*, III, 35.

20. "Sacred kingship" in India and in other cultures had been the topic of a congress of the International Association for the History of Religion. Cf. *Numen*, supplement no. 4, with C. M. Edsman's introductory essay, "Zum Sakralen Königtum in der Forschung der letzten hundert Jahre," 3–17. Important essays on this topic by M. Biardeau, R. Inden, and A. C. Mayer are also contained in T. N. Madan (ed.), *Way of Life: King, Householder, Renouncer—Essays in Honor of Louis Dumont*. The relationship between kingship and local temple cults is explored by R. Inden, "Hierarchies of Kings in Early Mediaeval India" in this work (99–125); and S. Gupta and R. Gombrich, "Kings, Power and the Goddess."

21. The term is *daṇḍa*, literally a stick, an instrument of punishment, as which the scepter has to be understood throughout in this tradition.

22. The term is *kheda*, meaning exhaustion; other manuscripts have *dhainya*.

23. *Śāntiparvan* 59, 12 ff.

24. *Viṣṇu Purāṇa* I, 13; *Bhāgavata Purāṇa* IV, 14.

25. *Viṣṇu Purāṇa* I, 13, 61–63.

26. One of the best examples is the *Rājadharma* section in the *Mahābhārata Śāntiparvan*, 1–128.

27. See *The Kauṭilīya Arthaśāstra*, R. P. Kangle, ed. and trans., 3 parts, containing the critical text, a translation, and a study. See also U. N. Ghosal, "Kauṭilīya."

28. The difference between the Kauṭilīyan idea of kingship and European absolutism is explored in N. P. Sil, "Political Morality vs. Political Necessity: Kauṭilya and Machiavelli Revisited."

29. The *Arthaśāstra* concludes with the maxim: "What humankind lives by that is *artha*, the science that deals with the means of conquering and possessing the earth is *arthaśāstra*."

30. *Jāti* is derived from the root *jā-*, "to be born," and is usually translated as "subcaste." In fact it is the *jātis* that determine the real place of a Hindu in society since every *varṇa* contains a hierarchy of numerous *jātis*.

31. Modernization is not necessarily Westernization: "Modernity, in that sense, is not new; it is a recurring historical force, a recurring opportunity 'which, taken at the flood, leads on to fortune, omitted, all the voyage of your life is bound in shallows and miseries.' Ultimately, we today are striving for the most strategic thing in our time, a new identity for ourselves and for the world. It is no less than an identity with the spirit of the age, the fulfillment of a new *karma*, and here the responsibility has lain squarely on the elites of history" (4).

32. Compare, e.g., the *prāyaścittas* for killing a cow and for killing a *caṇḍāla*.

33. The following letter to the editor of the *Times of India* (Bombay, March 20, 1968) on "Harijan's Plight" by Rajaram P. Mukane from Thana is quite telling: "Millions

of untouchables in this country continue to suffer shameful humiliations 20 years after independence. Almost every aspect of our life is infested with casteism and communalism. The Chief Minister of Andhra Pradesh disclosed in the Assembly last week that a Harijan youth was roasted alive on a charge of theft. The committee on untouchability constituted by the Union Government recently revealed that three untouchables were shot dead by caste Hindus for growing their moustaches upwards instead of downward, in keeping with the local Hindu tradition, and that an untouchable youth was killed in Mysore for walking along the street wearing chappals. Everyone remembers how in Maharastra three Harijan women were stripped naked and made to walk before the public on the roads. These are not isolated incidents. Such atrocities are perpetrated everywhere in our country due to the virus of casteism and untouchability, although the practice of the latter has been banned by law. The law against untouchability is almost inoperative because of the indifferent attitude of the so-called upper-caste Hindus holding key positions. For Hinduism the cow and other such things seem to occupy a more significant position than human dignity. . . ." More recent examples of injustices committed against the former outcastes can be found in A. George, *Social Ferment in India*, chapter 7: "The Scheduled Castes," 202 ff.

34. See B. R. Ambedkar, *What Congress and Gandhi Have Done to the Untouchables*. Dr. Ambedkar resented the appellation *Harijan* for the outcastes: it was a term used to designate the children of *devadāsis*, whose father was unknown.

35. Some idea of the issues that the Dalits are bringing up may be gathered from M. R. Anand and E. Zelliot (eds.), *An Anthology of Dalit Literature*. In New Delhi a (Christian) "Center for Dalit Studies" has opened in 2002 that is to develop a "Dalit theology." See A. King, "Dalit Theology: A Theology of Outrage." In I. Bocken, W. Dupre, P. van der Velde (eds.), *The Persistent Challenge*, 53–78. Nowadays Brahmins also have to perform lowly jobs such as riksha pullers and sanitation workers in order to make a living—there is not much left of the privileged position of former times! See Francois Gautier, "Are Brahmins the Dalits of Today?" http://in.rediff.com/news/2006/may/23.

## 21. *SAṂNYĀSA*: THE HIGHEST HINDU ASPIRATION

1. *Manusmṛti* X, 74 ff.

2. *Manusmṛti* VI, 37 threatens those with punishments in hell who take *saṃnyāsa* without having begotten a son and performed the proper rites. See also *Viṣṇusmṛti* V, 13.

3. More detailed background information can be found in I. C. Oman, *The Mystics, Ascetics and Saints of India* (first published in 1903); H. H. Wilson, *Religious Sects of the Hindus* (first published in *Asiatick Researches* XVI [1828] and XVII [1832]; S. Chattophadyaya, *The Evolution of Theistic Sects in Ancient India*; G. S. Ghurye, *Indian Sādhus*.

4. *Mahābhārata*, Anuśāsanaparvan, 141.

5. The *śikhā*, also called *choṭī*, is the little wisp of hair left at the place of the *brahmārandra*, where according to Vedic belief, the *ātman* leaves the body. It is never cut, while the rest of the head is shaved ritually quite often. It is, even today, a sign of Brahmanic orthodoxy and is cut off only if someone takes *saṃnyāsa*, whereby he technically ceases to belong to the community that observes *dharma*.

6. *Paramahaṃsa Upaniṣad*, condensed rendering from 108 *Upanisadeñ, Brahmā Vidyā Khaṇḍa*, no. 33, 526 ff.

7. P. Olivelle has edited and translated several classical texts relating to *saṃnyāsa*: *Vasudevāśrama's Yatidharmaprakāśa: A Treatise on World Renunciation*; *Rules and Regulations of Brahmanical Asceticism* [text and English translation of Yādavaprakāśas's *Yatidharmasamuccaya*]. See also his *Renunciation in Hinduism: A Medieval Debate*, which contrasts texts from the Śaṅkara and the Rāmānuja traditions.

8. Viśveśvarasarasvatī, *Yatidharmasaṅgraha*, V. G. Apte (ed.), 154.

9. *Vedārthasaṅgraha*, no. 251.

10. An early example is *Bṛhadāraṇyaka Upaniṣad* II, 6 mentioning fifty eight generations of gurus ending with "Parameṣṭhin from Brahman." Later sectarian sūtras carry lengthy lists of names, too.

11. *Upadeśasahasrī*, no. 6.

12. Concerning the legal aspects of *saṃnyāsa*, see P. V. Kane, *HDhS*, vol. 2 , part 2, 933 ff.

13. Ramdas Gaur, *Hindutva*, "*saṃpradāya khaṇḍa*," chapters 67–75.

14. On the life and work of Śaṅkara and the order founded by him see: W. Cenkner, *A Tradition of Teachers: Śaṅkara and the Jagadgurus Today*. Also: Yoshitsugu Sawai, "Śaṅkara's Theology of Saṃnyāsa."

15. Also some other ancient establishments claim to have been founded by Śaṅkarācārya and to possess his *guru paraṃparā*, expressed in the titles *jagadguru* and Śaṅkarācārya given to the resident chief ascetic. See, e.g., T. M. P. Mahadevan, *The Sage of Kanchi*, describing the life of Śrī Jagadguru Śaṅkarācārya of Kāmakothi Pīṭha, His Holiness Śrī Chandrasekharendra Sarasvatī on the completion of sixty years of spiritual rulership as the sixty-eighth Head of the Pīṭha. Śaṅkara is supposed to have founded a great many other *āśramas* like the Summeru and Paduka Maṭhas at Vārāṇasī and the Vadakkāri Madaur and Naduvilai Madaur in Kerala. Their *guru paraṃparā* is disputed. A reader of the first edition of the *Survey* who had made a special study of the succession of the Śaṅkara *maṭhas* informed me that today the *saṃnyāsi* names ending in Pūrī, Sāgara, Āśrama, Giri, Vāna, or Pārvata are rare, and the most frequently used are Bhārati, Tīrtha, and Sarasvatī. He mentioned that all the orders today greet each other or sign documents with the words *Iti Nārāyaṇasmaraṇam* or *Nārāyaṇasmṛtiḥ*. He also provided me with several pages of arguments, concluding that the Kāmakothi Pīṭha at Kāñchīpuram is not one of the four original *maṭhas* founded by Śaṅkara and that a 1979 meeting of the four undisputed *maṭhas* (called Chaturamnyāya Sammelan) did not mention Kāmakothi Pīṭha (letter by S. Vidyasankar, July 21, 1992).

16. In order to enhance their prestige non-Śaṇkarite *sādhus*, as e.g., the Neo-Caitanyas, also adopt these titles.

17. Cf. S. G. Ghurye, *Indian Sādhus*, chapter 6.

18. W. Cenkner, *A Tradition of Teachers*, 134.

19. S. G. Ghurye, *Indian Sādhus*, chapter 10.

20. Cf. T. M. P. Mahadevan, in *HCIP*, vol. 5, 458. See also H. H. Wilson, *Religious Sects*, 131 ff. and 142 ff. Rāmānuja, *Śrībhāṣya*, II, 2, 36; S. G. Ghurye, *Indian Sādhus*, 48 ff.

21. This group, founded in the early seventeenth century with centers in Banares, Gazipur, and Jaunpur, is classified as *sudhārak* (reformist) in Ramdas Gaur, *Hindutva*, 739. The traditional Aghoris are unapproachable to outsiders.

22. A. S. Raman, "Homage to Varanasi," *Illustrated Weekly of India* 85, nos. 6–7.

23. For a full-length monograph, see A. K. Banerjea, *The Philosophy of Gorakhnāth*.

24. Besides the information offered by Ramdas Gaur, see H. H. Wilson, *Religious Sects*, 148 ff.

25. Pandit Srinarayan Sastri Khiste, "Śrīvidyā," in *Kalyāṇa Devībhāgavatam Aṅgka*.

26. Ramdas Gaur, *Hindutva*, 730 ff.

27. W. S. Deming, *Rāmdās and the Rāmdāsis*.

28. Besides the text editions, translations, and works mentioned by C. Vaudeville in *Kabīr Granthavālī (Doha)*, G. H. Westcott, *Kabīr and the Kabīr Panth*, is still very recommendable.

29. Details in Ramdas Gaur, *Hindutva*, 735 ff.

30. Karpātrijī Mahārāj, *Rāmrājya aura Marksvāda* [in Hindī].

31. It was interesting to see the comments and reports in the dailies and weeklies of India in the days following the incident, especially the rather interesting opposite versions offered by the left-wing *Blitz* and the right-wing *Organizer*.

32. Cf. the Hindū Viśva Pariṣad publication *Viśva Hindū*, started in Bombay in 1964; special edition in January 1966, on occasion of a conference at the *Kumbha Melā* at Allahābad.

33. See K. Klostermaier, "Vaiṣṇavism and Politics: The New Dharma of Braj?" describing a meeting with Swāmi Vāmadeva and Swāmi Muktānanda, the present Secretary General of the organization. The appendix to the article offers a translation of a Hindī pamphlet containing the goals and demands of the movement.

34. As the Delhi paper *Pioneer* reports in its March 3, 1993, issue, the Sant Samiti appears to gain importance. The Sant Samiti, under the direction of Swāmi Vāmadeva, through frequently held *sant sammelans* (gatherings of *sādhus*), has taken up the task to continue the movement to "liberate" the major Hindu temple sites at Kāśī, Mathurā, and Delhi.

35. D. D. Kosambi has critically edited *The Epigrams Attributed to Bhartṛhari Including the Three Centuries*. The Advaita Āśrama Calcutta has brought out the text with translation of the *Vairāgya Śatakam* (1963) according to the rather heavily interpolated "vulgate" text. The extract here is from nos. 2–7 and 99–100.

36. Mādhava Ashish, "The Sādhu in Our Life."

## 22. *STRĪDHARMA*: THE POSITION OF WOMEN IN HINDUISM

1. Minoti Bhattacharyya, "Hindu Religion and Women's Rights."

2. *Ṛgveda* V, 28.

3. *Ṛgveda* VIII, 91, 1; I, 117, 7; X, 40, 1; X, 145, 16.

4. See also E. B. Findly, "Gārgī at the King's Court" and Uma Deshpande, "Some Ṛgvedic Poetesses: A Study."

5. *Ṛgveda* I, 116, 16.

6. *Ṛgveda* I, 48, 1.14–15.

7. *Ṛgveda* X, 125.3.4.5.

8. *Ṛgveda* V, 84.

9. A convenient collection of all *smṛti* references to *strīdharma* is provided in Sadhu Charan Prasad, *Dharmaśāstrasaṅgraha* [Sanskrit and Hindī], section 13, 209–22.

10. English translation by I. Julia Leslie.

11. *Manusmṛti* 5, 150–56; *Vyāsasmṛti* 2, 18–20.

12. *Manu* 2, 66–67.

13. *Manu* 5, 150–56. *Atrismṛti* 13, 3–137 goes one step further: like *Śūdras*, it says, women "fall" (i.e., they commit a sinful act) if they practice *japa*, *tapasya*, *samnyāsa*, mantras, *dhyāna*, or *devapūjā*.

14. *Manu* 9, 2–11.

15. See *Yājñavalkyasmṛti* 1, 70–82, for specifics, also *Manu* 11, 177–78.

16. *Manu* 9, 12 ff.

17. *Vyāsasmṛti* 2, 18–40.

18. *Aṅgirasasmṛti* 35–38.

19. See also *Vyāsasmṛti* 2, 38–40.

20. *Dakṣasmṛti*, 213.

21. In the *smṛtis*, *svayamvara* was the course of action to be taken if a father failed to find a husband for his daughter five years after she had attained puberty.

22. A. K. Majumdar, *Caitanya: His Life and Doctrine*, 290.

23. N. Chaudhuri, *Hinduism*, 286.

24. The most recent monograph of Āṇṭāl (also spelled Āndāl) containing a complete translation of her *Tiruppavai* and her *Nacciyar Tirumoli* (with notes) in contemporary idiomatic English is Vidyā Deheja, *Āṇṭāl and Her Path of Love*. The book also contains a good bibliography on *āḷvārs*.

25. See also D. Hudson, "Āṇṭāl Āḷvār: A Developing Hagiography."

26. See the traditional account of Mīrābāī's legend, together with a reproduction in the original languages of many of her poems and translations into English of a few of these, in Bankey Bihari, *Bhakta Mīrā*. See also: W. M. Callewaert, "The 'Earliest' Song of Mīrā (1503–1546)," with a good bibliography of editions of Mīrābāī's songs.

27. See "Śrī Ānandamayī," by Stephen (Umananda) Quong.

28. *Young India* (September 15, 1921).

29. *Young India* (October 21, 1926).

30. For detail and present-day discussion see A. Sharma, *Satī*. Also, Dorothy Stein, "Burning Widows, Burning Brides: The Perils of Daughterhood in India."

31. K. Klostermaier, "The Original Dakṣa Saga."

32. There is an extensive eyewitness description by J. Z. Holwell of a *satī* performed in 1742 in P. J. Marshall, *The British Discovery of Hinduism*, 94 ff.

33. G. H. R. Tillotson, "The Indian Travels of William Hodges."

34. D. Stein, "Burning Widows, Burning Brides," 483. *Spiegel Online* carried on September 21, 2006, a report about the *satī* of a 95-year-old woman that took place the previous day in Raipur, Madhya Pradesh.

35. For more detail, see Meena Khandelwal, *Women in Ochre Robes: Gendering Hindu Renunciation*, offering interesting narratives of Indian and non-Indian women renunciants. See also Catherine Ojha, "Feminine Asceticism in Hinduism: Its Tradition and Present Condition." Vishal Agarwal has compiled a website publication *Women in Hindu Dharma: A Tribute* (2004) for the Hindu Students Society of the University of Minnesota. www.hindurashtra.org/women-in-hinduism. A. Chowgule circulated on June 7, 2006, a news item about an *upanayana* of two girls performed at Shankar Krupa by Sudhakar Sharma of the Ārya Samāj of Bangalore.

36. March 12, 2005.

## 23. HINDU STRUCTURES OF THOUGHT: THE *ṢAḌDARŚANAS*

1. *Manusmṛti* II, 114 (Bühler's translation in *SBE* XXV).

2. *Manusmṛti* II, 156.

3. *Manusmṛti* II, 171.

4. Some interesting details are presented in a lighthearted manner by Kuppuswamy Sastri in a contribution to "The Library Movement" under the title "Kośavan ācāryah" (i.e., one who has a library is a teacher, or: a teacher is one who has a library). Reprinted in S. S. Janaki (ed.), *Kuppuswamy Sastri Birth Centenary Commemoration Volume*, Part I. This claim is also supported by the information on the scholastic engagement of the Śaṅkarācāryas past and present, in W. Cenkner, *A Tradition of Teachers*, especially chapter 4: "The Teaching Heritage After Śaṅkara," 84–106.

5. A popular maxim says: *Svadeśe pūjyate rājā vidvān sarvatrā pūjyate* i.e., while a king is honored in his own realm (only), a scholar is honored everywhere.

6. The thirty two different *vidyās* mentioned in the Upaniṣads can be seen as the beginning of different school traditions of Hinduism.

7. *Vādavāda*, a study of different viewpoints and polemics, became an integral part of traditional Indian learning. As T. R. V. Murti says: "polemic (*parapakṣanirākaraṇa*) is an integral part of each system" in "The Rise of the Philosophical Schools."

8. The text used as motto for this chapter provides the rationale for Śaṅkara to develop his extensive commentary on the *Brahmasūtras*.

9. Not only are a number of highly philosophical *stotras* ascribed to Śaṅkārācārya—hymns to different deities that are recited by ordinary Hindus in their daily worship—also the vernacular religious poetry of such favorites of contemporary Hindus like Tulsīdās, Kabīr, Sūrdās, Tukārām, and others is often highly speculative.

10. *Manusmṛti* II, 11.

11. *Tantravārttika* I, 3, 4.

12. S. Radhakrishnan mentions in *Indian Philosophy*, vol. 2, 20 n. 4, that Bhīmācārya in his *Nyāyakośa* included Sāṁkhya and Advaita Vedānta under the *nāstika*, i.e., unorthodox systems. He specifically quotes the sentence: *Māyāvādivedānti api nāstika eva paryavasāna sampadyate* ("In the end also the Vedāntin holding the opinion of illusionism [*māyāvāda*] turns out to be a *nāstika*, i.e., a non-believer in the Veda"). This sentence is not found in the fourth edition, revised by V. S. Abhyankar.

13. *Brahmasūtrabhāṣya* I, 1, 5.

14. S. Radhakrishnan, *Indian Philosophy*, vol. 2, 19.

15. Ibid., 20 ff.

16. Ibid., 24: "The six systems agree on certain essentials." In a footnote Radhakrishnan quotes Max Müller's statement—with reference to Vijñānabhikṣu, who in the fourteenth century attempted to bring about a unified *darśana*—"that there is behind the variety of the six systems a common fund of what may be called national or popular philosophy, a large *mānasa* lake of philosophical thought and language far away in the distant North and in the distant past, from which each thinker was allowed to draw for his own purposes." F. M. Müller, *The Six Systems of Indian Philosophy*, xvii. Radhakrishnan made a bold statement of the unity of Hindu philosophy in his popular *The Hindu View of Life*.

17. The term *darśana* has been common in India since the second century. Before that the term *anvīkṣikī*—later restricted to *logic* seems to have served. This issue is competently discussed by W. Halbfass in "Indien und die Geschichtsschreibung der Philosophie."

18. Thus the commentaries on Gaṅgeśa's *Tattvacintāmaṇi* were called *Didhiti*, *Gaṅgādhārī*, *Kārṣikā*, *Candrakālā*, *Nakṣatramālikā*, etc. See R. Thangasami Sarma, *Darśanamañjarī*, part 1, 64 ff.

19. The aforementioned author uses the titles *Nyāya*, *Vyākārana*, *Vedānta*, *Śiromaṇī*, showing that he is qualified in logic, grammar, and Vedānta.

20. Thus K. H. Potter, in his *Encyclopedia of Indian Philosophy*, restricts selections of text extracts to those portions that have a parallel in contemporary analytic Western philosophy.

21. K. H. Potter has assembled a very extensive *Bibliography of Indian Philosophies*, with additions published in *JIPh*. For professionals the as yet incomplete *New Catalogus Catalogorum*, appearing from the University of Madras (thirteen volumes so far), is the most valuable bibliographic resource, listing not only published editions and translations but also manuscripts and their location.

22. The text has been published several times (e.g., Pune: Bhandarkar Oriental Research Institute) and was translated into English, without *Śaṅkaradarśana*, more than a century ago by Cowell and Gough. This translation has been reprinted many times. See my translation of chapter 16: *Śaṁkaradarśana*, in *Brahmavidyā: The Adyar Library Bulletin*, vol. 61 (1997): 147–253.

23. See Kuppuswamy Sastri's introduction to his *Primer of Indian Logic*.

24. Ibid., 104.

25. D. Krishna et al. (eds.), *Saṃvāda: A Dialogue between Two Philosophical Traditions.*

## 24. HINDU LOGIC AND PHYSICS: NYĀYA-VAIŚEṢIKA

1. S. N. Dasgupta, *History of Indian Philosophy,* vol. 1, 282.

2. See the evidence offered by S. N. Dasgupta, Ibid.

3. It has only been preserved in a Chinese translation; this has been edited and translated and commented upon by H. Ui.

4. The best known may be the *Bhāṣāpariccheda* with *Siddhānta Muktāvalī* by Viśvanātha Nyāyapañcānana; ed. and trans. Swami Madhavananda.

5. K. Sastri, "Nyāya-Vaiśeṣika—Origin and Development," introduction to Kuppuswamy Sastri *Primer of Indian Logic,* 104.

6. In addition to sections on Nyāya and Vaiśeṣika in the major handbooks on Indian philosophy, besides the English-language works by S. N. Dasgupta and S. Radhakrishnan, the French works by L. Renou and J. Filliozat as well as M. Biardeau and S. Siauve, the German works by P. Deussen and E. Frauwallner, and the Sanskrit survey by Thiru Thanghasamy deserve consultation. The following specialized works will be found useful for more advanced students: D. H. H. Ingalls, *Materials for the Study of Navya-Nyāya Logic*; B. K. Matilal, *The Navya Nyāya Doctrine of Negation*; S. C. Chatterjee, *The Nyāya Theory of Knowledge*; U. Mishra, *The Conception of Matter According to Nyāya-Vaiśeṣika.* Some important and very informative essays on Nyāya-Vaiśeṣika are found in S. K. Maitra, *Fundamental Questions of Indian Metaphysics and Logic.* W. Halbfass, *On Being and What There Is,* subtitled "Classical Vaiśeṣika and the History of Indian Ontology," offers not only an up-to-date description of Vaiśeṣika research but also an incisive comparative study of ontology in the Greek and Indian contexts. An indispensable source is Sati Chandra Vidyabhusana, *A History of Indian Logic.* The most authentic representation of Nyāya and *Vaiśeṣika*—historically and doctrinally—is found in R. Thangaswami Sarma, *Darśanamañjarī,* Part I [in Sanskrit], which not only offers abundant information on the literature of Nyāya and *Vaiśeṣika* and their authors but also has many charts and diagrams illustrating the interconnection of works and concepts.

7. Early writers use the word Nyāya as a synonym with *Mīmāṃsā.*

8. *Arthaśāstra* 2, 30, a text often referred to in this connection. *Viṣṇu Purāṇa* I, 9, 121, has the same enumeration of sciences. In this text the Goddess (after the churning of the Milk Ocean) is addressed as the embodiment of all knowledge (*vidyā*) specifically of *anvīkṣikī, trayī, vārta,* and *daṇḍanīti.*

9. Kuppuswamy Sastri, "Nyāya-Vaiśeṣika," 107.

10. *Vaiśeṣikardarśana* by Anatalal Thakur, ed. and trans. N. Sinha.

11. W. Halbfass in an excursus "The Concept of Viśeṣa and the name of the Vaiśeṣika System" in *On Being,* 269–75, offers alternative suggestions.

12. *Padārthadharmasaṅgraha,* no. 156, trans. Ganganatha Jha.

13. Dasgupta, *HIPh,* vol. 1, 363.

14. These "nine things" are: *buddhi, sukha, duḥkha, icchā, dveṣa, prayatna, dharma, adharma, saṃskāra.*

15. *Nyāyasūtra* with *Vatsyāyana Bhāṣya*, ed., trans., and comm. Ganganatha Jha.

16. *Maṇikana, A Navya-Nyāya Manual*, ed. and trans. E. R. Sreekrishna Sarma, introduction, xvii.

17. *Nyāya Sūtra* I, 1, 22.

18. Ibid. IV, 1, 66.

19. See G. Chemparathy, *An Indian Rational Theology: Introduction to Udayaṅa's Nyāyakusumāñjalī.*

20. Udayanācārya's *Nyāyakusumāñjali*, with the commentary of Haridāsa Bhaṭṭācārya, trans. E. B. Cowell.

21. *Nyāya-bhāṣya* IV, 1, 21 ff.

22. *Tarkabhāṣā of Keśava Miśra*, ed. and trans. Ganganatha Jha.

## 25. HINDU METAPHYSICS AND PSYCHOLOGY: SĀṀKHYA-YOGA

1. The best-known text of Haṭha Yoga is the *Haṭhayogapradīpika* by Svātmārāma Yogīndra.

2. 2. See chapter 21.

3. E.g., *Bhāgavata Purāṇa* II, 25, 13 ff.; III, 28.

4. A. B. Keith, *The Sāṁkhya System*, 18. The most comprehensive recent study of *Sāṁkhya* is G. J. Larsen, *Classical Sāṁkhya*. See also H. Bakker, "On the Origin of the *Sāṁkhya* Psychology" with an extensive bibliography. G. J. Larsen makes an important point in his essay "The Format of Technical Philosophical Writing in Ancient India: Inadequacies of Conventional Translations." Comprehensive information on the development of *Sāṁkhya* is contained in E. Frauwallner, *Geschichte der Indischen Philosophie*, vol. 1, 228 ff. and 472 ff.

5. Dasgupta, *HIPh*, vol. 1, 264.

6. *Bhāgavata Purāṇa* III, 28.

7. The best edition and translation with ample comments is that by S. S. Suryanarayana Sastri. Also *Sāṁkhya Kārikā of Mahāmuni Śrī Īśvarakṛṣṇa*, with the commentary *Sārabodhinī* of Paṇḍit Sīvanārāyaṇa Śāstri with *Sāṅkhya Tattvakaumudī* of Vācaspati Miśra.

8. *Sāṁkhyadarśana*, ed. Pyarelal Prabhu Dayal and trans. J. R. Ballantyne.

9. Ed. and trans. under the title *The Yoga Upaniṣads*, by A. Mahadev Sastri and T. R. Srinivasa Ayyangar.

10. A good edition is that by Swāmi Vijñāna Āśrama. A complete English translation of Patañjali's *Yoga Sūtras* with Vyāsa's *Bhāṣya* and Vācaspati Miśra's *Tattva Vaicāradī* has been published by J. H. Woods in *HOS*, vol. 17. Students may find useful I. K. Taimni, *The Science of Yoga*, which offers the text and the translation of the *Yoga Sūtra* and a good running commentary that avoids the technicalities of the

classical commentaries. Valuable recent treatments of Yoga are: S. N. Dasgupta, *Yoga as Philosophy and Religion*; J. W. Hauer, *Der Yoga als Heilsweg*; G. Feuerstein, *The Philosophy of Classical Yoga*; G. M. Koelman, *Pātañjala Yoga: From Related Ego to Absolute Self*; I. Whicher, *The Integrity of Yoga*. Special problems connected with *Sāṁkhya*-Yoga are addressed in these recent papers: Swami Ranganathananda, "The Science of Consciousness in the Light of Vedānta and Yoga"; Mohan Singh, "Yoga and Yoga Symbolism"; S. Bhattacharya "The Concept of *Bideha* and *Prakṛti-Laya* in the *Sāṁkhya-Yoga* System"; C. T. Kenghe, "The Problem of the Pratyayasarga in *Sāṁkhya* and Its Relation with Yoga"; K. Werner, "Religious Practice and Yoga in the Time of the Vedas, Upaniṣads and Early Buddhism"; G. Oberhammer, "Das Transzendenzverständnis des Samkhyistischen Yoga als Strukturprinzip seiner Mystik"; G. Oberhammer, "Die Gotteserfahrung in der yogischen Meditation"; M. Eliade's *Yoga: Immortality and Freedom* has become a classic in its own right: it not only describes Patañjali Yoga but compares it to other phenomena and has an exhaustive bibliography of works up to 1964. Controversial new ideas on classical Yoga are advanced in G. Oberhammer, *Strukturen Yogischer Meditation*.

11. *Tejobindu Upaniṣad* VI, 107.

12. P. Hacker, "Śaṅkara der Yogin und Śaṅkara der Advaitin: Einige Beobachtungen." A full translation of the work has been made by James Legget.

13. *Sāṁkhya Kārikā*, 1.

14. This is the traditional interpretation given to *duḥkhatraya*.

15. *Sāṁkhya Kārikā*, 2.

16. Ibid., 18.

17. Ibid., 8.

18. Ibid., 63.

19. Ibid., 67.

20. *Yoga Sūtra* I, 5 ff.

21. Ibid. I, 23 ff.

22. Ibid. II, 5 ff.

23. According to Hatha Yoga the *utthita padmāsana* confers superhuman vision and cures troubles of the respiratory tract; *śupta padmāsana* cures illnesses of the digestive organs, *bhadrāsana* activates the mind, *dhastricāsana* regulates body temperature, cures fever, and purifies the blood, *guptāṅgāsana* cures venereal diseases, and so forth. There are centers in India, like the Yoga Research Institute at Lonavla, in which medical research is done on the effects of yoga on body and mind.

24. *Yoga Sūtra* II, 54.

25. Ibid. III, 1–3.

26. Ibid. III, 16 ff.

27. Ibid. IV, 34: *puruṣārthaśūnyānām guṇānām pratiprasavaḥ / kaivalam svarūpa pratiṣṭhā vā citiśaktir iti.*

28. These notions find a surprising parallel in contemporary scientific thought. See Prigogine-Stenger, *Order Out of Chaos*.

## 26. HINDU THEOLOGY, OLD AND NEW: MĪMĀṂSĀ AND VEDĀNTA

1. B. G. Apte (ed.), *Śābarabhāṣya*; English translation: Ganganatha Jha.

2. Prabhākara Miśra wrote a voluminous subcommentary to the *Śābarabhāṣya* called *Bṛhati*, S. K. Ramanatha Sastri (ed.), Kumārila Bhaṭṭa wrote the famous *Ślokavārtika*, another subcommentary on the first part of it, as well as the *Tantravārttika* and the *Tupṭīkā*, subcommentaries on the later parts, S. K. Ramanatha Sastri (ed.); Ganganatha Jha has published complete English translations of the *Ślokavārtika* and the *Tantravārtika*.

3. S. N. Dasgupta, *HIPh*, vol. 1, 371. Concerning the influence of Mīmāṃsā, Ganganatha Jha, *Pūrva-Mīmāṃsā in Its Sources*, chapter 33, has some interesting things to say. An important source for Mīmāṃsā studies is the seven-volume *Mīmāṃsākośa*, Kevalanda Sarasvatī (ed.). Important and relevant observations on this issue are also found in M. M. Deshpande, "Bhāṣā," chapter 22 of S. Mittal and G. Thursby (eds.), *The Hindu World*.

4. As W. Cenkner in *A Tradition of Teachers* reports, the study of Mīmāṃsā is one of the subjects that students in the schools associated with the present Śaṅkara *maṭhas* have to take. See also F. Staal (ed.), *A Reader on the Sanskrit Grammarians* and K. Kunjunni Raja, *Indian Theories of Meaning*. See also H. G. Coward and K. Kunjunni Raja (eds.), *The Philosophy of the Grammarians*, vol. 5 of *Encyclopedia of Indian Philosophies*.

5. *Jaimini Sūtras* I, 1, 2: *codanalakṣano'artho dharmaḥ*.

6. Ibid. I, 2, 1.

7. *Śābarabhāṣya* I, 1, 22: "There can be no creator of this relation because no soul is cognized as such by any of the means of cognition. If there had been such a creator, he could not have been forgotten." Cf. also: Kumārila Bhaṭṭa, *Ślokavārttika* XVI, 41 ff.

8. Ganganatha Jha, *Pūrva-Mīmāṃsā in Its Sources*, 178 ff.

9. *Jaimini Sūtras* VI, 1, 6 ff.

10. Ganganatha Jha, *Pūrva Mīmāṃsā*, 264 ff.

11. *Jaimini Sūtras* IV, 3, 15.

12. *Śābarabhāṣya* VI, 1, 1.

13. *Nyāyaratnākara*: "Liberation must consist in the destruction of the present body and the nonproduction of the future body." Quoted by G. Jha, *Pūrva-Mīmāṃsā*, 38.

14. *Prakāraṇapañcika*, *Tattvāloka*, 156.

15. O. Gächter, *Hermeneutics and Language in Pūrvamīmāṃsā: A Study in Śābara Bhāṣya* with bibliographic references to both Eastern and Western authors.

16. H. G. Coward, *The Sphoṭa Theory of Language: A Philosophical Analysis* with extensive bibliography. The complete text has been edited by Prof. K. V. Abhyankar and Acharya V. P. Limaye in the University of Poona Sanskrit and Prakrit Series.

17. Ramdas Gaur, *Hindutva*, 589.

18. According to S. K. Belvalkar, *Shree Gopal Basu Mallik Lectures on Vedanta Philosophy*, part 1, chapter 4: "Vedānta in the Brahmasūtras," (142), Jaimini, the author of the *Mīmāṃsāsūtra*, wrote a *Śarīrakasūtra* that sought to harmonize the teaching of

the *Sāmaveda Upaniṣads*, particularly the *Chāndogya Upaniṣad*, and this sutra was incorporated within and forms the main part of the present text of the *Brahma Sūtra*.

19. Among the widely recognized *Vedāntācāryas* are: Śaṅkara, Rāmānuja, Madhva, Vallabha, Bhāskara, Yadavaprakāśa, Keśava, Nīlakaṇṭha, Vijñānabhikṣu and Baladeva. They are the founders of separate branches of Vedānta philosophy. There are several comparative studies of the different schools of Vedānta such as V. S. Ghate, *The Vedānta* ; O. Lacombe, *L'absolu selon le Vedānta*.

20. Cf. Ramdas Gaur, *Hindutva*, 591 ff.

21. Other commentaries interpret Vedānta in the light of sectarian dogma under the names of Dvaitādvaita (Nimbārka), Śuddhādvaita (Vallabha), Acintyabhedābheda (Baladeva), and so forth.

22. Several attempts have been made to establish an earlier birth date for Śaṅkara: some Western scholars assign him to the seventh century CE, some Indian scholars believe that he was born in the sixth century BCE. See note 29.

23. A complete list with a critical analysis is given in S. K. Belvalkar, *Lectures on Vedānta Philosophy*, 218 ff. See also: R. T. Vyas, "Roots of Śaṅkara's Thought."

24. Swami Nikhilananda has brought out an English paraphrase of the *Māṇḍukyopaniṣad with Gauḍapāda's Kārikā and Śaṅkara's Commentary*. See also T. Vetter, "Die Gauḍapādīya-Kārikās: Zur Entstehung und zur Bedeutung von (A)dvaita."

25. *Maitrī Upaniṣad* VI, 15; *Muṇḍaka* II, 2, 8.

26. Contained in H. R. Bhagavat (ed.), *Minor Works of Śrī Śaṅkarācārya*, pp. 374–402.

27. Several complete English translations of the *Śaṅkarabhāṣya* are available: G. Thibaut (*SBE*, vols. 34 and 38); Swami Gambhirananda (Calcutta: Advaita Ashrama, 1965) makes use of some major classical commentaries. P. Deussen's German translation is still of importance. Out of the numerous publications dealing with Śaṅkara and his Advaita Vedānta a few may be mentioned: S. G. Mudgal, *Advaita of Śaṅkara: A Reappraisal*; Haripada Chakraborti, "Śaṅkārācarya," in *Asceticism in Ancient India*; D. N. Lorenzen, "The Life of Śaṅkarācārya," in F. Clothey and J. B. Long (eds.), *Experiencing Śiva*; P. Hacker, "Eigentümlichkeiten der Lehre und Terminologie Śaṅkaras: Avidyā, Nāmarūpa, Māyā, Īśvara" and *Vivarta: Studien zur Geschichte der illusionistischen Kosmologie und Erkenntnistheorie der Inder*; E. Deutsch, *Advaita Vedānta: A Philosophical Reconstruction* and E. Deutsch and J. A. B. van Buitenen (eds.), *A Source Book of Advaita Vedānta*. See also, R. V. Das, *Introduction to Śaṅkara*; K. S. Murty, *Revelation and Reason in Advaita Vedānta*. Authoritative and important studies on various aspects of Advaita Vedānta are also contained in the essays by S. K. Maitra, *Fundamental Questions of Indian Metaphysics and Logic*, and H. G. Coward (ed.), *Studies in Indian Thought: Collected Papers of Prof. T. R. V. Murti*. The most exhaustive survey of the source literature for Advaita Vedānta is R. Thangaswami, *A Bibliographical Survey of Advaita Vedānta Literature* [in Sanskrit].

28. Sureśvara in his *Naiṣkarmyasiddhi* refers to Śaṅkara as "the source of pure knowledge . . . and of illumination," calling him "omniscient," and "the guru of gurus," comparing him to Śiva himself: Śaṅkara is one of the popular names of Śiva. The *Naiṣkarmyasiddhi*, K. K. Venkatachari (ed. and trans.). For Sureśvara's teaching and his

relationship to Śaṅkara see the introduction to R. Balasubramanian (ed. and trans.), *The Taittirīyopaniṣad Bhāṣya-Vārtika of Sureśvara.*

29. A. Nataraja Aiyer and S. Lakshminarasimha Sastri, the authors of *The Traditional Age of Śrī Śaṅkarāchārya and the Maths,* not only provide the lists of all the successors to Śaṅkarācārya relying on eminent scholars who "have already proved that the date of Śaṅkara is 509–477 BC" (preface) but also bring excerpts from court cases that were initiated in the 20th century in order to settle the claims of candidates and counter-candidates to some *gaddis* (headships of *maṭhas*).

30. For biographical details see M. Yamunacarya, *Rāmānuja's Teachings in His Own Words,* 1–39; also J. B. Carman, *The Theology of Rāmānuja: An Essay in Interreligious Understanding,* chapter 2: "Rāmānuja's Life." For Rāmānuja speculative theology takes second place to active worship and self-surrender to Viṣṇu, described before in the context of the *bhaktimārga.* While Śaṅkara sees the highest human ideal in *saṃnyāsa* and objectless meditation, Śrī Vaiṣṇavism is family oriented and lays great importance on image worship and temple ceremonial.

31. See: K. D. Bharadwaj, *The Philosophy of Rāmānuja*; A. Sharma, *Viśiṣṭādvaita Vedānta: A Study.*

32. R. Balasubramanian, former head of the S. Radhakrishnan Institute for the Advanced Study in Philosophy at the University of Madras, which under T. M. P. Mahadevan's leadership had become the leading modern scholarly center for Advaita studies, responds to this criticism in *Some Problems in the Epistemology and Metaphysics of Rāmānuja.*

33. S. N. Dasgupta, *HIPh,* vol. 3, 471.

34. The last verse of the *Vedāntasūtra* meaning "no return, on account of the scripture words."

35. *Rāmānujabhāṣya* , G. Thibaut (trans.), *SBE,* vol. 48. Text edition: *Śrī Bhagavad Rāmānuja Granthamālā,* P. B. Annangaracharya Swami (ed.).

36. For details see: B. N. K. Sarma, *Madhva's Teachings in His Own Words,* 1–26, and also the major works of the same author: *Philosophy of Śrī Madhvācārya; A History of the Dvaita School of Vedānta and Its Literature,* 2 vols. A thorough study of Madhva's thought: S. Siauve, *La doctrine de Madhva.* See also: I. Puthiadam, *Viṣṇu the Ever Free: A Study of the Madhva Concept of God.*

37. Text and French translation with introduction and notes in: S. Siauve, *La voie vers la connaissance de Dieu sélon l'Aṇuvyākhyāna de Madhva.*

38. *Aṇuvyākhyāna,* 13.

39. *Mahānārāyaṇopaniṣad,* 1 ff.

40. R. Raghavendracharya (ed.), *Madhva Brahmasūtrabhāṣya with several commentaries*; S.S. Rao (trans.), *Madhva's Commentary on the Brahmasūtras.*

41. Swami Nikhilananda (ed. and trans.), *Ātmabodha*; Swami Jagagananda (ed. and trans.), *Upadeśasahasrī*; Swami Madhavananda (ed. and trans.), *Vivekacudāmaṇī.*

42. Swami Nikhilananda (ed. and trans.), *Vedāntasāra.*

43. Swami Swahananda (ed. and trans.), *Pañcadaśī.* Vidyāraṇya is assumed to be identical with Madhavācārya, the author of the famous *Sarvadarśanasaṃgraha,* head of

Śṛṅgerī Maṭha from 1377 to 1386. The nineteenth-century work *Vedāntasāgara* [Hindī] by Swami Niścaldas enjoys a very great reputation in India. A Sanskrit version of this work has also been published.

44. S. S. Suryanarayana Sastri (ed., trans., and comm.), *Vedāntaparibhāṣa*.

45. S. S. Raghavacar (ed. and trans.), *Vedārthasaṅgraha*.

46. Swami Adidevananda (ed. and trans.), *Yatīndramatadīpikā*.

47. V. Krsnamacarya (ed. and trans.), *Vedāntakarikāvalī*.

48. English translation by M. S. Rajagopala Aiyangar.

49. P. Nagaraja Rao (ed. and trans.), *Vādāvalī*.

50. Many of the aforementioned classics of Vedānta, especially the minor works of the great *ācāryas*, are being printed today in India with vernacular translations and commentaries in large editions by popular publishing houses. It is quite amazing to see the widespread interest in this philosophically quite sophisticated literature, which presupposes familiarity with the technical terminology of the medieval Vedānta tradition. It would be hard to find anything comparable in any Western country.

## 27. HINDUISM AND BUDDHISM

1. For more detail on the Buddha's life and teaching see K. Klostermaier, *Buddhism: A Short Introduction*.

2. P. V. Kane, *HDhS*, vol. 5, part 2 , 913 ff.

3. *Viṣṇu Purāṇa* III, 18.

4. *Ślokavārttika* I, 3, 7, Swami Dvarika Dass Sastri (ed.), Ganganatha Jha (trans.).

5. *Tattvasaṅgraha of Śāntarakṣita with the Commentary by Kāmalaśīla*, 2 vols., Swami Dvarika Dass Sastri (ed.), G. Jha (trans.).

6. *Vedāntasūtras* II, 2, 18–32.

7. *Śaṅkarabhāṣya* II, 2, 18–27 is directed against the Sarvāstivādis, 28–31a against the Vijñānavādis, and 31b–32 against the Śūnyavādis.

8. Trans. G. Thibaut, *SBE*, vol. 34, 427 ff.

9. *Selections from the Work of Swami Vivekananda*, 366.

10. Ibid., 494.

11. *Young India*, November 24, 1927.

12. Ibid.

13. Ibid.

14. *Young India*, December 8, 1927.

15. *Discovery of India*, 117.

16. Ibid., 120.

17. Jawaharlal Nehru, *Speeches 1953–1957*, 430 ff.: "Valedictory Address at the Seminar on Buddhism," New Delhi, November 29, 1956.

18. Marie Seton, *Panditji: A Portrait of Jawaharlal Nehru*, 454.

19. B. R. Ambedkar, *The Untouchables*.

20. D. Keer, *Dr. Ambedkar: Life and Mission*, 497.

21. Chandra Bharill, *Social and Political Ideas of B. R. Ambedkar*, 245.

22. Ibid., 256.

23. Ibid., 257.

24. *Journal of the Mahabodhi Society*, December 1959, 353.

25. Vir Savarkar, "Essentials of Hindutva," 12.

26. Ibid., 13.

27. Ibid., 15.

## 28. HINDUISM AND CHRISTIANITY IN INDIA

1. A. Chowgule, *Christianity in India*, 1 ff.

2. Much historical evidence supporting the historicity of the contents of the Acts of St. Thomas has been collected by Fr. Herman D'Souza, *In the Steps of St. Thomas*.

3. H. D'Souza mentions some fakirs in Sindh "who profess themselves as followers of Thuma Bhagat, i.e., Thomas the Saint. They practice a number of Christian rites and possess a book which they call the Gospel of St. Mathew," 17.

4. Quoted in S. C. Neill, *A History of Christianity in India: The Beginnings to* AD 1707, 146.

5. Ibid.

6. Sītā Ram Goel, *Catholic Ashrams: Samnyasis or Swindlers*, uses the example of de Nobili and his mission methods as an argument for his thesis that the indigenization of Christianity in India amounts to nothing but fraud and deception.

7. Early Protestant reformers, like Martin Luther, wrote about Judaism and Islam, the two non-Christian religions present in Europe at that time, albeit in a negative and defensive way.

8. The British East India Company was chartered in 1600 to carry out trade in India. It was dissolved when in 1874 the British Crown took over government in "British India." The Danish East India Company was chartered in 1616. It acquired a small strip of coastal land south of Madras (Tranquebar) and the settlement of Serampur (Śrīrāmpur) near Calcutta in 1755. Both were sold to the British East India Company in 1845.

9. Heinrich Ziegenbalg became the author of the first Tamil grammar in a European language. It was written in Latin and published in 1716 in Halle. He also translated three Tamil works into German.

10. It was finally edited and published by the Dutch Indologist Wilhelm Caland in 1926 at Amsterdam.

11. Quoted in: H. von Glasenapp, *Das Indienbild deutscher Denker*, 167.

12. Hans-Werner Gensichen, who devoted much energy to making Ziegenbalg's accomplishments known, calls it "an early example of a dialogue that plays out in the mutual readiness of an encounter on the human level" and that "attempts to understand the other as he understands himself." H. W. Gensichen, *Invitatio ad Fraternitatem*, 23 (my translation).

13. W. Carey, together with his entire family and some companions, had tried to embark for Calcutta in 1793 to begin missionary work there. Being without a royal permit, he was taken off the boat. A month later, having secured a royal permit from the king of Denmark, Frederick VI, he sailed on a Danish vessel and secured the protection of Colonel Bie, the Danish Governor, a friend of the famous German missionary W. Schwartz in Tranquebar. Ironically, it was the salary that the British East India Company paid to Carey in his capacity as instructor in Bengali and Sanskrit at the company college in Calcutta from 1801 onward that kept the Serampore enterprise alive.

14. For details see *The Story of Serampore and Its College*, published by the Council of Serampore College, n.d.

15. Quoted in R. D. Boyd, *An Introduction to Indian Christian Theology*, 41.

16. Ibid., 55.

17. E.g., the Kristakula Ashram in Tirupati (Andhra Pradesh), the Christavashram in Manganam (Kerala), and the Kristaseva Ashram in Pune (Mahārāṣṭra).

18. F. Heiler wrote a biography while Sundar Singh was still alive: *Sundar Singh: Apostel des Ostens und des Westens*. See also: A. J. Appasamy, *Sundar Singh: A Biography*.

19. K. L. Sheshagiri Rao, *Mahatma Gandhi and C. F. Andrews: A Study in Hindu-Christian Dialogue*.

20. Yisu Das Tiwari's youngest son, Dr. Ravi Tiwari, president of Serampore College, recently published a volume, *Yisu Das: The Witness of a Convert*, with a biography of Yisu Das, some autobiographical writings, and tributes by friends and colleagues.

21. J. N. Farquhar initiated a multivolume series, The Religious Life of India, which began appearing from 1920 onward from the (YMCA) Association Press in Calcutta, and which dealt with a great many different castes and sects in a scholarly manner. Justin Abbot produced a series, Poet Saints of Maharashtra, consisting of texts and translations of major Mahratti religious classics, published from 1926 onward in Poona by the Scottish Mission Industries Press in Poona. One of the most successful Christian enterprises in India has been the educational system established by various churches in the major centers. There are much sought-after Christian high schools and university colleges in Delhi, Kolkata, Mumbai, Chennai, and other cities frequented by a majority of Hindu students.

22. For a good summary see S. Wesley Ariarajah, *Hindus and Christians: A Century of Protestant Ecumenical Thought*, 17–31.

23. Ibid., 21.

24. Ibid., 20.

25. See ibid., 52–88.

26. R. Boyd, *An Introduction*, 163. See also: D. A. Thangasamy, *The Theology of Chenchiah*.

27. R. Boyd, *An Introduction*, 184.

28. Eric E. Sharpe, *Not to Destroy but to Fulfil*, 272 ff.

29. Thus, already, Warren Hastings, in a letter written in 1784, shortly after the appearance of the first English translation, had remarked that the *Bhagavadgītā* represented "a theology accurately corresponding with that of the Christian dispensation, and most powerfully illustrating its fundamental doctrines." Quoted in E. Sharpe, *The Universal Gita*, 8.

30. His autobiographical essay *My Theological Quest* appeared as the first booklet in the Indian Christian Thought Series from the CISRS Bangalore 1963.

31. Originally published in 1922 by Oxford University Press, it was reprinted by Motilal Banarsidass in Delhi in 1967. Farquhar also is the author of *Modern Religious Movements in India*, the first systematic attempt to describe nineteenth- and twentieth-century developments of Hinduism in an objective, sympathetic way. Published originally in 1914 by Oxford University Press, it was also reprinted by Motilal Banarsidass in 1967.

32. Cf. E. Sharpe, *Not to Destroy*. Farquhar, as previously mentioned, also initiated the series Religious Life of India.

33. Thus vol. 7, 3 and 4, are devoted to "The Christian and the Hindu Views Concerning Man," vol. 10, 1 to "Concepts of Love and Non-Violence," vol. 10, 3 to "Hindu and Christian Concepts of Ultimate Truth," with Christian as well as Hindu contributions in each.

34. For details see Ariarajah, *Hindus and Christians*, 133–165.

35. German translation *Hindus vor dem universalen Christus*.

36. For a report see *Religion and Society* 16, 2 (June 1969): 69–88.

37. *Viṣṇu-Nārāyaṇa: Texte zur indischen Gottesmystik*, Jena 1917.

38. Thus P. Lochhaas of the Lutheran Church of America. This and other such quotes can be found in Steven Gelberg, "Krishna and Christ: ISKCON's Encounter with Christianity in America," in H. Coward (ed.), *Hindu-Christian Dialogue*, 138–61.

39. It is interesting to note that Christian "de-programming" of youths who had joined the new religious movements was considered successful if they ate meat, drank liquor, and engaged in extramarital sexual relations.

40. References and more materials in S. Gelberg, "Krishna and Christ."

41. "Hindu Influence on Christian Spiritual Practice," in H. Coward (ed.), *Hindu-Christian Dialogue*, 198 ff. See also K. Klostermaier, "Samnyāsa: A Christian Way of Life in Today's India?" and "Hindu-Christian Dialogue: Revisiting the Tannirpalli Trinity's Original Vision."

42. The proceedings were published in *Hindu-Christian Dialogue: Perspectives and Encounters*. Motilal Banarsidass has published an Indian edition.

43. Under the joint editorship of Harold Coward and Anand Amaldass, the first issue appeared in Autumn 1988. It contains a major article by Coward: "Hindu-Christian Dialogue: A Review," 1–5, with a rich bibliography.

44. *Catholic Ashrams: Samnyasis or Swindlers?* The second, enlarged edition (1994) contains an exchange of open letters between Swami Devananda and Bede Griffith 1987–89.

45. Various websites submit the writings of American Hinduism scholars to critique from a Hindu standpoint.

46. In the essay "The Future of Hindu-Christian Dialogue," in H. Coward (ed.), *Hindu–Christian Dialogue*, 262–74, I have expressed myself on this issue in greater length.

47. In an Internet communication dated April 27, 2004, *Indians against Christian Aggression www.christreview.org*, vivid complaints are voiced against "The Hijacking of Hinduism," citing some quite outrageous instances of perverting Hindu scriptural texts and symbols.

## 29. HINDUS AND MUSLIMS IN INḌIA

1. See the report in *India Today* of April 8, 2002 "Secular Nemesis: A Communal Rage is Sweeping India."

2. See also the article "Islam in South Asia" by Peter Hardy in *ER*, vol. 7, 390–404.

3. E. C. Sachau, *Alberuni's India*, 22.

4. Riffat Hassan, "The Basis for a Hindu-Muslim Dialogue and Steps in That Direction from a Muslim Perspective," 129.

5. See also the article "Kabīr" by Charlotte Vaudeville in *ER* vol. 8, 226–27.

6. Muhammed Hedayetullah, *Kabīr: The Apostle of Hindu-Muslim Unity*. Kabīr scholarship has flourished in the last half century and as a result many doubts have been thrown on the authenticity of many sayings popularly attributed to Kabit. C. Vaudeville suspended indefinitely the projected second volume to her *Kabir I* (Oxford University Press) because of the uncertainty of authorship of many Kabīr texts.

7. Ibid., preface, xiii.

8. Quoted in Bikrama Jit Hasrat, *Dārā Shikūḥ: Life and Works*, 189.

9. Ibid, xxvi.

10. R. C. Majumdar, H. C. Raychaudhuri, K. Datta, *An Advanced History of India*, 728. See also the article "Sayyid Ahmad Khan" by C. W. Troll in *ER*, vol. 1, 155–57.

11. Rajmohan Gandhi, *Eight Lives: A Study of the Hindu-Muslim Encounter*, 19.

12. *Aligarh Institute Gazette*, June 12, 1897, quoted in R. Gandhi, *Eight Lives*, 45.

13. Rajmohan Gandhi, *Eight Lives*, 123.

14. The name *Pakistan* has been explained in several ways. Apparently it was the invention of some Indian students in England. According to some it means "Land of the Pure"; according to others it is a composite of the initial letters of the provinces out of which it was formed.

15. Volume 3 of the Gandhi Series, edited and published by Anand T. Hingorani.

16. Z. Haq, *Prophet Muhammad in Hindu Scripture*, 2.

17. *Dārā Shukūḥ: Life and Works.*

18. Although even Hasrat misquotes some titles of Sanskrit works, he is exceptionally well informed about Hinduism.

19. Azad Faruqi, *Sufism and Bhakti*, 44.

20. Ibid., 157.

21. http:/hinduforce.4t.com.

22. www.satyamevajayate.info.

## 30. HINDU REFORMS AND REFORMERS

1. I am thinking specifically of the Nātha movements, such as the Gorakhnātha and the Kabīr Panth, the Sikh community founded by Gurū Nānak and similar groups. See G. H. Wescott, *Kabīr and the Kabīrpanth*; M. A. Macauliffe, *The Sikh Religion: Its Gurus, Sacred Writings and Authors*, and more recent works by H. McLeod.

2. *India Hindu and India Christian*, 12.

3. Ibid., 40 ff. See also C. T. Jackson, *The Oriental Religions and American Thought*, chapter 5, "The Missionary View."

4. *Chips from a German Workshop*, vol. 2, 313.

5. Lecture in Westminster Abbey, December 3, 1873.

6. The first major work was J. N. Farquhar, *Modern Religious Movements in India*. Since then countless studies have been produced by Indian and foreign scholars. See N. S. Sarma, *Hindu Renaissance*.

7. *Complete Works of Swāmi Vivekānanda*, vol. 3, 151.

8. Ibid., vol. 5, 152.

9. S. C. Crawford, *Ram Mohan Roy: Social, Political and Religious Reform in Nineteenth-Century India*; see also the entry "Roy, Ram Mohan" by D. L. Haberman in *ER*, vol. 12, 479–80. As a source still indispensable is M. C. Parekh, *The Brahmo Samāj*.

10. A party of orthodox Brahmins, in an attempt to get the law rescinded, traveled to London to state their case; Ram Mohan Roy also journeyed there, dying in Bristol in 1833.

11. Important contemporary documents are collected in J. K. Majumdar, *Raja Rammohun Roy and Progressive Movements in India, Volume 1. A Selection from Records (1775–1845)*, 19, reproducing the list of names of those who voted for and against the abolition of *satī*.

12. The cover story of *India Today*, June 15, 1986, 26–33, "Female Infanticide: Born to Die." Also child marriages are still quite common in India as the feature article, "Wedding of the Dolls," (74–77) in the same magazine demonstrates.

13. See M. C. Parekh, *The Brahmo Samāj*.

14. The text with English translation by Hem Chandra Sarkar appeared as a centenary edition.

15. See M. C. Parekh, *Brahmarshi Keshub Chander Sen.*

16. See Lala Lajpat Rai, *The Ārya Samāj.* Major work on Dāyānanda Sarasvatī and the Ārya Samāj has recently been done by J. Jordens, whose findings are apt to revise some of the prevailing impressions. Dāyānanda's main work is *Satyārtha Prakāśa*, published first in the Aryan Era year of 1972949060 and reprinted many times (English translation Allahabad: Kal Press, 1947).

17. D. G. Tendulkar, *Mahātmā*, 8 vols.; Suresh Ram, *Vinoba and His Mission.*

18. *Young India*, October 6, 1921.

19. *Ibid.*

20. Modhi Prasad, *Kaka Kalelkar: A Gandhian Patriarch*, with a foreword by Lal Bahadur Shastri, 22.

21. The source of all books about Rāmakrishna is the voluminous *Gospel of Rāmakrishna*, an English rendering of the transcript by "M" of all the utterances of Rāmakrishna over many years. See Swāmi Nirvedānanda, "Śrī Rāmakrishna and Spiritual Renaissance," published by the Ramakrishna Mission Institute of Culture in Calcutta. There is a large amount of literature informing about the main figures of the Rāmakrishna Mission and its activities published by this movement. Jeffrey Kripal aroused the ire not only of members of the Rāmakrishna Order by his Freudian reading of the "Gospel" in his *Kālī's Child.*

22. *Collected Works*, vol. 3, 139.

23. *Ibid.* 27–29.

24. The Śrī Aurobindo Ashram Pondichéry has published all the writings of Śrī Aurobindo and informs through numerous magazines, films, and so forth also about its present activities.

25. An informative survey of the work of S. Radhakrishnan, together with an autobiographical sketch is given in: P. Schilpp (ed.), *The Philosophy of Sarvepalli Radhakrishnan.* His son, the historian S. Gopal, wrote a biography that is intimate as well as scholarly: *Radhakrishnan: A Biography.*

26. *Bunch of Thoughts*, 123.

27. *The Collected Works of Śrī Ramaṇa Maharṣi*, 8 vols., A. Osborne (ed.). A. Osborne, *Ramaṇa Maharṣi and the Path of Self-Knowledge.* See also Sing Kamath *Śrī Maharṣi: A Short Life-sketch*, with many photographs.

28. For his works consult the bibliography. About him see the brief biography of his successor, Svāmi Cidananda, *Light Fountain*, and K. S. Ramaswami Sastri, *Sivananda—The Modern World Prophet.*

29. The numerous and often reprinted books by Jiddu Krishnamurti are transcripts of his public addresses and questions and answers noted down by his numerous followers. One of the most popular is his *The First and Last Freedom* with a foreword by Aldous Huxley. One of the last, his *The Awakening of Intelligence*, Avon Books, 1976, contains a by now famous interview with physicist David Bohm. About him see Pupul Jayakar, *J. Krishnamurti: A Biography.*

30. See G. Das Gupta, *Mother As Revealed to Me.*

31. See *Autobiography of a Yogi* and the magazines of the Yoga Fellowship.

32. Martin Eban (ed.), *Maharishi the Guru: The Story of Maharishi Mahesh Yogi*. See also the numerous periodical publications of this movement.

33. See *Back to Godhead*, the magazine of the Hare Krishna Movement, which gives in each issue several times complete lists of the works of the founder guru. The movement has undergone severe stresses after the demise of its founder and was virtually split in half by the formation of the ISKCON Reform Movement (IRM), which claims the allegiance of a fair number of ISKCON centers.

34. His works have been collected under the title *Wanderings in the Himalayas*.

35. See his twelve-volume commentary on the *Bhagavadgītā* and his monthly publication, *Tapovan Prasad*, as well as the pamphlets issued in connection with the Sandeepany Sadhananlaya.

36. See *Satya Sai*, 6 vols.

37. H. Sunder Rao, "The Two Babas."

38. "Call to Revive Hinduism: Viswa Sammelan," *Times of India*, December 10, 1977.

39. Cf. M. N. Roy, *Materialism*. In the foreword to the second edition he wrote: "Since this book was written in 1934 and first published in 1940 religious revivalism has gained ground in philosophical thought. Mystic and irrationalistic tendencies have become more and more pronounced even in social philosophy and political theories. These developments are the symptoms of an intellectual crisis." See also his *New Humanism*.

40. P. C. Chatterji, *Secular Values for Secular India*.

41. *Illustrated Weekly of India* February 5, 1965. It must be kept in mind that this English-language weekly does not necessarily reflect the opinion of the traditional non-English-speaking Hindus.

42. *Seminar* 64, December 1964.

43. S. K. Haldar, Ibid., 20 ff.

44. J. D. M. Derret, *The Death of a Marriage Law: Epitaph for the Rishis*. A. S. Altekar blames this opposition on a misunderstanding: "This utter and pitiable ignorance of the real nature of Hinduism is at the root of the amazing opposition, which measures like the Hindu Code have evoked in the recent past even in educated circles. . . . Our ancient *rishis* never expected that the rules that they had laid down would be regarded as binding forever by their descendants. They themselves have pointed out the necessity of making periodical changes in them." ("Hinduism a Static Structure or a Dynamic Force?" in *Nehru Abhinandan Granth*, 421 ff.) Altekar refers here to *Manusmṛti* IV, 60.

45. As Peter Robb ("The Challenge of Gau Mata: British Policy and Religious Change in India, 1880–1916") has shown, the agitation against cow slaughter, which is a major political issue in today's India, has a rather long history.

46. V. K. Sinha, "Secularization."

47. T. N. Madan, "Secularism in Its Place."

48. See also P. C. Upadhaya, "The Politics of Indian Secularism."

49. See, e.g., the article "Nice People, Nasty Mood" by Madhu Jain.

50. More on this issue in: K. Klostermaier, "Truth and Tolerance in Contemporary Hinduism."

## 31. MAHĀTMĀ GANDHI: A TWENTIETH-CENTURY *KARMAYOGI*

1. The best and most detailed biography is D. G. Tendulkar: *Mahātmā: Life and Work of M. K. Gandhi*, with a preface by Pandit Nehru, 8 vols. The Government of India published Gandhi: Collected Works in 90 vols. 1958–86.

2. Several editions from Navajivan Publishing House, the literary heir of Gandhi's writings. It also appeared in a Penguin edition in 1986.

3. *Mahātmā* I, 39.

4. Ibid., 44.

5. Ibid., 71.

6. *Autobiography*, 365.

7. See *Mahātmā* I, 75–78.

8. *A Guide to Health*, Madras, 1930, 3: "The relation of the body and the mind is so intimate that if either of them got out of order, the whole system would suffer. Hence it follows, that a pure character is the foundation of health in the real sense of the term, and we may say that all evil thoughts and evil passions are but different forms of disease."

9. *Mahātmā* I, 103.

10. *Hind Swarāj or Indian Home Rule* appeared first serialized in *Indian Opinion*. As a separate booklet it appeared in Bombay in 1910. Edition used: Navajivan, 1944.

11. Gokhale on Gandhi: "A purer, a nobler, a braver and a more exalted spirit has never moved on this earth." *Mahātmā* I, 137.

12. Quoted according to the Navajivan edition, 1955.

13. *Mahātmā* II, 99.

14. *Young India*, December 31, 1931.

15. *Young India*, November 4, 1926.

16. *To the Students*, 46.

17. *Young India*, September 25, 1924.

18. *Mahātmā* II, 92.

19. *Mahātmā* II, 347.

20. *To the Students*, 47.

21. *Mahātmā* IV, 50 ff.

22. *To the Students*, 48.

23. *Harijan*, July 28, 1946.

24. *Constructive Program*, 13.

25. *Harijan*, July 20, 1947: "*Satyāgraha* can rid society of all evils, political, economic, and moral."

26. Preface to the English edition of *Hind Swarāj*, 1938.

27. Facsimile of Gandhi's "Talisman" in *Mahātmā* VIII.

28. *Constructive Program*, 12.

29. *Young India*, May 4, 1921.

30. *Harijan*, October 3, 1947.

## 32. *HINDŪTVA*—HINDUISM-HINDU *DHARMA*

1. There are notable exceptions. Journals like *Seminar* have long warned of "Hindu Fascism," and several scholars have studied the development of right-wing political Hinduism.

2. An extract (in translation) from *Ananadamaṭha* with the full text of the "Bande Mātaram" is provided in William Theodore de Bary (gen. ed.), *Sources of Indian Tradition*, vol. 2, 156 ff. The Akhil Bhāratiya Sant Samiti, an organization of *sādhus* in support of Hindu political parties, founded in 1989 by Svāmi Vāmadeva, advocates the readoption of the "Bande Mātaram" as the national anthem of India, because it considers the "Janaganamana," the present anthem, "a manifestation of slave-mentality . . . since it was sung at the welcoming ceremony of King George V in India." Translation of the manifesto of the Sant Samiti in *JVS* 1, 1 (1992): 176–79.

3. See M. J. Harvey, "The Secular as Sacred? The Religio-political Rationalization of B. G. Tilak."

4. The full text of the manifesto is reproduced in M. Pattabhiram (ed.), *General Elections in India 1967: An Exhaustive Study of Main Political Trends*, 217 ff.

5. Samagra Savarkar Wangmaya, *Hindū Raṣṭra Darśan*.

6. A very well-researched account of the background of N. Godse and the events up to and including Gandhi's assassination is given in L. Collins and D. Lapierre, *Freedom at Midnight*.

7. M. A. Jhangiani, *Jana Sangh and Swatantra: A Profile of the Rightist Parties in India*. Also V. P. Varma, *Modern Indian Political Thought* and S. Ghose, *Modern Indian Political Thought*.

8. Quoted in M. A. Jhangiani, Ibid., 10.

9. See the election manifesto in Pattabhiram, *General Elections in India*, 204 ff.; also Deendayal Upadhyaya, "Jana Sangh" and "A democratic alternative."

10. See K. Saxena, "The Janatā Party Politics in Uttar Pradesh (1977–79)." The vindictiveness of the Janatā government vis-à-vis the former congress leaders is quite vividly described in chapter 15 of the biography of the former president of India, *Giani Zail Singh*, by Surinder Singh Johar.

11. *India Today* (February 15, 1993), 59–63.

12. The *Viśva Hindū Pāriṣad* publishes a monthly *Hindū Viśva*. In a special issue, brought out before the Prayāga Sammelan January 1966, a number of prominent leaders

spelled out the essence of the movement in Hindī and English articles e.g., S. S. Apte, "Viśva Hindū Pariṣad. Confluence of Hindu Society."

13. The article in *India Today* quoted at the beginning of this chapter calls the Viśva Hindū Pariṣad "the intellectual arm of the RSS, with a million dedicated workers in 2,500 branches all over India."

14. Information on the origin and structure of the RSS is contained in literature mentioned in note 7. *Seminar* 151 (March 1972) had a major article on the RSS by D. R. Goyal and provided a fairly extensive bibliography (40 ff.). More recent publications are referred to in P. Dixit, "Hindu Nationalism." *The Illustrated Weekly of India's* cover story in its March 12, 1978, issue was "How Powerful is the RSS?" It also carried an interview with Balasaheb Deoras. The RSS is publishing a weekly magazine, *The Organiser*. See also C. P. Barathwal, "Rashtriya Swayamsevak Sangh: Origin, Structure and Ideology." "Open Offensive," *India Today*, (June 30, 1989), 58–61, claims that the RSS has over twenty-five thousand branches in almost twenty thousand cities and villages with about two million activists and five million members.

15. *Bunch of Thoughts*, chapter 1, "Our World Mission," 9 ff.

16. *Illustrated Weekly of India* (March 12, 1978), 11. See also L. Rattanani and Y. Ghimire's recent report on the RSS, "Manning All Battle Stations," *India Today* (January 15, 1993), 55.

17. His principles are laid down in *Rām Rājya aur Marxvād*.

18. Cf. K. P. Karunakaran, "Regionalism."

19. *The Illustrated Weekly of India* devoted its March 15, 1970 issue to the theme "Private Armies." Meanwhile much has been written on them.

20. See, e.g., A. George, *Social Ferment in India*. Also K. K. Gangadharan, "Shiv Sena."

21. P. C. Chatterji, "Secularism: Problems and Prospects," chapter 7 in *Secular Values for Secular India*, gives a fairly detailed account of some of the major recent communal riots and their genesis. See also S. P. Aiyar, *The Politics of Mass Violence in India*.

22. Louis Dumont, in a very incisive study, "Nationalism and Communalism" in *Religion/Politics and History in India*, 89–110, operates with a definition of *communalism* provided by W. C. Smith in *Modern Islam in India*, 185, as "that ideology which emphasizes as the social, political and economic unit the group of adherents of each religion, and emphasizes the distinction, even the antagonism, between such groups." *Communalism* is, in a certain sense, a specifically Indian phenomenon, large enough to make sure that the routine Western sociology and political science approach to Indian society is inadequate. Nirmal Mukarji, "The Hindu Problem."

23. Moin Shankar, "Social Roots of Communalism."

24. December 1991, 13/12, 1 and 4.

25. See also "Swāmis in Politics," *Hinduism Today* 13/7, July 1991, 25–26.

26. "Pilgrim's Protest," *India Today* (March 15, 1993), 74–76.

27. D. Upadhyaya, "A Democratic Alternative," 23: "Ideology-based parties and policy-oriented politics are desirable, for they alone can sublimate politics and distinguish

it from the game of self-aggrandizing power-hunting . . . an education of the people on an ideological and programmatic basis is necessary so that they are freed of caste-ism, communalism and regionalism."

28. See "One-Nation Challenge," *India Today*, February 15, 1993, 15.

29. See "Nice People, Nasty Mood," Ibid., 72–73.

30. Chaman Lal, in *Hindu America*, offers arguments for a long-standing naval connection between India and Central America.

31. R. C. Majumdar, in *Hindu Colonies in the Far East*, collected rich materials to document this expansion.

32. More detail on the Hindu heritage in South Asia in K. Klostermaier, "Hindu Missions in India and Abroad."

33. A. S. Altekar, "Hinduism, A Static Structure or a Dynamic Force," 425.

34. Somen Das, an Indian Christian theologian, critical of traditional Christianity, published in 1996 a series of essays, under the title *Dharma of the Twenty-first Century: Theological-Ethical Paradigm Shift*, that comes close to adopting the Hindu notion of *dharma*.

## 33. INDIA AND THE WEST

1. R. C. Majumdar, *The Classical Accounts of India.* Also J. Schwab, *The Oriental Renaissance: Europe's Rediscovery of India and the East, 1680–1880.*

2. Arrian's "Anabasis of Alexander" (second century CE) is based on the now lost writings of Aristobulos and Ptolemy, who had accompanied Alexander. See also Plutarch, *Life of Alexander*, ch. 64. English translations of these and other sources in R. C. Majumdar, *The Classical Accounts of India.* A standard work on this period is W.W. Tarn, *The Greeks in Bactria and India.*

3. Diodorus Siculus, *Historical Library*, vol. 17, 107.

4. Alisaunder, *Alexander: Alexander and Dindimus*, Latin text 10 ff.: my translation.

5. I. K. K. Menon, "Kerala's Early Foreign Contacts."

6. A famous Pāli work, *Milindapañha* describes questions placed before the Buddhist sage Nāgasena by Menander of Sagala in northwestern India. English translation: T. W. Rhys Davids, *The Questions of King Milinda.*

7. For details see J. Schwartzberg (ed.), *HASA*: "Campaign and Empire of Alexander the Great" and "India as Known to Early Greeks."

8. For more details see: E. Benz, *Indische Einflüsse auf die frühchristliche Theologie.*

9. A great many interesting articles on this subject are contained in R. Baine Harris (ed.), *Neoplatonism and Indian Thought.* See also E. Elintoff, "Pyrrho and India." An attempt to prove the independent origin of Greek philosophy over against those who assume an Indian influence was undertaken by H. J. Krämer, *Der Ursprung der Geistmetaphysik.*

10. For more details see: J. Filliozat, *Les rélations extèrieures de l'Inde*, 1. Les échanges de l'Inde et de l'Empire Romain aux premiérs siécles de l'ere chretienne, 2.

La doctrine brahmanique a Rome au IIleme siécle. See also Klaus Karttunen, "On the Contacts of South India with the Western World in Ancient Times, and the Mission of the Apostle Thomas."

11. The legend itself is of uncertain age. It found its expression in Nicolas Novotitch's *Life of Issa*, which is supposed to be the translation of a manuscript in a Tibetan monastery containing the life story of Jesus. Quite a few Indians have accepted it. See for instance Pundit Shunker Nath, *Christ: Who and What He Was*: Part 1. *Christ a Hindu Disciple, nay a Buddhist Saint*, Part 2. *Christ a Pure Vedāntist*. The Danish scholar Christian Lindtner goes even further by claiming that the Gospels of the New Testament are based on (inadequate) translations from Buddhist Sanskrit texts into Koine Greek. See his essay "Some Sanskritisms in the New Testament Gospels." Lindtner also announced a forthcoming monograph on the topic. See also the website www.jesusbuddha.com,

12. Tertullian, *Apologia versus gentes*, in *Migne Patrologia Latina*, vol. 1, 1080 ff.

13. *Migne Patrologia Latina*, vol. 17, 1167 ff.

14. Evidence of lively exchange between India and the Arab countries is collected in J. Duncan M. Derett's: "Greece and India Again: The Jaimini-Aśvamedha, the Alexander Romance and the Gospels." Interesting details are also presented in an Internet article, "India and Ancient Egypt," by www.arianuova.org. There is increasing interest in finding links between Hindu India and South America. Thus The Council of Elders of the Sacred Mayas, Guatemala held in 2005 a conference on "Hindu-Maya Cultural Similarities." BBC News 2006/08/03 carried an item "Peru link to Indian archeological find?"

15. Edward C. Sachau, trans., *Alberuni's India: An Account of the Religion, Philosophy, Literature, Geography, Chronology, Astronomy, Customs, Laws and Astrology of India about* A.D. 1030.

16. R. E. Latham (trans.), *The Travels of Marco Polo*. On India: 233–68. See also: Heimo Rau, "The Image of India in European Antiquity and the Middle Ages."

17. One of the most interesting accounts of South Indian Hinduism in the early eighteenth century is the recently discovered work by the Lutheran missionary Bartholomaeus Ziegenbalg (1682–1719), *Traktat vom Malabarischen Heidentum* (1711), which was never printed. See Hans-Werner Gensichen, "Abominable Heathenism—a Rediscovered Tract by Bartholomaeus Ziegenbalg." The work of Abbé Dubois (1770–1848), *Hindu Manners, Customs and Ceremonies*, first published by the East India Company in 1816, has become a classic in its own right and has been reprinted many times by Oxford University Press.

18. G. H. R. Tillotson, "The Indian Travels of William Hodges."

19. Ibid., 378 ff.

20. W. Leifer, *Indien und die Deutschen: 500 Jahre Begegnung und Partnerschaft*. Gita Dharampal compiled a bibliography of early German writing about India: "Frühe deutsche Indien-Berichte (1477–1750)."

21. *Systema Brahmanicum* (Rome: 1792); *Reise nach Ostindien* (Berlin: 1798).

22. P. J. Marshall (ed.), *The British Discovery of Hinduism in the Eighteenth Century*.

23. For more detail see G. H. Hampton, *Oriental Jones: A Biography of Sir William Jones 1746 1794* and *The Life and Mind of Oriental Jones: Sir William Jones, the Father of Modern Linguistics.*

24. For details on the *Ezour Vedam*, used as a source for Indian traditions by Voltaire, see M. Winternitz, *Geschichte der indischen Literatur*, vol. 1, 12 n. 1.

25. A brief history of French Indology is given in P. S. Filliozat's "The French Institute of Indology in Pondichery." A major contribution to Indian studies was also made by Russian and Polish scholars. In Russia especially, the study of Indian languages is flourishing today. Italian, Dutch, Belgian, and Finnish scholarship in Indian studies is alive, too, to a lesser degree perhaps in Spain and Latin American from where, however, some very good work has come out recently.

26. At the age of twenty five he wrote his epoch-making work: *Über das Conjugationsystem der Sanskrit Sprache in Vergleichung mit jenen der griechischen, lateinischen, persischen und germanischen Sprache. Nebst Episoden des Ramajan und Mahabharat in genau metrischen Übersetzungen aus dem Originaltexte und einigen Abschnitten aus den Vedas.* F. Staal, *A Reader on the Sanskrit Grammarians*, has assembled many valuable documents and comments on the history of Western Sanskrit scholarship.

27. The first complete translation of the Bible into Sanskrit was published by W. Carey from Serampore between 1808 and 1818; it was later improved upon by W. Yates and J. Wenger. For further details see: J. S. M. Hooper, *Bible Translation in India, Pakistan, Ceylon*, second edition: revised by W. J. Culshaw.

28. The *Sanskrit Wörterbuch* together with *Nachträge* has been reprinted by Motilal Banarsidass in 1991.

29. Published originally by Oxford University Press and reprinted several times by other publishers recently, the *Sacred Books of the East* have not yet been replaced as a standard work, although such series as *Sacred Books of the Buddhists, Sacred Books of the Jains*, and *Sacred Books of the Hindus* offer a larger number of text translations in the designated areas.

30. For more complete information consult: P. J. Chinmulgund and V. V. Mirashi (eds.), *Review of Indological Research in Last 75 Years.*

31. Hindu scholars like R. G. Bhandarkar, S. N. Dasgupta, S. Radhakrishnan, T. M. P. Mahadevan, and T. R. V. Murti, to name just a few, spent considerable time lecturing in the West.

32. For more details see: Dale Riepe, *The Philosophy of India and Its Impact on American Thought.* See also C. T. Jackson, *The Oriental Religions and American Thought: Nineteenth-Century Explorations.*

33. The journal *Philosophy East and West*, published by the University of Hawaii, has remained one of the principal instruments for the continued discussion of the conferences' issues.

34. Dale Riepe, *The Philosophy of India*, 275 ff.: "If the American empire meets with the fate of the British, if Americans cannot resolve their life-and-death struggle with the intelligent use of technology, if the alienation in American society cannot be alleviated, then a new attitude may gradually replace the 300-year reign of optimism.

Such eventualities may lead to more philosophers turning to contemplation, meditation and increased poring over the Hindu and Buddhist scriptures."

35. Ibid.

36. The case is well stated by Malati J. Shendge in her essay "The Interdisciplinary Approach to Indian Studies."

37. Ananda Coomaraswamy, *Transformation of Nature in Art*, 4.

38. *Indian and Western Philosophy: A Study in Contrasts*; *Facets of Indian Thought*.

39. *Philosophies of India*, J. Campbell (ed.); *Myths and Symbols in Indian Art and Civilization*.

40. *Nāma-Rūpa and Dharma-Rūpa: Origin and Aspects of an Ancient Indian Conception*.

41. *Introduction génerale a l'étude des doctrines hindoues*.

42. *The Hindu Temple*; *The Presence of Śiva*.

43. India and Europe: An Essay in Understanding," "On Being and What There Is: Classical Vaiśeṣika and the History of Indian Ontology."

44. The case has been convincingly stated by Jaideva Singh in his edition and translation of the *Pratyabhijñāhṛdayam* by the numerous references to the earlier translation of the text by K. F. Leidecker.

## 34. HINDUISM AND SCIENCE

1. The Chinese *Records of the Western World*, compiled between the seventh and tenth centuries (translated by S. Beal, *Si-yu-ki: Buddhist Records of the Western World*) contain a full description of this curriculum (*Si-yu-ki*, vol. 1, 78 ff.)

2. P. V. Kane has topically summarized in his monumental *History of Dharmaśāstra* the contents of this vast literature.

3. The most famous is the aforementioned Kauṭilya *Arthaśāstra*, ascribed to the prime minister at the Maurya court, who provides fascinating details of many departments in the vast administration of that empire.

4. Some important texts will be mentioned later.

5. One such text, the *Kṛṣi-Parāsara*, has been edited and translated by G. P. Majumdar and S. C. Banerji and published by the Asiatic Society Calcutta in 1960.

6. These high ethical demands were not only applicable to students of *adhyātma-vidyā*, as articulated by Śaṅkara in *Upadeśa-sahasrī*, 3 ff. but also to students in the professions, such as medicine, as stated in *Cāraka Saṃhitā* 8, 13 and others. [Cf. the Shree Gulabkunverba Ayurvedic Society's *The Cāraka Saṃhitā* (Jamnagar, 1949), vol. 1 (Introduction), 162–86.]

7. The success of modern Western science is based on reductionist analysis, that is, isolating parts of a complex whole that are treated as separate entities. Science-based technology similarly pursues limited objectives disregarding everything that does not pertain to a particular aim.

8. Betty Heimann, *Facets of Indian Thought*, 37 contrasts this notion with the Greek *kósmos*, idea: "*Ṛta*, the World-balance or World-course, is not as for instance

its equivalent in Greece, a purposeful order brought into the cosmos by a selective teleological plan laid down by the mastermind of a creator. Not before the things themselves come into being are they planned and then created . . . each single function is appropriate to the thing concerned, but serves at the same time to fulfil the purpose of the Whole."

9. *Taittirīya Upaniṣad* I, 7 S. Radhakrishnan (trans.), *The Principal Upaniṣads*, 535.

10. In the *Trimūrti*, the Hindu "Trinity," Viṣṇu has the role of "preserver."

11. See especially Prajāpati's teaching in *Chāndogya Upaniṣad* VIII, 7.

12. However, the intention with which the study was undertaken differed.

13. Translated into English by E. Sachau under the title *Alberuni's India.*

14. For more information on *Jyotiṣa Vedāṅga* see V. M. Apte, "The Vedāṅgas."

15. Besides these there were others, such as the *Kaśyapa Saṃhitā*.

16. Govinda Krishna Pillai in *Vedic History*, ix, writes: "The measuring rods used by Mohenjo Daro architects are still being used. Their limits and their proportions are still the guides for indigenous architects and builders."

17. See Guy Beck, *Sonic Theology.*

18. See W. Kaufmann, *Rāgas of North India.*

19. A succinct account of the development of Indian linguistics is provided in the historical resumé of *The Philosophy of the Grammarians*, G. Coward and K. Kunjunni Raja (eds.).

20. See Subhash Kak: "The Science of Consciousness in Ancient India" in T. S. R. Rao and S. Kak (eds.) *Computing Science in Ancient India*, pp. 91–106

21. See A. K. Biswas, "Brass and Zinc Metallurgy in the Ancient World: India's Primacy and the Technology Transfer to the West." The section "Indian Sciences." In G. Flood (ed.) *The Blackwell Companion to Hinduism*, 345–409 offers additional information on several of the areas mentioned.

## 35. HINDUISM AND ECOLOGY

1. In classical Hindu mythology, Yamunā is considered the sister, not the daughter, of Yama.

2. Anil Agarwal, "Can Hindu Beliefs Help India Meet Its Ecological Crisis," 175.

3. Ibid.

4. V. B. Mishra in an interview with David Suzuki in "Matrix of Life," Part 2 of the David Suzuki Video Series *The Sacred Balance* (2003).

5. Some examples of this can be found in K. Klostermaier, "Hinduism, Population, Consumption and the Environment."

6. David Lee, "The Natural History of the *Rāmāyaṇa*."

7. *Bhāgavata Purāṇa* (BhP) XI, 7–9.

8. Ibid. II, 7, 4.

9. Ibid. XI, 7, 19 ff.

10. Ibid. XI, 9, 27 ff.

11. By equating "the scriptural means of terminating misery" with the perceptible in which "there is no certainty or finality," it sets itself up against the "new religion" of post-Gupta, scripture-based Hinduism.

12. The question has been extensively addressed by E. Frauwallner in the first volume of his *Geschichte der Indischen Philosophie*.

13. On this see G. Feuerstein, *The Philosophy of Classical Yoga*, chapter VII, "Pātañjala Yoga and Classical Sāṁkhya."

14. Cf. *Bhagavadgītā* (*BG*) 5,6; 13, 29 ff.

15. *Kārikā* 59.

16. *BhP* III, 27, 12 ff.

17. J. H. Masui, "Introduction to the Study of Yoga," 19 ff.

18. G. J. Larson, "The Format of Technical Philosophical Writing in Ancient India: Inadequacies of Conventional Translations."

19. Cf. György Doczi, *The Power of Limits*.

20. *Pañcadaśī* (*PD*) IX, 89.

21. *PD* IV, 54 ff.

22. See M. Hiriyanna, "*Svabhāva-vāda* or Indian Naturalism."

23. *PD* VI, 144.

24. In the light of this, the following remark by J. A. Wheeler, a leading contemporary astrophysicist, is interesting: "The golden trail of science is surely not to end in nothingness . . . not machinery, but magic may be the better description of the treasure that is waiting." "From Relativity to Mutability," 203.

25. *PD* VI, 147.

26. *PD* V, 30.

27. Swami Prajnananda, *The Bases of Indian Culture*, 139 ff.

28. *PD* VI, 152.

29. *PD* VI, 160.

30. Satya Deva Mitra, "The Advaitic Concept of *Abhāsa*," 267 ff.

31. *PD* VI, 161.

32. *PD* VI, 165.

33. *PD* VI, 166.

34. *PD* VI, 183. I am using the words *implicate* and *explicate* so as to evoke an association with the way in which the physicist David Bohm (*Wholeness and the Implicate Order*) uses them, recalling Nicholas of Cusa's example.

35. *PD* VI, 211.

36. *PD* VI, 243.

37. *PD* VI, 252.

38. *Ṛgveda* X, 90, 13 and 14.

39. *Bhagavadgītā* XI, 7.

40. J. A. B. van Buitenen, *Rāmānuja on the Bhagavadgītā*, chapter 7, 4 ff.

41. Ibid., 7, 12.

42. Ibid.

43. *Yatīndramatadīpikā of Śrīnivāsadāsa*, Avatāra 7.

44. J. A. B. van Buitenen, *Rāmānuja on the Bhagavadgītā*, chapter 7, 13.

45. Ibid., 7, 14.

46. M. Yamunacharya, *Rāmānuja's Teachings in His Own Words*, 80 ff.

47. Śaṅkara on *Brahma Sūtra* I, 1, 2: "that omniscient, omnipotent cause from which proceed the origin, subsistence, and dissolution of this world—which is differentiated by names and forms, contains many agents and enjoyers, is the abode of the fruits of actions, these fruits having their definite places, times, and causes, and the nature of whose arrangement cannot even be conceived by the mind, that cause, we say, is Brahman." Rāmānuja on *Brahma Sūtra* I, 1, 2: "this entire world with its manifold wonderful arrangements, not to be comprehended by thought, and comprising within itself the aggregate of living souls from Brahmā down to blades of grass, all of which experience the fruits in definite places and at definite times."

48. See C. Deegan, "The Narmadā: Circumambulating a Landscape" and W. F. Fischer, "Sacred Rivers, Sacred Dams: Competing Visions of Social Justice and Sustainable Development along the Narmadā."

## 36. HINDU MEASURES OF TIME

1. P. V. Kane, *History of Dharmaśāstra*, vol. 5, part 1.

2. http://sanjayrath.tgripod.com/Article/hindu_calendar.htp

3. *Rāṣṭrīya Pañcāṅga*, published every year (in English and several Indian vernaculars), The Director General of Observatories, Government of India, New Delhi.

4. *Viśva Pañcāṅgam*, Kāśī Hindū Viśva Vidyālaya, (published every year in Hindī).

5. *Manusmṛti*.

6. *Viṣṇu Purāṇa*.

## 37. INDIAN CHRONOLOGY

1. Reported in *Spiegel Online*, May 31, 2005.

2. *MLBD Newsletter*, January 1993, 7.

3. See H. D. Sankalia, "Paleolithic, Neolithic and Copper Ages." Major archaeological research published by B. Allchin and F. R. Allchin, *The Rise of Civilization in India and Pakistan*. G. C. Possehl (ed.), *Harappan Civilisation: A Contemporary Perspective*. For locations of Stone Age archaeological sites in India, see *HASA*, plate II, 1; Neolithicum and Chalcolithicum plate II, 2 with reproductions of characteristic artifacts and appropriate text information, 263–66. For a map of locations of Harappan and other contemporary South Asian cultures see *HASA* plate II, 3 and text on 266 ff.

4. J. F. Jarrige, "Die frühesten Kulturen in Pakistan und ihre Entwicklung"; G. Quivron, "Die neolithische Siedlung von Mehrgarh."

5. *HASA* map "India as Revealed in the *Mahābhārata*," plate III A, 2. 164 ff. Text and bibliography: 266.

6. *HASA* map "India as Revealed in the *Rāmāyaṇa*," plate III A, 1, 164. Text and bibliography: 266.

7. *HASA* map "Vedic India," plate III A, 162 ff. Text and literature: 266.

8. J. G. Shaffer, "Prehistory" in "Addenda and Corrigenda," *HASA*, 265a.

9. See P. C. Sengupta, *Ancient Indian Chronology*, illustrating some of the most important astronomical methods. Also: S. C. Kak, "The Indus Tradition and the Indo-Āryans."

10. See A. D. Pusalker, "Historical Traditions," *HCIP*, vol. 1, 271–336. F. E. Pargiter, *Ancient Indian Historical Tradition*, starting from Purāṇic records, takes a notably different departure and assumes that the Aryans entered India from the mid-ranges of the Himālayas and settled around Banares ca. 2300 BCE before spreading westward and eastward.

11. P. C. Sengupta, *Ancient Indian Chronology*, 101 ff.

12. Internet communication April 5, 2005 IANS.

13. S. B. Roy, "Chronological Infrastructure of Indian Protohistory" and "Chronological Framework of Indian Protohistory—The Lower Limit."

14. S. Kalyanaraman in "Revival of the Legendary River Sarasvatī" reports on projects undertaken by the Indian government to bring the river system back to life after six thousand years of dormancy.

15. M. R. Mughal, "Recent Archaeological Research in the Cholistan Desert."

16. On this see H. Bechert, *On the Dating of the Historical Buddha*, and the reply by Dissanayake discussed in K. Klostermaier, *Buddhism: A Short Introduction*, 27, note 4.

17. About these and other eras used in India, see L. Renou and Jean Filliozat (eds.), *L'Inde Classique*, vol. 2., appendix 3, "Notions de chronologie," 720–38.

# Glossary

**abhāva** nonperception (in the Nyāya system); nonbeing (in the Vaiśeṣika system).

**abhaya** fearlessness; in iconology: *abhaya mudrā* is the hand gesture of a deity, inspiring confidence and trust.

**abhiniveṣa** desire; in the Yoga system: instinctive craving for life.

**abhiṣeka** anointment, part of installation ceremony of a king and an image of the deity.

**abhyāsa** exercise, practice, exertion.

**abhyudaya** rising of sun or other heavenly bodies; festival.

**ācamana** rinsing of mouth with water before worship and before meals.

**acara** immobile (an attribute of the Supreme Being).

**ācārya** master (used today as equivalent to MA).

**acetana** without consciousness (an attribute of matter).

**acintya** beyond intellectual understanding.

**ādāna** taking away.

**adbhuta** marvelous, miraculous.

**adharma** unrighteousness, evil.

**adhidevatā** a presiding deity.

**adhikāra** qualification (especially of students of religion).

**adhikāraṇa** section of a textbook; topic of a single work.

**adhiyajña** principal sacrifice.

**adhyāsa** superimposition; misidentification.

**adhyātma** supreme; spiritual; relating to the Supreme Being.

**adhyāya** chapter (of a treatise).

**aditi** Vedic Goddess, Mother Earth, mother of *adityas*.

**ādivāsi** original inhabitants; appellation of tribals.

**adṛṣṭa** invisible; important technical term in the Nyāya and Vaiśeṣika systems as well as in linguistic speculation.

**advaita** nonduality; name of a school of Vedānta.

**ādya prakṛti** primeval matter.

**āgama** source, beginning; name of a class of writings that are considered as revealed by the Śaivas.

**aghora** horrible: name of a sect of Śaivites.

**agni** fire; one of the foremost Vedic gods.

**agnicayana** a particular kind of Vedic fire sacrifice.

**agnihotra** a Vedic fire sacrifice.

**agniṣṭoma** fire sacrifice.

**ahaṁkāra** principle of individuation; egotism.

**ahiṃsā** not killing; nonviolence.

**ahita** improper, unwholesome, not propitious.

**aiśvarya** lordliness.

**aja** unborn (m); attribute of Supreme Being; he-goat.

**ajā** unborn (f), attribute of Primordial Matter; she-goat.

**akala** without parts; attribute of Supreme Being.

**akāma** without desire.

**ākāśa** ether (one of the five elements of Indian cosmology); space.

**ākhyāna bhāga** narrative part of a sacred text.

**akhāḍā** place of assembly; principal territorial center of some sects.

**akhila** undivided; complete.

**akṛti** uncreated; eternal principle underlying words, and so forth.

**akṣara** imperishable; syllable (letter); attribute of Supreme Being.

**alaṁkāra** ornament; technical term for ornate literature.

**amara** immortal.

**amarṣa** impatience; anger; passion.

**aṃbikā** mother; Mother Goddess.

**amṛta** nectar; draught of immortality.

**aṃśa** part, fragment.

**anādhāra** without support.

**anādi** without beginning; eternal.

**ānanda** bliss; used as last part of the proper name of many *samnyāsis* e.g., Vivekānanda: he who finds his bliss in discrimination.

**ananta** without end; proper name of the world snake upon which Viṣṇu rests.

**aṇava** veil; congenital ignorance concerning the ultimate; stain.

**aṅga** member, constituent part, e.g., of a major work.

**aṇimā** smallness; in Yoga the faculty to diminish one's size.

**aniruddha** free, without hindrance; proper name of one of the *vyūhas* of Viṣṇu.

**anitya** not permanent; transient.

**añjali** a handful, e.g., *puṣpāñjali*: a handful of flowers.

**aṅkuśa** goad; one of the divine weapons.

**anna** food, especially rice; formerly sixteenth part of a rupee.

**anṛta** against the (moral) law.

**anta** end, death.

**antarātman** conscience.

**antaryāmi** the "inner ruler," the Supreme Being as present in the heart.

**antyeṣṭi** last rites.

**aṇu** atom.

**anubhava** experience.

**anugraha** attraction; grace of God.

**anumāna** inference.

**apara** unsurpassed; attribute of the Supreme Being.

**aparādha** fault, sin.

**aparādha kṣamāpañca** prayer for forgiveness of faults.

**aparigraha** without having (and wanting) possessions.

**aparokṣa** immediate, present.

**apas** water.

**apāśraya** supportless.

**apauruṣeya** not human-made; technical term to describe the supernatural origin of the Veda in the Mīmāṃsā system.

**āpsara** nymph.

**apūrva** technical term in the Mīmāṃsā system to denote the not-yet realized effect of a sacrifice.

**araṇya** forest.

**arcā** rites of worship before an image.

**arcāvatāra** image of God, who took on this form in order to become an object of worship for the devotees.

**ardha** half.

**ardhanārīśvara** figurative representation of Śiva, in which one half shows a male figure, the other a female one.

**arghya** water to rinse hands before worship or before meals.

**arjuna** bright; proper name of hero in the *Bhagavadgītā*.

**arka** sun.

**artha** object; meaning; wealth.

**arthāpatti** inference, presumption.

**ārya** noble (man); self-designation of the Aryans.

**asaṃbaddha** unfettered; incoherent (talk).

**āsana** seat, sitting posture.

**asat** not true; "not real."

**āśīrvāda** (ritual) blessing.

**āsmitā** egoism; from *asmi*, "I am."

**aspṛha** without desire.

**āśrama** hermitage; stage in life; designation for a group of *samnyāsis*.

**aṣṭāgraha** a certain constellation of sun, moon, earth, and the five major planets.

**aṣṭāvaraṇa** the eight concealing (clouding) veils of the Self.

**asteya** not stealing.

**āstika** one who accepts the authority of the Veda; orthodox.

**aśubha** inauspicious.

**asuras** demons; class of superhuman beings.

**asūyā** indignation; envy, jealousy.

**aśvamedha** horse sacrifice.

**aśvatha** a tree: *ficus sacra*.

**aśvins** Vedic gods, a pair of brothers; astronomy: Castor and Pollux.

**ātmakūṭa** self-deceit.

**ātman** self, "soul."

**ātmanastuṣṭi** contentment.

**audarya** being in the womb, a son.

**audārya** generosity.

**āvāhana** invitation of the deity at worship.

**avatāra** descent (of God in a bodily form).

**avidyā** ignorance (of reality).

**avyakta** unmanifest.

**ayurveda** traditional Indian medicine; literally, "life knowledge."

**bābā(jī)** dear father; affectionate name for ascetics.

**bala** strength, power.

**bandha** bondage.

**bhadra** well, happy; blessing.

**bhāga** luck, fortune.

**bhagavān** lord; most general word for god.

**bhāī (Hindī)** brother; familiar title of courtesy.

**bhajana** devotional recitation.

**bhakti** love, devotion.

**bhasma** (sacred) ashes.

**bhāṣya** commentary.

**bhāva** condition; emotion; nature.

**bhaviṣya** future.

**bhaya** fear, terror; dread.

**bheda** difference.

**bhikṣu** mendicant; title of Buddhist monks.

**bhoga** enjoyment.

**bhū, bhūmī** earth; proper name of Viṣṇu's second consort.

**bhukti** enjoyment.

**bhūta** being, spirit, ghost.

**bibhatsa** trembling.

**bīja** seed.

**biṇḍu** dot, drop, globule.

**brahmā** (personal) creator god.

**brahmacāri** student; celibate.

**brahmacarya** first period in life, celibate studenthood.

**brahmaloka** world of Brahmā; highest abode.

**brahman** (impersonal) absolute.

**brāhmaṇa** member of the highest caste; class of ritual texts.

**brahmārandra** the place from where the soul departs at death (the backside of the cranium).

**buddhi** intelligence; in the Sāṁkhya system, name of the first product of the union of *puruṣa* and *prakṛti.*

**caitanya** spiritual, consciousness, also epithet for the Supreme; proper name of a Bengali saint of the sixteenth century.

**caitta** consciousness.

**cakra** circle, disc; centers in the body; one of Viṣṇu's weapons; discus.

**cakravarti** universal ruler.

**caṇḍa** moon; silver.

**caṇḍāla** wild; base; term for lowest caste; outcaste.

**caṇḍana** sandalwood.

**caṇḍī** fierce lady; proper name of Devī.

**capāti** bread; flat unleavened wheat breads.

**carita** biography; curriculum vitae.

**caryā** activity; mode of behavior.

**caturmukha** four-faced; epithet of Brahmā.

**caturvarṇāśrama** the four *varṇas* (castes) and stages of life.

**chāyā** shadow.

**choṭī** the wisp of hair left on the top of the head.

**cit** consciousness; spirit.

**citta** thought.

**daitya** a goblin, a slave, a demon.

**dakṣiṇa** sacrificial fees.

**dakṣiṇācāra** right-handed path.

**dāna** gift; charity.

**darśana** view; audience; theory; philosophical system.

**dāsa** servant; often part of proper name.

**daśanāmi** ten-named; proper name of a religious order.

**dasyu** slave.

**dayā** compassion.

**deva, devatā** divine (superior) being.

**devayāna** path of the gods.

**devī** goddess.

**dhairya** firmness.

**dhāma** realm; abode; body.

**dhāraṇa** support.

**dharma** "law," religion, basis, foundation support, and so forth.

**dharmaśāstra** (authoritative) law book.

**dharmakṣetra** "the field of righteousness."

**dhatṛ** giver; epithet of God.

**dhātu** element, mineral; in grammar: verbal root.

**dhṛti** firmness.

**dhūpa** incense.

**dhyāna** meditation; concentration in Yoga.

**digvijaya** conquest of the four quarters; appellation of the successful competition of a religious teacher.

**dīkṣā** initiation.

**dīpa** lamp.

**dohā** a couplet in Hindī poetics.

**dravya** substance; material (for sacrifice).

**droha** malice.

**duḥkha** sorrow, suffering.

**dvaita** duality; name of a school of Vedānta.

**dvaitādvaita vivarjita** beyond duality and nonduality.

**dvandva** pair of opposites (hot-cold, and so forth).

**dvāpara yuga** second era of each *kalpa*.

**dveṣa** hatred.

**dvijāti** twice-born; appellation of the three upper castes whose initiation is considered a second birth.

**dvīpa** island; continent.

**dyaus** resplendent; sky; Vedic high god.

**ekādaśī** eleventh day of each half-month; sacred to Vaiṣṇavas as a day of fasting and prayers.

**ekāgratā** one-pointedness, single-mindedness.

**ekoddiṣṭa** funeral ceremony for one deceased.

**ekaśṛṅga** one horn (unicorn); the fish descent (of Viṣṇu).

**gaddī** throne, seat, headship (as of a *maṭha*).

**gambhīrya** serenity; seriousness.

**gandharva** celestial musician.

**gaṇeśa** lord of the celestial armies; elephant-headed son of Śiva and Pārvatī.

**garbha** womb.

**garbha-gṛha** innermost sanctuary of the temples.

**gārhastya** second stage in the life of a Hindu (as householder).

**garuḍa** Viṣṇu's vehicle; griffin.

**gāyatrī** ancient Vedic formula that a Brahmin has to recite thrice a day.

**ghāṭ(a)** steps; especially flight of steps leading to a river.

**ghī** liquefied butter.

**gopī** milk maid.

**gopura** towerlike structure over the entrance into (South) Indian temple compounds.

**gośālā** old-age home for cows.

**gosvāmi** lord of cows; title for high-ranking Vaiṣṇavas of certain communities.

**gotra** stable; family, descent.

**grantha** (sacred) book; an ancient Indian script.

**gṛhasta** house father, male head of household.

**gṛhyasūtras** scriptures setting down the rituals to be performed in the home.

**guṇa** quality; elementary component of matter.

**guru** elder; spiritual master; teacher in general.

**gurukula** school according to the ancient Indian pattern.

**hala** plough.

**halāhala** poison churned up from the Milk Ocean, consumed by Śiva in order to save the world.

**hara** literally, "the one who takes away"; name of Śiva.

**hari** literally, "the yellowish green one"; name of Viṣṇu.

**harṣa** joy.

**hasyā** laughter.

**haṭhayoga** literally, "forced or violent Yoga"; physical exercises.

**hetu** cause.

**hiṃsā** violence, killing.

**hindūtva** "Hindūness," Hinduism as culture over against "Hindū-*dharma*" as religion.

**hiraṇyagarbha** literally, "golden womb"; the first being.

**hita** beneficial, good.

**hitavācana** well-intentioned speaking.

**hlādinī** enjoyment, bliss.

**holī** popular spring festival.

**homa** fire oblation.

**hotṛ** class of Vedic priests.

**hṛdaya** heart; core of something.

**icchā** wish, desire.

**iḍā** name of one of the main vessels in the body according to traditional Indian physiology.

**indriya** sense organs.

**īrṣyā** envy, jealousy.

**iṣṭa** preferred, wished for.

**iṣṭa-deva** the god of one's choice.

**īśvara** Lord; God.

**itihāsa** history; the epics; historical proof.

**jāgarita** waking consciousness.

**jagat** world.

**jagadguru** world-preceptor, title of Śaṅkarācāryas.

**jāl(a)** net (symbol for the world entangling the spirit).

**jana saṅgha** literally, "people, community"; name of former political party.

**janëu** sacred thread worn by the three upper castes.

**japa** repetition of the name of God or a mantra.

**jātakarma** rites performed at time of birth.

**jatī** birth; race, family, "subcaste."

**jaya** victory; also as greeting; "hail."

**jīva(-ātman)** life; individual living being.

**jīvanmukti** liberation while still in a body

**jñāna** knowledge.

**jñānaniṣṭha** the state of being firmly and irrevocably established in ultimate knowledge.

**jñānī** a knower (of the absolute).

**jyotiṣa** one of the auxiliary sciences of the Veda: astronomy and astrology.

**jyotiṣṭoma** a seasonal sacrifice for the departed.

**kaivalya** "aloneness"; ultimate aim of Yoga.

**kāla** time; black color; fate; death.

**kālamukha** black mouth; name of Śiva; name of a Śaivite sect.

**kālī** the "black one"; name of the terrible form of the Goddess.

**kaliyuga** age of strife; last period in each world era.

**kalki** the future (last) *avatāra* of Viṣṇu in the form of a white horse.

**kalpa** world era, Day of Brahmā; ritual; one of the auxiliary sciences of Veda.

**kalpa-sūtras** texts describing sacrificial rituals.

**kāma** desire, lust, love; name of god of love.

**kāmadhenu** wish fulfilling cow.

**kāṇḍa** major section of a literary work.

**kāpālika** literally, "one with a skull"; name of followers of certain Śaivite groups.

**kāraṇa** author; cause; title of the Supreme Being; God.

**karma** work; action; result of an action.

**karyā** worship of an image through various acts.

**kaṣṭa** evil; wrong; harsh.

**kaupina** small strip of cloth to cover private parts; the only garment worn by many ascetics.

**kavi** poet, wise man, omniscient.

**khadga** sword.

**khila-bhāga** supplement (of texts).

**kīrtaṇa** congregational religious singing.

**kleśa** suffering; pain.

**kośa** sheath; cover; treasury; lexicon.

**kriyā** activity; skill; exercise.

**krodha** anger.

**kṛpā** favor; grace; compassion.

**kṛṣṇa** black; name of the most famous *avatāra* of Viṣṇu.

**kṛtayuga** the first age in each world era; the golden age.

**kṣamā** forgiveness.

**kṣaṇa** moment; shortest time measure.

**kṣatriya** warrior; the second *varṇa*.

**kṣetra** field; also metaphorical.

**kubera** god of wealth, king of the *yakṣas*, friend of Śiva.

**kuṃbha** water pot; astronomically: sign of Aquarius.

**kumbhamelā** a great festal gathering at four specific holy places.

**kuṇḍalinī** serpent; in Tantricism: life energy.

**kūrma** tortoise; one of the *avatāras* of Viṣṇu.

**kuśa** a kind of grass that is required in Vedic rites.

**lajjā** modesty; shame.

**lakṣaṇa** characteristic; attribute; sign.

**līlā** play; sport.

**liṅga** characteristic sign; subtle nature; symbol of Śiva.

**lobha** greed.

**loka** world; sphere.

**loka-nātha** Lord of the world.

**lokasaṅgraha** universal welfare.

**mada** intoxication; dementia.

**mādhava** sweet like honey (*madhu*); epithet of Kṛṣṇa; proper name of several famous philosophers.

**madhurasa** "honey sentiment"; highest love and affection.

**madhuvidyā** "honey knowledge"; see: Upaniṣads.

**mahā** great.

**mahant(a)** head of a monastic establishment.

**maharṣi** great sage; honorific title.

**mahat** great; in Sāṁkhya: first evolved (intellect).

**mahātmā** great soul; honorific title.

**maheśvara** great lord; title of Śiva.

**mahiṣa** buffalo; proper name of a demon killed by Devī.

**maithuna** copulation; pair; astronomically; Gemini.

**makara** crocodile; alligator.

**mala** stain.

**mālā** garland; chain; rosary.

**maṃsa** meat.

**mānasa** mental.

**māna** pride; idea, concept; honor.

**manas** mind.

**māṇava** relating to Manu; human.

**mānava-dharma** laws given by Manu, valid for all humankind.

**maṇḍala** circle; section of *Ṛgveda*.

**maṇḍapa** covered hall; tent.

**mandira** palace; temple.

**maṅgala** auspicious, lucky.

**maṅgala-śloka** an opening verse or prayer of a text to ensure that the undertaking is auspicious.

**maṇi** jewel.

**mantra** word, formula (especially from scriptures).

**manu** progenitor of humankind.

**manvantara** an age of one (of fourteen) Manu.

**mārga** way; street; path of salvation.

**mārjāra** cat.

**markaṭa** monkey.

**maruta** wind; wind god.

**maṭha** monastic establishment.

**mātsara** jealous; selfish.

**matsya** fish.

**māyā** fiction, illusion.

**melā** fair, assembly.

**mīmāṃsā** inquisition; system; proper name of one *darśana.*

**mithyā** futility; false.

**mithyā-jñāna** false knowledge.

**mleccha** "barbarian"; foreigner not belonging to Aryan culture; one who does not speak Sanskrit.

**moha** delusion.

**mokṣa** liberation.

**mṛtyu** death.

**mudrā** pose; hand gesture.

**muhūrta** thirtieth part of day (about 45 minutes): an "hour."

**mukta** liberated.

**mukti** liberation.

**mukti-dātā** the giver of liberation, savior.

**mūla** root.

**mūla-prakṛti** primary matter.

**mūla-bera** the firmly installed image in a temple.

**mūla-saṃhitā** original text.

**mulayaka** name of demon, personification of evil, subdued by Śiva.

**mumukṣutva** desire for liberation.

**muni** literally, "one who keeps silence"; ascetic; "monk."

**mūñja** a kind of grass used in ritual contexts.

**mūrti** "embodiment"; figure; image.

**muśala** hammer.

**nāda** (loud) sound.

**nāḍī** (body) vessel, nerve.

**nāga** superior being; snake; naked, heretic.

**nagna** naked.

**naivedya** food offered to the image of God (prepared under certain conditions to ensure its purity).

**nāma-kīrtana** congregational singing where a name of God is constantly repeated.

**nāma-rūpa** name and form; individuality.

**namaskāra** greeting in a spirit of worship.

**nandi** Śiva's vehicle; a bull.

**naraka** hell.

**nāsadīya** title of a famous *Ṛgvedic* hymn beginning with *na-asad* ("there was not").

**nāstika** unorthodox; heretic who denies the authority of the Veda.

**nāstikya** irreligious.

**naṭarāja** title of Śiva the dancer.

**nātha** lord; *Viśva-nātha*: the Lord of the Universe.

**nigama** Veda; authoritative scripture.

**nigamana** quotation (from the Veda); in logic: deduction, conclusion.

**nīla** dark blue, *Śiva nīlakaṇṭha* is Śiva with a dark blue throat.

**nimeṣa** moment (shortest measure of time).

**nimitta** cause.

**nirguṇa** without qualities or attributes.

**nirukta** classical dictionary of etymology.

**niṣkala** without part; undivided, complete.

**niṣkāma** without desire.

**niṣkāma karma** action done without selfish motive.

**nīti** "ethics," rules of conduct.

**nitya** eternal.

**nivṛtti** withdrawal.

**niyama** (negative) commandment.

**nṛsinha** man-lion; one of the *avatāras* of Viṣṇu.

**nyāya** rule, method; motto; logic; syllogism.

**pada** foot; verse.

**pāda** section (passage) of a text.

**padārtha** category (in Vaiśeṣika system).

**padma** lotus.

**pādya** water for washing of feet in ritual.

**pañca** five; e.g., *pañcāgni*: five fires.

**pañcāṅga** the traditional Indian calendar.

**pañcagavya** the five products of the cow.

**pāñcarātra** branch of Vaiṣṇavism.

**pañcatantra** famous collection of allegorical animal stories.

**pañcāyat(a)** "council of five," the traditional caste or village authority.

**pañcāyātana-pūjā** worship of five gods.

**pāṇḍu** pale; proper name of father of the Pāṇḍavas.

**paṇḍa** family Brahmin who performs the traditional rituals.

**paṇḍit(a)** learned man; honorific title.

**pantha** path, way; e.g., *Kabīr-panth(a)* is the religious sect founded by Kabīr.

**pāpa** sin.

**para** beyond; transcending; supreme; liberation.

**paradravyābhīpsā** desiring another's property.

**paradroha** injurious in speech or deed.

**paramārthika** that which concerns ultimate reality.

**paraṃparā** (chain of) tradition.

**paraśurāma** Rāma with the battle-axe; an *avatāra* of Viṣṇu.

**paricaraṇa** attending; rendering service.

**parikrama** circumambulation.

**paritrāṇa** deliverance.

**paruṣa** harsh speech.

**pārvatī** daughter of the mountains; name of Śiva's consort.

**pāśa** fetter.

**pāṣaṇḍa** heretic; unbeliever; hypocrite.

**paśu** beast; cattle; in Śaiva Siddhānta: unliberated.

**paśupati** lord of the animals; name of Śiva.

**patra** "leaf," scripture, scroll.

**pattiśa** spear.

**pāvana** purifying; holy; fire.

**pavitra** ritually pure; holy.

**phala** fruit; result of an action.

**piṇḍa** small ball of rice offered to ancestors: oblation.

**piṅgalā** one of the major vessels in the body.

**piśāca** imp; ogre.

**pitāmahā** grandfather, often used as the proper name of Brahmā.

**pitṛ** ancestor, forefather.

**pitṛyāna** the path of the ancestor (followed by the departed).

**plakṣa** name of a tree (*ficus Indica*).

**prabhā** splendor.

**pradakṣinā** respect shown through certain actions.

**pradhāna** primary basis; source; in Sāṁkhya system, ground from which everything develops.

**prajāpati** Lord of creatures; creator.

**prakāśa** splendor.

**prakṛti** matter; nature.

**pralaya** dissolution of the world.

**pramāda** error.

**pramāṇa** logical proof; means of cognition.

**prāṇa** life breath.

**praṇava** the mantra OM.

**prāṇayama** breath control.

**prārabdha** remainder; karma left over from former births.

**prārthana** prayer.

**prasthāna trayī** triad of scriptural authorities (Upaniṣads, Bhagavadgītā, Brahmasūtras).

**pratibimba** reflection; mirror image.

**pratijñā** recognition; proposition.

**pratisarga** dissolution of the universe.

**pratisiddha maithuna** unlawful liaison.

**pratyabhijñā** recognition.

**pratyakṣa** immediate (sense) perception.

**pravṛtti** inclination; active liberation.

**prāyaścitta** atonement (through certain prescribed acts).

**prayatna** effort.

**premā** love; used as technical term for spiritual love.

**preta** soul of a deceased who has not received offerings.

**prīti** amity; love.

**priyavācana** gentle of speech.

**pṛthivī** earth.

**pūjā** worship.

**punarjanma** rebirth.

**punarmṛtyu** redeath.

**puṇḍarīkākṣa** lotus eyed.

**puṇya** merit.

**pura** fort.

**purāṇa** ancient; class of Hindu scriptures.

**pūrṇimā** full moon.

**purohita** class of Vedic priests.

**puruṣa** man; person; supreme being; spirit.

**puruṣārtha** aim of human life.

**puruṣottama** supreme person.

**puṣpa** flower.

**puṣṭi-mārga** special form of *bhakti*, "way of grace."

**putra** son.

**rāga** passion; in music; basic tune.

**rāgānuga bhakti** "passionate love"; special form of *bhakti*.

**rājanīti** statecraft, polity.

**rajas** excitement; one of the basic three *guṇas*.

**rājayoga** "royal way"; Patañjali's Yoga system.

**rajñī** splendor.

**rakṣasa** goblin.

**raktāṃbara** red clothed; an appellation for Buddhist monks.

**rāma** main hero of the *Rāmāyaṇa*; general name for God.

**rāmarājya** Rāma's rule; "kingdom of God."

**rasa** juice; sentiment.

**rathamelā** chariot feast.

**rati** pleasure; proper name of the consort of the god of Love.

**ratna** jewel; pearl; often used as an honorific title.

**rātri** night.

**romāñcā** horripilation; gooseflesh; enthusiasm.

**ṛk** hymn.

**ṛṣi** seer; wise man.

**ṛta** (Vedic) law of the world (moral and cosmic).

**ṛtvik** class of Vedic priests.

**rudra** reddish; name of Vedic god; name of Śiva, especially in his frightful aspect.

**rudrākṣa** "Rudra's eye"; rough, round seed of an Indian shrub, used in garlands by Śaivites.

**rukminī** Kṣṣṇa's spouse.

**śabda** sound; word; scriptural authority.

**saccidānanda** the Supreme Being (being, consciousness, bliss).

**sadācāra** morality; good behavior.

**ṣaḍdarśana** the six orthodox systems of Hindu philosophy.

**sādhana** means (to gain liberation).

**sādhaka** one who practices a *sādhana*.

**sādhāraṇa dharma** common law; religion common to all humankind.

**sādhu** "holy man"; mendicant.

**sādhvī** a female ascetic.

**sāgara** sea; great mass of things.

**saguṇa** with qualities.

**saguṇa brahman** *brahman* with attributes.

**sahaja** natural; innate.

**sahāmārga** one of the practices of Śaivasiddhānta.

**śākha** branch; a school of thought or practice.

**sākṣātkāra** bodily vision of the supreme.

**sākṣī** witness; the Supreme as present in humans.

**śākta** follower of Śakti cult.

**śakti** power; name of Śiva's consort.

**śālagrāma** ammonite; symbol under which Viṣṇu is worshipped.

**sālokya** sharing the same world; one of the stages of liberation.

**samādhī** deep concentration; death; memorial.

**sāman** Vedic tune.

**sāmānya** equality; category in Vaiśeṣika.

**samāvāya** similarity.

**samāveśa** togetherness.

**saṃbhoga** enjoyment.

**saṃdhyā** twilight; dusk and dawn; prayers recited at dawn.

**saṃdhyā-bhāṣā** words with double meaning.

**saṃhitā** collection; name of class of authoritative scriptures.

**samīpa** nearness; stage of liberation.

**samjñā** understanding.

**sāṁkhya** figure, number; name of philosophical system.

**saṁkīrtana** congregational chanting.

**samnyāsa** renunciation.

**samnyāsi** ascetic, homeless mendicant.

**sampat** wealth.

**saṃpradāya** a religious order or sect.

**saṃsāra** world; connoting constant cyclic change.

**saṃskāra** rites; "sacraments."

**saṃskṛta** artfully composed, refined, name of old Indian high language.

**saṃyama** concentration.

**sanātana dharma** eternal law; traditional designation of "Hinduism."

**śaṅkha** conch shell.

**sanmārga** "the true way"; highest stage in Śaivasiddhānta.

**saṇskṛti** culture.

**śānta** sentiment of peacefulness.

**santāpa** heat; compunction; atonement.

**śanti** peace.

**santoṣa** contentment.

**śaraṇāgatī** seeking refuge.

**sarga** creation; emanation.

**sāraṅga** bowstring.

**śarīra** body.

**sārūpa** of equal form.

**sarvauṣadhi** mixture of all (healing) herbs.

**śāstra** doctrine; treatise.

**śāstri** one who knows the traditional doctrine; BA.

**sat** being, truth.

**satī** "faithful"; wife who dies with deceased husband.

**śatasahasrasaṃhitā** collection of one hundred thousand verses; proper name for the *Mahābhārata*.

**satsaṅg(a)** "gathering of the righteous," religious meeting.

**sattva** being; nature; virtue; one of the three *guṇas*.

**satyam** truth; reality.

**śauca** purity.

**saulabhya** benevolence.

**sauśilya** kindness.

**śava** corpse; Śiva without *i* (*śakti*) is *śava*.

**savitṛ** sun god.

**sāyujya** togetherness.

**śeṣa** the endless, immortal world serpent upon which Viṣṇu rests.

**sevā** service.

**siddha** accomplished; saint.

**siddhi** accomplishment; in Yoga, extraordinary faculties.

**śikhā** tuft of hair on the crown of the head.

**śikhara** summit; spirelike apex over central sanctuary.

**śīkṣā** instruction.

**śīla** good behavior; morality.

**śirīṣa** a tree (acacia).

**sītā** furrow; proper name of Rāma's consort.

**śloka** double verse.

**smāsana** cremation ground.

**smṛti** what has been committed to memory; title of a certain class of scriptures.

**snāna** (ritual) bath.

**śoka** sorrow.

**soma** intoxicating drink used in Vedic sacrifices.

**spaṇḍaśāstra** school of Kāśmīra Śaivism; treatise on vibrations.

**sphoṭa** boil; idea; connection between letter and meaning.

**spṛhā** worldliness.

**śraddhā** faith.

**śrāddha** last rites.

**śrautasūtras** ritual texts dealing with public Vedic sacrifices.

**śravaṇa** listening to the recitation of religious texts.

**śrī** fortune; proper name of Viṣṇu's consort; sir.

**śrīvatsa** mark on Viṣṇu's body signifying Lakṣmī's presence.

**śṛṅgāra** feeling of erotic love.

**sṛṣṭhi** creation; emanation.

**śruti** what has been revealed and heard.

**steya** stealing.

**sthūla** gross material.

**stithi** maintenance.

**stotra** hymn in praise of God.

**strīdhana** dowry, a woman's personal property.

**śubha** auspicious.

**sūcanā** calumny.

**śuddha** pure.

**śuddhi** ritual of purification (readmission into caste).

**suṣila** bright.

**sūkṣma** subtle.

**sūkta** Vedic hymn.

**sūnā** activity (or place) where life is harmed.

**śūnya** zero; nothing; emptiness.

**sura** (inferior) divine being.

**surā** intoxicating drink.

**sūrya** sun.

**suṣumnā** one of the main vessels in the body.

**suṣupti** dreamless deep sleep.

**sūta** bard; charioteer.

**sūtra** aphoristic text; thread.

**svadharma** one's own duties.

**svādhyāya** (private) study of Vedic texts.

**svāhā** exclamation at offering to *devas*.

**svāmī** lord; Reverend.

**svapna** dream.

**svarga** heaven.

**svārtha** self-contained.

**svāstika** sign of auspiciousness.

**svatantra** free.

**svayambhū** being of itself; name for Supreme Being.

**śyāma** dusky; epithet of Kṛṣṇa.

**tamas** darkness; dullness; one of the three *guṇas*.

**tantra** loom; system of practices; branch of Hinduism.

**tapas** heat; energy.

**tapasvī** ascetic; one who has accumulated much merit through self-mortification.

**tarka** logic; debate.

**tarpaṇa** offering of water to ancestors.

**tat** that; designation of the Supreme Being.

**tat-etat** this is that; identity of Self and Supreme.

**tattva** principle; nature; reality, element.

**tejas** splendor; light; heat.

**ṭīkā** subcommentary.

**tīlaka** mark on forehead.

**tirobhāva** disappearance.

**ṭippaṇī** gloss.

**tīrtha** fording place; place of pilgrimage on holy river.

**tīrthayātra** pilgrimage.

**tiru** (Tamil) holy; also used as honorific: "Sir."

**tiru-kural** title of famous Tamil text.

**tithi** moon day.

**traividyā** knowledge of the three Vedas.

**tretāyuga** third world age.

**trilocana** three-eyed; name of Śiva.

**triloka** the three worlds.

**trimārga** literally, "three ways"; the collective name for the paths of works, devotion, knowledge.

**tripuṇḍra** Śiva's trident; sign on the forehead.

**triśaṇku** name of a constellation halfway between heaven and earth; name of a mythical king of Ayodhyā.

**tristhalī** the three most important places of pilgrimage, viz., Prayāga (Allahabad), Kāśī (Banares), and Gāyā (Bodhgaya).

**trivarga** the triad of *dharma*, *artha*, *kāma*.

**tṛṣṇa** thirst; greed for life.

**tulasī** a small tree (holy basil), sacred to Viṣṇu.

**turīya** the fourth; highest stage of consciousness.

**turyātīta** beyond the fourth; highest stage in some Hindu schools who claim to transcend the Vedāntic *turīya*.

**tyāgī** renouncer; ascetic.

**udāhāraṇa** example, illustration; part of Nyāya syllogism.

**udbhava** appearance.

**uḍaṃbara** Indian fig tree, sacred to Śiva.

**udyama** exertion; rising or lifting up.

**upadeśa** advice; religious instruction.

**upādhi** attribute; title; deceit.

**upagītā** "lesser Gītā."

**upamāna** analogy.

**upaṃśū** prayer uttered in a whisper.

**upanayana** initiation; investiture with sacred thread.

**upāṅga** auxiliary sciences or texts to Vedāṅgas.

**upaniṣad** class of authoritative scriptures; secret doctrine.

**upapurāṇa** lesser Purāṇa.

**upāsana** worship.

**upavāsa** (religious) fasting.

**ūrdhva** upwards.

**utsava bera** processional image.

**vācika** voiced audibly.

**vahana** conveyance.

**vaicitriya** manifoldness; distraction.

**vaidhi-bhakti** devotion expression itself through ritual worship.

**vaikuṇṭha** Viṣṇu's heaven.

**vairāgi(nī)** ascetic (f).

**vairāgya** asceticism.

**vaiśeṣika** name of a philosophical system.

**vaiśya** member of third varṇa.

**vajra** diamond; thunderbolt.

**vāk** voice; word.

**vālmīka** ant's hill.

**vāmācāra** left-handed way (in Tantra).

**vāmana** dwarf; one of the *avatāras* of Viṣṇu.

**vaṃśa** genealogy.

**vānaprastha** forest dweller; third stage in a Brahmin's life.

**varāha** boar; one of the *avatāras* of Viṣṇu.

**varṇāśramadharma** social system of the Hindus based on a partition into four classes and four stages of life.

**vāstuvidyā** architecture.

**vaṭa** the fig tree.

**vātsalya** love toward a child.

**vāyu** wind; wind god.

**veda** (sacred) knowledge; revelation; scripture.

**vedāṅga** limb of the Veda; auxiliary sciences.

**vedānta** end of the Veda; Upaniṣads; a philosophical system.

**vedī** altar for Vedic sacrifices.

**vibhava** emanation.

**vibhuti** supernatural power.

**videha** without a body.

**vidhi** ritual.

**vidyā** knowledge.

**vijñānamaya** made of knowledge.

**vinaya** discipline.

**vipra** learned, Brahmin.

**vīra** hero.

**viraja** pure, free from passion.

**virāṭ** first product of Brahman; universe.

**vīrya** heroism.

**viṣāda** despair.

**viśeṣa** propriety.

**viśiṣṭa** qualification.

**viśvarūpa** universal form.

**vitarka** debate; logical argument.

**viveka** discrimination.

**vrata** vow; celebration.

**vrātya** mendicant; ethnic group; Supreme Being.

**vṛddhi** growth, increase.

**vṛtti** being; condition; fluctuation; activity, means of subsistence.

**vyākaraṇa** grammar.

**vyakta** manifest; revealed.

**vyāpāra** function.

**vyāsa** arranger; proper name of Vedic sage credited with the compilation of the Vedas, the *Mahābhārata*, and the Purāṇas.

**vyavahāra** livelihood; the world of senses.

**vyūha** emanation; special manifestation of Viṣṇu.

**yajña** Vedic sacrifice.

**yajñopavīta** sacred thread.

**yajus** rites.

**yakṣa** goblin; tree-spirit.

**yama** god of the netherworld; restraint (Yoga).

**yantra** machine; meditation device.

**yatanīya** something to be accomplished.

**yati** wandering ascetic.

**yatidharma** rules for ascetics.

**yātrā** pilgrimage, festival.

**yoga** yoke; name of a practical philosophical system.

**yojana** "league" (either four, five, or nine miles).

**yoni** source; womb.

**yuga** world era.

# Bibliography


Abbot, J. E. (ed. and trans.) *The Poet Saints of Maharastra*, 12 vols. Poona: Scottish Mission Industries, 1926–41.

Abhyankar, V. S. (rev. and ed.) *Nyāyakośa* by Bhīmācārya. Pune: Bhandarkar Oriental Research Institute, 1978.

*Āgama Prāmānyam* by Yamunācārya. J. A. B. van Buitenen (ed. and trans.) Madras Ramanuja Research Society 1971.

Agarwal, A. "Can Hindu Beliefs and Values Help India Meet its Ecological Crisis?" In C. K. Chapple and M. E. Tucker (eds.) *Hinduism and Ecology*, 165–79.

Agarwal, V. "A Reply to Michael Witzel's 'Ein Fremdling im Ṛgveda.'" *www.voiceofdharma.org.*

Id. "The Aryan Migration Theory: Fabricating Literary Evidence." *www.bharatvani.org.*

Agrawal, D. P. "The Technology of the Indus Civilization." In R. K. Sharma (ed.), *Indian Archeology, New Perspectives*, 83–91. Delhi: Agam Kala Prakashan, 1982.

Agrawala, V. S. *India as Known to Pāṇini*, 2d ed. Varanasi: Prithvi Prakasan, 1963.

Id. *Matsya-Purāṇa: A Study*. Varanasi: All-India Kashiraj Trust, 1963.

Id. "Mother Earth." In *Nehru Abhinandan Granth*, 490 ff. Calcutta: Nehru Abhinandan Granth Committee, 1949.

*Ahirbhudhnyasaṃhitā*, 2 vols. M. D. Ramanujacarya (ed.); 2d rev. ed. V. Krishṅamacharya (ed.). Adyar: Adyar Library, 1966.

*Agni Purāṇa*. Poona: Anandashram, 1957.

*Agni Purāṇa*, 2 vols., M. N. Dutt (trans.). Reprint Varanasi: Chowkhambha, 1967.

Aiyangar, S. K. *Some Contributions of South India to Indian Culture*. Calcutta: Calcutta University, 1942.

Aiyar, C. P. Ramaswamy. *Fundamentals of Hindu Faith and Culture*. Trivandrum: Government Press, 1944.

Aiyar, S. P. *The Politics of Mass Violence in India*. Bombay: Manaktalas, 1967.

Aiyer, A. Nataraja, and S. Lakshminarasimha Shastri. *The Traditional Age of Śrī Śaṅkarāchārya and the Maths*. Madras: private publication, 1962.

Aiyer, V. G. R. *The Economy of a South Indian Temple*. Annamalai: Annamalai University, 1946.

*Ajitāgama*, 2 vols., N. R. Bhatt (ed.). Pondichery: Institut Français d'Indologie, 1964–1967.
Ali, S. *The Congress Ideology and Programme*. New Delhi: People's Publishing House, 1958.
Ali, S. M. *The Geography of the Purāṇas*. New Delhi: People's Publishing House, 1966.
Alisaunder. *Alexander and Dindimus*. W. W. Skeat, (ed.) Latin text. Early English Text Society: Extra Series No. 31, 1876; reprint 1930.
Allchin, B. and R. Allchin. *The Rise of Civilization in India and Pakistan*. Cambridge: Cambridge University Press, 1982.
Alper, H. P. "Śiva and the Ubiquity of Consciousness," *JIPH* (1976): pp. 345–407.
Alsdorf, L. *Varuṇa und die Wasser*. Göttingen: Vandenhoek and Ruprecht, 1951.
Id. *Varuṇa und das Ṛta*. Göttingen: Vandenhoek and Ruprecht, 1959.
Altekar, A. D. "Hinduism, A Static Structure or a Dynamic Force?" In: *Nehru Abhinandan Granth*, 421–425. Calcutta: NAG Committee 1949.
Id. *The Position of Women in Hindu Civilization from Prehistoric Times to the Present Day*. Banares: Motilal Banarsidass, 1956.
Id. *Sources of Hindu Dharma in Its Socio-Religious Aspect*. Sholapur: Institute of Public Administration, 1952.
Id. *State and Government in Ancient India*, 4th ed.Delhi: Motilal Banarsidass, 1962.
Ambedkar, B. R. *What Congress and Gandhi Have Done to the Untouchables*, 2nd ed. Bombay: Thacker and Co., 1946.
Id. *Buddha and His Dharma*. Bombay: Siddhartha College Publications, 1957.
Id. *The Untouchables*. Bombay: Thacker and Co. 1948.
Amore, R. C., and L. D. Shinn. *Lustful Maidens and Ascetic Kings: Buddhist and Hindu Stories of Life*, New York: Oxford University Press, 1981.
Anand, Mulk Raj. *The Hindu View of Art*, Bombay: Popular, 1957.
Id. *Coolie*. Bombay: Kutub, 1957.
Id. *Untouchable*. Bombay: Jaico, 1956.
*Ancient Indian Tradition and Mythology*. (English translation of all the *Mahāpurāṇas*.) Delhi: Motilal Banarsidass, 1971H.
Anderson, W. K. and S. D. Dhamle. *The Brotherhood in Saffron: The Rāṣṭrīya Swayamesevak Sangh and Hindu Revivalism*. Boulder, Colo.: Westview Press, 1987.
Animananda, B. *The Blade: Life and Work of Brahmabhandav Upadhyaya*. Calcutta: Roy and Son, n.d.
*Aṇuvākhyāna of Madhva*. Bombay: Nirnaya Sagara Press. S. S. Rao, trans. 2d ed. Tirupati: 1936.
*Aparoksānubhūti of Śaṅkarācārya*, 2d ed. Swami Vimuktananda (trans.). Calcutta: Ramakrishna Math, 1955.
Appadorai, A. *Economic Conditions in Southern India 1000–1500* AD, 2 vols. Madras: University of Madras, 1936.
Appasamy, A. J. *Sundar Singh: A Biography*. Madras: CLS, 1966.
Apte, S. S. "Viśva Hindū Pariṣad: Confluence of Hindu Society," *Hindū Viśva* (January 1966): 87–89.
Apte, V. M. *Ṛgvedic Mantras in Their Ritual Setting in the Gṛhyasūtras*, Poona: Deccan College Research Institute, 1950.
Id. "The Vedāṇgas." CHI vol. 1:289–92.

Arapura, J. G. *Hermeneutical Essays on Vedāntic Topics*. Delhi: Motilal Banarsidass, 1986.
Archer, W. G. *India and Modern Art*. London: Allan and Unwin, 1959.
Id. *Indian Miniatures*. Greenwich: New York Graphic Society, 1960.
Id. *The Loves of Krishna in Indian Painting and Poetry*. London: Allen and Unwin, 1957. New York: Grove Press (pb), 1957.
Ariarajah, S. W. *Hindus and Christians: A Century of Protestant Ecumenical Thought*. Grand Rapids: Eerdmans, 1991.
Armadio, B. A. "The World Made of Sound: Whitehead and Pythagorean Harmonics in the Context of Veda and the Science of Mantra." *Journal of Dharma* 17, 3 (1992):233–266.
*Arthapañcaka* by Lokācārya Pillai. T. Bheemacarya (ed. and trans.). Indore: Bharati Printing Press, 1972.
*Arthasaṅgraha of Laugākṣī Bhāskara*. D.V. Gokhale (trans.). Poona: Oriental Book Agency, 1932.
Ashish, M. "The *Sādhu* in Our Life." *Seminar* 200 (April 1976):12–18.
Assisi, Francis C. "The Hinduization of America." Indolink, June 2005.
Athalye, D. *Life of Lokmanya Tilak*. Poona: A. Chiploonkar, 1921.
Id. *Neo-Hinduism*. Bombay: Tareporevala, 1932.
*Atharvaveda*, 2 vols. W. D. Whitney (trans.). In *HOS*, 1902. Reprint Varanasi: Chowkhamba, 1962.
*The Atharvaveda Saṃhitā*. R. Roth and W. D. Whitney (eds.). Berlin: 1856.
*Ātmabodha of Śaṅkarācārya*, 2d ed. Swami Nikhilananda (trans.). Mylapore: Ramakrishna Math, 1962.
Atreya, B. L. *The Philosophy of the Yogavāsiṣṭha*. Adyar: Adyar Library, 1936.
Auboyer, J. *Daily Life in Ancient India from Approximately 200 BC to AD 700*. New York: Macmillan, 1965.
Aufrecht, T. *Die Hymnen des Ṛgveda*, 2d ed. Bonn: A. Marcus, 1877.
Aurobindo, Śrī. *Essays on the Gītā*, Pondichery: Sri Aurobindo Ashram, 1928.
Ayrookuzhiel, A. M. A. *The Sacred in Popular Hinduism: An Empirical Study in Chirakkal, North Malabar*. Madras: CLS 1983.
Ayyar, C. V. N. *Origin and Early History of Śaivism in South India*. Madras: University of Madras, 1936.
Ayyar, P. V. J. *South Indian Festivities*. Madras: Higginbothams, 1921.
Baden-Powell, B. H. *The Indian Village Community*. Reprint New Haven: Yale University Press, 1958.
Id. *Land Systems of British India*, 3 vols. Oxford: Oxford University Press, 1892.
Bailey, G. M. "Brahmā, Pṛthu and the Theme of the Earth-Milker in Hindu Mythology." *Indo-Iranian Journal* 23 (1981):105–16.
Id. "Notes on the Worship of Brahmā in Ancient India." *Annali dell' Istituto Orientale di Napoli* 39 (1979): 1–170.
Baird, R. D., (ed.). *Religion in Modern India*. Delhi: Manohar, 1981.
Bakker, H. "On the Origin of the Sāṁkhya Psychology." *WZKSA* 26 (1982): 117–48.
*Bālarāma Vedāntasūtrabhāṣya*, B. D. Basu, (trans.). *SBH*, vol. 5. Allahabad: Panini Office, 1934.
Balasubramanian, R. *Advaita Vedānta*. Madras: University of Madras, 1976.
Id. *The Mysticism of Poygai Āḷvār*. Madras: Vedanta Publications, 1976.

Id. *Some Problems in the Epistemology and Metaphysics of Rāmānuja*. Professor L. Venkataraman Endowment Lectures 1975–76, Madras: University of Madras, 1978.

Id. (ed. and trans.). *The Taittirīyopaniṣad Bhāṣya-Vārtika of Sureśvara*, Madras: Radhakrishnan Institute for the Advanced Study of Philosophy, University of Madras, 1984.

Balasundaram, T. S. *The Golden Anthology of Ancient Tamil Literature*, 3 vols. Madras: South India Śaiva Siddhānta Book Publishing Society, 1959–1960.

Balsara, J. F. *Problems of Rapid Urbanization in India*. Bombay: Manaktala, 1964.

Banerjea, A. K. *Philosophy of Gorakhnāth*. Gorakhpur: Mahant Dig Vijai Nath Trust, Gorakhnath Temple, 1962.

Banerjea, J. N. *The Development of Hindu Iconography*, 2d ed. Calcutta: University of Calcutta, 1956.

Banerjea, S. C. *Dharma Sūtras: A Study of Their Origin and Development*. Calcutta: Punthi Pustak, 1962.

Banerjee, G. N. *Hellenism in Ancient India*, Delhi: Munshiram Manoharlal, 1961.

Banerjee, N. V. *The Spirit of Indian Philosophy*. New Delhi: Arnold-Heinemann, 1958.

Barthwal, C. P. "Rashtriya Swayamsevak Sangh: Origin, Structure and Ideology." *Indian Political Science Review* (December 1983): 23–37.

Barua, B. M. *History of Pre-Buddhistic Indian Philosophy*. Calcutta: Calcutta University, 1921.

de Bary, W. T. (gen. ed.). *Sources of Indian Tradition*. New York: Columbia University Press, 1958.

Barz, R. K. *The Bhakti Sect of Vallabhācārya*. Faridabad: Thompson Press, 1976.

Id. "Vallabha." *ER*, vol. 15, 183 f.

Id. and M. Thiel-Horstmann (eds.). *Living Texts from India*. Wiesbaden: Harrassowitz, 1989

Basham, A. L. *History and Doctrines of the Ajīvikas*. London: Luzac, 1951.

Id. *The Wonder That Was India*. New York: Grove Press, 1959.

Baynes, A. *Indian Ethnography: Castes and Tribes*. London: 1912.

Beal, S. *Si-Yu-Ki: Buddhist Records of the Western World*. London: 1884; reprint Delhi: Oriental Books Reprint Corporation, 1969.

Beals, A. R. *Gopalpur: A South Indian Village*, New York: Holt Rinehart and Winston, 1965.

Beane, W. C. Myth, *Cult and Symbols in Śākta Hinduism: A Study of the Indian Mother Goddess*. Leiden: Brill, 1977.

Bechert, H. *The Dating of the Historical Buddha*. Goettingen: Vandenhoek and Ruprecht, 1991.

Bechert, H. and G. von Simson. *Einführung in die Indologie*. Darmstadt: Wissenschaftliche Buchgesellschaft, 1979.

Beck, B. (ed.). *Folktales of India*. Chicago: University of Chicago Press, 1987.

Beck, G. *Sonic Theology: Hinduism and Sacred Sound*. University of South Carolina Press, 1993.

Belvalkar, S. K. *Shree Gopal Basu Malik Lectures on Vedānta Philosophy*. Poona: Bilvakunja, 1929.

Belvalkar, S. K. and R. D. Ranade. *History of Indian Philosophy Volume II: The Creative Period. Volume III:* Mysticism in *Mahārāṣtra*. Poona: Bilvakunja, 1927 and 1932.

*Bengali Religious Lyrics: Śākta*, E. J. Thompson and A. M. Spencer (trans.). Calcutta: Association Press, 1923.

Benz, E. *Indische Einflüsse auf die frühchristliche Theologie*. Mainz: Mainzer Akademie der Wissenschaften, 1951.

Bernard, T. *Haṭha Yoga*. New York: S. Weiser, 1944.

Bernstorff, D. "Das Kastensystem im Wandel." E. Weber and R. Töpelman (eds.), In *Indien in Deutschland*, 29–51. Frankfurt am Main: Peter Lang, 1990.

Berreman, G. D. *Hindus of the Himālayas*. Berkeley: University of California Press, 1963.

Besant, A., *Hindu Ideals*. Adyar: Theosophical Publishing House, 1904.

Id. *Wake Up, India*. Adyar: Theosophical Publishing House, 1913.

Id. *Theosophy and World Problems*. Adyar: Theosophical Publishing House, 1922.

Id and Bhagavan Das, *Advanced Textbook of Hindu Religion and Ethics*. Adyar: Theosophical Publishing House, 1913.

Beteille, A. *Caste, Class and Power: Changing Patterns of Stratification in a Tanjore Village*. Berkeley: University of California Press, 1965.

Id. *Castes, Old and New*, New York: Asia Publishing House, 1969.

Betty, L. S. (trans.). *Vādirāja's Refutation of Śaṅkara's Non-Dualism: Clearing the Way for Theism*. Delhi: Motilal Banarsidass, 1978.

*Bhagavadgītā*. F. Edgerton (trans.). Cambridge, Mass.: Harvard University Press, 1944.

*Bhagavadgītā*. S. Radhakrishnan. (trans.). London: Allen and Unwin, 1956.

*Bhagavadgītā*. R. C. Zaehner. (trans.) Oxford University Press, 1969.

*Bhagavadgītābhāṣya* by Madhvācārya. Subba Rao (trans.). Madras, 1906.

Bhagavat, H. R. (ed.). *Minor Works of Śrī Śaṅkarācārya*, 2d ed. Poona Oriental Series No. 8. Poona: Oriental Book Agency, 1952.

*Bhāgavata Purāṇa*, 2 vols. (Sanskrit text and English trans.) Gorakhpur: Gita-Press, 1952–60.

*Bhaktidarśana*. Swami Jnanandaji Maharaj (ed.) Bombay: Nirnaya Sagara Press, Sake 1844.

*Bhaktirasāmṛtasindhu of Rūpa Goswāmi*. Vijendra Snataka (ed.). Delhi: Dilli Visvavidyalaya, 1963; Swami Bon Maharaj (trans.). 3 vols. Vṛndāvana: Institute of Oriental Philosophy, 1964–78. New trans. D. Haberman. Delhi: Motilal Banarsidass, 2003.

*The Bhāmatī of Vācaspati on Śaṅkara's Brahmasūtrabhāsya*. S. S. Suryanarayana Sastri and C. Kunhan Raja (eds. and trans.). Adyar: Theosophical Publishing House, 1933.

Bhandarkar, R. G. *Vaiṣṇavism, Śaivism and Minor Religious Systems*. Reprint Varanasi: Indological Book House, 1965.

Bharadwaj, K. D. *The Philosophy of Rāmānuja*. New Delhi: Sir Sankar Lall Charitable Trust Society, 1958.

Bharati, Agehananda (L. Fischer). *The Ochre Robe*. Seattle: University of Washington Press, 1962.

Id. "Psychological Approaches to Indian Studies: More Cons than Pros," *The Indian Review* 1, 1 (1978): 71–75.

Id. *The Tantric Tradition*. London: Rider and Company, 1965.

Bhardwaj, Surinder Mohan. *Hindu Places of Pilgrimage in India: A Study in Cultural Geography*. Berkeley: University of California Press, 1973.

Bharill, C. *Social and Political Ideas of B. R. Ambedkar.* Jaipur: Aalekh Publications, 1977.
*Bhartrhaṛi: Vākyapādīya*, K. V. Abhyankar and Acharya V. P. Limaye (eds.). University of Poona Sanskrit and Prakrit Series. Poona: University of Poona, 1965.
*Bhāṣapariccheda with Siddhānta Muktāvalī of Viśvanātha Nyāyapañcānana.* Swami Madhavananda (trans.), Calcutta: Advaita Ashrama, 1954.
Bhatt, G. H. "The School of Vallabha." CHI, vol. 3, 348.
Bhatt, G. P. *The Epistemology of the Bhaṭṭa School of Pūrva Mīmāṃsā.* Banares: Chowkhamba, 1954.
Bhattacharji, S. *The Indian Theogony: A Comparative Study of Indian Mythology from the Vedas to the Purāṇas.* Cambridge: Cambridge University Press, 1970.
Bhattacharya, H. (gen. ed.). *The Cultural Heritage of India*, 6 vols., 2d ed. Calcutta: Ramakrishna Mission Institute of Culture, 1957–62.
Bhattacharya, H. D. "Tantrik Religion." In *HCIP*, vol. 4.
Bhattacharya, K. C. *Studies in Vedāntism.* Calcutta: University of Calcutta, 1909.
Id. *Studies in Philosophy*, 2 vols. Calcutta: Progressive Publishers, 1956.
Bhattacharya, S. "The Concept of *Bideha* and *Prakṛti-Laya* in the Sāṁkhya-Yoga System." *ABORI* 48–49 (1968): 305–12.
Bhattacharya, T. *The Canons of Indian Art: A Study of Vāstuvīdya*, 2d ed. Calcutta: Firma K. L. Mukhopadhyay, 1963.
Id. *The Cult of Brahmā.* Patna: C. Bhatacarya, 1957.
Bhattacharyya, M. "Hindu Religion and Women's Rights." *Religion and Society* 35, 1 (1988): 52–61.
Bhattacharyya, N. N. *History of the Tantric Religion.* Delhi: Manohar, 1982.
*Bhattojī-Dīksita: Siddhānta Kaumudī*, 2 vols. Srisa Candra Vasu, (ed. and trans.). Reprint Delhi: Motilal Banarsidass, 1964.
Bhave, Vinoba. *Bhoodan-Yajna.* Ahmedabad: Navajivan, 1954.
Id. *Sarvodaya and Communism.* Tanjore: Sarvodaya Prachuralaya, 1957.
Bhujle, S. and M. N. Vahia, "Calculation of *Tithis*: An Extension of *Sūryasiddhānta* Formalism." IJHSc 41.2 (June 2006): 133–150.
Biardeau, M. *Théorie de la connaissance et philosophie de la parole dans le brahmanisme classique.* Paris: Mouton, 1964.
Bihari, B., *Minstrels of God*, 2 vols. Bombay: Bharatiya Vidya Bhavan, 1956.
Id. *Bhakta Mīrā*, Bombay: Bharatiya Vidya Bhavan, 1961.
Id. *Sufis, Mystics and Yogis of India.* Bombay: Bharatiya Vidya Bhavan, 1962.
Bishop, D. H. (ed.). *Indian Thought: An Introduction.* New York: John Wiley and Sons, 1975.
Id. (ed.). *Thinkers of the Indian Renaissance.* New York: Wiley Eastern, 1982.
Biswas, A. K. "Brass and Zink Metallurgy in the Ancient and mediaeval World: India's Primacy and the Technology Transfer to the West." IJHSc 41.2 (June 2006):159–174.
Blasi, A. J. "Ritual as a Form of the Religious Mentality." *Sociological Analysis* 46, 1 (1985): 59–72.
Bloomfield, M. *The Religion of the Veda.* New York: G. B. Putnam's, 1908.
Id. *Vedic Concordance.* Reprint Delhi: Motilal Banarsidass, 1996.
Boethlingk, O. and R. Roth (eds.). *Sanskrit Wörterbuch*, 7 vols. Originally published in St. Petersburg 1853–1875, second edition 1879, reprint Delhi: Motilal Banarsidass 1991.

Bohm, D. *Wholeness and the Implicate Order*. London: Routledge and Keegan Paul, 1980.

Bolle, K. W. (trans.). *The Bhagavadgītā, a New Translation*. Berkeley: University of California Press, 1979.

Boner, A., S. R. Sarma and R. P. Das. *New Light on the Sun Temple of Koṇārka: Four Unpublished Manuscripts Relating to Construction History and Ritual of This Temple*. Varanasi: Chowkhambha Sanskrit Series Office, 1972.

Bose, D. N. *Tantras: Their Philosophy and Occult Secrets*, 3rd ed. Calcutta: Oriental Publishing Co., 1956.

Bose, N. K. "The Geographical Background of Indian Culture." In *CHI*, vol. 1, 3–16.

Id. *Peasant Life in India: A Study in Indian Unity and Diversity*. Calcutta: Anthropological Survey of India, 1961.

Bose, N. K. and D. Sen. "The Stone Age in India." In *CHI*, vol. 1, 2d ed., 1958, 93–109.

Boyd, R., *An Introduction to Indian Christian Theology*. Madras: Christian Literature Society, 1977.

Brahma, N. K. *Philosophy of Hindu Sādhana*. London: Trübner, 1932.

Brecher, M. *Nehru: A Political Biography*. London: Oxford University Press, 1959.

*Bṛhadāraṇyakopaniṣadbhāṣya* by Madhvācārya. Srisa Chandra Vasu (trans). In SBH, vol. 14. Allahabad: Panini Office, 1916.

*Bṛhaddevatā*. A. A. Macdonell (ed. and trans.). Reprint Delhi: Motilal Banarsidass, 1965.

*Bṛhati: Prabhākara Miśra's Subcommentary to the Śābarabhāsya*. (ed.) 3 vols. S. K. Ramanatha Sastri. Madras: University of Madras, 1931–33.

*Bṛhatsaṃhitā of Varāhamihira*. Pandit Acutyananda Jha Sarmana (ed. and Hindī trans.). Varanasi: Motilal Banarsidass, 1959.

*Bṛhatstotratnakara*, Bombay: Sri Venkatesvar Press, 1952.

Briggs, G. W. *The Chamars*, Calcutta: Association Press, 1920.

Id. *Gorakhanātha and Kānphaṭa Yogis*. Calcutta: Association Press, 1938.

Brockington, J. "The Sanskrit Epics." In G. Flood (ed.) *The Blackwell Companion to Hinduism*. 116–128.

Bronkhorst, J. and M. M. Deshpande (eds.). *Āryan and Non-Āryan in South Asia: Evidence, Interpretation and Ideology*. Columbia, Miss.: South Asia Books, 1999.

Brown, C. M. *God as Mother: A Feminine Theology in India: An Historical and Theological Study of the Brahmavaivarta Purāṇa*. Hartford, Vt: Claude Stark, 1974.

Id. "The Origin and Transmission of the Two *Bhāgavata Purāṇas*: A Canonical and Theological Dilemma." *JAAR* 51, 4 (1983):67–76

Brown, L. W. *The Indian Christians of St. Thomas*. London: Cambridge University Press, 1956.

Brown, P. *Indian Painting*, Calcutta: YMCA Publishing House, 1960.

Id. *Indian Architecture*, 4th ed. 2 vols. Bombay: Taraporevala, 1964.

Brown, W. N. *Man in the Universe: Some Continuities in Indian Thought*. Berkeley: University of California Press, 1966.

Id. *The United States and India and Pakistan*. Cambridge: Harvard University Press, 1963.

Id. *India and Indology: Selected Articles*. Rosane Rocher (ed.). Delhi: Motilal Banarsidass, 1978.

Brunton, P. *Maharsi and His Message*. London: Rider and Co., 1952.
Brzezinski, "Prabodhānananda Saraswatī: From Banaras to Braj." *BSOAS* 55,1(1992):52–75.
Id. "Prabodhānanda, Hita Harivamśa and the Rādhārasasudhānidhi." *BSOAS* 55,2 (1992):472–97.
Buck, H. M. and G. E. Yocum (eds.). *Structural Approaches to South Indian Studies*. Chambersburg: Wilson Books, 1974.
Buddhiraja, S. *The Bhagavadgītā: A Study*. Madras: Ganesh and Co., 1927.
Bühler, G. *Grundriss der indo-arischen Altertumskunde*. Strassburg: Trübner, 1847ff.
Id. (trans.). *The Laws of Manu*. SBE vol. 25, Reprint Delhi: Motilal Banarsidass, 1962.
Id.(ed.). *Encyclopedia of Indo-Aryan Research*.(1897). Reprint Varanasi: Indological Bookhouse, 1963.
Id. trans. *The Sacred Laws of the Āryas*. In *SBE*, vols. 2,14. Reprint Delhi: Motilal Banarsidass, 1964.
van Buitenen, J. A. B. *Tales of Ancient India*. New York: Bantam Books, 1961.
Id. "The Name Pāñcarātra." *HR* 1,2 (1961): 291–99.
Id. *Rāmānuja on the Bhagavadgītā*. Delhi: Motilal Banarsidass, 1965.
Bulcke, C. *Rāmakathā* [in Hindi]. Prayaga: Hindī Pariṣad Viśvavidyālaya, 1956.
Burrow, T. *The Sanskrit Language*. London: Faber and Faber, 1965.
Bussabarger, R. F. and B. D. Robins. *The Everyday Art of India*. New York: Dover, 1968.
Caitanya, K. *A New History of Sanskrit Literature*. Calcutta: KLM, 1964.
*Caitanyacaritāmṛta of Kṛṣṇadāsa Goswāmi*. 17 vols. A. C. Bhaktivedānta (ed. and trans.) Los Angeles: BBT 1974–75
*Śrī Caitanyacaritāmṛtam*, 2d ed., 3 vols. S. K. Chaudhuri (trans.). Calcutta: Gaudia-Math, 1959.
Cakravarttī, Viśvanātha. "*Bhaktirasāmṛtasindhubinduh*." K. Klostermaier (trans.), *JAOS* 1 (1974):96–107.
Caland, W. and V. Henry. *L'Agniṣṭoma: Description compléte de la forme normals du sacrifice de Soma dans le culte védique*, 2 vols. Paris: E. Leroux, 1906–1907.
Callewaert, W. M. and S. Hemraj; *Bhagavadgītānuvāda: A Study in Transcultural Translation*. Ranchi: Sathya Bharati Publication, 1983.
Id. "The Earliest Song of Mīrā (1503–1546)." *JOIB* 39,3–4 (1990): 239–53.
Campbell, A. *The Heart of India*. New York: Knopf, 1958.
Caṇḍīdāsa, B. *Singing the Glory of Lord Krishna,*. M. H. Klaiman (trans.). Chico 3rd ed.: Scholars Press, 1984.
*Cārakasaṃhitā*, T. Y. Sarma (ed.) (English translation published by the Shree Gulabkunverba Ayurvedic Society Jamnagar 1949.) Bombay: Nirnaya Sagara Press, 1933.
Carman, J. B. *The Theology of Rāmānuja: An Essay in Inter religious Understanding*. New Haven and London: Yale University Press, 1974.
Id. and A. Marglin (eds.). *Purity and Auspiciousness in Indian Society*. Leiden: Brill, 1985.
Carpenter, J. E. *Theism in Mediaeval India*. London: Constable and Co., 1921.
Carstairs, G. M. *The Twice-Born*. London: Hogarth Press, 1957.

Cenkner, W. *A Tradition of Teachers: Śaṅkara and the Jagadgurus Today*. Delhi: Motilal Banarsidass, 1983.
Chaitanya, K. *Sanskrit Poetics*. Bombay: Asia, 1965.
Chakladar, H. C. *Social Life in Ancient India*, 2d ed. Calcutta: Greater India Society, 1954.
Chakraborti, H., "Śaṅkarācārya." In *Asceticism in Ancient India*. Calcutta: Punthi Pustak, 1973.
Chakravarti, C. *Tantras: Studies on Their Religion and Literature*. Calcutta: Punthi Pustak, 1963.
Chakravarti, S. C. *The Philosophy of the Upaniṣads*. Calcutta: University of Calcutta, 1935.
Chand, T. *Influence of Islam on Indian Culture*. Allahabad: The Indian Press, 1963.
Chandavarkar, B. D. *A Manual of Hindu Ethics*, 3rd ed. Poona: Oriental Book Agency, 1965.
Chapple, C. K. and M. E. Tucker (eds.). *Hinduism and Ecology: The Intersection of Earth, Sky and Water*. Cambridge, Mass.: Harvard University Press, 2000.
Chatterji, C. *Hindu Realism*. Allahabad: The Indian Press, 1952.
Chatterjee, B. R. "The *Rāmāyaṇa* and the *Mahābhārata* in Southeast Asia." In *CHI*, vol. 2, 119 ff.
Chatterjee, M. *Gandhi's Religious Thought*. South Bend, Ind.: University of Notre Dame Press, 1983.
Chatterjee, S. *The Nyāya Theory of Knowledge*, 3rd ed. Calcutta: University of Calcutta, 1965.
Chatterji, P. C. *Secular Values for Secular India*. New Delhi: Lola Chatterji, 1986.
Chatterji, S. and D. M. Datta. *An Introduction to Indian Philosophy*, 7th ed. Calcutta: University of Calcutta, 1968.
Chatterji, S. K. "Contributions from Different Language-Culture Groups." In *CHI*, vol. 1, 76–90.
Id. *Languages and Literatures of Modern India*. Calcutta: 1963.
Id. "Race Movements and Prehistoric Culture." In *HCIP*, vol.1, 164 ff.
Chattopadhyaya, S., *Reflections on the Tantras*. Delhi: Motilal Banarsidass, 1978.
Id. *Some Early Dynasties of South India*. Delhi: Motilal Banarsidass, 1974.
Chattopadhaya, S. *The Evolution of Theistic Sects in Ancient India*. Calcutta: Progressive Publishers, 1963.
Chaudhuri, N. *That Compassionate Touch of Ma Anandamayee*. Reprint Delhi: Motilal Banarsidass, 2006.
Chaudhuri, N. C. *Autobiography of an Unknown Indian*. London: Macmillan, 1951.
Id. *The Continent of Circe*. Bombay: Jaico, 1966.
Id. *The Intellectual in India*. New Delhi: Vir Publishing House, 1967.
Id. *Hinduism*. London: Chatto and Windus, 1979.
Chaudhuri, R., "The Nimbārka School of Vedānta." In *CHI*, vol. 3, 333 ff.
Id. *Doctrine of Śrīkaṇṭha*, 2 vols. Calcutta: Pracyavani, 1959–1960.
Chemparathy, G. *An Indian Rational Theology: Introduction to Udayana's Nyāyakusumañjalī*. Vienna: De Nobili Research Library, 1972.
Chengappa, R. "The Himālayas: Startling Discoveries." *India Today* (March 15, 1993): 90–101.

Chethimattam, J. B. *Consciousness and Reality: An Indian Approach to Metaphysics.* Bangalore: Dharmaram Publications, 1967.

Id. (ed.). *Unique and Universal: Fundamental Problems of an Indian Theology.* Bangalore: Dharmaram Publications, 1972.

Chinmulgund, P. J., and V. V. Mirashi (eds.). *Review of Indological Research in Last 75 Years.* Poona: Bharatiya Charitrakosha Mandal, 1967.

Choudhuri, D. C. R. *Temples and Legends of Bihar.* Bombay: Bharatiya Vidya Bhavan, 1965.

Choudhury, B. "Love Sentiment and Its Spiritual Implications in Gaudīya Vaiṣṇavism." In D. T. O'Connel (ed.), *Bengal Vaiṣṇavism, Orientalism, Society and the Arts,* South Asia Series Occasional Papers No. 35. East Lansing: Asian Studies Center, Michigan State University, 1985.

Chowgule, A. V. *Christianity in India: The Hindutva Perspective.* Mumbai: Hindu Vivek Kendra, 1999.

Cidananda, Swāmi. *Light Fountain.* Rishikesh: Divine Light Society, 1967.

Clooney, F. X. *Theology After Vedānta: An Experiment in Comparative Theology.* Albany: State University of New York Press, 1993.

Id. "What's a God? The Quest for the Right Understanding of *Devata* in Brahmanical Ritual Theory (*Mīmāṃsā*)." *IJHS,* 1,2 (Aug. 1997):337–385.

Id. *Divine Mother, Blessed Mother: Hindu Goddesses and the Virgin Mary.* New York: Oxford University Press, 2005.

Clothey, F. W. *The Many Faces of Murukan: The History and Meaning of a South Indian God.* RS, no. 6. The Hague: Mouton, 1978.

Id. "Tamil Religion." ER, vol. 12, 260 ff.

Id. "Murukan." ER, vol. 10,160–161.

Id. "Pilgrimage Centers in the Tamil Cultus of Murukan." *JAAR,* 40 (1972): 79–95.

Clothey, F. M. and J. B. Lond (eds.). *Experiencing Śiva.* Columbia, Mo.: South Asian Books, 1983.

Coburn, T. B. *Devī Māhātmya: The Crystallization of the Goddess Tradition.* Delhi: Motilal Banarsidass, 1984.

Cohn, B. *India: The Social Anthropology of a Civilization.* Englewood Cliffs, N.Y.: Prentice Hall, 1971.

Colebrook, T. "On the Vedas, or Sacred Writings of the Hindus." *Asiatic Researches* 8:369–476.

Collins, L. and D. Lapierre. *Freedom at Midnight.* New York: Simon and Schuster 1975. Reprint New York: Avon Books, 1980.

Coomaraswamy, A. *The Dance of Śiva,* 3rd ed. Bombay: Asia Publishing House, 1956.

Id. *History of Indian and Indonesian Art.* Reprint New York: Dover, 1965.

Id. *The Transformation of Nature in Art.* Reprint New York: Dover, 1956.

Coomaraswamy, A. and Sister Nivedita. *Myths of the Hindus and Buddhists.* Reprint New York: Dover, 1967.

Cormack, M. L. *She Who Rides a Peacock: Indian Students and Social Change.* New York: Praeger, 1962.

Courtright, P. B. *Ganeśa: Lord of Obstacles, Lord of Beginnings.* New York: Oxford University Press, 1985.

Coward, H. G., *Bhartṛhari.* Boston: Twayne Publishers, 1976.

Id. *Jung and Eastern Thought.* Albany: State University of New York Press, 1985.

Id. (ed.). *Language in Indian Philosophy and Religion*. SR Supplements. Waterloo, Ont.: Wilfrid Laurier University Press, 1978.
Id. (ed.). *Population, Consumption and the Environment*. Albany: State University of New York Press. 1995.
Id. *The Sphoṭa Theory of Language: A Philosophical Analysis*. Delhi: Motilal Banarsidass, 1981.
Id. (ed.). *Studies in Indian Thought: Collected Papers of Prof. T. R. V. Murti*. Delhi: Motilal Banarsidass, 1984.
Id. (ed.). *Hindu-Christian Dialogue: Perspectives and Encounters*, New York: Orbis Books, 1990.
Id. and W. Goa, *Mantra*. Chambersburg, Pa.: Anima Publications, 1991.
Id. and K. Kunjunni Raja, *The Philosophy of the Grammarians*, vol. 5 of *Encyclopedia of Indian Philosophy*, Karl Potter (gen. ed.). Princeton University Press, 1990.
Id. and J. R. Hinnells, R. B. Williams. *The South Asian Diaspora in Britain, Canada and the United States*. Albany: State University of New York Press, 2000.
Id. and K. Śivaraman (eds.). *Revelation in Indian Thought*. Emeryville: Dharma Publishing, 1977.
Crawford, S. C. *The Evolution of Hindu Ethical Ideals*, revised edition. Honolulu: University of Hawaii Press, 1982.
Id. *Ram Mohan Roy: Social, Political and Religious Reform in Nineteenth-Century India*. New York: Paragon House, 1987.
Creel, A. B. *Dharma in Hindu Ethics*. Columbia, Mo.: South Asia Books, 1977.
Cronin, V. A. *Pearl to India: The Life of Roberto de Nobili*. London: Darton, Longman and Todd, 1966.
Crooke, W. *Popular Religion and Folklore in Northern India*, 2 vols. 1896. Reprint Delhi: Munshiram Manoharlal. 1968.
Cunningham, A. *Ancient Geography of India*. Calcutta: Archaeological Survey of India, 1924.
Cuttat, J. A. *Encounter of Religions*. New York: Desclee and Co., 1962.
Dandekar, R. N. "Ancient Indian Polity." *Indo-Asia Culture*. 11,4 (April 1963):323–32.
Id. *Some Aspects of the History of Hinduism*. Poona: University of Poona, 1967.
Id. *Universe in Hindu Thought*. Bangalore: University of Bangalore, 1972.
Id. (ed.).*V. Raghavan Felicitation Volume: Sanskrit and Indological Studies*. Delhi: Motital Banarasidass, 1975.
Id. *Vedic Bibliography*, vol. 1. Bombay: Karnatak Publishing House,1946; vol. 2, Poona: University of Poona, 1967.
Id. "Vṛtrahā Indra." *ABORI* 30,1 (1951):1–55.
Id. and G. R. Welbon. "Vaiṣnavism." ER vol. 15, 168–71.
Daniélou, A. *Hindu Polytheism*. London: Routledge and Kegan Paul, 1963.
Id. *Yoga: The Method of Reintegration*. New York: University Books, 1956.
Danielson, H. (trans.). *Adiśeṣa: The Essence of Supreme Truth (Paramārthasāra)*. Nisaba: Religious Texts Translation Series. Leiden: Brill, 1980.
Das, B. *Kṛṣṇa: A Study in the Theory of Avatāras*. Bombay: Bharatiya Vidya Bhavan, 1962.
Das, R. V. *Introduction to Śaṅkara*. Calcutta: Punthi Pustak, 1968.
*Daśapadārtha Śāstra*. (1917) H. Ui (ed. and trans.). Reprint Chowkhambha Sanskrit Series, Varanasi: Chowkhamba, 1962.

Das, S. *Dharma of the Twenty-first Century: Theological-Ethical Paradigm Shift*. Calcutta: Punthi Pustak, 1996.
DasGupta, G. *Mother as Revealed to Me*. Banares: 2d ed. Shree Shree Anandamayi Sangha, 1954.
Dasgupta, S. H., *Obscure Religious Cults*, Calcutta: Firma K. L. Mukhopadhyay, 1962.
Dasgupta, S. N. *Development of Moral Philosophy in India*. Bombay: 1961.
Id. *Hindu Mysticism*. Chicago: Open Court, 1927.
Id. *History of Indian Philosophy*, 3rd ed., 5 vols. Cambridge: Cambridge University Press, 1961–1962.
Id. *A Study of Patañjali*. Calcutta: Firma K. L. 1930.
Id. *Yoga as Philosophy and Religion*. 1924. Reprint Delhi: Motilal Banarsidass, 1973.
Dass, A. C. "The Origin of Brahmanical Image Worship and the Iconogenic Properties in *Ṛg Veda*." *JOIB* 34,1–2 (1984):1–11.
Datta, B. and Singh, A. N. *History of Hindu Mathematics: A Source Book*, (2 parts). Bombay-Calcutta-New Delhi: Asia Publishing House, 1962.
Dave, J. H. *Immortal India*, 2d ed., (4 parts). Bombay: Bharatiya Vidya Bhavan, 1959–1962.
Davis, K. *The Population of India and Pakistan*. Princeton: Princeton University Press, 1951.
Day, T. P. *The Conception of Punishment in Early Indian Literature*. Waterloo, Ont.: Wilfrid Laurier University Press, 1982.
De, S. K. *Early History of the Vaiṣṇava Faith and Movement in Bengal*, 2d ed. Calcutta: Firma K. L. Mukhopadhyay, 1961.
Id. *Sanskrit Poetics as a Study of Aesthetic*. Berkeley: University of California Press, 1963.
"De-anglicizing Asian Academia." *Hinduism Today* (July 1997):27.
Deegan, C. "The Narmadā: Circumambulating a Landscape." In C. L. Chapple and M. E. Tucker (eds.) *Hinduism and Ecology*, 389–99.
Deheja, V. *Āntāl and Her Path of Love*. Albany: State University of New York Press, 1990
Id. *Devī: The Great Goddess*. Washington, DC: Smithsonian Institution, 1999.
Delmonico, N. "Rūpa Goswāmi: His Life, Family and Early Vraja Commentators" *JVS* I,2 (1993):133–57.
Deming, W. S. *Rāmdās and Rāmdāsis*. The Religious Life of India Series. Oxford: Oxford University Press, 1928.
Derret, J. D. M. *Critique of Modern Hindu Law*. Bombay: N. M. Tripathi, 1970.
Id. *The Death of a Marriage Law: Epitaph for the Rishis*. Durham, N.C.: Academic Press, 1978.
Id. "The Concept of Duty in Ancient Indian Jurisprudence: The Problem of Ascertainment." In W. D. O' Flaherty and J. D. M. Derret (eds.), *The Concept of Duty in Southeast Asia*, 18–65. New Delhi: Vikas, 1978.
Id. *Essays in Classical and Modern Hindu Law*, 3 vols. Leiden: Brill, 1976–1977.
Id. "Greece and India: The Milindapañha, the Alexander Romance and the Gospels." *ZRGG* 19 (1967):33–64.
Id. "Greece and India Again: The Jaimini-Aśvamedha, the Alexander Romance and the Gospels," *ZRGG* 22, 1 (1970): 19–44.
Id. *Hindu Law Past and Present*. Calcutta: A. Mukherjee, 1957.
Id. *History of Indian Law (Dharmaśāstra)*. Leiden: Brill, 1973.

Id. *Introduction to Modern Hindu Law*. Calcutta: A. Mukherjee, 1963.
Desai,M. *The Gītā According to Gandhi*. Ahmedabad: Navajivan, 1946.
Deshpande, M. M. "Changing Conceptions of the Veda: From Speech-Acts to Magical Sounds." *ALB* 54 (1990): 1–41.
Deshpande, U. "Some Ṛgvedic Poetesses: A Study." *Bharatiya Vidya* 48,1 (1988):1–5.
Deussen, P. *The Philosophy of the Upaniṣads*. 1905. Reprint New York: Dover, 1966.
Id. *The Philosophy of the Veda*. Edinburgh: Clark, 1908.
Deutsch, E. *Advaita Vedānta: A Philosophical Reconstruction*. Honolulu: University of Hawaii, 1969.
Deutsch, E., and J. A. B. van Buitenen. *A Source Book of Advaita Vedānta*. Honolulu: University of Hawaii, 1971.
Devanandan, P. D. *The Concept of Māyā*. Calcutta: YMCA Publishing House, 1954.
Devasenapathy, V. A. *Śaiva Siddhānta as Expounded in the Śivajñana Siddhiyar and Its Six Commentaries*. Madras: University of Madras, 1960.
*Devī-Bhāgavata Purāṇa*. Swami Vijnananda(ed.) Varanasi: Pandit Pustakalaya. 1962 (Trans.) 2 vols. SBH Allahabad: Panini Office, 1923.
Dharampal, G. "Frühe deutsche Indien Berichte (1477–1750)." *ZDMG* 134, 2 (1984): 23–67.
*Dharmaśāstrasaṅgraha*. Bombay: Śrī Venkatesvar Press, 1970 (Samvat).
Dhatta, A. K. *Bhaktiyoga*. Bombay: Bharatiya Vidya Bhavan, 1959.
Dhavamony, M. *Classical Hinduism*. Roma: Universitá Gregoriana Editrice, 1982.
Id. *Love of God According to Śaiva Siddhānta: A Study in the Mysticism and Theology of Śaivism*. Oxford: Clarendon Press, 1971.
Dhingra, B. *Asia through Asian Eyes*. Bombay: Asia Publishing House, 1959.
Diehl, C. G. *Instrument and Purpose: Studies on Rites and Rituals in South India*. Lund: Gletup, 1956.
Diksitar, V. R. *Studies in Tamil Literature and History*. London: Luzac, 1930.
Dimmit, C.,and J. A. B. van Buitenen (eds. and trans.). *Classical Hindu Mythology: A Reader in the Sanskrit Purāṇas*. Philadelphia: Temple University Press, 1978.
Dimock, E. C. (trans.). *The Thief of Love: Bengali Tales*. Chicago: University of Chicago Press, 1963.
Dixit, P. "Hindu Nationalism." *Seminar* 216 (August 1977): 27–36.
*Doctrine of Śrīkaṇṭha*, 2 vols. R. Chaudhuri (trans.) Calcutta 1959 ff.
Doczi, G. *The Power of Limits: Proportional Harmonies in Nature, Art and Architecture*. Boulder and London: Shambala, 1981.
Dold, P. "The Mahāvidyās at Kāmarūpa: Dynamics of Transformation in Hinduism." *Religious Studies and Theology* 23,1 (2004):89–122.
Dom, H. "The English Invention of Hinduism." *www.raceandhistory.com*
Dowson, J. *A Classical Dictionary of Hindu Mythology and Religion, Geography, History and Literature*. London: Routledge and Kegan Paul, 1961.
Drekmeier, C. *Kingship and Community in Early India*. Stanford: Stanford University Press, 1962.
D'Souza, H. *In the Steps of St. Thomas*. 2d ed. Poona: Yeravda Prison Press, 1964.
Dube, S. C. *India's Changing Villages*. London: Routledge and Kegan Paul, 1958.
Id. *Indian Villages*. New York: Harper and Row, 1967.
Dubois, Abbé. *Hindu Manners, Customs and Ceremonies*, 3rd ed. Reprint Oxford: Oxford University Press, 1959.

Dumont, L. "A Fundamental Problem." In *Religion, Politics and History in India*. The Hague: Mouton, 1970. [Ecole Pratique des Hautes Etudes; Sorbonne, VIe section: sciences économiques et sociales: "Le Monde d'Outre-Mer-Passè et Présent" Première Série, Etudes XXXXIV].

Id. *Religion, Politics and History in India: Collected Papers in Indian Sociology*. The Hague: Mouton, 1970.

Id. *Homo hierarchicus: Essai sur le systéme des castes*. Paris: Gallimard 1966; English trans. Chicago: University of Chicago Press, 1970.

Dumont, P. E. *L'Aśvamedha*. Paris: Geuthner, 1927.

Dutt, P. R. *India Today and Tomorrow*. Delhi: People's Publishing House, 1955.

Dutt, R. C. *Economic History of India 1757–1900*, 2 vols. Reprint Delhi: Publications Division, Government of India, 1960.

Dutt, S. *Buddhist Monks and Monasteries in India: Their History and Their Contribution to Indian Culture*. London: Allen and Unwin, 1962.

Eban, M. (ed.). *Maharishi the Guru: The Story of Maharishi Mahesh Yogi*. Bombay: Pear Publications, 1968.

Eck, D. L. *Banaras: City of Light*. Princeton: Princeton University Press, 1983.

Id. *Darśan: Seeing the Divine Image in India*, 2d ed. Chambersburg, Pa.: Anima Books, 1985.

Edsman, C. M. "Zum sakralen Königtum in der Forschung der letzten hundert Jahre." *Numen Supplement* 4:3–17.

Edwardes, S. M., and H. O. O. Garrett. *Mughal Rule in India*. Reprint Delhi: S. Chand, 1962.

Eidlitz, W. *Kṛṣṇa-Caitanya, Sein Leben und Seine Lehre*. Stockholm Studies in Comparative Religion 7. Stockholm: Almquist and Wiksell, 1968.

Einstein, A. *Ideas and Opinions*. New York: Crown, 1985.

Eisenstadt, S. N., R. Kahane, and D. Shulman (eds.). *Orthodoxy, Heterodoxy and Dissent in India*. Leiden: Walter de Gruyter, 1984.

Elder, J. W. (ed.). *Lectures in Indian Civilization*. Dubuque: Kendall Hunt Publishing Co., 1970.

Eliade, M. *From Primitives to Zen*. New York: Harper and Row, 1967.

Id. *Yoga: Immortality and Freedom*, 2d ed. Bollingen Series 41. Princeton: Princeton University Press, 1969.

Elintoff, E. "Pyrrho and India." *Phronesis* 1980. 1: 88–108.

Elliot, H. M. and J. Dowson. *The History of India as Told by Its Own Historians: The Mohammedan Period*, 8 vols. Reprint Delhi: 1964.

Elkman, S. M. *Jīva Goswāmi's Tattvasandarbha*. Delhi: Motilal Banarsidass, 1986.

Elmore, W. T. *Dravidian Gods in Hinduism*, Lincoln: The University Studies of the University of Nebraska, 1915.

Elwin, V. *The Religion of an Indian Tribe*. London: Oxford University Press, 1955.

Endl, K. M. "Śākta." In S. Mittal and G. Thursby (eds.) *The Hindu World*, 140–61. New York and London: Routledge, 2004.

Erikson, E. H. *Gandhi's Truth*. New York: W.W. Norton, 1970.

*Essentials of Hinduism*. Allahabad: The Leader, n.d.

Esteller, A. "The Quest for the Original *Ṛgveda*," *ABORI* 507 (1969): 1–40.

Id. "The *Ṛgveda Saṃhitā* as a 'Palimpsest'." *Indian Antiquary* (Third Series) 4,1 (January 1967): 1–23.

Fairservis, W. A. *The Harappan Cilization and Its Writing*. Leyden: Brill, 1992.
Id. "The Harappan Civilization and the Ṛgveda." In M. Witzel (ed.), *Inside the Texts—Beyond the Texts*, 61–68.
Falk, H. "Die Legende von Sunaḥśepa vor ihrem rituellen Hintergrund." ZDMG 134, 1, (1984): 115–135.
Falk, M. *Nāma-rupa and Dharma-rūpa; Origin and Aspects of an Ancient Indian Conception*. Calcutta: University of Calcutta, 1943.
Fakirbhai, D. *Khristopaniṣad*. Bangalore: C. I. S. R. S., 1966.
Farquhar, J. N. *Modern Religious Movements in India*. Oxford: Oxford University Press, 1914; reprint Varanasi: 1967.
Id. *An Outline of the Religious Literature of India*. Reprint Varanasi: Motilal Banarsidass, 1967.
Faruqi, A. *Sufism and Bhakti: Mawlana Rumi and Sri Ramakrishna*, New Delhi: Abhinav, 1984.
Feldhaus, A. (trans. and annotator). *The Deeds of God in Riddhipur* New York: Oxford University Press, 1984.
Fergusson, J. *Tree and Serpent Worship*. London: W. H. Allen, 1868.
Feuerstein, G. *The Philosophy of Classical Yoga*. Manchester: University of Manchester Press, 1982.
Id. *Encyclopedic Dictionary of Yoga*. New York: Paragon House, 1990.
Id. *The Yoga Tradition*. Prescott, Ariz.: Home Press, 1998.
Id., and Jeanine Miller. *Yoga and Beyond: Essays in Indian Philosophy*. New York: Schocken Books, 1972.
Id., S. Kak and D. Frawley, *In Search of the Cradle of Civilization*. Wheaton, Ill.: The Theosophical Publishing House, 1995.
Filliozat, J. "Les Āgamas Çivaites." Introduction in *Rauravāgama*, N. R. Bhatt (ed.). Pondichery: Institute Français d'Indologie, 1961.
Id. *The Classical Doctrine of Indian Medicine: Its Origins and Its Greek Parallels*. D. R. Chanama, (trans.). Delhi: Munshiram Manoharlal, 1964.
Id. "The French Institute of Indology in Pondichery," *WZKSA* 28 (1984): 133–147.
Id. *Les rélations extérieures de l'Inde*. Pondichery: Institute Français d'Indologie, 1956.
Findly, E. B. "Gārgī at the King's Court: Women and Philosophic Innovation in Ancient India." In *Women, Religion, and Social Change*, Y. Y. Haddad and E. B. Findly, (eds.), Albany: State University of New York Press, 1985, 37–85.
Fischer, L. *The Life of Mahatma Gandhi*. Reprint Bombay: Bharatiya Vidya Bhavan, 1959.
Fischer, W. F. "Sacred Rivers, Sacred Dams: Competing Visions of Social Justice and Sustainable Development along the Narmadā." In C. L. Chapple and M. E. Tucker (eds.) *Hinduism and Ecology*. 401–21.
Fitzgerald, James L. "The Great Epic of India as Religious Rhetoric A Fresh Look at the Mahābhārata." *JAAR* 51, 4 (1986): 611–30.
Flood, G. (ed.) *The Blackwell Companion to Hinduism*. Blackwell Publishing, 2003.
Fonseca, R. "Constructive Geometry and the Śrī-Cakra Diagram." *Religion* 16, 1 (1986): 33–49.
Forbes, G. *Women in Modern India*. Cambridge: Cambridge University Press, 1996.
Frauwallner, E. *Geschichte der indischen Philosophie*, 2 vols. Salzburg: Otto Müller Verlag, 1953.

Id. *History of Indian Philosophy*, 2 vols. V. M. Bedekar, (trans.), Delhi: Motilal Banarsidass, 1983–1984.
Frawley, D. *Gods, Sages and Kings: Vedic Secrets of Ancient Civilization*. Salt Lake City: Passage Press, 1991.
French, H. W., and A. Sharma. *Religious Ferment in Modern India*. New York: St. Martin's Press, 1981.
Frykenberg, R. E. (ed.). *Land Control and Social Structure in Indian History*. Madison: University of Wisconsin Press, 1969.
Fuller, C. J. *Servants of the Goddess: The Priests of a South Indian Temple*. Cambridge: Cambridge University Press, 1984.
Id. *The Camphor Flame: Popular Hinduism and Society in India*. Princeton: Princeton University Press, 1992.
Gächter, O. *Hermeneutics and Language in Pūrvamīmāṃsa: A Study in Śābara Bhāṣya*. Delhi: Motilal Banarsidass, 1983.
Gandhi, M. K. *Collected Works*, 90 vols. Delhi: Government of India, 1958–1984.
Id. *Autobiography or the Story of My Experiments with Truth*. 2nd revised and authorized edition, Ahmedabad:Navajivan Publishing House, 1940.
Gandhi, R. *Eight Lives: A Study of the Hindu-Muslim Encounter*. Albany: State University Press, 1986.
Gangadharan, K. K. "Shiv Sena." *Seminar* 151 (March 1972): 26–32.
Gangadharan, N. *Liṅgapurāṇa: A Study*. Delhi: Ajanta Books International, 1980.
Garbe, B. *Die Bhagavadgītā*, 2d ed. Leipzig: H. Haessel, 1921.
Gatwood, L. E. *Devī and the Spouse Goddess: Women, Sexuality and Marriage in India*. Delhi: Manohar, 1985.
Gaur, R. *Hindutva* (Hindī). Kasi: Visvaprasad Gupta, 1995 (samvat).
Gaur, R. C. *Excavations in Atranjikhera: Early Civilization of the Upper Gaṅgā Basin*. Delhi: Archeological Survey of India, 1983.
*Gautama's Nyāyasūtras with Vātsyāyana Bhāṣya*, 2 vols. Ganganatha Jha, Sanskrit (ed.) and English (trans.) Poona: Oriental Book Depot, 1939.
Gayal, S. R. *A History of the Imperial Guptas*. Allahabad: Kitab Mahal, 1967.
*Gazetteer of India*, 4 vols. Reprint, Delhi: Ministry for Information and Braodcasting, 1965.
Gelberg, S. J. (ed.) *Hare Krishna, Hare Krishna: Five Distinguished Scholars on the Krishna Movement in the West*. New York: Grove Press, 1983.
Geldner, H. F. *Ṛgveda deutsch*, 5 vols. Cambridge, Mass.: Harvard University Press, 1955–1957.
Gensichen, H-W. "Abominable Heathenism: A Rediscovered Tract by Bartholomaeus Ziegenbalg." *Indian Church History Review* 1, 1 (1967):29–40.
Id. *Invitatio ad Fraternitatem*. Münster and Hamburg: LIT; 1993.
George, A. *Social Ferment in India*. London: The Athlone Press, 1986.
Getty, A. *Gaṇeśa*. Oxford: Oxford University Press, 1936.
Ghate, V. S. *The Vedānta*. Poona: B. O. R. I., 1926; reprint 1960.
*Gheraṇḍasaṃhitā*. S. C. Vasu (trans.). Allahabad: Panini Office, 1914.
Ghose, Aurobindo. *Śrī Aurobindo*. Birth Centenary Library 30 vols. Pondichery: Śrī Aurobindo Ashram, 1972–1975.
Id. *The Secret of the Veda*. Pondichery: Sri Aurobindo Ashram, 1953.

Id. *Sri Aurobindo on Himself and on the Mother*. Pondichery, Sri Aurobindo Ashram 1955.

Ghose, S. K. *Lord Gaurāṅga*. Bombay: 1961.

Id. *Modern Indian Political Thought*. New Delhi: Allied Publishers, 1984.

Ghosh, B. K. "The Āryan Problem." In *HCIP*, vol. 1, 205–21.

Id. "The Origin of the Indo-Āryans." In *CHI*, vol. 1, 129–43.

Ghoshal, U. N. *A History of Indian Political Ideas: The Ancient Period and the Period of Transition to the Middle Ages* 3rd ed., Oxford: Oxford University Press, 1959.

Id. "Kautilīya." *Encyclopedia of Social Sciences* 10th ed., vol. 3. 1953, vol. 3, 473 ff.

Ghurye, G. S. *Caste, Class and Occupation*, 3rd ed. Bombay: Popular Book Depot, 1961.

Id. *Gods and Men*. Bombay: Popular Book Depot, 1962.

Id. *Indian Sādhus*, 2d ed. Bombay: Popular Prakashan, 1964.

Gibb, H. A. R. (ed.). *Ibn Battuta: Travels in Asia and Africa*, 2d ed. London: Routledge and Kegan Paul, 1957.

*Gītārthasaṁgraha by Yamunācārya*. Swami Adidevananda (ed. and trans.). Madras: Ramakrishna Math Mylapore, 1950.

Glasenapp, H. von. *Das Indienbild deutscher Denker*. Stuttgart: Köhler, 1960.

Glucklich, A. "Karma and Pollution in the Dharmaśāstra." *JOIB* 35,1–2 (1985):49–60.

Gode, P. K. "The Aśvamedha Performed by Śevai Jayasingh of Amber 1699–1744 AD." In *Studies in Indian Literary History*, 292–306. Bombay: Bharatiya Vidya Bhavan, 1954.

Godman, D. (ed.). *Be As You Are: The Teachings of Ramana Maharsi*. Boston: Arkana, 1985.

Goel, S. R. *Catholic Ashrams: Samnyasins or Swindlers?* 2d ed. New Delhi: Voice of India, 1994.

Id. *History of Hindu-Christian Encounters*. New Delhi: Voice of India, 1989.

Goetz, H. *The Art of India*. New York: Crown Publishers, 1964.

Gold, D. *The Lord as Guru: Hindī Saints in the Northern Indian Tradition*. New York: Oxford University Press, 1987.

Goldman, R. P. (trans.). *The Rāmāyaṇa of Vālmīki: An Epic of Ancient India*, 6 vols. Princeton: Princeton University Press, 1984 ff.

Golwalkar, M. S. *Bunch of Thoughts*, 2d ed. Bangalore: 1966.

Gonda, J. *Aspects of Early Viṣṇuism*. Utrecht: 1954; reprint Delhi: Motilal Banarsidass, 1965.

Id. "The Historical Background of the Name 'Satya' Assigned to the Highest Being." *ABORI* 48–49 (1968): 83–93.

Id. *Die Religionen Indiens*, 2 vols. Stuttgart: Kohlhammer, 1960–1963.

Id. *The Ritual Functions and Significance of Grasses in the Religion of the Veda*. Amsterdam: North-Holland Publ., 1985.

Id. *The Ritual Sūtras*. In *HIL*, vol. 1. Wiesbaden: Harrassowitz, 1975.

Id. *Vedic Literature (Saṃhitās and Brāhmaṇas)*. In *HIL*, vol. 1. Wiesbaden: Harrassowitz, 1975.

Id. *Vedic Ritual: The Non-solemn Rites*. Amsterdam: North-Holland Publishing, 1980.

Id. *The Indra Hymns of the Ṛgveda*. Leiden: Brill, 1989.

Gopal, R. *British Rule in India: An Assessment*. New York: Asia Publishing House, 1963.

Id. *Indian Muslims*. New York: 1959.

Gopi, Krishna. *The Biological Basis of Religion and Genius*. New York: Harper and Row, 1972.

Gordon, D. H. *The Prehistoric Background of Indian Culture*. Bombay: N. M. Tripathi, 1960.

Gordon, S. "Hindus, Muslims, and the Other in Eighteenth-Century India." *IJHS* 3,3 (Dec. 1999): 221–239.

Goudriaan, T. *Māyā Divine and Human: A Study of Magic and Its Religious Foundations in Sanskrit Texts, with Particular Attention to a Fragment on Viṣṇu's Māyā Preserved in Bali*. Delhi: Motilal Banarsidass, 1978.

Govindacharya, A. *The Divine Wisdom of the Dravida Saints*. Madras: C. N. Press, 1902.

Id. *The Life of Rāmānuja*. Madras: C. N. Press, 1906.

Griffith, R. T. H. *The Texts of the White Yajurveda*. (3rd ed.) Reprint Banares: Chowkhamba, 1957.

Id. (trans.) *Hymns of the Ṛgveda*, 2 vols., 4th ed. Reprint, Banares: 1963.

Id. (trans.) *Hymns of the Yajurveda*. Reprint, Banares: 1957.

Id. (trans.) *Hymns of the Sāmaveda*, Reprint, Varanasi: Chowkhambha Sanskrit Series, 1963.

*Grihyasūtras*. H. Oldenberg and F. Müller (trans.) in *SBE*, vols. 29 and 30.

Griswold, H. D. *Religion of the Rigveda*. Delhi: Motilal Banarsidass, n.d.

Guénon, Rene. *Introduction génerale a l'étude des doctrines hindoues*, 5th ed. Paris: Les editions Vega, 1964.

Günther, H. V. *Yuganādha: The Tantric View of Life*. Banares: 1952; reprint Boulder: Shambhala, 1976.

Gupta, S. and R. Gombrich. "Kings, Power and the Goddess." *South Asia Research* 6,2 (1986): 123–38.

Gupta, S., D. J. Hoens, and T. Goudriaan. *Hindu Tantrism: Handbuch der Orientalistik*. B. Spuler (general ed.). Leiden: Brill, 1979.

Gyana, S. G. *Agni Purāṇa: A Study* 2d ed. Banares: Chowkhamba, 1966.

Habermann, D. L. "On Trial: The Love of Sixteen Thousand Gopees," *HR* 33,1 (1993), 44–70.

Hacker, P. "Eigentümlichkeiten der Lehre und Terminologie Śaṅkaras: *Avidyā, Nāmarūpa, Māyā, Īśvara*," *ZDMG* 100 (1950): 246–86.

Id. "Śaṅkara der Yogin und Śaṅkara der Advaitin: Einige Beobachtungen." *WZKSA* 12–13 (1968): 119–148.

Id. *Vivārta: Studien zur Geschichte der Illusionistischen Kosmologie und Erkenntnistheorie der Inder*. Wiesbaden: Akademie der Wissenschaften Mainz, 1953.

Id. "Zur Entwicklung der Avatāralehre." *WZKSA* 4 (1960): 47–70.

Halbfass, W. "Indien und die Geschichtsschreibung der Philosophie." *Philosophische Rundschau* 23, 1–2 (1976): 104–31.

Id. *India and Europe: An Essay in Understanding*. Albany: State University Press of New York Press 1988.

Id. *On Being and What There Is: Classical Vaiśeṣika and the History of Indian Ontology*. Albany: State University of New York Press, 1992.

Hampton, G. H. *The Life and Mind of Oriental Jones: Sir William Jones, the Father of Modern Linguistics*. Cambridge: Cambridge University Press, 1990.

Id. *Oriental Jones: A Biography of Sir William Jones 1746–1794*. Bombay: Asia Publishing House, 1964.

Handelman, D., "Myths of Murukan: Asymmetry and Hierarchy in a South Indian Purāṇic Cosmology." *HR*, 27, 2 (1987): 133–70.

Haq, M. U. *Islam in Secular India*. Simla: Indian Institute of Advanced Studies, 1972.

Id. *Muslim Politics in Modern India*. Meerut: Meenakshi Publications, 1970.

Haq, Z. *Prophet Mohammed in Hindu Scripture*. http://cyberistan.org/islamic/prophets.html.

Hardgrave, R. L. *The Dravidian Movement*. Bombay: Popular Prakashan, 1965.

Hardy, E. T. *Viraha Bhakti* Delhi: Oxford University Press, 1983.

Hardy, P. "Islam in South Asia." ER, vol. 7:390–404.

Harle, J. C. *The Art and Architecture of the Indian Subcontinent*. Harmondsworth: Penguin, 1987.

Harper, E. B. (ed.) *Religion in South Asia*. Seattle: University of Washington Press, 1964.

Harper, M. H. *Gurus, Swāmis, and Avatāras: Spiritual Masters and Their American Disciples*. Philadelphia: Westminster Press, 1972.

Harris, I. C. *Radhakrishnan: The Profile of a Universalist*. Columbia, Mo.: South Asia Books, 1982.

Harris, R. B. (ed.). *Neoplatonism and Indian Thought: Studies in Neoplatonism Ancient and Modern*, vol. 2. Albany: State University of New York Press, 1982.

Harrison, S. S. *India: The Most Dangerous Decade*. Oxford: Oxford University Press, 1960.

Harvey, M. J. "The Secular as Sacred? The Religio-political Rationalization of B. G. Tilak." *Modern Asian Studies* 20, 2 (1986): 321–31.

Hasrat, B. J. *Dārā Shikūh: Life and Works*. Delhi: Manoharlal, 1982.

Hassan, R. "The Basis for a Hindu-Muslim Dialogue and Steps in That Direction from a Muslim Perspective." In L. Swidler (ed.), *Religious Liberty and Human Rights in Nations and Religions*, Philadelphia: Ecumenical Press, 1985.

*Haṭhayogapradīpikā by Svātamarāma Yogīndra*. Adyar: Theosophical Publishing House, 1933. Srinivasa Iyengar, English (trans.), 2d ed. Adyar: Theosophical Publishing House, 1933.

Hauer, J. W. *Der Vrātya: Untersuchungen über die nichtbrahmanische Religion Altindiens*. Stuttgart: Kohlhammer, 1927.

Id. *Der Yoga als Heilsweg*. Stuttgart: W. Kohlhammer, 1932.

Havell, E. B. *Banares, The Sacred City: Sketches of Hindu Life and Religion*. London: W. Thacker and Co., 1905.

Hawley, J. S. *Kṛṣṇa the Butter Thief*. Princeton: Princeton University Press, 1983.

Id. *At Play with Krishna: Prilgrimage Dramas from Brindavan*. Princeton: Princeton University Press, 1981.

Id. *Saints and Virtues*. Berkeley: University of California Press, 1987.

Id. *Sūrdās: Poet, Singer, Saint*. Seattle: University of Washington Press, 1985.

Id. "Why Sūrdās Went Blind" *Journal of Vaisnavism*. 1, 2 (1993): 62–78.

Id. "Author and Authority in the Bhakti Poetry of North India," *JAS* 47, 2 (1988): 269–90.

Hawley, J. S. and D. M. Wulff (eds.). *The Divine Consort: Rādhā and the Goddesses of India*. Berkeley: University of California Press, 1982.
Hazra, R. C. "The Purāṇas." In *CHI*, vol. 2, 240 ff.
Id. *Studies in the Purāṇic Records of Hindu Rites and Customs*. Dacca: University of Dacca, 1940; reprint Delhi: 1968.
Id. *Studies in the Upapurāṇas*, 2 vols. Calcutta: Sanskrit College, 1958–63.
Hedayetullah, M. *Kabir: The Apostle of Hindu-Muslim Unity*. Delhi: Motilal Banarsidass, 1978.
Heesterman, J. C. *The Inner Conflict of Tradition: Essays in Indian Ritual, Kingship and Society*. Chicago: University of Chicago Press, 1985.
Id. "On the Origin of the Nāstika." *WZKSA* 12,13 (1968–69): 171–85.
Hegel, G. W. F. *Vorlesungen über die Philosophie der Weltgeschichte*, vol.2. G. Larsson (ed.). Hamburg, 1968.
Heiler, F. *Sundar Singh: Apostel des Ostens und Westens*. München: Reinhardt, 1924.
Heimann, B. *Facets of Indian Thought*. London: Allen and Unwin, 1964.
Id. *Indian and Western Philosophy: A Study in Contrasts*. London: Allen and Unwin, 1937.
Heimsath, C. H. *Indian Nationalism and Hindu Social Reform*. Princeton: Princeton University Press, 1968.
Hein, N. *The Miracle Plays of Mathurā*. New Haven: Yale University Press, 1972.
Id. "A Revolution in Kṛṣṇaism: The Cult of Gopāla." *HR* 26, 3 (1986): 296–317.
Hellman, S. *Rādhā: Diary of a Woman's Search*. Porthill: Timeless Books, 1981.
Hija, J. A. "The Gita of J. Robert Oppenheimer." *Proceedings of the American Philosophical Society* 144:2 (June 2000): 123–67.
Hiltebeitel, A. *The Ritual of Battle: Krishna in the Mahābhārata*. Ithaca: Cornell University Press, 1976.
Hingorani, A. T. (ed.) *Gandhi Series*. Karachi: T. Hingorani, 1952.
Hiriyanna, M. *Outlines of Indian Philosophy*, 4th ed. London: George Allen and Unwin, 41958.
Id. "*Svabhāva-vāda* or Indian Naturalism." *Indian Philosophical Studies*. Mysore University: Mysore 1957. 71–8.
Id. *Indian Conception of Values*. Mysore: Kavyalaya Publishers, 1975.
Hocart, A. M. *Caste: A Comparative Study*. New York: Russell, 1950.
Holland, B., (compiler). *Popular Hinduism and Hindu Mythology: An Annotated Bibliography*. Westport: Greenwood Press, 1979.
"Holy War in India" *Newsweek* (21 Dec. 1992):46–47.
Hooper, J. S. M. *Bible Translation in India, Pakistan and Ceylon*, 2nd ed. rev. by W. J. Culshaw. Oxford: Oxford University Press, 1963.
Id. *Hymns of the Āḷvārs*. Calcutta: Association Press, 1929.
Hopkins, E. W. *Epic Mythology*. Strassburg: Trübner, 1915.
Id. *Ethics of India*. New Haven: Yale University Press, 1924.
Id. *The Great Epic of India*. New York: 1902; reprint Calcutta: Punthi Pustak, 1969.
Hopkins, T. J. *The Hindu Religious Tradition*. Belmont: Dickenson, 1971.
Hronzny, B. *Über die älteste Völkerwanderung und über das Problem der Proto-indischen Zivilisation*. Prague: Orientalisches Institut, 1939.
Hudson, D. "Āṇṭāl Āḷvār: A Developing Hagiography." *Journal of Vaiṣṇava Studies* 1, (1993): 27–61.

Hume, R. (trans.). *The Principal Upaniṣads*. Oxford: Oxford University Press, 1921.

Hunashal, S. M. *The Vīraśaiva Social Philosophy*. Raichur: Amaravani Printing Press, 1957.

Hutton, J. H. *Caste in India: Its Nature, Function and Origins*, 3rd ed. Oxford: Oxford University Press, 1961.

Inden, R. "Hierarchies of Kings in early Medieval India." In T. N. Madan (ed.) *Way of Life, King, Householder, Renouncer. Essays in honour of Louis Dumont*, 99–125. Delhi: Vikas Publishing House, 1982.

Id. "Orientalist Constructions of India." *Modern Asian Studies*, 20, 3 (1986): 401–46.

*India Hindu and India Christian*. 2nd ed. Madras: Christian Literary Society for India, 1900.

Indich, W. M. *Consciousness in Advaita Vedānta*. Delhi: Motilal Banarsidass, 1980.

Indradeva, S. "Cultural Interaction Between Ancient India and Iran." *Diogenes* 111 (1980): 83–109.

Ingalls, D. H. H. *Materials for the Study of Navya-Nyāya Logic*. *HOS*, no. 40. Cambridge, Mass.: Harvard University Press, 1968.

Ions, V. *Indian Mythology*. London: Paul Hamlyn, 1967.

Isaacs, H. R. *India's Ex-Untouchables*. New York: John Day, 1965.

Isacco, E. and A. L. Dallapiccola (eds.). *Krishna, the Divine Lover: Myth and Legend Through Indian Art*. Boston: Serindia Publications and David R. Godine, 1982.

Israel, B. J. *The Bene Israel of India, Some Studies*, Bombay: Orient Longman, 1984.

Iyengar, N. (ed. and trans.). *Mumukṣupadī of Lokācārya*. Madras: 1962.

Iyer, L. K. A. *The Mysore Tribes and Castes*, 4 vol. Mysore: Mysore University, 1928–1935.

Iyer, M. K. V. *Advaita Vedānta*. Bombay: Asia Publishing House, 1964.

Jacobi, H. *Das Rāmāyaṇa*. Bonn: 1893; rev. ed. Darmstadt: Wissenschaftliche Buchgesellschaft, 1970.

Jacobsen, D., and S. Wadley (eds.). *Women in India: Two Perspectives*. Delhi: Manohar Book Service, 1974.

Jacobsen, K. A. *Prakṛti in Sāṁkhya-Yoga: Material Principle, Religious Experience, Ethical Implications*. New York: Peter Lang, 1999.

Jackson, C. T. *The Oriental Religions and American Thought: Nineteenth-Century Explorations*. Westport: Greenwood Press, 1981.

*Jaimini's Mīmāṃsāsūtra with Śābara's Commentary and Notes*, 3 vols. Ganganatha Jha (trans.). Gaekwad Oriental Series. Baroda: 1933–36; reprint Oriental Institute, 1973–1974.

Jain, M. "Nice People, Nasty Mood." *India Today* (15 February 1993): 72–3.

Jaipaul, R. "Kurukshetra Revisited." *Indian and Foreign Review* (1 March 1981): 27.

Jamison, S. W. *Sacrificed Wife / Sacrificer's Wife: Women, ritual and Hospitality in Ancient India*. New York: Oxford University Press, 1996.

Janaki, S. S. (ed.). *Kuppuswamy Sastri Birth Centenary Commemoration Volume*, 2 parts. Madras: Kuppuswamy Sastri Research Institute, 1981.

Jarrige, J. F. "Die frühesten Kulturen in Pakistan und ihre Entwicklung." In: P. von Zabern (ed.), *Vergessene Städte am Indus: Frühe Kulturen in Pakistan vom 8. bis zum 2. Jahrtausend*. Mainz: Verlag P. von Zabern, 1987.

Jarrell, H. R. *International Yoga Bibliography, 1950–1980*. Metuchen: Scarecrow Press, n.d.

Jayakar, P. *J. Krishnamurthi: a Biography*. Delhi: Penguin India, 1987.
Jayaswal, K. P. *Hindu Polity*, 4th ed. Bangalore: Bangalore Press, 1967.
Jesudason, C. S. H. *A History of Tamil Literature*. Heritage of India Series. Calcutta: Y.M.C.A. Publishing House, 1961.
Jha, G. *Pūrva-Mīmāṃsā in Its Sources*. Banares: Banares Hindu University, 1942; reprint Delhi: 1981.
Jha, M. (ed.). *Dimensions of Pilgrimage*. New Delhi: Inter-Indian Publications, 1985.
Jhangiani, M. A. *Jana Sangh and Swatantra: A Profile of the Rightist Parties in India*. Bombay: Manaktalas, 1969.
Jindal, K. B. *A History of Hindī Literature*. Allahabad: Kitab Mahal, 1955.
Johar, S. S. *Giani Zail Singh*. New Delhi: Gaurav Publishing House, 1984.
Johnson, C. (ed.). *Vedānta: An Anthology of Hindu Scripture, Commentary, and Poetry*. New York: Harper and Row, 1971.
Johnston, E. H. *Early Sāṁkhya*. Delhi: Motilal Banarsidass, 1969.
Jolly, J. *Hindu Law and Custom*. Calcutta: Greater India Society, 1928.
Joshi, L. S. "Moral Foundations of Indian Society." in *Nehru Abhinandan Granth*, 464–69. Calcutta: N. A. G. Committee, 1949.
Joshi, M. V. "The Concept of Brahman in Vallabha Vedānta," *JBOI* 22, 4 (June 1973): 474–83.
Joshi, R. V. *Le rituel de la dévotion Kṛṣṇaite*, Pondichery: Institute Français d'Indologie, 1959.
Kak, S. C. "Astronomy of the Vedic Altar." *Vistas in Astronomy* 36 (1993): 1–26.
Id. "The Astronomy of the Vedic Altar and the Ṛgveda," *Mankind Quarterly* 33, 1 (Fall 1992):43–55.
Id. "On the Chronology of Ancient India." *Indian Journal of History of Science* 22, 3 (1987): 222–34.
Id. "The Indus Tradition and the Indo-Aryans" *The Mankind Quarterly* 32, 3 (1992): 195–213.
Id. *The Astronomical Code of the Ṛgveda*, Munshiram Manoharlal: New Delhi, 2000.
Kakati, B. K. *The Mother Goddess Kāmākhyā*. Gauhati: Lawyers' Book Stall, 1948.
Kale, M. R. *A Higher Sanskrit Grammar*. Reprint Delhi: Motilal Banarsidass, 1961.
Kalyanaraman, S. "Revival of the Legendary River Sarasvatī." *ALB*, (1999) 17–21.
Id. *Sarasvatī*, 7 vols. Bangalore: Babasaheb (Umakanta Keshav) Apte Smarak Samiti, 2003.
Kane, P. V. *History of Dharmaśāstra*, 5 vols. (7 parts). Poona: Bhandarkar Oriental Research Institute, 1930–1962.
Id. *History of Sanskrit Poetics*, 3rd ed. Delhi: Motilal Banarsidass, 1961.
Kapadia, K. M. *Marriage and Family in India*, 2d ed. Oxford: Oxford University Press, 1959.
Karmarkar, A. P. "Religion and Philosophy of the Epics." In *CHI*, vol. 2, 80 ff.
Id. *The Religions of India*. Lonavla: Mira Publishing House, 1950.
Karpatriji Maharaj. *Rāmrājya aura Marksvāda* (in Hindī) Gorakhpur: Gītā Press, 1964.
Karttunen, K. "On the Contacts of South India with the Western World in Ancient Times." In A. Parpola and B. S. Hansen (eds.) *South Asian Religion and Society*, 189–204. London: Kurzon Press, 1986.
Karunakaran, K. P. "Regionalism." *Seminar* 87 (November 1966): 21–25.

Karve, I. *Hindu Society: An Interpretation*. Poona: Deshmukh Prakashan, 1961.
Id. *Kinship Organisation in India*. New York: Asia Publishing House, 1965.
Katre, S. M. *Introduction to Textual Criticism*. Poona: Deccan College, 1954.
Kaufmann, W. *The Rāgas of North India*. Oxford University Press, 1968.
*Kauṭilīya's Arthaśāstra*. R. P. Kangle (ed. and trans.), 3 parts. Bombay: University of Bombay, 1960–1961.
Kaylor, R. D. "The Concept of Grace in the Hymns of Nammāḷvār." *JAAR* 44 (1976): 649–60.
Kazanas, N. "Indigenous Indo-Āryans and the *Rigveda*." *Journal of Indo-European Studies* 30,3and4 (Fall/Winter 2002):275–334.
Id. "Final Reply." *Journal of Indo-European Studies* 31,1 and 2 (Spring/Summer 2003): 171–231
Keay, F. E. *Hindī Literature*, 3rd ed. Calcutta: YMCA Publishing House, 1960.
Id. *Kabīr and His Followers*. London: 1931.
Keer, D. *Dr. Ambedkar: Life and Mission*. Bombay: Popular Prakashan, 1962.
Keith, A. B. *The Age of the Ṛgveda*. Cambridge, Mass.: Harvard University Press, 1922.
Id. *A History of Sanskrit Literature*. London: Oxford University Press, 1920.
Id. *Indian Logic and Atomism*. Oxford: Clarendon Press, 1921.
Id. *The Karma Mīmāṃsā*. Calcutta: Association Press, 1921.
Id. *The Religion and Philosophy of the Veda and Upaniṣads*. Cambridge, Mass.: Harvard University Press, 1925.
Id. *The Sāṁkhya System*, 3rd ed. Heritage of India Series. Calcutta: YMCA Publishing House, 1949.
Id. *The Sanskrit Drama*. Reprint Oxford: Oxford University Press, 1924.
Keller, C. A. "Aspiration collective et éxperience individuelle dans la bhakti shivaite de l'Inde du sud." *Numen* 31, 1 (July 1984): 1–21.
Kenghe, C. T. "The Problem of Pratyayasarga in Sāṁkhya and its Relation to Yoga." *ABORI* 48–49 (1968): 365–73.
Kennedy, M. T. *The Chaitanya Movement* Calcutta: Association Press, 1925.
Khandelwal, M. *Women in Ochre Robes: Gendering Hindu Renunciation*. Albany: State University of New York Press, 2004.
Khiste, P. S. S. "Śrīvidyā." In *Kalyāna Devībhāgavatam Aṅgka*, 689–96. Gorakhpur: Gita Press, 1960, 689–96.
Kingsbury, F. and G. E. Philips (trans.). *Hymns of the Tamil Śaivite Saints*. Calcutta: Association Press, 1921.
Kinsley, D. *Hindu Goddesses*. Berkeley: University of California Press, 1986.
Id. *Hinduism: A Cultural Perspective*. Englewood Cliffs: Prentice Hall, 1982.
Id. *The Sword and the Flute: Kālī and Kṛṣṇa, Dark Visions of the Terrible and the Sublime in Hindu Mythology*. Berkeley: University of California Press, 1975.
Kipphardt, H. *In the Matter of Robert J. Oppenheimer*. London: Methuen, 1967.
Kirfel, W. D. *Purāṇa Pañcalakṣana*. Banares: Motilal Banarsidass, 1963.
Klaiman, M. H. (trans.). "Singing the Glory of Lord Krishna." In *The Śrī Kṛṣṇa Kīrtana of Baru Cāṇḍīdāsa*. Chico: Scholars Press, n.d.
Klimkeit, H. J. *Der politische Hinduismus, Indische Denker zwischen religiöser Reform und politischem Erwachen*. Wiesbaden: Harrassowitz, 1984.
Kloppenborg, Ria (ed.). *Selected Studies on Ritual in the Indian Religions. Essays to D. J. Hoens.Supplements to Numen* 45. Leiden: Brill, 1983.

Klostermaier, K. "Hindu Views of Buddhism." In R. Amore, (ed.), *Canadian Contributions to Buddhist Studies*, 60–82. Waterloo, Ont.: Wilfred Laurier University Press, 1980.

Id. "Hinduism in Bombay." *Religion* (UK) 1, 2 (1972): 83–91.

Id. *Hinduismus*. Cologne: Bachem, 1965.

Id. *In the Paradise of Kṛṣṇa*. Philadelphia: Westminster, 1971.

Id. *Mythologies and Philosophies of Salvation in the Theistic Traditions of India*. Waterloo, Ont.: Wilfred Laurier University Press, 1984.

Id. "Śaṁkaradarśanam." In *ALB* 61 (1997), 151–253 (Also published as a book with the Sanskrit text by the Theosophical Society, Adyar 2001)

Id. "The Original Dakṣa Saga." *Journal of South Asian Literature* 20, 1 (1985): 93–107.

Id. "*Sādhana*." *Religion and Society* 16, 2 (1969): 36–50.

Id. "Vaiṣṇavism and Politics." *JVS* 1: 1 (1992): 166–82.

Id. *A Concise Encyclopedia of Hinduism*, Oneworld: Oxford, 1998

Id. *Hindu Writings: A Short Introduction to the Major Sources*, Oxford: Oneworld, 2001.

Id. "Himsā and Ahimsā Traditions in Hinduism." In H. Dueck (ed.), *The Pacifist Impulse in Historical Perspective*, 227–239. University of Toronto Press, 1995.

Id. "Hinduism, Population, Consumption and the Environment." In H. Coward (ed.), *Population, Consumption, and the Environment*, 137–153. Albany: State University of New York Press, 1995.

Id. "Charity in Hinduism." In M. Benad (ed.), *Diakonie der Religionen* 1, 111–118. Frankfurt a. M.: P. Lang, 1996,

Id. "Gauḍīya Vaiṣṇavism: The Education of Human Emotions." In K. Iswaran (ed.), *Ascetic Culture: Renunciation and Worldly Engagement*, 127–138. Brill: Leiden, 1999.

Id. "Bhakti, Ahimsā and Ecology." *Journal of Dharma* (Bangalore) 16, 3: 246–54.

Id. "Questioning the Āryan Invasion Theory and Revising Ancient Indian History." *International Quarterly of Indian Philosophy*, Special Issue, June 2001, 63–78.

Id. "Hindu-Christian Dialogue: Revisiting the Tannirpalli Trinity's Original Vision." *Hindu-Christian Studies Bulletin*, 16 (2003): 3–11.

Id. "Hinduism and Science." In J. W. Vrede von Huysteen (ed.), *Encyclopaedia of Science and Religion*, vol. 1: 305–10. Macmillan, 2003.

Id. "Truth and Tolerance in Contemporary Hinduism." In: E. Furcha (ed.), *Papers from the 1990 Symposium on Truth and Tolerance*. Montreal: McGill University, 1990

Id. "Remembering Vṛndāvana." In A. McDowall and A. Sharma (ed.), *Vignettes of Vṛndāvana*. New Delhi: Books and Books, 1987.

Id. "Hindu Missions in India and Abroad." In: J. S. Scott and G. Griffith (eds.), *Mixed Messages: Materiality, Textuality, Misions*, 173–202. New York: Palgrave Macmillan, 2005.

Id. "Hinduism in Bombay." *Religion* 1,2 (1972):83–91.

Id. "Samnyāsa: A Christian Way of Life in Today's India?" *Indian Ecclesiastical Studies* 7, 1 (1968):8–40.

Id. "Mokṣa." In S. Mittal and G. Thursby (eds.). *The Hindu World*: 288–305. New York—London. Routledge, 2004.

Id. "A Universe of Feelings." In P. Billimoria and P. Fenner (eds.), *Religion and Comparative Thought*, 123–39. Delhi: Śrī Satguru Publications, 1989.

Id. *Buddhism: A Short Introduction*, Oxford: Oneworld, 1999.
Knipe, D. M. *In the Image of Fire: Vedic Experiences of Heat.* Delhi: Motilal Banarsidass, 1975.
Id. *Hinduism: Experiments in the Sacred.* San Francisco: Harper, 1991.
Koelman, G. M. *Patañjala Yoga; From Related Ego to Absolute Self.* Poona: Papal Athenaeum, 1970.
Koestler, A. *The Lotus and the Robot.* New York: Harper and Row, 1961.
Kölver, B. "Stages in the Evolution of a World Picture." *Numen* 32, 2, 131–168.
van Kooij, K. R. "Protective Covering (*Kavaca*)," In *Selected Studies on Ritual in the Indian Religions*; 118–129. R. Kloppenburg, (ed.) Leiden: Brill, 1983.
Kopf, D. *The Brahmo Samāj and the Shaping of the Modern Indian Mind.* Princeton: Princeton University Press, 1979.
Kosambi, D. D. (ed.). *The Epigrams Attributed to Bhartṛhari Including the Three Centuries.* Singhi Jain Series. Bombay: Bharatiya Vidya Bhavan, 1948.
Id. *An Introduction to the Study of Indian History.* Bombay: Popular Book Depot, 1956.
Id. *Myth and Reality: A Study in the Foundations of Indian Culture.* Bombay: Popular Prakashan, 1961.
Kothari, R. *Caste in Indian Politics.* New Delhi: Orient Longman, 1970.
Krämer, H J. *Der Ursprung der Geistmetaphysik*, 2d ed. Amsterdam: B. R. Bruner, 1967.
Kramrisch, S. *The Art of India: Traditions of Indian Sculpture, Painting and Architecture.* London: Phaidon, 1954.
Id. *The Hindu Temple*, 2 vols. Calcutta: University of Calcutta 1946; reprint Delhi: Motilal Banarsidass, 1977.
Id. "The Image of Mahādeva in the Cave Temple on Elephanta Island." *Ancient India* 2 (1946): 4–8.
Id. *Indian Sculpture* (1933); reprint Delhi: Motilal Banarsidass, 1981.
Id. *The Presence of Śiva*, Princeton: Princeton University Press, 1981.
Id. "The Triple Structure of Creation in the *Ṛgveda.*" *HR* 2, 1–2 (1962): 140–75 and 256–85.
Krick, H. "Der Vanistusava und Indras Offenbarung." *WZKSA* 19 (1975): 25–74.
Kripal, J. *Kali's Child: The Mystical and the Erotic in the Life and Teaching of Ramakrishna.* Chicago: The Univeristy of Chicago Press, 1995.
Krishna, D. et al. *Samvāda: A Dialogue between Two Philosophical Traditions.* Delhi: Indian Council of Philosophical Research, 1991.
Krishna, G. *The Awakening of Kuṇḍalinī.* New York: E. P. Dutton, 1975.
Krishnamurti, J. *The Awakening of Intelligence.* New York: Avon Books, 1976.
Id. *The First and Last Freedom.* London: V. Gollancz, 1967 (1954).
*Kṛṣṇakarnāmṛta of Līlāsūka*, M. A. Acharya, (ed. and trans.). Madras: V. Ramaswamy Sastrulu, 1958.
Kuiper, F. B. J. *Ancient Indian Cosmogony.* New Dehli: Vikas, 1983.
Kulkarni, R. "Vāstupādamaṇḍala." *JOIB* 28:3–4 (March-June 1979): 107–38.
Kumar, G. D. "The Ethnic Components of the Builders of the Indus Civilization and the Advent of the Āryans." *Journal of Indo-European Studies* 1, 1 (1973): 66–80.
Kumarappa, B. *The Hindu Conception of the Deity.* London: Luzac, 1934.
Kumari, V. (trans.). *The Nīlamata Purāṇa.* Srinagar: J and K Academy of Art, Culture and Language, 1968.

Kunst, A. "Use and Misuse of the Dharma." In W. D. O'Flaherty and J. D. M. Derret (eds.), *The Concept of Duty in Southeast Asia*, 3–17.

Kuppuswamy, B. *Dharma and Society: A Study in Social Values*. Columbia, Mo.: South Asia Books, 1977.

Kuppuswamy, G., and M. Hariharan. "Bhajana Tradition in South India," *Sangeet Natak* 64–65 (April-September 1982): 32–50.

Id., (eds.). *Jayadeva and Gītāgovinda: A Study*. Trivandrum: College Book House, 1980.

Lacombe, O. *L'absolu sélon le Vedānta*. Paris: 1957; reprint Geuthner, 1966.

*Laghusiddhāntakaumudī of Vāradarāja*. J. R. Ballantyne (ed. and trans.). Reprint Delhi: Motilal Banarsidass, 1961.

Lal, B. B. "The Indus Script: Some Observations Based on Archaeology," in: *JRAS* 1975: 2: 173–209.

Id. "Reading the Indus Script." *IFR* (15 April 1983): 33–36.

Lal, C. *Hindu America*. Bombay: Bharatiya Vidya Bhavan, 1961.

Lal, K. *Holy Cities of India*. Delhi: Asia Press, 1961.

Lamb, B. P. *India: A World in Transition*, 3rd ed. New York: Praeger, 1968.

Lannoy, R. *The Speaking Tree*. Oxford: Oxford University Press, 1971.

Larson, G. J. "The *Bhagavad-Gītā* as Cross-Cultural Process: Toward an Analysis of the Social Locations of a Religious Text." *JAAR* 43 (1975): 651–669.

Id. *Classical Sāṅkhya*. Delhi: Motilal Banarsidass, 1969.

Id. "The Format of Technical Philosophical Writing in ancient India: Inadequacies of Conventional Translations," *Philosophy of East and West* 30, 3 (1980): 375–80.

Latham, R. E. (trans.). *The Travels of Marco Polo*. Harmondsworth, U.K.: Penguin, 1958.

Lee, D. "The Natural History of the Rāmāyaṇa." In C. K. Chapple and M. E. Tucker (eds.). *Hinduism and Ecology*, 245–68.

Legget, T. (trans.) *The Complete Commentary by Śaṅkara on the Yoga Sūtras: A Full Translation of the Newly Discovered Text*. London: Kegan Paul, 1990.

Leifer, W. *Indien und die Deutschen: 500 Jahre Begegnung und Partnerschaft*. Tübingen and Basel: Horst Erdmann Verlag, 1969.

LeMay, R. *The Culture of South-East Asia: The Heritage of India*. London: Allen and Unwin, 1954.

Lester, R. C. *Rāmānuja on the Yoga*. Madras: The Adyar Library and Research Centre, 1976.

Lévi, S. *La doctrine du sacrifice dans le Brāhmaṇas*. Paris: 1898; reprint Presses Universitaires de France, 1966.

Liebert, G. *Iconographic Dictionary of the Indian Religions: Hinduism, Buddhism, Jainism*. Leiden: Brill, 1976.

Lindtner, C. "Some Sanskritisms in the New Testament Gospels." *Brahmavidyā*, 65 (2002): 101–110.

Lipner, J. *The Face of Truth*. Albany: State University of New York Press, 1986.

Id. *Hindus: Their Religious Beliefs and Practices*, London: Routledge, 1994.

Long, J. B. "Festival of Repentance: A Study of Mahāśivarātrī," *JBOI* 22, 1–2 (September-December 1972): 15–38.

Lorenzen, D. N. *The Kāpālikas and Kālamukhas: Two Lost Śaivite Sects*. Berkeley: University of California Press, 1972.

Id. "The Life of Śaṅkarācārya." In *Experiencing Śiva*, F. Clothey and J. B. Long, (eds.) Columbia, Mo.: South Asia Books, 1983.

Id. "Who Invented Hinduism?," *Comparative Studies in Society and History* 41.1 (Oct. 1999) 630–59.

Lott, E. J. *God and the Universe in the Vedantic Theology of Rāmānuja: A Study in His Use of the Self-Body Analogy*. Madras: Rāmānuja Research Society, 1976.

Lupsa, M. *Chants á Kālī de Rāmprasād*. Pondichery: Institute Français d'Indologie, 1967.

Lüders, H. *Varuṇa*, 2 vols. L. Alsdorf (ed.). Göttingen: Vandenhoeck and Ruprecht, 1951–59.

Lütt, Jürgen, *Hindu-Nationalismus in Uttar Pradeś 1867–1900*. Stuttgart: Ernst Klett Verlag, 1970.

Macauliffe, M. A. *The Sikh Religion: Its Gurus, Sacred Writings and Authors*, 3 vols. Reprint Delhi: S. Chand, 1963.

Macdonnell, A. A. *A History of Sanskrit Literature*, 2d ed. Reprint Delhi: Motilal Banarsidass, 21961

Id. *Vedic Mythology*. Reprint Varanasi: Indological Bookhouse, 1963.

Id. "Vedic Religion." In *Encyclopedia of Religion and Ethics*. E. Hastings, (3rd ed.) 1954, vol. 12, 601–18.

Id., and A. B. Keith. *Vedic Index of Names and Subjects*, 2 vols. Reprint Delhi: Motilal Banarsidass, 1958.

McKean, L. *Divine Enterprise: Gurus and the Hindu Nationalist Movement*. Chicago: University of Chicago Press, 1996.

Mackichan, D. "Vallabha." *ERE*, vol. 12, 580–83.

Maclagan, D. *Creation Myths: Man's Introduction to the World*. London: Thames and Hudson, 1977.

Macnicol, N. *Indian Theism*. London: Oxford University Press, 1915.

Id. *Psalms of the Maratha Saints*. Heritage of India Series. Calcutta: Association Press, 1919.

Madan, T. N. (ed.). *Way of Life: King, Householder, Renouncer—Essays in Honor of Louis Dumont*. Delhi: Vikas Publishing House, 1982.

Id. "Secularism in Its Place." *JAS* 64, 4 (1987):747–59.

Id., and G. Sarana. *Indian Anthropology*. New York: Asia Publishing House, 1962.

*Mahābhārata* (short summary). C. Rajagopalachari (ed.). Bombay: Bharatiya Vidya Bhavan, 1958.

*Mahābhārata*, P. C. Roy. 12 vols (trans.). Calcutta: 1884–96 (several reprints: Calcutta Oriental without date).

*Mahābhārata*, Books 1–5. J. A. B. van Buitenen, (trans.) 3 vols. Chicago: Chicago University Press, 1973–1978.

*Mahābhārata, Critical Edition*, 22 vols. Poona: Bhandarkar Oriental Research Institute, 1933–1966.

Mahadevan, T. M. P. *Outline of Hinduism*, 2d ed. Bombay: Cetana, 1960.

Id. *Ramana Maharsi and His Philosophy of Existence*. Annamalai: 1951.

Id. *The Sage of Kanchi*. Secunderabad: 1967.

Id. "Śaivism." In *HCIP*, vol. 2, 433 ff.

Id. *Ten Saints of India*. Bombay: Bharatiya Vidya Bhavan, 1961.

Id. (ed. and trans.). *Hymns of Śaṅkara*. Madras: 1970.

Mahadevananda, Swāmi (trans.). *Devotional Songs of Narsi Mehta*. Delhi: Motilal Banarsidass, 1985.

Maitra, S. K. *The Ethics of the Hindus*, 3rd ed. Calcutta: University of Calcutta, 1963.

Id. *Fundamental Questions of Indian Metaphysics and Logics*, 2 vols. Calcutta: Chuckervertty, Chatterjee and Co., 1956–1961.

Maitra, S. *An Introduction to the Philosophy of Sri Aurobindo*, 2d ed. Banares: Banares Hindu University, 1945.

Majumdar, A. K. *Caitanya: His Life and Doctrine*. Bombay: Bharatiya Vidya Bhavan, 1969.

Majumdar, D. N. *Caste and Communication in an Indian Village*, 3rd ed. Bombay: Asia Publishing House, 1962.

Id. *Races and Cultures of India*. Bombay: Asia Publishing House, 1964.

Majumdar, G. P. and S. C. Banerjea (eds. and translators). *Kṛṣi-Parāśara*. Calcutta, Asiatic Society, 1960.

Majumdar, J. K. *Rājā Rammohan Roy and Progressive Movements in India, Volume 1. A Selection from Records (1774–1845)*. Calcutta: Brahmo Mission Press, n.d.

Majumdar, R. C. *The Classical Accounts of India*. Calcutta: Firma K. L. Mukhopadhyay, 1960.

Id. "Kāpāla and Kālamukha Sects." HCIP vol. 5, 458–59.

Id. *Hindu Colonies in the Far East*, 2d ed. Calcutta: Firma K. L. Mukhopadhyay, 1963.

Id. (gen. ed.). *The History and Culture of the Indian People*. Bombay: Bharatiya Vidya Bhavan, 1945–1978.

Majumdar, R. C., H. C. Raychaudhuri, and K. Datta. *An Advanced History of India*, 3rd ed. London: Macmillan, 1965.

Malamoud, C. "On the Rhetoric and Semantics of Puruṣārtha." In *Way of Life*, T. N. Madan, (ed.) Delhi: Vikas Publishing House, 33–52.

Malkovsky, B. J. *The Role of Divine Grace in the Soteriology of Śaṁkarācārya*. Leiden: Brill, 2001.

Maloney, C. *Peoples of South Asia*. New York: Holt, Rhinehart and Winston, 1974.

*Mānameyodaya*. C. Kunhan Raja (trans.). Adyar: Theosophical Publishing House, 1933.

*Mānasāra*. P. K. Acharya (trans.). 1934; reprint New Delhi: Motilal Banarsidass, 1980.

*Mānava Dharma Śāstra*. J. Jolly (trans.). London: 1887.

*Mānava Śrauta Sūtra*, J. M. van Gelder (trans.). New Delhi: International Academy of Indian Culture, 1963.

*Māndūkyopaniṣad with Gauḍapāda's Kārikā and Śaṅkara's Commentary*, 4th ed., Swāmi Nihkilananda (trans.). Mysore: Ramakrishna Math, 1955.

Manickam, V. S. *The Tamil Concept of Love*. Madras: South Indian Śaiva Siddhānta Works Publishing Society, 1962.

*Maṇikana, A Navya-Nyāya Manual*, E. R. Sreekrishna Sarma (ed. and trans.). Adyar: Adyar Library, 1960.

*Manusmṛti*. Pandit Hargovind Sastri (ed.). Varanasi: Chowkhamba Sanskrit Series, 1952. G. Buehler (trans.), *SBE* vol. 25: *The Laws of Manu*.

Marfatia, M. I. *The Philosophy of Vallabhācārya*. Delhi: Munshiram Manoharlal, 1967.

*Mārkaṇḍeya Purāṇa*, 3rd ed. Bombay: Venkatesvar Steam Press, 1910; F. E. Pargiter (trans.), reprint Delhi: Indological Book House, 1969.

Marriott, McKim (ed.). *Village India: Studies in the Little Community*. Chicago: University of Chicago Press, 1963.

Marshall, J. *Mohenjo Daro and the Indus Civilization*, 3 vols. London: University of Oxford Press, 1931.

Marshall, P. J. (ed.). *The British Discovery of Hinduism in the Eighteenth Century*. European Understanding of India Series. Cambridge: 1971.

Masani, M. R. *The Communist Party of India*. London: Derek Versdroyle, 1954.

Masui, J. H. " Introduction to the Study of Yoga." In P. A. Sorokin (ed.). *Forms and Techniques of Altruistic and Spiritual Growth*, 19–31.

Mate, M. S. *Temples and Legends of Mahārāṣṭra*. Bombay: Bharatiya Vidya Bhavan, 1962.

Mathur, S. K. *Caste and Ritual in a Malwa Village*. New York: Asia Publishing House, 1964.

Matilal, B. K. *Logic, Language and Reality*. Delhi: Motilal Banarsidass, 1985.

Id. *The Navya Nyāya Doctrine of Negation*. Harvard Oriental Series, 46. Cambridge, Mass.: Harvard University Press, 1972.

*Mayamata*. B. Dagens, French (trans.), 2 vols. Pondichery: Institut Français d'Indologie, 1970–1976.

Mayer, A. C. *Caste and Kinship in Central India: A Village and Its Religion*. Berkeley: University of California Press, 1965.

Mayr, E. *Toward a New Philosophy of Biology*. Cambridge: Harvard University Press, 1988.

McDowall, A. and A. Sharma (eds.). *Vignettes of Vṛndāvana*. New Delhi: Books and Books, 1987.

McKenzie, J. *Hindu Ehtics*. Oxford: Oxford University Press, 1922.

Meenaksisundaram, T. P. *A History of Tamil Literature*. Annamalainagar: Annamalai University, 1965.

Mehendale, M. A. "Purāṇas." In *HCIP*, vol. 3, 291–99.

Mehra, J. (ed.). The Physicists Conception of Nature, Dordrecht: Reidel, 1973.

Mehta, M. "The Evolution of the Suparṇa Saga in the *Mahābhārata*." *JOIB* 1971: 41–65.

Id. "The Problem of the Double Introduction to the *Mahābhārata*," *JAOS* 93, 4 (1973): 547–50.

Meister, M. W. "Hindu Temples." In *Encyclopedia of Religion*, M. Eliade (ed.), vol. 14, 368–73.

Id. "Maṇḍala and Practice in Nāgara Architecture in North India," *JAOS* 99 (1979): 204–219.

Id. "Measurement and Proportion in Hindu Architecture." *Interdisciplinary Science Reviews* 10 (1985): 248–258.

Id. (ed.). *Encyclopedia of Indian Temple Architecture*, vol.1, South India. New Delhi: American Institute of Indian Studies, 1983.

Id. (ed.). *Discourses on Śiva*, Philadelphia: University of Pennsylvania Press, 1984.

Menon, I. K. K. "Kerala's Early Foreign Contacts." *IFR* (15 July 1980): 13 ff.

Menski, W. F. *Hindu Law: Beyond Tradition and Modernity*. Dehli: Oxford University Press, 2003.

Miller, D. M. and D. C. Wertz. *Hindu Monastic Life: The Monks and Monasteries of Bhubaneswar*. Montreal: McGill-Queen's University Press, 1976.

*Mīmāṃsākośa*, 7 vols. Kevalananda Sarasvati (ed.). Wai: Dharmakosamandala, 1952–1966.
*Mīmāṃsāparibhāṣa of Kṛṣṇa Yajvan*. Swāmi Madhavanand (ed. and trans.). Belur Math: The Ramakrishna Mission Sarada Pitha, 1948.
*Minor Lawbooks*. J. Jolly (trans.). In *SBE*, vol. 33.
Minor, R. (ed.). *Modern Indian Interpretation of the Bhagavadgītā*. Albany: State University of New York Press, 1986.
Minor, R. *Bhagavad-Gītā: An Exegetical Commentary*. Columbia, Mo.: South Asia Books, 1982.
Minz, N. "Anthropology and the Deprived." *Religion and Society* 32, 4 (1985): 3–19.
Mishra, V. *The Conception of Matter According to Nyāya-Vaiśeṣika*. Reprint Delhi: Gian Publishers, 1983.
Id. *Hinduism and Economic Growth*. Oxford: Oxford University Press, 1963.
Id. "Prehistory and Protohistory." In *Review of Indological Research in Last 75 Years*, P.J. Chinmulgund and V.V. Mirashi, (eds.) Poona: Bharatiya Charitra Kosha Mandal, 1967, 353–415.
Misra, Om Prakash. *Mother Goddess in Central India*. Delhi: Agam Kala Prakashan, 1985.
Mitra, A. M. *India as Seen in the Bṛhatsamhitā of Varāhamihira*. Delhi: Motilal Banarsidass, n.d.
Mitra, S. D. "The Advaitic Concept of Abhāsa." In R. N. Dandekar (ed.) V. Raghavan Felicitation Volume, 267–89.
Mittal, S. and G. Thursby (eds.). *The Hindu World*. New York and London: Routledge, 2005.
Mollat, M. "The Importance of Maritime Traffic to Cultural Contacts in the Indian Ocean." *Diogenes* 3 (1980): 1–18.
Möller, V. *Götter und Mythen des indischen Subkontinents*, vol. 5 of H. W. Haussig (ed.). *Wörterbuch der Mythologie*. Stuttgart: Klett-Cotta, 1972.
Monier-Williams, M. *Dictionary, English and Sanskrit*. Originally published in London 1851, reprint Varanasi: Chowkhambha Sanskrit Series Office, 1965.
Mookerjee, A., and M. Khanna. *The Tantric Way: Art—Science—Ritual*. London: Thames and Hudson, 1977.
Morinis, E. A. *Pilgrimage in the Hindu Tradition: A Case Study of West Bengal*. South Asian Studies Series. New York and New Delhi: Oxford University Press, 1984.
Morris-Jones, W. H. *The Government and Politics of India*. London: Hutchinson University Library, 1964.
Mudgal, S. G. *Advaita of Śaṅkara: A Reappraisal*. Delhi: Motilal Banarsidass, 1975.
Mughal, M. R. "Recent Archeological Discoveries in the Cholistan Desert." In G. Possehl (ed.). *Harappan Civilisation*, Warminster: Aris and Philips, 1982.
Mukarji, Nirmal. "The Hindu Problem," *Seminar* 269 (January 1982): 37–40.
Mulji, K. *History of the Sect of the Mahajaras or Vallabhacaryas in Western India*, Bombay, 1865.
Müller, M. (ed.). *Ṛgveda with the Commentary of Sāyaṇa*, 4 vols., 2d ed. London: 1892; reprint: Varanasi: Chowkhambha Sanskrit Office, 1966.
Id. (ed.). *Ṛgveda pratiśākhya* by Śaunaka. Leipzig 1856.

Id. *The Six Systems of Indian Philosophy*. Reprint Varanasi: Chowkhamba, 1962.

*Mumukṣupatti of Pillai Lokācārya with Manacalamuni's Commentary* (trans.). P. Y. Mumme. Anantacharya Indological Research Series, 19. Bombay, 1988.

Mundaden, A. M. *St. Thomas Christians and the Portuguese*. Bangalore: Dharmaram Studies, 1970.

Id. *The Traditions of St. Thomas Christians*. Bangalore: Dharmaram Studies, 1972.

Murti, G. Srinivasa. "Introduction." In *Śrī Pāñcarātra Rakṣa of Śrī Vedānta Deśika*. [M.D. Aiyangar and T. Venugopalacharya, (eds.),] Madras: Adyar Library, 1942.

Murti, T. R. V. "The Rise of the Philosophical Schools." In *CHI*, vol. 3, 32.

Murty, K. S. *Revelation and Reason in Advaita Vedānta*. Waltair: Waltair University, 1959.

Nagendra, D. *Indian Literature*. Agra: Lakshmi Narain Agarwal, 1959.

Nair, K. *Blossoms in the Dust*, 2d ed. London: Duckworth, 1962.

*Naiṣkarmyasiddhi* of Sureśvara. K. K. Venkatachari (ed. and trans.). Adyar: Adyar Library, 1982.

*Nālaḍiyār*. G. U. Pope (trans.). Oxford: Oxford University Press, 1893.

Nandimath, S. C. *Handbook of Vīraśaivism*. Dharwar: L. E. Association, 1941.

*Nārada Bhakti Sūtras: Aphorisms on the Gospel of Divine Love*, 3rd ed. Swāmi Tyagisananda (trans.). Mylapore: Ramakrishna Math, 1955.

Narayan, J. *From Socialism to Sarvodaya*. Kashi: Sarva Seva Sangh Prakashan, n.d.

Narayanan, V. "Gender and Priesthood in the Hindu Traditions." *Journal of Hindu-Christian Studies*, 18 (2005): 22–31.

Nath, Pundit Shunker. *Christ: Who and What He Was*: Part 1. *Christ a Hindu Disciple, nay a Buddhist Saint*: Part 2. *Christ a Pure Vedāntist*. Calcutta: Calcutta Dayamoy Printing Works, 1927–1928.

Nayar, T. Balakrishnan. *The Problem of Dravidian Origins—A Linguistic, Anthropological and Archeological Approach*. Madras: University of Madras, 1977.

Neevel, W. G. Jr. *Yamuna's Vedānta and Pāñcarātra: Integrating the Classical and the Popular*. Chico Calif.: Scholar's Press, 1977.

Nehru, J. *Autobiography*. London 1936; Indian (ed.) New Delhi: Allied Publishers, 1962.

Id. *The Discovery of India*. London: 1946; reprint Meridian Books, 1960.

Neill, S. *A History of Christianity in India: The Beginnings to* AD *1707*. Cambridge: Cambridge University Press, 1984.

Neog, M. *Early History of the Vaiṣṇava Faith and Movement inAssam Śaṅkaradeva and His Time*, 2d ed. Delhi: Motilal Banarsidass, 1985.

Neufeldt, R. F. *Max Müller and the Ṛg-Veda: A Study of Its Role in His Work and Thought*. Columbia, Mo.: South Asia Books, 1980.

Id. (ed.) *Karma and Rebirth: Post-classical Developments*. Albany: State University of New York Press, 1986.

Neuman, E. *An Analysis of the Archetype The Great Mother*. R. Manheim (trans.). Princeton: Bollingen, 1955.

Neumayer, E. *Prehistoric Indian Rock Paintings*. Delhi: Oxford University Press, 1983.

de Nicolás, A. T. *Avatāra: The Humanization of Philosophy Through the Bhagavad Gītā*. New York: Nicholas Hays, 1976.

Swāmi Nikhilananda (trans.). *Gospel of Sri Ramakrishna*. Calcutta: 1930.

*Nimbārka. Vedānta Parijāta Saurabha and Vedānta Kausthubha of Śrīnivāsa*, R. Bose, (trans.) 3 vols. Calcutta: Royal Asiatic Society of Bengal, 1940–1943.
Nirvedananda, Swāmi. "Śrī Rāmakrishna and Spiritual Renaissance." In *CHI*, vol. 4, 653–728.
"No Holds Barred Battle" *India Today* (15 March 1987): 56–57.
Nooten, B. A. van. *The Mahābhārata*. New York: 1971.
*Nyāsavimśati by Vedānta Deśika*, D. Ramaswamy Aiyangar (ed. and trans.). Mylapore-Madras: Vishishtadvaita Pracharini Sabha, 1979.
*Nyāyakusumañjali of Udāyana*. E. G. Cowell, (ed. and trans.). Calcutta: 1864.
Oberhammer, G. "Die Gotteserfahrung in der yogischen Meditation." In *Offenbarung als Heilserfahrung in Christentum, Hinduismus and Buddhismus*. W. Strolz and S. Ueda (eds.). Freiburg-Basel-Vienna: Herder, 1982, pp. 146–66.
Id. *Strukturen Yogischer Meditation*. Vienna: Österreichische Akademie der Wissenschaften, 1977.
Id. "Das Transzendenzverständis des Sāṁkhyistischen Yoga als Strukturprinzip seiner Mystik." In *Transzendenzerfahrung, Vollzugshorizont des Heils*, G. Oberhammer, (ed.) Vienna: De Nobili Research Library, 1978, 15–28.
Oberlies, T. "Die Śvetāsvatara Upaniṣad: Eine Studie ihrer Gotteslehre." *WZKS* 32 (1988): 35–62.
O'Connell, J. T. "Historicity in the Biographies of Caitanya." *JVS* 1,2 (1993): 102–32.
O'Flaherty, W. D. *Asceticism and Eroticism in the Mythology of Śiva*. London: Oxford University Press, 1973.
Id. *The Origins of Evil in Hindu Mythology*. Berkeley: University of California Press, 1976.
Id. "The Origin of Heresy in Hindu Mythology." *HR* 10 (May 1971): 271–333.
Id. *Śiva: The Erotic Ascetic*. New York: Oxford University Press, 1981.
Id. (ed.). *Karma and Rebirth in Classical Indian Traditions*. Berkeley: University of California Press, 1980.
O'Flaherty, W. D. and Derret, J. D. M. (eds.). *The Concept of Duty in Southeast Asia*. New Delhi: Vikas, 1978.
Oguibenine, B. "Cosmic Tree in Vedic and Tamil Mythology: Contrastive Analysis." *Journal of Indo-European Studies* 12,3–4 (1984): 367–374.
Ojha, C. "Feminine Asceticism in Hinduism: Its Tradition and Present Condition." *Man in India*, 61, 3 (1981): 254–85.
Oldenberg, H. *Das Mahābhārata*. Göttingen: Vandenhoeck and Ruprecht, 1922.
Oldmeadow, H. *Journeys East: Twentieth-Century Western Encounters with Eastern Religions*. Bloomington, Ind.: World Wisdom, 2004.
Olivelle, P. (ed. and trans.). *Vasudevāśrama's Yatidharmaprakāśa: A Treatise on World Renunciation*, 2 vols. Vienna: De Nobili Library, 1977.
Id. "Contributions to the Semantic History of Samnyāsa," in *JAOS* 101 (1981): 265–74.
Id. *Renunciation in Hinduism: A Medieval Debate*, 2 vols.. Vienna: Institute of Indology University of Vienna, 1986–87.
Id. (ed. and trans.). *Rules and Regulations of Brahmanical Asceticism: Yatidharmasamuccaya of Yādava Prakāśa*, Albany: State University of New York Press, 1995.
O'Malley, L. S. *Popular Hinduism: The Religion of the Masses*. Oxford: Oxford University Press, 1941.

Oman, I. C. *The Mystics, Ascetics and Saints of India*. Reprint Delhi: Oriental Publishers, 1973.

O'Neil, L. T. *Māyā in Śaṅkara: Measuring the Immeasurable*. Delhi: Motilal Banarsidass, 1980.

Osborne, A. *Ramaṇa Maharṣi and the Path of Self-Knowledge*, 2d ed. Bombay: Jaico, 1962.

Id. (ed.). *The Collected Works of Ramaṇa Maharṣi*. New York: S. Weiser, 1959.

Ostor, A. *The Play of the Gods: Locality, Ideology, Structure and Time in the Festivals of a Bengali Town*. Chicago: University of Chicago Press, 1980.

Otto, R. *Mysticism East and West*. New York: Macmillan, 1957.

Overstreet, L., and M. Windmiller. *Communism in India*. Berkeley: University of California Press, 1959.

*Pañcadaśī of Vidyāraṇya*. Swāmi Swahananda (ed. and trans.). Madras: Ramakrishna Math, 1967.

*Pāñcarātra Rakṣā of Śrī Vedānta Deśika*, M. Duraiswami Aiyanjar and T. Venugopalacharya (eds.) with notes and variant readings, introduction by G. Srinivasa Murti. Adyar: Adyar Library, 1942.

*Pañcatantra*, 2d ed. A. W. Ryder (trans.). Reprint Bombay: Jaico, 1962.

*Pañcaviṃśa Brāhmaṇa*, W. Caland (trans.). Calcutta: Asiatic Society of Bengal, 1931.

Pandey, R. B. *Hindu Saṃskāras: Socio-religious Study of the Hindu Sacraments*. Banares: Vikrama Publications, 1949.

Pandeya, L. P. *Sun Worship in Ancient India*. Delhi: Motilal Banarsidass, 1972.

Panikkar, W. C. Sastri (ed.). *One Hundred and Eight Upanisads*. Bombay: Nirnaya Sagar Press, 1932.

Panikkar, K. M. *Asia and Western Dominance*, 3rd ed. London: Allen and Unwin, 1955.

Id. *Geographical Factors in Indian History*. Bombay: Bharatiya Vidya Bhavan, 1955.

Id. *Hindu Society at Cross Roads*. Bombay: Asia Publishing House, 1956.

Id. *Hinduism and the Modern World*. Bombay: Bharatiya Vidya Bhavan, 1956.

Id. *A Survey of Indian History*. Bombay: Asia Publishing House, 1947.

Pannikkar, R. (ed. and trans.). *The Vedic Experience: Mantramañjari—An Anthology of the Vedas for Modern Man and Contemporary Celebration*. Berkeley: University of California Press, 1977.

Id. *Kerygma und Indien*. Hamburg: Evangelischer Verlag, 1967.

*Pāniṇi's Aṣṭādhyāyī*, Sastri Devaprakasa Patanjala, (ed.). Delhi: Motilal Banarsidass, 1954.

*Pāniṇi's Aṣṭādhyāyī*, 2 vols. S. C. Vasu (ed. and trans.). Reprint Delhi: Motilal Banarsidass, 1961.

*Paramārtha Sopāna*. R. D. Ranade, Allahabad: Adhyātma Vidyā Mandir, 1954.

Paramesvaran, M. R. *Studies in Śrivaiṣṇavism*, Winnipeg: Larkuma 2005.

Paranjoti, V. *Śaiva Siddhānta*, 2d ed. London: Luzac, 1954.

Parekh, M. C. *Brahmarshi Keshub Chander Sen*. Rajkot: Bhagavat Dharma Mission, 1926.

Id. *The Brahmo Samāj*. Calcutta: Brahmo Samāj, 1922.

Id. *A Hindu's Portrait of Jesus Christ*. Rajkot: Bhagavat Dharma Mission, 1953.

Id. *Śrī Swāmi Nārāyaṇa*. Rajkot: Bhagavat Dharma Mission, 1936.

Id. *Vallabhācārya*. Rajkot: Bhagavat Dharma Mission, 1936.

Pargiter, F. E. *Ancient Indian Historical Tradition*. Reprint Delhi: Motilal Banarsidass, 1962.

Id. *The Purāṇa Texts of the Dynasties of the Kaliage*. Oxford: Oxford University Press, 1913.

Parpola, A. *The Sky Garment: A Study of the Harappan Religion and the Relation to the Mesopotamian and Later Indian Religions*. Helsinki: Finnish Oriental Society, 1985.

Id. *Deciphering the Indus Script*, Cambridge: Cambridge University Press, 1994.

Id. (ed.) with B. S. Hansen. *South Asian Religion and Society*. Studies on Asian Topics No. 11, Scandinavian Institute of Asian Studies. London: Curzon Press, 1986.

Parthasarathi, J. "The Dravida Veda-Vedāṅga: A Revolutionary Crosscurrent," *Śrī Rāmānuja Vānī* (April 1981): 47–68.

Parsons, J. *The Remains of Japhet, Being Historical Inquiries into the Affinity and Origins of the European Languages*. London: L. Davis and Co. 1767.

Parvathamma, C. *Politics and Religion*. New Delhi: Sterling Publishers, 1971.

*Patañjali Mahābhāsya*. 10 vols. Vedavrata Snataka (ed.). Gurukul Jhajjar (Rohtak): Haryana Sahitya Samsthan, 1961–1964.

*Patañjali's Yogasūtra*. Swāmi Vijnana Asrama (ed. and trans.). Ajmer: Śrī Madanlal Laksminivas Chandak, 1961.

Pathak, P. V. "Tectonic Upheavals in the Indus Region and Some Ṛgvedic Hymns." *ABORI* 64 (1983): 227–32.

Patil, D. R. *Cultural History of Vāyu Purāṇa*. Delhi: Motilal Banarsidass, n.d.

Patthabhiram, M. (ed.). *General Elections in India 1967: An Exhaustive Study of Main Political Trends*. Bombay: Allied Publishers, 1967.

Payne, A. A. *The Śāktas*. Calcutta: YMCA Publishing House, 1933.

Pechilis, K. (ed.). *The Graceful Guru: Hindu Female Gurus in India and the United States*. Oxford: Oxford University Press, 2004.

Pereira, J. (ed.). *Hindu Theology: A Reader*. Garden City: Doubleday, 1976.

Piggott, S. *Prehistoric India*. Baltimore: Penguin Books, 1961.

Pillai, G. K. *Vedic History*. Allahabad: Kitabistan, 1959.

Pillai, G. S. *Introduction and History of Śaiva Siddhānta*. Annamalai: Annamalai University, 1948.

Pillai, K. K. "The Caste System in Tamil Nadu." *Journal of the Madras University* 49, 2 (1977): 1–89.

Id. "The Non-Brahmin Movement in South India." In S.P. Sen (ed.) *Social Contents of Indian Religious Reform Movements*, 411–25. Calcutta: Institute of Historical Studies, 1978.

Id. *A Social History of the Tamils*, 2d ed.,vol. 1. Madras: University of Madras, 1973.

Pillai, S. S. "The Śaiva Saints of South India." In *CHI*, vol. 4, 339 ff.

Podgorski, F. R. *Hinduism: A Beautiful Mosaic*. South Bend, Ind.: Foundations Press of Notre Dame, 1983.

Popley, H. A. *The Music of India*. Calcutta: YMCA Publishing House, 1950.

Possehl, G. C. (ed.). *Harappan Civilisation: A Contemporary Perspective*. Warminster: Aris and Philips, 1982.

Potter, K. *Bibliography of Indian Philosophies*. Delhi: Motilal Banarsidass, 1970.

Id. (gen. ed.) *The Encyclopedia of Indian Philosophies*. Varanasi: Motilal Banarsidass, 1970–.

Id. *Presuppositions of India's Philosophies*. Englewood Cliffs: Prentice Hall, 1963.
Powell-Price, J. C. *A History of India*. London: T. Nelson, 1955.
Prabhananda, Svāmi. "Who Gave the Name Ramakrishna and When?" *The Vedanta Kesari* 74 (1987): 107–12.
Prabhu, P. H. *Hindu Social Organisation: A Study in Socio-Psychological and Ideological Foundations*, 4th ed. Bombay: Popular Prakashan, 1963.
Prabhu, R. K. and U. R. Rao (eds.). *The Mind of Mahatma Gandhi*. Ahmedabad: Nava Jivan, 1967
Prajnananada, Svāmi, *The Bases of Indian Culture*. Ramakrishna Ashram: Calcutta, 1972.
Prakash, O. *Political Ideas in the Puraṇas*. Allahabad: Panchanda Publications, 1977.
*Prameyaratnavalī by Baladeva*. Chandra Vasu Vidyarnava (trans). *SBH*, Allahabad: Panini Press, 1934.
Prasad, M. *Kaka Kalelkar: A Gandhian Patriarch*. Bombay: Popular Prakashan, 1965.
Prasad, S. *Dharmaśāstrasaṅgraha*. Bombay: Nirnaya Sagara Press, 1931.
*Pratyabhijñāhṛdayam*. J. Singh (ed. and trans.). Delhi: Motilal Banarsidass, 1963.
Presler, F. A. "The Structure and Consequences of Temple Policy in Tamiḷnādu, 1967–81." *Pacific Affairs* (Summer 1983): 232–46.
"Priestly Protest." *India Today* (15 December 1986): 111.
"Procedure of Reciting *Śrimad Bhāgavata*" *Kalyāṇa Kalpatāru* vol. 18/1 (August 1952): 6–8.
"Purāṇic India (Bhārata)." *HASA* 27.
Pusalker, A. D. "Aryan Settlements in India." In *HCIP*, vol. 1, 245–267.
Id. "Historical Traditions." In *HCIP*, vol. 1, 271–336.
Id. "Historicity of Kṛṣṇa." In *Studies in Epics and Purāṇas of India*,49–81. Bombay: Bharatiya Vidya Bhavan, 1955.
Id. "The Indus Valley Civilization." In *HCIP*, vol. 1, 172–202.
Id. "The *Mahābhārata*: Its History and Character." In *CHI*, vol. 2, 51 f 71.
Id. "Purāṇic Studies." *Review of Indological Research in the Last 75 Years*: 689–773. Poona: Bharatiya Charitrakosha Mandal, 1967.
Id. "The *Rāmāyaṇa*: Its History and Character." In *CHI*, vol. 2, 14 ff.
Id. *Studies in Epics and Purāṇas of India*. Bombay: Bharatiya Vidya Bhavan, 1955.
Id. "Traditional History from the Earliest Time to the Accession of Parikshit." In *The Vedic Age, HCIP*, vol. 1, 171–322.
Puthiadan, I. *Viṣṇu the Ever Free: A Study of the Madhva Concept of God*. Dialogue Series, No. 5. Madurai: Dialogue Publications, 1985.
Putnam, J. J. "The Ganges, River of Faith," with photography by Raghubir Singh. *National Geographic Magazine* (October 1971): 445–83.
Quong, S. "Śrī Ānandamāyī." *Hinduism Today* (Sept.–Oct. 1999): 7–8.
Radhakrishnan, S. *The Bhagavadgītā*. London: Allen and Unwin, 1948.
Id. *The Brahmasūtra*. London: Allen and Unwin, 1961.
Id. *Eastern Religions and Western Thought*. New York: Oxford University Press, 1964.
Id. *The Hindu View of Life*. New York: Macmillan, 1962.
Id. *Indian Philosophy*, 2d ed., 2 vols. London: Allen and Unwin, 1948.
Id. *My Search for Truth*. Agra: Agrawala, 1946.
Id. *The Principal Upaniṣads*. London: Allen and Unwin, 1953.
Id. *Religion and Society*. London: Allen and Unwin, 1947.

Id. *Religion in a Changing World*. London: Allen and Unwin, 1967.
Id. and C. A. Moore. *A Sourcebook in Indian Philosophy*. Princeton: Princeton University Press, 1957.
Raghavan, V. *The Great Integrators: The Saint Singers of India*. Delhi: Ministry of Information and Broadcasting, 1966.
Id. *The Indian Heritage*. Bangalore: Indian Institute of Culture, 1956.
*Rahasyatrayasāram by Vedānta Deśika* M. S. Rajagopala Ayangar; Agnihothram Ramanuja Thathachariar, Kumbakonam, 1956.
Rai, L. *The Ārya Samāj*. London: Longman, 1915.
Raj, D. *L'ésclavage dans l'Inde ancienne d'apres les textes Palis et Sanskrits*. Pondichery: Institute Français d'Indologie, 1957.
Raja, C. K. "Vedic Culture." In *CHI*, vol. 1, 199–220.
Raja, K. K. *Indian Theories of Meaning*. Adyar: The Adyar Library and Research Centre, 1963.
Rajagopalachari, R. C. *Hinduism: Doctrine and Way of Life*. Bombay: Bharatiya Vidya Bhavan, 1959.
Rajagopalan, V. "The Śrī Vaiṣṇava Understanding of Bhakti and Prapatti." Thesis: University of Bombay, 1978.
Raju, P. T. *The Philosophical Traditions of India*. London: Allen and Unwin, 1971.
Id. *Idealistic Thought of India*. London: Allen and Unwin, 1953.
Id. *Structural Depths of Indian Thought*. Albany: State University of New York Press, 1985.
Ralston, H. *Christian Ashrams: A New Religious Movement in Contemporary India*, Lewiston/Queenston: The Edwin Mellon Press, 1987.
Ram, S. *Vinoba and His Mission*, 3rd ed. Kasi: Akhil Bharata Sarva Seva Sangh, Rajghat, 1962.
Rama Tirtha, S. *Words of Godrealization*. Sarnath: Rama Tirtha Pratisthan, 1956.
*Rāmacaritamānasa by Tulsīdās*. Gorakhpur: Gītā Press, 1968.
*Śrī Bhagavad Rāmānuja Granthamālā*, P. B. Annangaracharya Swāmi (ed.). Kanchipuram: Granthamala Office, 1956.
*Rāmānuja's Vedārthasaṅgraha*. S. S. Raghavachar. (ed. and trans.) Mysore: Ramakrishna Ashrama, 1956.
Ramanujan, A. K. (trans.) *Speaking of Śiva*. Harmondsworth: Penguin Books, 1973.
*Rāmāyaṇa* (brief summary), 4th ed. C. Rajagopalachari (ed.). Bombay: Bharatiya Vidya Bhavan, 1962.
*The Rāmāyaṇa*, 3 vols. M. N. Dutt (trans.) 3 vols. Reprint Calcutta: Oriental Publishing Co., 1960.
*Rāmāyaṇa of Vālmīki*, 3rd ed. R. T. H. Griffith (trans.) Reprint Varanasi: Chowkhamba, 1963.
*Rāmāyaṇa, Critical Edition*, 7 vols. Baroda: Oriental Institute, 1960–1975.
Ramdas, Swāmi. *God-Experience*. Bombay: Bharatiya Vidya Bhavan, 1963.
Ramesan, R. *Temples and Legends of Andhra Pradesh*. Bombay: Bharatiya Vidya Bhavan, 1962.
Ranade, R. D. *Bhagavadgītā as a Philosophy of God-Realization, Being a Clue through the Labyrinth of Modern Interpretations*, 2d ed., Bombay: Bharatiya Vidya Bhavan, 1965.

Id. *A Constructive Survey of Upaniṣadic Philosophy*. Reprint Bombay: Bharatiya Vidya Bhavan, 1968.

Id. *Pathway to God in Hindī Literature*. Bombay: Bharatiya Vidya Bhavan, 1959.

Id. *Pathway to God in Kannaḍa Literature*. Bombay: Bharatiya Vidya Bhavan, 1960.

Id. *Pathway to God in Marathī Literature*. Bombay: Bharatiya Vidya Bhavan, 1961.

Ranganathananda, Swāmi. "The Science of Consciousness in the Light of Vedānta and Yoga," *Prabuddha Bharata* (June 1982): 257–63.

Rao, H. S. "The Two Babas." *Illustrated Weekly of India* (21 November 1965).

Rao, S. G. *Mahātmā Gandhi and C. F. Andrews: A Study in Hindu-Christian Dialogue*. Patiala: Punjabi University, 1969.

Rao, S. R. "Deciphering the Indus Valley Script." *Indian and Foreign Review* (15 November 1979): 13–18.

Id. *The Decipherment of the Indus Script*. Bombay: Asia Publishing House, 1982.

Id. "Krishna's Dwarka." *Indian and Foreign Review* (15 March 1980): 15–19.

Rao, T. A. G. *Elements of Hindu Iconography*, 4 vols. Reprint New York: Paragon, 1968.

Rao, T. S. R, and S. Kak (eds.). *Computing Science in Ancient India*, Lafayette: University of Lousiana, 1998.

Rapson, E. I., (gen. ed.). *Cambridge History of India*, 6 vols. Reprint Delhi: S. Chand, 1964.

Rau, C. V. S. *A Glossary of Philosophical Terms* (Sanskrit-English), Madras: University of Madras, 1941.

Rau, H. "The Image of India in European Antiquity and the Middle Ages." In *India and the West: Proceedings of a Seminar Dedicated to the Memory of Hermann Goetz*. 197–208. J. Deppert, (ed.) New Delhi: Manohar, 1983.

Ray, N. R. "Sculpture" *HCIP*, vol. 2, 506 ff.

Ray, R. K. "The Kahar Chronicle." *Modern Asian Studies* 21, 4 (1987): 711–749.

Raychaudhuri, R. "The *Mahābhārata*: Some Aspects of Its Culture." *CHI*, vol. 2, 71 ff.

Reddy, Y. G. "The Svargabrahma Temple of Alampur: Iconographical Study." *Journal of Indian History* 55, 1–2 (1977): 103–17.

Renou, L. *Le déstin du Veda dans l'Inde*. Paris: Adrien Maisonneuve, 1960. English trans. *Destiny of the Veda in India*. Delhi: Motilal Banarsidass, 1968.

Id. *Les écoles védiques et la formation du Veda*. Paris: Adrien Maisonneuve, 1947.

Id. *Hinduism*. New York: Washington Square Press, 1964.

Id. *Indian Literature*. New York: Praeger, 1965.

Id. *Religions of Ancient India*. London: Athlone Press, 1953.

Id. *Vedic India*. Calcutta: Sunil Gupta, 1957.

Id., and J. Filliozat (eds.). *L'Inde Classique*, 3 vols. Paris Hanoi: Imprimerie Nationale, 1953.

Rhys Davids, T. W. (trans.). *The Questions of King Milinda*. In *SBE*, vols. 25 and 26.

Rice, E.P. *Kanarese Literature*. Calcutta: Association Press, 1921.

Riepe, D. *The Naturalistic Tradition in Indian Thought*. Seattle: University of Washington Press, 1961.

Id. *The Philosophy of India and Its Impact on American Thought*. Springfield, Ill.: Charles C. Thomas, 1970.

Rinehart, R. "A Message Without an Audience: Svami Rama Tirtha's 'Practical Vedanta.'" *IJHS* 2, 2 (Aug. 1998): 185–221.
Risley, H. H. *The Peoples of India*. 2d ed. London: W. Thacker, 1915.
Rizvi, S. A. A. *A History of Sufism in India*, 2 vols. Delhi: Manoharlal, 1978.
Robb, P. "The Challenge of Gau Mata: British Policy and Religious Change in India, 1880–1916." *Modern Asian Studies* 20, 2 (1986): 285–319.
Robins, R. H. "The Evolution of Historical Linguistics." *JRAS*(1986): 5–20.
Rocher, L. "The Purāṇas." *HIL*, vol. 2/3. Wiesbaden: Otto Harrassowitz, 1986.
Id. "The Dharmaśāstras." In G. Flood (ed.). *The Blackwell Companion to Hinduism*. 102–115.
Roland, A. "The Uses (and Miuses) of Psychoanalysis in South Asian Studies: Mysticism and Child Development." www.sulekha.com, 8/5/03.
Ross, A. D. *The Hindu Family in its Urban Setting*. Toronto: University of Toronto Press, 1962.
Rosser, Y. G. "The Groan: Loss of Scholarship and High Drama in 'South Asian' Studies." www.sulekha.com.
Rowland, B. *The Art and Architecture of India: Buddhist, Hindu, Jain*, 2d ed. Baltimore: Penguin Books, 1967.
Roy, Ajit, "Communalism—Its Political Roots." *Religion and Society* 31, 4 (1984): 14–23.
Roy, D. K., and J. Devi. *Kumbha: India's Ageless Festival*. Bombay: Bharatiya Vidya Bhavan, 1955.
Roy, M. N. *India's Message*. Calcutta: Renaissance Publishers, 1950.
Id. *Materialism*, 2nd ed. Calcutta: Renaissance Publishers, 1951.
Id. *New Humanism*, 2d rev. ed. Calcutta: Renaissance Publishers, 1953.
Roy, S. B. "Chronological Framework of Indian Protohistory—The Lower Limit." *JBOI* 32, 3–4 (March-June 1983): 254–74.
Id. "Chronological Infrastructure of Indian Protohistory." *JBRS* 32 (1972): 44–78.
Ruben, W. *Materialismus im Leben des Alten Indien*. *Acta Orientalia* 13. Leiden: Brill, 1935.
Rudolph, L. I. and S. H. Rudolph. *The Modernity of Tradition*. Chicago: Chicago University Press, 1967.
Ruhela, S. P. and D. Robinson (eds.). *Sāī Bābā and His Message*. Delhi: Vikas, 1976.
Rukmani, T. S. "Samnyāsa and Some Indian Reform Movements in the Eighteenth, Nineteenth and Twentieth Centuries." *ALB* 62 (1998): 23–50.
Id. (ed.). *Hindu Diaspora: Global Perspectives*. Montreal: McGill University, 2003.
Ryerson, C. A. "Meaning and Modernization in Tamil Nadu: Tamil Nationalism and Religious Culture." *RS* 17,4 (1970): 1–16.
*Śābarabhāṣya*, with contemporary Sanskrit commentary by B. G. Apte, 6 vols. Poona: Anandasrama, 1931–1934.
*Śabdakalpadruma*, by Raja Radha Kanta Deva, 5 vols. Varanasi: Chowkhamba Series Office, 1961.
Sachau, Edward C. (trans.). *Alberuni's India: An Account of the Religion, Philosophy, Literature, Geography, Chronology, Astronomy, Customs, Laws and Astrology of India about* AD 1030. Trübner's Oriental Series. Reprint Delhi: 1964.
Sādhucaranprasād, Vaikunthavāsi Śrī Babu. *Dharmaśāstrasaṅgraha*. Bombay: Śrī Venkatesvar Stim Mudranayantralaya, 1913.

Sāī Bābā (Śrī Sathya). *Satya Sāī Speaks*, 7 vols. Kadugodi: Śrī Sathya Sai Education and Publication Foundation, 1972–76.

*Śaiva-upaniṣads*. A. M. Sastri (ed.). Madras: The Adyar Library, 1960.

*Śaiva-upaniṣads*. T. R. Srinivasa Ayyangar (trans.). Madras: The Adyar Library, 1955.

Sakare, M. R. *History and Philosophy of the Liṅgāyata Religion*. Belgaum: Published by the author, 1942.

*Śākta, Vaiṣṇava, Yoga, Śaiva, Saṃnyavedānta, and Minor Upaniṣads*. P. M. Sastri (ed. and trans.). Adyar: Adyar Library, 1912–38.

Saletore, B. A. *Ancient Indian Political Thought and Institutions*. Bombay: Asia Publishing House, 1963.

Salomon, R. (ed. and trans.). *The Bridge to the Three Holy Cities, the Samāyaṇa-Praghaṭṭaka of Nārāyaṇa Bhaṭṭa's Triṣṭhalīsetu*. Delhi: Motilal Banarsidass, 1985.

Samartha, S. J. *Hindus vor dem universalen Christus*. Stuttgart: Evangelisches Verlagswerk, 1970.

*Sāmaveda*, 2nd ed. Ram Sarma Acarya (ed.). Bareilly: Samskrit Samsthana 1962; R. T. H. Griffith (trans.), reprint Varanasi: Chowkhamba, 1963.

*Sāṁkhyakārikā*, 4th ed. S. S. Suryanarayana Sastri (ed. and trans.). Madras: University of Madras, 1948.

*Sāṁkhya Kārikā of Mahamuni Śrī Īśvarakṛṣṇa*, with the commentary of Pandit Swanarayana Sastri and *Sāṅkhya Tattvakaumudī of Vācaspati Miśra*. Bombay: Nirnaya Sagar Press, 1940.

Saṅgani, N. P. "*Sanātana dharma hi sarvabhauma dharma yā mānava dharma hai.*" *Dharmāṅka, Kalyāna* 30, 1 (January 1966): 242–49.

Sankalia, H. D. *Indian Archeology Today*. New York: Asia Publishing House, 1962.

Id. "Paleolithic, Neolithic and Copper Ages." In *HCIP*, vol. 1, 125–42.

Id. *Prehistoric Art in India*. Delhi: Vikas Publishing House, 1978.

Id. *Prehistory and Protohistory in Indian and Pakistan*. Bombay: University of Bombay, 1961.

*Sankalpa Sūryodaya by Vedānta Deśika*, R. Rajagopala Aiyangar (trans.), Tirupati: Tirumalai Tirupati Devasthanam, 1965.

*Śaṅkarabhāsya*. Swāmi Gambhirananda (trans.). Calcutta: Advaita Ashrama, 1965.

Sankarananda, Swāmi. *Hindu States of Sumeria*. Calcutta: Firma K. L. Mukhopadhyay, 1962.

Sankaranarayan, P. *The Call of the Jagadguru*. Madras: Akhila Bharata Sankara Seva Samiti, 1958.

*Saṅkhāyana Śrautasūtra*. S. W. Caland (trans.). Nagpur: The International Academy of Indian Culture, 1953.

Santucci, J. A. *An Outline of Vedic Literature*. The American Academy of Religion Aids to the Study of Religion Series. Missoula: Scholar's Press, 1977.

Sarasvati, Dayananda. *Satyārtha Prakāśa*. Allahabad: Kal Press, 1947.

Sarkar, B. K. *The Positive Background of Hindu Sociology*, 3 vols. In *SBH*, vols. 18, 25, 32. Allahabad: Panini Press, 1914–37.

Sarkar, S. *The Aboriginal Races of India*. Calcutta: Bookland, 1954.

Sarma, D. S. *Hinduism Through the Ages*, rev. ed. Bombay: Bharatiya Vidya Bhavan, 1958.

Id. *The Renaissance of Hinduism*. Banares: 1958.

Id. "Sanātana Dharma," *Kalyāṇa* 40,1 (1966): 238–41.

Sarma, N. S. *Hindu Renaissance*. Banares: 1944.
Sarma, R. Thangasami. *Darśanamañjarī*, part 1. Madras: University of Madras, 1985.
*Sarvadarśanasaṁgraha of Mādhava*, 3rd ed. V. S. Abhyankar (ed.). Poona: BORI, 1978; E. B. Cowell and A. E. Gough (trans.) (incomplete), 1892; reprint Varanasi: Chowkhamba, 1960.
Sastri, G. *A Study in the Dialectics of Sphoṭa*. Delhi: Motilal Banarsidass, 1981.
Sastri, K. A. N. *The Colas*, 3 vols. Madras: University of Madras, 1935.
Id. *The Culture and History of the Tamils*. Calcutta: Firma K. L. Mukhopadhyay, 1964.
Id. *History of South India*. Madras: Oxford University Press, 1955.
Sastri, K. S. R. *Śivānanda: The Modern World Prophet*. Rishikesh: Divine Light Society, 1953.
Sastri, Kuppuswami. "Kośavan ācāryaḥ." Reprinted in *KSBCCV*, S. S. Janaki (ed.). Madras: Kupppuswami Research Institute, 1981, part 1.
Id. "Nyāya-Vaiśeṣika—Origin and Development." Introduction to K. Sastri, *Primer of Indian Logic*. 1932; reprinted in *KSBCCV*, S.S. Janaki (ed.). Madras: 1981.
Sastri M. and T. R. Srinivasa Ayyangar (ed. and trans.) *The Yoga Upaniṣads*. Adyar: Theosophical Publishing House, 1952.
Sastri, P. D. *The Doctrine of Māyā in Vedānta*. London: 1911.
Sastri, S. S. "Vṛṣakapi." *Bharatiya Vidya* 10:145–59.
Sastry, R. A. (trans.). *Viṣṇusahasranāma: With the Bhāṣya of Śrī Śaṁkarācārya*. Adyar Library General Series. Adyar: Adyar Library and Research Centre, 1980.
*Śatapathabrāhmaṇa*, 5 vols. J. Eggeling (ed. and trans.). In *SBE*, vols. 12, 26, 41, 43 and 44.
Savarkar, V. "Essentials of Hindutva." *Samagra Savarkar Waṅgmaya, Hindū Rāṣṭra Darshan*, vol.6. Poona: Maharashtra Prantik Hindusabha, 1964.
Sawai, Y. "Śaṅkaras Theology of Samnyāsa." *Journal of Indian Philosophy* 14 (1986): 371–87.
Sax, W. S. "Conquering the Quarters: Religion and Politics in Hinduism." *International Journal of Hindu Studies* 4,1 (April 2000): 39–60.
Saxena, K. "The Janatā Party Politics in Uttar Pradesh (1977–79)." *Indian Political Science Review* (July 1983): 172–87.
Scharfe, H. *The State in Indian Tradition*. Leiden: Brill, 1989.
Schilpp, P. A. (ed.). *The Philosophy of Sarvepalli Radhakrishnan*. New York: Tudor Publishing Co., 1952.
Schlingloff, D. *Die altindische Stadt*. Wiesbaden: Harrassowitz, 1969.
Schneider, U. "Kṛṣṇa's postumer Aufstieg: zur Frühgeschichte der Bhaktibewegung." *Saeculum* 33, 1 (1982): 38–49.
Schour, K. and McLeod, W. H. (eds.) *The Saints: Studies in a Devotional Tradition of India*. Delhi: Motilal Banarsidass, 1987.
Schrader, F. O. *Introduction to the Pāñcarātra and the Ahirbudhnya Saṃhitā*. Adyar: Adyar Library and Research Centre, 1916.
Schroedinger, E. "Der Geist der Naturwissenschaft." In *Eranos Jahrbuch 1946*, 491–520.
Schwab, J. *Das indische Tieropfer*. Erlangen: Deichert, 1896.
Schwab, R. *La Rénaissance Orientale*, 1950. English: *The Oriental Renaissance: Europe's Rediscovery of India and the East, 1680–1880*. G. Patterson-Black and V. Reinking (trans.). New York: Columbia University Press, 1984.

Schwartzberg, J. E. (ed.) *Historical Atlas of India*. Chicago: University of Chicago Press, 1978. 2nd rev.ed. 1990.
Seal, A. *The Emergence of Indian Nationalism*. Cambridge: 1968.
Seal, B. N. *Comparative Studies in Vaishnavism and Christianity with an Examination of the Mahābhārata Legend about Nārada's Pilgrimage to Śvetadvīpa and an Introduction on the Historico-Comparative Method*. Calcutta: Private publication, 1899.
Id. *The Positive Sciences of the Hindus*. Reprint Delhi: Motilal Banarsidass, 1958.
"Secret Societies." *Seminar* 151 (March 1972).
"Secular Nemesis: A Communal Rage is Sweeping India." *India Today* (8 April 2002): 23–26.
Seemann, R. "Versuch zu einer Theorie des Avatāra. Mensch gewordener Gott oder Gott gewordener Mensch?" *Numen* 33,1 (1986): 90–140.
Segal, J. G. "White and Black Jews at Cochin, the Story of a Controversy." *JRAS* 1983,2: 228–52.
Segal, R. *The Crisis of India*. Penguin: Harmondsworth, 1965.
Seidenberg, A. "The Geometry of the Vedic Rituals." In F. Staal (ed.), *Agni: The Vedic Ritual of the Fire Altar*, vol. 2, 95–126.
Sen, N. "The Influence of the Epics on Indian Life and Literature." In *CHI*, vol. 2, 117 ff.
Sen, S. P. *Social Contents of Indian Religious Reform Movements*. Calcutta: Institute of Historical Studies, 1978.
Sengupta, N. C. *Evolution of Ancient Indian Law*. London: Probsthain, 1953.
Sengupta, P. C. *Ancient Indian Chronology*. Calcutta: University of Calcutta, 1941.
Seton, M. *Panditji: A Portrait of Jawaharlal Nehru*. New York: Taplinger, 1967.
Shankar, M. "Social Roots of Communalism." *RS* 31,4 (1984: 24–44.
Shaffer, J. G. and D. A. Lichtenstein, "Migration, Philosophy and South Asian Archeology." In M. Witzel. (ed.) *Inside the Texts—Beyond the Texts*: 239–60.
Shah, A. *The Bījak of Kabīr*, Hamirpur: A. Shah, 1917.
Sharma, A. *The Hindu Gītā: Ancient and Classical Interpretations of the Bhagavadgītā*. Lasalle: Open Court, 1986.
Id. *The Puruṣārthas: A Study in Hindu Axiology*. East Lansing: Asian Studies Center, Michigan State University, 1982.
Id. *Viśiṣṭādvaita Vedānta: A Study*. New Delhi: Heritage Press, 1978.
Id. (ed.) *The Study of Hinduism*. Columbia: University of South Carolina Press, 2003.
Id. *Satī*. Delhi: Motilal Banarsidass, 1989.
Sharma, B. N. K. *The Brahmasūtras and Their Principal Commentaries: A Critical Exposition*, 2 vols. Bombay: Bharatiya Vidya Bhavan, 1971–74.
Id. *A History of Dvaita School of Vedānta and Its Literature*, 2 vols. Bombay: Booksellers Publishing Co., 1960–61.
Id. *Madhva's Teaching in His Own Words*. Bombay: Bhavan's Book University, 1961.
Id. *Philosophy of Śrī Madhvācārya*. Bombay: Bharatiya Vidya Bhavan, 1962.
Sharma, H. D. *Brahmanical Asceticism*. Poona: Oriental Book Agency, 1939.
Sharma, K. *Bhakti and the Bhakti Movements*. Delhi: Manohar Lal, 2nd ed. 2003.
Sharma, R. K. (ed.). *Indian Archeology: New Perspectives*. Delhi: Agam Kala Prakashan, 1982.
Sharma, R. S. *Śūdras in Ancient India*. Delhi: Motilal Banarsidass, 1958.

Sharma, S. R. *Swāmi Rama Tirtha*. Bombay: Vidya Bhavan, 1961.
Sharpe, E. J. *The Univeral Gītā: Western Images of the Bhagavadgītā, A Bicentenary Survey*. La Salle: Open Court, 1985.
Id. *Not to Destroy but to Fulfil*. Uppsala: Gleerup, 1965.
Shastri, A. M. *India as Seen in the Bṛhatsaṃhitā of Varāhamihira*. Delhi: Motilal Banarsidass, 1969.
Shastri, D. R. *Short History of Indian Materialism*. Calcutta: The Book Company, 1930.
Shendge, M. J. "The Interdisciplinary Approach to Indian Studies." *ABORI* 63 (1982): 63–98.
Id. *The Civilized Demons: The Harappans in Ṛgveda*. New Delhi: Abhinav, 1977.
Sheth, N. *The Divinity of Krishna*. Delhi: Munshiram Manoharlal Publishers, 1984.
Shils, E. A. *The Intellectual Between Tradition and Modernity: The Indian Situation*. The Hague: Mouton, 1961.
Shinn, L. D. *The Dark Lord: Cult Images and the Hare Krishnas in America*. Philadelphia: Westminster, 1987.
Shourie, A. *Hinduism: Essence and Consequence—A Study of the Upaniṣads, the Gītā and the Brahma-Sūtras*. New Delhi: Vikas Publishing House, 1980.
Shulman, D. D. *Tamil Temple Myths: Sacrifice and Divine Marriage in the South Indian Śaiva Tradition*. Princeton: Princeton University Press, 1980.
Siauve, S. *La doctrine de Madhva*. Pondichery: Institut Français d'Indologie, 1968.
Id. *La voie vers la connaissance de Dieu sélon l'Aṇuvyākhyāna de Madhva*. Pondichery: Institute Français d'Indologie, 1957.
*Siddhitraya by Yamunācārya*. R. Ramanujachari and K. Srinivasacarya (ed. and trans.). Annamalai: Annamalai University, 1943.
Siegel, L. *Fires of Love—Waters of Peace: Passion and Renunciation in Indian Culture*. Honolulu: University of Hawaii Press, 1983.
Id. *Sacred and Profane Dimensions of Love in Indian Traditions as Exemplified in the Gītāgovinda of Jayadeva*. Oxford: Oxford University Press, 1978.
*Śīksādivedaṣadaṅgāṇi* (loose leaf), Pandurang Jawaji (ed.). Bombay: Venkatesvara Steam Press, 1934.
Sil, N. P. "Political Morality vs. Political Necessity: Kautilya and Machiavelli Revisited." *Journal of Asian History* 19, 2 (1985): 101–42.
Singer, M. (ed.). *Krishna: Myths, Rites and Attitudes*. Chicago: University of Chicago Press, 1969.
Id. (ed.). *Traditional India: Structure and Change*. Philadelphia: American Folklore Society, 1959.
Singh, G. P. "The Purāṇic Tradition of Historiography in India." *The Indian Historical Review* 31,1–2 (2004): 1–17.
Singh, K. *India: A Mirror for its Monsters and Monstrosities*. Bombay: Pearl, 1970.
Singh, M. "Yoga and Yoga Symbolism." *Symbolon: Jahrbuch für Symbolforschung* Band 2 (1959): 121–43.
Singh, N. K. "Ānand Mārg." *Seminar* 151 (March 1972): 21–25.
Singh, S. *Vedāntadeśika*. Varanasi: Chowkhamba, 1958.
Sinha, J. *History of Indian Philosophy*, 2 vols. Calcutta: Sinha Publishing House, 1956–61.
Id. *Indian Psychology*, 2 vols. Calcutta: Sinha Publishing House, 1958–60.

Id. *Indian Realism*. London: K. Paul, French, Trübner and Co., 1938.
Singhal, D. P. "Naturalism and Science in Ancient India." In *India and World Civilisations*, vol.1, 1969.
Sinha, P. N. *A Study of the Bhāgavata Purāṅa*, 2nd ed. Madras: Theosophical Society, 1950.
Sinha, V. K. "Secularization." *Seminar* 269 (January 1982): 37–40.
Sirkar, D. C. *The Śākta Pīṭhas*, rev. ed. Delhi: Motilal Banarsidass, 1948.
Id. "Viṣṇu." *Quarterly Journal of the Mythological Society* 25 (1935): 120 ff.
Śivapadasundaram, S. *The Śaivaschool of Hinduism*. London: Allen and Unwin, 1934.
*Śiva-Purāna*. Banares: Pandit Pustakalaya, 1962; J. L. Shastri (trans.), 4 vols. Delhi: Motilal Banarsidass, 1970–71.
Śivaramamurti, C. *Indian Bronzes*. Bombay: Taraporevala, 1960.
Śivaraman, K. *Śaivism in Philosophical Perspective*. Delhi: Motilal Banarsidass, 1973.
Id. "The Word as a Category of Revelation." In H. Coward and K. Śivaraman, (eds.), *Revelation in Indian Thought, A Festschrift in Honor of Professor T. R. V. Murti*, 45–64. Emeryville: Dharma Publishing, 1977.
*Śivasaṃhitā*, S. C. Vasu (trans.). Allahabad: Panini Office, 1923.
*Ślokavārtika of Kumārila Bhaṭṭa with the commentary Nyāyaratnakāra of Parthasarathi Misra*. Swāmi Dvārikādāsa Śāstrī (ed.). Varanasi: Tara Publications, 1978. Ganganatha Jha (trans.), Calcutta: Asiatic Society, 1907.
Smart, N. *Doctrine and Argument in Indian Philosophy*. London: Allen and Unwin, 1964.
Smith, B. K. "Ritual, Knowledge, and Being: Initiation and Veda Study in Ancient India." *Numen* 33,1 (1986): 65–89.
Id. *Classifying the Universe: The Ancient Indian Varṇa System and the Origins of Caste*. New York: Oxford University Press, 1994.
Id. "Questioning Authority: Constructions and Deconstructions of Hinduism." *IJHS* 2,3 (December 1998): 313–40.
Smith, B. L. (ed.). *Religion and the Legitimation of Power in South Asia*. International Studies in Sociology and Social Anthropology. Leiden: Brill, 1978.
Smith, B. D. (ed.). *Hinduism: New Essays on the History of Religions*. Leiden: Brill, 1976.
Smith, D. E. *India as a Secular State*. Princeton: Princeton University Press, 1967.
Smith, F. M. "Financing the Vedic Ritual: The *Mūlādhyāyapariśiṣṭa* of Katyāyana." *WZKS*, 32 (1989): 63–75.
Smith, V. *History of India*. Oxford: Oxford University Press, 1955.
Smith, W. C. *Modern Islam in India*, 3rd ed. Lahore: Mohammed Ashraf, 1963.
*Somaśambhupaddhatī*, 2 vols. H. Brunner-Lachaux (ed.) French (trans.). Pondichery: Institut Français d'Indologie, 1963–68.
Sorokin, P. A. (ed.) *Forms and Techniques of Altruistic and Spiritual Growth*. Boston: Beacon Press, 1954.
Sørenson, M. *Index of Subjects in the Mahābhārata*. Reprint Delhi: Motilal Banarsidass, 1962.
Spate, O. H. K. *India and Pakistan: A General and Regional Geography*. New York: Dutton, rev. ed. 1963.
Spellman, J. W. *Political Theory of Ancient India*. New York: Oxford University Press, 1964.

*Śrīmad-Viṣṇu-Tattva-Vinirṇaya of Madhva*. S. S. Raghavachar (ed. and trans.), Mangalore: Ramakrishna Ashrama, 1954.

Srinivas, M. N. *Caste and Ohter Essays*, 2nd ed. Bombay: Asia Publishing House, 1965.

Id. *India's Villages*. Bombay: Asia Publishing House, 1960.

Id. *Religion and Society among the Coorgs*, 2nd ed. Bombay: Asia Publishing House, 1965.

Srinivasacari, P. *The Philosophy of Viśiṣṭādvaita*. Adyar: Theosophical Society, 1946.

Srinivasan, D. "Unhinging Śiva from the Indus Civilization." *JRAS* 1 (1984): 77–89.

Srinivasan, D. M. (ed.). *Mathurā: The Cultural Heritage*. New Delhi: American Institute of Indian Studies, 1989.

*Śrī Parameśvara Saṃhitā*. Sri Govindacarya (ed.). Srirangam: Kodandaramasannidhi, 1953.

*Śrīpati's Śrīkāra Bhāṣya*. Hayavadana Rao (ed.). Bangalore: 1936.

Staal, J. F. *Advaita and Neoplatonism*. Madras: University of Madras, 1961.

Id. *Agni: The Vedic Ritual of the Fire Altar*, 2 vols. Berkeley: University of California Press, 1983.

Id. "Exchange with a Reviewer of *Agni*." *JAS* 46,1 (1987): 105–10.

Id. "Language and Ritual." In *KSBCCV*, 51–62. Madras: Kuppuswami Research Institute, 1985, part 2.

Id. "The Meaninglessness of Ritual." *Numen* 26 (1979): 2–22.

Id. *The Science of Ritual*. Poona: Deccan Institute, 1982.

Id. "The Sound of Religion." *Numen* 33 (1986): 33–64, 185–224.

id (ed.). *A Reader on the Sanskrit Grammarians*. Cambridge, Mass.: MIT Press, 1972.

Stein, D. "Burning Widows, Burning Brides: The Perils of Daughterhood in India." *Pacific Affairs* 61,3 (1988): 465–85.

Stevenson, I. *Cases of the Reincarnation Type*, 4 vols. Charlottesville University Press of Virginia, 1972–76.

Stevenson, M. *The Rites of the Twice Born*. Oxford: Oxford University Press, 1920.

von Stietencron, H. "Dämonen und Gegengötter: Überlegungen zur Typologie von Antagonismen." *Saeculum* 34,3–4 (1983): 372–83.

Id. "Die Göttin Durgā Mahiṣāsuramārdiṇī: Mythos, Darstellung und geschichtliche Rolle bei der Hinduisierung Indiens." In *Visible Religion: Annual for Religious Iconography*, vol. 23, 11–166. Leiden: Brill, 1983.

Id. *Gaṅgā und Yamunā*. Wiesbaden: Harrrassowitz, 1972.

Id. *Indische Sonnenpriester: Sāmba und die Śākasdiśpīya Brāhmaṇa*. Wiesbaden: Harrrassowitz, 1966.

Id. "Suicide as a Religious Institution." *Bharatiya Vidya* 27 (1967): 7–24.

Stoler-Miller, B. *Love Song of the Dark Lord*. New York: Columbia University Press, 1977.

Id. "Rādhā: Consort of Kṛṣṇa's Vernal Passion." *JAOS* 95,4 (1975): 655–71.

Id. "Stella Kramrisch: A Biographical Essay." In *Exploring India's Sacred Art*, B. Stoler-Miller, (ed.) Philadelphia: Uṇiversity of Pennsylvania, 1983, 3–33.

Strickmann, M. (ed.). *Classical Asian Rituals and the Theory of Ritual*. Berlin: Springer, 1986.

*Stotraratna by Yamunācārya*. Swami Adidevanada (ed. and trans.). Madras: Ramakrishna Math, Mylapore 1960.

Subbarao, B. *The Personality of India*. Baroda: University of Baroda, 1959.
*Subhodinī by Vallabhācārya*. J. D. Redington (ed. and trans.). Delhi: Motilal Banarsidass, 1983.
Subramaniyaswami, Sivaya. *Dancing with Śiva: A Hindu Catechism*. Hawaii: Himalayan Academy, 1993.
Id. *How to Become a(better)Hindu*. Hawaii: Himalayan Academy, 2000.
Id. *Living with Śiva: Hinduism's Nandināthan Sūtra*, Hawaii: Himalayan Academy, 1998.
*Śukra Nītisāra*, 2nd ed. B. K. Sarkar (trans.). Allahabad: Panini Office, 21923.
Sukthankar, V. S. *On the Meaning of the Mahābhārata*. Bombay: Asiatic Society, 1957.
Sundaram, P. K. *Advaita Epistemology*. Madras: University of Madras, 1968.
Sundaresan, V. "Conflicting Hagiogaphies and History: The Place of Śaṅkaravijaya Texts in Advaita tradition." *IJHS* 4,2 (August 2000): 109–148.
Swarup, B. *Theory of Indian Music*, 2nd ed. Allahabad: Swamy Brothers, 1958.
Tagore, R. *Sādhana*. Calcutta: Macmillan, 1950.
Id. *Creative Unity*. Calcutta: Macmillan, 1959.
Taimni, I. K. *The Science of Yoga.*, 3rd ed. Wheaton: Theosophical Publishing House, 1972.
Talbot, P. and S. L. Poplai. *India and America: A Study of Their Religions*. New York: Harper and Row, 1959.
Tandon, P. *Punjabi Century*. Berkeley: University of California, 1968.
Taposwami Maharaj, Swāmi. *Wanderings in the Himālayas*. Madras: Ganesh, 1960.
*Tarkabhāṣa of Keśava Miśra*, 2nd ed. G. Jha (ed. and trans.). Poona: Oriental Book Agency, 1949.
Tarn, W. W. *The Greeks in Bactria and India*. Cambridge: Cambridge University Press, 1951; reprint 1966.
*Tattvatrayam by Pillai Lokācārya*. M. B. Narasimha Iyengar (trans.). Madras: M.C. Krishna, 1974.
Tendulkar, D. G. *Mahātmā: Life and Work of* M. K. *Gandhi*, 8 vols. Bombay: V. K. Jhaveri, 1951–58.
Thangasamy, D. A. *The Theology of Chenchiah*. Bangalore: YMCA/CISRS, 1966.
Thangaswami, R. *A Bibliographical Survey of Advaita Vedānta Literature* (in Sanskrit). Madras: University of Madras, 1980.
Id. *Darśanamañjarī*. Madras: University of Madras, 1985.
Thapar, R. *A History of India*, 2 vols. Baltimore: Penguin Books, 1966.
Id. *India in Transition*. Bombay: Asia Publishing House, 1956.
Thomas, M. M. *The Acknowledged Christ of the Indian Renaissance*. London: SCM Press, 1969.
Thomas, P. *Epics, Myths and Legends of India*. Bombay: Taraporevala, 1961.
Id. *Hindu Religion, Custom and Manners*. Bombay: 1961.
Thompson, E. J. and A. M. Spencer. *Bengali Religious Lyrics, Śākta*. Calcutta: Association Press, 1923.
Thurston, E. and K. Rangachari. *Tribes and Castes of South India*, 4 vols. Madras: Government Press, 1929.
Tilak, B. G. *The Arctic Home in the Vedas*. Reprint Poona: Tilak Bros., 1956.
Id. *Gītā rahasya*, 2 vols. Reprint. Poona: Tilak Brothers, 1956.
Id. *Orion or Researches into the Antiquity of the Veda*. Bombay: Sagoon, 1893. Reprint Poona: Tilak Brothers, 1955.

Id. *Vedic Chronology*. Poona: 1909.
Tillotson, G. H. R. "The Indian Travels of William Hodges." *JRAS* (London), Series 3, 2, 3 (1992): 377–98.
Timberg, T. A. (ed.). *Jews in India*. New York: Advent Books, 1986.
Timm, J. R. "Vallabha, Vaiṣṇavism and the Western Hegemony of Indian Thought." *Journal of Dharma* 14,1 (1989): 6–36.
Tirtha, Swami Bharati Krishna. *Sanātana Dharma*. Bombay: Bharatiya Vidya Bhavan, 1964.
*The Tirukkural* (in Tamil). G. U. Pope, W. H. Drew, J. Lazarus and F. W. Ellis (trans.). Tinnelvelly: South India Śaiva Siddhānta Works Publishing Society, 1962.
*Tiruvācagam*, G. U. Pope (ed. and trans.). 1900; reprint Madras: University of Madras, 1970.
*Tiruvācakam*. Ratna Navaratnam (trans.). Bombay: Bharatiya Vidya Bhavan, 1963.
Titus, M. T. *Islam in India and Pakistan*. Calcutta: YMCA. Publishing House, 1959.
Tiwari, R. *Yisu Das: The Witness of a Convert*. Delhi: ISPCK, 2000.
Tod, J. *Annals and Antiquities of Rajasthan*. 3 vols. William Crooke (ed.). Delhi: Motilal Banarsidass, n.d.
Tripathi, G. C. "Das Indradhvaja Fest in Orissa: Die Überreste der Indra-Verehrung in Ostindien, *ADMG Supplement* 3, 2 (1977).
*Tripurā Rahasya*. A. U. Vasaveda (trans.). Varanasi: Chowkhamba, 1965.
*Tripurārahasyam*. Swāmi Sanatanadevaji Maharaja (ed.). Varanasi: Chowkhamba, 1967.
Trivedi, M. M. "Citsukha's View on Self-Luminosity." *JIPh* 15 (1987): 115–23.
Troll, C. W. "Sayyid Ahmad Khan." *ER*, vol. 1:155–57.
Tyagisananda, Swāmi (ed. and trans.). *Aphorisms on the Gospel of Divine Love or Nārada Bhaktisūtras*, 5th ed. Madras: Ramakrishna Math, 1972.
Underhill, M. M. *The Hindu Religious Year*. Calcutta: Association Press, 1921.
*Upadeśasahasrī of Śaṅkarācārya*, 3rd ed. Swami Jagadananda (ed. and trans.) Madras: Ramakrishna Math, 1962.
Upadhyaya, D. "A Democratic Alternative." *Seminar* 80 (April 1966): 21–24.
Id. "Another Path." *Seminar* 17 (January 1961): 38–43.
Id. "Jana Sangh." *Seminar* 89 (January 1967): 34–37.
Upadhyaya, K. D. *Studies in Indian Folk Culture*. Calcutta: Indian Publications, 1964.
Upadhyaya, P. C. "The Politics of Secularism." MAS 26,4 (1992): 815–35.
Upadhye, P. M. "Manusmṛti—Its Relevance in Modern India." *JOIB* 35, 1–2 (1985): 43–48.
*Vadāvalī of Nagojī Bhaṭṭa*. N. Rao (ed. and trans.). Adyar: Adyar Library, 1943.
Vaidyanathan, K. R. *Śrī Krishna, the Lord of Guruvayur*. Bombay: Bharatiya Vidya Bhavan, 1974.
*Vaiśeṣikardarśana*, A. Thakur (ed. and trans.). Darbhanga: Mithila Institute, 1957.
*Vaiśeṣikasūtras of Kaṇāda*. N. Sinha (trans.). Allahabad: Panini Office, 1911.
*Vārāṇasī at a Glance*. A souvenir issued on the eve of the twenty-fourth session of the All Indian Oriental Conference. October 1968. Vārāṇasī: Vārāṇaseya Sanskrit Viśvavidyālaya, 1968.
Varma, K. C. "The Iron Age, the Veda and the Historical Urbanization." In *Indian Archeology, New Perspectives*, R. K. Sharma, (ed.) New Delhi: Indian Archeological Survey, 1982, 155–183.

Varma, L. A. Ravi, "Rituals of Worship." In *CHI*, vol. 4, 445–63.
Varma, V. P. *Modern Indian Political Thought*, 4th ed. Agra: Laksmi Narain Agarwala, 1968.
Vasu, S. C. (ed. and trans.). *Pāṇinī's Aṣṭādhyayī*. 2 vols. Reprint Delhi: Motilal Banarsidass, 1961.
Vatsyayan, Kapila. "Prehistoric Paintings." *Sangeet Natak, Journal of the Sangeet Natak Akademi* 66 (October-December 1981): 5–18.
Vaudeville, C. *Kabīr Granthāvalī* (Doha). Pondichery: Institut Français d'Indologie, 1957.
Id. "Kabir." *ER*, vol. 8: 226–27.
*Vedāntakarikāvalī of Venkatācārya*. V. Krisnamacarya (ed. and trans.). Adyar: Adyar Library, 1950.
*Vedāntaparibhāṣa by Dharmarāja*. S. S. Suryanarayana Sastri (ed. and trans.). Adyar: Adyar Library, 1942.
*Vedānta Parijāta Saurabha by Nimbārka with Vedānta Kaustubha by Śrīnivāsa*. Roma Bose (trans.). Calcutta: Asiatic Society of Bengal, 1940.
*Vedāntasāra of Sadānanda Yogīndra*, 4th ed. Swāmi Nikhilananda (ed. and trans.) Calcutta: Ramakrishna Math, 1959.
*Vedāntasūtras with the Commentary of Bāladeva*, 2nd ed. S. C. Vasu Vidyaranava (trans.). *SBH*. Allahabad: Panini Office, 1934.
*Vedāntasūtras with the Commentary of Madhva*, 2nd ed. S. S. Rao (trans.). Tirupati: Sri Vyasa Press, 1936.
*Vedāntasūtras with Rāmānuja's Commentary*. G. Thibaut (trans.). In *SBE*, vol. 48.
*Vedāntasūtras with Śaṅkarācārya's Commentary*, 2 vols. G. Thibaut (trans.). In *SBE*, vols. 34 and 38.
*Vedārthasaṁgraha of Rāmānuja*. S. S. Ragavacar (ed. and trans.). Mysore: Ramakrishna Ashrama, 1956.
Vetter, T. "Die Gauḍapadīya-Kārikās: Zur Entstehung und zur Bedeutung von [A]dvaita." *WZKSA* 22 (1978): 95–131.
Vidyabhusana, S. C. *A History of Indian Logic*. Calcutta: University of Calcutta, 1921.
Vidyarthi, L. P. *Aspects of Religion in Indian Society*. Meerut: Vednat Nath Rammath, 1962.
Vidyarthi, P. B. *Knowledge, Self and God in Rāmānuja*. New Delhi: Motilal Banarsidass, 1978.
Viennot, O. *Le culte de l'arbre dans l'Inde ancienne*. Paris: 1954.
*Viṣṇu Purāṇa*. H. H. Wilson (trans.). Reprint Calcutta: Punthi Pustak, 1961.
*Viśva Hindū Viśesāṇgka*. Bombay: World Council of Hindus, 1966.
*Viśvakarma Vāstuśāstra*. K. V. Sastri and N. B. Gadre (eds.). Tanjore Sarasvati Mahal Series No. 85, 1958.
*Viśveśvarasaraswatī's Yatidharmasaṅgraha*, V. G. Apte, (ed.) Poona: Anandasrama, 1928.
*Vivekacudāmaṇī of Śaṅkarācārya*, 6th ed. Swami Madhavananda (ed. and trans.). Calcutta: Ramakrishna Math, 61957.
Vivekānanda, Swāmi. *Complete Works of Swāmi Vivekānanda*, 8 vols. Calcutta: Advaita Ashrama, 1970–1971.
Vogel, J. P. *Indian Serpent Lore*. London: Probsthain, 1926.
Volwahsen, A. *Living Architecture: Indian*. New York: Grosset and Dunlap, 1969.

Vyas, K. C. *The Social Renaissance in India*. Bombay: Asia Publishing House, 1957.
Vyas, R. T. "Roots of Śaṅkara's Thought." *JOIB* 32, 1–2 (1982): 35–49.
Vyas, S. N. *India in the Rāmāyaṇa Age*. Delhi: Atura Ram and Sons, 1967.
Waghorne, J. P. and N. Cutler (eds.). *Gods of Flesh/Gods of Stone: The Embodiment of Divinity in India*. Chambersburg: Anima Publications, 1985.
Walker, B. *The Hindu World: An Encyclopedic Survey of Hinduism*, 2 vols. New York: Praeger, 1968.
Warder, A. K. *Outline of Indian Philosophy*. Delhi: Motilal Banarsidass, 1968.
Wasson, R. G. "The Soma of the *Rig Veda*: What Was It?" *JAOS* 91, 2 (1971): 169–91.
Weber, A. "Über das Menschenopfer bei den Indern der vedischen Zeit." *Indische Streifen* I, vol. 1, 54–89. Berlin: Nicolai, 1968.
Weber, M. *The Religion of India: The Sociology of Hinduism and Buddhism*. Reprint New York: Free Press, 1967.
Weightman, S. and S. M. Pandey, "*Dharm* and *Kartavy* in Modern Hindī." In W. D. O'Flaherty and J. D. M. Derret (eds.), *The Concept of Duty in Southeast Asia*: 223–45. New Delhi: Vikas, 1978.
Weiss, B. "Meditations in the Myth of Savitri." *JAAR* 53, 2: 259–70.
von Weizsäcker, C. F. and Gopi Krishna. *Biologische Basis religiöser Erfahrung*. Weilheim: Otto Wilhelm Barth Verlag, 1971.
Welbon, G. and G. E. Yocum, (eds.) *Religious Festivals in South India and Śrī Laṅkā*. Delhi: Manohar, 1985.
Werner, K. "A Note on Karma and Rebirth in the Vedas." *Hinduism* 83 (1978): 1–4.
Id. "Religious Practice and Yoga in the Time of the Vedas, Upaniṣads and Early Buddhism." *ABORI* 56 (1975): 179–94.
Id. "The Vedic Concept of Human Personality and Its Destiny," *JIPh* 5 (1978): 275–89.
Westcott, G. H. *Kabīr and the Kabīr Panth*, 2d ed. Reprint Calcutta: Susil Gupta, 1953.
Whaling, F. *The Rise of the Religious Significance of Rāma*. Delhi: Motilal Banarsidass, 1980.
Wheeler, J. A. " From Relativity to Mutability." In J. Mehra (ed.). *The Physicist's Conception of Nature*. 202–47.
Wheeler, M. *The Indus Civilization*. Cambridge: Cambridge University Press, 1953.
Wheelock, W. T. "Patterns of Mantra Use in a Vedic Ritual." *Numen* 32, 2 (1986): 169–93.
Whicher, I. *The Integrity of the Yoga Darśana: A Reconsideration of Classical Yoga*. Albany: State University of New York Press, 1998.
White, S. J. "Kṛṣṇa as Divine Child." *HR* 12,2 (1972): 156–77.
Whitehead, H. *The Village Gods of South India*, 2d ed. Religious Life of India Series. Calcutta: Association Press, 1921.
Whitney, W. D. (ed. and trans.).*The Atharvaveda Saṃhitā*. 2 vols. Reprint Dehli: Motilal Banarsidass, 1963.
Williams, R. B. *A New Face of Hinduism: The Swaminarayan Religion*. Cambridge: Cambridge University Press, 1984.
Wilson, H. H. *Essays and Lectures on the Religion of the Hindus*, 2 vols. London: Trübner, 1862.
Id. *Religious Sects of the Hindus*. 1861. Reprint, Calcutta: Punthi Pustak, 1958.

Winternitz, M. *Geschichte der indischen Literatur*, vol. I. 1905, reprint: Stuttgart, K. F. Kohler, 1968. English Translation: *A History of Indian Literature*, 3 vols. S. Ketkar and H. Kohn (trans.). Reprint, Calcutta: University of Calcutta, 1927–1967.

Wiser, W. H. *Behind Mud Walls 1930–60*. Berkeley: University of California, 1963.

Id. *The Hindu Jajmani System*. Lucknow: Lucknow Publishing House, 1958.

Witzel, M. "Ein Fremdling im *Ṛgveda*." *JIES* 31, 1 and 2 (2003): 107–85

Id. (ed.) *Inside the Texts—Beyond the Texts*. Columbia, Mo.: South Asia Books, 1997.

Woodroffe, J. (Arthur Avalon). *Introduction to Tantra Śāstra*, 4th ed. Madras: Ganesh and Co., 1963.

Id. *Mahānirvāṇatantra: The Great Liberation*, 4th ed. Madras: Ganesh and Co., 1963.

Id. *Principles of Tantra*, 3rd ed. Madras: Ganesh and Co., 1960.

Woods, J. H. (trans.). *Patañjali's Yogasūtra, with Vyāsa's Bhāṣya and Vācaspati Miśra's Tattva Vaiśāradī*. Harvard Oriental Series 17. Cambridge, Mass.: Harvard University Press, 1914.

Wright, M. and N. "Bāladeva Vidyābhūṣana: The Gauḍīya Vedāntist." *JVS* 1, 2 (1993): 158–84.

Wyatt, N. "*Aśvamedha* and *Puruṣamedha* in Ancient India." *Religion* (1989): 1–11.

Yadav, B. S. "Vaiṣṇavism on Hans Küng: A Hindu Theology of Religious Pluralism." *Religion and Society* 27,2 (1980): 32–64.

*Yajurveda Vājasaneyasaṃhitā*, 2 vols. A. Weber (ed.), Leipzig: Indische Studien, 1871–1872.

Yamunacarya, M. *Rāmānuja's Teachings in His Own Words*. Bombay: Bharatiya Vidya Bhavan, 1963.

*Yatidharmasaṅgraha of Viśveśvarasaraswatī*, V. G. Apte (ed.) Poona: Anandasrama, 1928.

*Yatīndramatadīpikā of Śrīnivāsadāsa*. Swami Adidevananda (ed. and trans.). Madras: Ramakrishna Math, 1949.

Yatiswarananda, Swāmi. *The Divine Life*. Mylapore: 1964.

Id. (ed.) *Universal Prayers*. Mylapore: Ramakrishna Math, 1956.

Yocum, G. E. "The Goddess in a Tamil Śaiva Devotional Text: Manikkavācakar's Tiruvācakam." *JAAR* Supplement 45 (1977): 367–88.

Id. *Hymns to the Dancing Śiva: A Study of Manikkavācakar's Tiruvācakam*. Columbia, Mo.: South Asia Books, 1982.

Id. "Shrines, Shamanism, and Love Poetry: Elements in the Emergence of Popular Tamil Bhakti." *JAAR*, 41 (1973): 3–17.

Yogananda, Paramahamsa. *Autobiography of a Yogi*. Bombay: Jaico, 1960.

*Yogavaśiṣṭha Rāmāyaṇa*. 2 vols. D. N. Bose (trans.), 2 vols. Calcutta: Oriental Publishing Co., 1958.

Young, K., and A. Sharma. *Images of the Feminine—Mythic, Philosophic and Human—in the Buddhist, Hindu and Islamic Traditions: A Biography of Women in India*. Chico, Calif.: New Horizons Press, 1974.

Young, R. F. *Resistant Hinduism: Sanskrit Sources on Anti-Christian Apologetics in Early Nineteenth-Century India*. Vienna: Indologisches Institut der Universität Wien, 1981.

Younger, P. "A Temple Festival of Mariyamman." *JAAR* 48 (1980): 493–517.

Zabern, Phillip von (ed.). *Vergessene Städte am Indus: Frühe Kulturen in Pakistan vom 8. bis zum 2. Jahrtausend v. Chr.*, Mainz: Verlag von Zabern, 1987.
Zaehner, H. *Hinduism*. Oxford: Oxford University Press, 1962.
Zelliot, E. "The Medieval Bhakti Movement in History: An Essay on the Literature in English." In B.L. Smith, (ed.), 173–68, *Hinduism: New Essays in the History of Religions*, Leiden: Brill, l976.
Zimmer, H. *The Art of Indian Asia*, 2 vols. New York: Bollingen Foundation, 1955.
Id. *Artistic Form and Yoga in the Sacred Images of India*. Gerald Chapple and James B. Lawson (trans.). Princeton: Princeton University Press, 1984.
Id. *The King and the Corpse*. New York: Pantheon, 1947.
Id. *Myths and Symbols in Indian Art and Civilization*, 4th ed. New York: Harper and Row, 1963.
Id. *Philosophies of India*. J. Campbell (ed.). Princeton: Bollingen Foundation, 1951.
Zvelebil, K. V. *Tiru Murugan*. Madras: International Institute of Tamil Studies, 1982.
Id. "Some Tamil Folklore Texts." *JRAS* 64,2 (1989): 290–303.

# Index